AF413376

Art
Unpacked

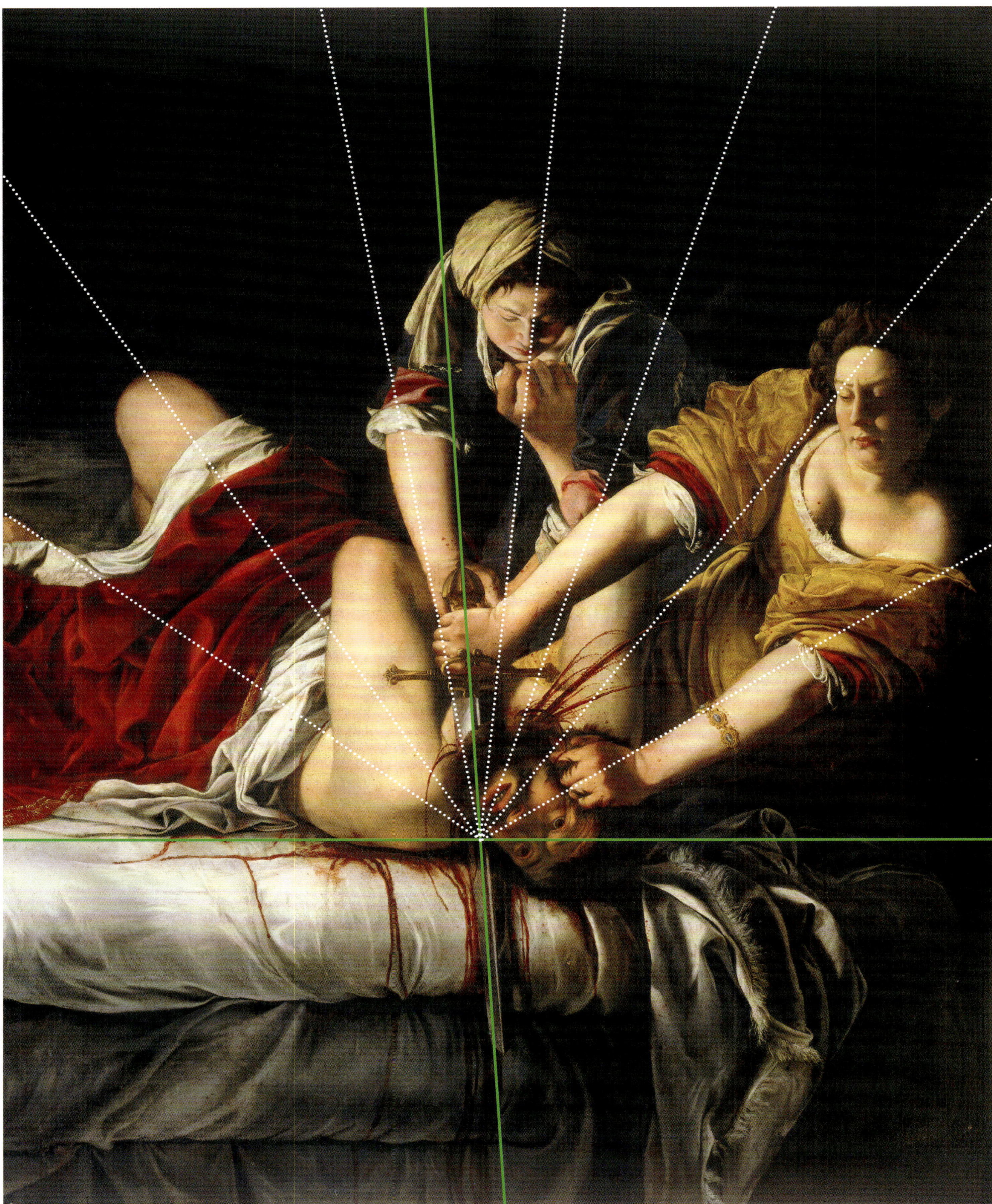

Matthew Wilson

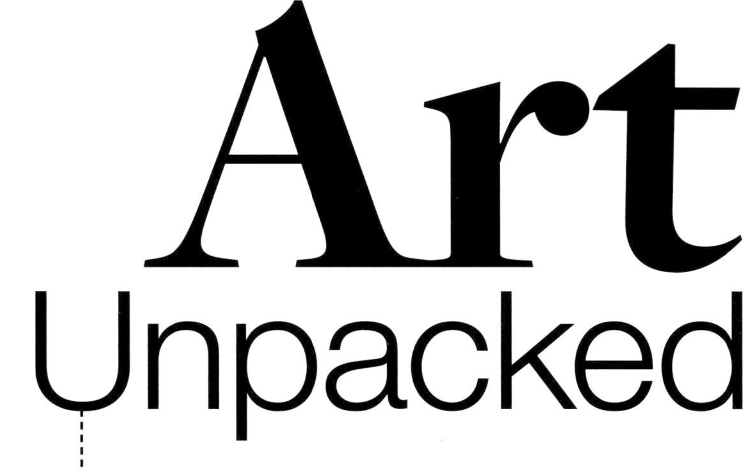

50 Works of Art: *Uncovered, Explored, Explained*

with over 850 images

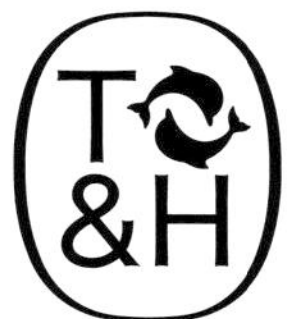

Contents

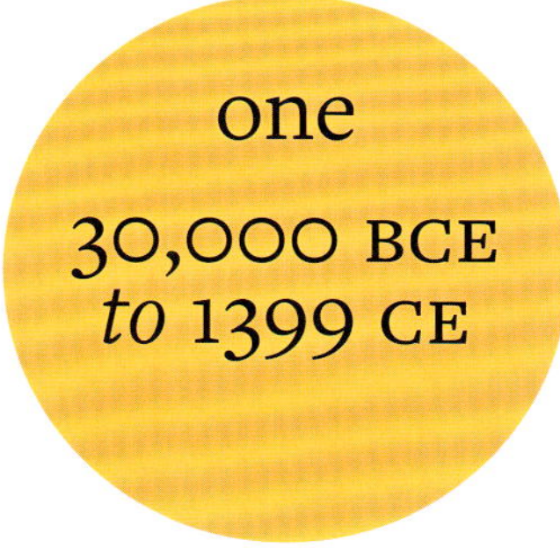

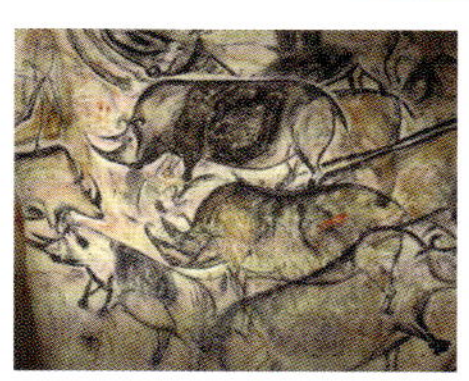

1 **Animal Magic**
France, Aurignacian
Rhinoceros panel
c. 30,000 BCE

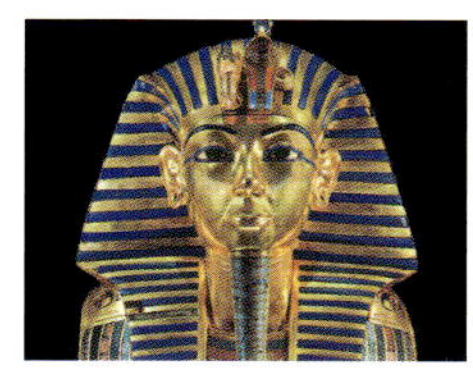

2 **Art for the Afterlife**
Egypt, New Kingdom
Funerary mask of Tutankhamun, 1327–18 BCE

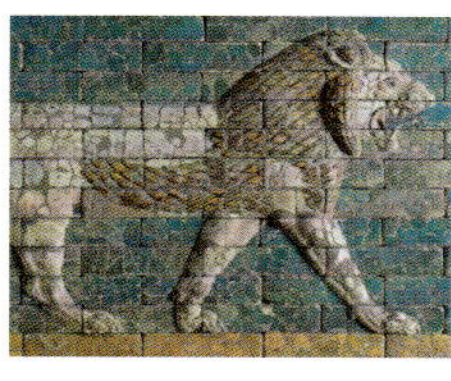

3 **Guardians of Ceremony**
Iraq, Neo-Babylonian
Panel with striding lion
c. 604–562 BCE

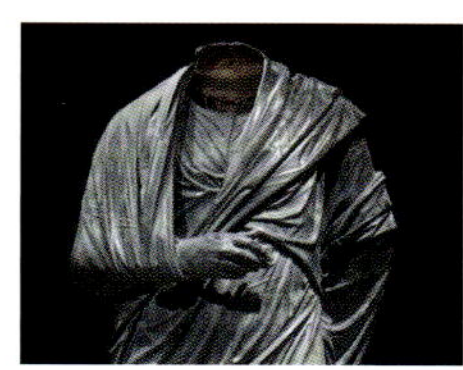

4 **Man and Superman**
Turkey, Roman
The Emperor as Philosopher
c. 180–200 CE

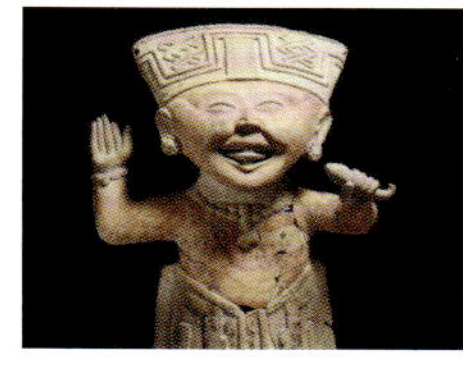

5 **Spiritual Rapture**
Mexico, Remojadas
'Smiling' figure
7th–8th century

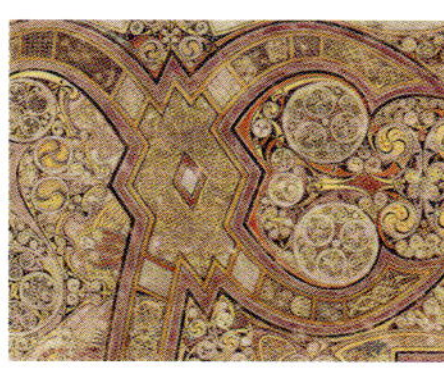

6 **Patterns of the Mind**
Scotland, Hiberno-Saxon
Chi-Rho-Iota page, Book of Kells
c. 800

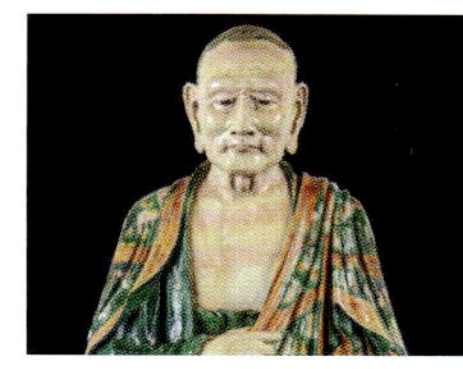

7 **Elevated Wisdom**
China, Liao dynasty
Arhat (*Luohan*)
c. 1000

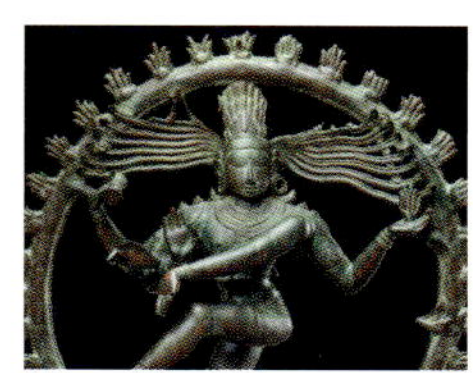

8 **Cosmic Dancing**
India, Chola dynasty
Shiva as Lord of the Dance (*Nataraja*), c. 11th century

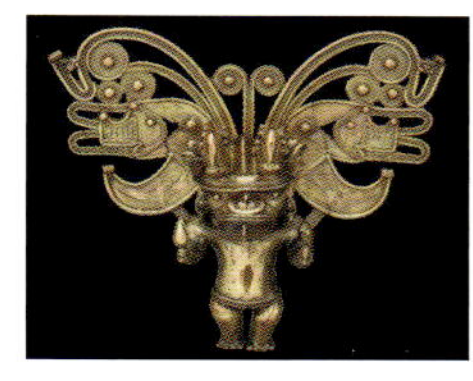

9 **Supernatural Powers**
Colombia, Tairona
Figure pendant
10th–16th century

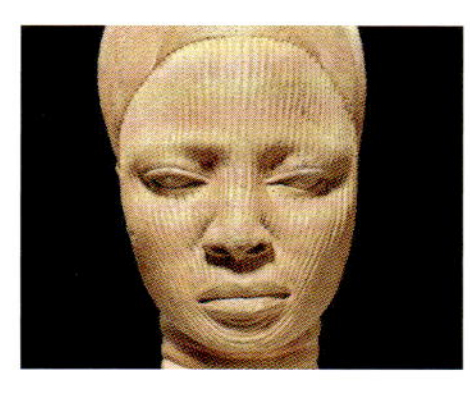

10 **Immortalizing Humanity**
Nigeria, Yoruba
Shrine head
12th–14th century

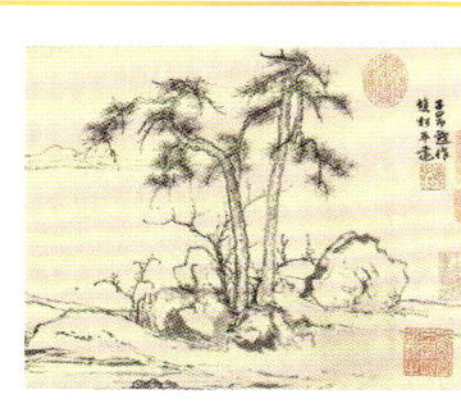

11 **Landscapes of the Mind**
Zhao Mengfu
Twin Pines, Level Distance
c. 1310

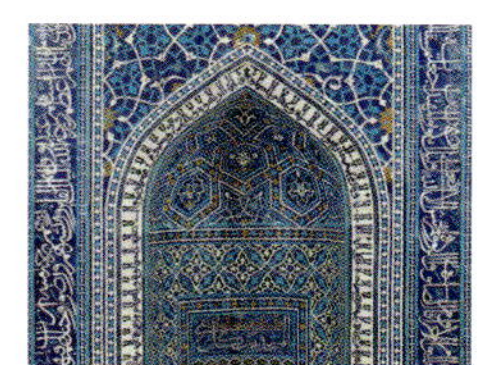

12 **Glorifying Words**
Iran, Islamic
Mihrab (*prayer niche*)
c. 1354–55

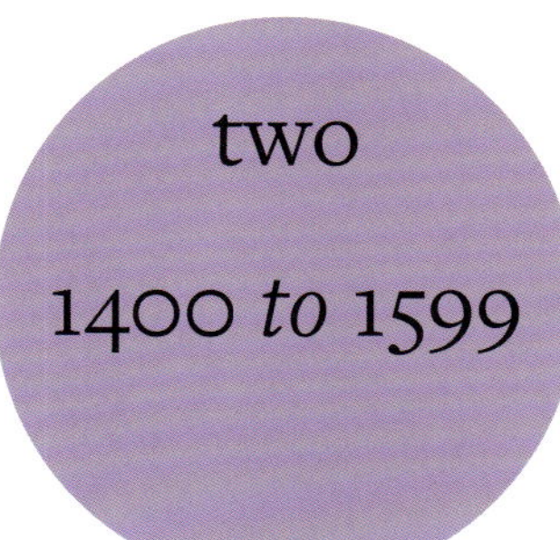

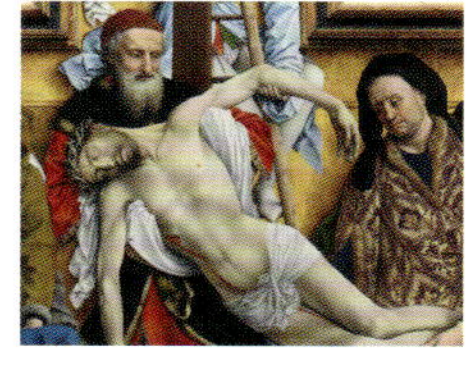

13 **Faith and Feeling**
Rogier van der Weyden
The Descent from the Cross
before 1443

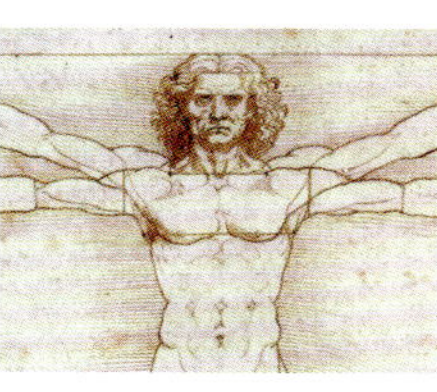

14 **Creating the Ideal**
Leonardo da Vinci
Vitruvian Man
c. 1490

Introduction—
how art works

Art Unpacked is for anyone who may be baffled by art, but is also curious about how it works. It is a friendly introduction to the history of visual culture, giving access to new types of art and providing a fresh look at familiar objects. The 50 works presented here span a vast range, from the earliest known images created by humans some 30,000 years ago (p. 12) to an installation at the US/Mexico border from 2017 (p. 228). They are not intended to represent pivotal masterpieces of history, but to suggest different approaches to the creation process, demonstrating just how varied the making and meaning of art itself can be.

My first ambition when writing this book was to dissolve boundaries between types of cultural artefacts, so that paintings and sculptures – often considered the traditional art forms – are examined alongside drawings, photographs, prints, ornaments, masks, book illustrations and posters. My second aim was to create links between 'western' art and the art of the rest of the world. With this in mind, I chose a core of relatively well-known artworks and familiar genres and set them alongside examples from global traditions to highlight some common aims and aspirations, while recognizing the cultural differences that give the works their character and make them unique.

Art-viewing toolkit

There are a few essential ways of seeing that can help unlock any work of art. Often referred to as 'formal analysis', these are the basic tools for appreciating art. One of these is form, the shape of a work or the shapes that are used within it. Another is colour, which can be utilized in a variety of ways: to describe action, show emotion, symbolize an idea, and so on. Primary colours are the boldest, while secondary and tertiary colours are often used to create a calmer atmosphere.

Composition is the arrangement of elements within an artwork. A composition can be orderly or disordered, equipoised or asymmetrical, diagonal, vertical or horizontal. Artists use composition to create works that are proportionate, harmonious and symmetrical, or unbalanced and visually discordant. Your gaze might follow the lines around shapes, or directional lines that guide the eye to a certain point for emphasis. In three-dimensional artworks, volume, mass and texture can be evaluated. In two-dimensional works that depict realistic scenes, the representation of space may be judged through the artist's use of perspective.

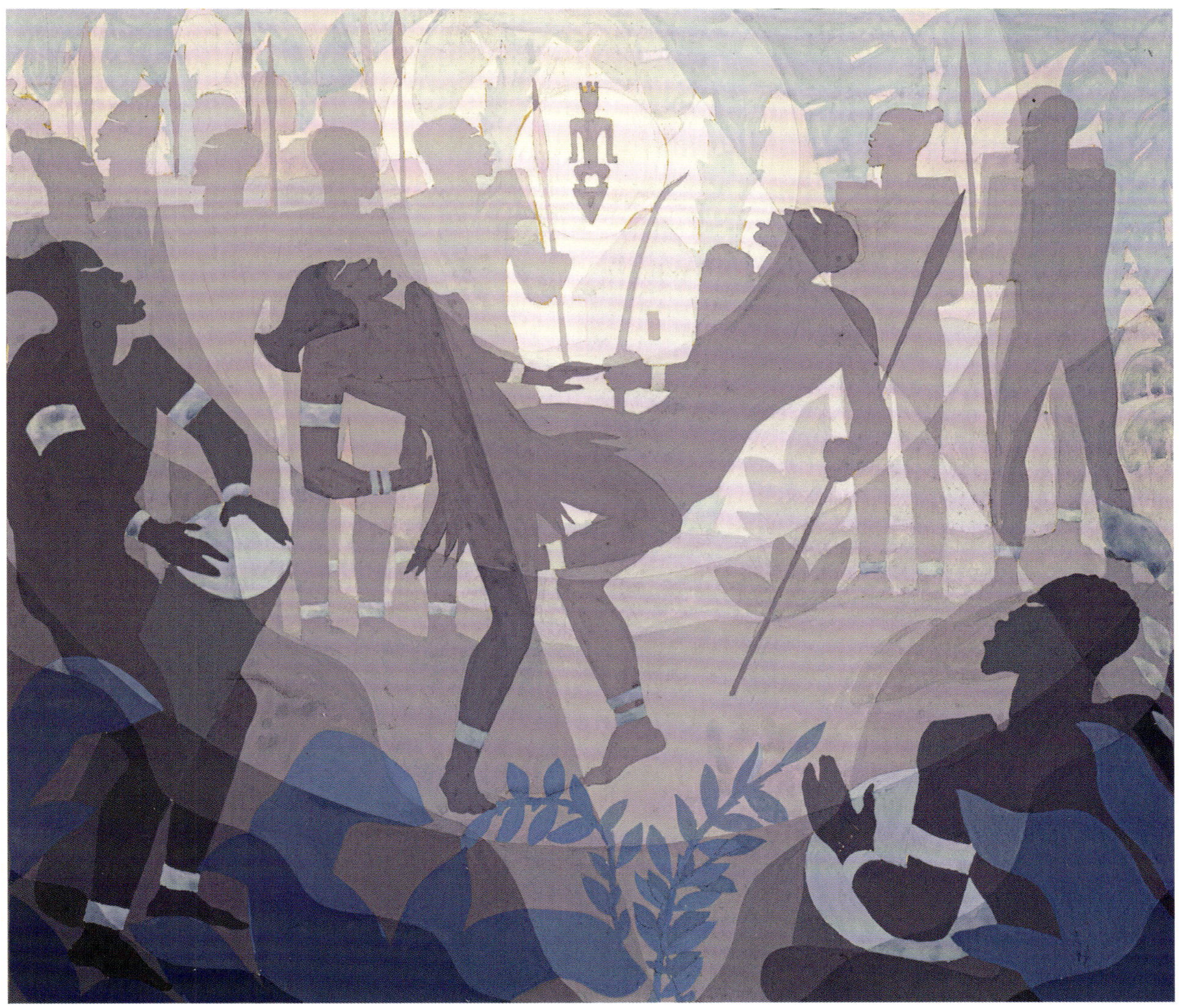

Aaron Douglas, *Study for Aspects of Negro Life: The Negro in an African Setting*, 1934.
Gouache, with touches of graphite, on illustration board, 37.2 × 40.6 cm, 14¾ × 16 in.

We can see how these elements help us to appreciate the principles behind many works of art. For example, in *Study for Aspects of Negro Life: The Negro in an African Setting* by Aaron Douglas (above), an artist who was a key figure of the Harlem Renaissance, a couple dance to the tempo of drums. The composition is made stable by translucent and symmetrical concentric circles positioned centrally within the composition, while the diagonal lines of the central couple introduce an element of dynamism. Tertiary colours (violet and amber) soften the action, making the whole scene seem like a vision, or a memory of a far-off time.

In Claude Monet's *The Bridge at Argenteuil* (ill. overleaf), fat clouds amble across a summer sky, boats glide beneath a stone bridge and sunlight breaks across the rippling water in a mosaic of colour. At first glance, it appears to be a scene that was captured spontaneously, and it is easy to miss Monet's visual structure. Repeated vertical forms like the masts and bridge piers create a steady rhythm across the composition, and intersect with the horizontal lines

Claude Monet, *The Bridge at Argenteuil*, 1874. Oil on canvas, 60 × 79.7 cm, 23½ × 31¼ in.

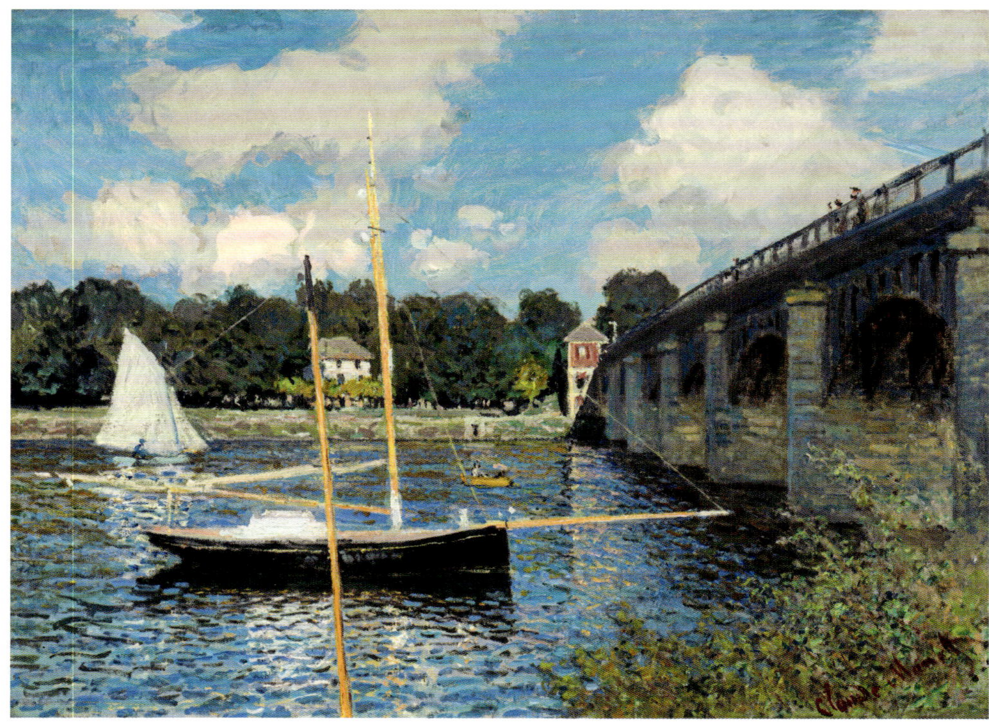

Key junctures in the painting correspond to a 5-by-5 grid, giving the work a subtle consistency and hidden logic. To establish linear perspective, straight lines (shown in white) extending away from the viewer seem to converge at a vanishing point in the distance. The space between the planes (in red) established by the bridge's piers appear to get closer together.

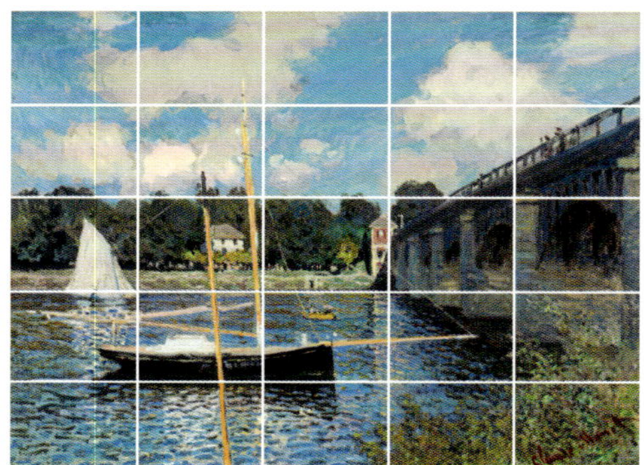

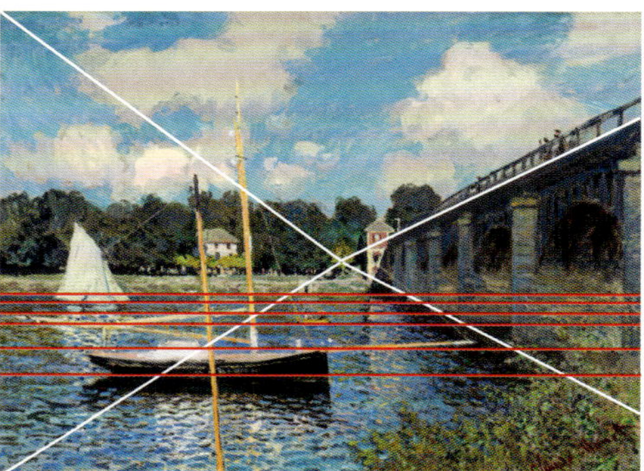

established by the riverbanks and tree line. The bridge is positioned so that it occupies almost exactly two-fifths of the scene from the right side, with the mast of the largest boat marking two-fifths from the left. This creates a stable visual architecture that underpins the composition. The angle of the bridge indicates depth through the application of the mathematical laws of linear perspective devised in the Renaissance. The lines of the bridge appear to converge at the 'vanishing point', as do the equally spaced horizontal lines (or planes) as they approach the horizon.

Even abstract artworks, like Joan Mitchell's *Piano mécanique* (opposite), can be appreciated using the same methods. Mitchell's brush marks have a steady cadence, swelling in shape at the lower centre and becoming more horizontal and compacted at the top, suggesting a landscape and the sensation of receding space. The colours, mainly primary tones, seem random at first, but have an inner connection: the blues swoop up from the bottom left, reds burn across the upper third, and yellows flicker over the surface level like dust on a car windscreen.

Roles, functions and uses

In the process of researching and writing about the 50 extraordinary works of art presented here, I have been reminded of just how diverse art is, and how many different roles it can fulfil. The examples in this book concern subjects ranging from power, science, nature, politics and spiritual beliefs to sorrow, perfection, violence, protection and personal identity. They were created for an incredible array of functions: to hang in people's homes, to complement the written word, to advertise products and ideas, to explain current affairs, to provoke, entertain, impress or shock. Some were designed to be gazed at; others to be worn, embody a divinity or sat upon.

Asking why a work of art was made and what its original function was is the gateway to a deeper understanding of the object in question. Discovering who commissioned it unlocks the dimension of patronage; probing into its historical context reveals fundamental aspects of the artist's political and social concerns, and curiosity about their race, gender, ethnicity or upbringing may give meaning to the style or subject matter. We might ask where such works were seen originally, or how and why they later came to be put on public view.

These kinds of questions broaden and deepen our relationship with art, enriching our appreciation of the facts of its creation and history, and our personal interaction with it. I hope that the following 50 works of art from around the world will help you gain a greater understanding of art, inspire your curiosity and spark your enjoyment of art in all its forms.

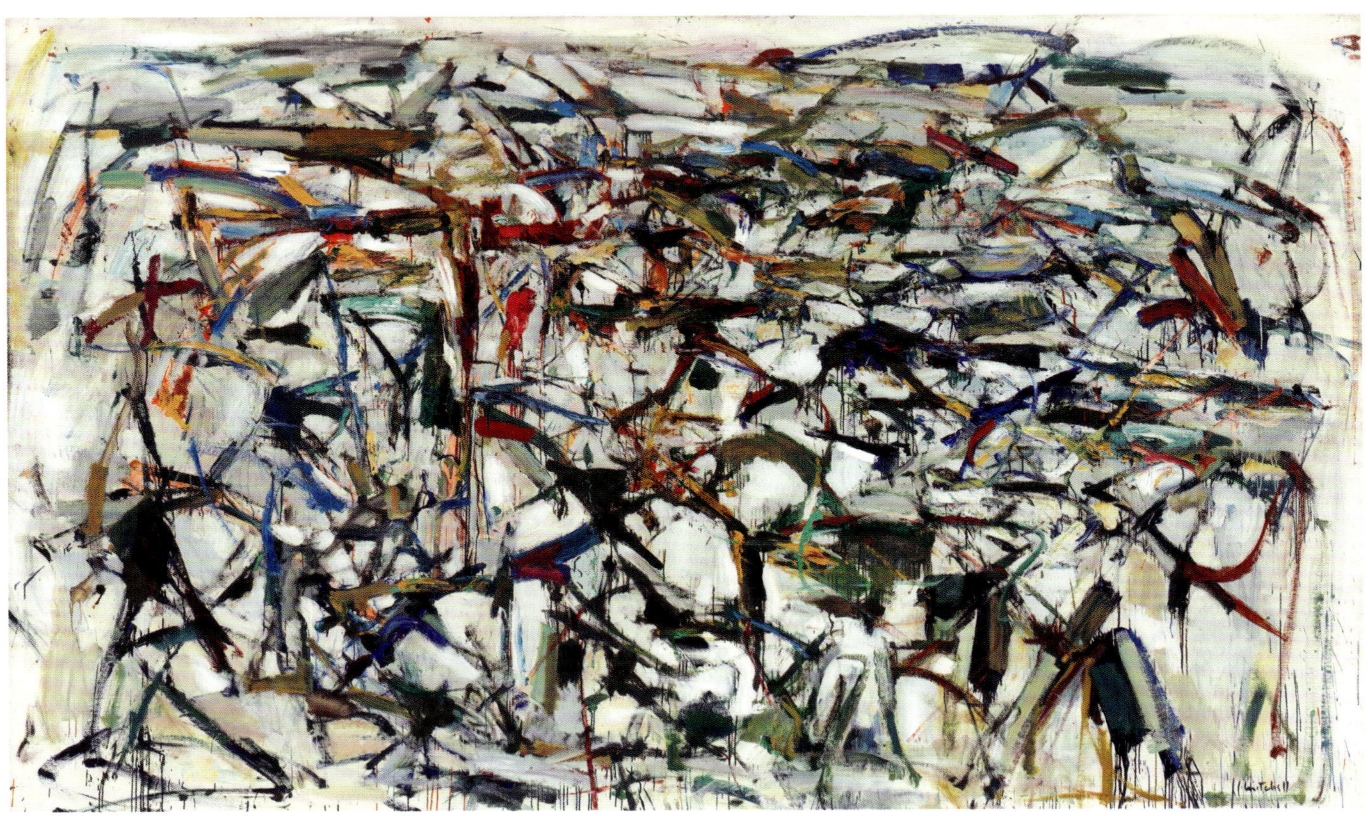

Joan Mitchell, *Piano mécanique*, 1958. Oil on canvas, 198.1 × 318.8 cm, 78 × 125½ in.

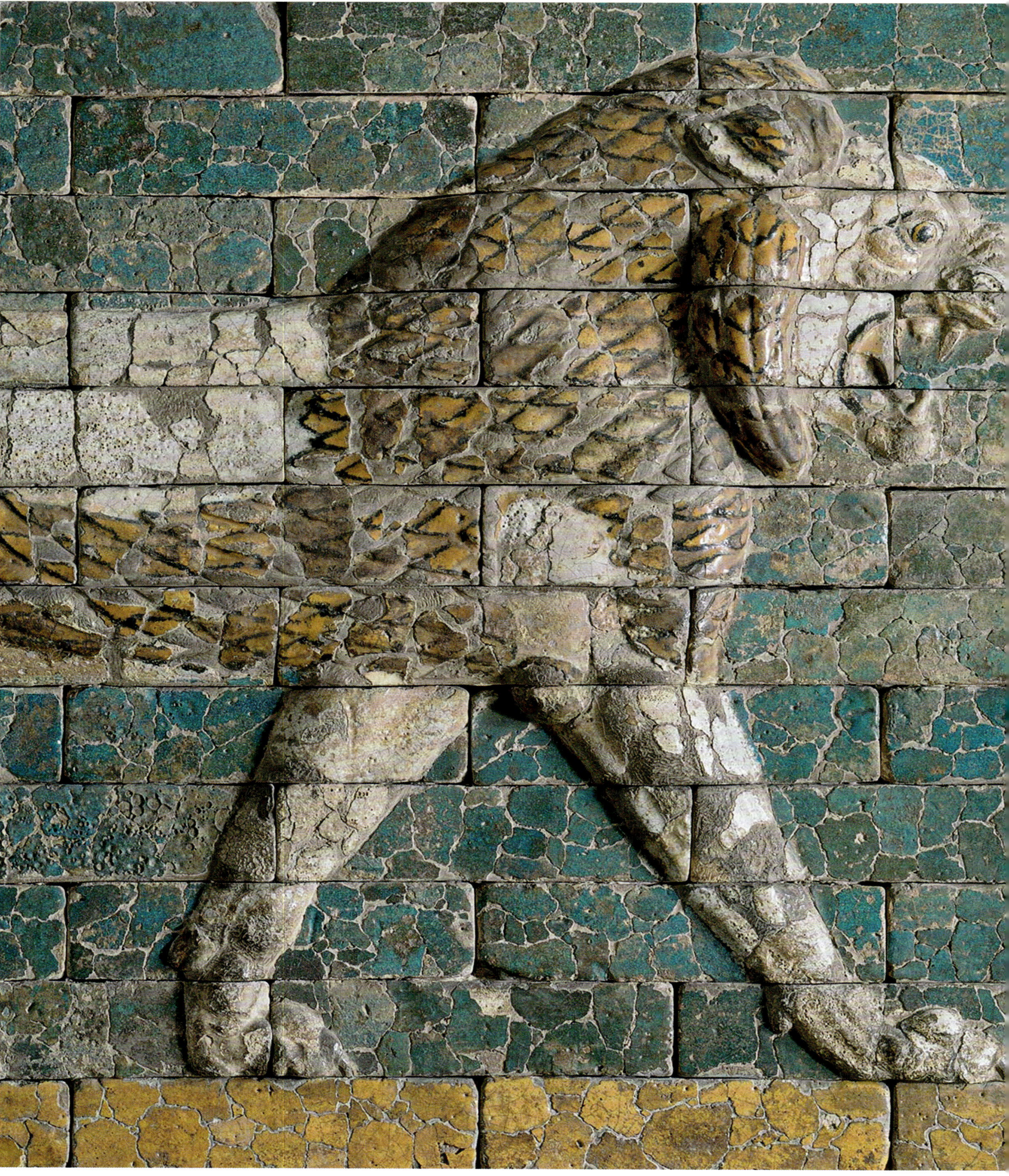

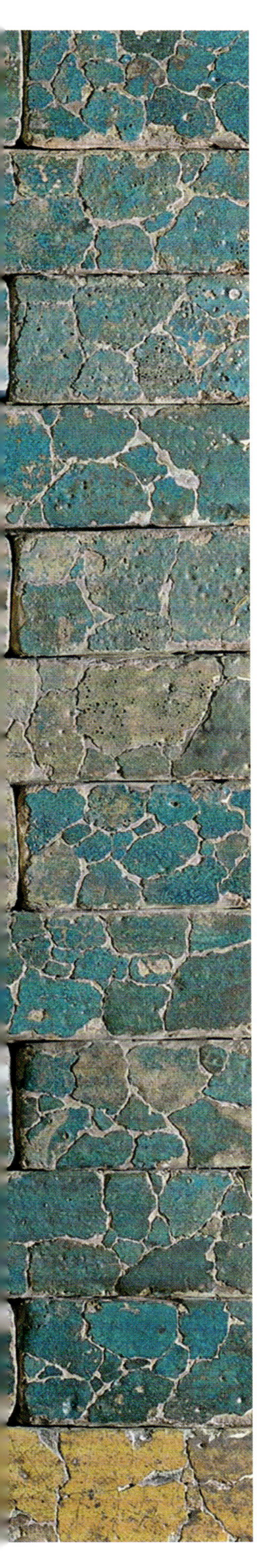

1. The *roots* of art

30,000 BCE *to* 1399 CE

The oldest surviving works of art are found in Palaeolithic sites. The best preserved, however, are from the world's first cities, demonstrating the far-reaching power of ancient empires and religions. These works became a wellspring of inspiration for the artists of the future, and the roots of long-lasting artistic traditions.

30,000 BCE *to* 1399 CE

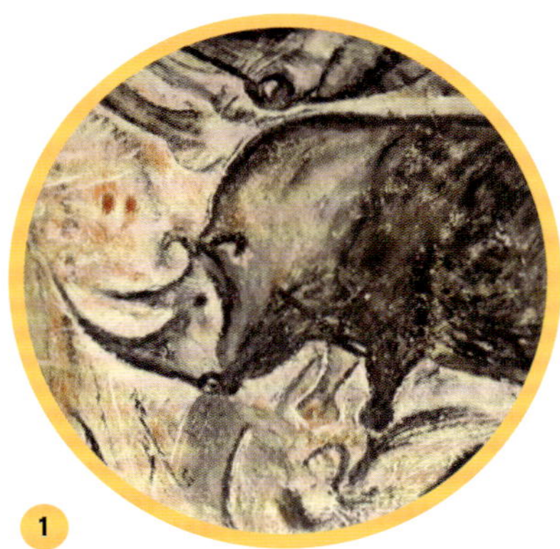

1

Animal Magic

France, Aurignacian
Rhinoceros panel
c. 30,000 BCE

Art for the Afterlife

Egypt, New Kingdom
Funerary mask of Tutankhamun
1327–18 BCE

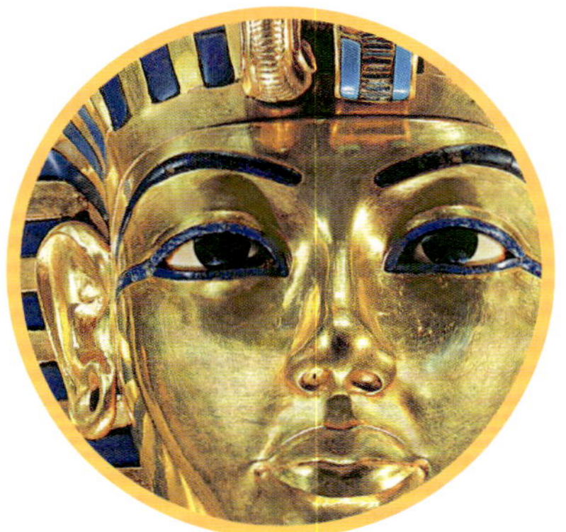

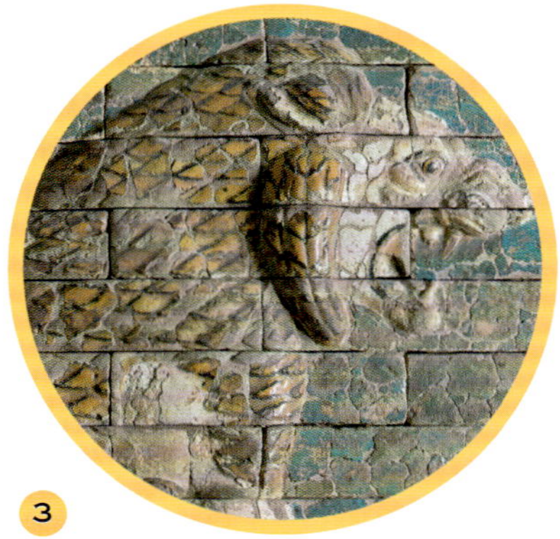

3

Guardians of Ceremony

Iraq, Neo-Babylonian
Panel with striding lion
c. 604–562 BCE

4

Man and Superman

Turkey, Roman
The Emperor as Philosopher
c. 180–200 CE

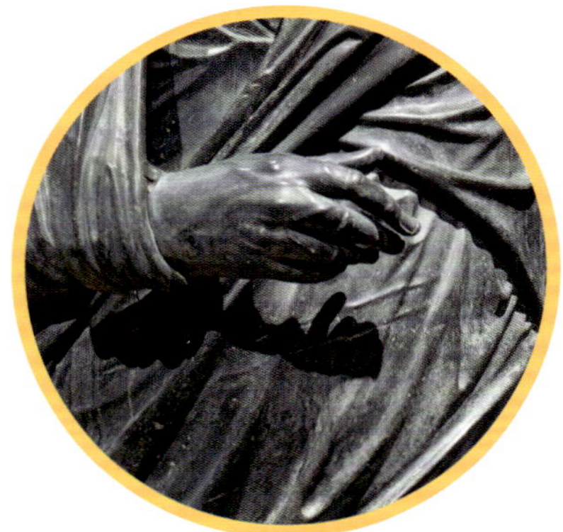

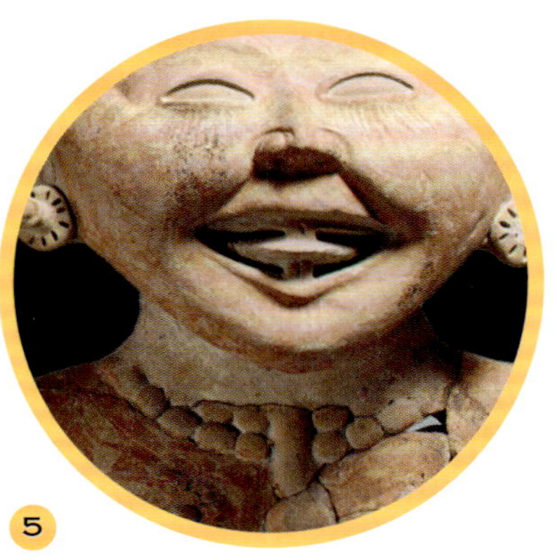

5

Spiritual Rapture

Mexico, Remojadas
'Smiling' figure
7th–8th century

Patterns of the Mind

Scotland, Hiberno-Saxon
Chi-Rho-Iota page, Book of Kells
c. 800

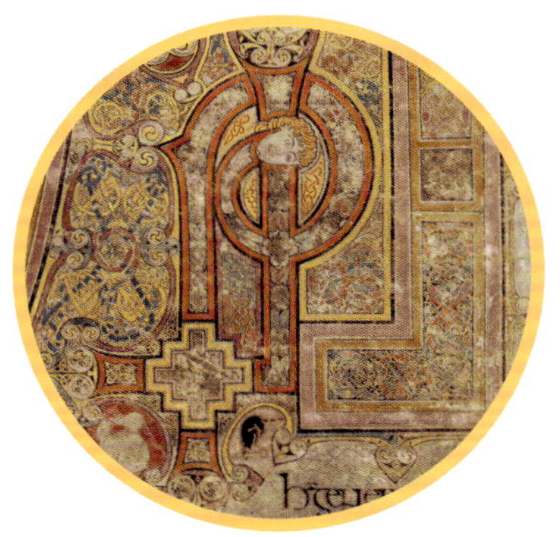

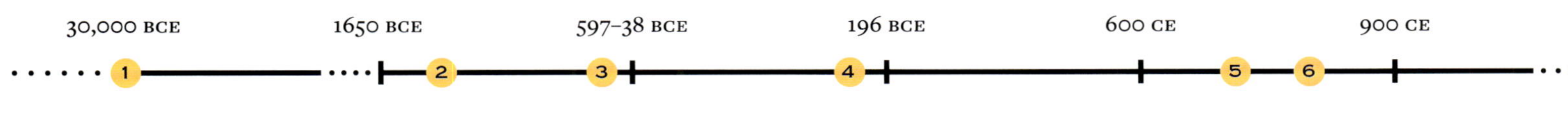

30,000 BCE — Neanderthals become extinct in Europe

1650 BCE — The Mycenaean civilization emerges in mainland Greece

597–38 BCE — The Babylonian captivity of the Jews

196 BCE — The Rosetta Stone is carved

600 CE — Porcelain is invented in China

900 CE — The lost-wax method is introduced to Mesoamerica

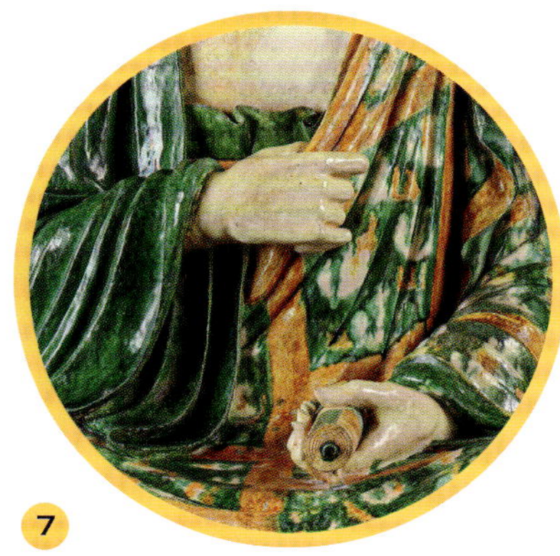

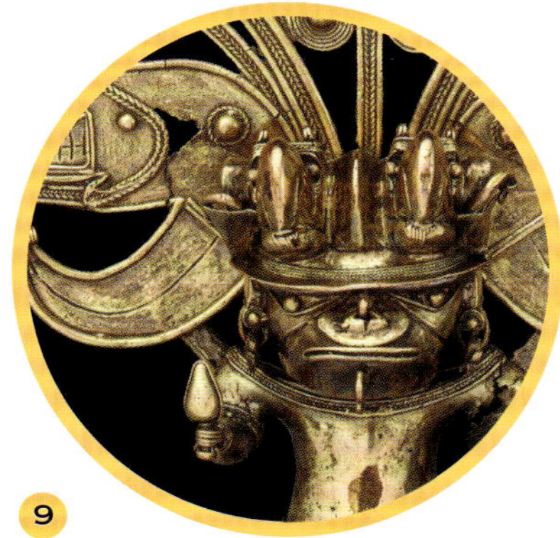

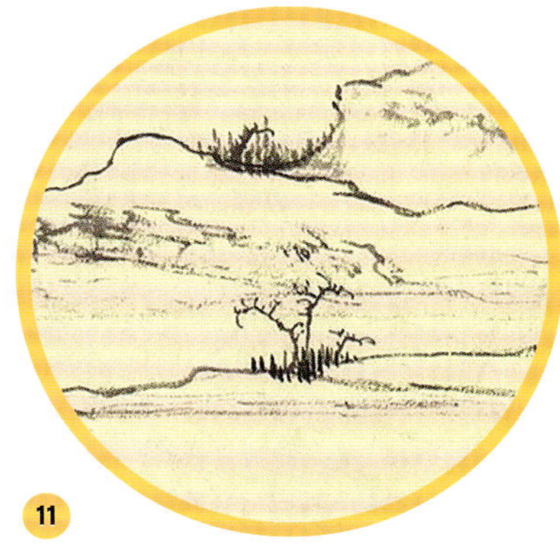

7

Elevated Wisdom
China, Liao dynasty
Arhat (Luohan)
c. 1000

9

Supernatural Powers
Colombia, Tairona
Figure pendant
10th–16th century

11

Landscapes of the Mind
Zhao Mengfu
Twin Pines, Level Distance
c. 1310

Cosmic Dancing
India, Chola dynasty
Shiva as Lord of the Dance (Nataraja), *c.* 11th century

10

Immortalizing Humanity
Nigeria, Yoruba
Shrine head
12th–14th century

Glorifying Words
Iran, Islamic
Mihrab (prayer niche)
c. 1354–55

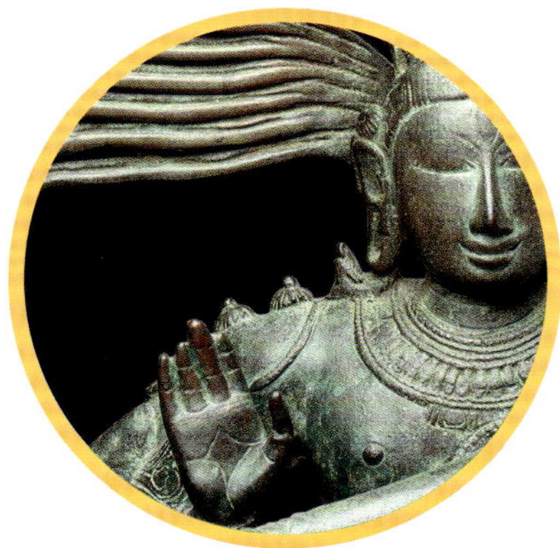

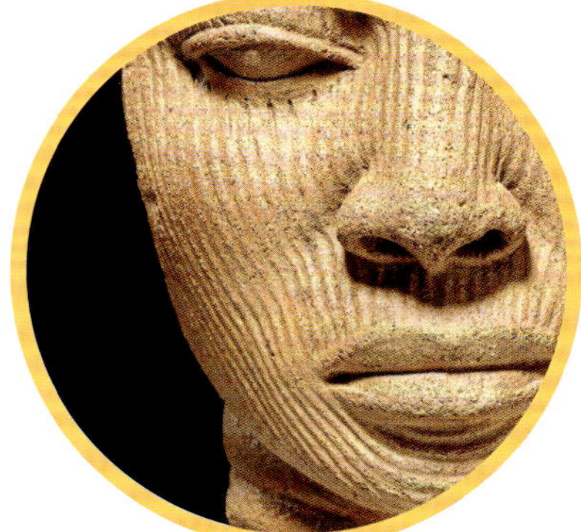

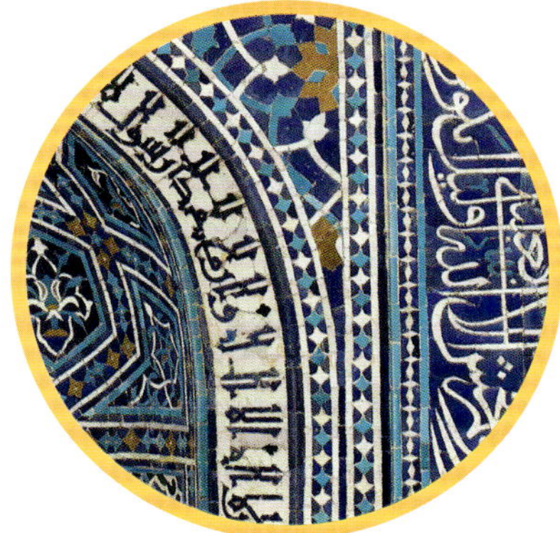

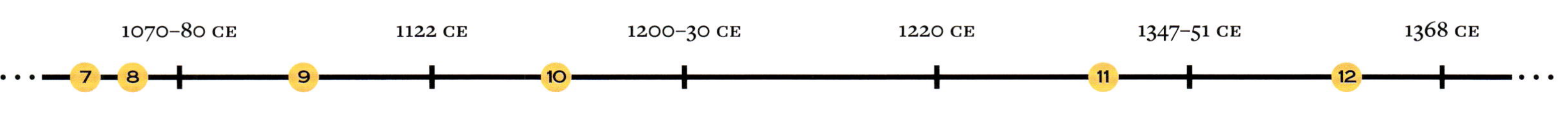

The Bayeaux Tapestry is created

Construction begins at Angkor Wat, Cambodia

The first Icelandic family sagas are written

The kingdom of Great Zimbabwe emerges in southern Africa

The Black Death kills a third of Europe's population

The Mongols are expelled from China

1. Animal Magic

Over 30,000 years ago, aided only by the dim, guttering light of an animal-fat lamp, an artist working deep inside a cave in the Ardèche valley in France brought a group of rhinoceros and other animals to life on a wall of rock.

Light must have been the most important material for the artists working in those deep, dark spaces. Without it, their inscriptions and marks in charcoal, ochre or haematite (iron oxide) could not be drawn, nor could they become 'art' through the act of being seen by someone else. A rockslide at Chauvet later ensured that no form of light or other people would enter the cave for thousands of years. The next humans to bring both light and appreciative eyes to this scene – and the hundreds of others that surround it – were three cave explorers in December 1994. The discovery kickstarted an ongoing dialogue about the artistic sophistication of these ancient images, and what they would have meant to the people who made them.

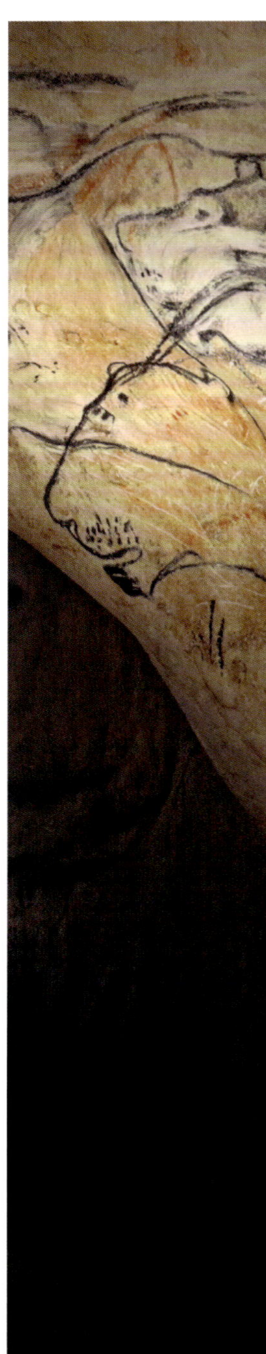

Charcoal and ochre on rock
Chauvet cave, Ardèche

France, Aurignacian
Rhinoceros panel
c. 30,000 BCE

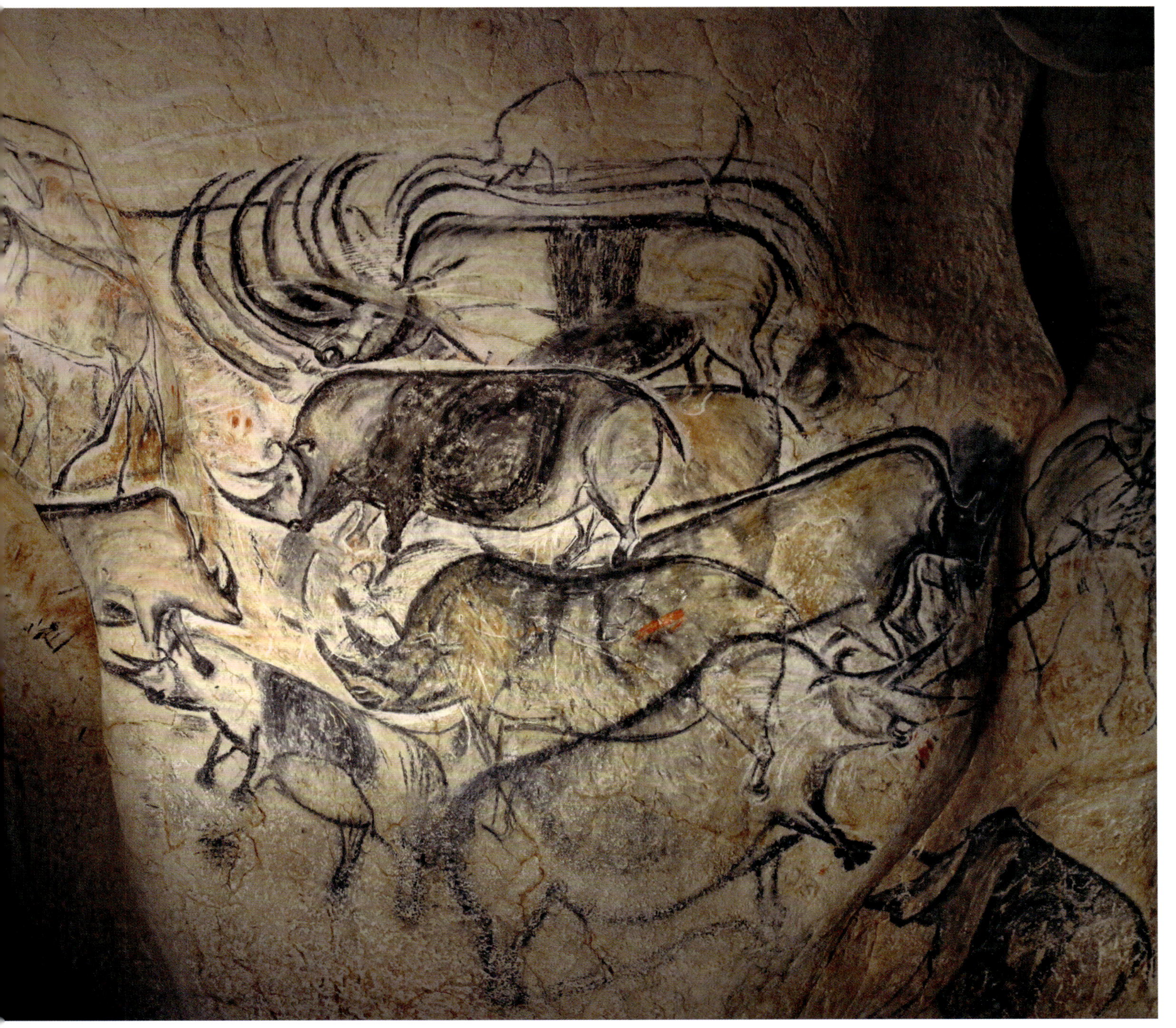

❶ Parallel lines

A blur of furious activity draws our eye to the middle distance. Is it a throng of rhinos, or one animal whose crashing momentum leaves an echo of repeated lines in its wake?

❷ Wild beasts

Works of art from the Palaeolithic era show that their creators were fascinated by the animal world. Wild animals were a vital source of food and materials, and knowing how to track and hunt them was critical for survival. Rhinoceros, however, were not killed for food and were probably regarded as exotic or exalted beasts, seldom seen and thus perhaps more revered.

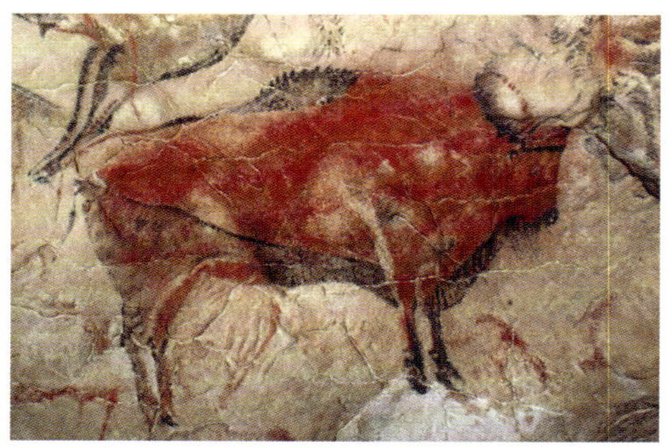

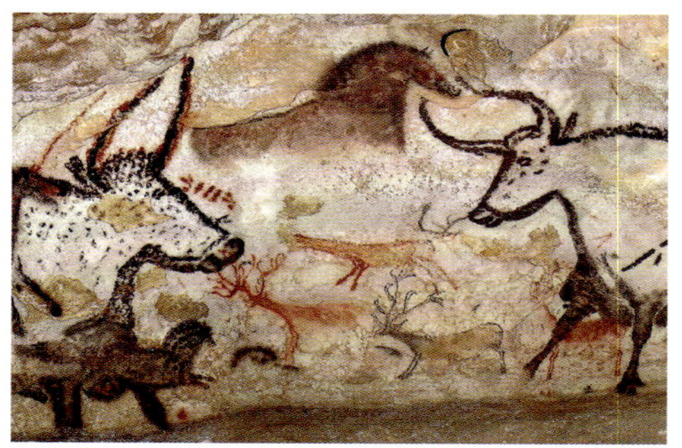

↑ Hall of Bulls, *c.* 15,000 BCE. Lascaux cave, Dordogne, France

↑↑ Herd of bison from the ceiling of the main hall, *c.* 12,500 BCE. Altamira cave, Spain

❸ Purpose

What was the original intent of paintings like these at the Chauvet caves and at other sites, including the caves at Altamira in Spain and Lascaux in France? Given the enormous time span that lies between us and their creation, it is unlikely we will ever know. Several theories have been put forward about their meaning, including:

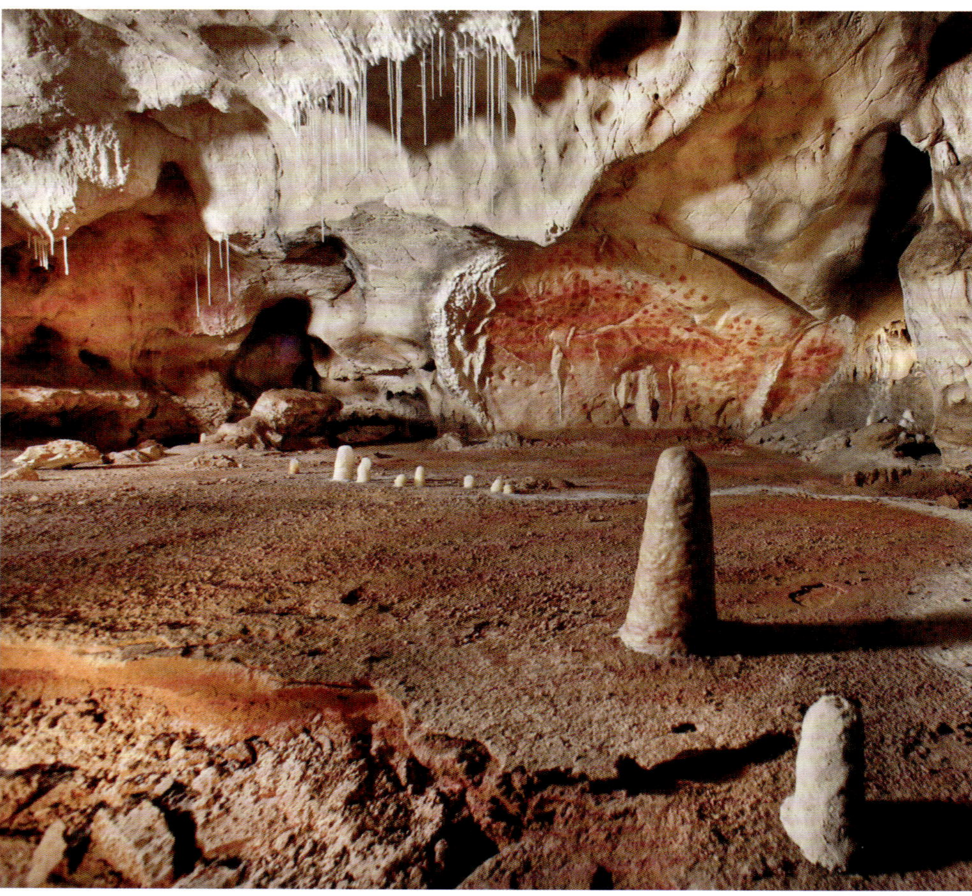

- The paintings depict the wars of ancient tribes, represented by their animal totems (Max Raphael).
- They are concerned with fertility, as they show species during their reproductive season (Norbert Aujoulat, referring to the Lascaux paintings).
- They illustrate epic stories about the 'mythic universe' of the artists' belief system (Carole Fritz and Gilles Tosello).
- They were used in religious ceremonies to unify humans with a spirit world represented by animals (David Lewis-Williams and Jean Clottes).[1]

❹ Proportion

It is extraordinary that these artists were able to represent animals with such accurate proportions. They must have been painted from memory, as the artists would not have been able to draw the animals from life.

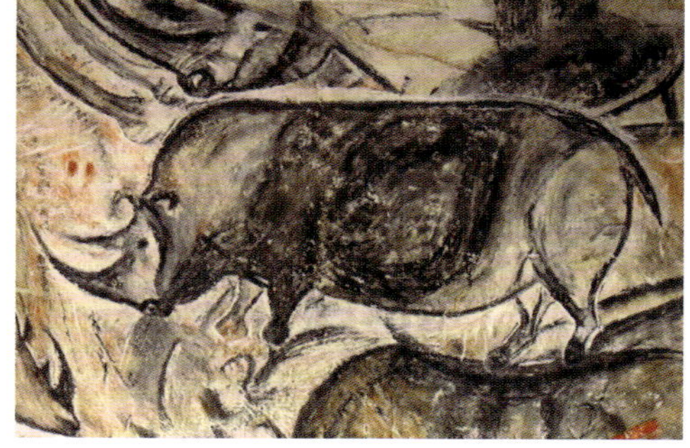

❺ Creative revolution

It is believed that the paintings stem from a period of creative evolution in the minds of *Homo sapiens*. They are evidence that in around 40,000 to 30,000 BCE humans discovered the power of imagination and developed a sophisticated art culture that communicated through vivid and emotive visual storytelling.

❻ Meeting places

This period of development is known as the Aurignacian. It is possible that the people who lived then used sites like Chauvet, Altamira and Lascaux as gathering places, much like a temple or cathedral, where they would assemble at significant moments during the year.

7 Surface

The artists made use of the shape of the cave walls to enhance their drawings. Sometimes they would draw the animals' bodies onto bulging areas of the rock face to make them seem even more three-dimensional. In other places, they would deliberately depict the animals as if they were emerging from the natural crevasses of the cave walls.

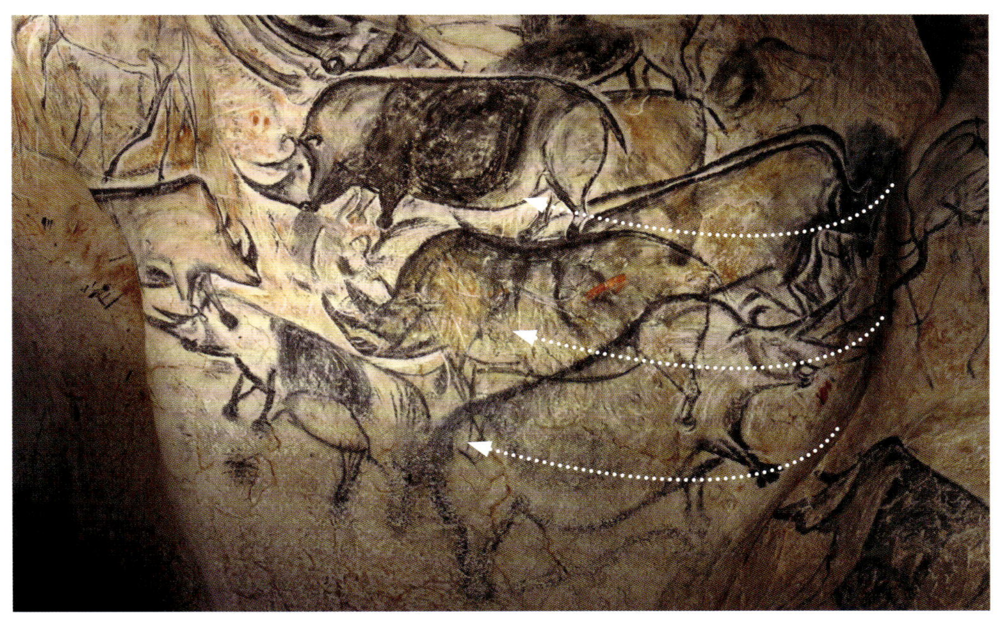

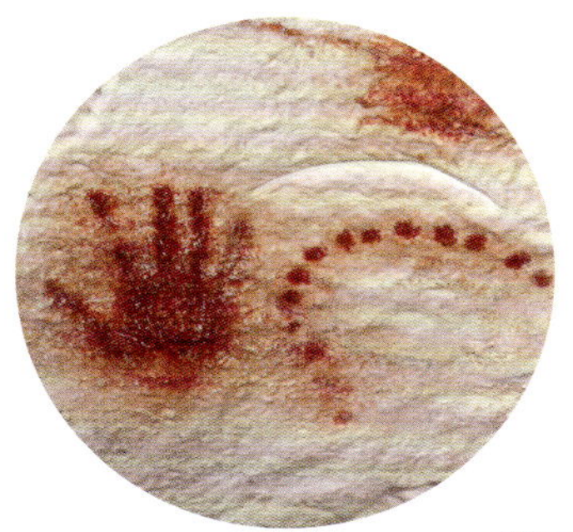

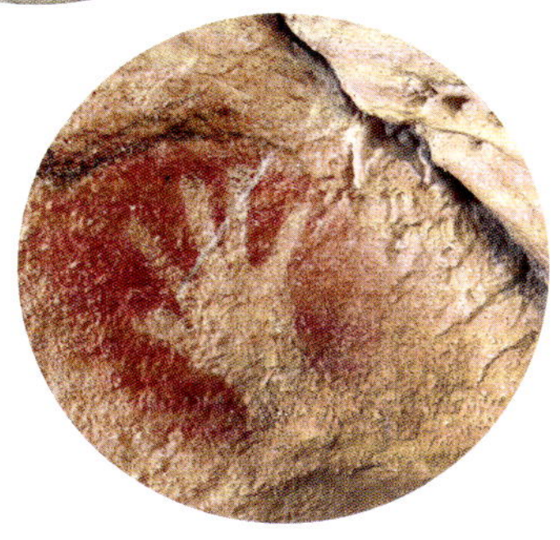

Hand stencils, *c.* 30,000 BCE. Chauvet cave, Ardèche, France

8 Light

Apart from charcoal, flint and red ochre, another key material used in the caves was light. The artists would have needed fire to work, whether in hand-held lamps made using animal fat and a wick, or in hearths on the cave floor. It would have allowed the paintings to be seen and displayed via the atmospheric, flickering illumination of fire.

9 Technique

The works show a sophisticated knowledge of shading – with thicker outlines to suggest shadow, and smudging of the charcoal to create a sense of volume – and perspective. The overlapping forms also give the impression of animals that are represented realistically, as if from the vantage point of a stationary viewer in daylight.

10 Mark-making

Charcoal, made from the wood of a pine tree, is the main medium, used in combination with areas inscribed with stone tools. In other places, red ochre was used. There are also palm prints where a paint-daubed hand has been pressed onto the rock face, and areas where powdered pigment was blown through tubes onto hands to create stencils (above). Researchers have even discovered brushes and pieces of haematite shaped into hand-held drawing tools.[2]

11 Impact

When cave paintings were rediscovered at the end of the 19th century, they were believed by some scholars to be fakes, as the makers' knowledge of art techniques seemed too advanced. It had previously been thought that shading and perspective were invented much later, in cultures such as ancient Egypt, Mesopotamia and Greece.

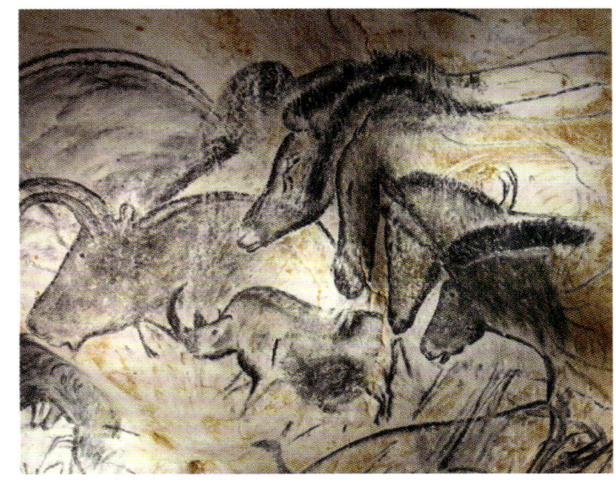

Frieze of horses, rhinoceros and aurochs, *c.* 30,000 BCE. Chauvet cave, Ardèche, France

12 Dating

Radiocarbon dating has determined that the works in the Chauvet cave date to two distinct periods. The oldest were made around 36,000 years ago, with a second group of artists adding additional paintings some 5,000 years later. The discovery of the true age of these artworks has led to a reappraisal of human artistic cultivation as occurring much further back in history than previously thought.

LINKED PRACTITIONERS

UPPER PALAEOLITHIC ART:

Artists of Gabarnmung (*c.* 42,000 BCE), AUSTRALIA
Artists of the Maros-Pangkep caves (*c.* 41,000 BCE), INDONESIA
Artist of the Lion-man (*c.* 40,000–35,000 BCE), GERMANY
Artist of the Venus of Willendorf (*c.* 30,000–25,000 BCE), AUSTRIA

MOTION LINES:

Diego Velázquez (1599–1660), SPAIN
Giacomo Balla (1871–1958), ITALY
Marcel Duchamp (1887–1968), FRANCE
Harold Edgerton (1903–1990), USA
Roy Lichtenstein (1923–1997), USA

CHARCOAL:

Leonardo da Vinci (1452–1519), ITALY
J.A.M. Whistler (1834–1903), USA/UK
Odilon Redon (1840–1916), FRANCE
Suzanne Valadon (1865–1938), FRANCE
Lee Krasner (1908–1984), USA

2. Art for the Afterlife

When this beautiful mask was made, the artists were creating an object that would last for eternity. Yet despite the skill and expensive materials that went into its production, the mask remained hidden away for over 3,000 years, sealed inside three coffins, deep within a burial chamber carved in the rock.

In the innermost sarcophagus was the mummy of Tutankhamun, pharaoh of the two kingdoms of Egypt, who had died aged 19. After his death, the body had been dried out with salt and wrapped in linen, then placed inside its tomb. These elaborate precautions were intended to ensure the deceased pharaoh a safe journey into the afterlife. Such matters were of overwhelming significance for the people of ancient Egypt, and the impetus behind their dramatic artistic and architectural output. 'The Egyptians say that their houses are only temporary lodgings,' wrote the Greek historian Diodorus Siculus in the 1st century BCE, 'and their graves are their houses.'

Gold, lapis lazuli, glass paste, obsidian and turquoise
54 × 39.3 cm, 21¼ × 15½ in.
The Egyptian Museum, Cairo

Egypt, New Kingdom
Funerary mask of Tutankhamun
1327–18 BCE

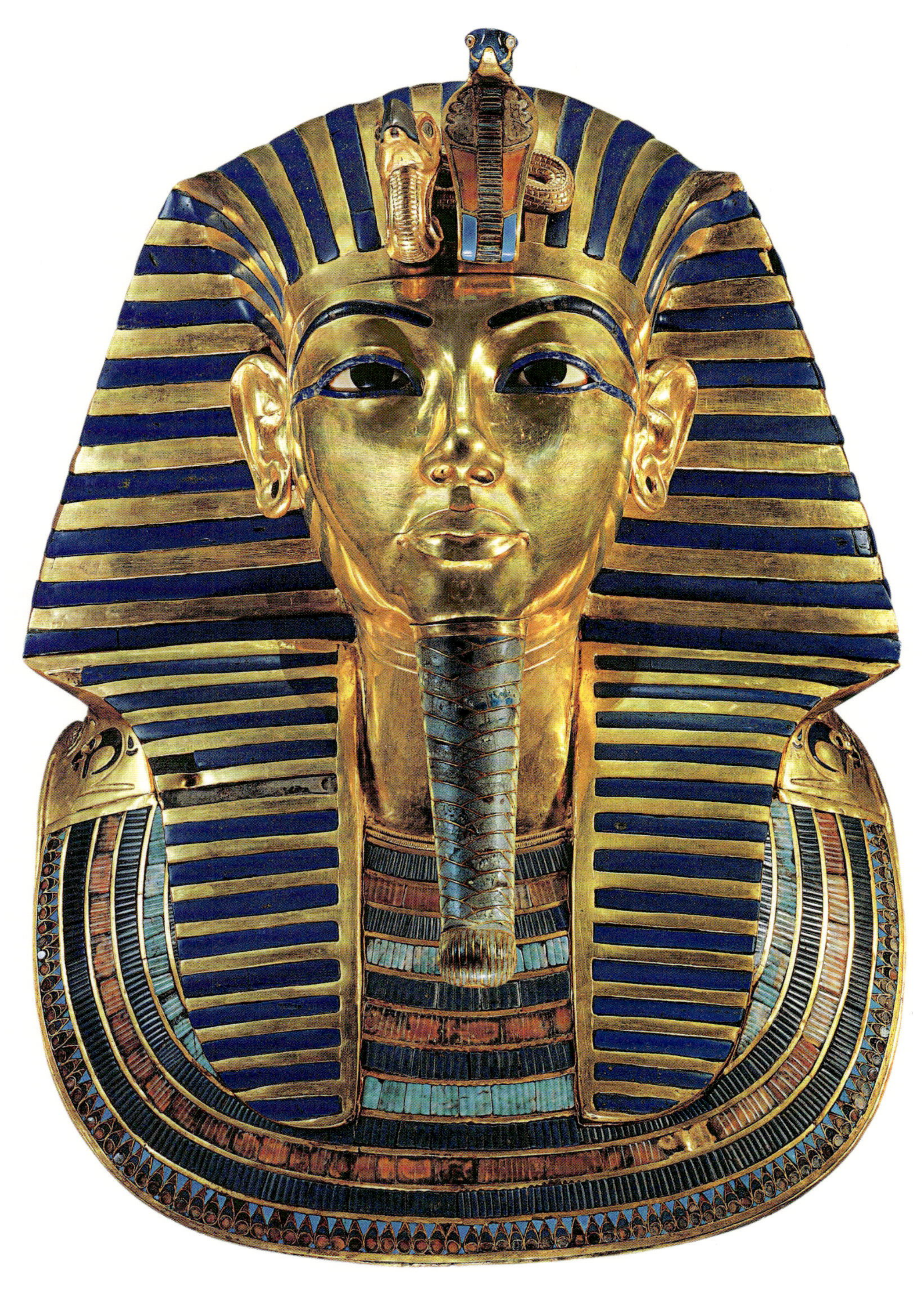

❶ *Nemes* headdress

Tutankhamun is shown wearing a *nemes* headdress, a piece of striped and pleated cloth fixed to a band, worn across the forehead and incorporating two flaps, or lapets, which hang down over the shoulders. The headdress is represented with strips of gold and blue glass.

❷ Divine ruler

Ancient Egyptians believed that the pharaohs possessed semi-divine powers. In keeping with representations of the gods, Tutankhamun has hair made from lapis lazuli and skin of gold, perhaps to align himself with Osiris, the god of the dead and weigher of souls, who will allow him to rule in the kingdom of the afterlife.

❸ Make-up

Lapis lazuli inlays around the eyes of the mask imitate the make-up the pharaoh would have worn in life. The pupils are made from obsidian, and the whites of the eyes from quartz.

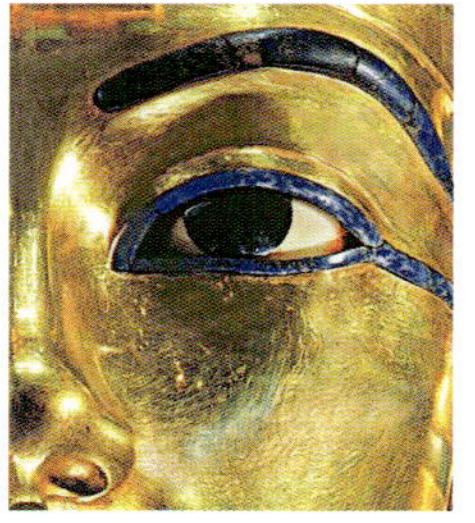

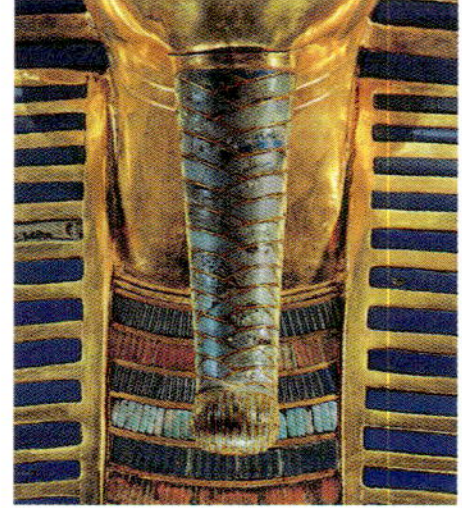

❹ Beard

Along with the hair of lapis lazuli and skin of gold, the false beard was another indicator of the pharaoh as a god, further reinforcing the idea of divinity.[3]

❺ A time of change

Tutankhamun was probably the son of the previous pharaoh, Akhenaten, a controversial figure who replaced the existing belief system of multiple gods with a single deity – the sun god Aten – and moved the religious capital to Amarna. After Akhenaten's death, Tutankhamun restored the old religion and the focus of worship to the god Amun, and returned the capital to Thebes.

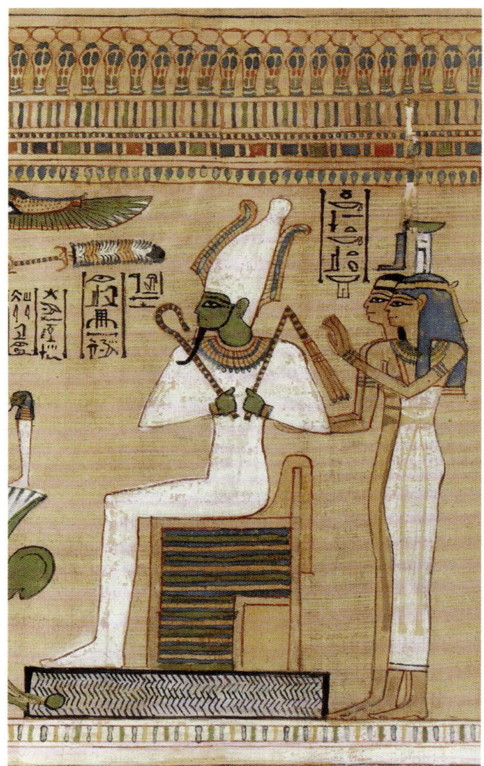

Book of the Dead of Hunefer (detail), Egypt, 19th dynasty, *c.* 13th century BCE. Papyrus, overall 38.9 × 550 cm, 15¼ × 216½ in.

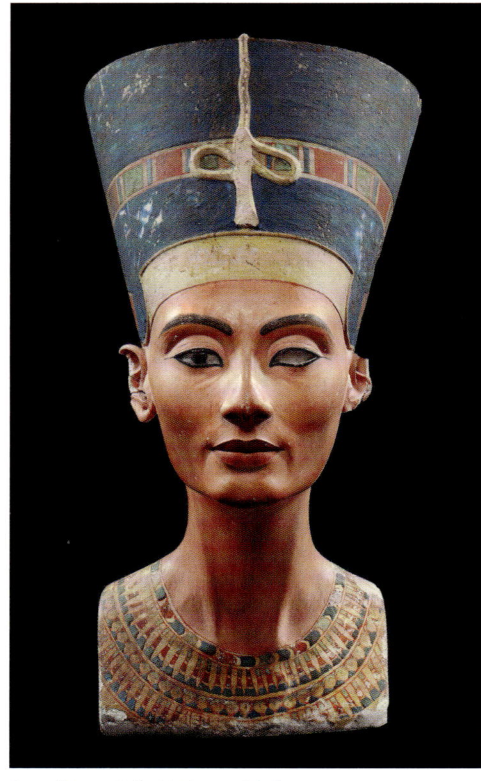

Bust of Queen Nefertiti, Egypt, 18th dynasty, *c.* 1351–34 BCE. Limestone, painted stucco, quartz and wax, 49 × 24.5 × 35 cm, 19¼ × 9¾ × 13¾ in.

❻ Authority

Tutankhamun became pharaoh at the age of nine, and died ten years later. He was ruler of Upper Egypt in the south and Lower Egypt in the north, nearest the Mediterranean Sea. The two figures on the headdress are the guardians of Upper and Lower Egypt: Nekhbet (symbolized by a vulture) and Wadjet (a snake). Together, they represent the unification of the two regions of the kingdom.

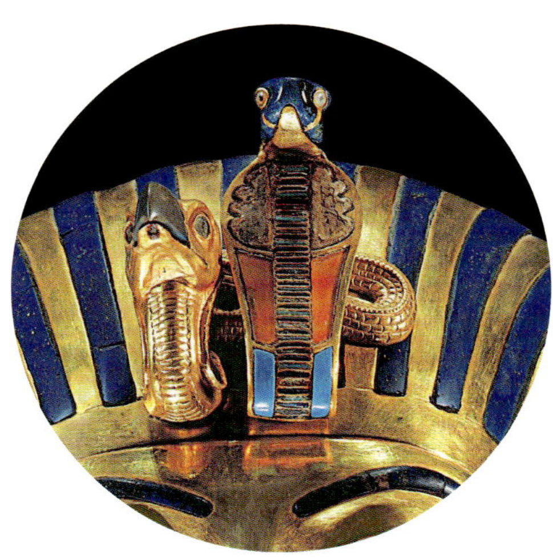

❼ Tutankhamun?

The face of the mask is similar to other representations in the tomb of the boy king. But some scholars have speculated that the *nemes* headdress may have been reused from another burial mask, perhaps that of Nefertiti (above), the wife of Akhenaten (and possibly Tutankhamun's mother). This is, in part, because of the different qualities of gold in the face (23.2 kt) and the headdress (23.5 kt).

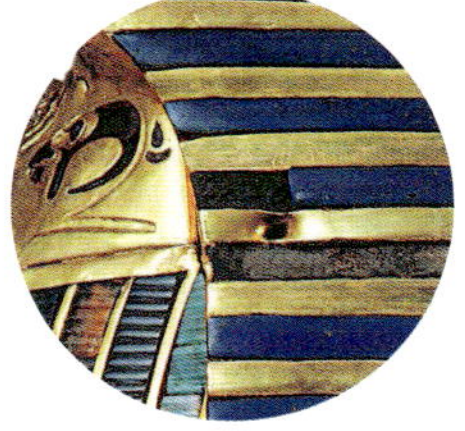

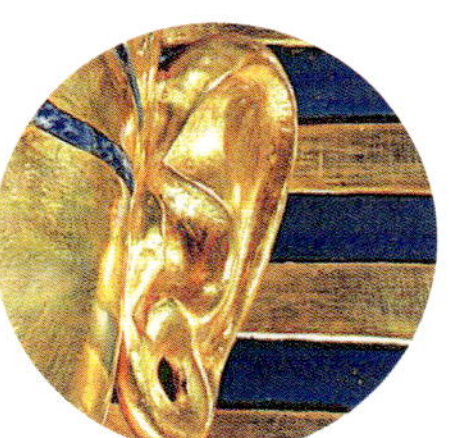

❽ Holes

There are several holes in the mask. A wire would have been threaded through the hole in the left lapet to hold the crook and flail in place. The holes for earrings in the earlobes have since been filled in with gold foil.

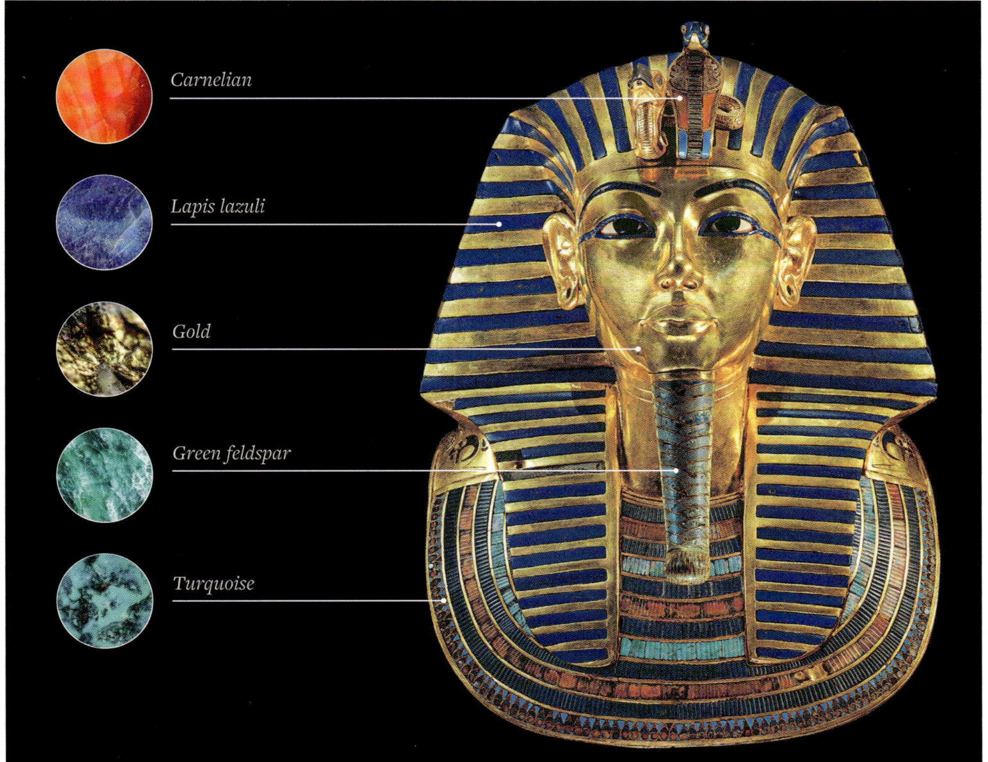

❾ Gold

The mask is made of solid gold, a material associated with Ra, another sun god. Weighing 10 kg (over 22 lbs), it was constructed from two sections of flat gold, hammered into shape and further decorated with inlaid precious stones such as carnelian, green feldspar, turquoise and lapis lazuli. The gold used for the face has a slightly lighter tone than that used for the headdress.

❿ Land of the Dead

On the back of the mask is a tract of hieroglyphic text relaying Spell 151b from the Book of the Dead (below). This incantation explains how to protect the body in the afterlife.

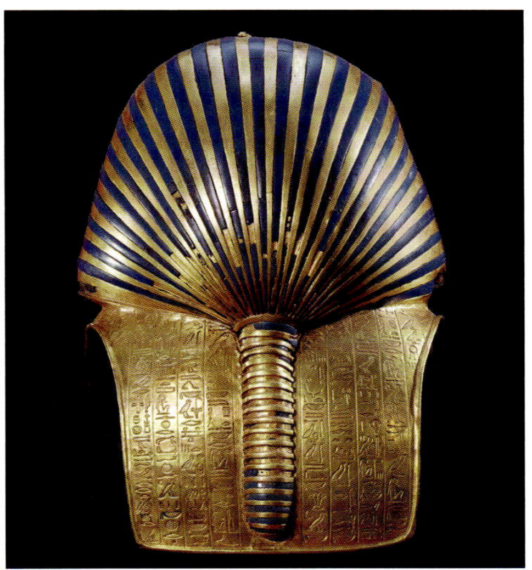

⓫ Discovery

After being sealed, the tomb remained undisturbed for over 3,000 years until it was rediscovered by Howard Carter in 1922. After a period of investigation, the coffins were opened in 1925.

⓬ Russian doll

A photograph by Harry Burton from the time captures Howard Carter examining the innermost sarcophagus of Tutankhamun. The middle and outer coffins were both made from wood and gilded, and further decorated with precious materials such as multicoloured glass, lapis lazuli and turquoise.[4]

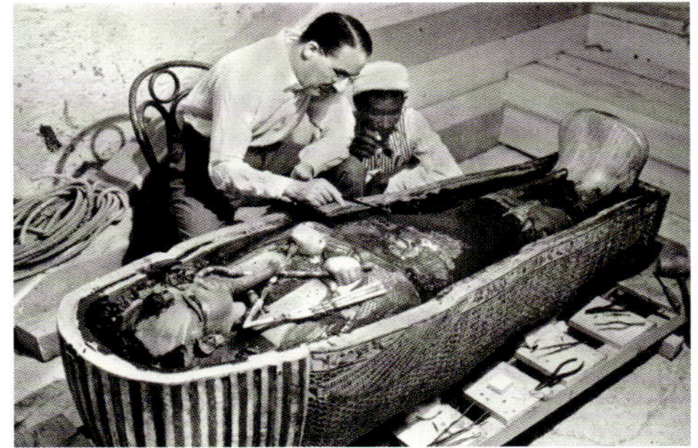

⓭ In need of a clean

When it was discovered, the mask was not in the pristine condition we see today. Covering it were large quantities of the black anointing liquid used in the royal funeral ceremony.

⓮ Falcons

Falcons are depicted on each shoulder. These were prestigious birds in ancient Egypt, associated with the deity Horus (who had a falcon's head) and with the pharaoh himself.

LINKED PRACTITIONERS

EGYPTIAN ART AND ARTEFACTS:

Artist of the Seated Scribe (*c.* 2620–2500 BCE), LOUVRE, PARIS
Artist of Hippopotamus 'William' (*c.* 1961–1878 BCE), METROPOLITAN MUSEUM OF ART, NEW YORK
Artist of the Bust of Queen Nefertiti (*c.* 1351–34 BCE), NEUES MUSEUM, BERLIN
Artist of the Younger Memnon (1270 BCE), BRITISH MUSEUM, LONDON
Artist of the Rosetta Stone (196 BCE), BRITISH MUSEUM, LONDON

FALCONS:

Artist of Plaque depicting a falcon, probably the god Horus (*c.* 664–525 BCE), SMITHSONIAN, WASHINGTON, DC
Artist of the Bayeux Tapestry (11th century), BAYEUX MUSEUM, NORMANDY
Hans Holbein the Younger (1497–1543), GERMANY
Artist of Falconer with two ladies, a page and a foot soldier (*c.* 1500–30), METROPOLITAN MUSEUM OF ART, NEW YORK
Artist of A mounted man hunting birds with a falcon (early 18th century), SMITHSONIAN, WASHINGTON, DC

FUNEREAL ART:

Artist of the Sarcophagus of the spouses (*c.* 530–10 BCE), NATIONAL ETRUSCAN MUSEUM, ROME
Artist of the Sarcophagus of Junius Bassus (359 CE), MUSEO DEL TESORO, ROME
Artists of the Sutton Hoo artefacts (6th–7th centuries), BRITISH MUSEUM, LONDON
Artist of the Tomb of Philippe Pot (*c.* 1477–80), LOUVRE, PARIS
Ustad Ahmad Lahori (fl. 1632–1653), INDIA

3. Guardians of Ceremony

Once a year, the people of the ancient city of Babylon would walk along a processional route lined with 120 identical lions to the Ishtar Gate, before arriving at the Bit Akitu temple.

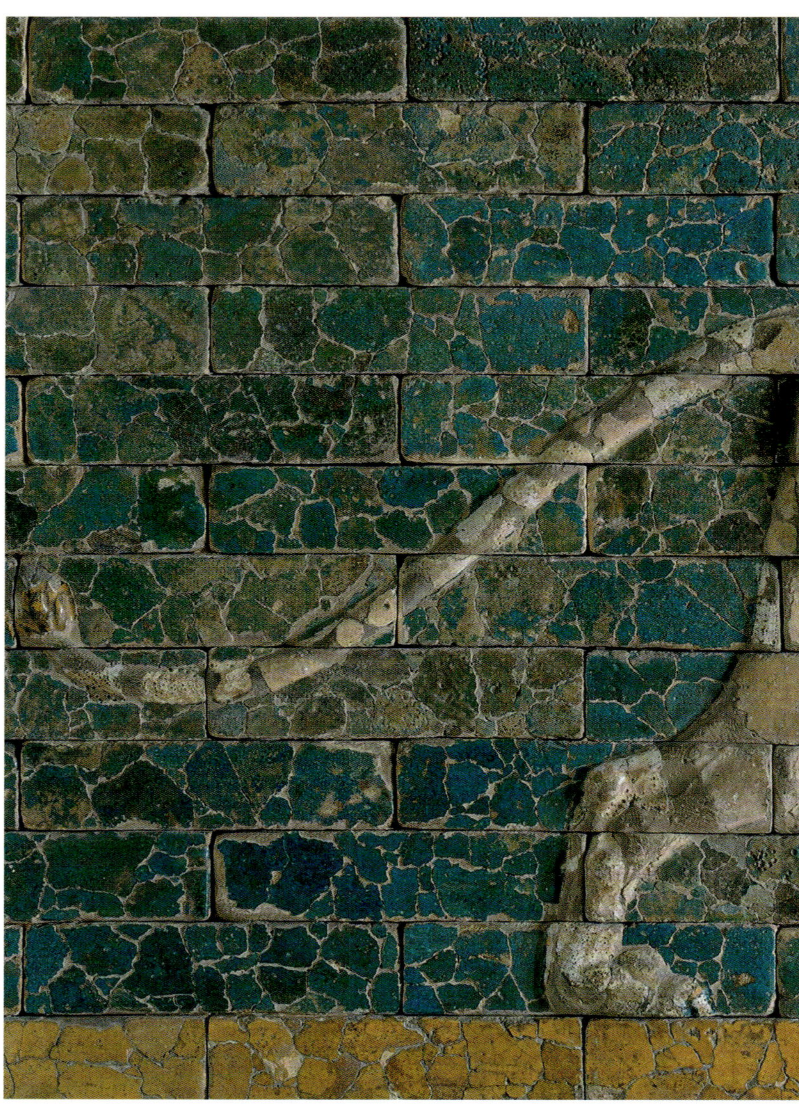

Ceramic, glaze
99.7 × 230.5 cm, 39¼ × 90¾ in.
Metropolitan Museum of Art,
New York

Iraq, Neo-Babylonian

Panel with striding lion

c. 604–562 BCE

At 180 m (over 590 ft) in length, this parade of lions – their snarling teeth flickering in the light of thousands of candles and torches – was a miraculous sight in a city of miracles. Babylon, the largest in the world with over 200,000 citizens, was also home to the Tower of Babel and the Hanging Gardens, built by the mighty Nebuchadnezzar II (r. 604–562 BCE).

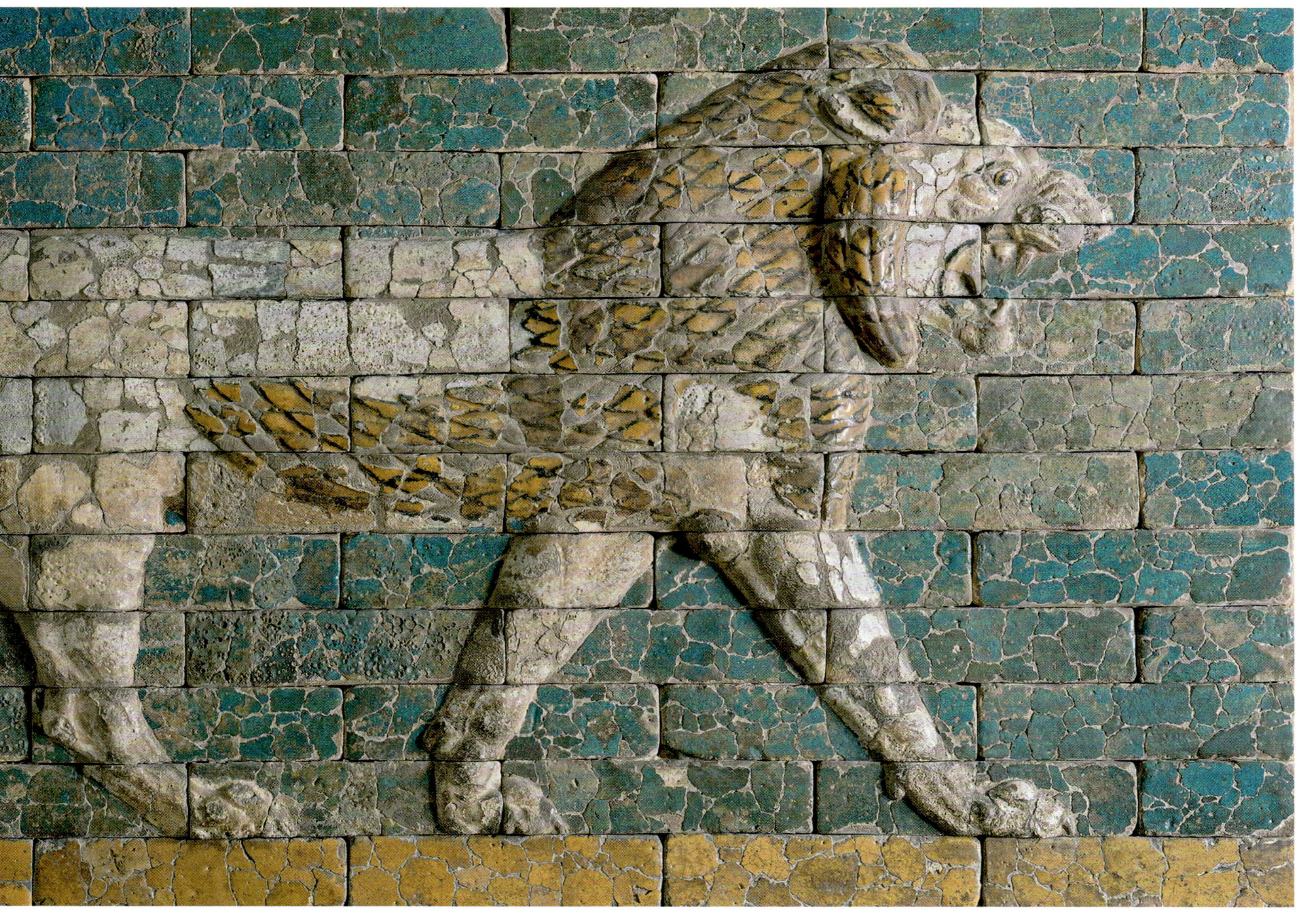

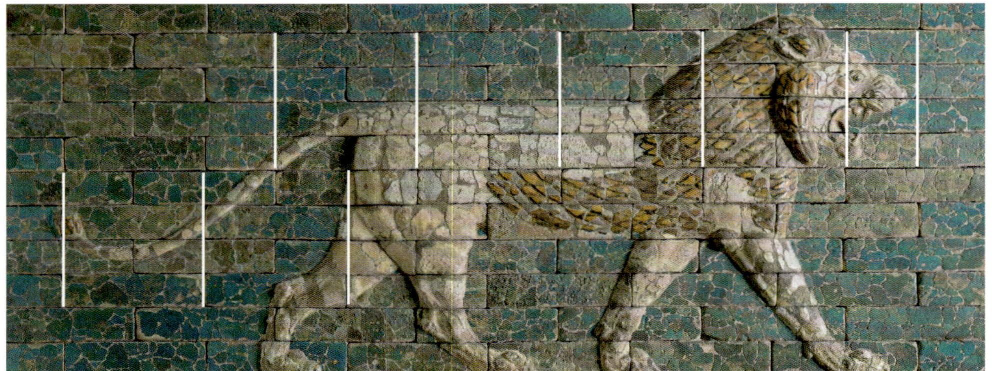

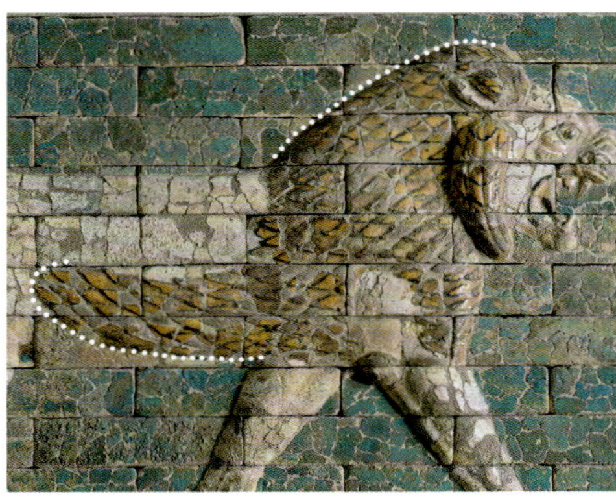

❶ Holy lion

Lions were linked with Ishtar, the Babylonian goddess of love and war, and the 120 lions that lined the route were a powerful reinforcement of her authority. At one end was the Ishtar Gate, decorated with hundreds more lions, as well as mythical dragon-like creatures known as *mušhuššus* (below).

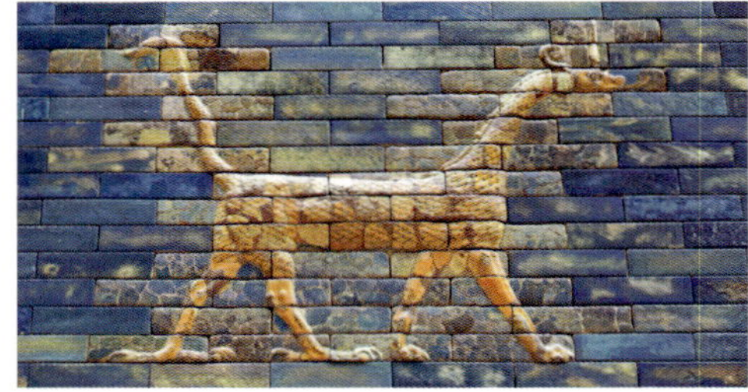

Snake dragon (*mušhuššu*) on the Ishtar Gate of Babylon, reconstruction, original 6th century BCE

❷ Standardization

The identical reliefs of the lions were made by pressing clay bricks into reusable moulds, with 70 separate moulds used for each animal. The repetition of majestic beasts would have reinforced the disciplined regimentation of Nebuchadnezzar II's city.[5]

❹ Babylon

The king's authority emerged in the wake of a power vacuum. Nearly three decades earlier, the once-mighty Assyrian Empire collapsed after the death of its charismatic king, Ashurbanipal, in 631 BCE. This led to the rebirth of the ancient city of Babylon under Nabopolassar (r. 625–605 BCE), and especially his son, Nebuchadnezzar II.

❸ Supernatural

The lions' long manes sweep back to their sides like flowing hair, reflecting their connection to Ishtar.[6] The Processional Way ends at the Ishtar Gate, where an inscription proclaims the goddess as 'the one who defeats her enemies'.[7]

❺ From the earth

In Babylonian mythology, the first humans were formed out of clay. For the city's architects and artisans, therefore, their work echoed the very act of creation. There was also a political dimension to the use of clay bricks in the city's buildings, as each one was stamped with the name of the king.

❻ Bricks

The lions lining the route were also made from clay bricks, to which coloured glazes, including the intense blue of the background, and the gold beneath their paws were added. The size and shape of the bricks define the animals' proportions: the bodies are four-and-a-half bricks in length, and the tails are two bricks.

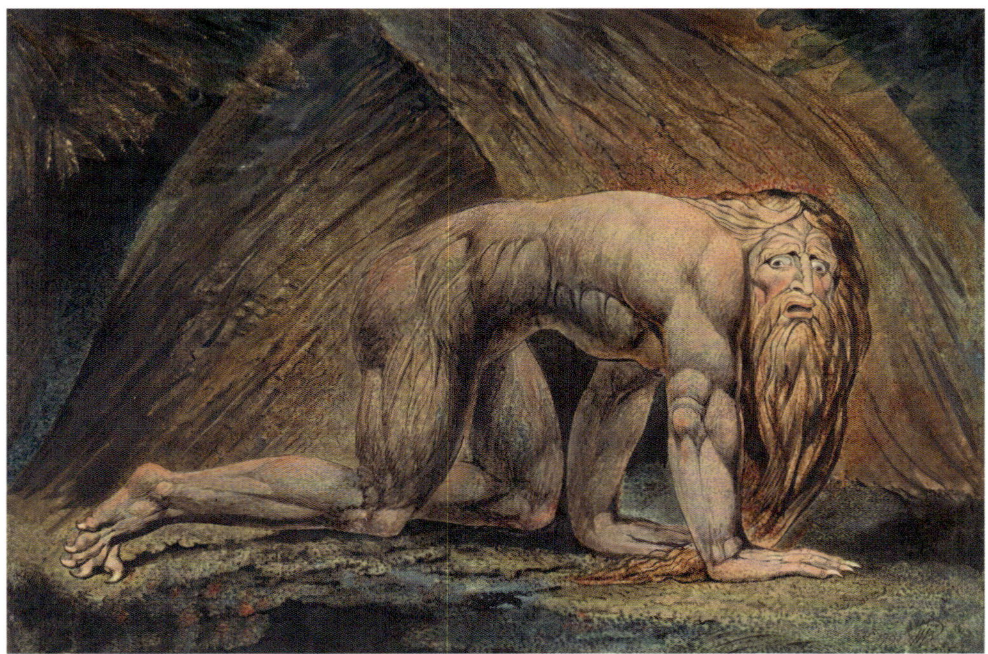

William Blake, *Nebuchadnezzar*, 1795–1805. Colour print, ink and watercolour on paper, 44.5 × 61.9 cm, 17½ × 24¼ in.

Fired-clay brick of Nebuchadnezzar II, Neo-Babylonian dynasty, 604–562 BCE. Fired clay, 32.5 × 32 cm, 12¾ × 12½ in.

7 Profile

The lion's face is shown in profile, allowing a clear view of its powerfully rounded muscles, with a single, bulging eye that appears to be fixed on the spectators. This side-on view is also indebted to older styles in Mesopotamia, including Assyrian sculpted reliefs (right).

8 City of legend

Babylon was already 1,500 years old when Nebuchadnezzar II set about his programme of rebuilding the city. The ancient city has been associated with the biblical Tower of Babel (identified with Etemenanki, a ziggurat dedicated to the god Marduk) and the mysterious Hanging Gardens. It had a gridded street system, with a main road that led to the Ishtar Gate and the Bit Akitu temple beyond.

9 Heavenly and earthly power

The Babylonians believed that their city stood at the centre of the world and marked the place where humankind was created. The Processional Way and the Ishtar Gate were conceived as a zone in which gods and humans could confront one another. By building these structures, Nebuchadnezzar II was not only reinforcing the power of the priesthood, but also his own rule.[8]

10 Renewal

The Processional Way was used for celebrations to mark the start of the agricultural year, with statues of the various gods paraded to the Bit Akitu temple where rituals to ensure renewal and fertility would be performed.

11 Owning history

Excavations of the Ishtar Gate and the Processional Way began in 1899. Fragments of these monuments ended up all over the world, including the Pergamon Museum in Berlin, where the Ishtar Gate can be seen in its reconstructed state (below). In the 1980s, the Iraqi leader Saddam Hussein began rebuilding Babylon on the foundations of the ancient city, but the project was never completed.

→ Human-headed winged lion (*lamassu*), Assyrian, *c.* 883–59 BCE. Gypsum, 311.2 × 62.2 × 276.9 cm, 122½ × 24½ × 109 in.

↓ Ruins of the North Palace of Nebuchadnezzar II, Hillah, Iraq, 6th century BCE

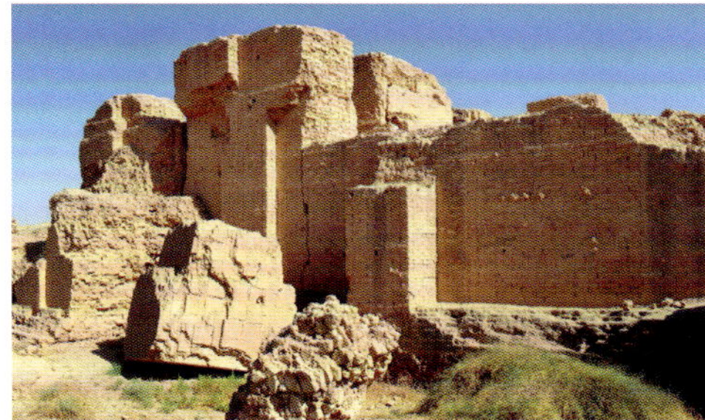

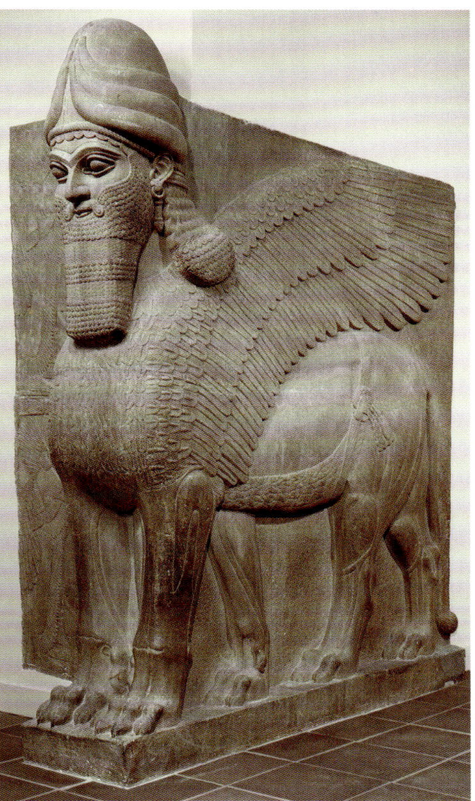

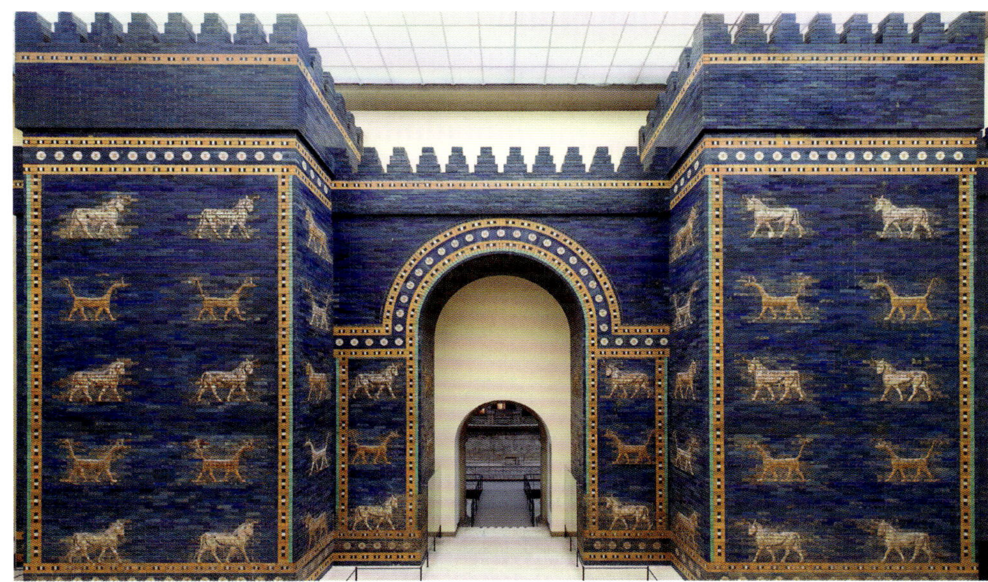

Ishtar Gate of Babylon, reconstruction, original 6th century BCE

LINKED PRACTITIONERS

LIONS:

Artist of the Human-headed winged lion (883–59 BCE), METROPOLITAN MUSEUM OF ART, NEW YORK
Artists of the Lion Capital of Ashoka (*c.* 250 BCE), SARNATH MUSEUM, INDIA
George Stubbs (1724–1806), UK
Henri Rousseau (1844–1910), FRANCE
Carel Weight (1908–1997), UK

TILES AND BRICKS:

Artists of the Wall tiles in the Palace of Darius (550–486 BCE), PERGAMON MUSEUM, BERLIN
Artists of the Mihrab (1354–55), METROPOLITAN MUSEUM OF ART, NEW YORK
Carl Andre (born 1935), USA
Antony Gormley (born 1950), UK
Jorge Méndez Blake (born 1974), MEXICO

PROCESSIONS:

Phidias (*c.* 480–430 BCE), GREECE
Pieter Bruegel the Younger (1564–1638), BELGIUM
Artist of Envoys from vassal states and foreign countries presenting tribute to the emperor (1761), PALACE MUSEUM, BEIJING
L.S. Lowry (1887–1976), UK
Ellis Wilson (1899–1977), USA

4. Man and Superman

The sculptor of this statue wanted it to look like a recognizably human figure, but also to possess something of the superhuman. At the time it was made, the Roman Empire extended to Syria, Africa, Spain and England. At its eastern reaches in Byzantium, belief in the divinity of the emperor had a strong following and it is possible that the statue was made there.

Cult temples dedicated to this belief system needed images to communicate the idea of a figure who was half-man, half-deity. The pose and costume are suggestive of a Greek philosopher, which has led to the statue's association with the emperor Marcus Aurelius (r. 161–80 CE), the final emperor of Pax Romana, a period of peace that lasted for about two hundred years, and the last of the 'five good emperors' named by Machiavelli in the 16th century.

Bronze, hollow cast in several pieces and joined
Height: 193 cm, 76 in.
Cleveland Museum of Art, Ohio

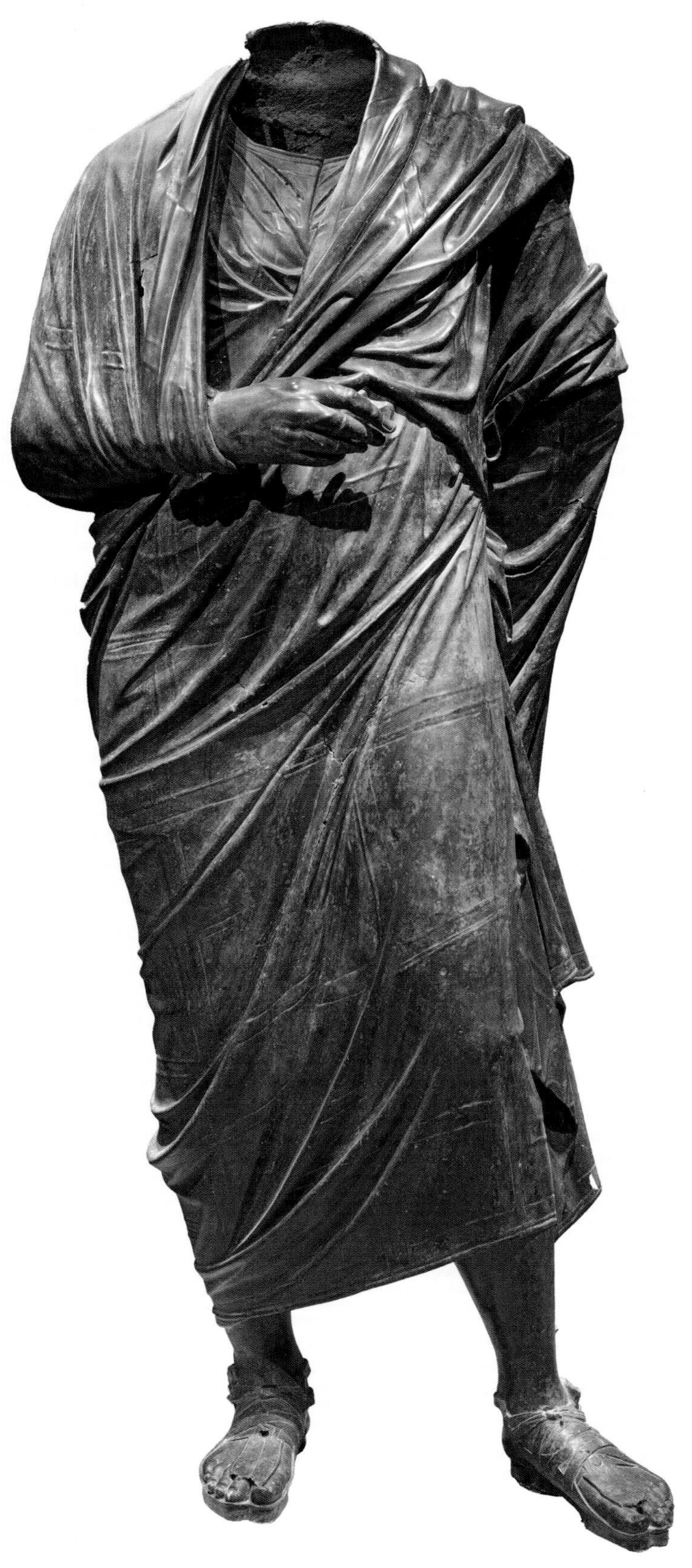

Turkey, Roman
The Emperor as Philosopher, probably Marcus Aurelius
c. 180–200 CE

❶ Hand

Our eye is drawn automatically to the hand, which stands out against the expansive folds of drapery. Its extraordinary realism has been achieved through careful analysis of three aspects of the human anatomy: the surface, expressed through the wrinkles of the skin and cuticles of the fingernails; the substructure, the muscles and veins visible on the back of the hand; and the skeletal system, articulated by the knuckle bones that catch the light.

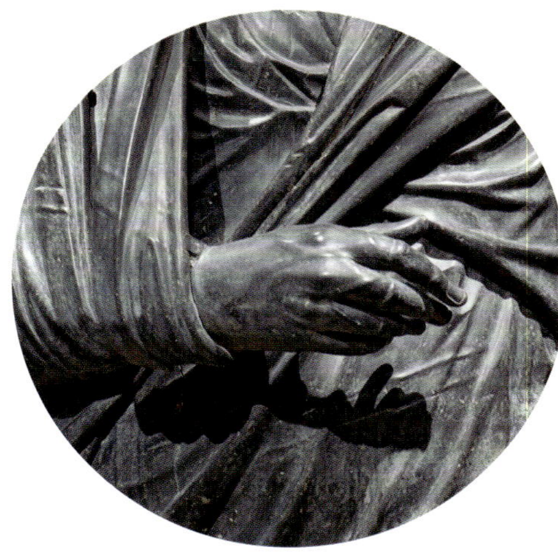

❷ Oration

The raised hand suggests that the figure is in mid-speech, possibly in the process of addressing an audience or a crowd. The gesture is typical of an ancient Greek philosopher, revived centuries later in this Roman sculpture.

❸ Emperor

The pose, costume and date of the late 2nd century CE all indicate that the statue is of Marcus Aurelius. The emperor was known to be a follower of the Greek philosophy of Stoicism, and the pose would have been in keeping with this practice. Another bronze sculpture from the Roman period also depicts Marcus Aurelius gesturing with his hand (right), as if he is addressing a group of people.

❹ Deity

It is possible that the sculpture is one of a group of surviving bronze statues discovered in Turkey (ancient Byzantium) of emperors and their families. The group was probably created for an imperial cult temple that depicted them as deities.

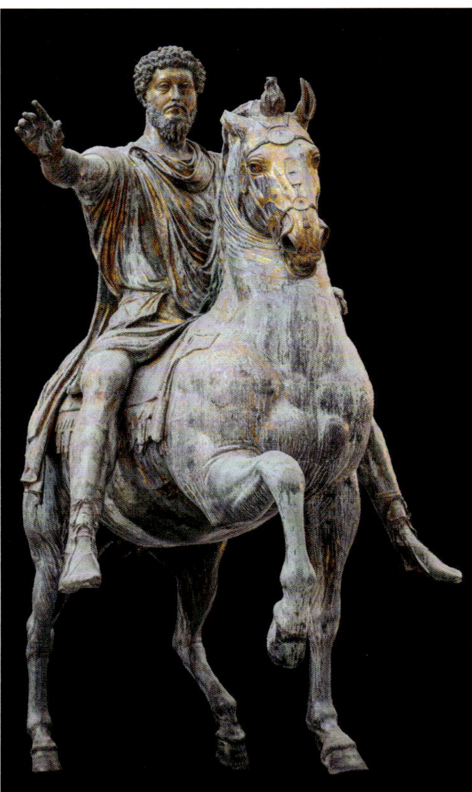

Equestrian statue of Marcus Aurelius, *c.* 161–80 CE. Bronze, height: 424 cm, 167 in.

❺ Textiles

The representation of fabric masterfully replicates the fall of drapery across the body, as well as creating dynamic diagonal lines. Raised sections across the surface of the material even suggest a hem and a checked pattern embroidered on it.

❻ Retro

The sculpture was made in the Roman Empire, but the style of dress replicates the much earlier fashions of ancient Greece, comprising a short under-tunic (*chiton*) and a longer over-cloak (*himation*). Even the footwear (*trochades*, a kind of walking sandal) is Greek, of the type worn some 500 years before the sculpture was made. This retro fashion choice is one of the reasons that scholars identify the figure as the emperor Marcus Aurelius.

❼ Suggested volume

Only a tiny percentage of the figure's body is visible, with the rest merely suggested by the folds of the drapery.

❽ Pose

With one hand, the figure draws his robe aside to advance his left leg slightly forward, setting the hips at a tilt. This subtle stance gives the appearance that the weight is on one leg and a sense of understated movement. The pose (contrapposto) was devised and much used by the sculptors of ancient Greece.

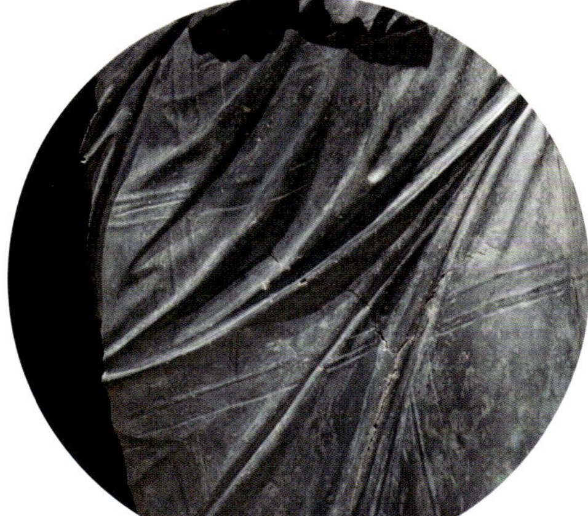

❾ Missing head

How did the statue lose its head? No one knows, although it appears that at some point it was deliberately removed by vandals. The head would have been created separately and attached to the body, allowing it to be easily detached. Although the sculpture appears to be a single piece of bronze, in fact it is made from 29 separately cast sections.

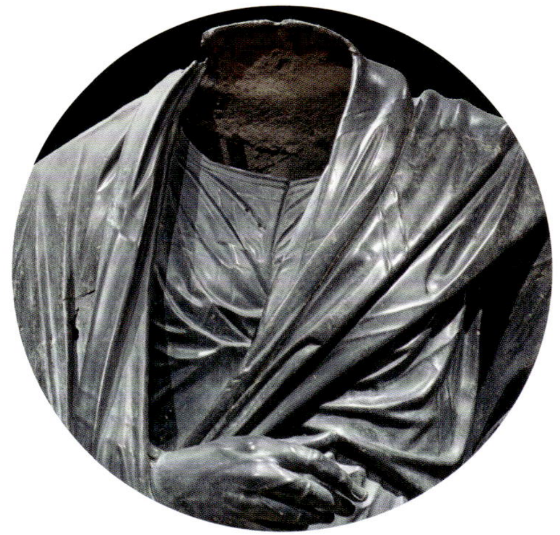

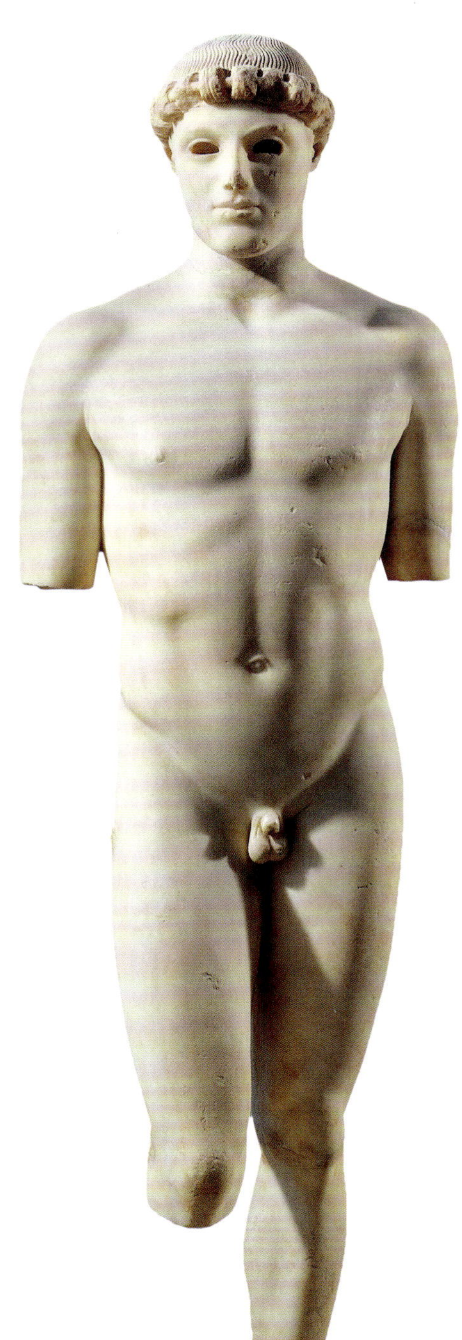

⑩ Technique

The artist used the lost-wax technique, an ancient method of creating hollow statues from metal, thus saving on materials and making the works much lighter. The process required specialist equipment and a team of experts to create the moulds and manipulate the molten bronze, which would reach temperatures of around 1,000°C (1,832°F). The lost-wax method was used in the creation of the Riace Warriors (below right), two full-sized bronze statues discovered in 1972.

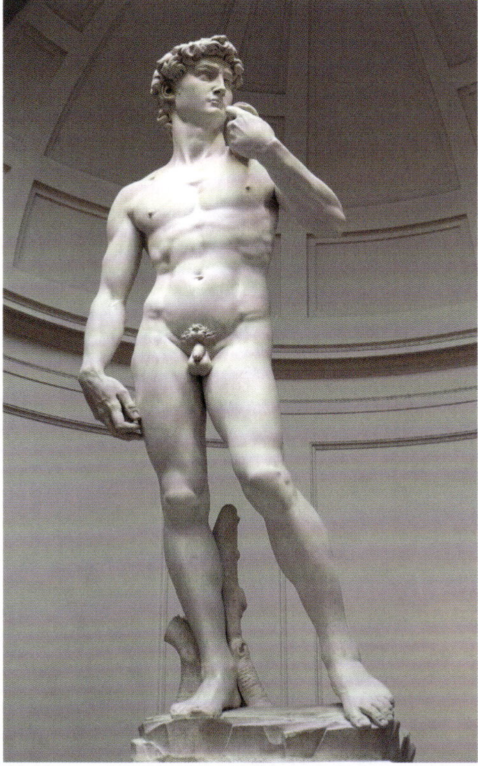

↑ Michelangelo, *David*, c. 1501–4.
Marble, height: 517 cm, 203½ in.

← *The Kritios Boy*, c. 480 BCE.
Marble, height: 120 cm, 47¼ in.

→ *Riace Warrior*, c. 460–50 BCE.
Bronze, height: 198 cm, 78 in.

⑪ Bronze

Since at least the 4th century BCE, metallurgists have combined the weaker metals of tin and copper in exact proportions to produce bronze, a material that is exponentially stronger than the sum of its parts. Because of its durability, it became a favoured material in sculpture. In the present statue, the proportion of metals is approximately 71 per cent copper, 8 per cent tin and 21 per cent lead.

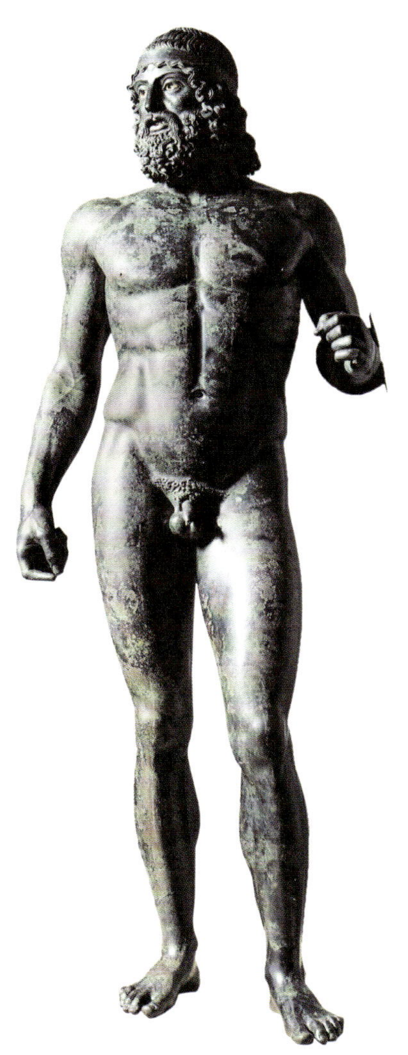

LINKED PRACTITIONERS

CONTRAPPOSTO:

Polykleitos (480–420 BCE), GREECE
Praxiteles (395–330 BCE), GREECE
Alexandros of Antioch (2nd–1st century BCE), GREECE
Michelangelo (1475–1564), ITALY
Rineke Dijkstra (born 1959), NETHERLANDS

INFLUENCE OF CLASSICAL SCULPTURE:

Lorenzo Ghiberti (1378–1455), ITALY
Michelangelo (1475–1564), ITALY
Antonio Canova (1757–1822), ITALY
Auguste Rodin (1840–1917), FRANCE
Camille Claudel (1864–1943), FRANCE

LOST-WAX TECHNIQUE:

Artist of the Riace Warriors (c. 460–50 BCE), MUSEO NAZIONALE DELLA MAGNA GRECIA, REGGIO CALABRIA
Artist of the Bronze Head from Ife (12th–14th century), BRITISH MUSEUM, LONDON
Donatello (1386–1466), ITALY
Aristide Maillol (1861–1944), FRANCE
Louise Bourgeois (1911–2010), FRANCE/USA

5. Spiritual Rapture

Some 1,300 years ago, an artist of the Remojadas culture of Mesoamerica produced this squat, engaging figure, with its large head and broad smile. It was made from clay, a material that was readily available, using a series of moulds to form the various body parts, and then painted and placed inside a tomb.

The Remojadas people lived and worked in what is today the Veracruz region of southern Mexico, and the art they produced presents a conundrum for historians. Very little is known about their society and the true function of their artistic output, so any theories must be based on reasoned conjecture. The figure appears to be merrily dancing, perhaps to evoke the spirit of a carnival. The fact that it was placed in a burial chamber, along with its carefree pose and euphoric abandon, has led some to believe that it symbolizes renewal in nature.

Ceramic
47.5 × 29.9 × 15.9 cm, 18¾ × 11¾ × 6¼ in.
Metropolitan Museum of Art, New York

Mexico, Remojadas
'Smiling' figure
7th–8th century

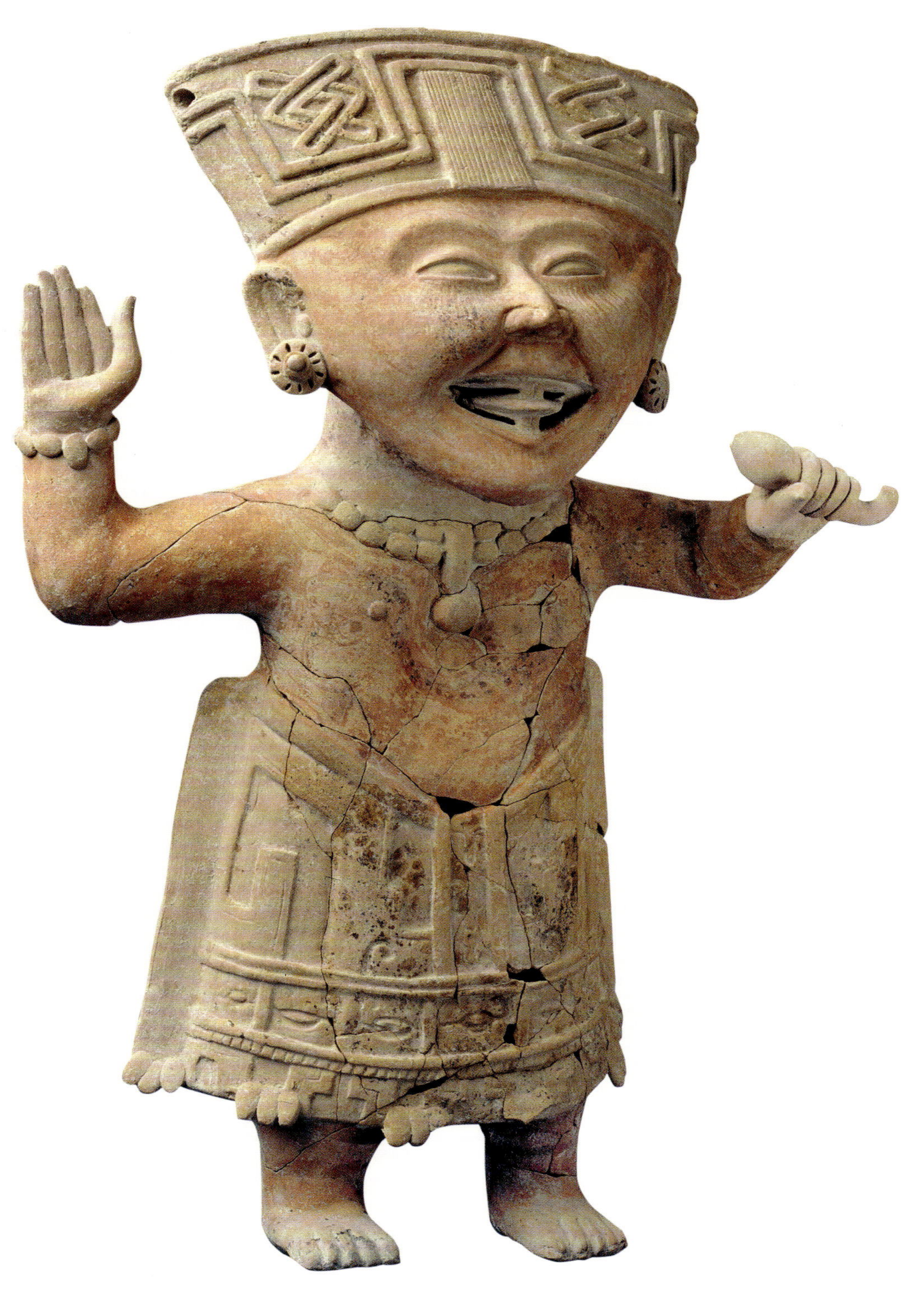

❶ Rattle and roll

The pose of the figure is almost symmetrical, but this near-perfect balance is disrupted by what is happening in its left hand. It clutches a gourd, possibly for use as a rattle, extending it outwards. The raised right hand suggests that the figure is dancing.

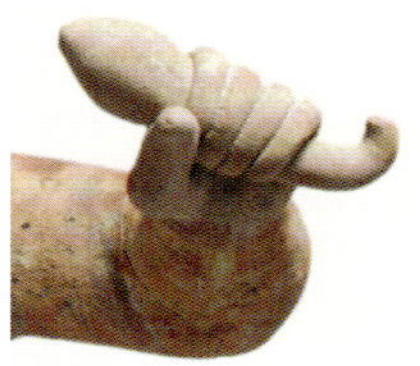

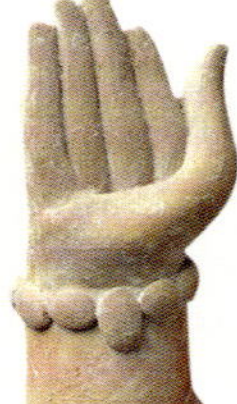

❷ Sound and vision

In what is otherwise a purely visual work of art, the presence of the rattle helps us to imagine an accompanying sound. The rhythmic beat would be joined by other sounds produced by the bells on the figure's bracelets.

❸ A celebration of music

This sculpture type was made repeatedly by the Remojadas people of Pre-Columbian Mesoamerica. Some versions were functional, serving as bells or whistles.

❹ Goddess of dance

The dance-like pose suggests a link to the goddess Tlazōlteōtl, who represented music, dance, laughter and inebriation, and embodied nature's vitality and rejuvenation.[9]

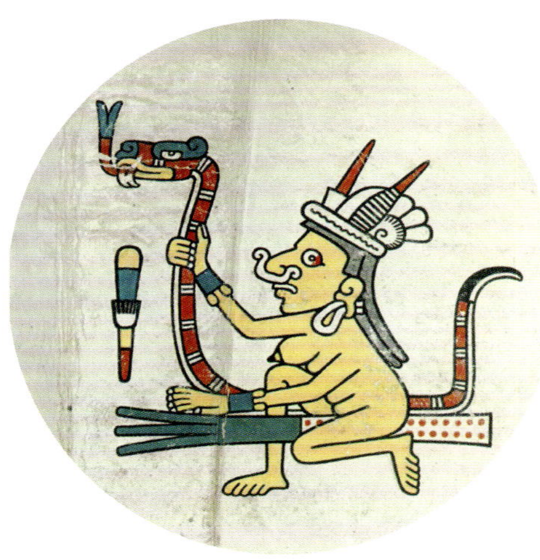

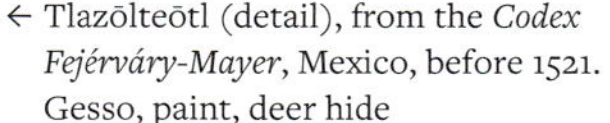

← Tlazōlteōtl (detail), from the *Codex Fejérváry-Mayer*, Mexico, before 1521. Gesso, paint, deer hide

❺ Smile

The artist, or artists, has successfully emulated how the face transforms when smiling, and has evidently studied the physical effects produced by a broad grin: the wrinkling of the skin on the temples and sides of the nose, and crinkling of the eyes. This style of figurine is known as a *sonriente*, or 'smiling' figure.

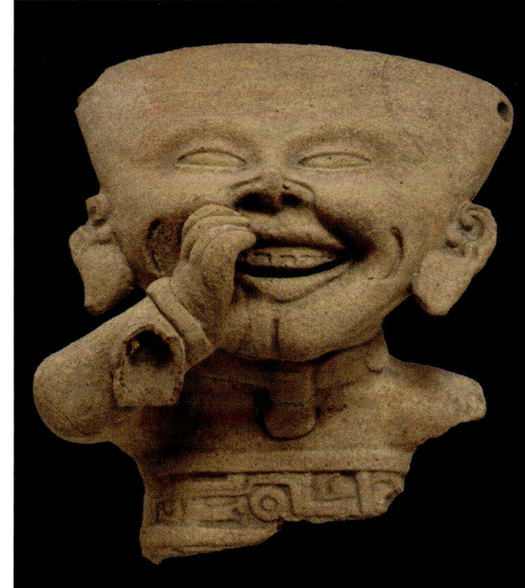

Fragmentary smiling figure, Mexico, Remojadas, 6th–9th century. Ceramic, 21.3 × 16.8 × 12.1 cm, 8½ × 6½ × 4¾ in.

❻ Rarity

It is unusual to see animated expressions on sculpture from this period. Typically, examples are straight-faced and impassive to convey the dignity of the sitter.

❼ Function

Sonrientes have been discovered in burial chambers, and are believed to be offerings to the dead. They were made over a 900-year period, from around 0 to 900 CE, but intact examples are rare. Although celebrated for their mastery of ceramics, the Remojadas are an otherwise little-understood culture.

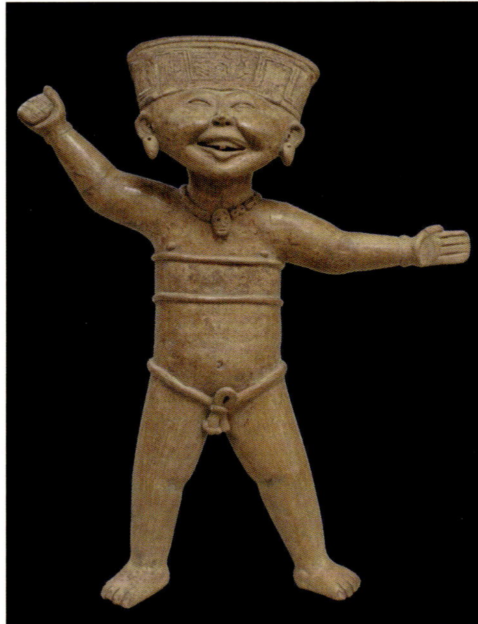

Standing smiling figure, Mexico, Remojadas, 7th–9th century. Ceramic, 51.9 × 42.6 × 10.2 cm, 20½ × 16¾ × 4 in.

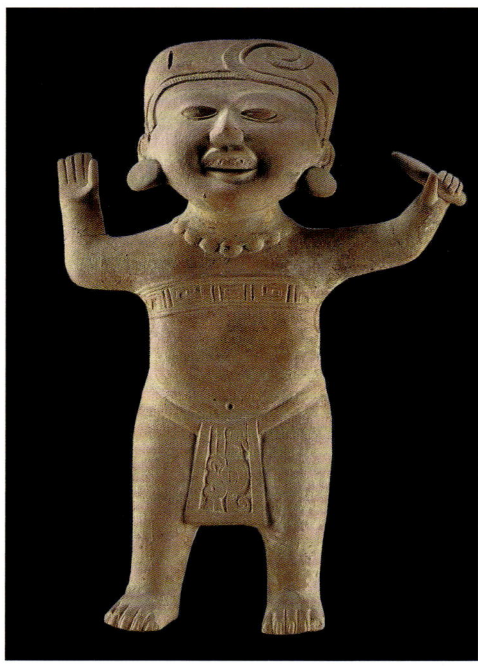

Smiling figure, Veracruz, Mexico, 200–600. Ceramic, 36.8 × 25.1 cm, 14½ × 10 in.

❽ Creation

The figure is hollow, made from fired clay, and probably had a slip applied to the surface. The body parts were not handmade, but shaped in pre-existing moulds and then joined together. This process suggests that they were made quickly, perhaps in great quantities.

9 Children?

As the many hundreds of statues from the region attest, the artists of the time were adept at representing accurate body proportions. *Sonrientes*, however, have enlarged heads and stocky bodies. Could they, in fact, represent children?

10 Servants of the underworld

Another theory is that these figures are mythical servants of the god of afterlife, known as *chaneque*. This interpretation tallies with the fact that *sonrientes* are found in burial chambers.

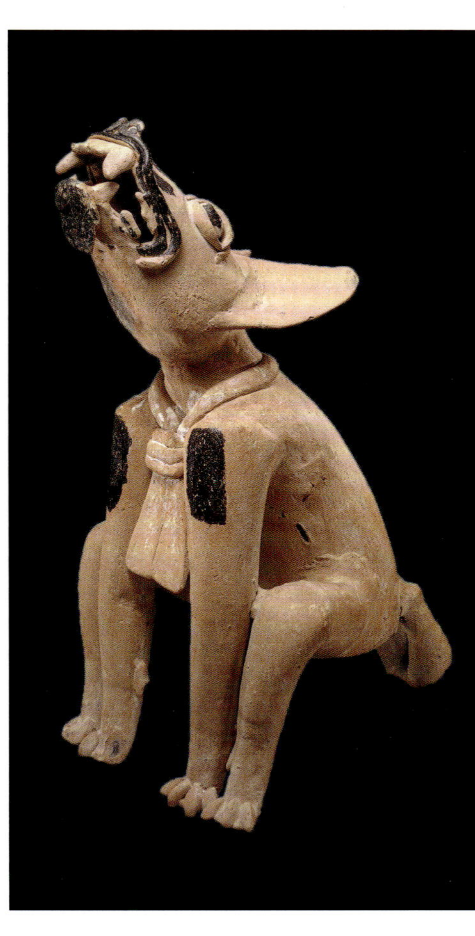

11 Gender

The gender of the figure is uncertain. Women are generally portrayed in Mesoamerican art as wearing skirts, but with their upper bodies covered. It is generally accepted, therefore, that *sonrientes* depict men.

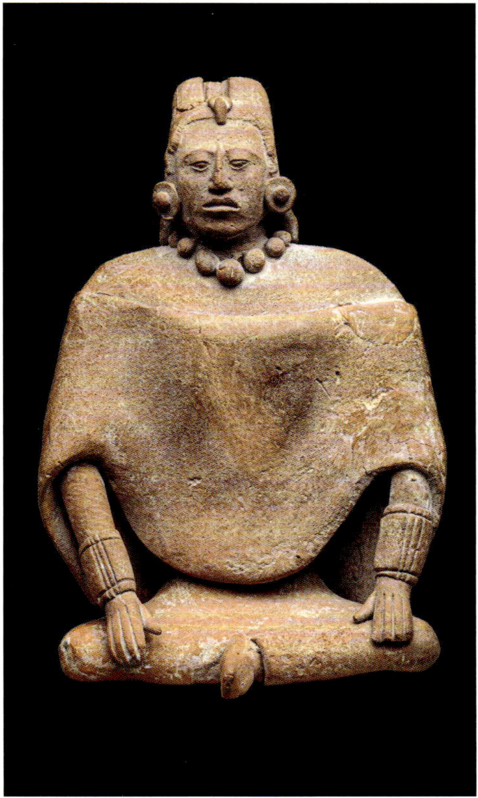

Seated female figure,
Mexico, Mayan,
6th–9th century. Ceramic,
18.2 × 12.7 × 8.9 cm,
7¼ × 5 × 3½ in.

Howling canine,
Mexico, Remojadas,
5th–6th century. Ceramic,
50.8 × 26 × 40.6 cm,
20 × 10¼ × 16 in.

↓ *red marks under the eye*

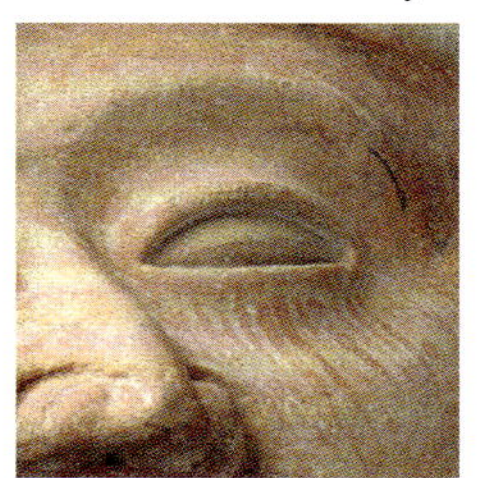

↓ *red marks on the chin*

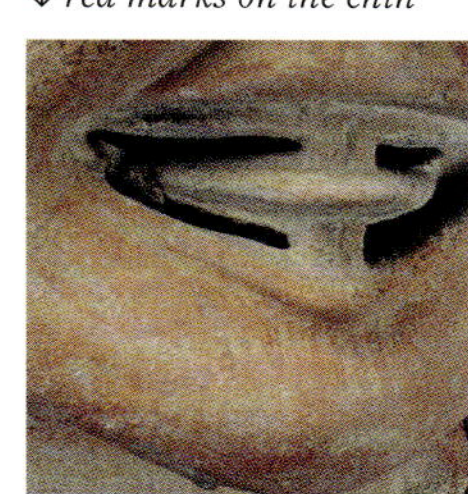

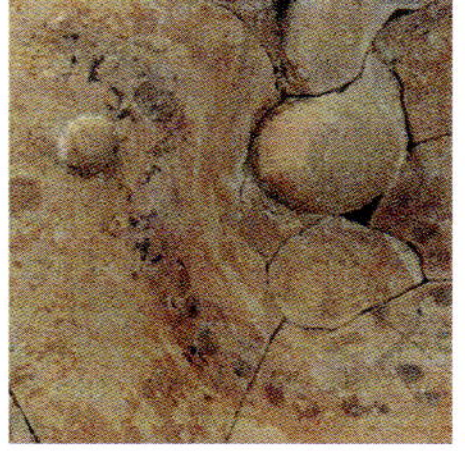

↑ *black marks on the chest*

↑ *traces of paint*

12 Tattoos and pattern

There are traces of black tar paint on the torso, and red marks below the eyes and on the chin, which could represent tattoos or make-up. Traces of paint on the costume suggest that the figure may once have been decorated with a vibrant design.

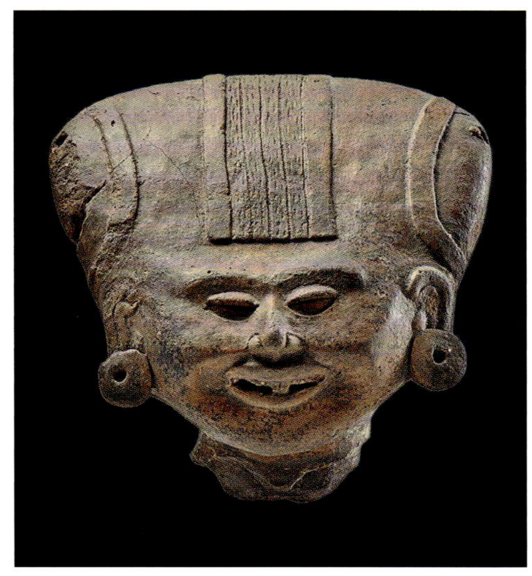

Smiling figure,
Veracruz, Mexico,
600–900. Ceramic,
16.2 × 17 × 12.3 cm,
6¼ × 6¾ × 4¾ in.

LINKED PRACTITIONERS

SMILES:

Antonello da Messina (1430–1479), ITALY
Leonardo da Vinci (1452–1519), ITALY
Frans Hals (1582–1666), NETHERLANDS
Élisabeth Vigée Le Brun (1755–1842), FRANCE
Yue Minjun (born 1962), CHINA

MUSIC:

Artist of the Wall painting from Room H, Villa of P. Fannius Synistor (*c.* 50–40 BCE), ITALY
Caravaggio (1571–1610), ITALY
Judith Leyster (1609–1660), NETHERLANDS
Wassily Kandinsky (1866–1944), RUSSIA/FRANCE
Pablo Picasso (1881–1973), SPAIN

TATTOOS:

Gottfried Lindauer (1839–1926), CZECHIA/NEW ZEALAND
Peter Blake (born 1932), UK
Don Ed Hardy (born 1945), USA
Huang Yan (born 1966), CHINA
Paul Binnie (born 1967), UK

6. Patterns of the Mind

At the abbey of Iona, a remote island off Scotland's west coast, a scribe decorated this sheet of calfskin vellum: the first page of the Gospel of Matthew, known as the 'Chi Rho'. Working in his scriptorium, it would have taken months of painstaking labour and skill to complete.

It is difficult to imagine the levels of devotion that would bring people to such a desolate place. Christ had urged his followers to take his message 'unto the uttermost part of the earth' (Acts 1:8) – which is exactly what the Inner Hebrides were. But the abbey's residents had other things on their minds than just isolation: Vikings had raided the island in three successive attacks, in 795, 802 and 806. Made at a time of intense strife and spirituality, this work of great beauty is an ingenious blend of word and image, and testament to faith and the human imagination.

Ink and tempera on vellum
32.5 × 24 cm, 12¾ × 9½ in.
Trinity College, Dublin

Scotland, Hiberno-Saxon

Chi-Rho-Iota page, Book of Kells

c. 800

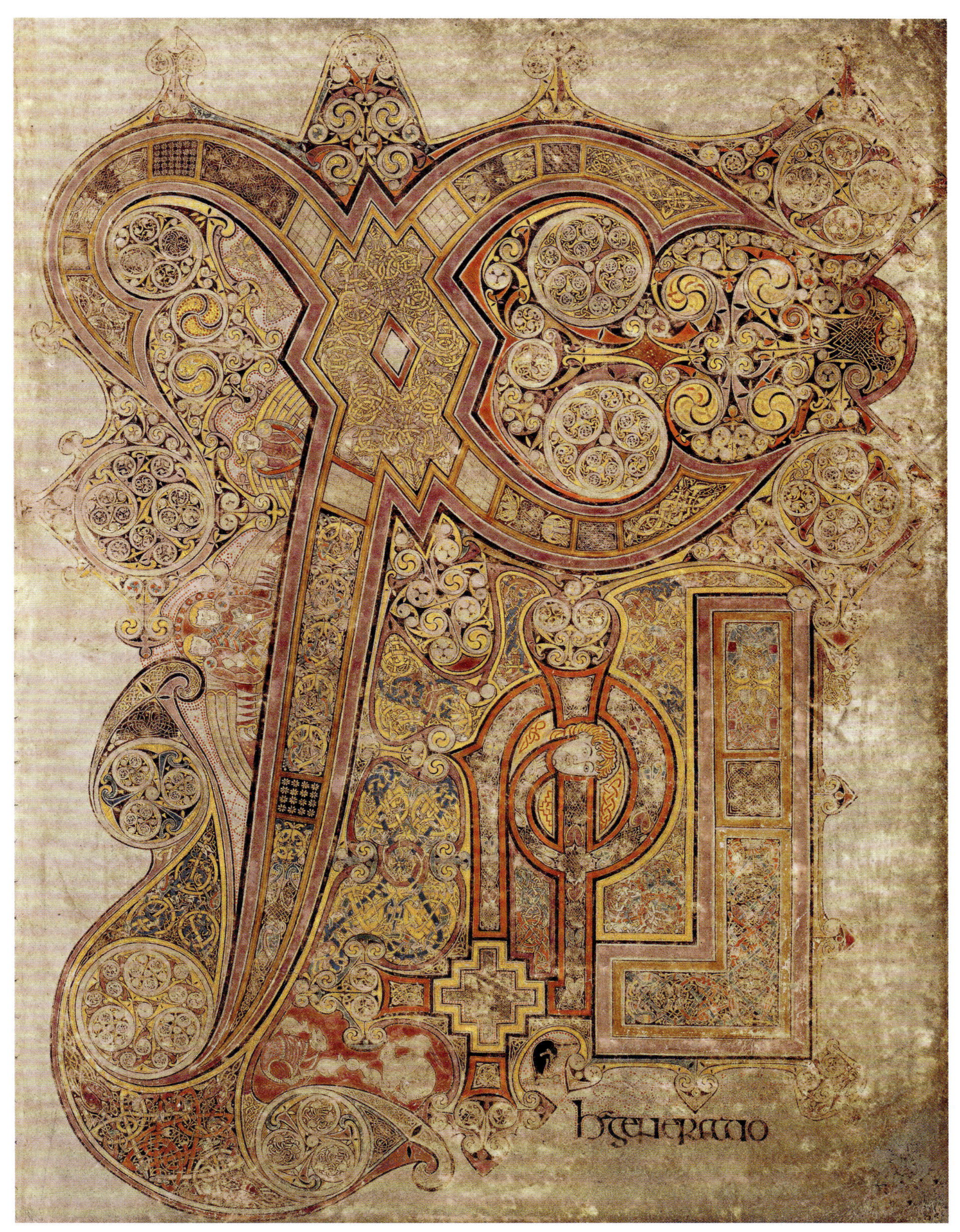

❶ Shapes

The shapes forming the core of the design are the Greek letters (Chi and Rho), signifying the beginning of the Gospel of Matthew: *Christi autem generatio*, 'the birth of Christ'. Here, the focus is on the first two letters of the word 'Christ' as it is written in ancient Greek: ΧΡΙΣΤΟΣ. The Chi Rho (ΧΡ), one of the oldest symbols for Jesus, is usually represented by superimposing the two letters. Here, however, one leg of the X is stretched downwards, so that it resembles an X and P simultaneously. A separate P and I (Iota) are below. Two forms of communication – word and image – are fused together on the page. It's hard to see where one ends and the other begins.

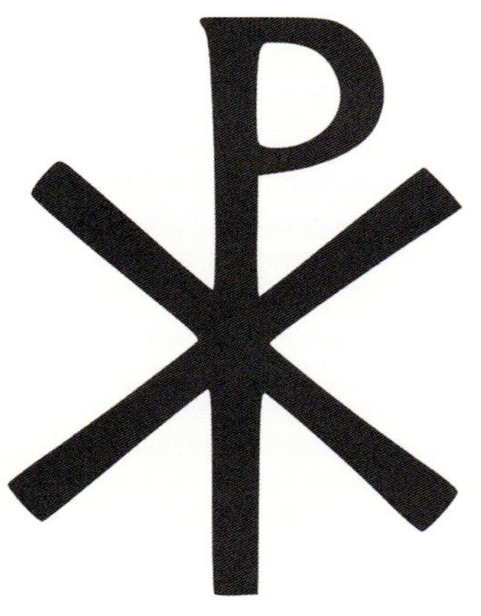

Chi Rho symbol, with letters superimposed

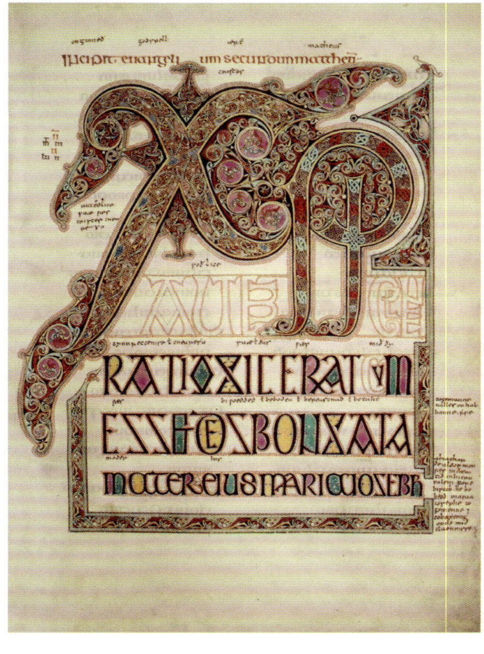

Chi Rho page of the Gospel of Matthew, *Lindisfarne Gospels*, 710–21. Parchment, 36.5 × 27.5 cm, 14¼ × 10¾ in.

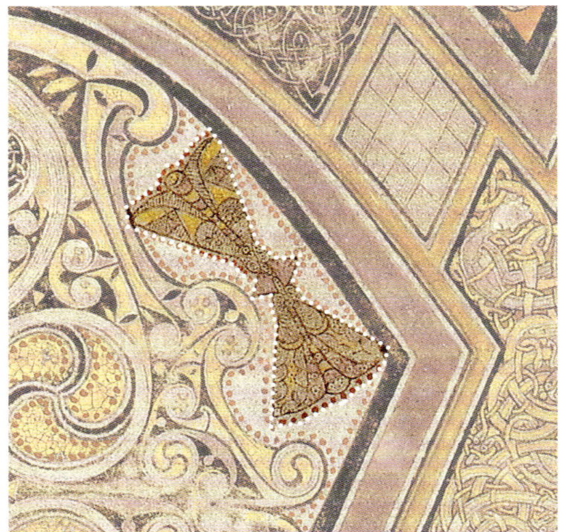

❷ Moths of heaven

Hidden among the decorative patterns are various animals, including two moths at the upper left, beneath the spandrel of the Chi. Because butterflies hatch from the chrysalis of a caterpillar, they were likened to the spirit escaping from the tomb after death.[10] It is placed high in the composition, perhaps to symbolize the creatures of the air.

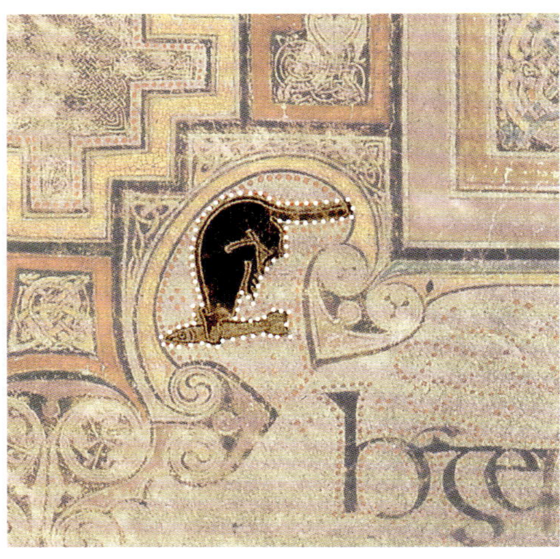

❸ Fish of holiness

In the lower right, a fish is devoured by an otter – a scene that was probably often witnessed by the monks of Iona along the island's coast. The association of fish with Christ stems from the biblical tale of feeding the five thousand, in which two fish multiply miraculously to provide enough food for all – symbolic of the ability of the word of God to feed the souls of the faithful.

❺ What was it for?

The page is from the *Book of Kells*. Books were a relatively new technology for storing and disseminating knowledge, replacing papyrus scrolls in about the 5th century. The process of decorating the pages of these books quickly became a new art form. This page was probably not meant to be read aloud from, but to be displayed and admired, or even worshipped for its exquisite artistry.

❻ What does it mean?

The page appears at the point that the Incarnation of Christ (i.e. the turning into flesh) is first mentioned. The Chi Rho symbol looks as if it is bursting into existence before our eyes, like the tendrils of a plant uncoiling from a seed pod. At the bottom left-hand corner, the letter X appears to emerge from a cluster of circular microcosms, and the eye is led diagonally upwards as new patterns bubble into existence.

❼ Why decorate so much?

In other biblical texts like the *Vespasian Psalter*, decorations were confined to the borders and kept separate from the text. Here in the *Book of Kells*, the two are joined. The extravagant patterning doesn't have a meaning in itself, but to the faithful embodies the infinite complexities of God.

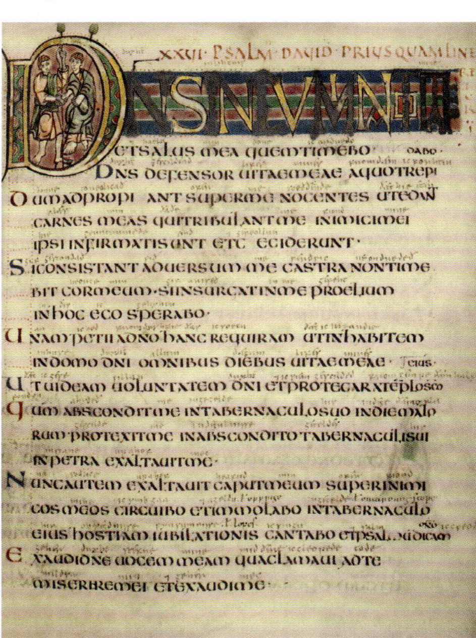

Vespasian Psalter, folio 31, *c.* 725–850. Parchment, 24 × 19 cm, 9½ × 7½ in.

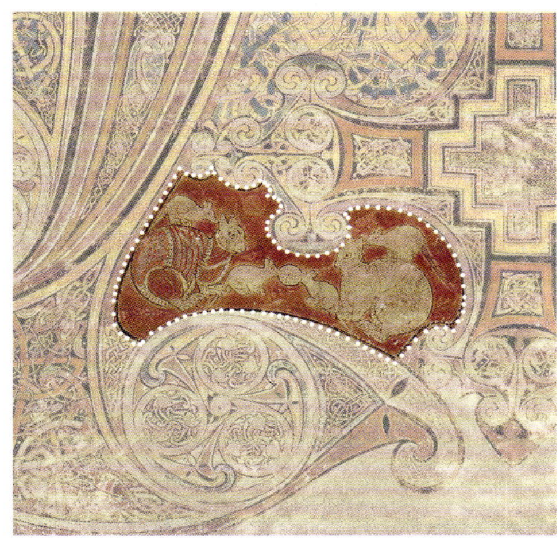

4 Cats of evil

Two mice nibble on a communion wafer, symbolizing the body of Christ. Behind them, a pair of cats watch intently, poised to spring. Although many animals are referenced in the Bible, cats are not – they were seen as symbols of the devil, and in the Middle Ages in Europe were associated with witchcraft. Like the otter, the cats and mice represent the beasts of the land and sea, and so are at the bottom of the composition.

8 An international style

Art historians believe that this type of design, known as Hiberno-Saxon or Insular (from the Latin *insula*, or 'island'), was influenced by the Coptic textile designs of North Africa.[11] The interlace pattern appears to be inherited from Anglo-Saxon design, while the repeated depiction of animals recalls the art of the Scythians from the Eurasian Steppes.[12] The scribe of the *Book of Kells* was working in an original style, but one built on centuries of experimentation with pattern and ornament.

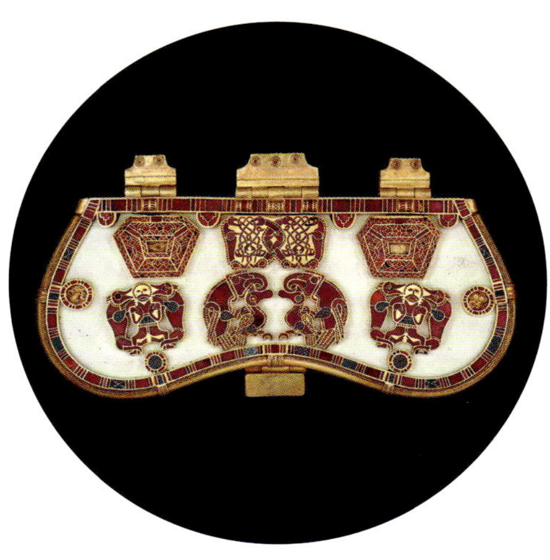

The Sutton Hoo purse-lid, early Anglo-Saxon, early 7th century. Gold, garnet, glass, length: 19 cm, 7½ in.

9 The work of an angel

Around the Chi Rho is a labyrinth of lines and shapes. There is no single focal point in the decoration, encouraging the reader's eye to meander across the page. The design appears spontaneous, but the level of detail indicates careful planning. Although we know that the scribe wouldn't have had a magnifying glass, it seems impossible that he could have achieved such detail without one. Even crafting a quill with a fine enough tip to produce such work required great skill.[13] To the first people who saw the page, it would have seemed miraculous. It certainly was to Gerald of Wales, who saw the *Book of Kells* – or a very similar manuscript – a few centuries later and wrote:

> *Look more keenly at it and you will penetrate to the very shrine of art. You will make out intricacies, so delicate and so subtle, so full of knots and links, with colours so fresh and vivid, that you might say that all this were the work of an angel, and not of a man.*

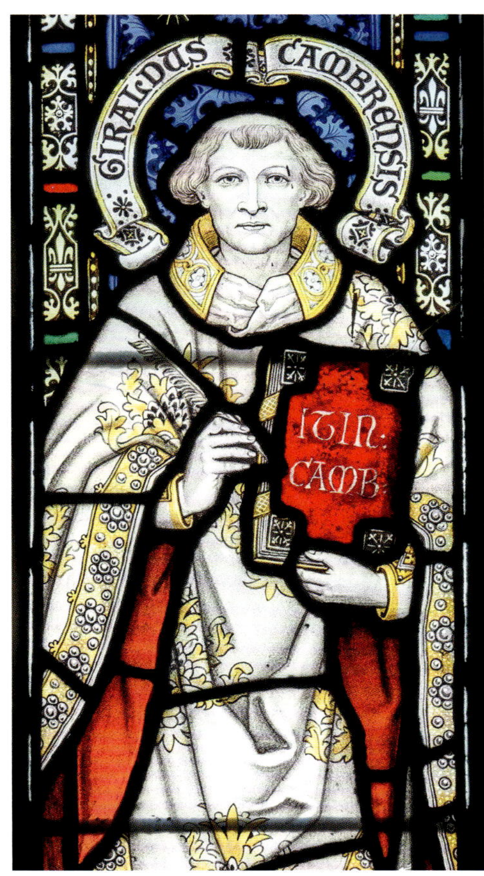

← *Gerald of Wales*, from the Church of St James, Manorbier, Pembrokeshire, 1915. Stained glass

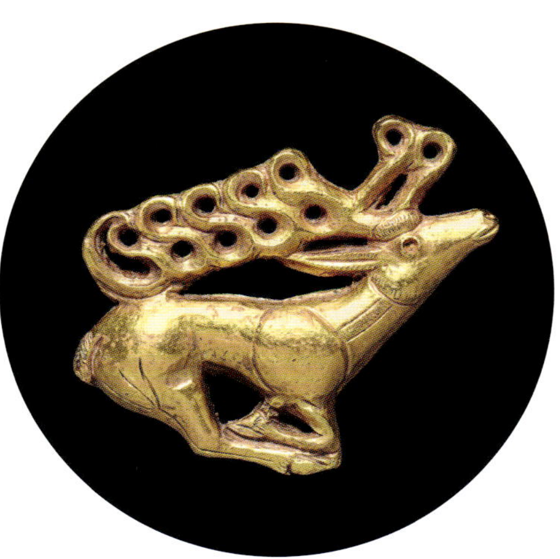

Stag plaque, Scythian, 5th–4th century BCE. Gold, cast in shell mould, overall: 4.1 cm, 1½ in.

LINKED PRACTITIONERS

INSULAR ART:

Artists of the Cathach of St Columba (6th century), ROYAL IRISH ACADEMY, DUBLIN
Artists of the Codex Usserianus Primus (early 7th century), TRINITY COLLEGE DUBLIN
Artists of the Gospel Book Fragment (*c.* 650), DURHAM CATHEDRAL LIBRARY
Artists of the Book of Durrow (*c.* 700), TRINITY COLLEGE DUBLIN
Artists of the Lindisfarne Gospels (*c.* 715–20), BRITISH LIBRARY, LONDON

MOTHS AND BUTTERFLIES:

Maria van Oosterwijck (1630–1693), NETHERLANDS
François Gérard (1770–1837), FRANCE
Jean Dubuffet (1901–1985), FRANCE
Hunt Slonem (born 1951), USA
Damien Hirst (born 1965), UK

CATS:

Artists of Bastet (*c.* 664–30 BCE), EGYPT
Zhu Ling (fl. *c.* 1820–1850), CHINA
Édouard Manet (1832–1883), FRANCE
Takahashi Hiroaki (1871–1945), JAPAN
Aubrey Beardsley (1872–1898), UK

7. Elevated Wisdom

In this statue of a seated figure, the artist set out to portray a noble protector of knowledge. In Buddhism, these arhats *(Sanskrit for 'one who is worthy'; the Chinese word is* luohan*) were believed to have achieved a higher plane of enlightenment – higher than that of mere mortals, but less than Buddha's own perfect state of understanding.*

Despite the *luohans*' role as the guardians of supreme knowledge, this figure of this statue has not been represented as if he is different from any other man. Instead, he is portrayed in a surprisingly human way, as an elderly, careworn monk with the sagging features that betray his age and a far-away expression, absent-mindedly adjusting his robes.

Stoneware with three-colour glaze
104.8 × 91.4 × 83.8 cm, 41¼ × 36 × 33 in.
Metropolitan Museum of Art, New York

China, Liao dynasty
Arhat (Luohan)
c. 1000

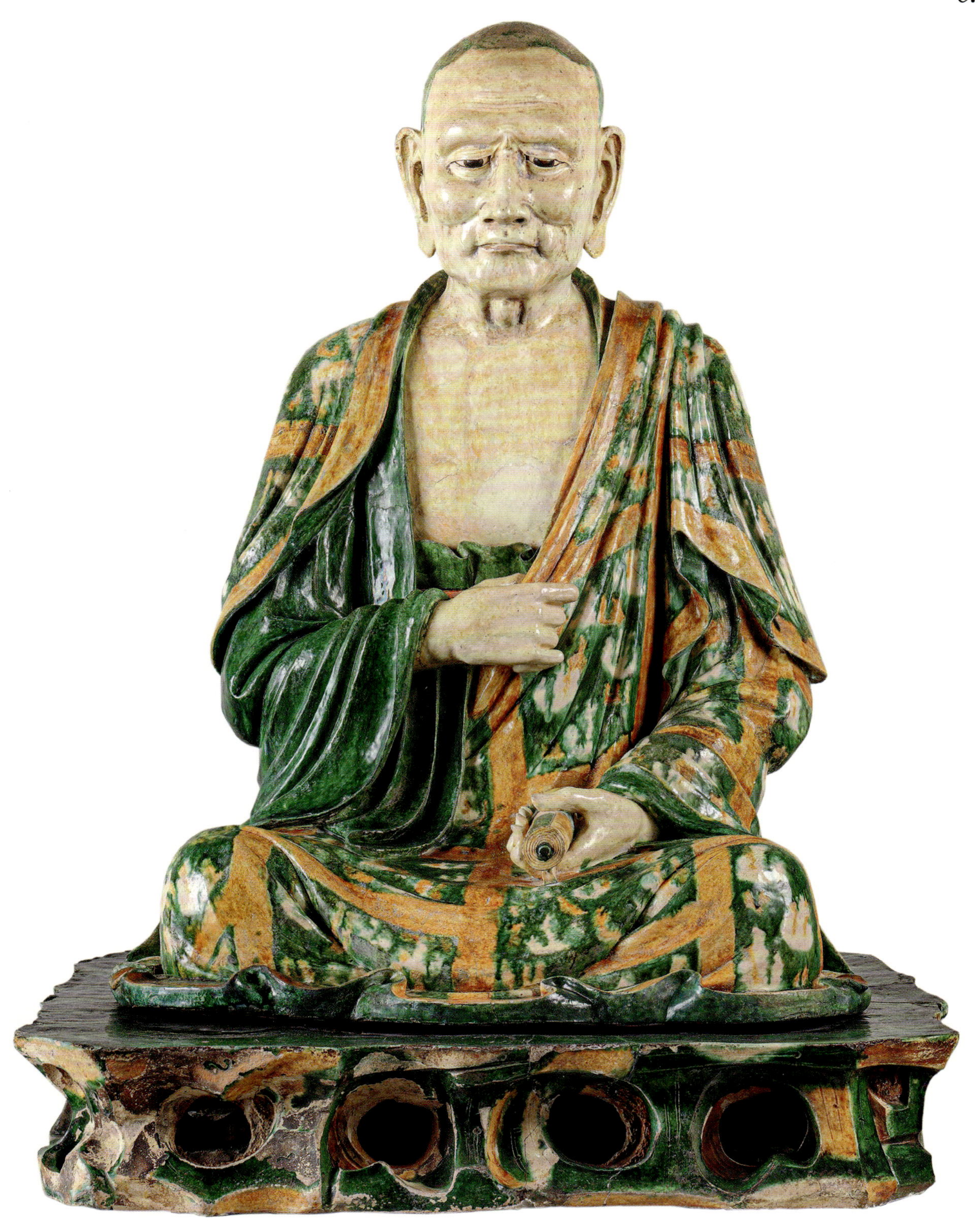

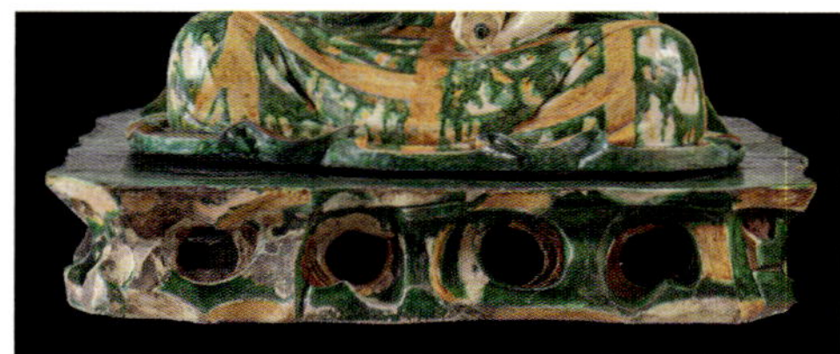

❶ Holy mountain

The figure sits on a plinth, which was created to resemble a rocky mountain top, punctuated at the front with four stylized caves. In Chinese art, mountains are often portrayed as the home of wise men and ascetics.

❷ *Luohans*

Luohans were disciples of the Buddha and guardians of his teachings. They are often described as living a hermit-like existence in caves.

❸ Buddhism

The Buddha – also known as Shakyamuni, Siddhartha or Gautama – was an ascetic and teacher who lived in South East Asia in the 6th and 5th centuries BCE. The Buddhist religion is based on his teachings, including the achievement of enlightenment through perfect mental and physical control, ultimately leading to the relinquishment of desire, attachment and ignorance.[14]

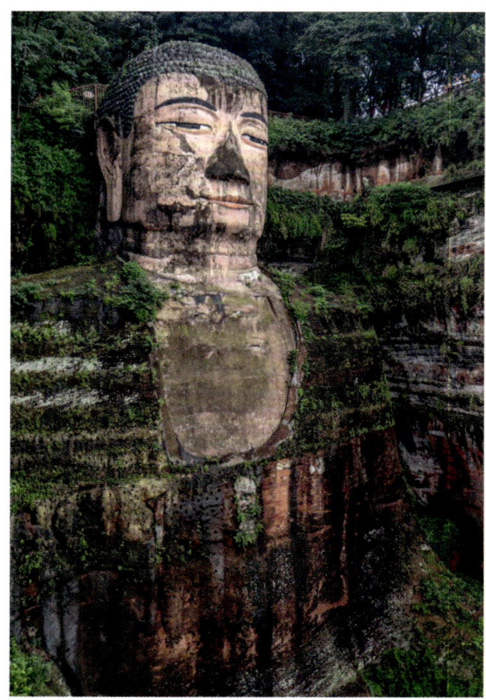

❹ Wisdom

The *luohan* is holding a scroll in his hand, indicating that he is a scholar or teacher, as if he has just finished reading from it to a student.

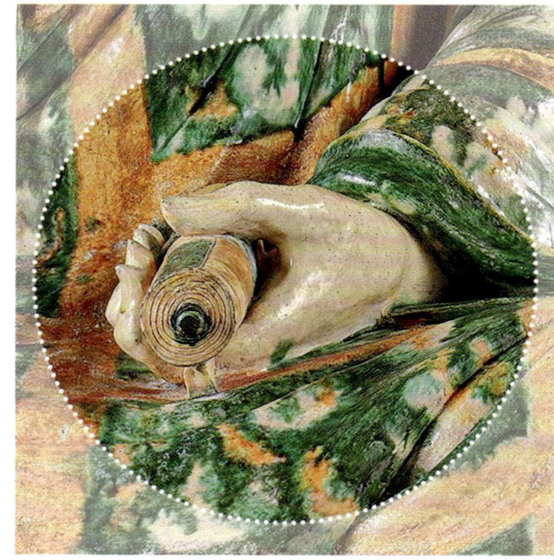

❼ Holy stories?

Buddhism does not have a sacred text in the same way that other religions do. Its teachings were passed down from monk to student, and not written down until about 400 years after the Buddha's death in the 5th century BCE. This *luohan* appears to be in the middle of a lesson, representing the bond between teacher and pupil in monasteries across Asia.

❽ Broken links

Buddhists acknowledge that the original lessons of the Buddha may have been forgotten or diluted over time. Some *luohans* are believed to have been alive during his lifetime, and symbolize the protection of his pure wisdom.

❾ Persecution

The persecution of Buddhists in China at the time this sculpture was made led to the cult of the *luohans* and their guardianship of the Buddha's teachings.[15] It was believed that they would enter Nirvana at the coming of the future Buddha (Maitreya), so *luohans* also represent the salvation of the true believer.

Lehan Giant Buddha, China, Tang dynasty, 713–803. Stone, height: 71 m, 233 ft

Fengdongyan kiln site at Dayao, Longquan, China

❺ Confucianism

To represent a monk as a learned scholar would have had added resonance in China. Followers of the Chinese philosophy of Confucianism admired academic discipline and learning.

❻ Spirituality and realism

This *luohan* has elongated earlobes, which in Buddhism are seen as a symbol of heightened enlightenment and wisdom. His face is not idealized, with the brow wrinkled in thought, and deeply etched lines around the eyes. His cheekbones protrude prominently, suggesting a lifetime of restraint from excess, while the sagging flesh at the corners of his mouth indicate the smiling of serene contentment.

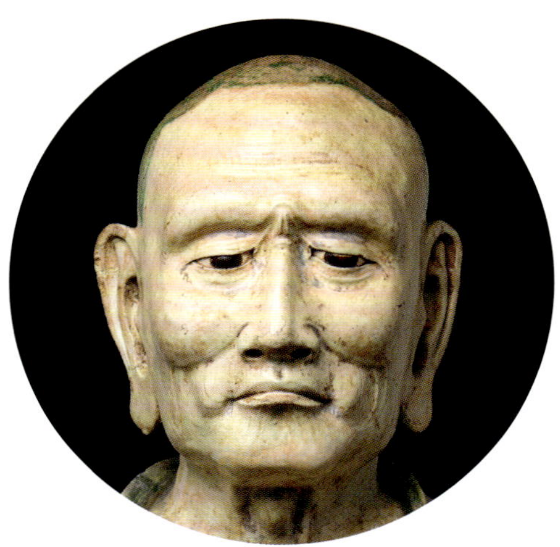

❿ Technique

The statue was probably made at the Longquan kilns outside Beijing. The process would have involved biscuit-firing at temperatures of up to 1010°C (1850°F), before glazing with colours and firing again.[16]

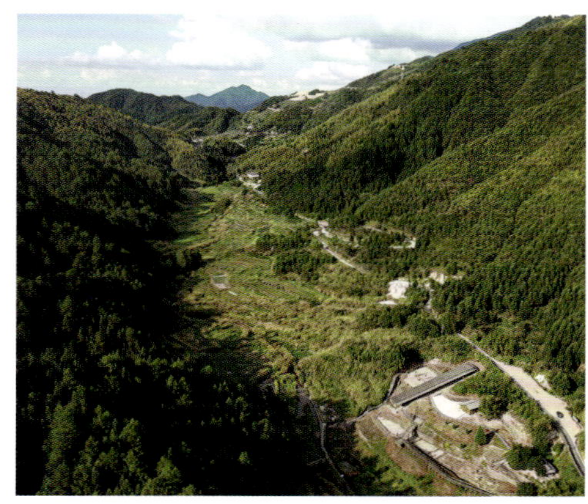

⓫ Pose

The *luohan* is slightly hunched with a frail body, as evidenced by his wasted chest and veined hands. His cross-legged pose is reminiscent of the lotus position in yoga, which evolved in tandem with Buddhism.

⓬ Exchange of ideas

Buddhism arrived in China in the 1st century CE from India, travelling east along the Silk Road, an ancient network of trade routes that connected Europe and the Far East. Monasteries were often located at stopping-off points along the routes.

⓭ Discovery

This figure was part of a set of statues, 16 or 18 in total, discovered in 1913 and depicting *luohans* (below). It is believed that they were found in the caves of the Yixian region in Hebei Province. One remains in China, with the rest dispersed in museums and collections around the world.

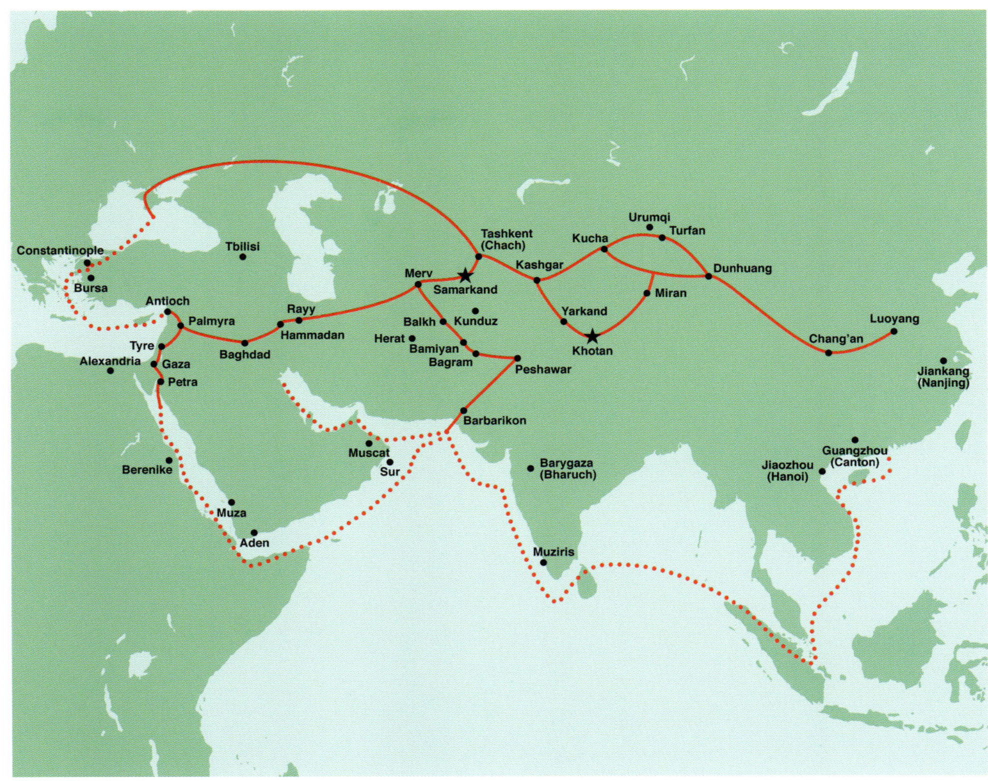

Silk Routes, by land and sea

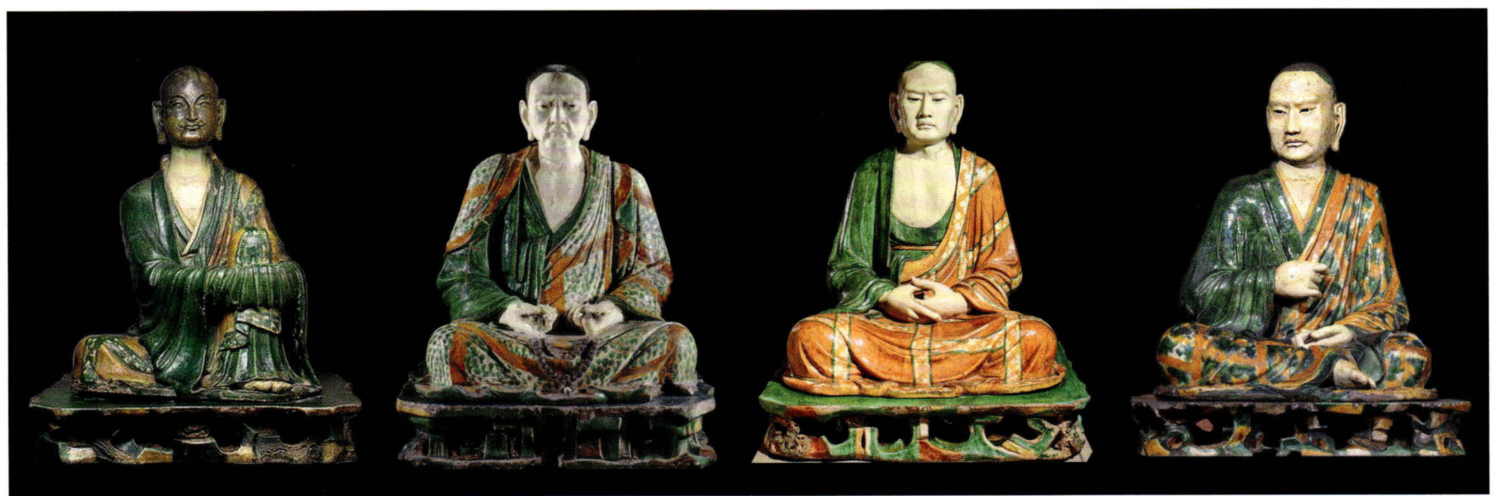

Figure of a *luohan*, China, Liao-Jin dynasty, 11th century. Moulded earthenware with glaze, height: 126.5 cm, 49¾ in.

Statue of the *luohan* Tamrabhadra, China, Liao-Jin dynasty, 10th–13th century. Glazed terracotta, height: 123 cm, 48½ in.

Seated figure of a *luohan*, China, Liao-Jin dynasty, 907–1125. Stoneware, height: 103 cm, 40½ in.

Seated figure of a *luohan*, China, Liao-Jin dynasty, 10th–13th century. Glazed terracotta, height: 105 cm, 41¼ in.

LINKED PRACTITIONERS

POLYCHROME SCULPTURE:

Phidias (c. 480–430 BCE), GREECE
Juan Martínez Montañés (1568–1649), SPAIN
Gregorio Fernández (1576–1636), SPAIN
Sir Anthony Caro (1924–2013), UK
Ron Mueck (born 1958), AUSTRALIA

BUDDHIST ART:

Artist of the Standing Buddha (3rd–4th century), PAKISTAN
Artist of the Buddha head (530–80), CHINA
Artist of the Leshan Giant Buddha (713–803), CHINA
Artist of Borobudur Buddha Head (800–99), INDONESIA

OLD AGE:

Artist of the Old Drunkard (3rd century BCE), GREECE
Domenico Ghirlandaio (1448–1494), ITALY
El Greco (1541–1614), SPAIN
Rembrandt van Rijn (1606–1669), NETHERLANDS
Alice Neel (1900–1984), USA

8. Cosmic Dancing

Around 1,000 years ago, a team of artists working in what is now Tamil Nadu, at the tip of southern India, created this sculpture of the Shiva Nataraja, a depiction of the Hindu deity as 'lord of the dance'. The dance's pulsating rhythm identifies Shiva as master of the creation, preservation and destruction of the universe, symbolizing time as a perpetual cycle of annihilation and rebirth.

These are ideas on a cosmic scale, communicated by the artist through a graceful piece of choreography. Each of Shiva's gestures – from beating the *damru*, which signals the act of creation, to holding the fire of destruction and stamping out illusion – is a symbol of the possibility of enlightenment and salvation. The statue as a whole is rhythmic, elegant and perfectly balanced – elements that have kept the Shiva Nataraja as a focus of worship in the Hindu religion to the present day.

Copper alloy
Height: 68.3 cm, 27 in.
Metropolitan Museum of Art, New York

India, Chola dynasty
Shiva as Lord of the Dance (*Nataraja*)
c. 11th century

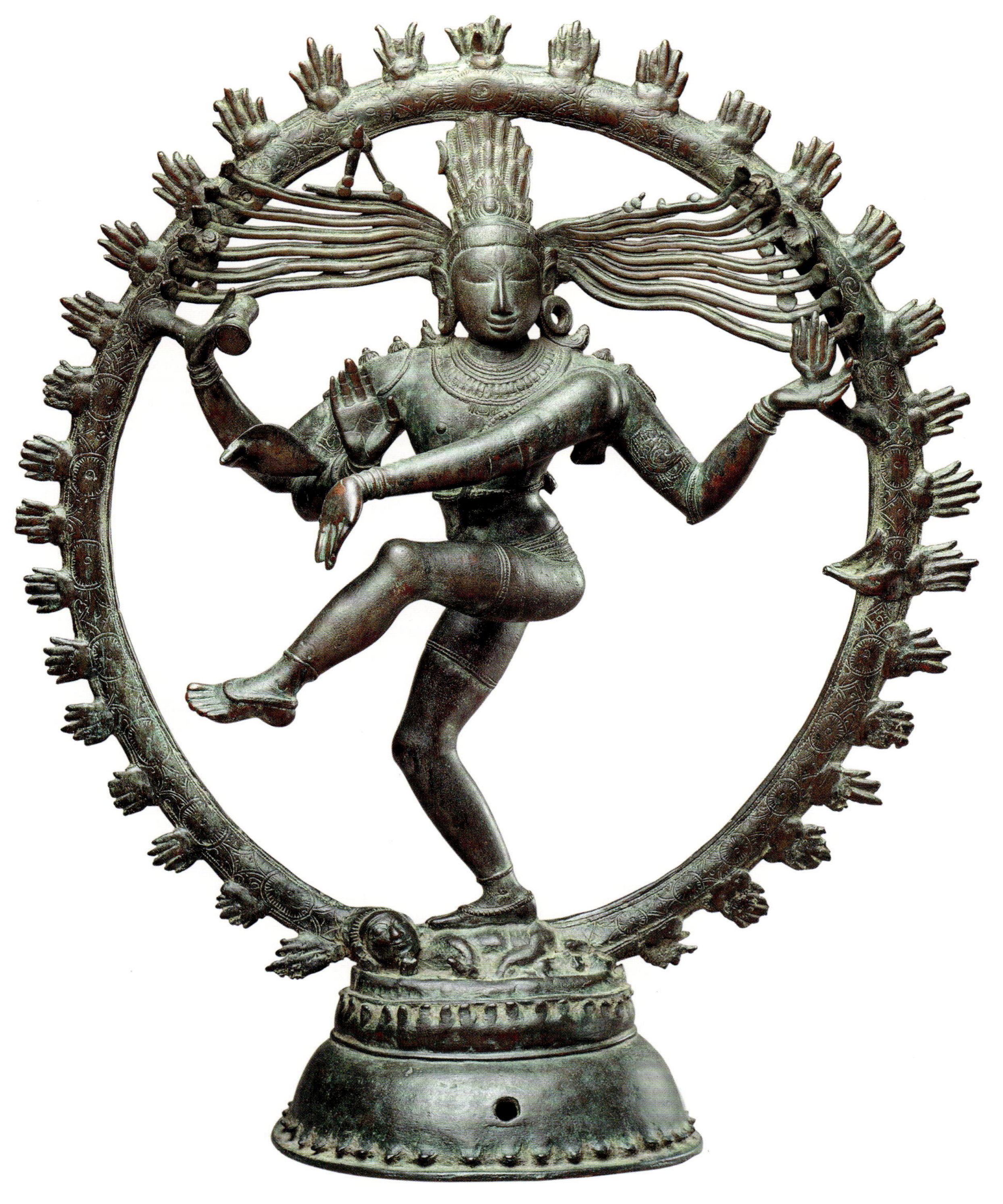

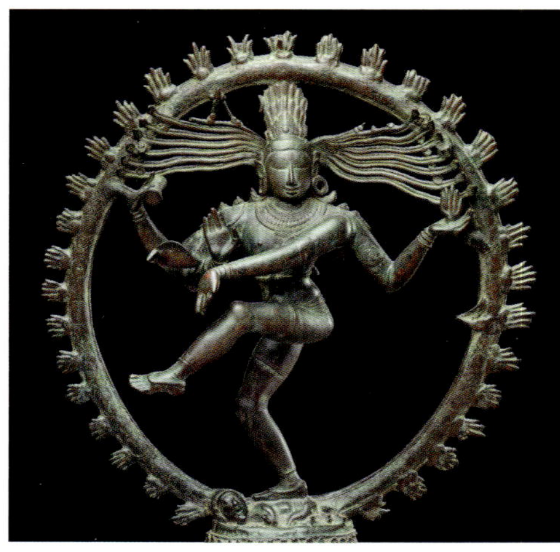

❶ Frame

The circle surrounding Shiva is a flaming halo, or *prabhamandala*, meaning 'circle of light'. It provides a frame for his body, but also demonstrates Shiva's divinity and symbolizes the outer limits of the universe.[17]

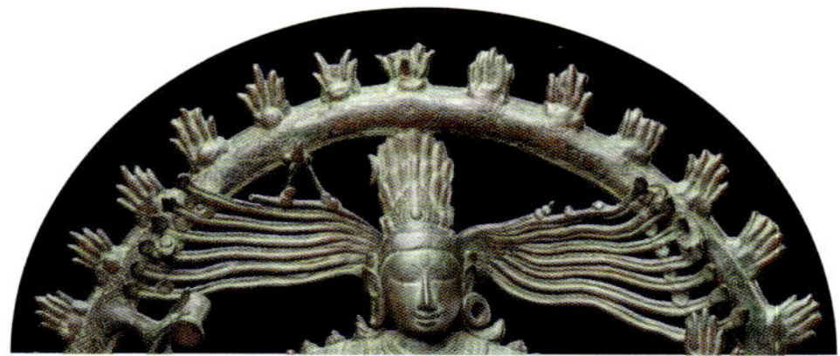

❷ Cycles of time

The halo and the flames emitted from it with such centrifugal energy symbolize the recurrent rotation of time. Fire destroys the cosmos so that it can be reborn again.

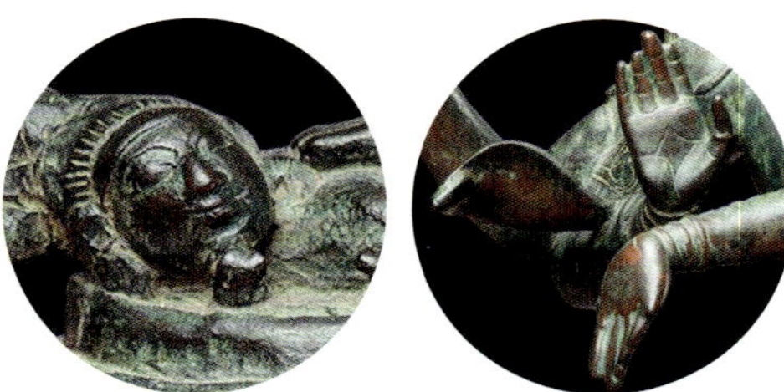

❸ Ignorance

The small figure beneath Shiva's feet is the demon of ignorance, Apasarma, who represents the selfishness and seductions of the illusory material world. Shiva performed his dance in the forests of Chidambaram in southern India to silence the dissent of unenlightened priests, who sent the malevolent Apasarma and a snake (visible in the deity's outstretched arm) to attack Shiva.

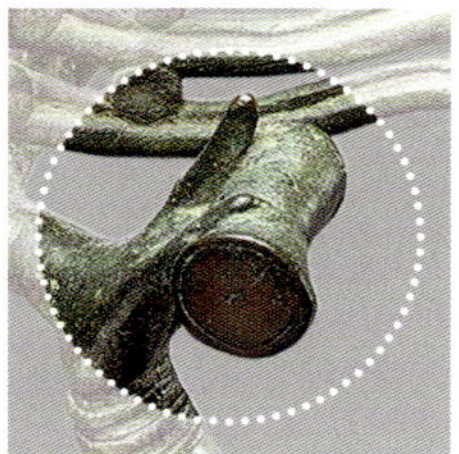

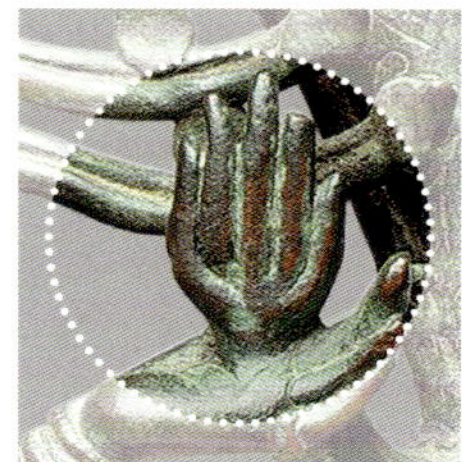

❹ Creation

The beat of Shiva's drum was the first sound heard in the universe, setting the rhythm for its heartbeat. It symbolizes a divine act of creation. *Agni*, the flame of destruction, is held in Shiva's raised hand.

❺ Intelligence

If Apasarma represents ignorance, Shiva represents insight. During religious ceremonies, the all-comprehending Shiva inhabits the sculpture, which was made using the lost-wax technique, a complex process for creating hollow metal sculptures. This hollowness meant that the statue could be easily lifted, but also creates space inside for the deity to be present within the artwork.

❻ Gestures

Shiva has four arms that express his supernatural powers. The two lower hands are set in codified gestures, with the one on the right displaying *abhayamudra*, signifying protection from fear, and the left hand pointing to the lifted left leg, indicating that the route from ignorance and illusion is through worship of Shiva.

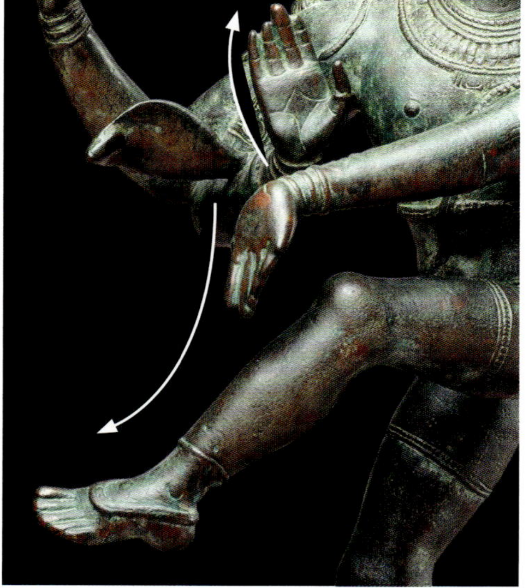

❼ Proportion

The bodily proportions were all designed to convey Shiva's divinity by being perfect. They correspond to a set of rules of proportions, based on ideal shapes and mathematical ratios, recorded in the *Shilpa Shastras*. These are texts that stipulate the *tala* (measurements), *mana* (proportions) and the relationship of parts.

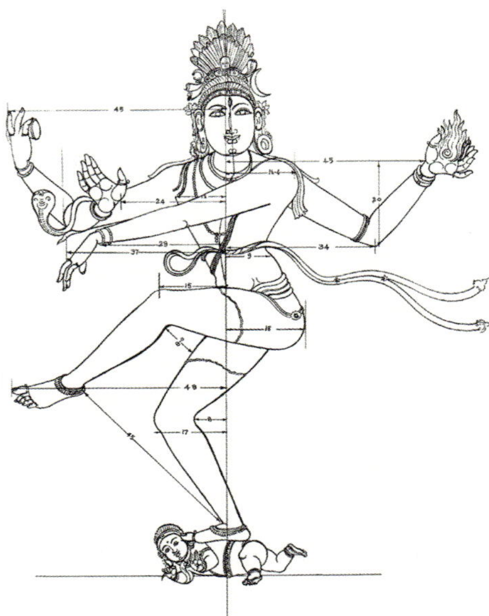

Vaidyanatha Ganapati Sthapati, measurements for the form of Shiva Nataraja, 2002

❽ Body

Shiva's body is adorned with the kind of jewelry normally worn by a Brahmin priest. The left earring is of a type worn by women, alluding to the representation of Shiva in other Hindu sculptures as having male and female attributes.

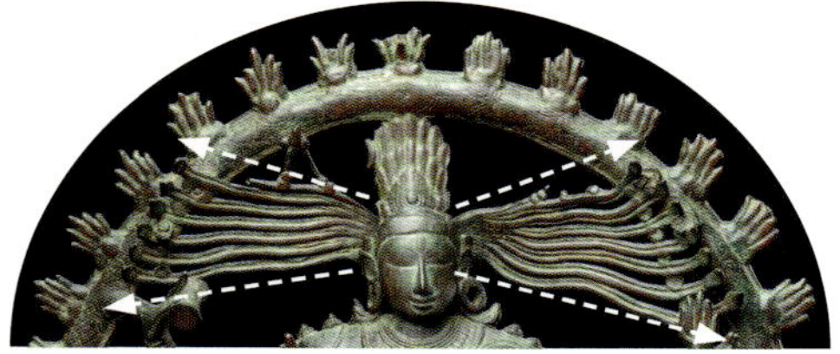

❾ Motion

The hair is plaited into dreadlocks, which fly outwards during the dance. The statue successfully juxtaposes dynamic movement with Shiva's calm expression and the precise gestures of arms, legs and hands. It has equipoise and visual repetition without being monotonous.

⑩ Chola dynasty

Sculptures of Shiva in various manifestations had been made in India for centuries. The representation of Shiva mid-dance as Nataraja emerged during the Chola dynasty, which began in the 3rd century BCE and finally ended in 1279 CE. At its height, the Chola ruled an empire that extended throughout South East Asia. This expansion brought a blossoming of artistic development, and the dynasty's power and prestige is reflected in this graceful representation of Shiva.

Shiva Nataraja, Badami cave temple, India, Chalukya dynasty, 6th–7th century. Height: 152.4 cm, 60 in.

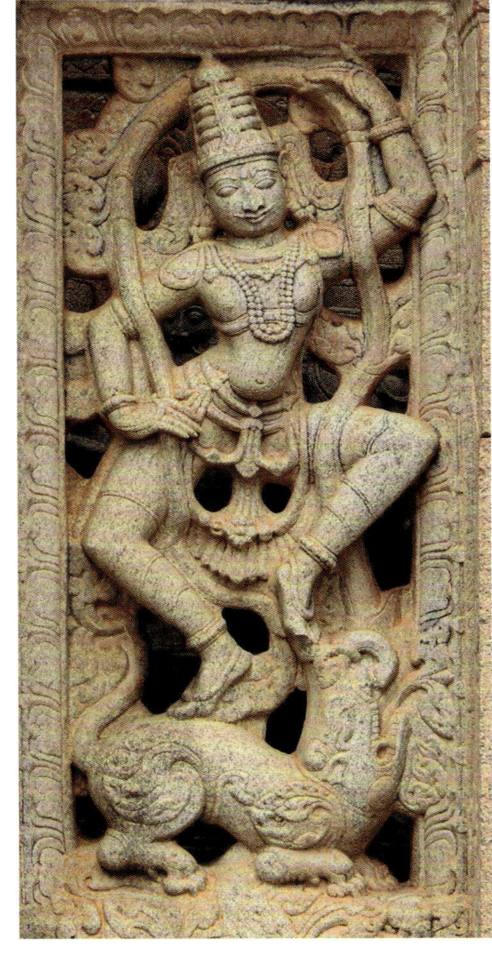

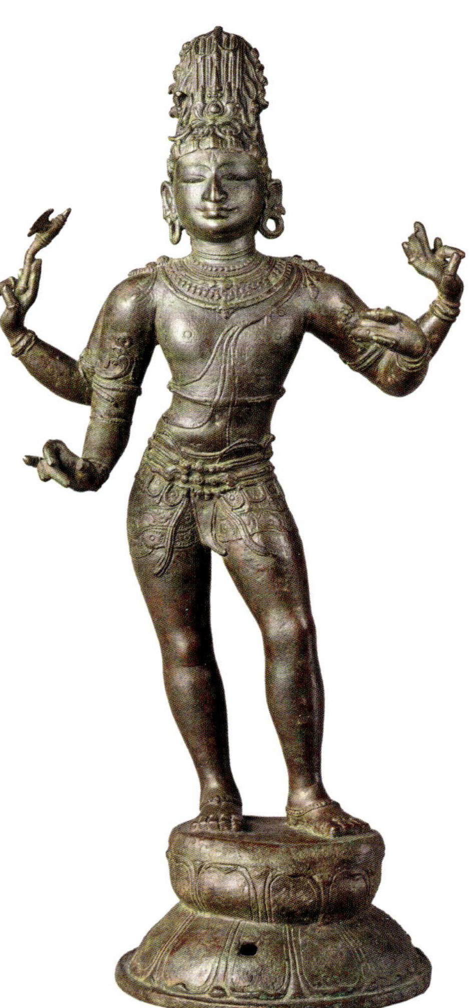

Shiva Nataraja, Bhoganandishwara temple, India, Chola dynasty, 9th–10th century

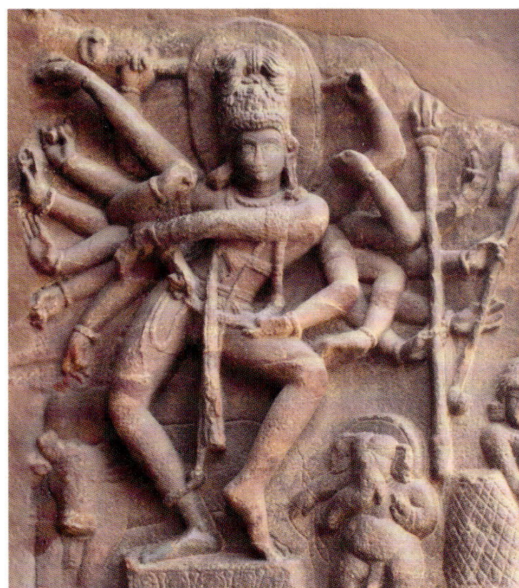

⑪ Movement

Stone sculptures of Shiva can be found in large numbers in Hindu temples, but this lightweight metal version could be carried around in processions, perhaps draped with fabric and flowers. The pose of Shiva Nataraja echoes the ritual dances that would take place in the temples. During festivals, when the statue would be paraded through the streets, the dance would be given added momentum.[18]

↑ *Shiva as Vanquisher of the Three Cities (Shiva Tripuravijaya)*, India, Chola dynasty, *c.* 1000–20. Copper alloy, height: 57.2 cm, 22½ in.

→ *Shiva as Mahesha*, India, Chola dynasty, 10th century. Granite, height: 147.3 cm, 58 in.

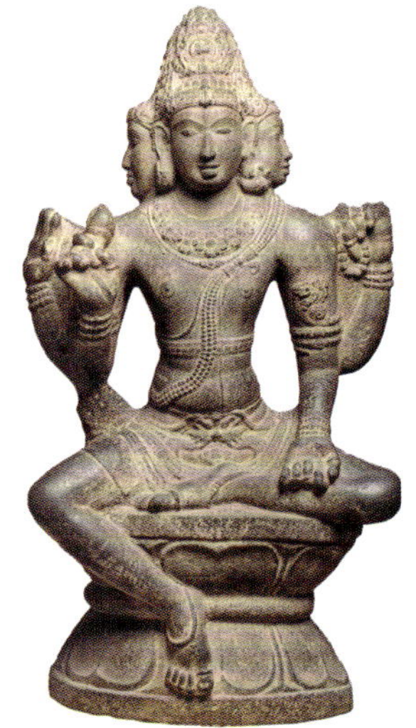

⑫ Flow of life

In other representations of Shiva Nataraja, the hair is depicted to resemble the flowing waters of the river Ganges, with the deity Ganga floating within it.

LINKED PRACTITIONERS

CIRCLES:	DANCE:	FIRE:
Giotto di Bondone (*c.* 1267–1337), ITALY	*Artist of the* 'Smiling' figure (7th–8th century), MEXICO	*Hieronymus Bosch* (1450–1516), NETHERLANDS
Wassily Kandinsky (1866–1944), RUSSIA	*Nicolas Poussin* (1594–1665), FRANCE	*John Martin* (1789–1854), UK
Sonia Delaunay (1885–1979), FRANCE	*Edgar Degas* (1834–1917), FRANCE	*Anselm Kiefer* (born 1945), GERMANY
Benedetta Cappa (1897–1977), ITALY	*Henri Matisse* (1869–1954), FRANCE	*Cai Guo-Qiang* (born 1957), CHINA
Tom Phillips (1937–2022), UK	*Gillian Wearing* (born 1963), UK	*K Foundation* (established 1993), UK

9. Supernatural Powers

The artists behind this exquisite pendant were expert metalworkers capable of articulating fine detail on a small scale and using the lost-wax technique with consummate skill. They belonged to the Tairona people of what is now northern Colombia, and this item of jewelry provides some evidence of their worldview.

The pendant would have been made as a high-status item, possibly worn by a member of the social elite, and the figure at the centre may represent a leader of some kind, whether political or religious. The imaginative interplay of animal forms in the headdress indicates a connection with nature and adds to the figure's assertive presence.

Gold
13.7 × 16.8 × 5.1 cm, 5½ × 6½ × 2 in.
Metropolitan Museum of Art, New York

Colombia, Tairona
Figure pendant
10th–16th century

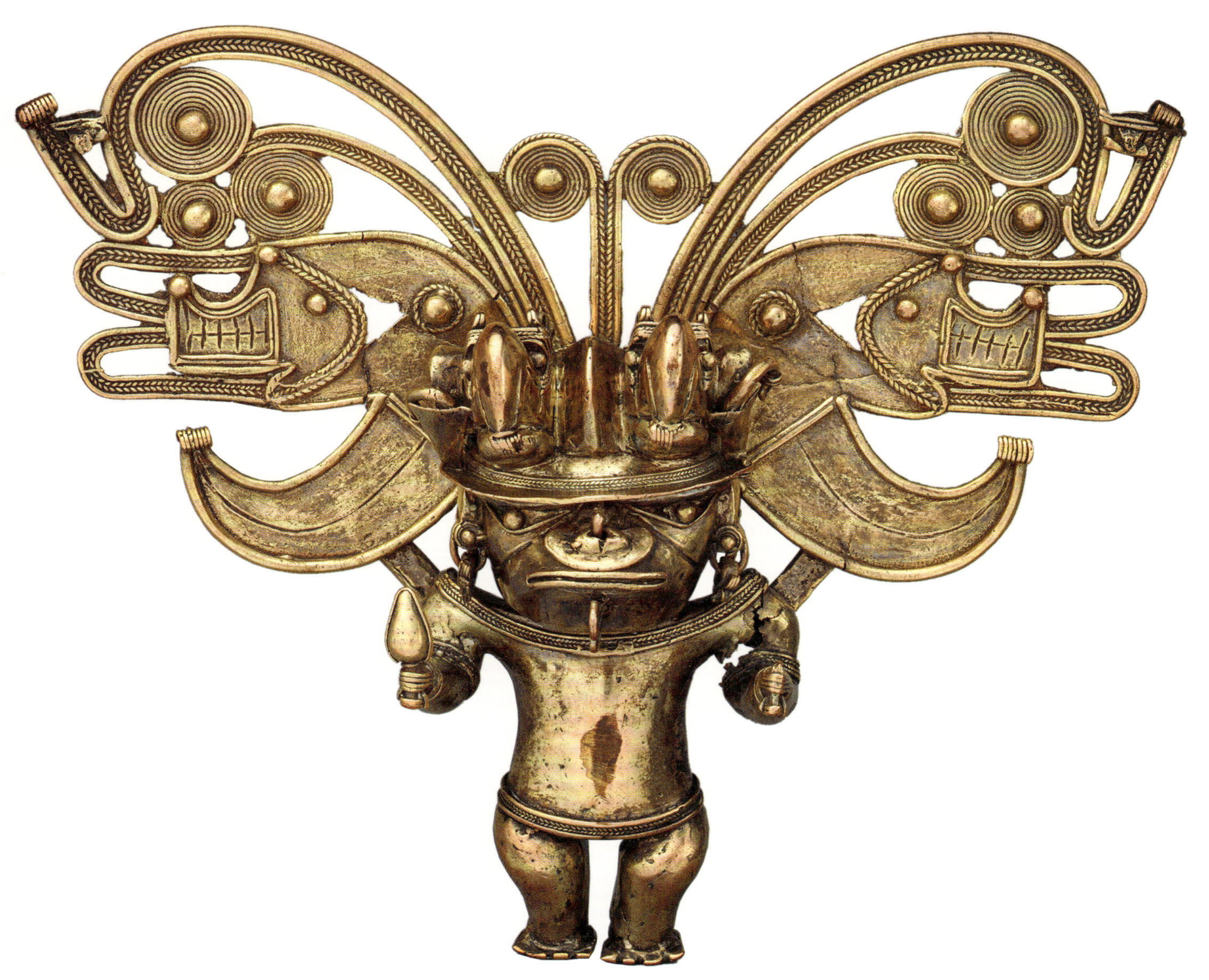

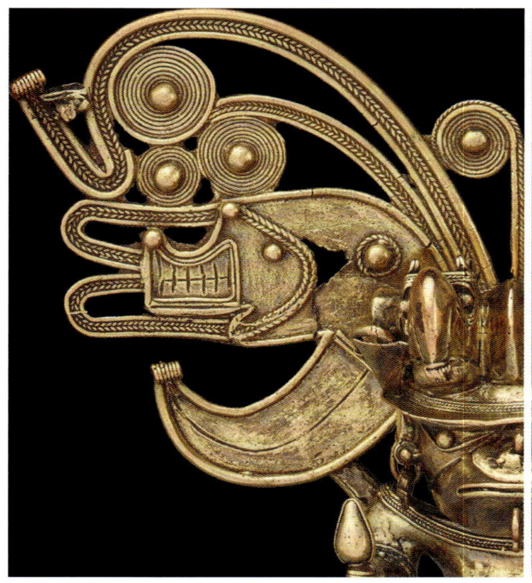
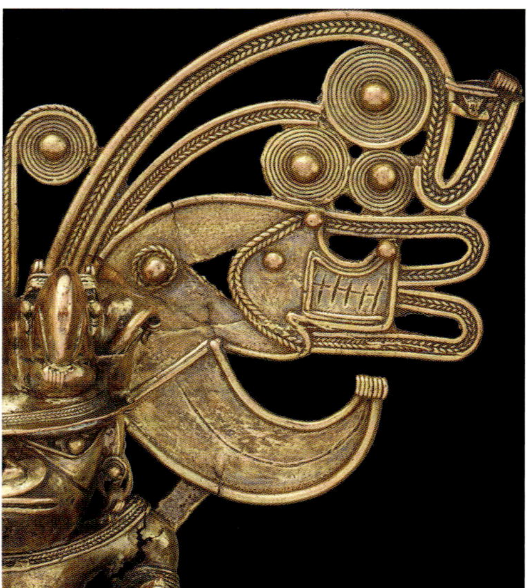

❶ Symmetry

The bilateral symmetry of the pendant means that each feature on the left is mirrored on the right. This gives the work an ornamental and pictographic quality, more reminiscent of an insect than of a human body.

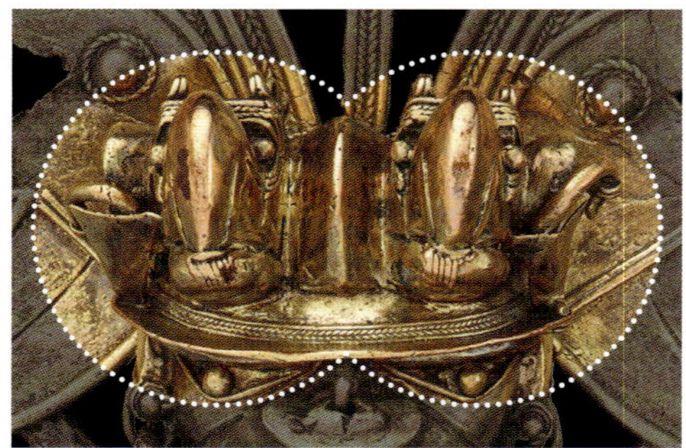
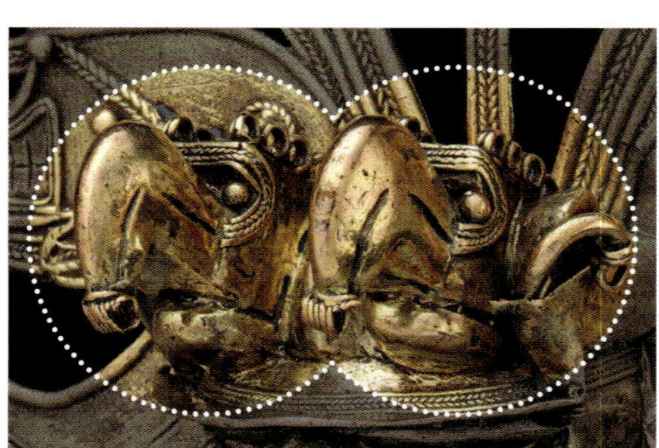

❹ Animal energy

Two ornamental birds sit atop the figure's crown. The headdress resembles a butterfly or bird, with outstretched wings and crocodile-like snouts. The animals may have been symbols of political power, or represented affiliation to a particular clan.

❷ Scale

At just under 14 cm (5½ in.) tall, the pendant is about the height of a smartphone. Its small size suggests that it was worn as a piece of jewelry, perhaps passed down through successive generations as a prized personal item.

❸ A language of symbols

Birds – who inhabit the heavens and possess the skills of speed and agility – are natural symbols of political or religious authority. They and other animals appear as decoration on many other Tairona artefacts, including a series of bells (opposite), suggesting that a common system of symbols was used by the various groups within their culture.[19]

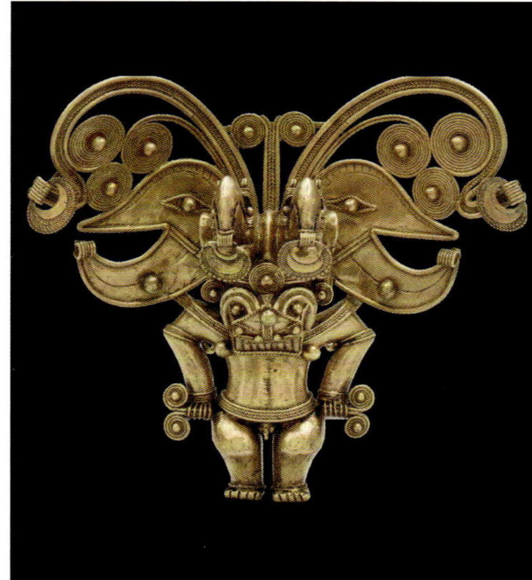

Masked figure pendant, Colombia, Tairona, 10th–16th century. Gold, 13.3 × 14.6 × 5.1 cm, 5¼ × 5¾ × 2 in.

❺ Tairona people

We know that the work was created by the Tairona people, a Pre-Columbian culture living at the northern tip of South America. The term 'Tairona' describes a diverse group of societies who inhabited the Sierra Nevada de Santa Marta mountain region. Their craft skills are preserved in many artefacts, particularly in cast gold ornaments, which demonstrate a centuries-old tradition of metalworking.

❻ Caribbean cultures

Scholars believe that the Tairona had historic connections with other peoples of Central and South America and the Greater and Lesser Antilles islands in the Caribbean, including Mayan-speaking communities and those from the Ulúa Valley, Honduras, and Veraguas, Panama.

❼ Colonization

Knowledge of the art of the wider Caribbean region was disrupted by European colonization. Following Christopher Columbus's arrival in 1492, local communities were obliterated by subsequent waves of invaders through warfare and the spread of disease.

❽ The face of power

The figure's enlarged head focuses our attention on its expressive facial features. In other, similar sculptures, the figure has an animal face, but here it is fully human.

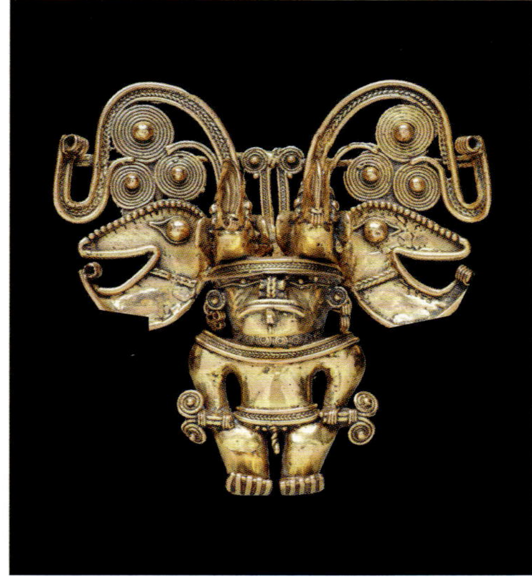

Masked figure pendant, Colombia, Tairona, 10th–15th century. Gold, 13 × 13 × 4 cm, 5 × 5 × 1½ in.

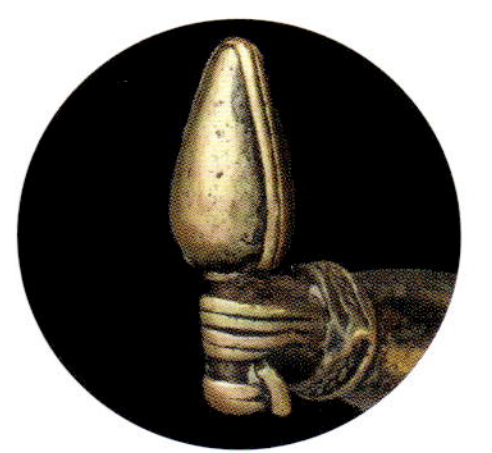

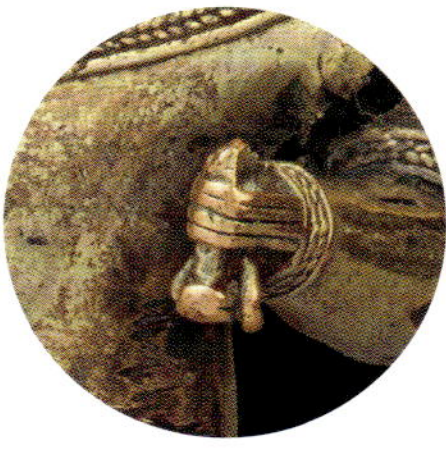

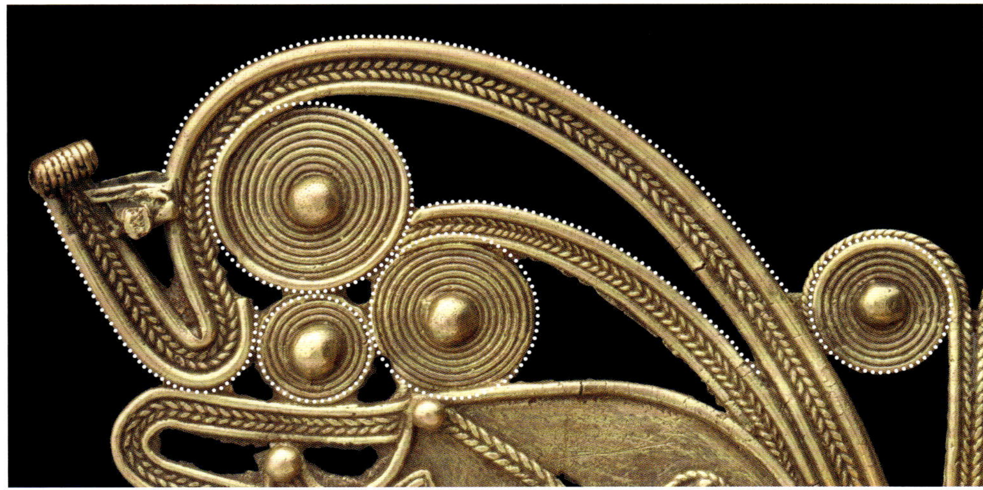

❾ Power pose

The figure's pose, with arms upraised and hands clutched around unknown objects, indicates a ceremonial activity. Its identity and the purpose of the ritual are mysterious, but it is likely to represent a person of high importance, possibly a ruler, a shaman or a powerful ancestor.[20]

❿ Gold

Gold is a soft material, impractical for use as tools and weapons, but its rich colour and rarity made it precious to early civilizations. The Tairona were highly skilled goldsmiths and produced some of the most complex and intricate objects made from gold in history. We don't know if they attributed religious symbolism to the material – like the ancient Egyptians, who believed that gold was the sacred fire of the sun – but it was reserved for representing significant figures. In this figure, the gold has been alloyed with copper to make a substance known as tumbaga.

⓫ Piercings

The face contains various facial piercings including a disc-shaped nose ornament, a labret (a piercing in the lower lip) and ornate earrings.

⓬ The language of clothing

The elaborate patterns on the headdress, armbands, necklace and belt are evidence of another craft skill of the Tairona culture: textile production.

⓭ *Caciques*

Tairona sculptures of this type are known as *caciques*, or 'chieftains'.

⓮ Hollow

This hollow figure, like the Roman statue of an emperor as philosopher (p. 28) and the figure of Shiva Nataraja (p. 44), was made using the lost-wax technique. This method had the advantage of using less precious materials. A wax sculpture with a solid core would be coated with plaster or similar casting material, then heated. The wax would then melt out, leaving a void for molten metal to be poured into, and creating a hollow metal sculpture.

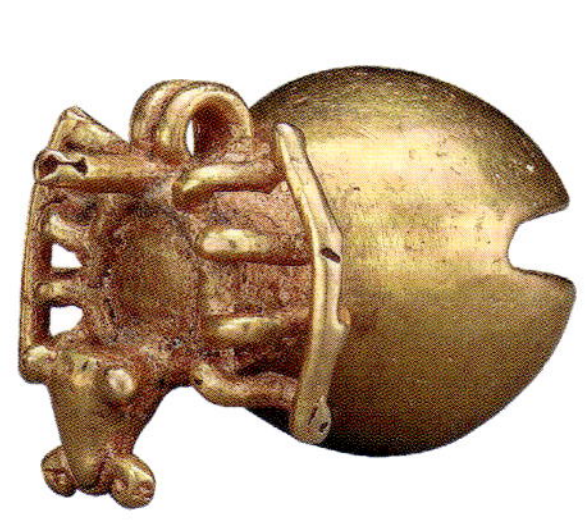

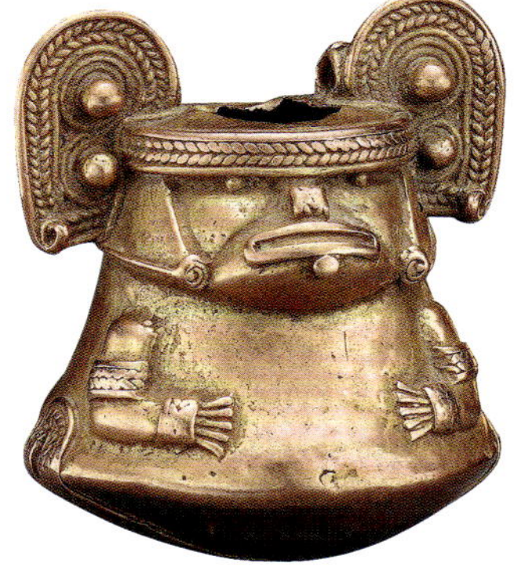

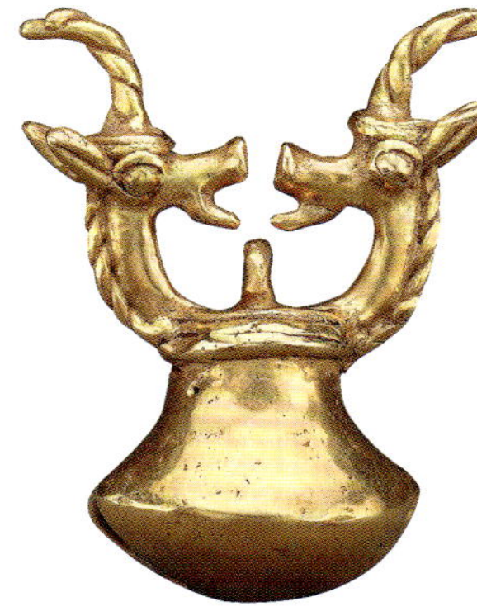

Bells, Colombia, Tairona, 1000–1500 CE. Tumbaga (alloy of gold and copper), 4.4 × 4 × 3.8 cm, 1¾ × 1½ × 1½ in.

LINKED PRACTITIONERS

PATTERNS FOUND IN NATURE:

Artist of the Chi-Rho-Iota page, Book of Kells (*c.* 800)
Artist of the Leopard caryatid stool (possibly 1800s)
William Morris (1834–1896), UK
Lita Albuquerque (born 1946), USA
Maya Lin (born 1959), USA

SYMMETRY:

Artist of Funerary mask of Tutankhamun (*c.* 1327–18 BCE)
Pietro Perugino (1446–1523), ITALY
Hilma af Klint (1862–1944), SWEDEN
Frank Stella (born 1936), USA
Rachel Whiteread (born 1963), UK

SMALL-SCALE WORKS OF ART:

Artists of Pectoral and necklace of Sithathoryunet (1887–78 BCE)
Limbourg Brothers (fl. 1385–1416), NETHERLANDS
Isaac Oliver (*c.* 1565–1617), UK
Matthew Simmonds (born 1963), UK
Rosa de Jong (born 1987), NETHERLANDS

10. Immortalizing Humanity

This naturalistic sculpture of a head was made around 800 years ago by an artist of the Yoruba people in the ancient city of Ife, now part of Nigeria. It is one of a large number of such heads, all made with similar skill, but whose purpose is largely unknown.

The original function of these objects remains shrouded in mystery, in part because they were buried and dug up repeatedly over the centuries for ceremonial reasons. They were relatively unknown to the wider world until the 1910s, and the revelation of a hitherto undiscovered sophisticated artistic tradition had a profound effect on the understanding and appreciation of the art and history of Africa as a whole.

Terracotta
31.1 × 14.6 × 18.4 cm, 12¼ × 5¾ × 7¼ in.
Minneapolis Institute of Art

Nigeria, Yoruba
Shrine head
12th–14th century

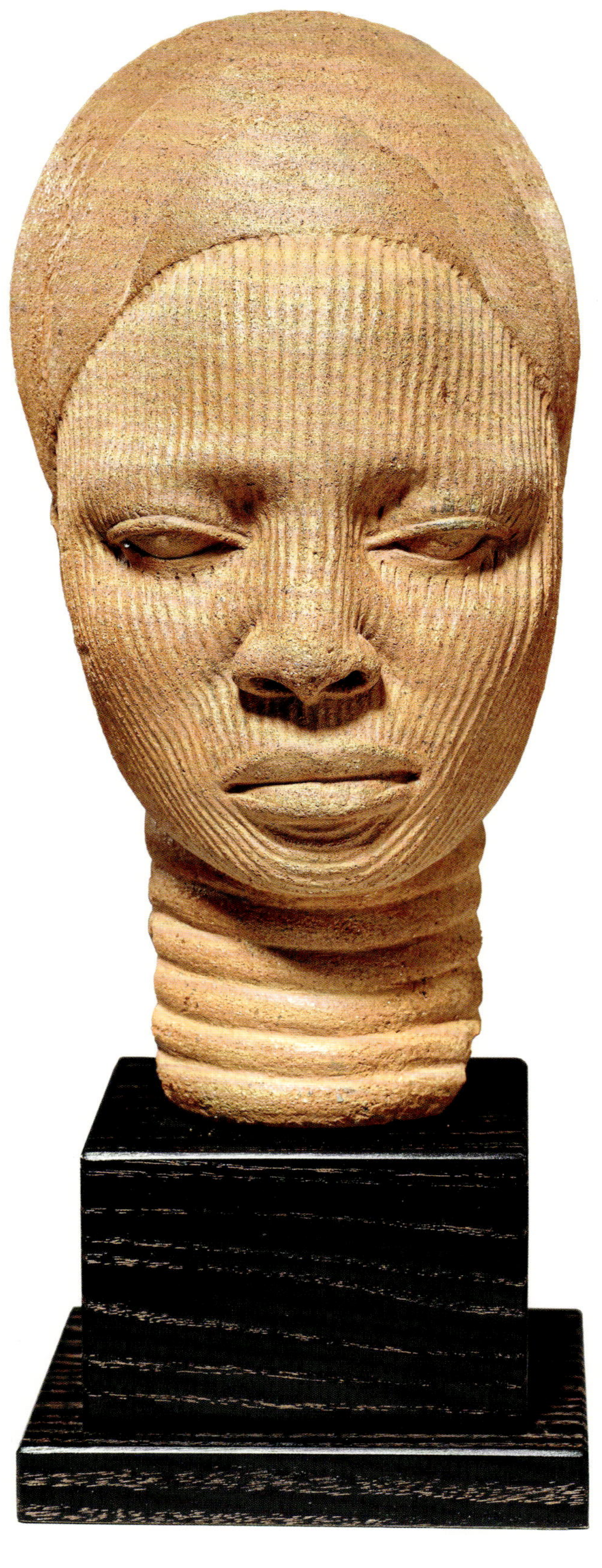

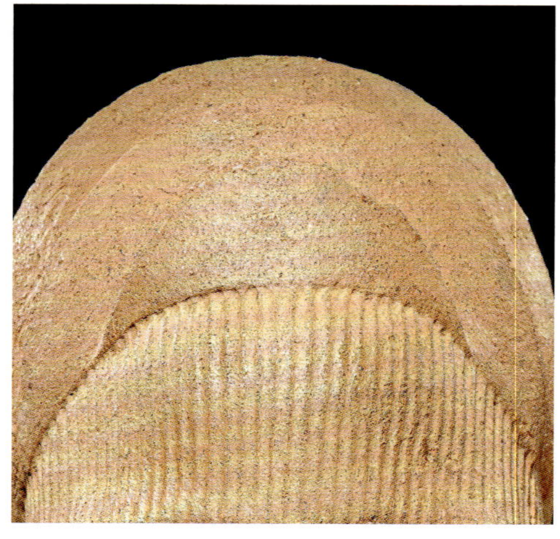

❶ Hair

The hair on the figure is stylized into a series of ridges, resembling a crown.

❷ What was it made for?

The exact purpose of this and similar heads made from terracotta, bronze and other materials is not fully known. It is possible they were ceremonial stands for headgear belonging to high-ranking figures in Ife. Works like these were buried in sacred sites and dug up again periodically at important moments for ritual or ceremonial purposes.[21]

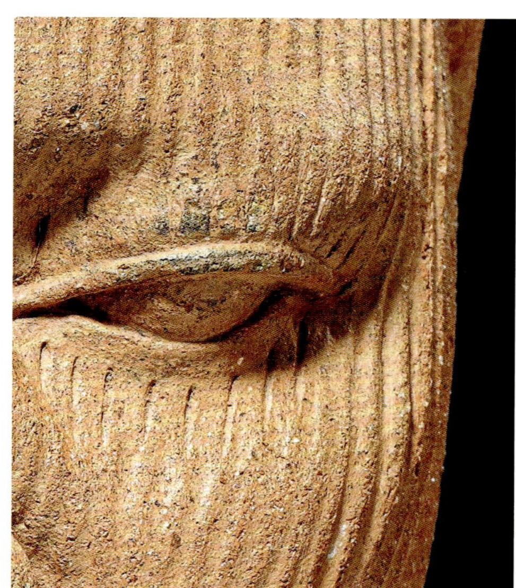

❸ Realism

The head is very naturalistic, with details like the crease of the eyelids and the bulging flesh between eyebrows and eyes represented with a high degree of realism.

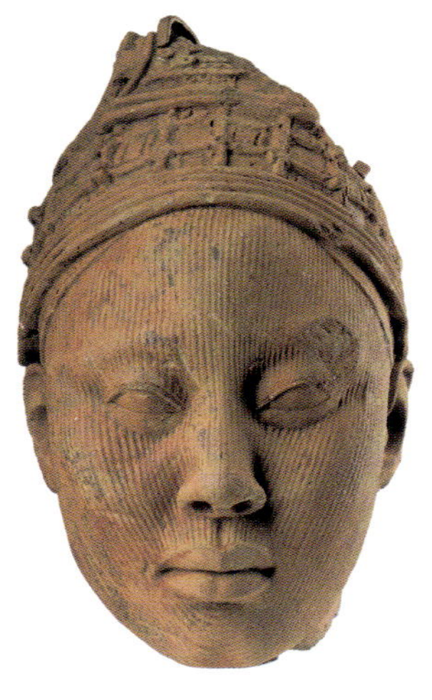

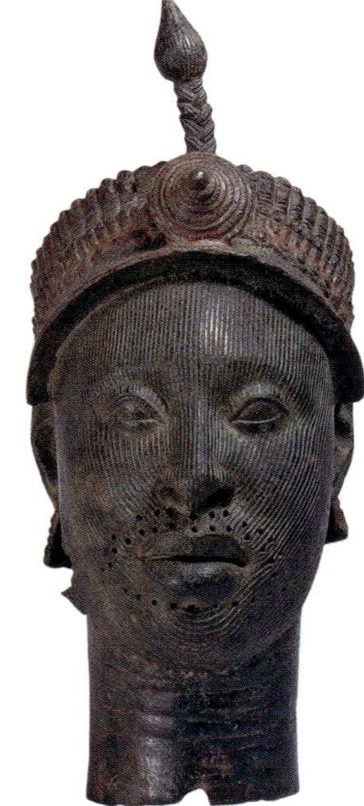

← Head, possibly a king, Nigeria, Yoruba, 12th–14th century. Terracotta with residue of red pigment and traces of mica, height: 26.7 cm, 10½ in.

← Ife head, Nigeria, Yoruba, 14th–15th century. Brass, height: 35 cm, 13¾ in.

↓ Head, Nigeria, Yoruba, 12th–15th century. Terracotta, height: 17.5 cm, 7 in.

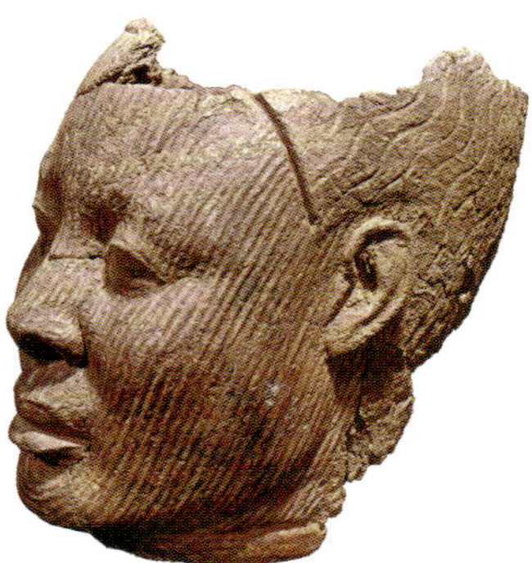

❹ A regal pose

The face of this head and others like it have similar serene expressions. They are not impersonal or formulaic, however, with each one having distinctive features and personalities.[22]

❺ Significance of the head

According to the beliefs of the Yoruba people, the head was where an individual's identity was contained, comprising the *iwa* (character) and *ase* (life spirit). Humans have their destinies established by the god Ajala, a divine craftsman who designs people's heads and sets their fate in motion.[23]

❻ Skilled artist

The sculptor of this head has replicated the appearance of the flesh of the lips with great skill, noting particularly the indentation where the corner of the mouth sinks inwards.

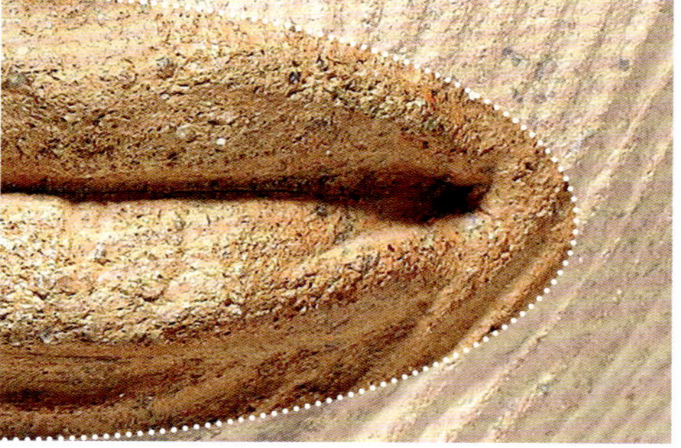

❼ Figurative and abstract

There is evidence that these figurative sculptures were buried alongside more abstract representations of the human face, possibly symbolizing the two dimensions of reality: *ori ode* (outer) and *ori inu* (inner). The outer, physical world is conveyed with a powerful realism, and the inner, or spiritual, world by more abstract forms. This way of representing the human experience is unique to Ife sculpture.

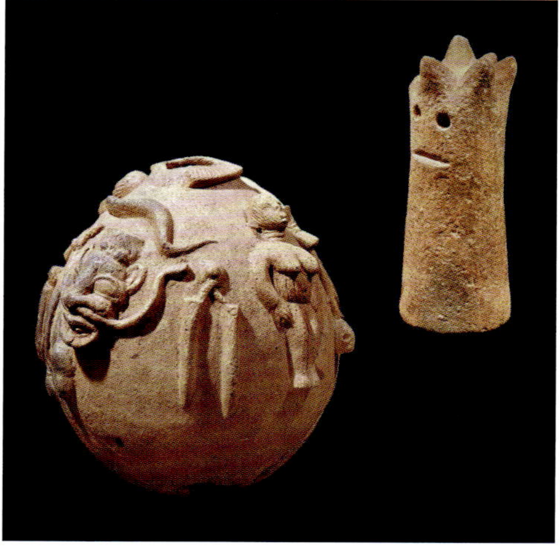

Ritual vessel from Obalara's Land, Nigeria, Yoruba, 13th–14th century. Terracotta, height: 24.8 cm, 9¾ in.

Cylindrical representation of a human head, Nigeria, Yoruba, 13th–14th century. Terracotta, height: 16.2 cm, 6¼ in.

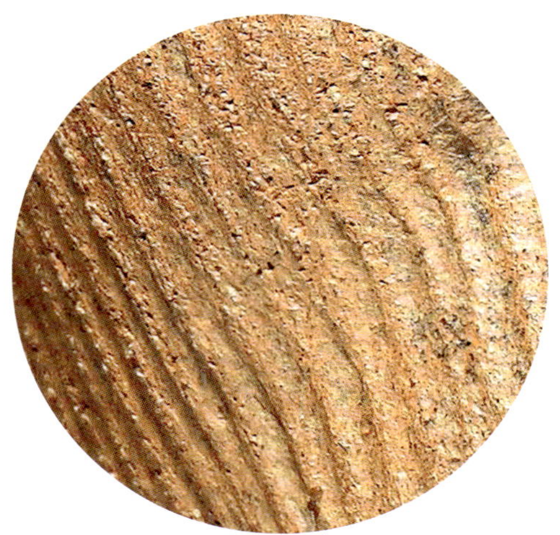

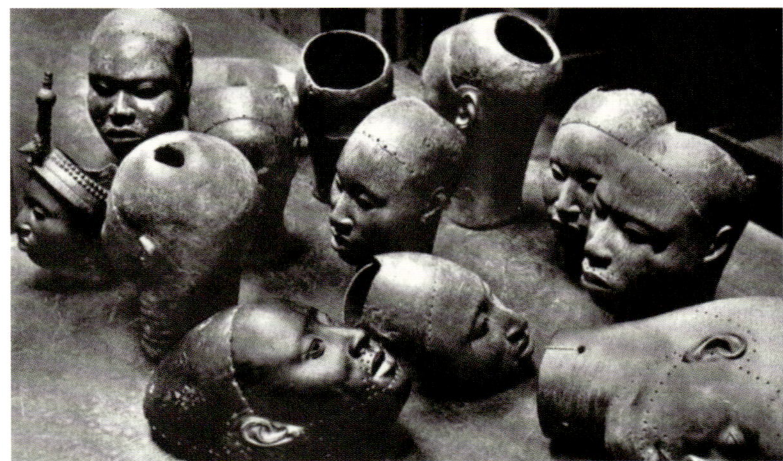

The Wunmonije heads at the British Museum, London, 1948

8 Facial marks

The lines running down the face are probably scarification marks, made by cutting the skin so that the scar tissue formed ridge-like surfaces on the skin.[24] As well as being signs of high rank, the lines also help to accentuate the three-dimensionality of the face.

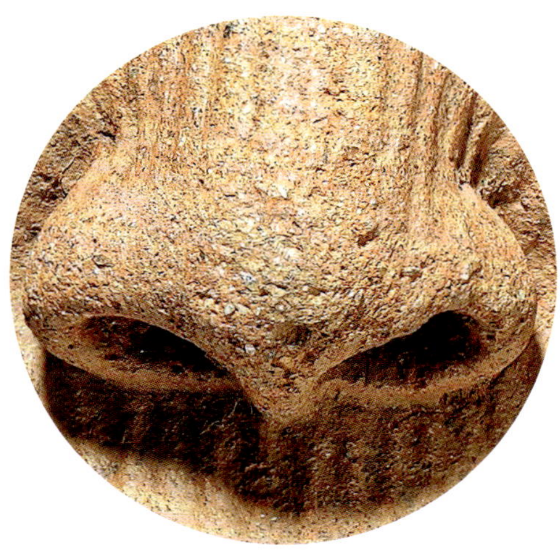

9 What makes it glitter?

The sparkling granules on the surface are specks of mica that have been combined into the clay.

10 Technique

The head was made using coils of clay, still visible at the back, which overlap one another as the shape is built up. It was then left in the sun to partially dry before being modelled using various tools; the artist would then wet certain areas to allow the terracotta to be manipulated. Finally, the sculpture was put into a high-temperature kiln – with the temperature carefully regulated and vents to allow hot air to escape – until it solidified.

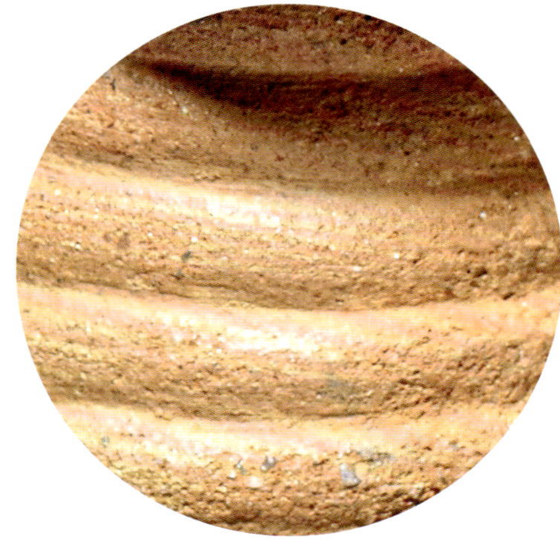

11 Who made this?

The name of the individual who made this head is unknown, but there is some speculation about the artists who created this example and others like it. As metallurgy was a male specialism in Ife, it has been assumed that the artists of the bronze heads were men. Women were specialists in terracotta production, leading scholars to speculate that this head and other clay examples were made by female artists.

12 Artistic heritage

The heads from Ife have attracted a great deal of interest from art historians, and been described as 'belonging to the highest levels of the artistic heritage of mankind as a whole'.[25] When they were discovered by the ethnologist Leo Frobentius in 1910, he erroneously concluded they were evidence of an ancient Greek colony in West Africa.

LINKED PRACTITIONERS

NATURALISTIC PORTRAITS:

Artist of the Head of a Roman patrician (early 1st century BCE), ITALY
Michel Sittow (1469–1525), ESTONIA
Diego Velázquez (1599–1660), SPAIN
Rembrandt van Rijn (1606–1669), NETHERLANDS
Chuck Close (1940–2021), USA

TERRACOTTA:

Artist of the Terracotta statuette of a draped woman (3rd century BCE), GREECE
Artists of the Terracotta warriors (late 3rd century BCE), CHINA
Luca della Robbia (1400–1482), ITALY
Alessandro Algardi (1598–1654), ITALY
Augustin Pajou (1730–1809), FRANCE

OTHER IFE HEADS AND THEIR LOCATIONS:

Copper mask for King Obalufon II (*c.* 1300), IFE NATIONAL MUSEUM
Fragment of an Ife head (12th–15th century), BROOKLYN MUSEUM, NEW YORK
Bust of a king or dignitary (12th–15th century), BERLIN ETHNOLOGICAL MUSEUM
Ife head (14th–15th century), BRITISH MUSEUM, LONDON

11. Landscapes of the Mind

The artist and calligrapher of this scroll, Zhao Mengfu (1254–1322), probably painted it while working as a government scribe in Dadu (in what is now Beijing), the capital of the Yuan dynasty, many miles from his home in Huzhou, Zhejiang province.

Zhao Mengfu

Twin Pines, Level Distance

c. 1310

The painting conveys a subtle sense of the artist's frustrations and fears. Although it emulates a traditional landscape composition, Zhao Mengfu pioneered a radical style by using his brush as if writing, rather than painting, thus producing a relatively harsher and more austere atmosphere. This blending of art forms was revolutionary, and would prove to be highly influential in Chinese landscape painting. It also reflects the inner turmoil of the artist's mind.

Handscroll, ink on paper
26.8 × 107.5 cm, 10½ × 42¼ in.
Metropolitan Museum of Art, New York

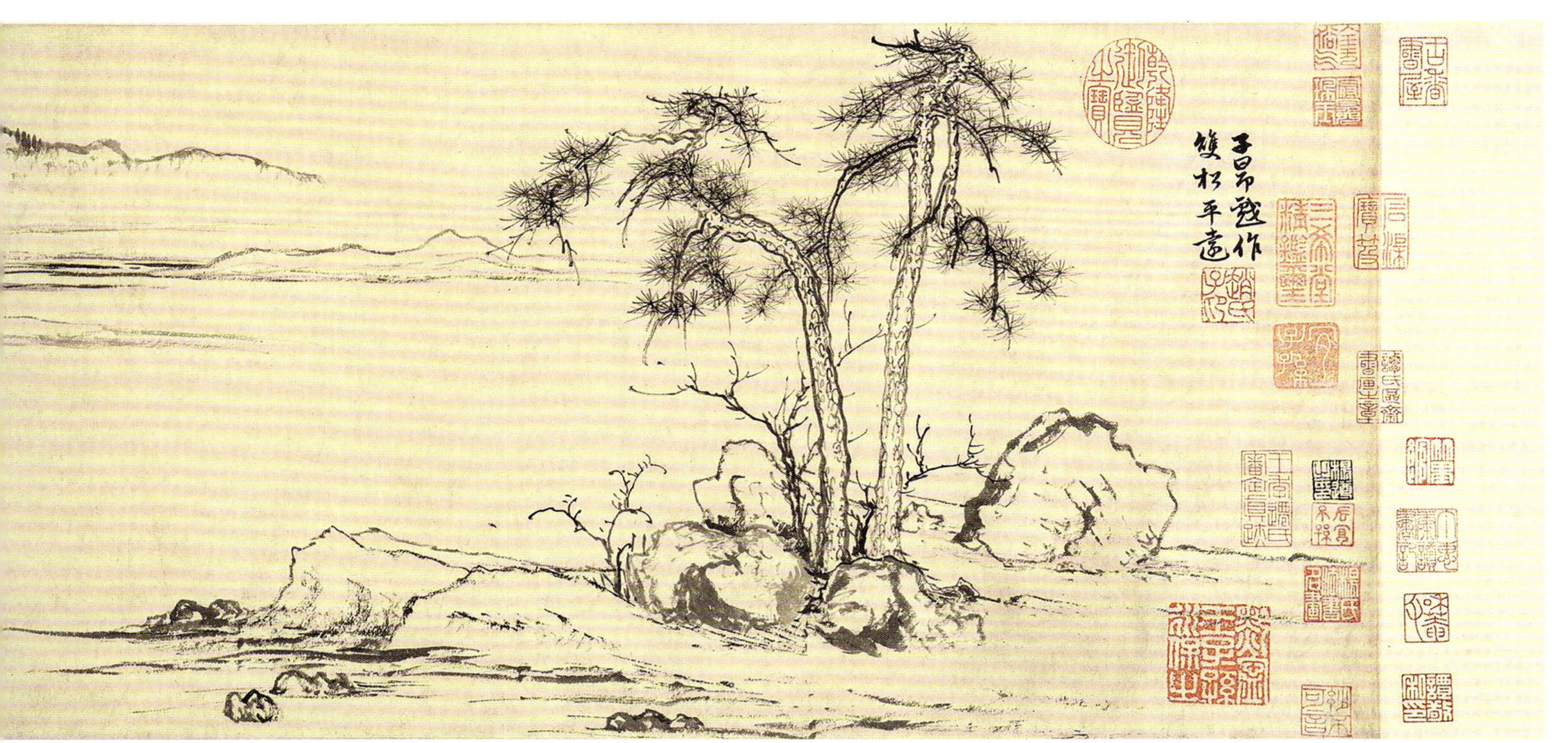

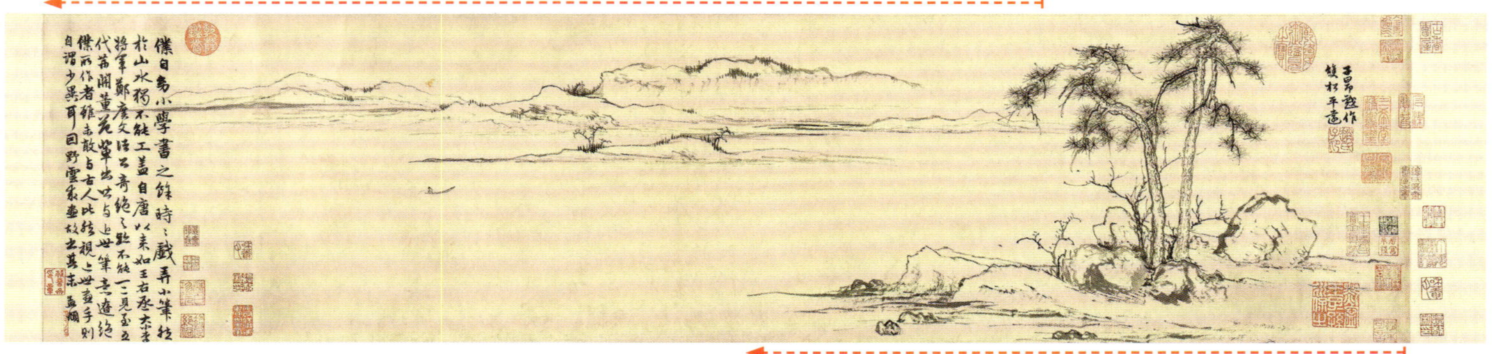

❶ Direction of travel

The landscape is designed to be read from right to left, so that we begin 'reading' the scene from the group of pine trees in the foreground.

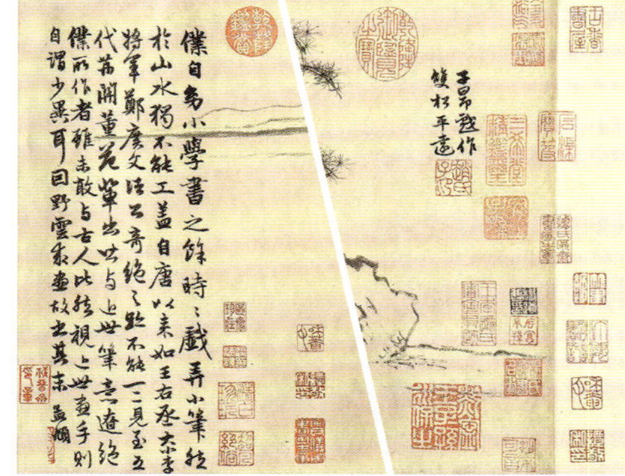

❷ Collector's seals

The red stamps are the seals of various collectors, evidence of those who have owned and admired this landscape scene over the centuries.

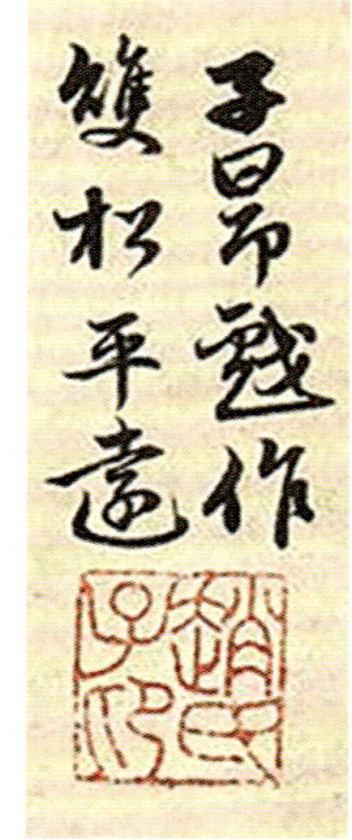

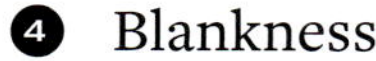

❸ Rolling hills

The work is part of a long scroll that must be unrolled to be seen in its entirety. Viewers would unroll one section at a time, creating an experience similar to walking through a landscape. To either side of the central image are poems written by later hands, which, like the collector's seals, indicate the various owners of the past.

❹ Blankness

Unusually for the time, a large amount of empty space has been left in the middle of the drawing. Zhao Mengfu adhered to the principles of traditional Chinese landscape painting, but unlike his predecessors, including Guo Xi and Li Cheng, he did not use ink washes. The result is an image that is dramatically stark and austere.

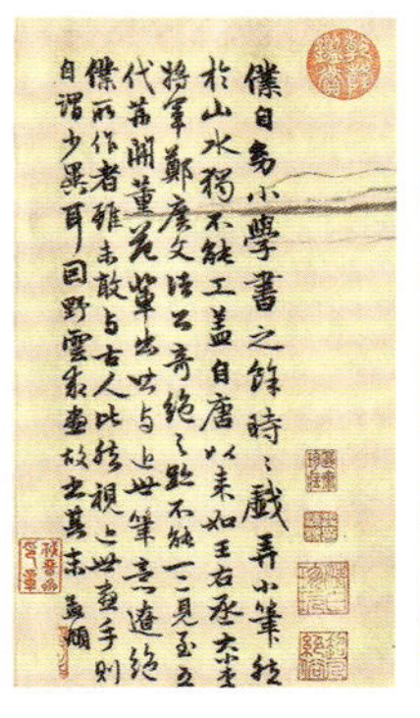

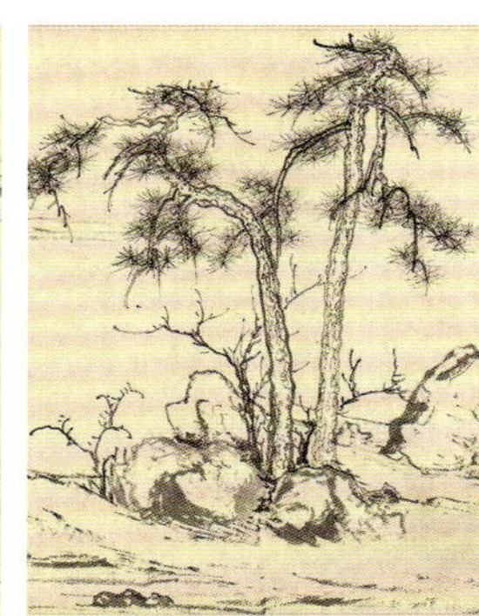

❺ Composition

Zhao Mengfu achieved a balanced composition by placing text at the left side of the work to echo the pine trees on the right side.[26]

❻ Revolution and tradition

The artist wrote a colophon about Guo Xi's *Old Trees, Level Distance* (below), painted nearly 250 years earlier, in which he honours this past master of Chinese landscape painting:

> *My whole life I have followed his lofty message of forests and streams;*
> *Constrained by petty official duties, I have been unable to achieve it.*[27]

❼ Text

In the colophon, Zhao Mengfu also passes judgment on Chinese landscape tradition. His painting is indeed very different in terms of technique:

> *What I paint may not rank with the work of ancient masters, but compared with recent paintings, I daresay mine are quite different.*[28]

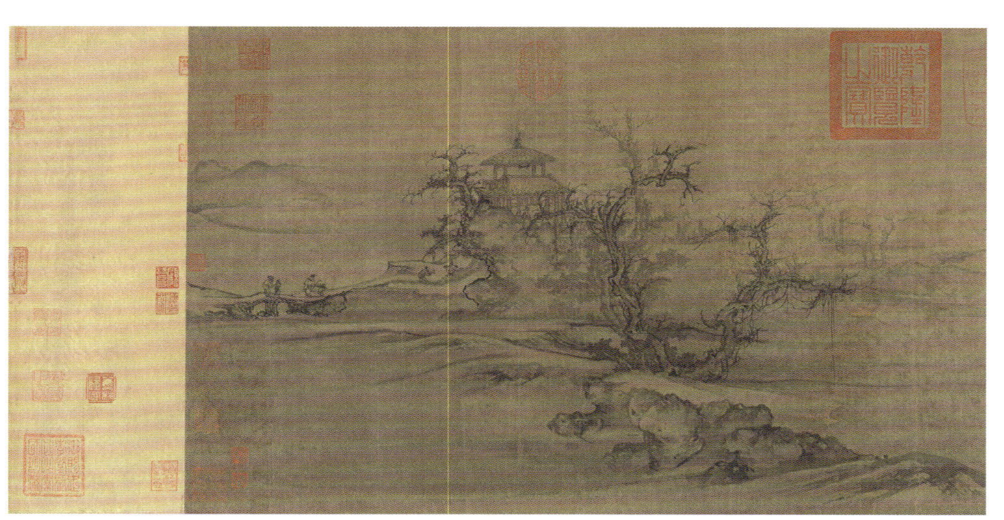

Guo Xi, *Old Trees, Level Distance*, c. 1080.
Handscroll, ink and colour on silk,
35.6 × 104.4 cm, 14 × 41 in.

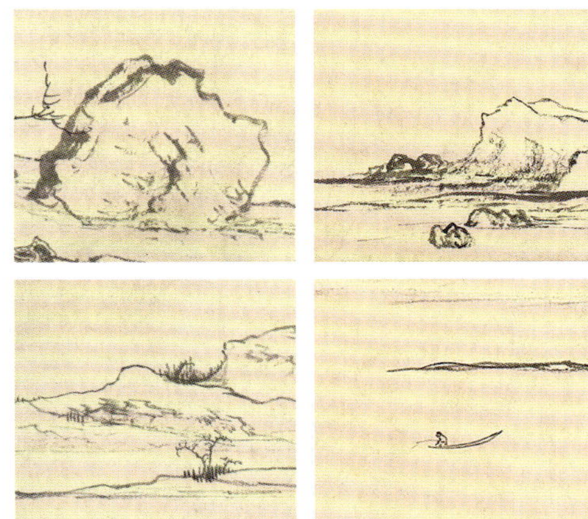

❽ Ink style

Zhao Mengfu is celebrated for his innovative technique. He used his brush in a manner that is closer to calligraphy than to drawing. Features in the landscape – the rocks, mountains and trees, as well as the tiny fishing boat – are defined with a bare minimum of lines, deliberately applied to create a scene as clear as a few simple words on a blank page.

❾ Twin pines

In Chinese painting, pine trees are symbols of endurance. The two saplings in front of the trees at the right suggest the stages of maturity, or successive generations. On the far island is an identical grouping of pines. This visual rhyme connects our gaze from the foreground to the middle ground of the composition.

❿ Word art

Three types of brushwork are visible. The patterns on the trees and pine needles are similar to the bold, rounded style of seal script, while the largest boulder displays the gestural 'flying white' style. Finally, the branches of the saplings are drawn in clear standard script. As Zhao Mengfu himself noted: 'Calligraphy and painting have always been the same.'[29]

⓫ Influential

This new style was to have a lasting influence on Chinese painting, and many later artists followed Zhao Mengfu's calligraphically abbreviated drawing technique.

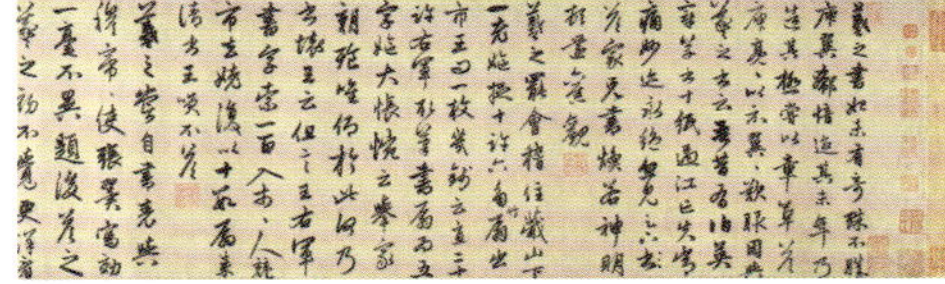

Four Anecdotes from the Life of Wang Xizhi, 1310s. Handscroll, ink on paper, 24.4 × 117 cm, 9½ × 46 in.

⓬ Level distance

Zhao Mengfu used the traditional system of 'three distances': foreground, middle ground and background. This is established through diminishing scale and ink tone, with elements depicted in ever-fainter ink as the scene recedes into the distance.

⓭ Fisherman

The blank space in the middle of the composition is completely ambiguous, with no rippling waves or swimming fish to tell us that it represents water. The lone boat and fisherman are the only elements of human interaction in the entire scene, adding to the feeling of distance and serene detachment in nature.

⓮ Calm before the storm

Unrolling the scroll reveals a poem by one of Zhao Mengfu's friends about a storm:

As the tiny boat tries to advance upriver,
Mighty mountain trees are suddenly swept
into a tumult
Swiftly heavy wind and rain pour through
the night,
Clapping waves against the sky – making
the oars hard to control.

⓯ Art imitating life

The poem seems to be a description of a tempest heading towards this serene idyll, or conditions further upstream. These hardships might have been inserted to reflect the artist's circumstances. During his lifetime, China was ruled by Mongol overlords. Although a descendant of the Song dynasty, Zhao Mengfu served grudgingly at the court of these foreign leaders.

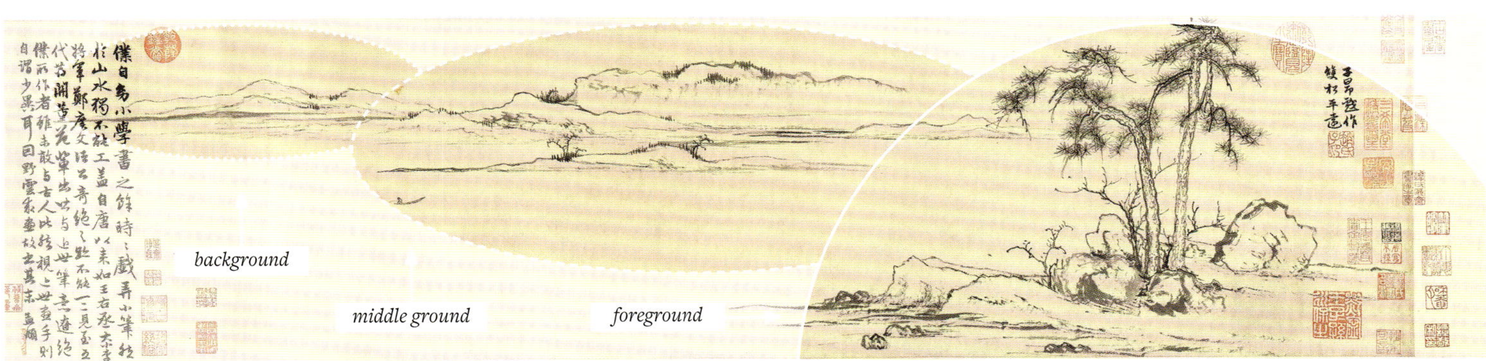

LINKED PRACTITIONERS

YUAN DYNASTY ARTISTS:

Qian Xuan (1235–1305), CHINA
Huang Gongwang (1269–1354), CHINA
Wu Zhen (1280–1354), CHINA
Ni Zan (1301–1374), CHINA
Wang Meng (1308–1385), CHINA

CHINESE CALLIGRAPHY:

Wang Dongling (born 1945), CHINA
Liu Youju (born 1955), CHINA
Xu Bing (born 1955), CHINA
Wang Tiande (born 1960), CHINA
Cao Jun (born 1966), CHINA

TREES:

John Constable (1776–1837), UK
Utagawa Hiroshige (1797–1858), JAPAN
Albert Bierstadt (1830–1902), GERMANY/USA
Vincent van Gogh (1853–1890), NETHERLANDS
Michael Craig-Martin (born 1941), UK

12. Glorifying Words

In this prayer niche built in the city of Isfahan during the 14th century, words have been integrated into the decorative pattern. They were written onto pieces of shaped glazed tiles that were then tessellated together, a technique developed during the Ilkhanid period of the Mongol dynasty, and orchestrated into rhythmic ribbons of colour.

At the time, calligraphy was more usually written onto paper, but here it has been incorporated directly onto the lustrous, multicoloured surface, mimicking the appearance of looping, inked letters from a pen. Words have a central importance in Islam as the means of human communication with the divine, with the Prophet Mohammed as the gateway. The words both frame the design and define its existence, as well as echo the tempo of colours and patterns that dance across the surface of the *mihrab*.

Mosaic of polychrome-glazed cut tiles
on a stonepaste body, set into mortar
343.1 × 288.7 cm, 135 × 113¾ in.
Metropolitan Museum of Art, New York

Iran,
Islamic
Mihrab
(*prayer niche*)
c. 1354–55

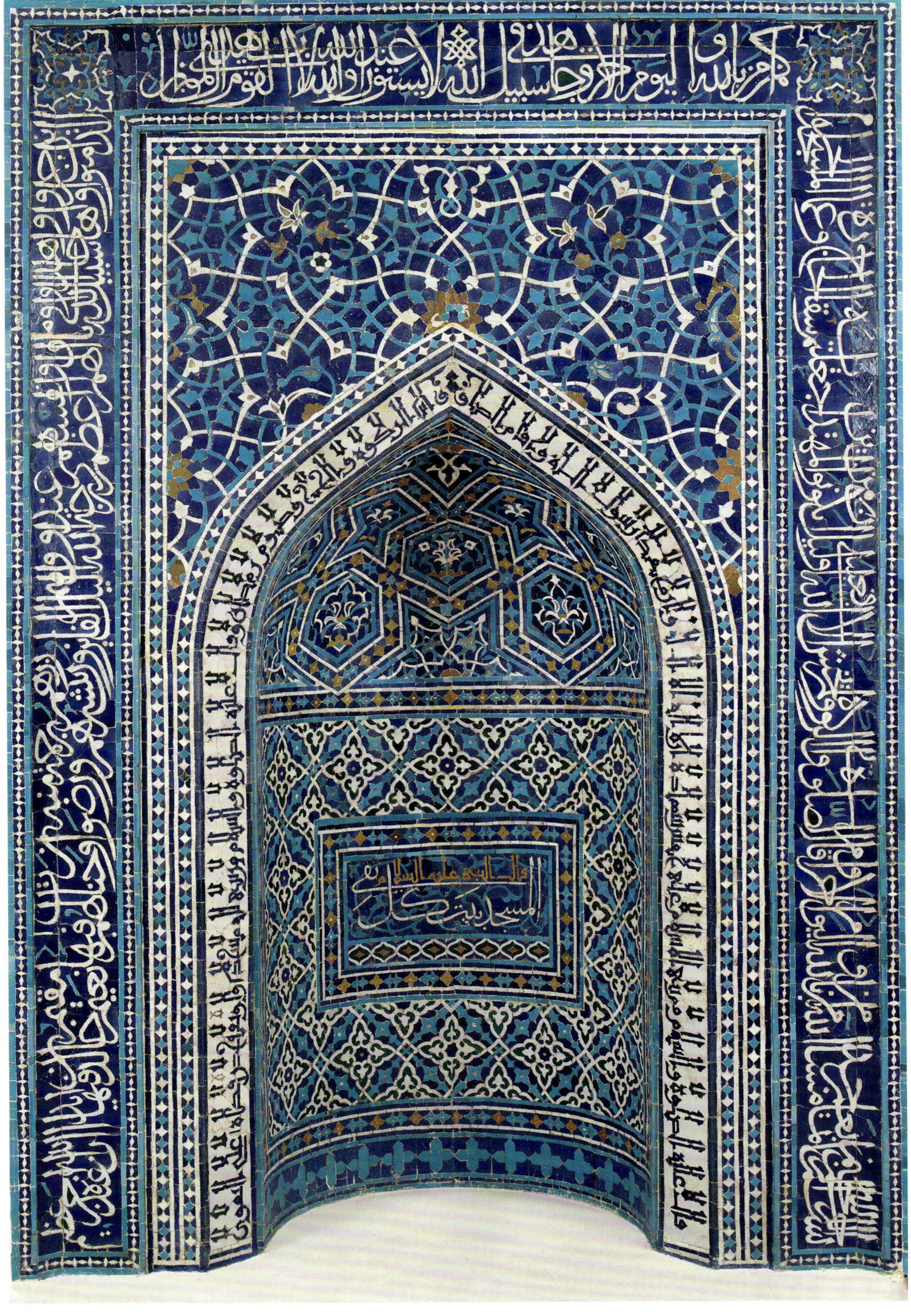

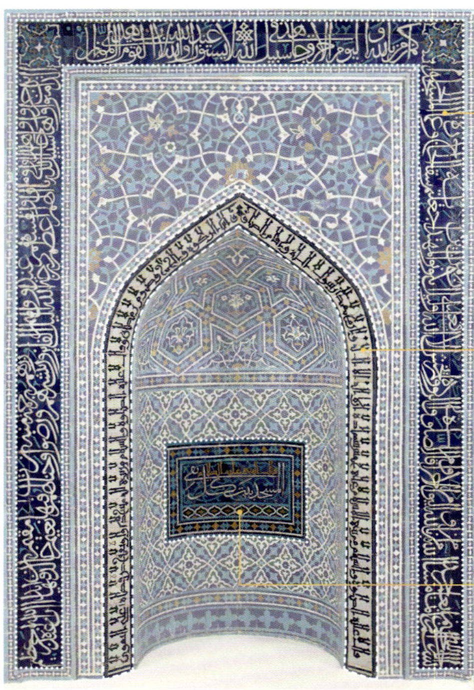

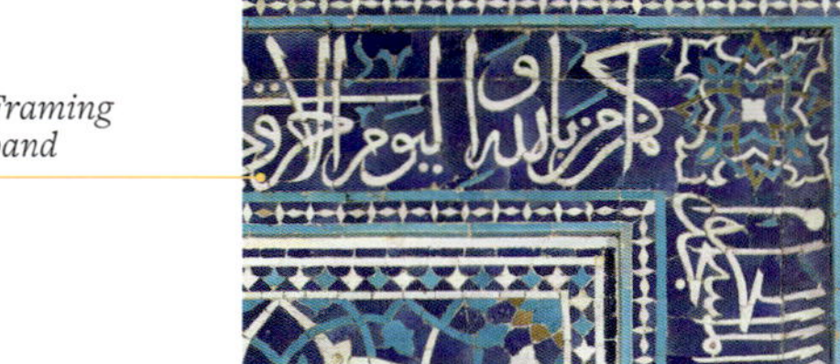

Framing band

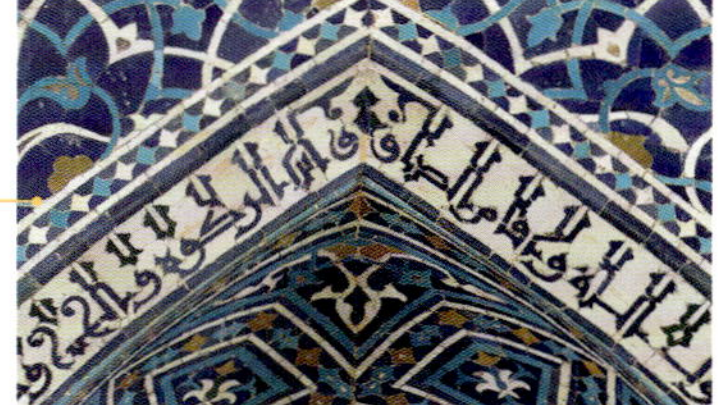

Inner border

Rectangular panel

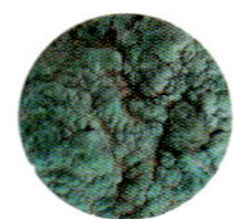

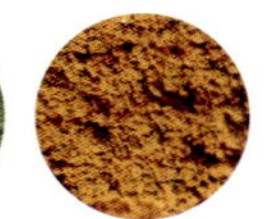

8 Colour

The artists used four coloured glazes, in addition to white, throughout the composition: cobalt blue, turquoise, green and yellow ochre.

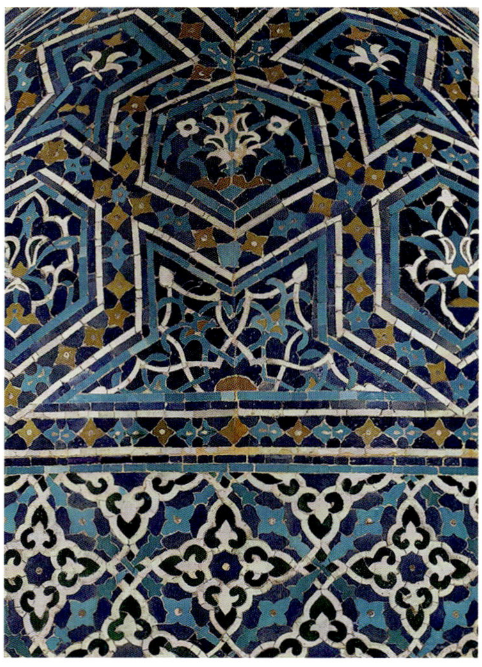

1 Central focus

The rectangular panel at the centre of the niche contains two types of Arabic: *kufic* and *muhaqqaq*. The way that the tile pieces have been cut and fit into place creates a three-dimensional effect, with the white *muhaqqaq* script appearing to overlap the decorative pattern below. Some of the extended lines of the letters also seem to lie on top of one another.

2 Significance of the mosque

The words on the tablet read: *The Prophet, may peace be upon him, said: the mosque is the abode of the pious.*[30]

3 Framing band

The framing band is written in the *muhaqqaq* script, one of six writing styles defined by Ibn Muqla during the Abbasid Caliphate in the 10th century (opposite, below). The others are *naskh*, *rayhani*, *riqa'*, *tawqi'* and *thuluth*.

4 The holiness of building

The inscription describes the auspiciousness of building mosques. This is echoed in the *mihrab* itself, which exemplifies the ingenuity and creativity seen in its patterns, graceful script and vivid colour.

5 Inner border

Kufic script, a more old-fashioned style of calligraphy, runs around the inner border of the niche. The tops of the letters are unified to add pattern and rhythm to the text.

6 Five Pillars of Islam

The text of the inner border comes from the *Book of Hadith*, the sayings of the Prophet. It relates to the Five Pillars of Islam: profession of faith (*shahada*), prayer (*salat*), alms (*zakat*), fasting (*sawm*) and pilgrimage (*hajj*).[31]

7 Natural forms

The pattern, known as vegetal decoration, may look symmetrical at first, but closer inspection reveals subtly disguised imperfections. Based on observations of plant forms, it is highly stylized and influenced by pattern motifs that featured in older works by artists of the Sasanian Empire and in Greco-Roman culture.

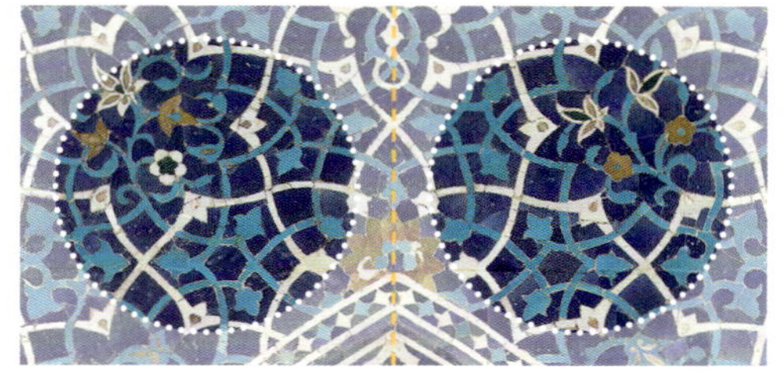

9 Materials

The design is like a mosaic, comprising hundreds of glazed tiles that have been cut and fit together. When the *madrasah* was lit with the flames of torches and candles, the tiles would have reflected the flickering light, giving the whole niche a sparkling quality.

10 Mecca

The Prophet Mohammed once lived in Mecca, but was exiled to Medina, where he resided in a house that faced his hometown. *Mihrabs*, therefore, face Mecca.

11 Direction of prayer

The *mihrab* was originally placed within an Islamic religious school: the Madrasah-i Imami, in Isfahan (opposite, above). It indicated the direction of prayer towards Mecca, providing the faithful with a focal point for their devotion.

View of the courtyard of the Mesdjid-i-Shah, Isfahan, from Xavier Pascal Coste's *Monuments modernes de la Perse mesurés, dessinés et décrits*, 1867

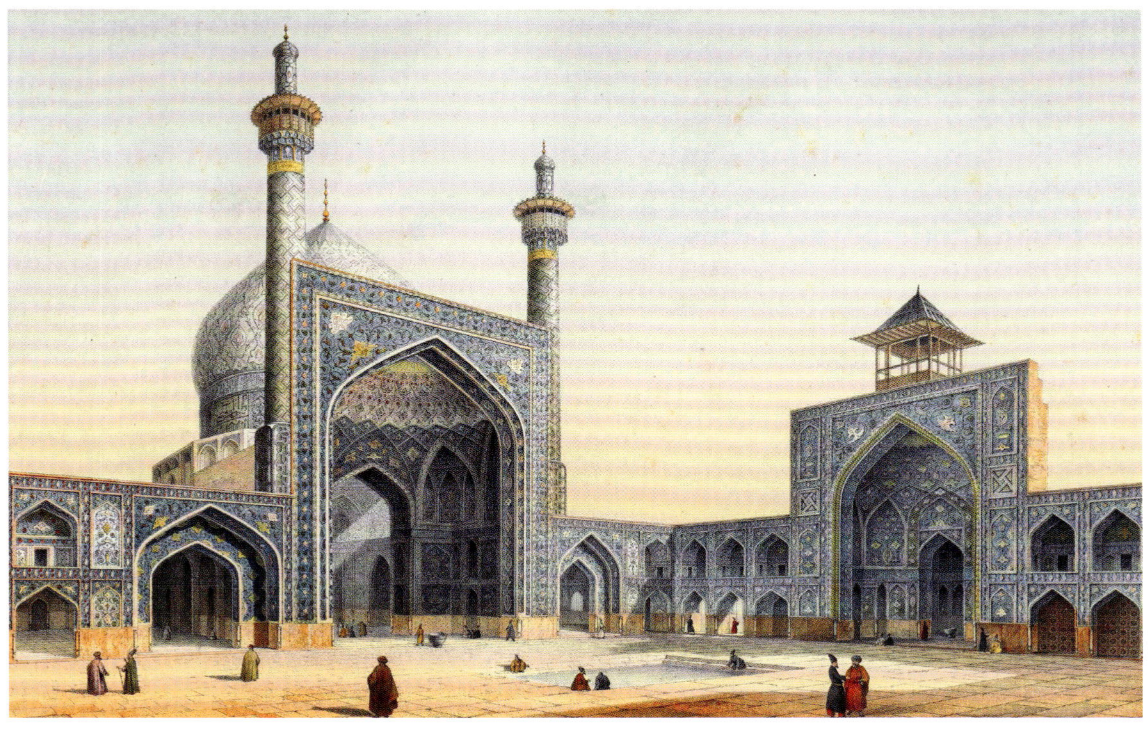

SIX CALLIGRAPHIC STYLES DEFINED BY IBN MUQLA

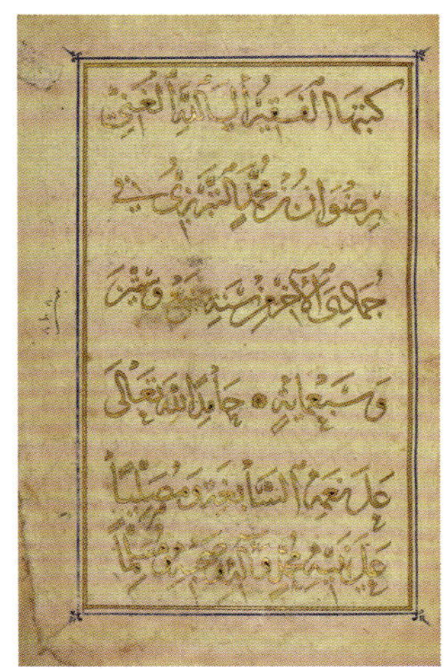

Ridwan ibn Muhammad al-Tabizi (scribe), colophon in gold *tawqi'* script, *c.* 1366

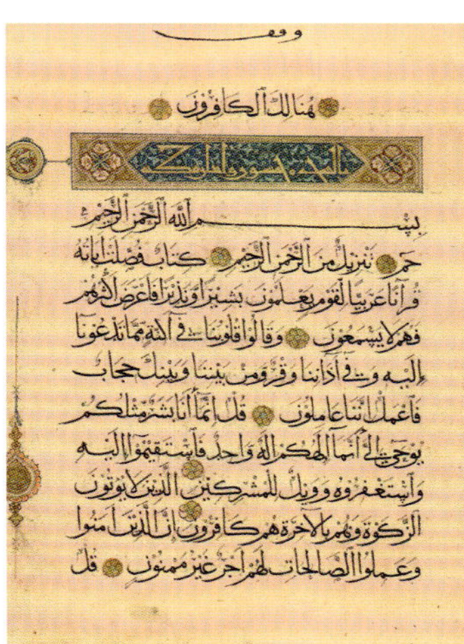

Qur'an leaf in *muhaqqaq* script, *c.* 1327

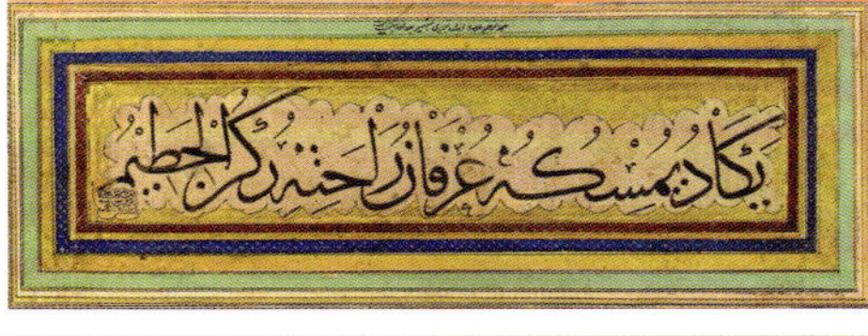

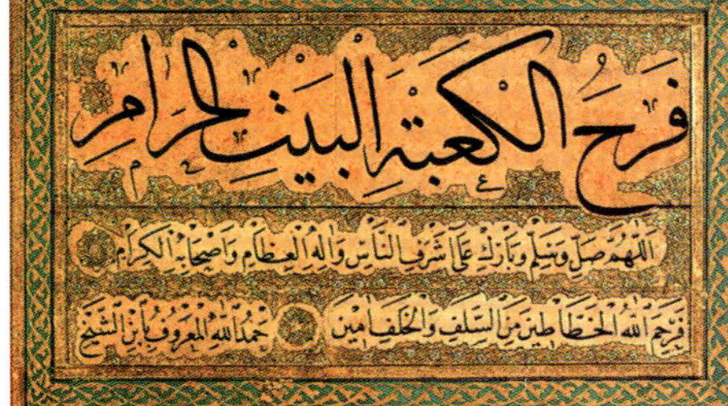

↑ Page from calligraphy album in *naskh* script

↑↑ Attributed to Ala' al-Din Tabrizi (calligrapher), Arabic prayer in *thuluth* script, 16th century

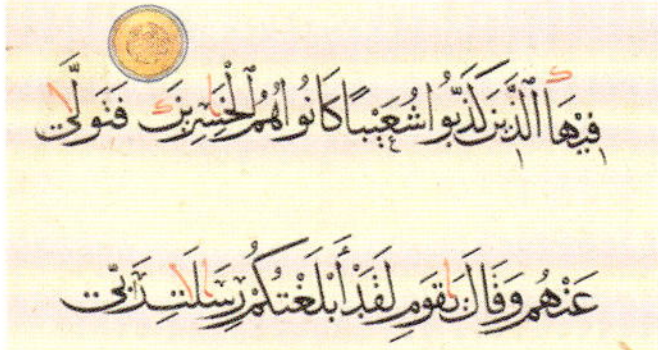

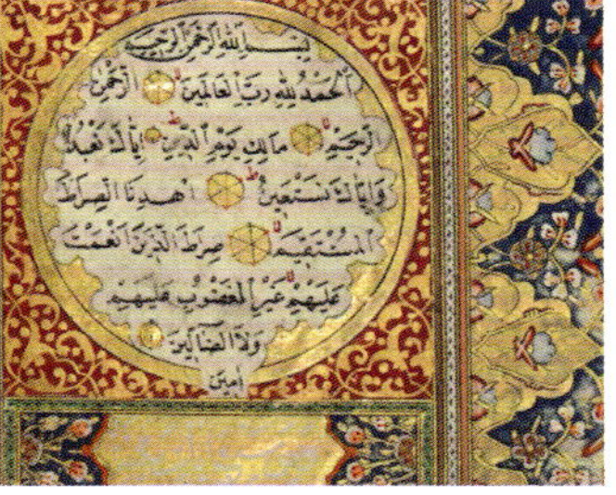

↑ Muhammad ibn Mustafa Izmiri (scribe), folio from illuminated Qur'an manuscript in *riqa'* script, *c.* 1865–66

↑↑ Attributed to Ali ibn Muhammad al-Mukattib al-Ashrafi (calligrapher), double page from a manuscript of the Qur'an in *rayhani* script, *c.* 1370–75

LINKED PRACTITIONERS

MUHAQQAQ SCRIPT:

Ibn Muqla (886–940), IRAQ
Ibn al-Bawwāb (died 1022), IRAQ
Yaqut al-Musta'simi (died 1298), TURKEY
Ahmad al-Suhrawardi (1256–1340), IRAQ
Hâfiz Osman (1642–1698), TURKEY

VEGETAL DECORATION:

Bishandas (17th century), INDIA
Artist of the Tughra of Sultan Süleiman the Magnificent (*c.* 1555–60)
Artist of Rosette bearing the names and titles of Shah Jahan (*c.* 1630–40)

INSPIRED BY ISLAMIC ARTS:

Jean-Léon Gérôme (1824–1904), FRANCE
Frederic Leighton (1830–1896), UK
William De Morgan (1839–1917), UK
Lalla Essaydi (born 1956), MOROCCO
Inci Eviner (born 1956), TURKEY

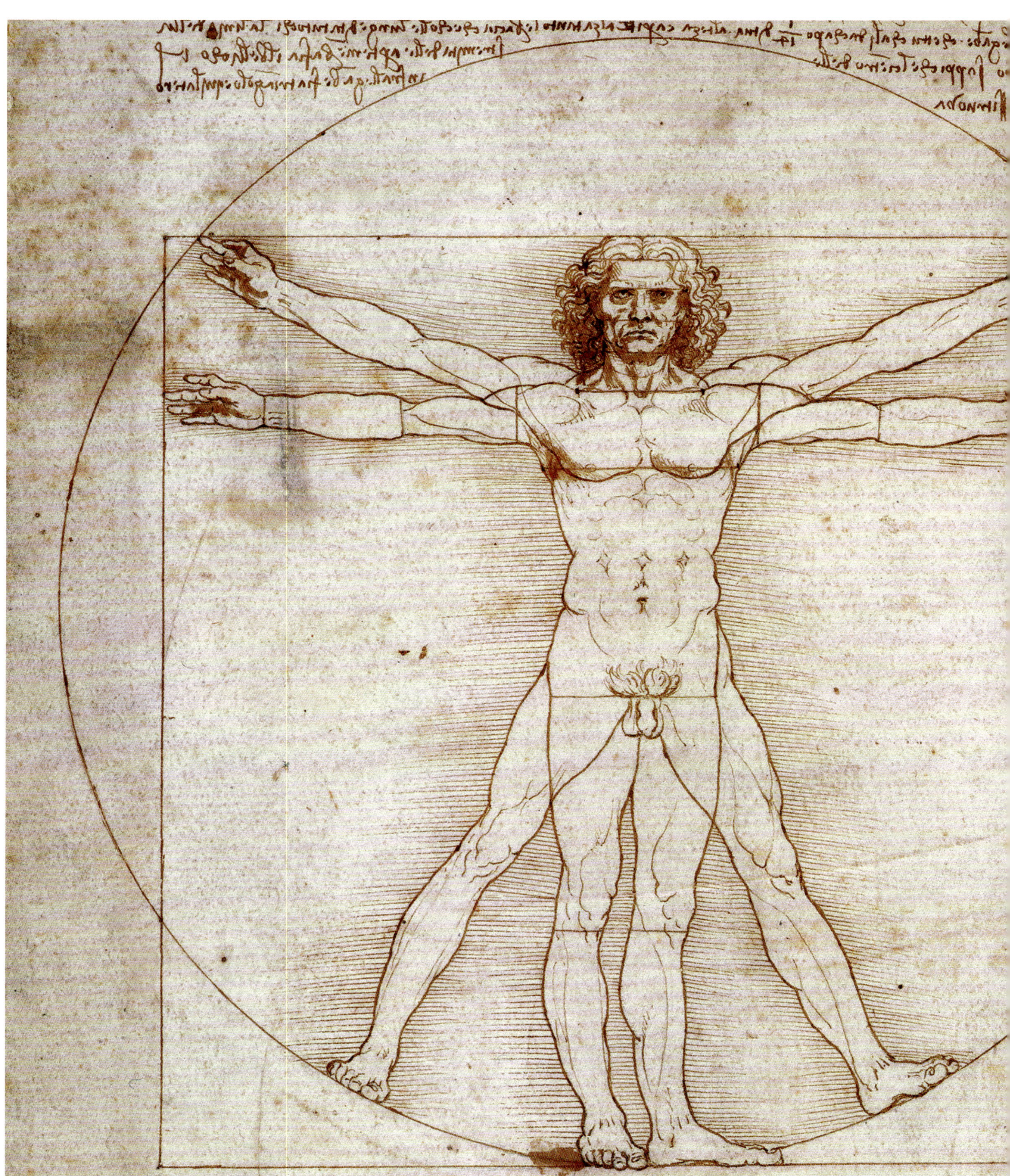

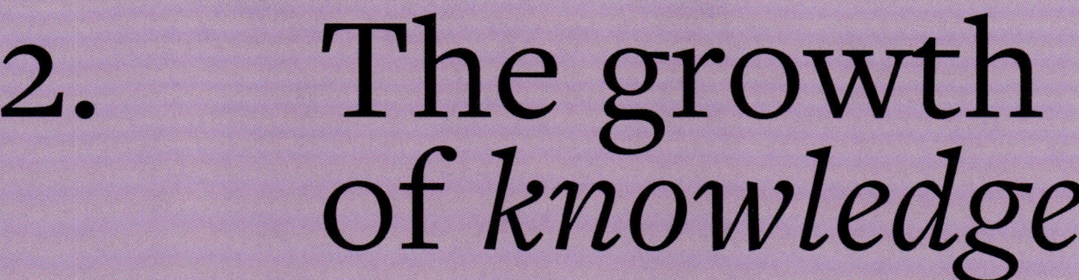

2. The growth of *knowledge*

1400 *to* 1599

In the 15th and 16th centuries, art underwent a revolution. Artists continued to refine the techniques and styles of the past, but new ways of seeing were emerging, driven by discoveries in mathematics, human anatomy and physics, as well as contact for the first time between previously separate cultures.

1400 *to* 1599

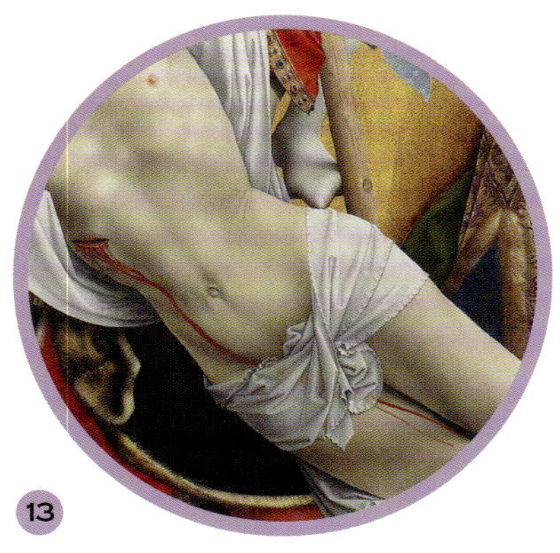

13

Faith and Feeling

Rogier van der Weyden
The Descent from the Cross
before 1443

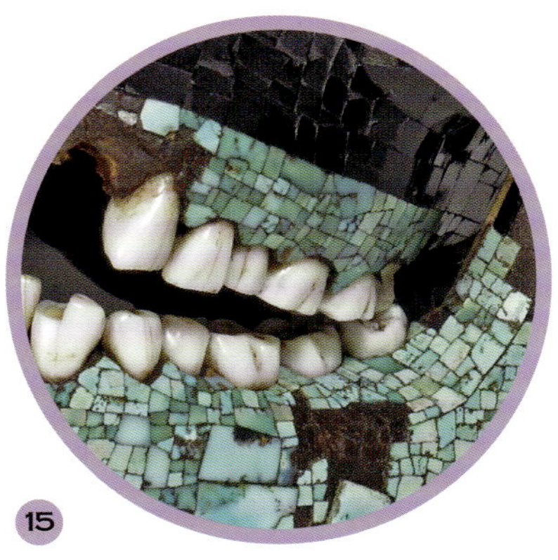

15

Spirit Worlds

Mexico, Aztec
Mosaic skull of Tezcatlipoca
1400–1521

14

Creating the Ideal

Leonardo da Vinci
Vitruvian Man
c. 1490

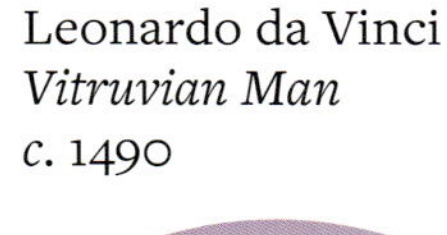

16

Cultural Interactions

Sierra Leone, Sapi-Portuguese
Hunting horn
late 15th century

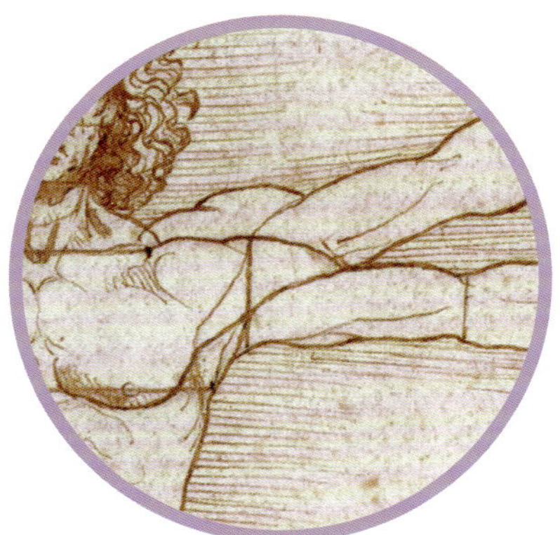

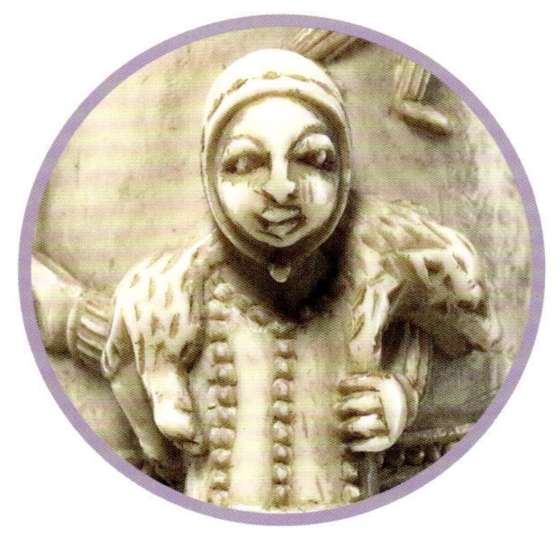

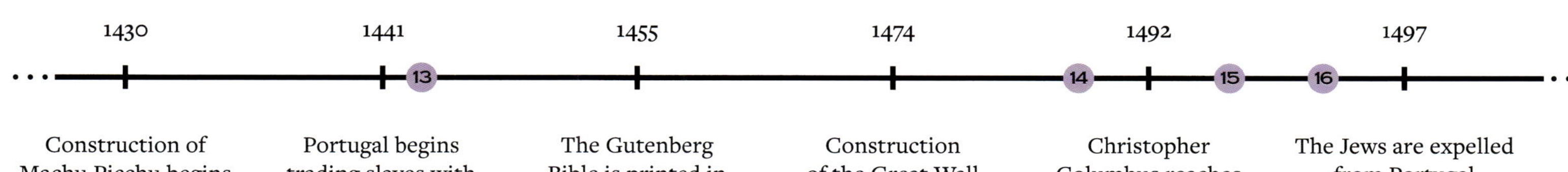

1430 — Construction of Machu Picchu begins

1441 — Portugal begins trading slaves with West Africa

1455 — The Gutenberg Bible is printed in Mainz, Germany

1474 — Construction of the Great Wall of China begins

1492 — Christopher Columbus reaches the New World

1497 — The Jews are expelled from Portugal

Timeline of events, artworks 13–21

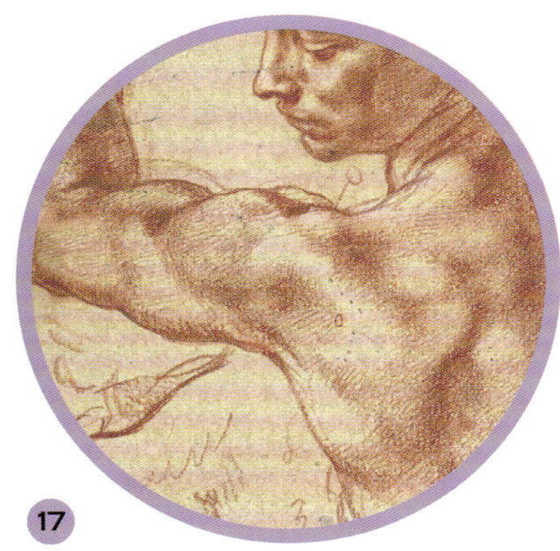

17

Proper Preparations

Michelangelo
Studies for the Libyan Sibyl
c. 1510–11

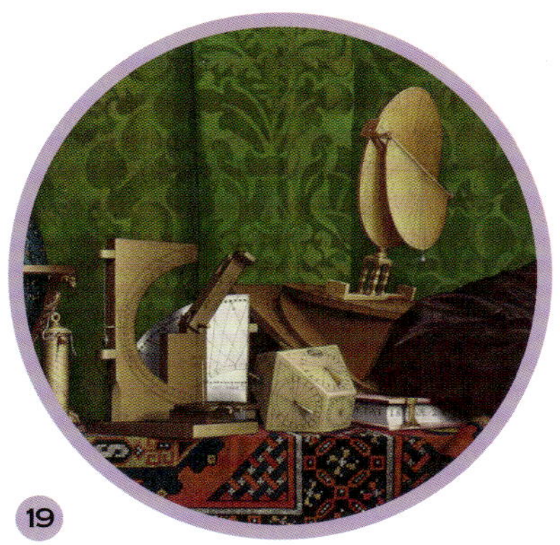

19

A Multilayered Portrait

Hans Holbein the Younger
The Ambassadors
1533

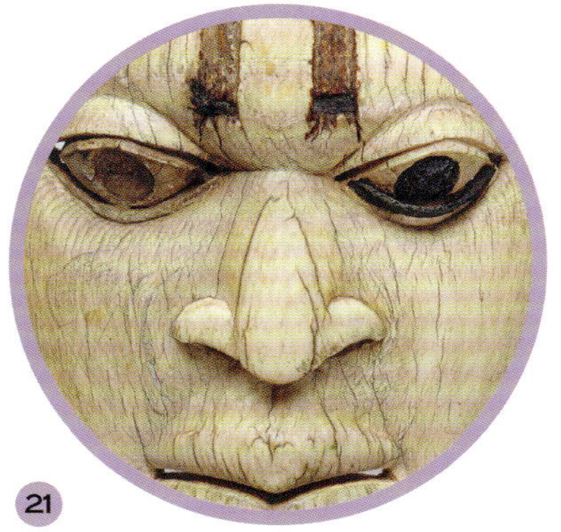

21

Protection and Command

Nigeria, Edo
Queen mother pendant mask
16th century

18

Stories Within Stories

Master of James IV of Scotland, *Deathbed Scene* and *Office of the Dead*, *c.* 1510–20

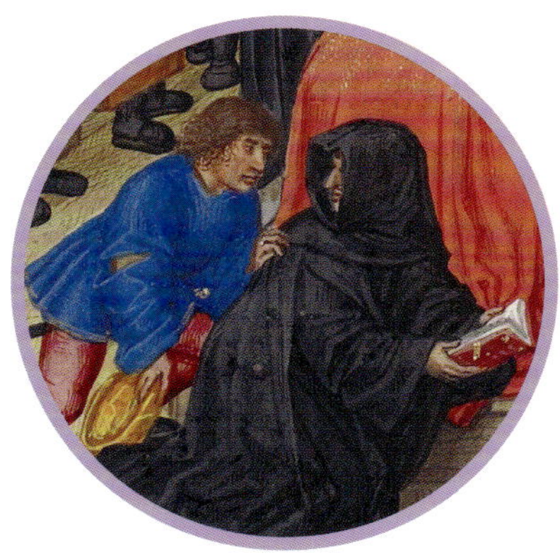

20

Signature Styles

Turkey, Ottoman
Tughra of Süleiman the Magnificent
c. 1555–60

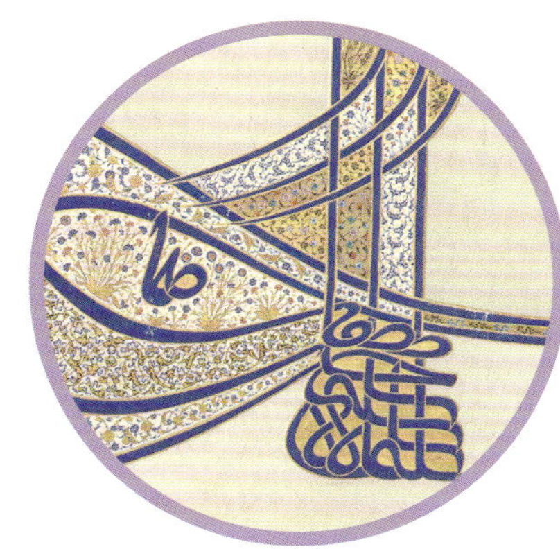

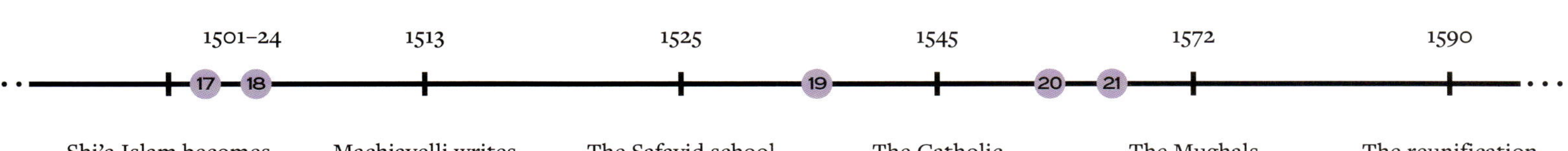

1501–24: Shi'a Islam becomes the state religion of Persia

1513: Machiavelli writes *The Prince* (published in 1532)

1525: The Safavid school of manuscript illumination begins

1545: The Catholic Counter-Reformation is launched

1572: The Mughals conquer Gujarat in western India

1590: The reunification of Japan is complete

13. Faith and Feeling

When Rogier van der Weyden (1399–1464) painted this altarpiece in 15th-century Flanders, he set out to portray the crucifixion, the climactic event in the Bible, in the clearest, most impactful way possible. Already a master of oil-painting techniques, his aim was to achieve new and even greater heights of realism.

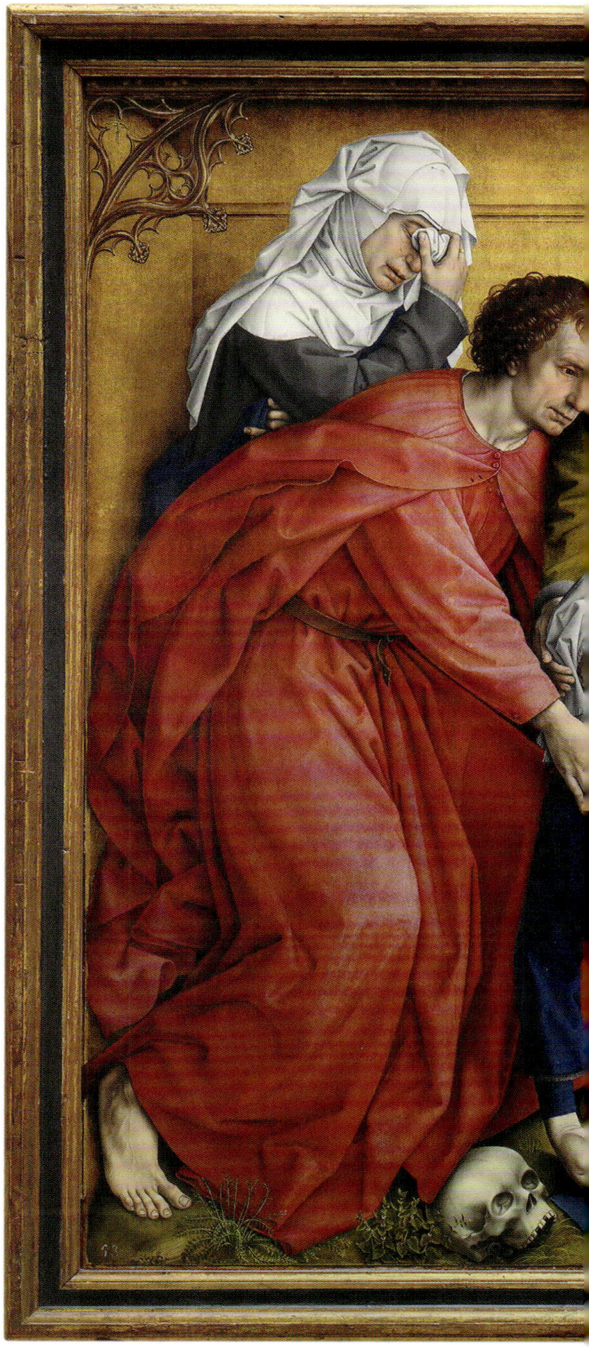

That level of hyper-realism that Van der Weyden sought – and mastered – is on display here, from the articulation of tears running down the figures' cheeks to the swollen eyelids and wrinkled skin of their faces, to the individual bristles that stand out on unshaven faces. But the power of the work is not simply due to its naturalism. Van der Weyden's understanding of psychology, symbolism, colour and composition all played a part in the creation of a work of art that has lasting emotional intensity.

Oil on panel
204.5 × 261.5 cm, 80½ × 103 in.
Museo del Prado, Madrid

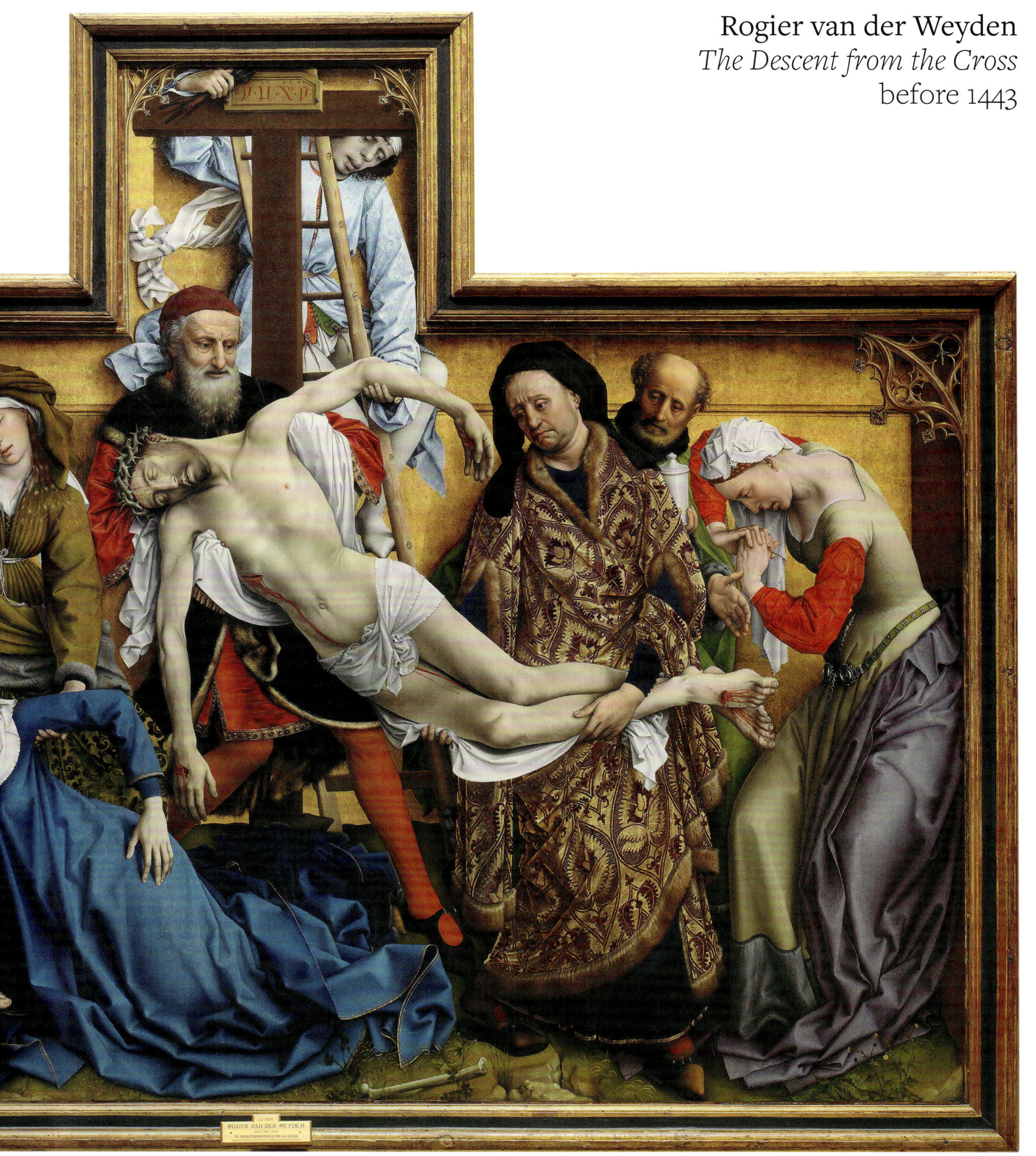

Rogier van der Weyden
The Descent from the Cross
before 1443

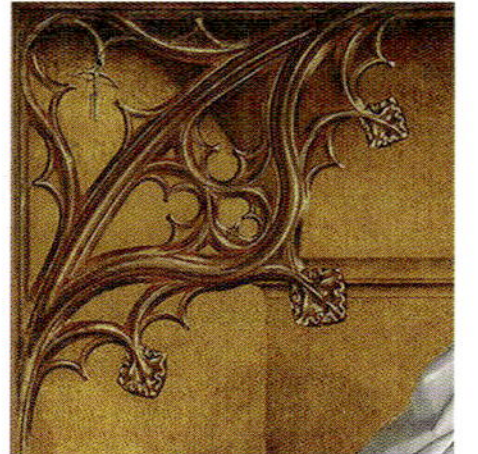

❶ Architecture

The altarpiece contains realistic representations of illusionistic Gothic tracery.

❷ Hidden symbols

Within these tracery designs are crossbows, a reference to the original commission. The altarpiece was painted for the Greater Guild of Crossbowmen for the Chapel of Our Lady Outside the Walls in Leuven, Belgium. Christ's body is arranged to resemble a crossbow.

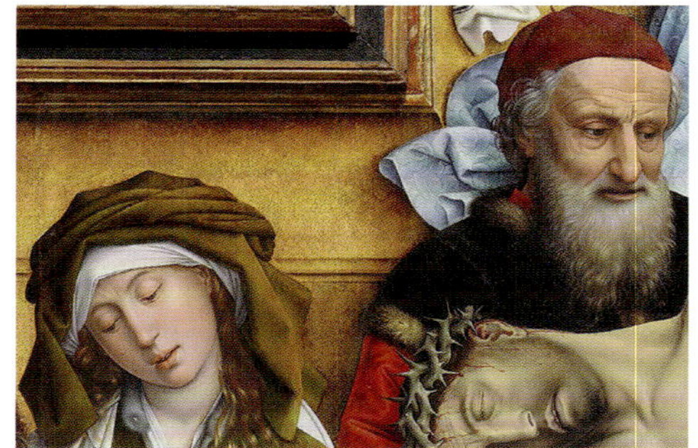

❸ Gold

The figures stand on a realistic ground, but there is no similarly realistic landscape behind them. Instead, they appear to be standing inside a gold box. The use of gold heightens the splendour of the scene, but also reminds us that we are looking at an artwork, not reality.

❹ Distortion

On closer inspection, the space portrayed in the painting is distorted. The ground seems to extend back some distance, but the box-like space at the top is very shallow. The top of the cross appears to be directly behind the tracery in the upper corners, but its base is set far back, behind the Virgin's blue dress. Together, these inconsistencies create a sense of unreality and reinforce a feeling of unease in the viewer. It is a perfect tactic for an image that sets out to convey discomfort.

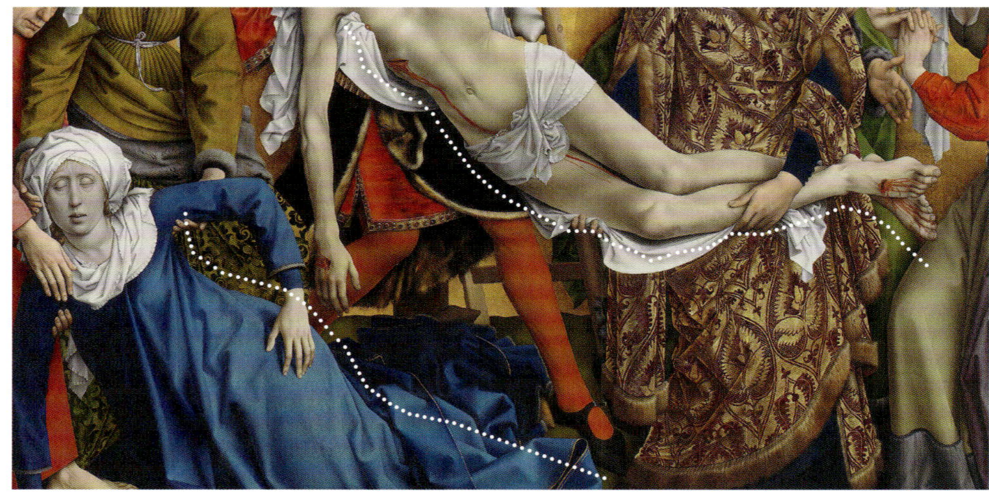

❺ Echoes

The shape of Christ's body is repeated in that of the Virgin, echoing the emotional bond between mother and son and heightening the tragedy of the events unfolding.

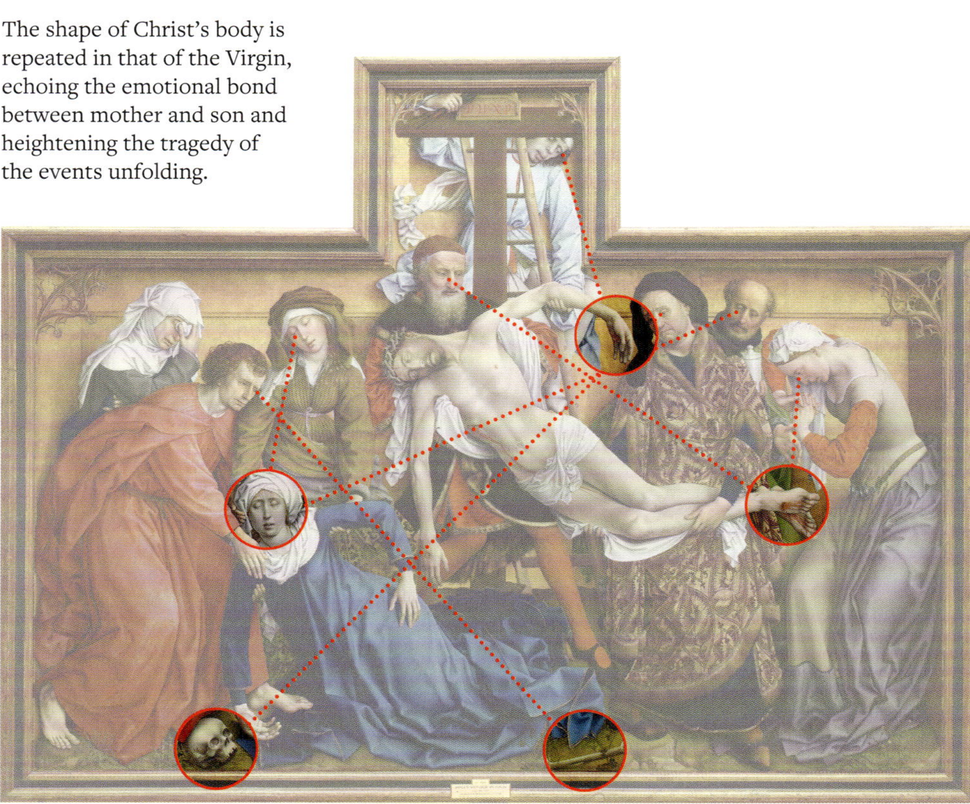

❻ Sightlines

Following the gaze of each figure leads to five zones of interest: the Virgin's grief-stricken face; the skeletal remains on the ground; and the wounds on Christ's body. To place the focus on the Virgin's face, the figure at the right – a servant – looks 'through' the wound on Christ's side. In front of him, Joseph of Arimathea similarly looks 'through' the wound on Christ's right hand.

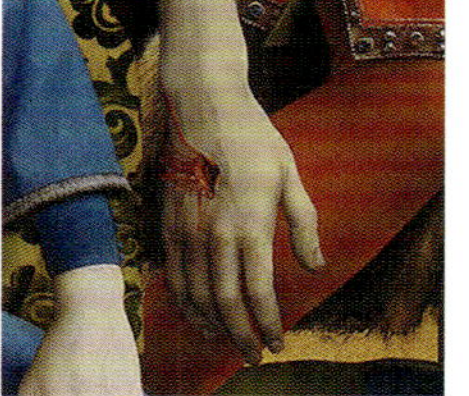

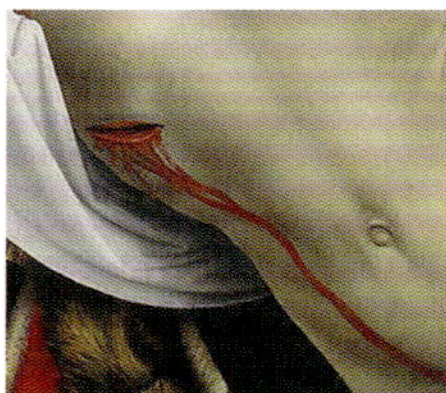

❼ Tears of blood

Christ's wounds have been painted to resemble weeping eyes, mirroring the bereft spectators.

❽ Figures

The figure directly above Christ is Nicodemus; above him is the servant who takes Christ's body down from the cross. The man wearing a golden cloak is Joseph of Arimathea; to the right is Mary Magdalene and behind them is another servant. The Virgin, in blue, has collapsed on the ground. Above her are Mary Cleophas, St John the Evangelist and Mary Salome.

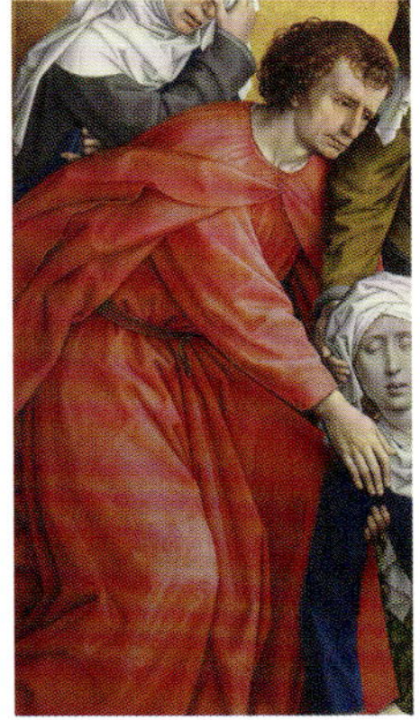

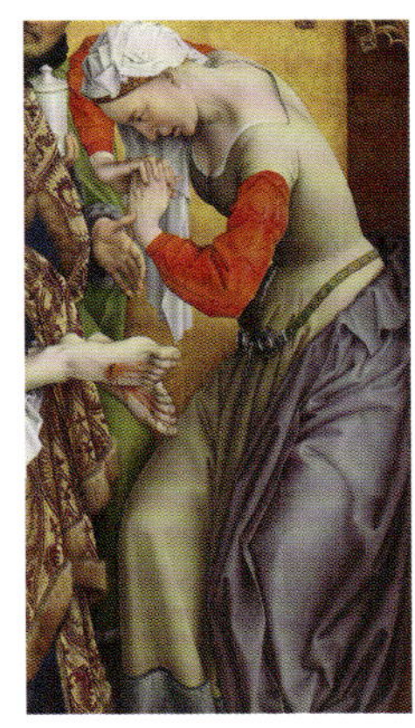

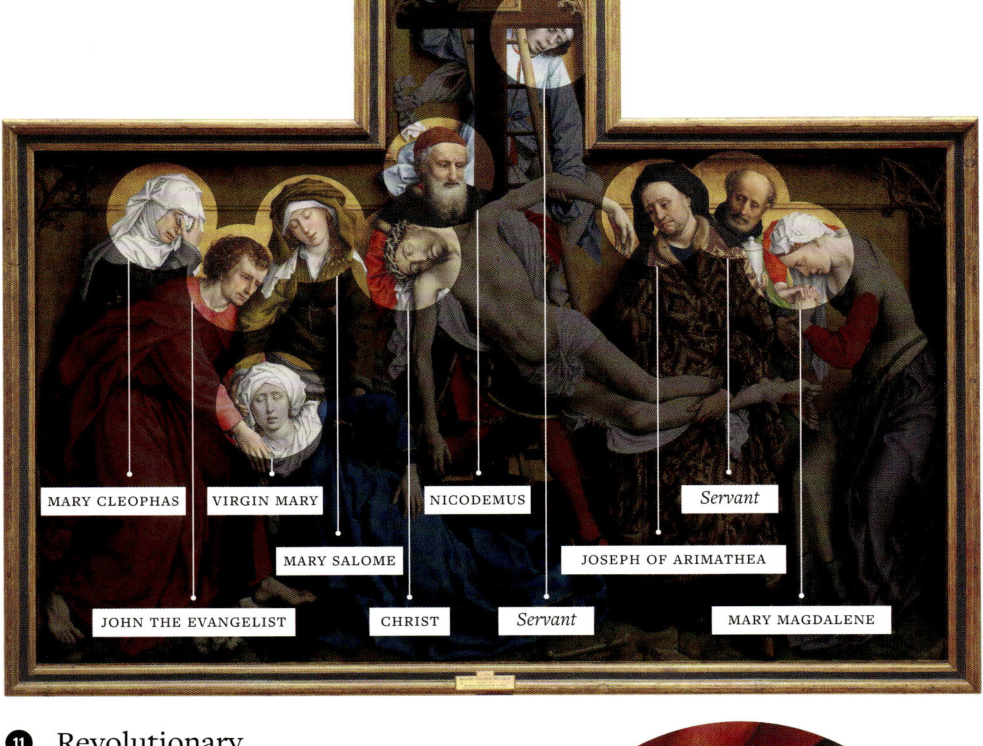

❾ More echoes

Mary Magdalene and St John the Evangelist stand at the outer edges of the composition, balancing the scene with their mirrored poses.

❿ Emotion

The act of grief is represented in detail, suggesting that Van der Weyden studied the effect of emotion on body language. The painting is large in scale, but its microscopic level of detail draws the viewer in to examine it at close range.

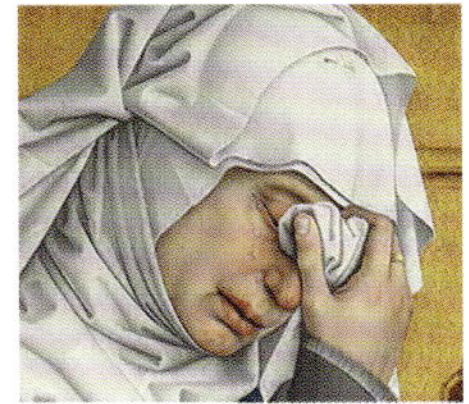

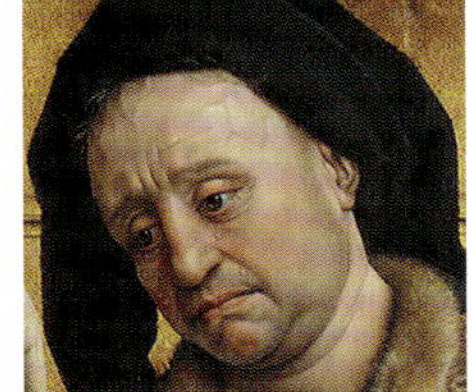

⓫ Revolutionary

The artist's successful representation of human psychology was noticed by his peers. The 15th-century humanist and antiquarian Cyriacus of Ancona wrote how the figures 'cry with great grief' and 'breathe as though alive'.[32]

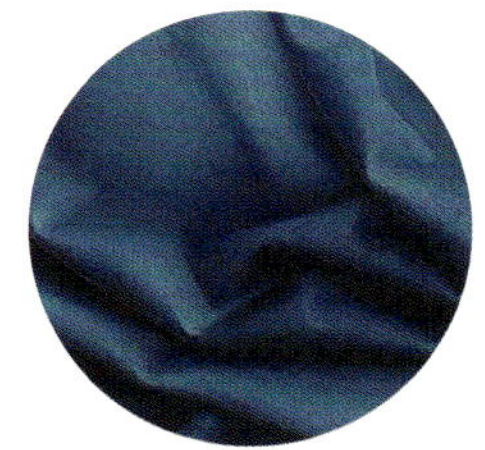

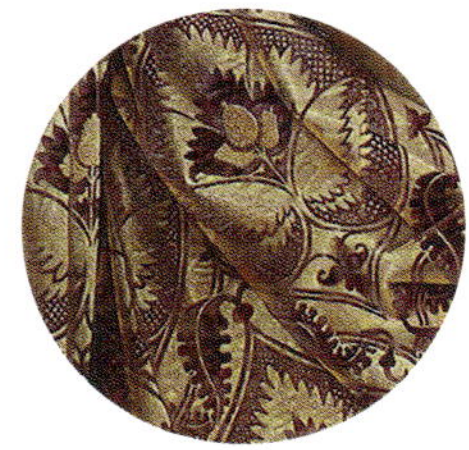

⓬ Technique

The heightened degree of realism is the result of the materials and techniques used: oil paint provides intense colour, and allows for more detail and convincing effects of shading.

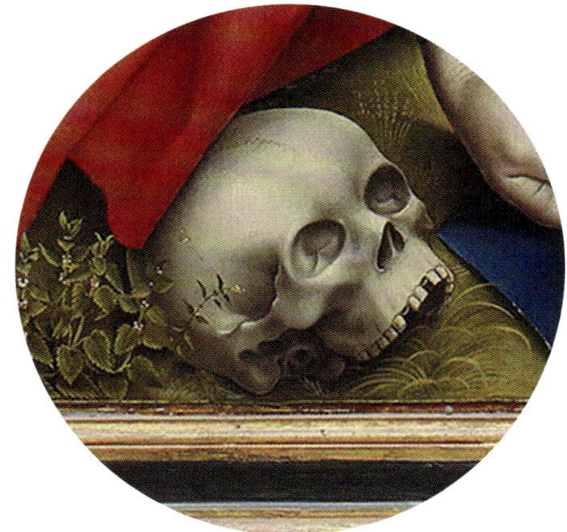

⓭ Skull

The figures look down on Christ and the Virgin, leading our gaze to the skull at the bottom of the painting. This *memento mori*, an artistic or symbolic reminder of death, represents the body of Adam, the first man, who is believed to be buried in the same location as Christ's crucifixion: Golgotha ('the place of the skull').[33]

LINKED PRACTITIONERS

THE NORTHERN RENAISSANCE:

Hugo van der Goes (1440–1482), BELGIUM
Veit Stoss (1447–1533), GERMANY
Albrecht Dürer (1471–1528), GERMANY
Hans Holbein the Younger (1497–1543), GERMANY/UK
Catharina van Hemessen (1528–1565), BELGIUM

REALISM IN PAINTING:

Hugo van der Goes (1440–1482), BELGIUM
Juan Sánchez Cotán (1560–1627), SPAIN
Richard Estes (born 1932), USA
Charles Bell (1935–1995), USA
Chuck Close (1940–2021), USA

ALTARPIECES:

Jan van Eyck (1390–1441), BELGIUM
Giovanni Bellini (1430–1516), ITALY
Andrea Mantegna (1431–1506), ITALY
Tilman Riemenschneider (1460–1531), GERMANY
Peter Paul Rubens (1577–1640), BELGIUM

14. Creating the Ideal

Leonardo da Vinci (1452–1519) *had journeyed to Milan from Florence in 1482 at the behest of his patron, Lorenzo de' Medici, and would remain there for the next 17 years. While in Milan, he undertook two commissions, the* Virgin of the Rocks *and the* Last Supper, *pictures that would eventually be among his most recognizable works. It was also during this time that he probably drew this study of a nude male figure.*

Inserted between written notes, the figure faces us, arms outstretched, touching the edges of a square and a circle with his feet and fingertips. The concepts that inspired Leonardo to draw such an image derive from centuries-old theories about how the individual relates to the wider cosmos, and have their basis in eternal geometries and mathematical principles.

Metalpoint, pen and ink,
touches of watercolour on white paper
34.6 × 25.5 cm, 13½ × 10 in.
Galleria dell'Accademia, Venice

Leonardo da Vinci

Study of the proportions of the human body, known as the Vitruvian Man, c. 1490

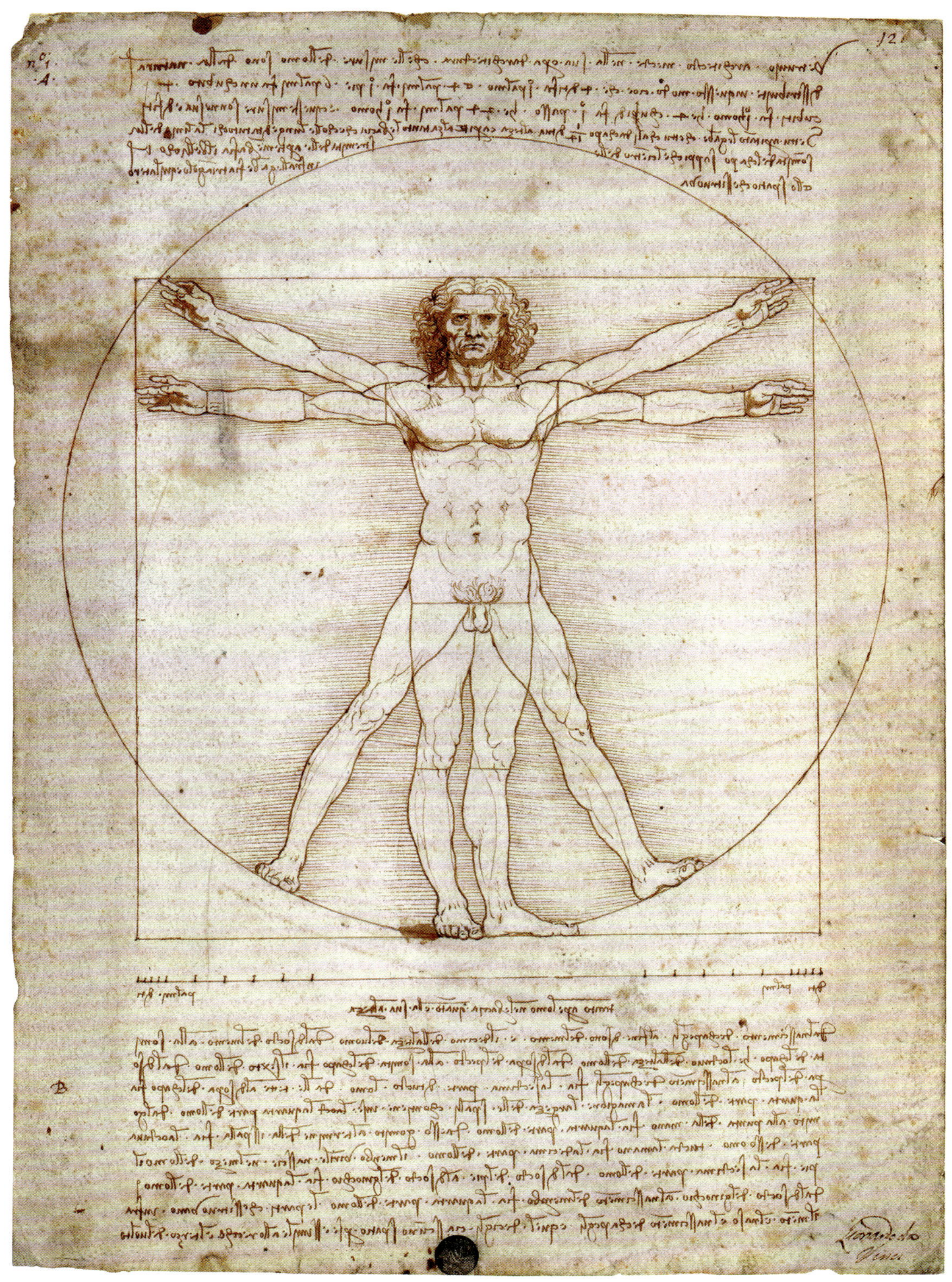

❶ Centre point #1

In Leonardo's drawing, the tips of the man's fingers and the soles of his feet define the circumference of a circle, with the centre marked by his navel.

❷ Centre point #2

The outstretched arms and legs touch the perimeter of a perfect square, with the centre marked by the top of the figure's groin. Several artists before had tried to capture the human body fitting perfectly into a square and circle (below, right). What made Leonardo's version original was that he arranged the shapes so that they didn't share the same centre point.

❸ Art and science

Leonardo combined the disciplines of art and science, using geometry to define the ideal proportions and beauty of the human form.

❹ A thorough analysis

The drawing is reminiscent of the artist's anatomical drawings (below), which explore the structures of human bodies below the surface.

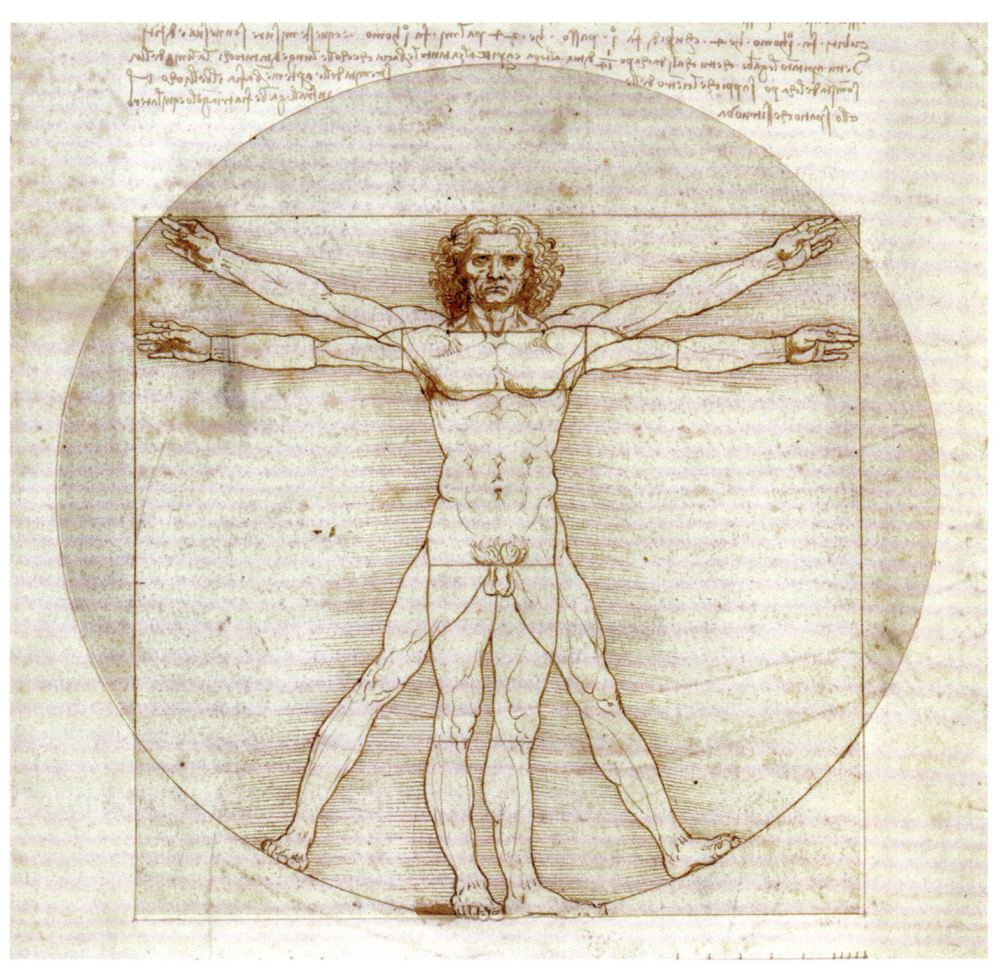

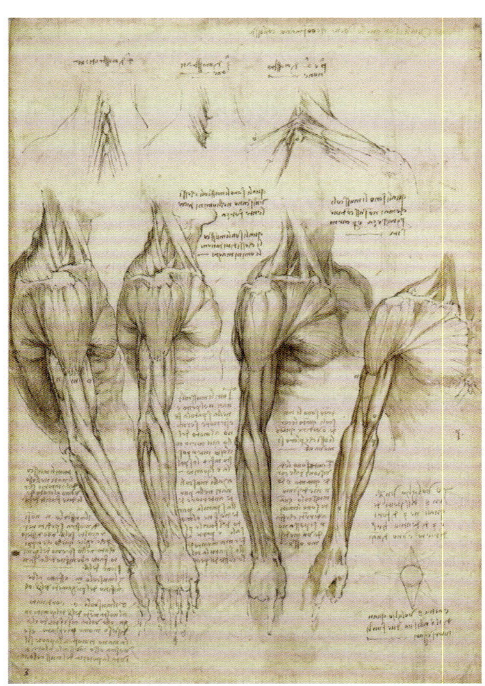

The muscles of the shoulder, arm and neck, c. 1510–11. Black chalk, pen and ink, wash, 28.8 × 20.2 cm, 11¼ × 8 in.

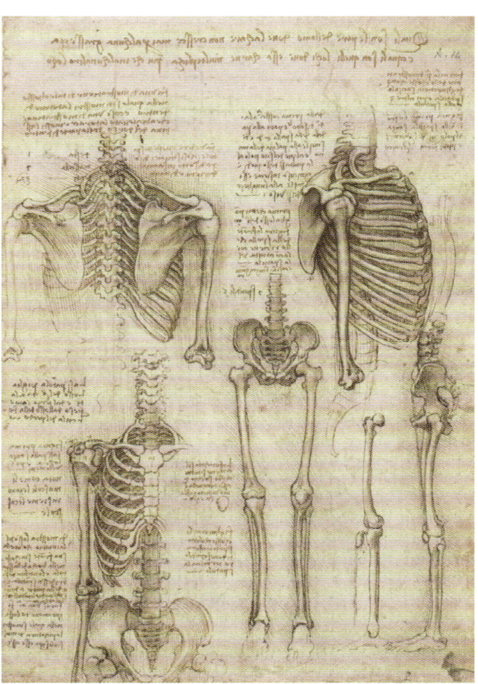

The skeleton, c. 1510–11. Black chalk, pen and ink, wash, 28.8 × 20 cm, 11¼ × 7¾ in.

❺ The measure of all things?

The centre of the square is marked by the top of the man's penis. This may be of special significance, as in Europe at the time male bodies were considered to be the ideal in terms of beauty. This was partly due to religious reasons: in the Book of Genesis Adam was created first with Eve as an afterthought. In the text of the drawing is a sentence that reads: *Il membro virile nascie nel mezo dell'omo* ('the virile member rises in the centre of man').[34]

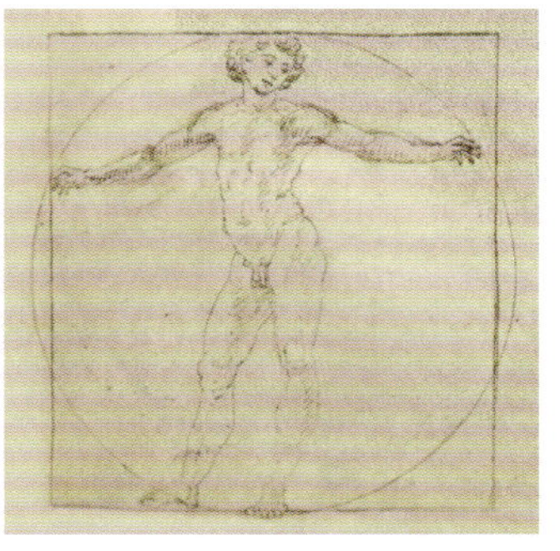

Francesco di Giorgio Martini, *L'Homo ad circolum*, MS Ashburnham 361, f. 5r

→ Michelangelo, *The Creation of Adam*, 1511. Fresco, 230.1 × 480.1 cm, 90½ × 189 in.

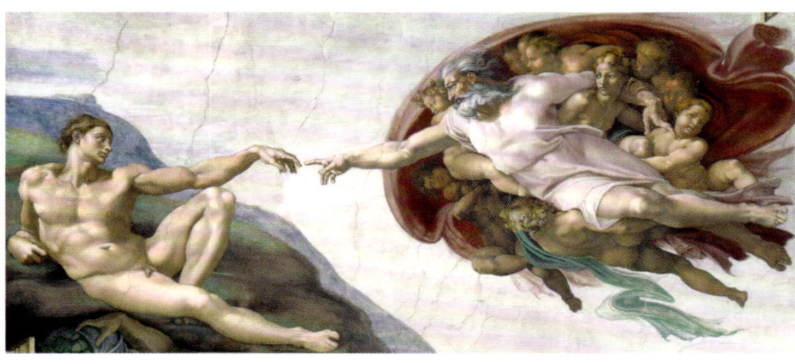

↓ *Perspectival study for the Adoration of the Magi*, c. 1481. Pen and ink, traces of silverpoint and white on paper, 16.3 × 29 cm, 6½ × 11½ in.

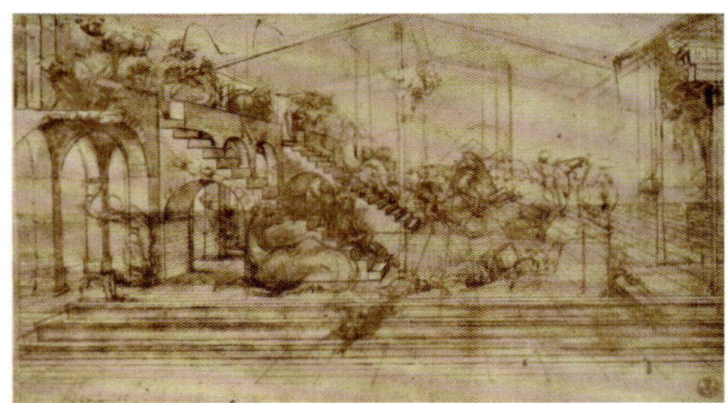

❻ Divine harmonies

According to the Greek philosopher Pythagoras, the mathematical structure of harmonics in music denotes a universal system of divine harmonies that point the way to ideal beauty.[35] This concept was revived in Europe during the Renaissance, where the beauty of an object (a building, for example) lay in the harmonious proportions of its parts, such as the height of its columns in relation to its height, or the width to the length of the floorplan.

❼ Ideal v. nature

Leonardo was not convinced by the idea that a set of mathematical paradigms could define ideal proportion. In other drawings, he emphasized the aberrations, variety and multiplicity of the human body.

❽ Circle and square

According to symbolism devised in the Middle Ages, the circle was a symbol of the sky and infinity and the square a symbol of the earth.

❾ Alberti?

Even though the drawing is popularly known as the *Vitruvian Man*, Leonardo likely never read Vitruvius' multi-volume tome *De archittura* (1st century BCE) in the original Latin.[36] His system of proportions corresponds more closely to those set out by Leon Battista Alberti in his treatise *On Sculpture* (c. 1450).

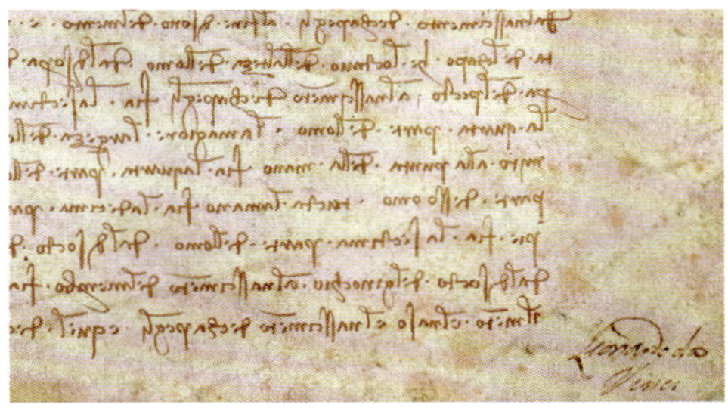

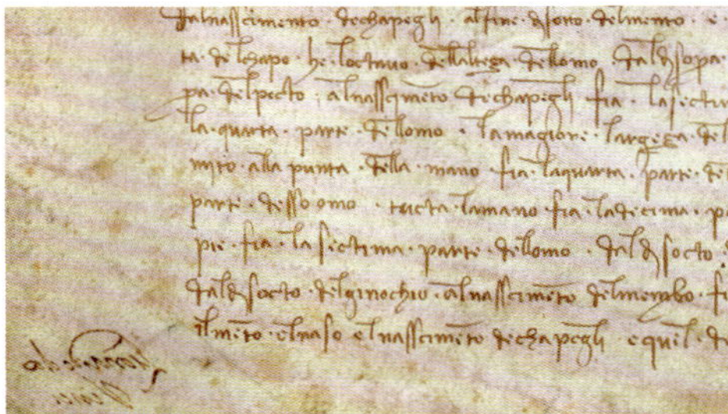

❿ Vitruvius?

The text is written backwards, decipherable only by holding it up to a mirror. It is based on Vitruvius' anatomical theory, in which the dimensions of the body are measured by units such as the foot or the head. The bottom section reads, in part:

The length of the outspread arms is equal to the height of a man; from the hairline to the bottom of the chin is one-tenth of the height of a man; from below the chin to the top of the head is one-eighth of the height of a man.

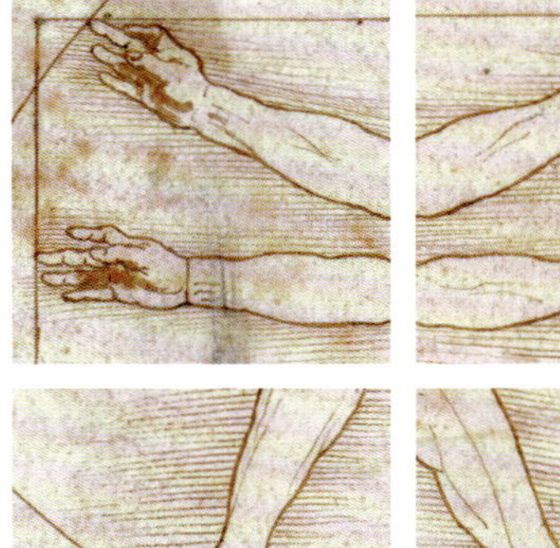

⓫ Asymmetry

The visual power of the drawing lies in its bold, simple shapes, the clear outlines of the forms and the commanding stare of the man at the centre. Although his frame fits perfectly into the symmetrical geometric circle, Leonardo has been careful to avoid too much precision: the hands of the figure are all in subtly different positions.

⓬ Purpose

Historians are not entirely clear if there was a specific reason why Leonardo made the drawing. It may have been conceived as a title page for a new version of Alberti's *On Sculpture*, or possibly was drawn as an aid to discussion about ideal proportions with a group of friends with shared intellectual interests. The drawing was owned by Cesare Monti, the Archbishop of Milan, then the De Pagave family, and then the painter Giuseppe Bossi, before ending up in the collection of the Galleria dell'Accademia in Venice, where it is rarely on display owing to its fragility.

LINKED PRACTITIONERS

EXPLORING ANATOMY:

Antonio del Pollaiuolo (1433–1498), ITALY
Filippino Lippi (1457–1504), ITALY
Spike Walker (born 1933), UK
Orlan (born 1947), FRANCE
Rebecca D. Harris (born 1977), UK

WORKS ON PAPER:

Habiballah of Sava (fl. c. 1590–1610), IRAN
Tsukioka Yoshitoshi (1839–1892), JAPAN
Sol LeWitt (1928–2007), USA
Fung Ming Chip (born 1951), CHINA
Imran Qureshi (born 1972), PAKISTAN

GEOMETRY:

Nicolas Poussin (1594–1665), FRANCE
Piet Mondrian (1872–1944), NETHERLANDS
Josef Albers (1888–1976), GERMANY
Agnes Martin (1912–2004), USA
Dóra Maurer (born 1937), HUNGARY

15. # Spirit Worlds

This striking mask was made somewhere in the Aztec empire, in the capital Tenochtitlan (Mexico City) or in a provincial centre like Oaxaca. The original function of the so-called 'mosaic skull of Tezcatlipoca' is unknown, as is the story of how it came to Europe. Despite the mysteries surrounding its origins, what is beyond question is the level of skill and artistry on display.

The surface of the mask is a jigsaw of minuscule pieces of precious materials, all perfectly fitted together. Its shimmering beauty makes us forget that underneath is a real human skull, complete with a hinge on the jaw so that the mouth can be opened and closed. It is possible that it represents Tezcatlipoca, a major deity in the Aztec religion, who was celebrated in rites that included human sacrifice.

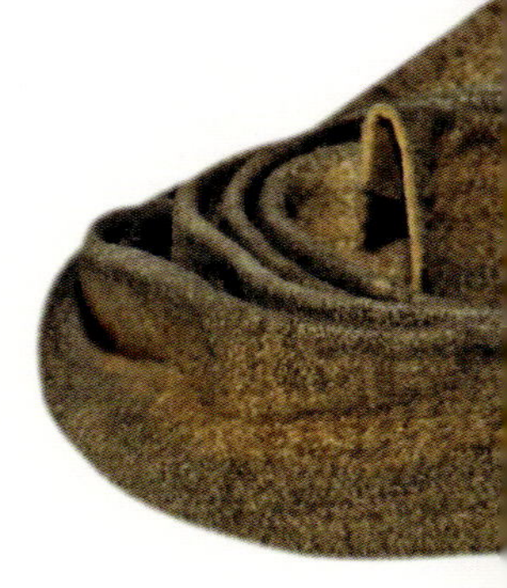

Human bone, turquoise, conch shell, pyrite, deer skin, lignite, pine and agave
Height: 19 cm, 7½ in.
British Museum, London

Mexico, Aztec
Mosaic skull of Tezcatlipoca
1400–1521

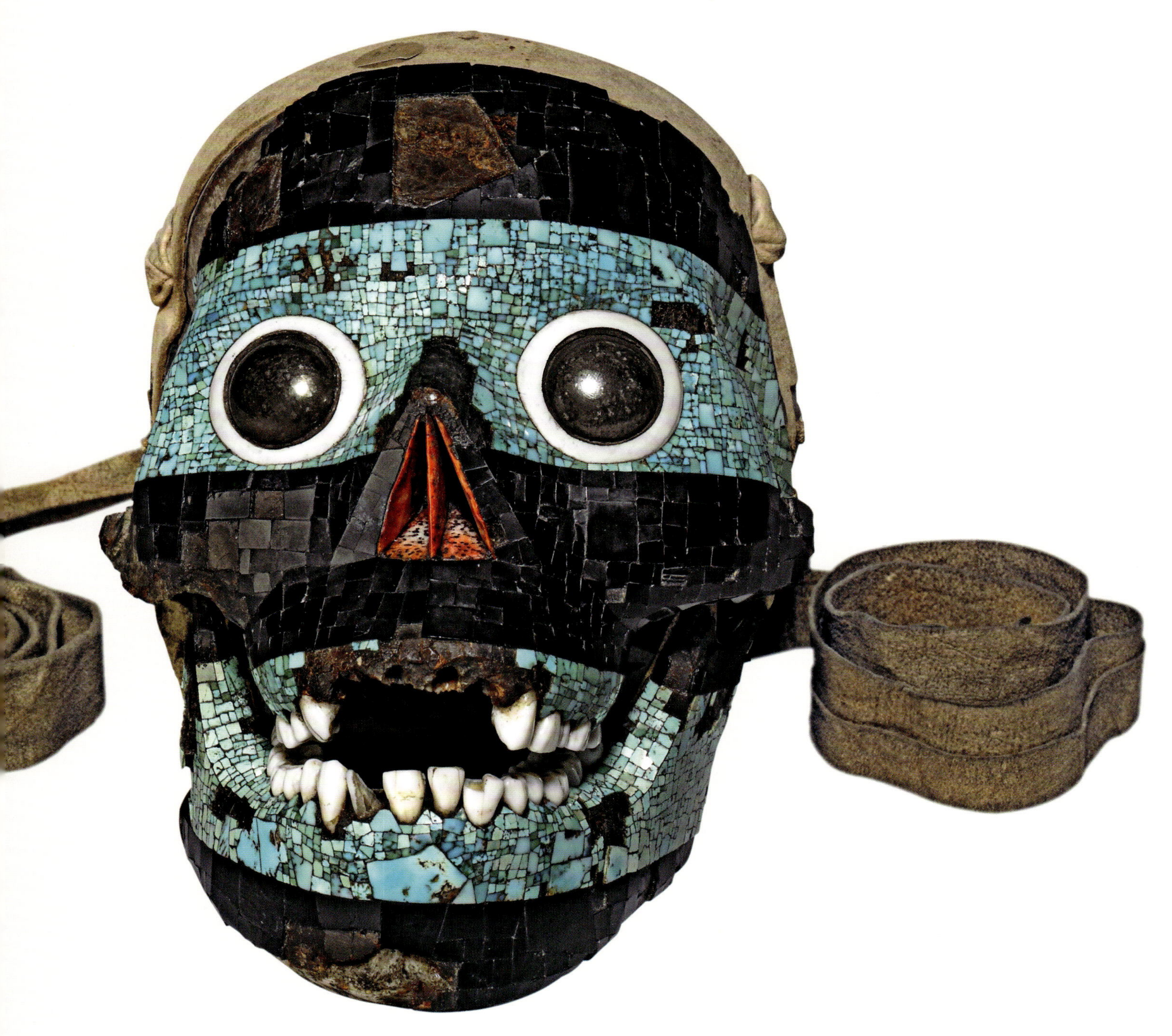

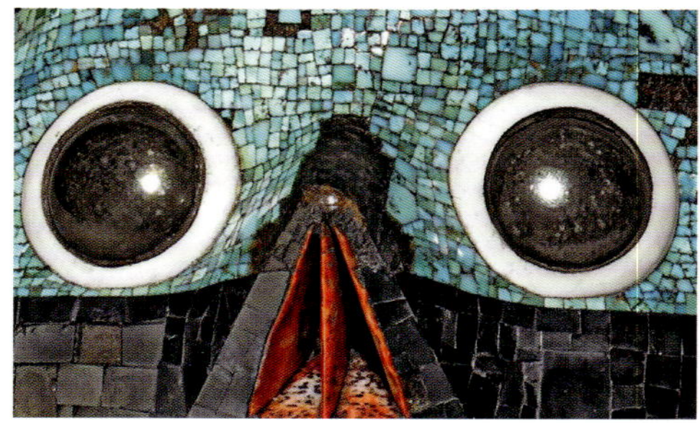

❶ Mirror eyes

The eyes are made of polished iron pyrite, known as 'fool's gold' for its dull lustre and colour, encircled by white conch shell. The pyrite has been polished to reflect the light, so that it hazily mirrors its surroundings, like the surface of a real human eye.

❷ Surface pattern

The surface pattern on the face is decorated with bands of turquoise and black. These are formed by the arrangement of tiny bits of lignite and turquoise like a mosaic.

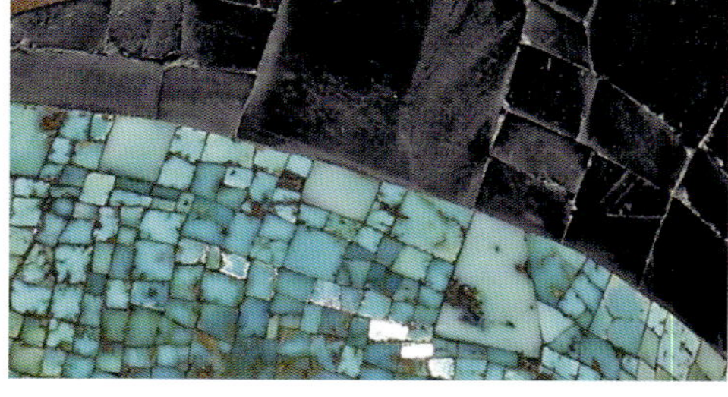

❸ Black mirrors

The Aztecs used mirrors made from obsidian (volcanic glass, formed from cooling magma) to view the spirit world and predict the future. After contact, some Europeans, including the occultist John Dee (1527–1608/9), believed these 'black mirrors' could be used to contact angels and other celestial beings from the spiritual world.

❹ Gods of creation

Obsidian mirrors were a symbol of the Aztec deity Tezcatlipoca, whose name means 'smoking mirror'. Tezcatlipoca was one of the Aztec world's four gods of creation, and could see into the souls of humans, knowing their past and predicting their future. He is represented with a black streak across his face, and usually a black mirror on his head or at his foot.

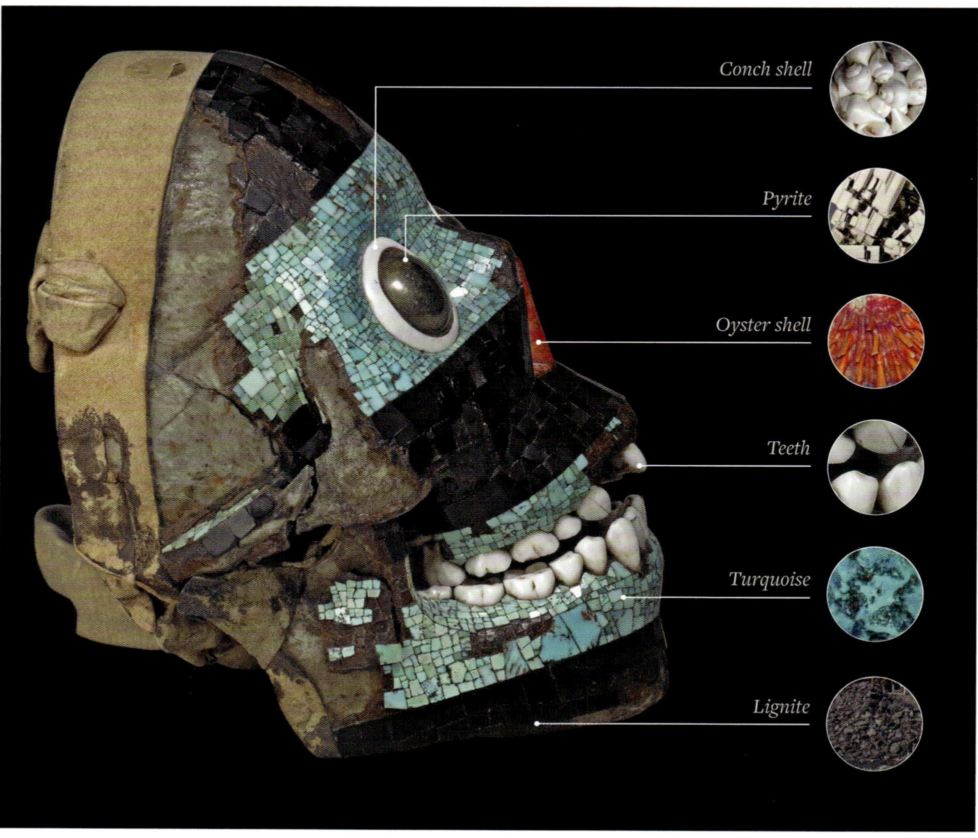

❺ The spoils of empire #1

The materials used in the mask came from all over the Aztec empire. The turquoise is from the southern United States, the white conch shell from the Gulf of Mexico and the red thorny oyster shell (inside the nose) may have been collected from as far away as Peru – evidence of the might and scale of the Aztec world at its height.

❻ The spoils of empire #2

Spanish conquistadors, led by Hernán Cortés, arrived in 1519. The emperor of the Aztecs, Montezuma II, invited Cortés to Tenochtitlan and offered him gifts, perhaps including this skull. Some artefacts made their way to Europe, where they were seen by Albrecht Dürer in 1520. 'I marvelled over the subtle ingenuity of the men in these distant lands,' he said. 'Indeed, I cannot say enough about the things which were there before me.'

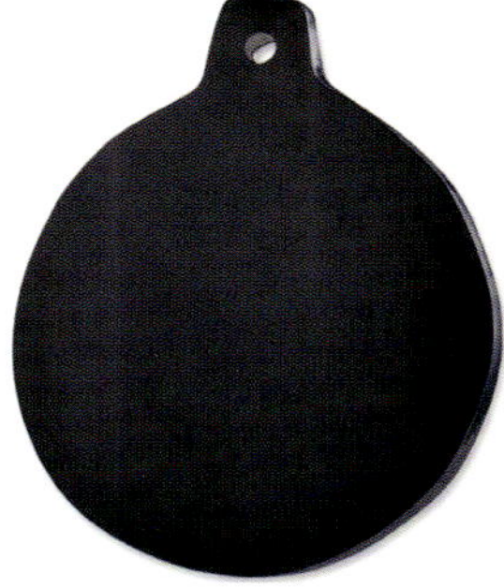

↑ Magical mirror of John Dee, Mexico, 14th–16th century (?). Obsidian, wood, leather, diameter: 18.4 cm, 7¼ in.

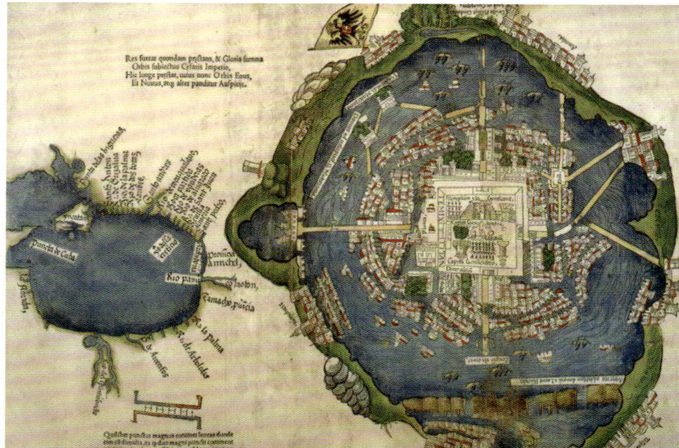

→ Hernán Cortés, map of Tenochtitlan (detail), published in Nuremberg, 1524

7 Craftsmanship

It would have taken an extraordinary level of skill to cut and bevel each of the hundreds of individually shaped pieces of lignite and turquoise that cover the surface of the mask. Many of these pieces are minute in scale, and manipulating them into position and fixing them with resin to the skull would have required the most dexterous of manoeuvres.

8 Teeth and nose

The mask is symmetrical apart from the teeth, which betray the fact that it was made from a real human skull. The hole for the nose has been inset with the red shell of a thorny oyster (*Spondylus princeps*).

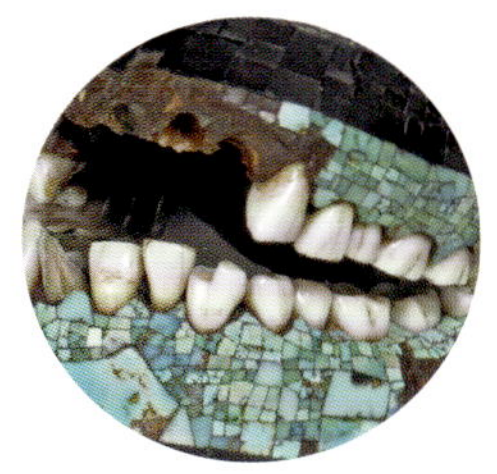

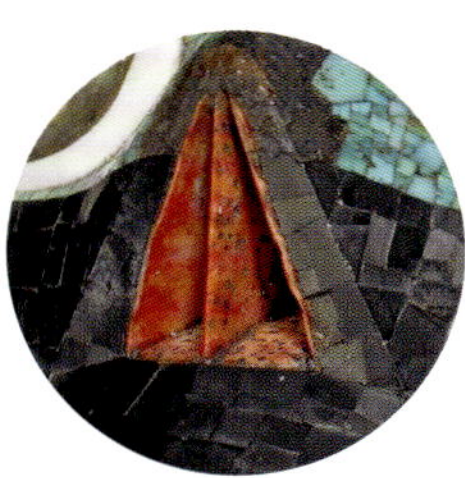

9 A work of art for wearing

The reverse of the mask shows how it was worn. Deerskin straps were attached to the sides and used to fasten the mask to the wearer. From behind, you can see the inside of the skull, which was also lined with deerskin.

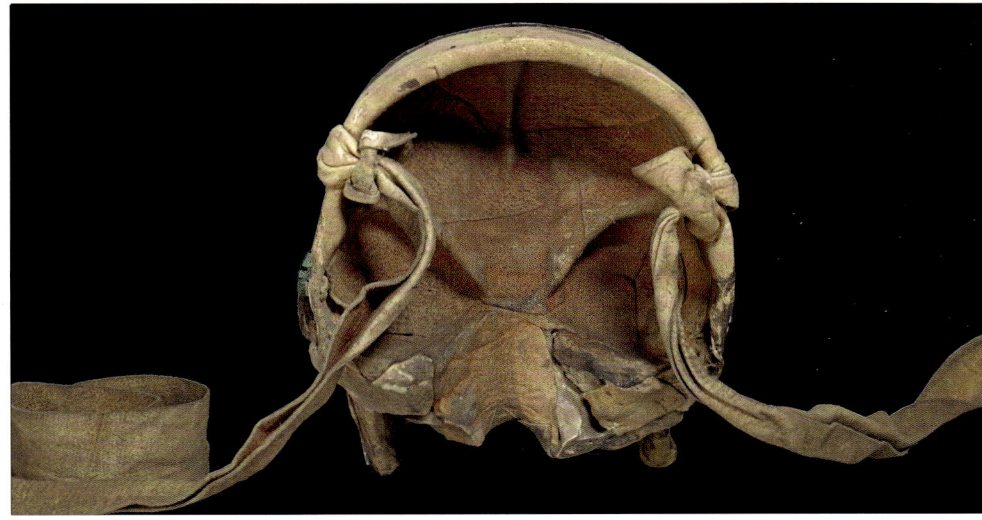

10 Symbol of authority

The length of the strap indicates that it was probably worn around the waist, possibly at the back, by a priest.

11 Sacrifice

The skull may have come from Templo Mayor, the largest temple in Tenochtitlan. The Aztecs believed that the spilling of human blood was a way of appeasing the gods and perpetuating the cycle of the seasons, and the temple was the site of many human sacrifices, with the skulls of the victims displayed on racks. Archaeologists have uncovered several of these monuments, known as *tzompantli*, which contain hundreds of human skulls cemented into the towers and walls of temples.

Tzompantli displayed at the Museo del Templo Mayor, Mexico City

LINKED PRACTITIONERS

AZTEC ART:

Artist of Coatlicue, *c.* 1500, NATIONAL MUSEUM OF ANTHROPOLOGY, MEXICO CITY
Artists of the Zouche-Nuttal Codex, *c.* 1200–1521, BRITISH MUSEUM, LONDON
Artist of the Double-headed Serpent, *c.* 15th–16th century, BRITISH MUSEUM, LONDON
Artist of the Aztec Eagle Warrior, *c.* 13th–15th century, NATIONAL MUSEUM OF ANTHROPOLOGY, MEXICO CITY
Artist of the Sun Stone, *c.* 1502–20, NATIONAL MUSEUM OF ANTHROPOLOGY, MEXICO CITY

MIRRORS:

Diego Velázquez (1599–1660), SPAIN
Parmigianino (1503–1540), ITALY
Johannes Vermeer (1632–1675), NETHERLANDS
Paul Delvaux (1897–1994), BELGIUM
Joan Jonas (born 1936), USA

MOSAICS:

Lluís Brú (1868–1952), SPAIN
Isaiah Zagar (born 1939), USA
Emma Biggs (born 1956), UK
Carrie Reichardt (born 1966), UK
Anne Schwegmann-Fielding (born 1967), UK

16. Cultural Interactions

This ornamental ivory horn was made in what is now Sierra Leone. The carving is among the finest of the period, but the decorative scheme is even more extraordinary. Despite being made thousands of miles away, it bears the coats of arms of two of Europe's most powerful dynasties – in Spain and Portugal – and some of the scenes echo illustrations from a book published several years earlier in France.

The incorporation of this type of imagery into a work produced in western Africa is evidence of an early form of globalization based on trade and the local capitalization of the demands of the European luxury-goods market. Portuguese explorers had arrived on the western coast of Africa in the 14th century, followed by traders who acquired objects made from ivory by the Sapi people for export. The fusion of these two art traditions created an Afro-European hybrid art form known as Sapi-Portuguese.

Ivory and metal
64.2 × 16.4 × 9 cm, 25¼ × 6½ × 3½ in.
National Museum of African Art,
Smithsonian, Washington, DC

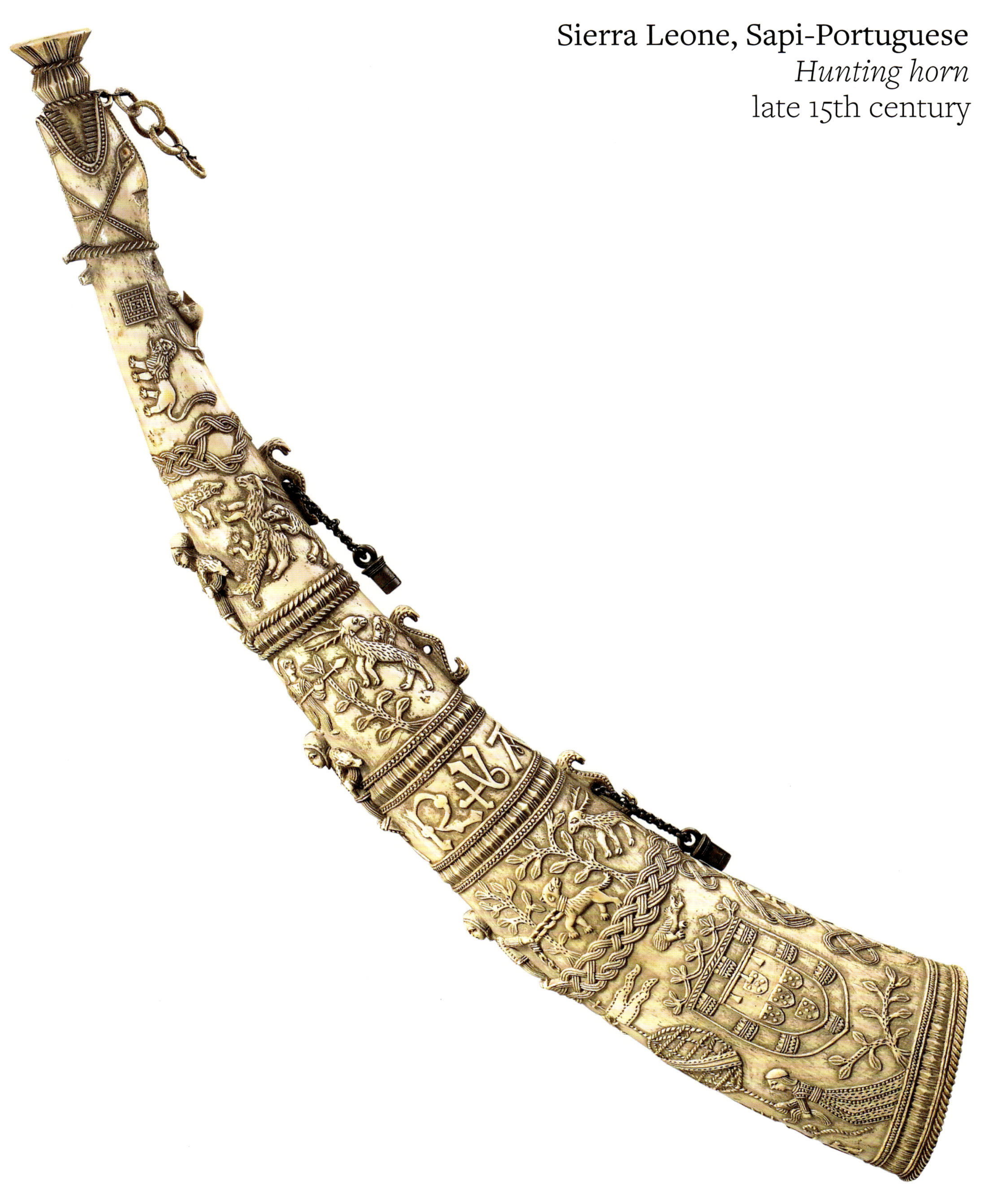

Sierra Leone, Sapi-Portuguese
Hunting horn
late 15th century

❶ Coats of arms

The largest decorative motifs on the horn appear at its base. On one side is the royal coat of arms of Portugal; on the other is that of the Spanish kingdoms of Aragon and Castile.

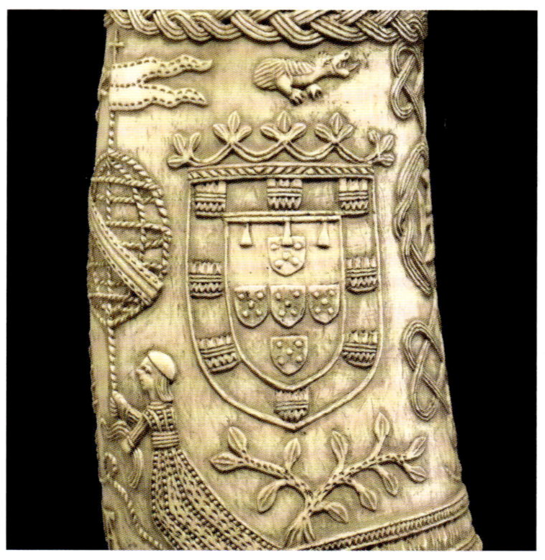

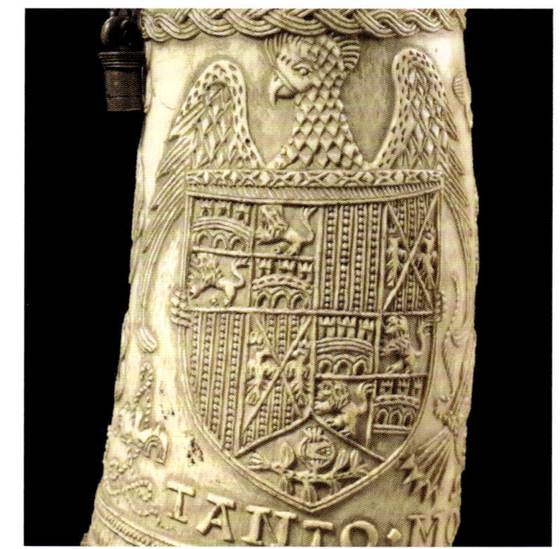

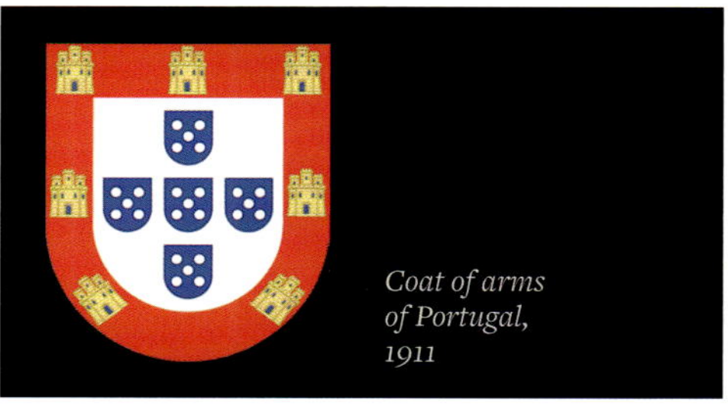

Coat of arms of Portugal, 1911

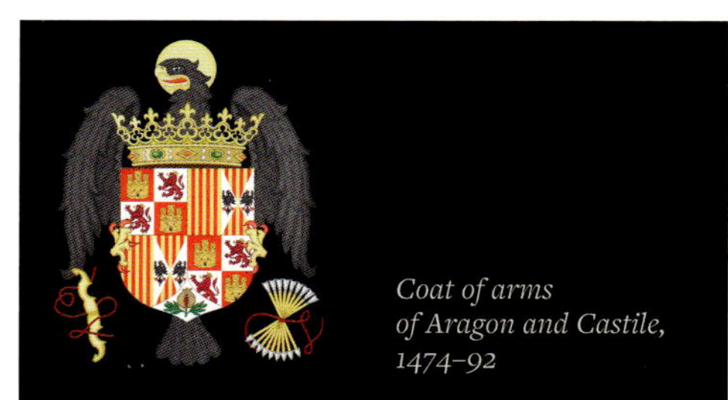

Coat of arms of Aragon and Castile, 1474–92

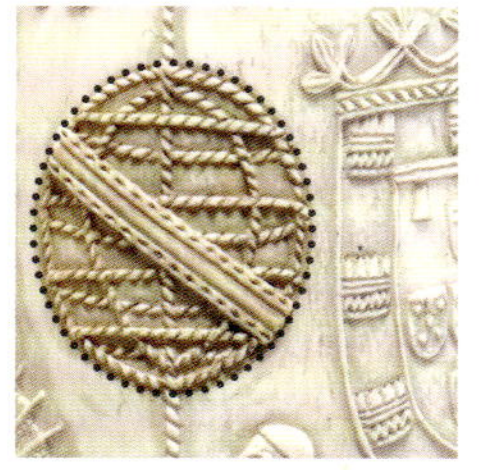

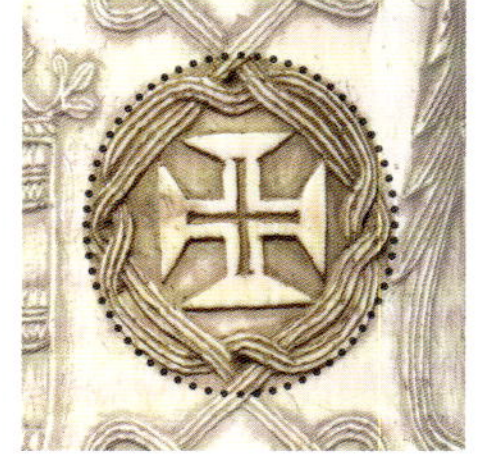

❷ Emblems of Manuel I

Between the coats of arms on one side is an armillary sphere (a 3D model of the planets), which was on the personal flag of Manuel I of Portugal (r. 1495–1521) and has featured on the country's flag ever since. On the other is another emblem of Manuel I: the cross of the Military Order of Christ.

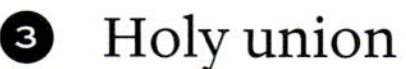

❸ Holy union

While many Sapi-Portuguese artefacts feature the coat of arms of Portugal, this horn is unusual in that it also bears the arms of Aragon and Castile. It is possible that it was a gift from Manuel I to Ferdinand II of Aragon and Isabella of Castile on the occasion of his marriage to their daughter Isabella in 1497.

❹ The hunt

Some of the decoration features scenes of deer hunting. Although not an exact copy, they appear to be closely related to the *Horae Beatus Mariae Virginis* (*Hours of the Blessed Virgin Mary*), published in 1498 in Paris by Philippe Pigouchet and Thielman Kerver.

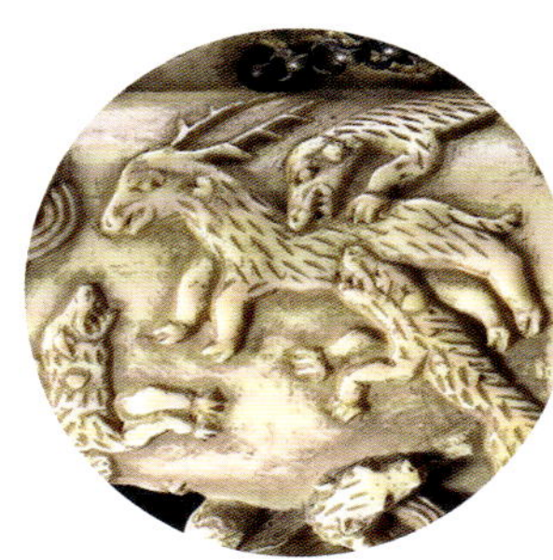

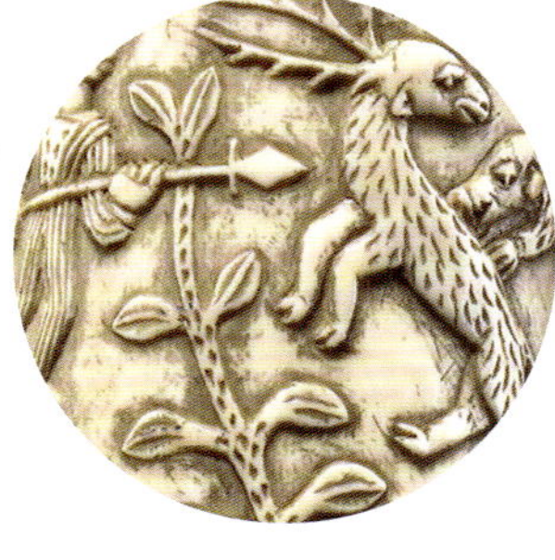

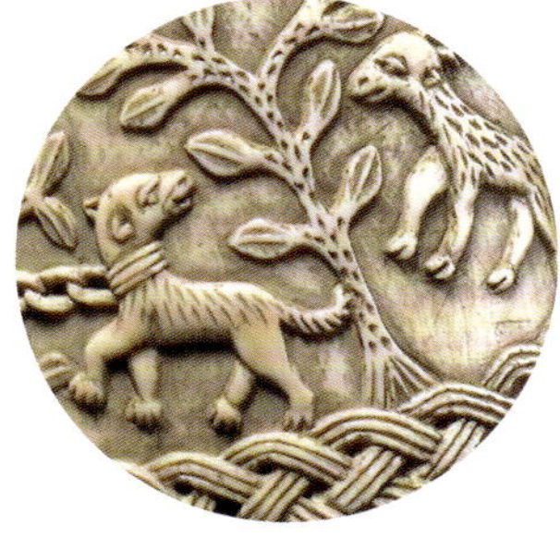

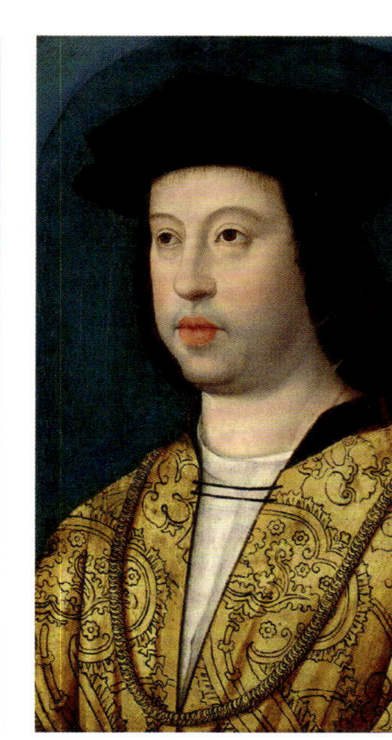

← *Ferdinand V of Spain, King of Aragon*, c. 1470–1520. Oil on panel, 37 × 27 cm, 14½ × 10½ in.

⇇ *Isabella I of Spain, Queen of Castile*, c. 1470–1520. Oil on panel, 37.5 × 26.9 cm, 14¾ × 10½ in.

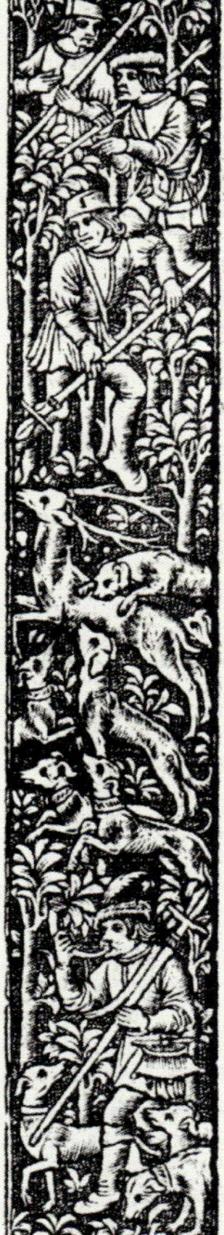

⇉ Workshop of Philippe Pigouchet, *The hunt of the stag*, from *Horae Beatus Mariae Virginis*, 1498

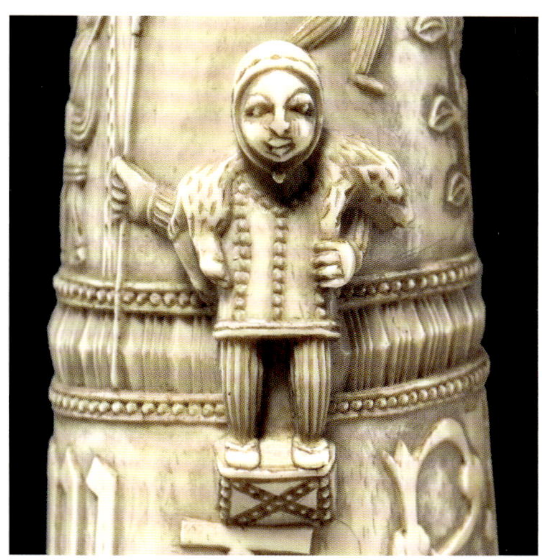

5 The Good Shepherd

A figure shown carrying an animal over his shoulders is an echo of the Christian motif of Christ as the Good Shepherd. This vignette captures the horn's hybrid nature, with European scenes meeting African techniques.

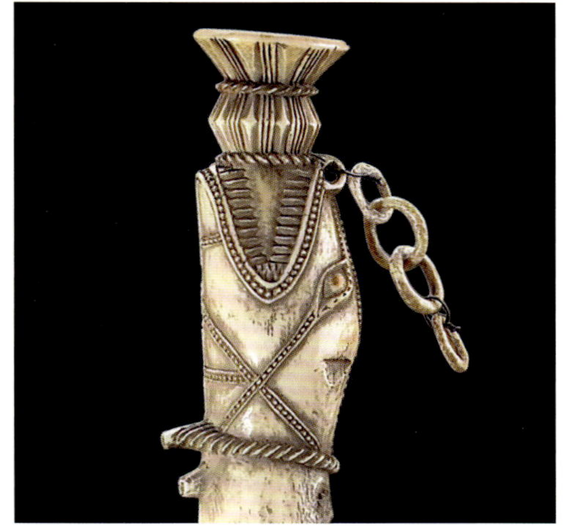

6 Sacred snake

The mouthpiece is gripped in the jaws of a beast resembling a serpent, which commonly appear on European cannon barrels. Serpents often appear in the decoration of Sapi-Portuguese artefacts.

7 International contact

In the 15th century, Portuguese explorers came into contact with tribes along the coast of modern-day Sierra Leone, collectively knows as the Sapi people, while searching for new routes to India. They began to commission works from the local artists, which would be among the first commodities to arrive in Europe from Africa. These Afro-European artefacts are an early example of African art produced specifically for a European market.

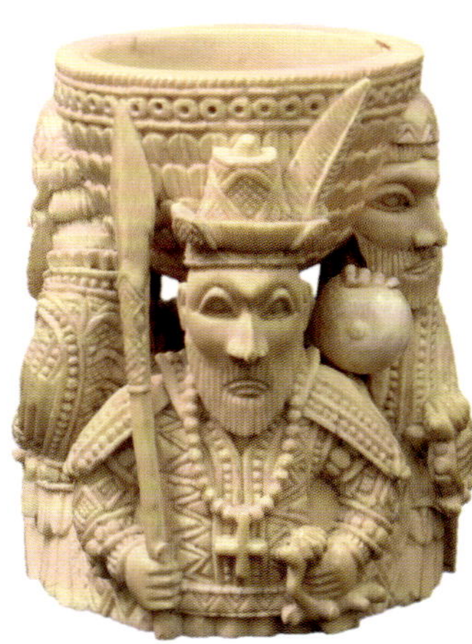

Saltcellar, Afro-Portuguese, *c.* 1526–1600. Ivory, 10 × 8.3 cm, 4 × 3¼ in.

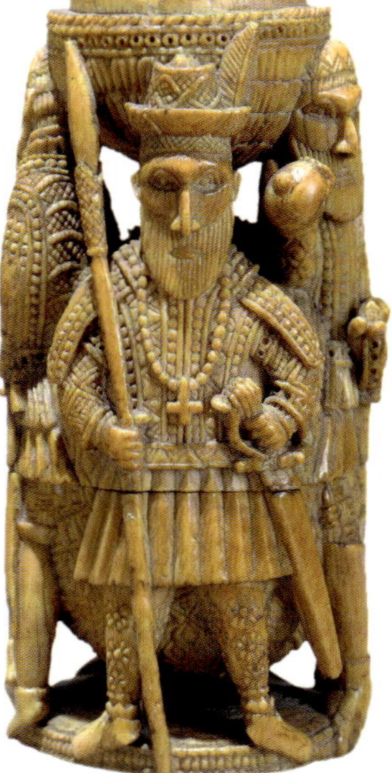

Master of the Heraldic Ship (Court of Owo or Benin, Nigerian), saltcellar with Portuguese figures, *c.* 1525–1600. Ivory, 19.1 × 7.6 × 8.3 cm, 7½ × 3 × 3¼ in.

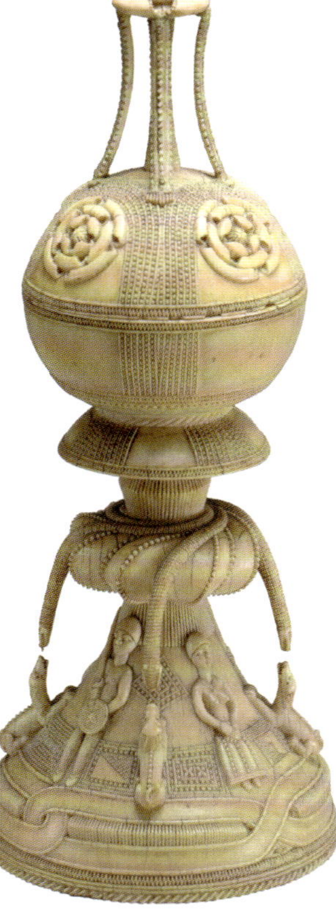

Lidded saltcellar, Sapi-Portuguese, 15th–16th century. Ivory, 29.8 × 10.8 cm, 11¾ × 4¼ in.

8 The fate of the Sapi

The Sapi were invaded by neighbouring peoples in the mid-16th century. Most traces of their culture have been irrevocably lost.

9 Neglect and rediscovery

Many Sapi-Portuguese ivory artefacts were stored away and forgotten. It was not until the publication in 1959 of *Afro-Portuguese Ivories* by William Fagg that they came to more widespread attention.

10 Ivory

The horn was made from ivory, a material that would have been a natural choice for Sapi artists. Today, elephant populations have declined drastically and trade in ivory is banned, as are works of art made from it.

11 Oliphants

Hunting horns like this were known as 'oliphants', a corruption of the word 'elephant', the source of ivory.

LINKED PRACTITIONERS

ARTISTS FROM SIERRA LEONE:

Alphonso Lisk-Carew (1887–1969), SIERRA LEONE
Esteban Arriaga (1922–2009), SIERRA LEONE
John Goba (1944–2019), SIERRA LEONE
Abu Bakarr Mansaray (born 1970), SIERRA LEONE
Lamin Fofana (born 1982), SIERRA LEONE

HUNTING:

Paolo Uccello (1397–1475), ITALY
Pieter Bruegel the Elder (*c.*1525/30–1569), NETHERLANDS
Anthony van Dyck (1599–1641), BELGIUM
Eugène Delacroix (1798–1863), FRANCE
Frida Kahlo (1907–1954), MEXICO

MARRIAGE:

Jan van Eyck (*c.* 1390–1441), NETHERLANDS
Pieter Bruegel the Elder (*c.*1525/30–1569), NETHERLANDS
Paolo Veronese (1528–1588), ITALY
William Hogarth (1697–1764), UK
Marc Chagall (1887–1985), RUSSIA/FRANCE

17. Proper Preparations

In 1508, Michelangelo Buonarroti (1475–1564) was engaged by his patron Pope Julius II, one of the world's most powerful figures at the time, to undertake an important commission: painting the ceiling of the Sistine Chapel in Rome. The main narrative of the vast scheme was to be taken from the Book of Genesis, from the formation of the planets to the story of Noah.

This drawing in red chalk, done using a young man as a model, was made in preparation for the female Libyan sibyl, one of the 10 prophets and sibyls flanking the main panels. It captures a moment of artistic experimentation, showing Michelangelo in the act of working out how to accurately represent on a two-dimensional surface the complex pose of a figure rotating away from the viewer to occupy a three-dimensional space.

Red chalk, with small accents of white chalk
on the left shoulder of the figure in the main study
28.9 × 21.4 cm, 11¼ × 8½ in.
Metropolitan Museum of Art, New York

Michelangelo
Studies for the Libyan Sibyl
c. 1510–11

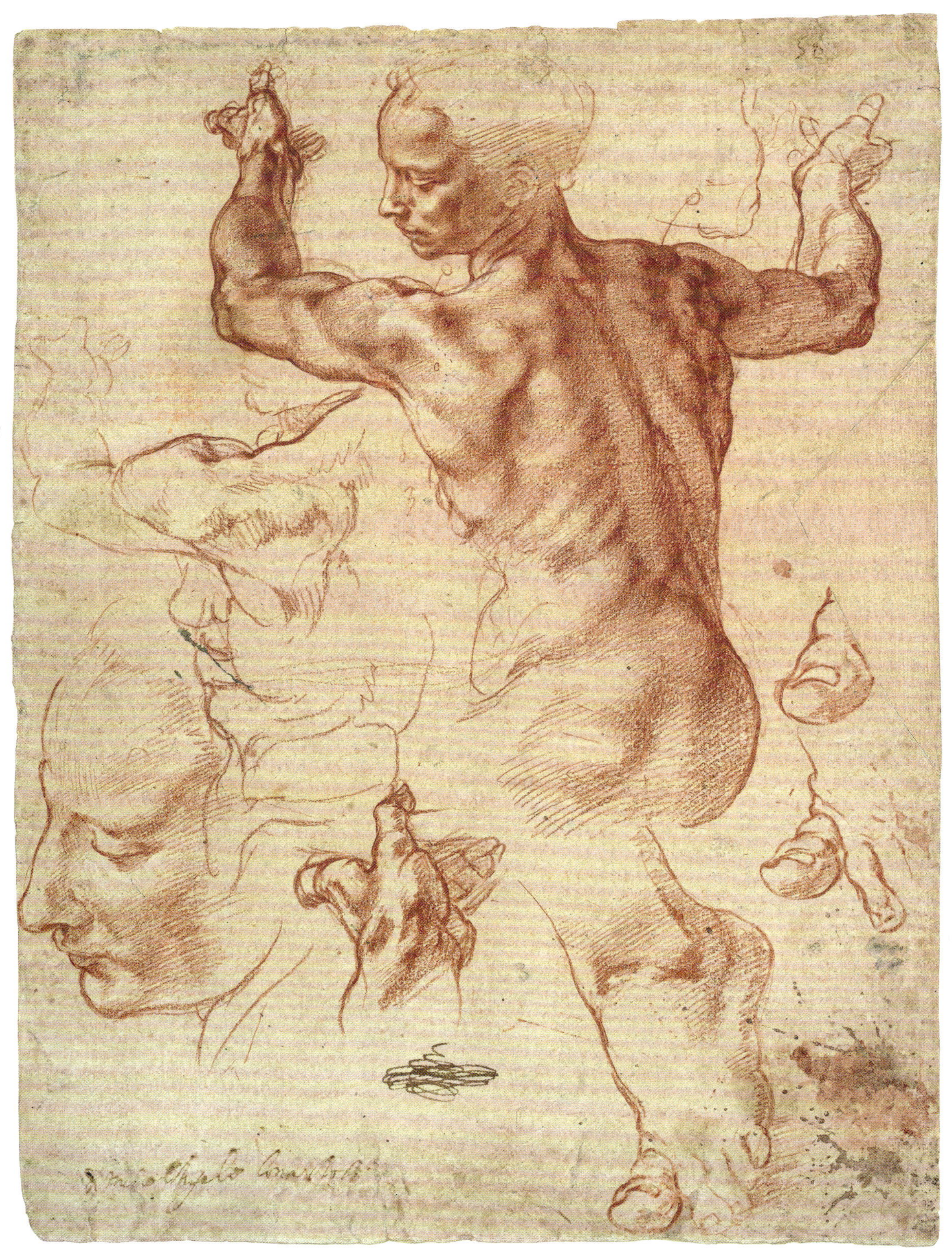

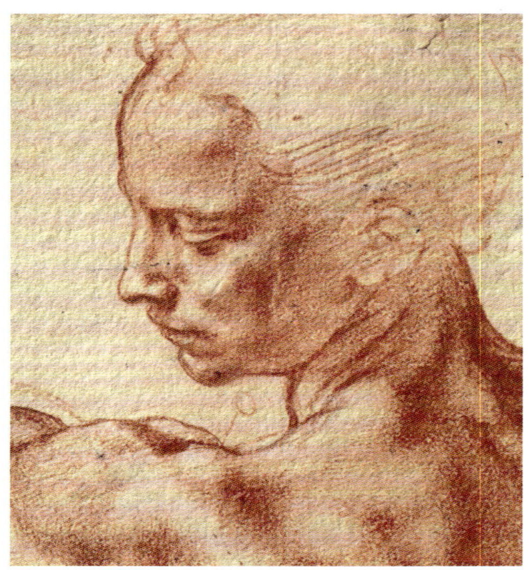

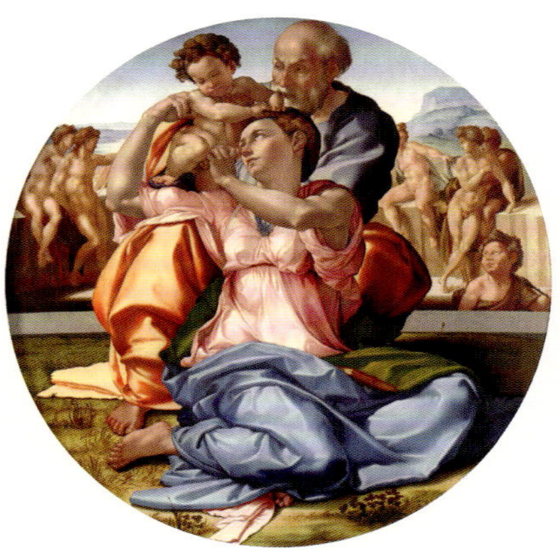

Doni Tondo, 1505–6.
Tempera on panel, diameter: 120 cm, 47¼ in.

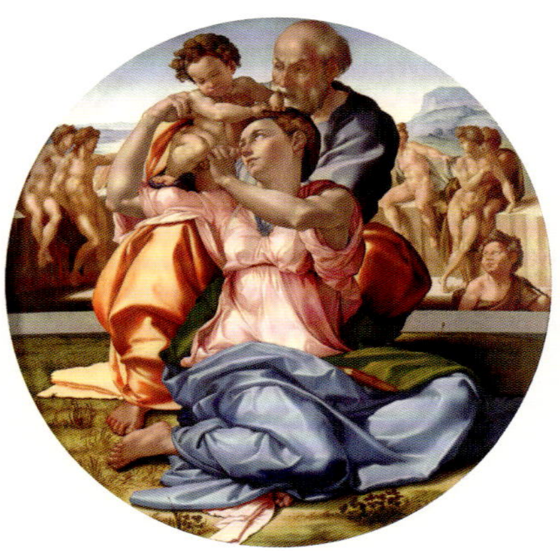

Taddei Tondo, 1504–5.
Marble, diameter: 106.8 cm, 42 in.

❶ Light and shade

Michelangelo emphasized the highlights and shading on the sibyl's face by using the technique of tonal modelling to establish the three-dimensionality of the form.

❸ Sculptural

Michelangelo was a painter, architect and sculptor, as well as a draughtsman, but was perhaps most inspired by the last of these disciplines. His method of establishing deep shadows with the red chalk has often been compared to the way a sculptor carves into the marble with a chisel.

❹ Disegno

Sketching was a vital component of the art-making process in the Renaissance. This was particularly the case in Florence, where *disegno* – referring to both drawing and the broader artistic intelligence required to create harmonious designs – was highly prized.[38] The art of Florence at this time was more concerned with the contours of forms than with colour or atmospheric effects, which held particular interest for artists in Venice.

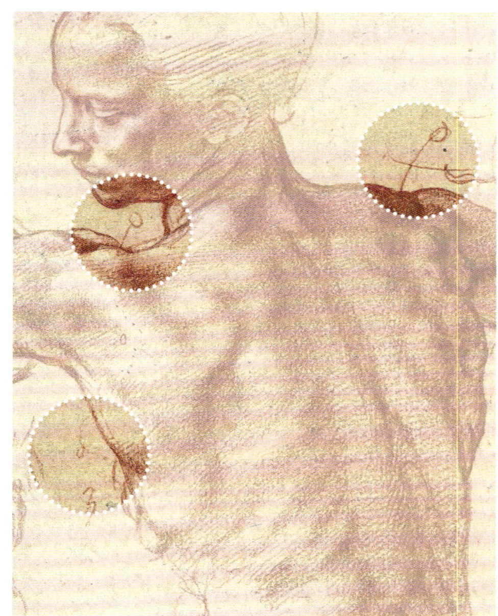

Study for the Battle of Cascina, c. 1504.
Pencil and silverpoint on paper,
23.5 × 35.6 cm, 9¼ × 14 in.

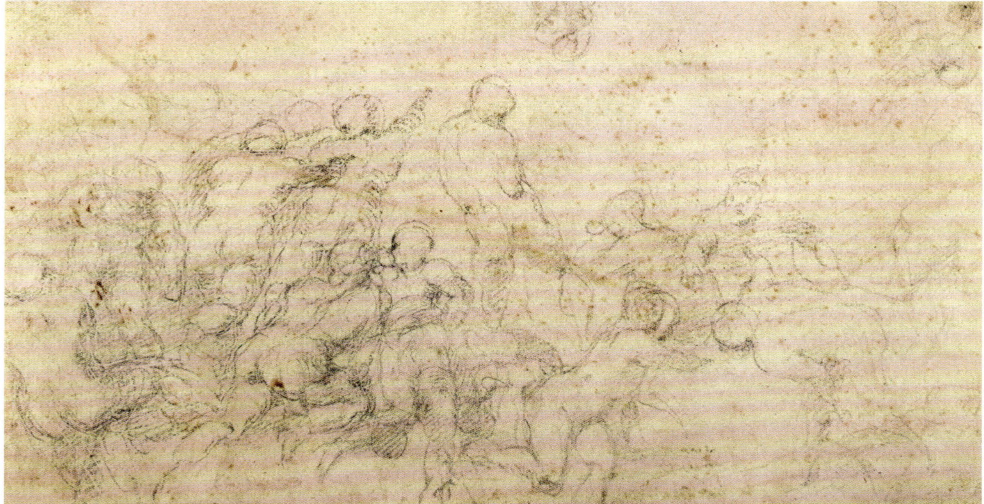

❷ Notations

Michelangelo added lines that extend from the shoulders and end in a circle. A third line points towards the armpit.[37] It is not known for certain what they represent, but he may have added them as notes to himself about the lightest to darkest areas of shading, or to point out certain muscles to students or colleagues.

❺ Anatomy

The back of the figure reveals the extraordinary attention Michelangelo paid to specific muscles and skeletal elements in the human body. He was known to have attended dissections to better understand the structures that lie beneath the skin.

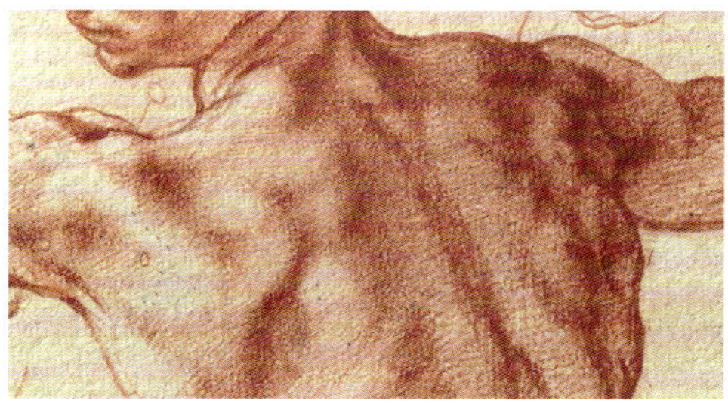

❻ Pose

The figure strikes a balletic pose, rotating with arms aloft. In the final work (below, right), we can see the intention: to show the sibyl closing a book, while simultaneously stepping down from an altar and turning to face the viewer.

❼ Part of an epic scene

Michelangelo made the drawing in the latter stages of his work on the Sistine Chapel ceiling. The ceiling as a whole represents the story of creation in the Book of Genesis, from Adam and Eve to Noah and the flood. It had a profound impact on art history, and remains one of the most iconic artworks in the world, particularly the scene representing the creation of Adam (ill. p. 75). The Libyan Sibyl is located at the northeast end of the ceiling, next to an image of God dividing light from darkness.

❽ Gender

In the final painting, the figure is a woman: Phemonoe, a legendary priestess from classical history who could predict the future. Even though she is supposed to be female, Michelangelo used a male model for his sketch. In the painting, the sibyl looks androgynous, a body type considered by scholars in the Italian Renaissance as the ideal, one that blended the best of male and female elements (see also pp. 72–5).

❾ Final result

The final painting looks dramatic but also disjointed, with the legs and torso appearing disconnected. The reason for this has its roots in Michelangelo's sketch, where scrutiny is paid to individual parts of the body, rather than to the whole.

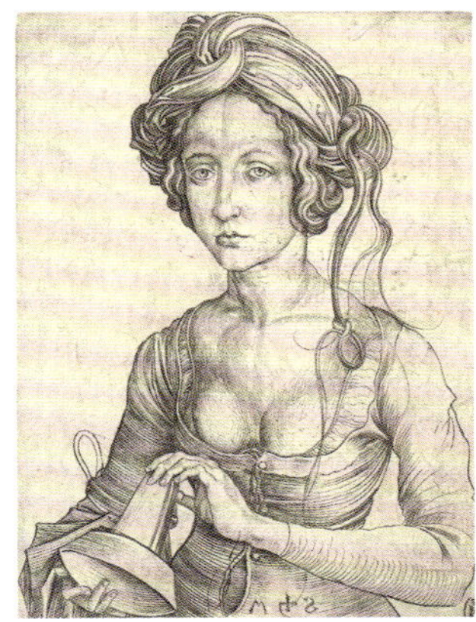

Martin Schongauer, *A Foolish Virgin in Half-Figure*, 1470–91. Engraving, 14.7 × 10.8 cm, 5¾ × 4¼ in.

❿ Sketching technique

The application of chalk with different degrees of pressure is clearly visible in the variety of weighted contours, as is the cross-hatching used to express texture, volume and light effects. Michelangelo was impressed by the shading found in prints and engravings from northern Europe, particularly those of Martin Schongauer (above).[39]

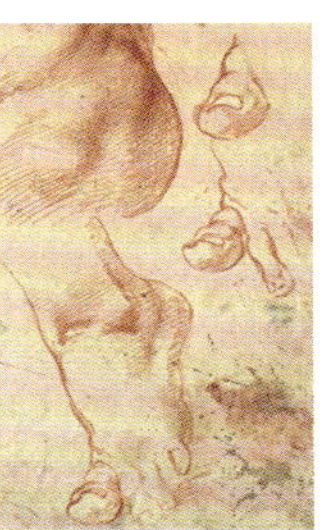

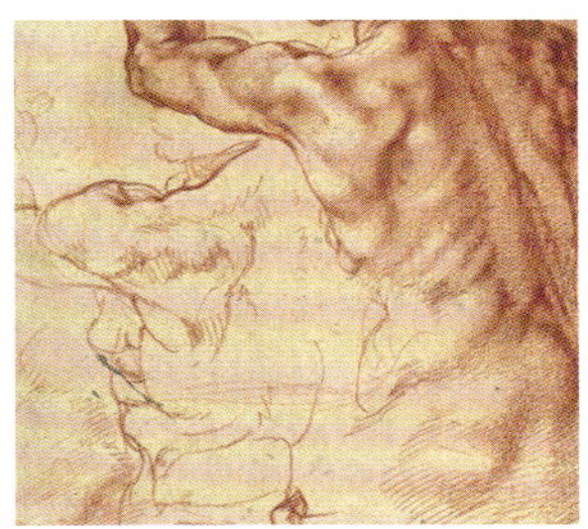

⓫ Multiple forms

The drawing is evidence of Michelangelo's exploratory mind, as we see him trying out a number of poses with the male model in preparation for the final work.

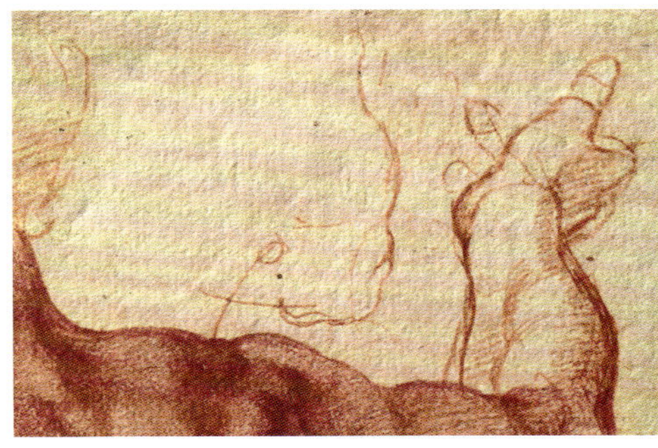

⓬ Visual echo

The detail of the splayed toe reveals Michelangelo's interest in repeating forms. In the final painting, the toes form an inverted imitation of the 'V' of the open book.

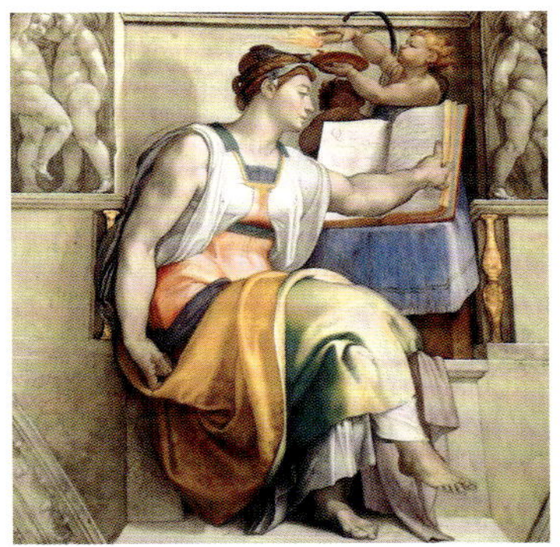

The Erythraean Sibyl, 1509.
Fresco, 360 × 380 cm, 141¾ × 149½ in.

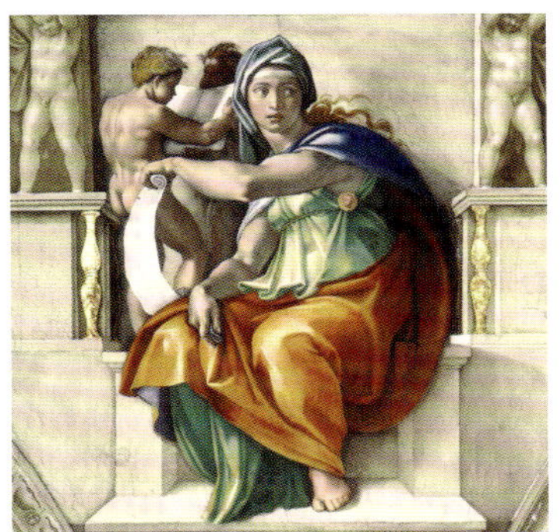

The Delphic Sibyl, 1509.
Fresco, 350 × 380 cm, 137¾ × 149½ in.

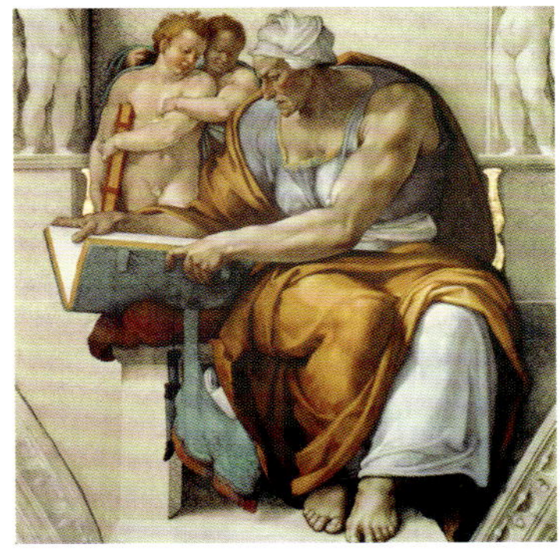

The Cumaean Sibyl, 1510.
Fresco, 375 × 380 cm, 147½ × 149½ in.

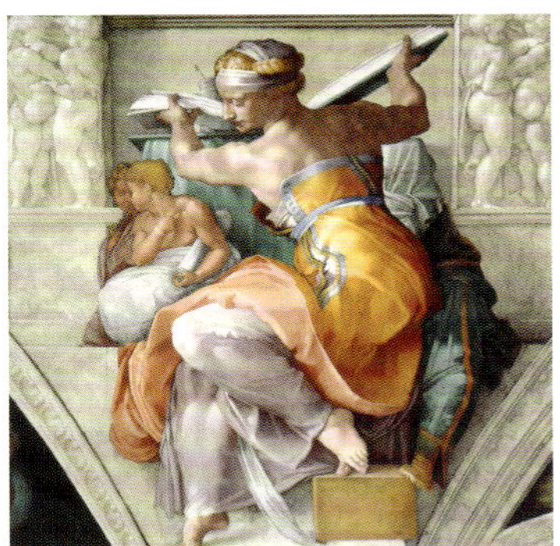

The Libyan Sibyl, c. 1508–12
Fresco, 395 × 380 cm, 155½ × 149½ in.

LINKED PRACTITIONERS

SKETCHES:

Albrecht Dürer (1471–1528), GERMANY
Rembrandt van Rijn (1606–1669), NETHERLANDS
Jean-Antoine Watteau (1684–1721), FRANCE
Käthe Kollwitz (1867–1945), GERMANY
Tracey Emin (born 1963), UK

THE NUDE:

Praxiteles (395–330 BCE), GREECE
Henri Matisse (1869–1954), FRANCE
Paula Modersohn-Becker (1876–1907), GERMANY
Brassaï (1899–1984), FRANCE
Carolee Schneemann (1939–2019), USA

OTHER SISTINE CHAPEL ARTISTS:

Cosimo Rosselli (1439–1507), ITALY
Luca Signorelli (1441–1523), ITALY
Sandro Botticelli (1445–1510), ITALY
Pietro Perugino (1446–1523), ITALY
Domenico Ghirlandaio (1448–1494), ITALY

18. Stories Within Stories

These two extraordinarily detailed and narrative-rich folios from the Spinola Hours *were probably made in a workshop in Ghent, perhaps for Margaret of Austria, Duchess of Savoy, who also owned the* Très Riches Heures, *decorated by the Limbourg Brothers.*

The miniatures were created for a Book of Hours, a type of devotional text that was intended to inspire spiritual reflection and give readers a personal engagement with religious ideas. Here, the subject is death and the rituals that accompany a funeral. The artist has used some astoundingly innovative techniques to appeal to readers' hearts and minds.

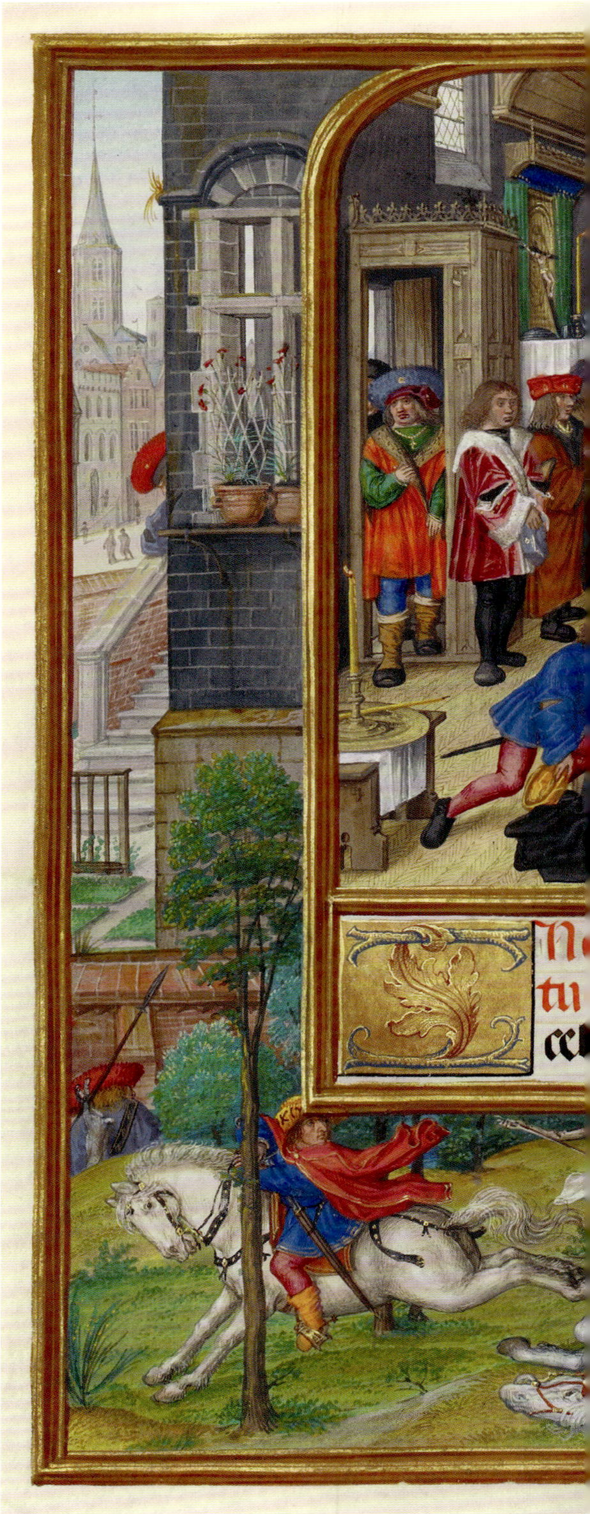

Tempera colours, gold and ink
23.2 × 16.7 cm, 9¼ × 6½ in. (each)
The J. Paul Getty Museum, Los Angeles

Master of James IV of Scotland
Deathbed Scene and *Office of the Dead*
Spinola Hours, c. 1510–20

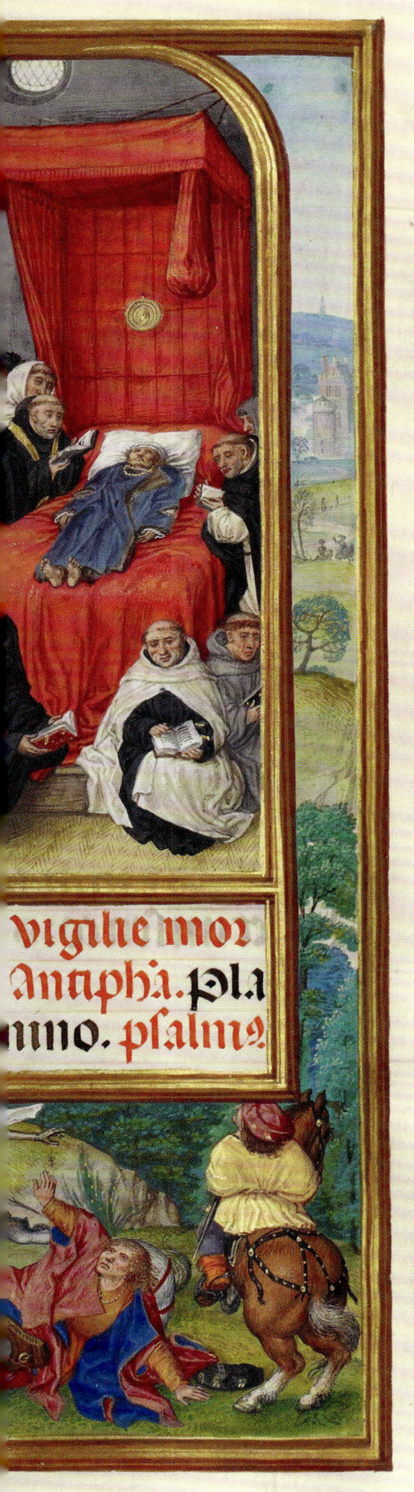

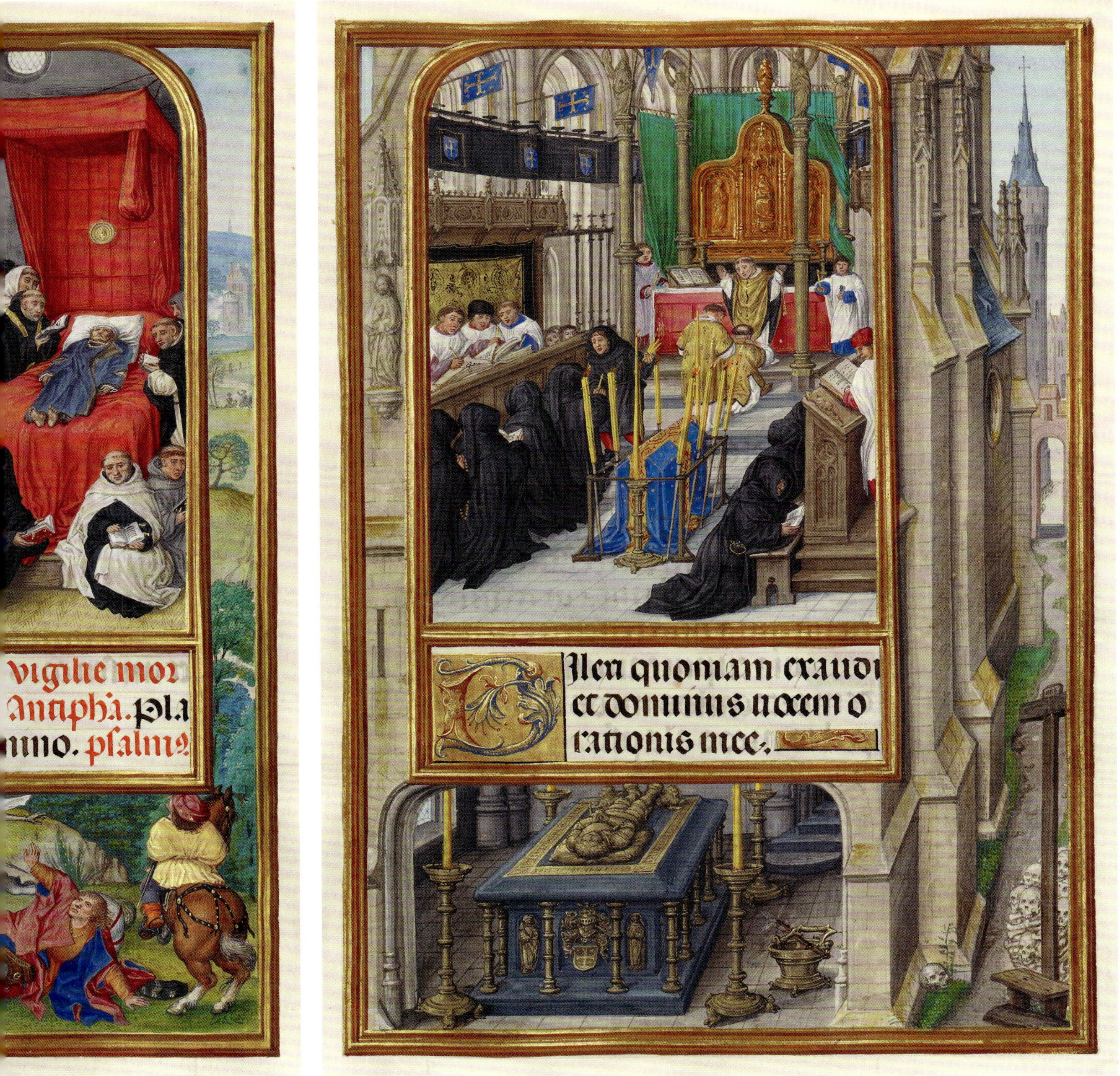

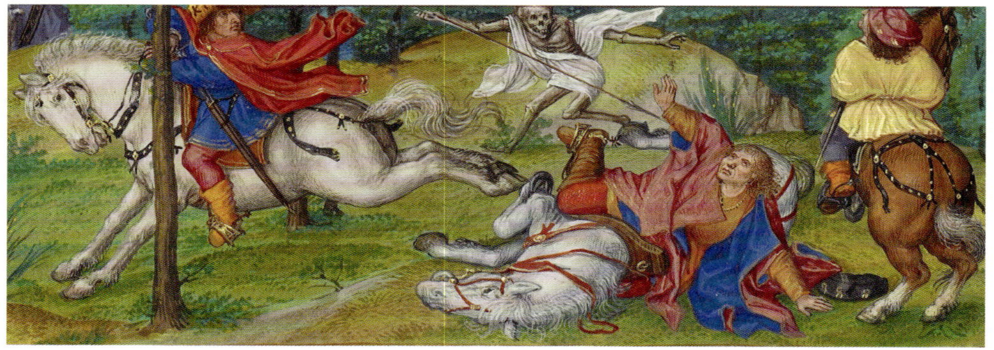

❶ Death

The two folios tell a story that begins with the hunting scene at the bottom of the left page. A young man is killed while riding his horse by Death, wielding a spear. The scene, known as the 'Three Living and the Three Dead', is a familiar one in medieval art, in which three young men encounter three skeletons while out hunting, who warn them to behave well in life as death may suddenly appear.[40]

❷ Real events?

Death was a popular subject in medieval art, reflecting the perilous conditions of the time, affected by warfare, disease and failed harvests. Here, it may have had personal significance as the illuminations may have been made for Margaret of Austria, whose husband Philibert II, Duke of Savoy, died suddenly while hunting in 1504.[41] Death appears to mock the dying man by mimicking his outstretched arms.

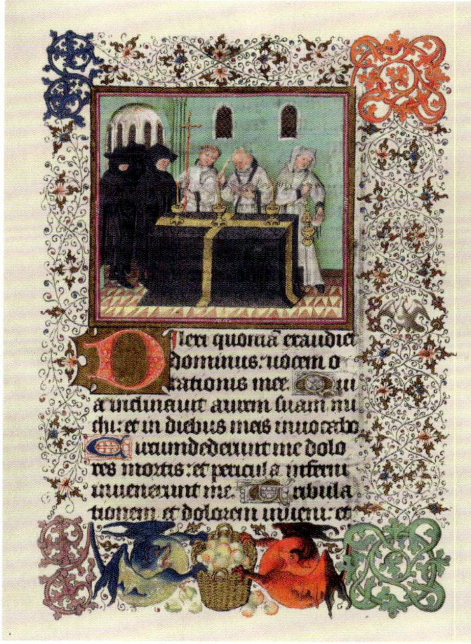

Master of Catherine of Cleves,
Final Absolution, folio 169r,
from the *Hours of Catherine of Cleves*, c. 1440

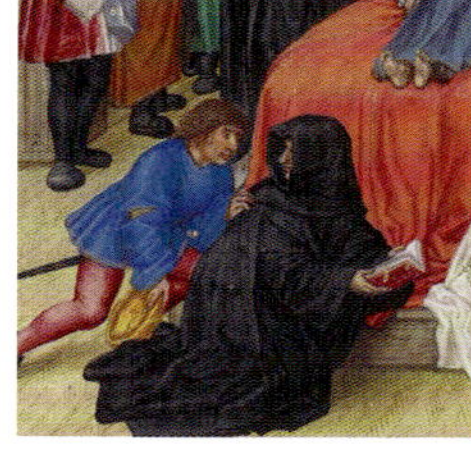
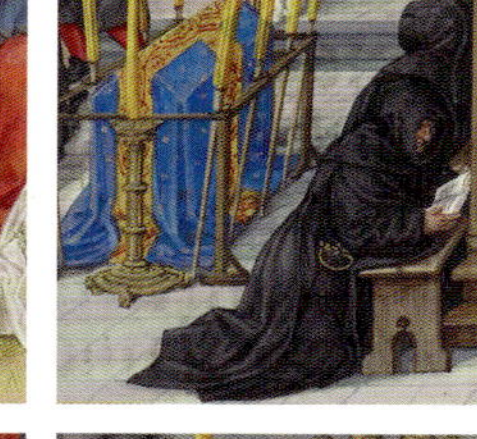
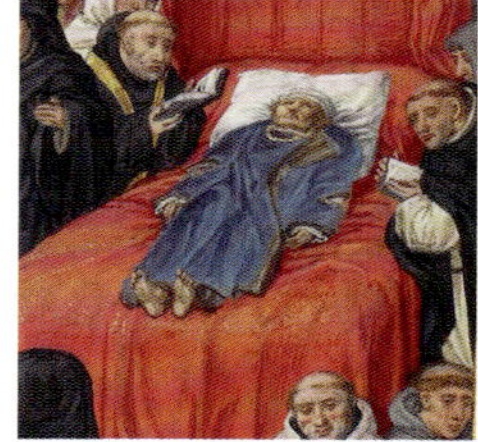
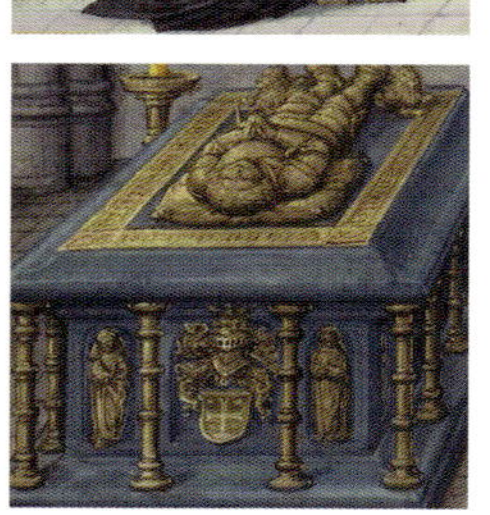

❸ Visual links

The repetition of gestures is one of many visual echoes between the two paintings. A kneeling monk who appears in the left folio is mirrored by a kneeling monk on the right. Similarly, the recumbent effigy at the bottom of the right folio is an echo of the man on his deathbed in the upper section of the left page.

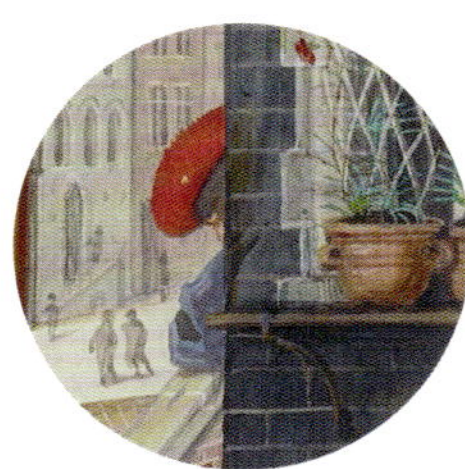
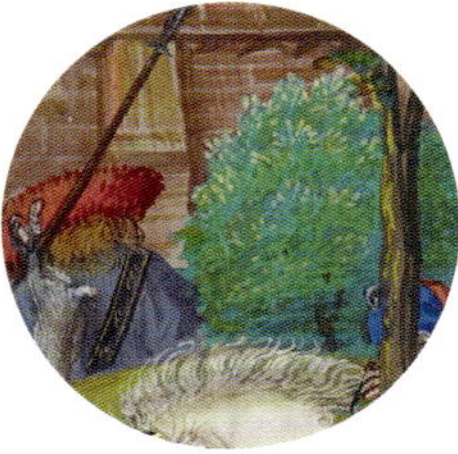

❹ Mystery man

On the left page, the hunting scene at the bottom is linked to the mourning ritual above by a mysterious figure in a red hat who witnesses the death of the man from behind a tree, and again outside the door of the house.

❺ Miniature and border

As we follow the progression of the narrative, our gaze moves between the exterior scenes and the interior scenes framed in gold. This arrangement follows a traditional composition of illuminated manuscripts, in which a decorative border surrounds a separate but related vignette. One of the innovations on display here is how both miniature and border are incorporated into a unified composition.

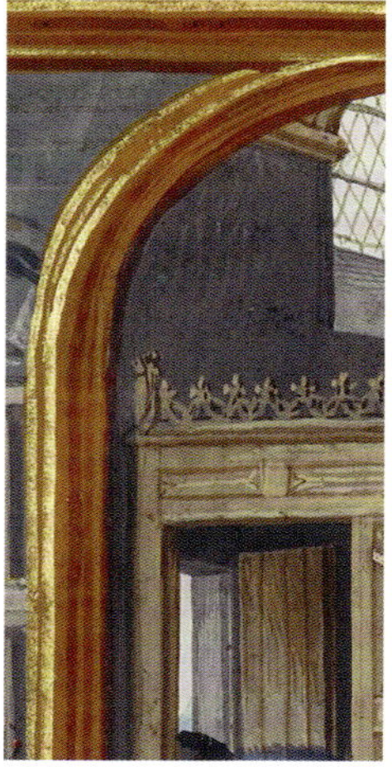
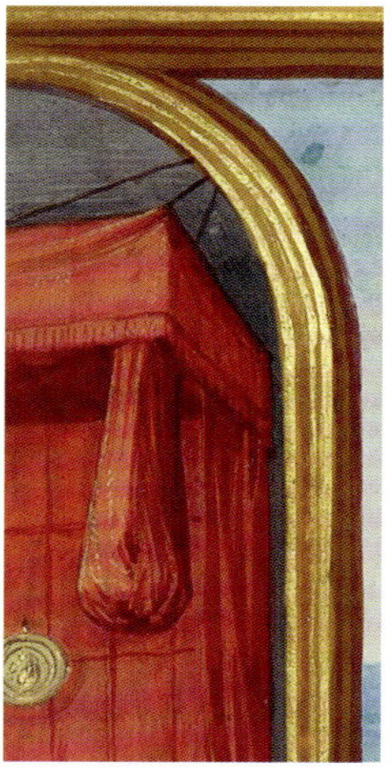

❻ Frames

The gold frames have been given shading to suggest three-dimensionality. As well as distinguishing the various stages of the story, they also reveal the interiors of buildings, as if they had x-ray powers.

❼ Last rites and prayers

The interior scene of the left folio shows the deceased surrounded by mourners, who read the Office of the Dead over his corpse on the eve of his burial. On the right folio, the interior scene shows a requiem mass taking place within a sumptuous private chapel.[42]

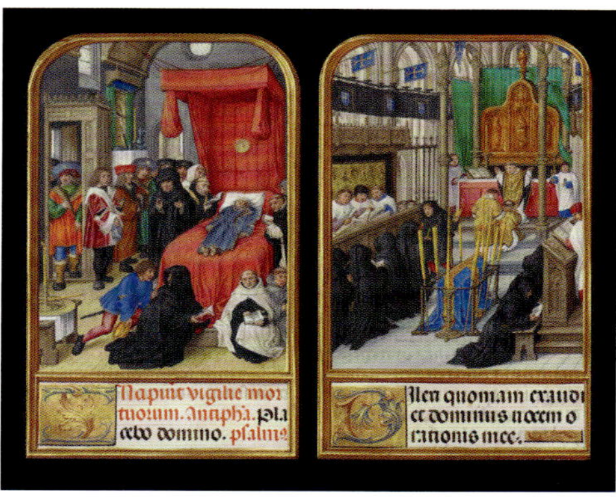

❽ Book of Hours

The Office of the Dead is one section of a Book of Hours, of which the *Spinola Hours* is an exceptionally decorative example, created as a luxury item for a very wealthy individual.

❾ Words

The Book of Hours is a devotional text with prayers in Latin for various times of the day, along with a yearly calendar of religious dates and other texts to encourage devoutness and reflection. It was intended to be read by anyone – not just nuns, monks or priests – and was a bestseller in medieval Europe, with more copies produced than any other book, even the Bible.[43]

❿ Illusionism

One of the most inventive aspects of the *Spinola Hours* is the integration of text and pictures. Using ingenious illusionistic trompe-l'oeil effects, the text is set in places on a hinged panel, as if it is meant to swing open over the paintings; in others, words appear as if pinned to the manuscript on a scrap of paper.

⓫ Resting place

The crypt is linked to the upper chapel above by a set of stairs. Here the story ends, with the Office of the Dead complete and the dead man's soul finally departed from the world of the living.

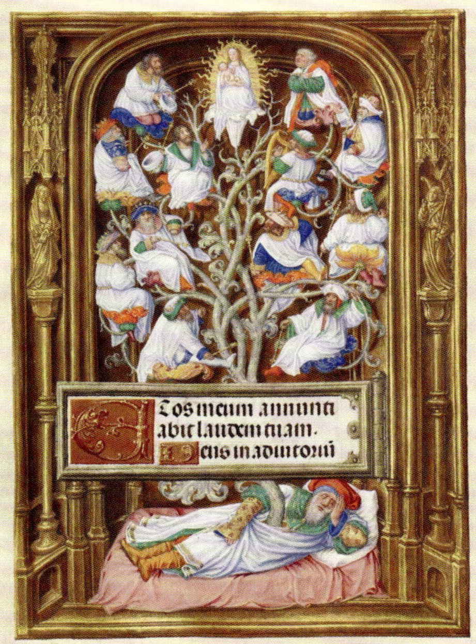

The Tree of Jesse, folio 10v, from the *Spinola Hours*, c. 1510–20. Tempera, gold and ink, 23.2 × 16.7 cm, 9¼ × 6½ in.

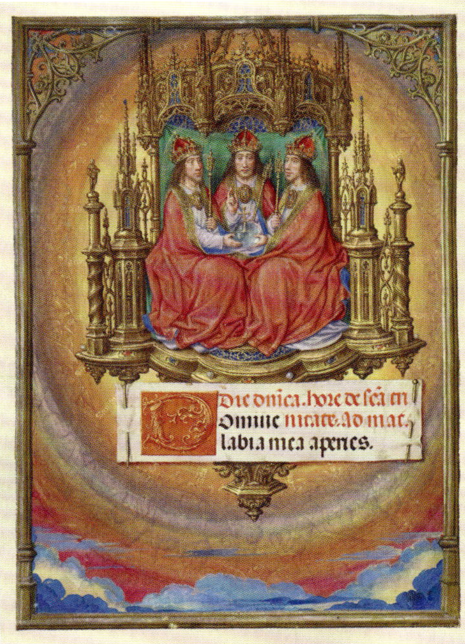

The Holy Trinity Enthroned, folio 10v, from the *Spinola Hours*, c. 1510–20. Tempera, gold and ink, 23.2 × 16.7 cm, 9¼ × 6½ in.

⓬ Vivid detail

When the first readers of the *Spinola Hours* read the Office of the Dead, they would have imagined that the funeral illustrated could be their own. The Book of Hours encouraged meditation on the omnipresence of death, and how to lead a good life. To appeal more directly to readers, the artist has included such vivid details as the stains on the walls of the church caused by leaky drainage.

⓭ Artistry

Although small, the paintings contain an extraordinary level of realistic detail. The artist worked in minute dabs of diluted but fast-drying paint, building layers of tone to replicate texture, space and the effects of light.[44] The identity of the artist is unknown; he is called the Master of James IV of Scotland after a portrait he painted of the king (right), and is widely believed to be the Flemish miniaturist Gerard Horenbout (1465–1541).

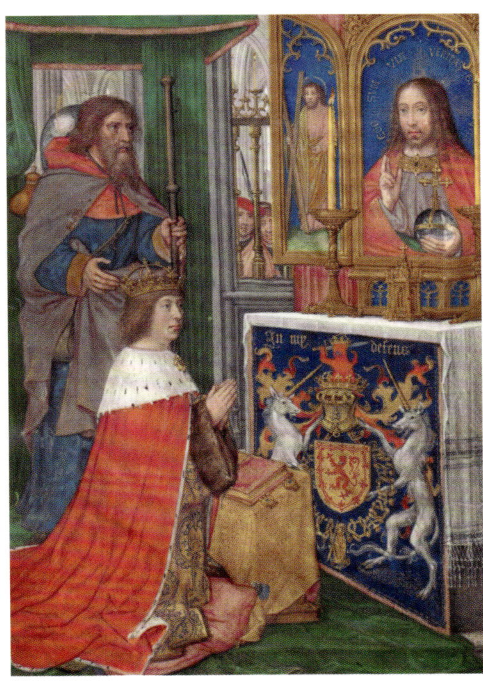

James IV at Prayer (detail), folio 24v, from the *Hours of James IV of Scotland*, c. 1502

LINKED PRACTITIONERS

DEATH PERSONIFIED:

Hieronymus Bosch (1450–1516), NETHERLANDS
Arnold Böcklin (1827–1901), SWITZERLAND
Gustave Doré (1832–1883), FRANCE
José Guadalupe Posada (1852–1913), MEXICO
Janis Rozentāls (1866–1916), FINLAND

BOOKS OF HOURS:

Jean Pucelle (fl. 1320–1355), FRANCE
Giovannino dei Grassi (1350–1398), ITALY
Limbourg Brothers (fl. 1385–1416), NETHERLANDS
Gerard David (1460–1523), BELGIUM
Giulio Clovio (1498–1578), ITALY

FUNERALS:

El Greco (1541–1614), GREECE/SPAIN
Gustav Courbet (1819–1877), FRANCE
Édouard Manet (1832–1883), FRANCE
Anna Ancher (1859–1935), DENMARK
George Grosz (1893–1959), GERMANY

19. A Multilayered Portrait

When Hans Holbein the Younger (1497–1543) painted this work in London in 1533, he had never before undertaken a full-length double portrait. The highly unusual painting was commissioned by Jean de Dinteville, the French ambassador to the court of Henry VIII, to commemorate his friendship with Georges de Selve, Bishop of Lavaur.

The final work includes an astonishing amount of specific detail, possibly the result of consultation between artist and sitters. Along with the ambassador, the bishop and their sumptuous garments, we are also shown an enigmatic interior and an assortment of objects, including scientific and musical instruments, globes and books, which seem to have a collective meaning. When decoded, they could unlock a deeper understanding of the sitters' shared political, intellectual and religious beliefs.

Oil on panel
207 × 209.5 cm, 81½ × 82½ in.
National Gallery, London

Hans Holbein the Younger
The Ambassadors
1533

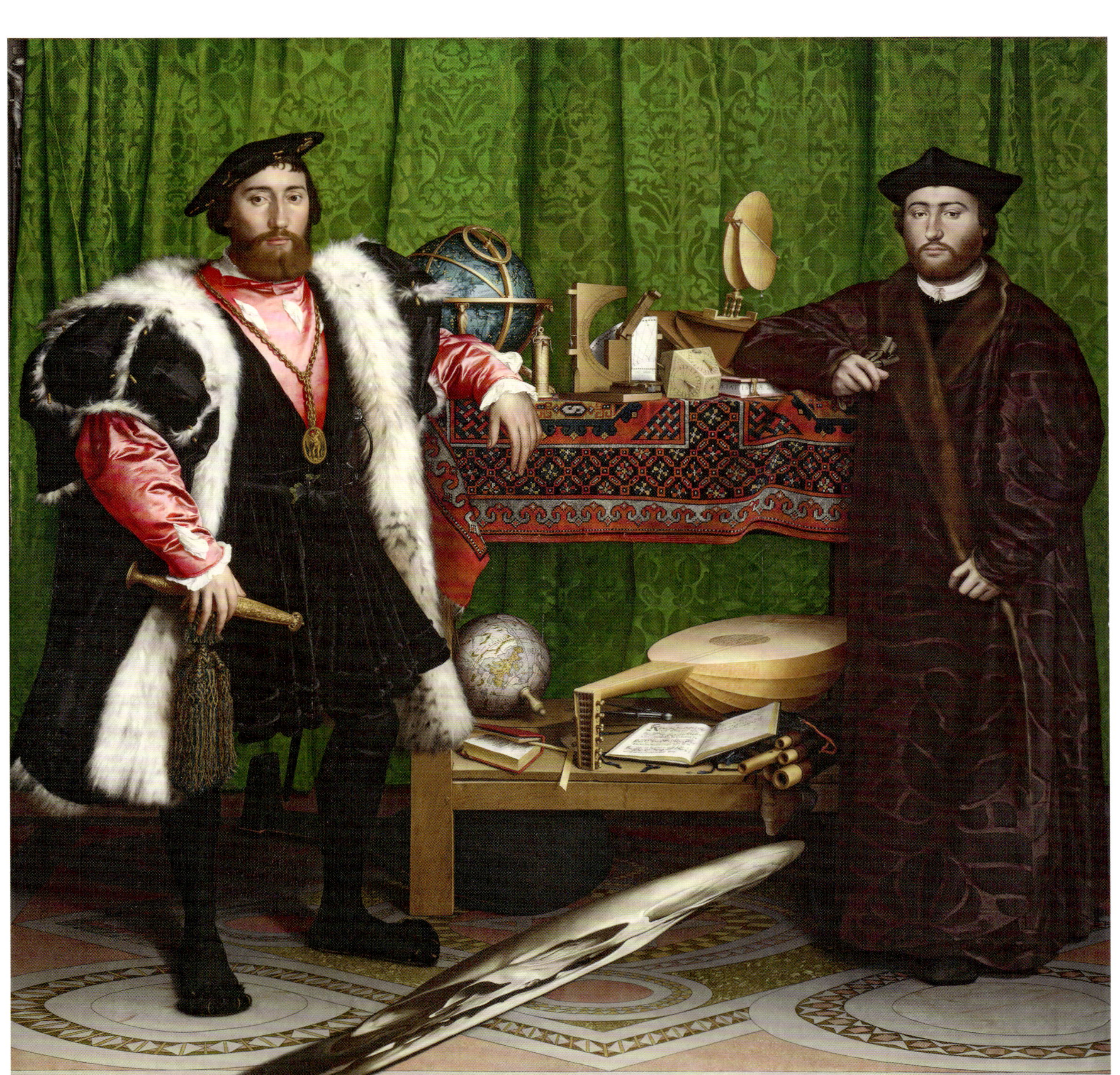

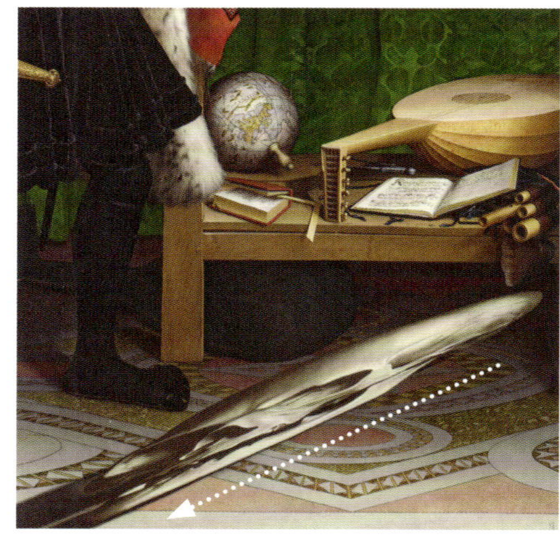

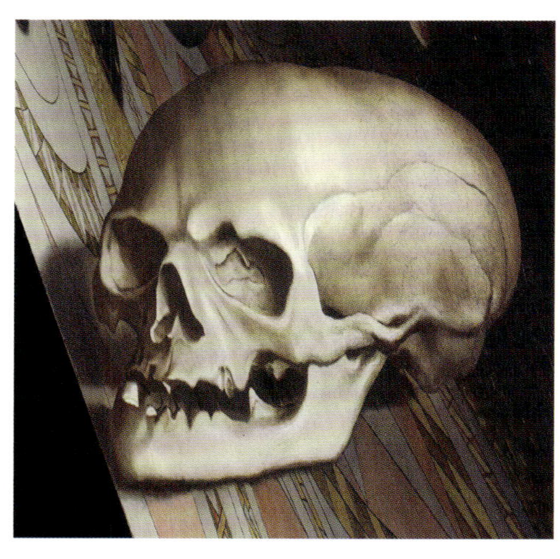

❶ Skull

In the 19th century, a curator at the National Gallery in London expressed his belief that the strange shape at the base of the painting was the bone of a cuttlefish. By standing at the right of the portrait and looking down at a raking angle, however, the object reveals itself to be a skull. This effect of optical distortion is known as anamorphic perspective.

❷ Memento mori

The skull may be a *memento mori*, or reminder of death. The idea had become popular in the 16th century: people who owned paintings or sculptures containing such symbols were seen as humble and recognizing the futility of leading a materialistic life. A woodcut made by Holbein some years earlier for the *Dance of Death* series illustrated exactly this theme, with a similar composition of two figures and a skull between them. Here, the purpose of using anamorphic perspective may have been to show that death is incomprehensible in life, but when death is seen clearly, life itself is incomprehensible.[45]

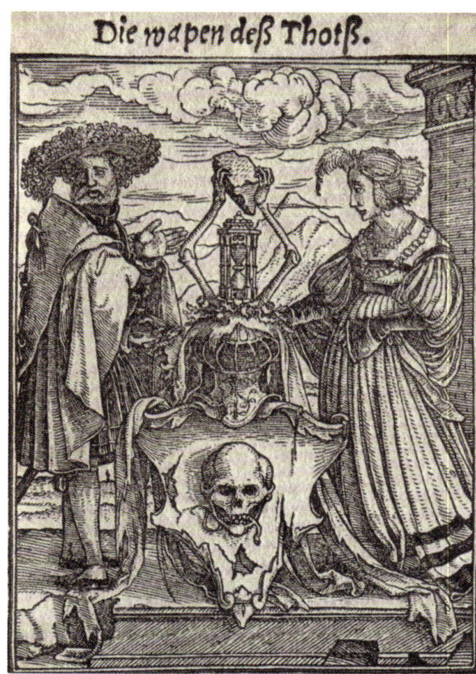

The Coat of Arms of Death, from the *Dance of Death* series, *c.* 1526. Woodcut, 6.5 × 4.9 cm, 2½ × 2 in.

❸ Insignia

Close inspection of the ambassador's beret reveals that his cap badge is also a skull: the personal insignia of Jean de Dinteville.

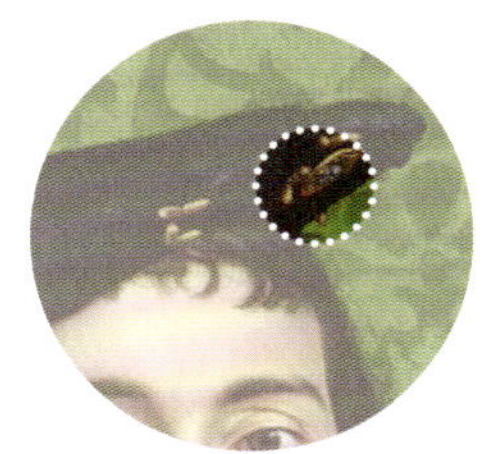

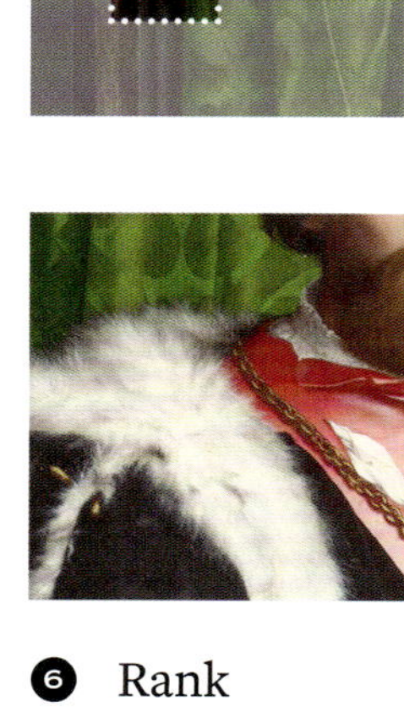

❺ Salvation

At the top left of the portrait a silver crucifix is visible, half-hidden behind a green curtain. This subtle addition may allude to salvation, the redemption of the purest souls on the day of judgment.

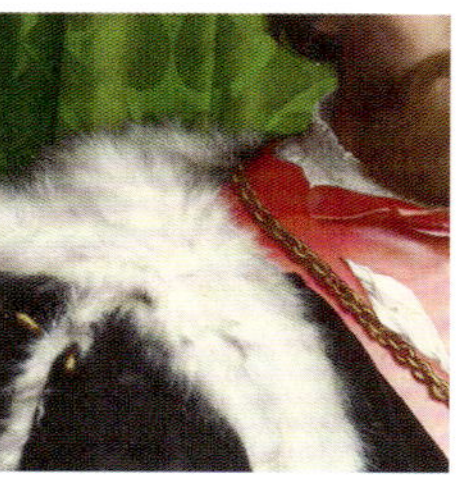

❻ Rank

The clothing of the men tells its own story. Jean de Dinteville wears a coat in black velvet, lined with expensive lynx fur, over a doublet of equally costly pink satin. Georges de Selve, however, wears a long, slightly less ostentatious brown robe.

❹ Leading man

Holbein's composition places Jean de Dinteville as the more commanding presence in the portrait. The ambassador's right foot is further forwards than the bishop's, and is placed in the centre of a circle on the floor.

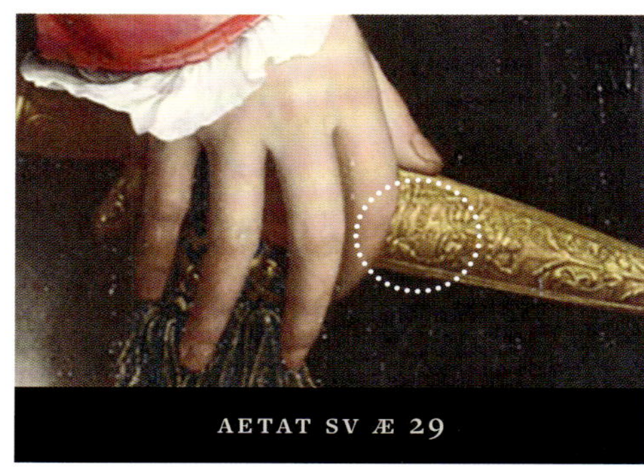

AETAT SV Æ 29

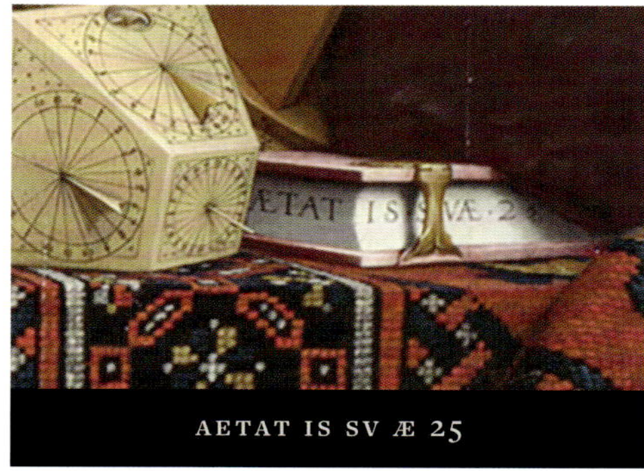

AETAT IS SV Æ 25

❼ Personalized details

The gold dagger is held by the ambassador in such a way that the number '29', signifying his age, is prominently displayed. The age of his companion (25th year) is visible on the pages of the book the bishop leans on.

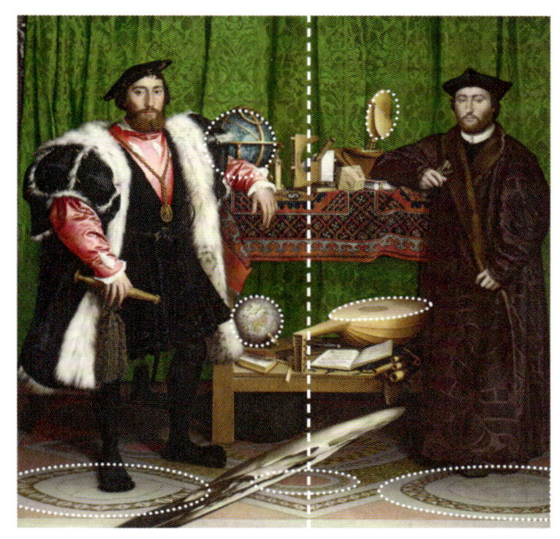

8 Spheres of influence

The arrangement of the composition shows repeated circular shapes that follow a roughly symmetrical pattern, establishing an ordered and rational atmosphere in the scene.

9 Technique

Holbein recorded the individual threads of the tassel of Jean de Dinteville's dagger and the hairs of Georges de Selve's beard in meticulous detail. He used real gold in places, including the tassel, brushing gold leaf over glue to secure it onto the surface of the painting.

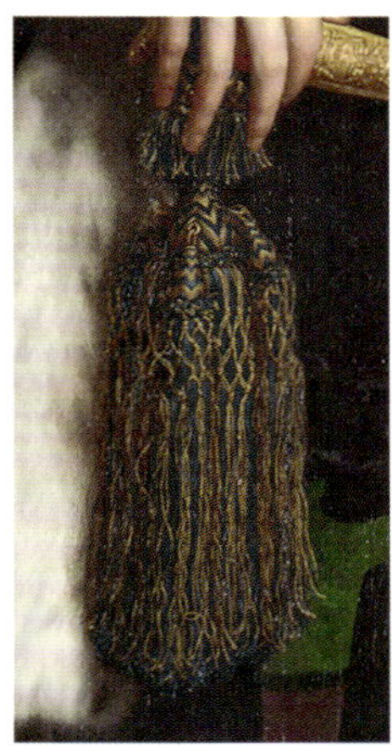

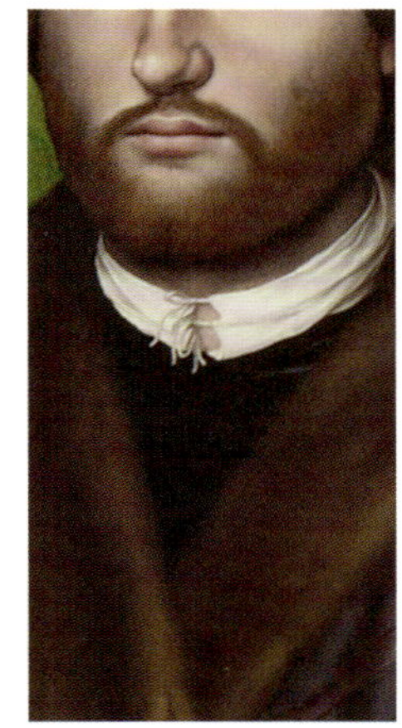

10 Restoration

The current appearance of the painting is the result of various periods of restoration, most recently in 1998. Photographs taken during the process reveal the oak planks forming the base and the extent of damage to the original paintwork. Much of the version we see today is the work of modern restorers.

Portrait of Nicolaus Kratzer, 1528. Tempera on oak, 83 × 67 cm, 32¾ × 26¼ in.

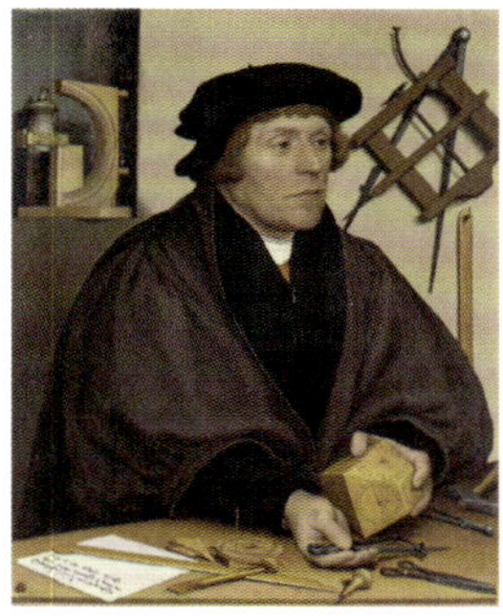

11 Renaissance knowledge

On top of the cabinet between the two men are objects that relate to the sky. These include a globe showing the constellations of the stars, and instruments for measuring time that rely on the sun's position, including cylindrical and polyhedral sundials and a torquetum. The theme of the passage of time is related to the skull at the bottom of the painting, which represents what occurs at the end of an individual's allotted time on earth.

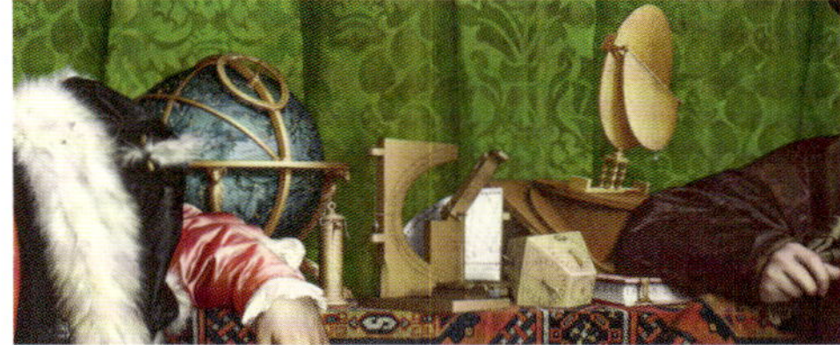

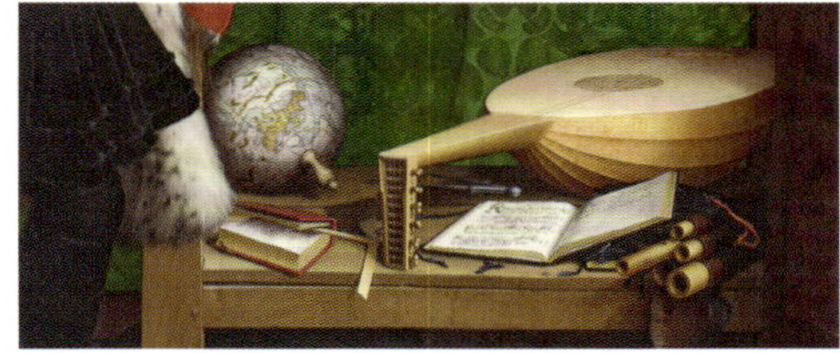

12 Worldly things

On the lower shelf are items related to how we experience the world around us: the earth, mathematics, music and religion. The globe is rotated to highlight Jean de Dinteville's hometown of Polisy, France, where he took the portrait on his departure from England.

13 Cutting-edge science

The instruments on display may have been observed by Holbein in the collection of Henry VIII's chief astronomer, Nicolaus Kratzer. A portrait of Kratzer (left) painted by Holbein five years earlier shows similar instruments.

14 Navigation

Interest in navigational instruments and the mapping of the world in the Renaissance reveals a fascination with exploration and international trade. Christopher Columbus arrived in the New World in 1492, and the first circumnavigation of the world was completed by Ferdinand Magellan in 1522.

15 Divisions and discord

There are two books on the lower shelf of the cabinet: a German book of mathematics on the left, and on the right a Lutheran hymnal. The presence of the hymnal alludes to a contemporary upheaval in Europe: the splitting of the church into Catholic and Protestant, triggered by the radical cleric Martin Luther in 1517. The fact that the book of mathematics has been opened at the section describing division may not be a coincidence.

16 Ambassador's work

The year that Holbein painted *The Ambassadors* – 1933 – was a pivotal one in the history of religion in Europe. Henry VIII divorced Catherine of Aragon to marry Anne Boleyn without the approval of Pope Clement VII, and from that point on, religion in England was separate from the Catholic faith with the monarch the head of the new Anglican church. Jean de Dinteville was at the centre of these events, representing the interests of King Francis I of France as the power relationships in Europe shifted dramatically.

LINKED PRACTITIONERS

DOUBLE PORTRAITS:

Jan van Eyck (1390–1441), NETHERLANDS
Piero della Francesca (1415–1492), ITALY
Anthony van Dyck (1599–1641), BELGIUM
Thomas Gainsborough (1727–1788), UK
David Hockney (born 1937), UK

SKULLS:

Jacques de Gheyn II (1565–1629), NETHERLANDS
Harmen Steenwyck (1612–1656), NETHERLANDS
Georgia O'Keeffe (1887–1986), USA
Andy Warhol (1928–1987), USA
Damien Hirst (born 1965), UK

RENAISSANCE ARTISTS:

Donatello (1386–1466), ITALY
Sandro Botticelli (1445–1510), ITALY
Leonardo da Vinci (1452–1519), ITALY
Raphael (1483–1520), ITALY
Titian (c. 1488/90–1576), ITALY

20. Signature Styles

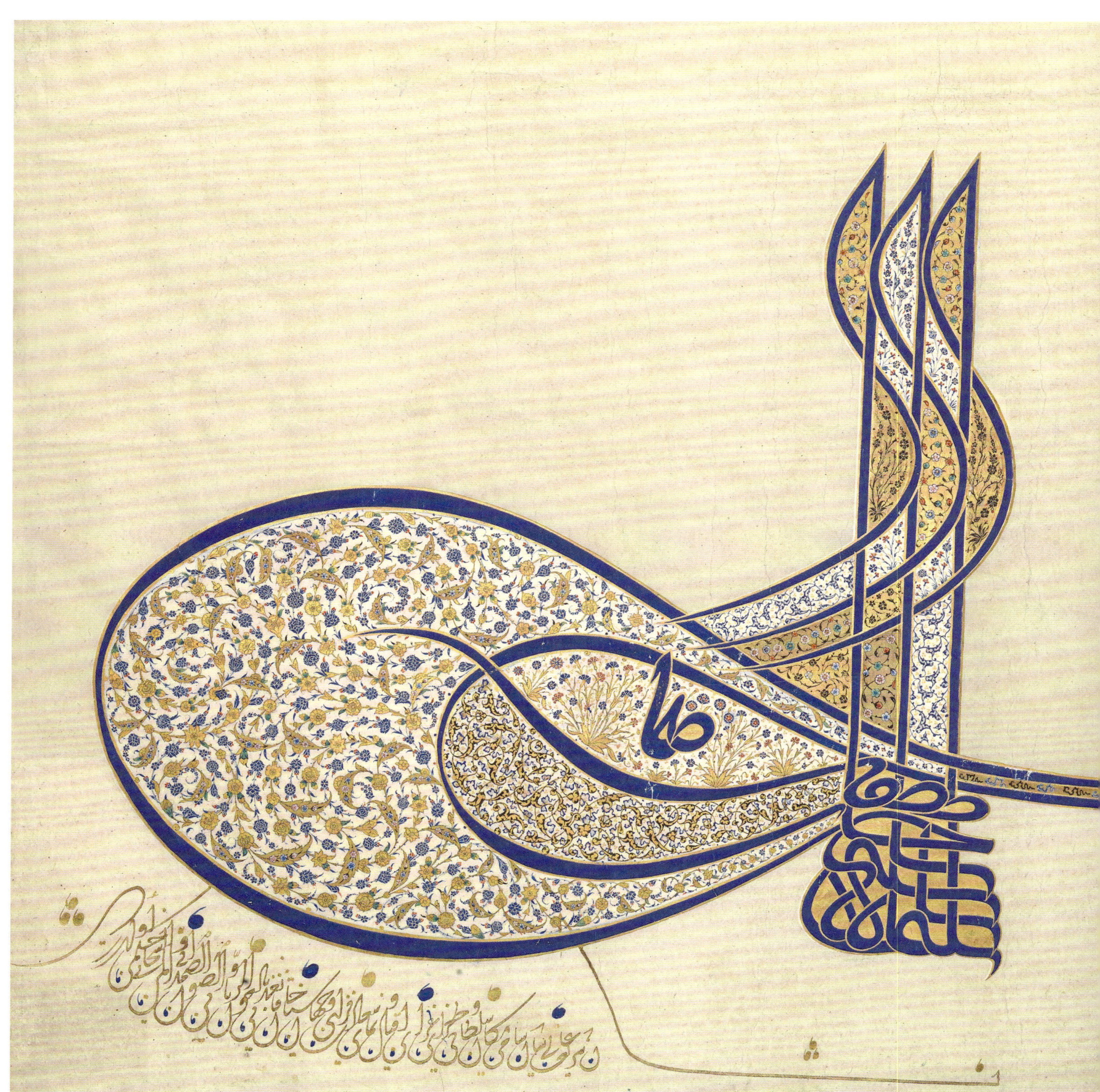

Turkey, Ottoman

Tughra of Süleiman the Magnificent

c. 1555–60

Working in collaboration at the Topkapi Palace in Istanbul, an elite calligrapher and a highly trained illuminator created this sinuous composition to symbolize the authority of the Sultan of the Ottoman Empire: Süleiman the Magnificent (r. 1520–66).

Tughras are the ceremonial signatures of the Ottoman sultans. First used in a more simplified form in 1324, by the time of Süleiman's rule in the 16th century they had evolved into vividly intricate designs. *Tughras* would have been fixed to the top of official documents as a seal of the sultan's authority, delivered with a swirl of organic shapes, billowing lines and eye-popping colours – made deliberately complex to avoid imitation.

Ink, opaque watercolour and gold on paper
52.1 × 64.5 cm, 20½ × 25½ in.
Metropolitan Museum of Art, New York

1 Microscopic detail

This *tughra* is the work of more than one highly trained artist. The writing in cobalt blue would have been set down by a specialist calligrapher – one of the highest officials in the court – with the decorative elements filled in by a painter using watercolour with black and gold inks. The type of script, *diwani*, was a specifically Ottoman style of writing. Calligraphers would spend a lifetime learning to master the art, as the resulting design had to be elaborate enough to avoid being forged.

2 Flower power

Hundreds of individual flowers and other floral motifs fill the spaces in and around the letters. Roses, carnations, split palmettes and peonies are all represented, although they probably were not symbolic – such decoration had been a feature of Islamic design for generations. The flowers are not static but are placed to give the appearance of naturalism, as if they are spiralling and flowing, creating a feeling of dynamism.

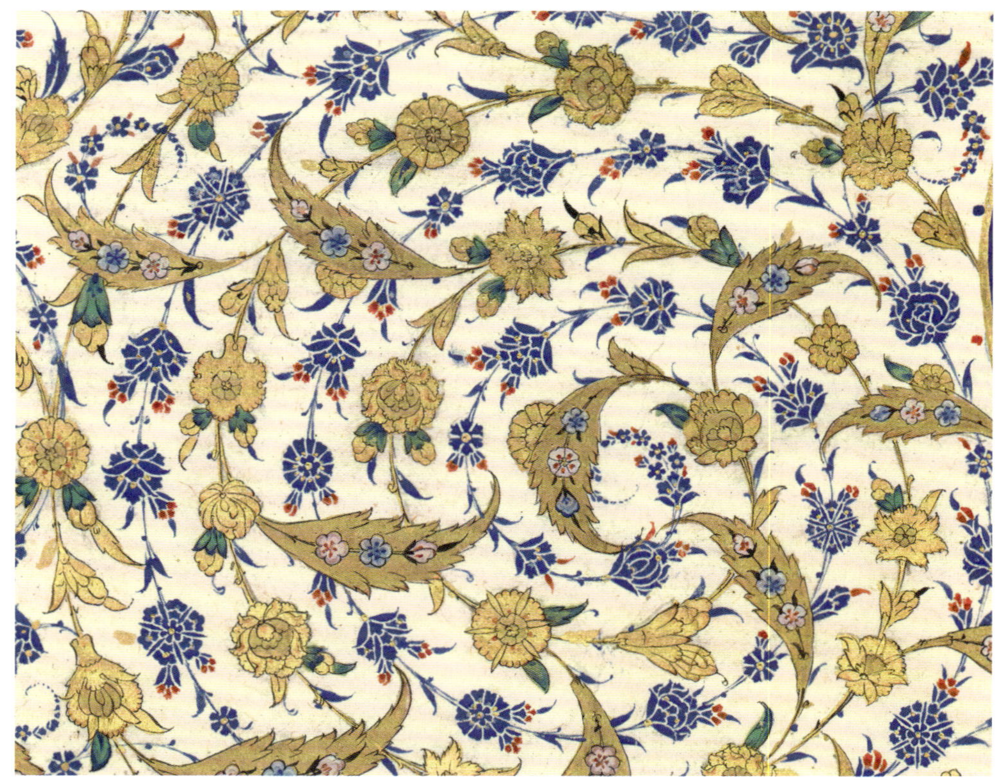

3 Pattern

The names of Süleiman the Magnificent and his father Selim I appear at the lower right of the main image, below three vertical lines. At the centre of the inner oval is another motif, a word meaning 'the victorious forever'. It is encircled by two ovals that, like the vertical lines, are traditional features of a *tughra*.

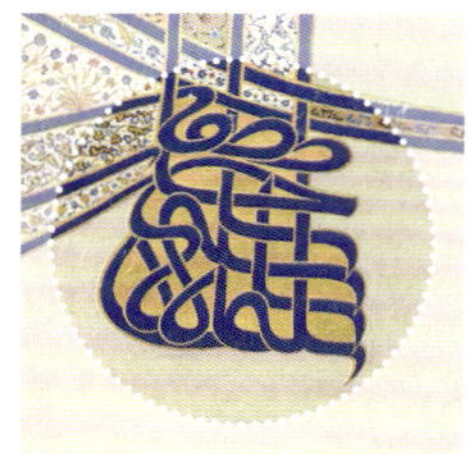

5 Depth

Although the work appears flat, the three vertical elements appear to overlap, giving a subtle suggestion of three-dimensionality.

6 Noble, exalted, brilliant

A *tughra* would have been attached to the top of official documents issued by the Sultan. The lettering in gold at the bottom would lead the reader into whatever text follows, whether a legal writ or a communiqué to an ambassador. It reads:

> *This is the noble, exalted, brilliant sign-manual, the world-illuminating and adoring monogram of the Sultan. May it be made efficient by the aid of the Lord and the protection of the Eternal. His order is that ...*

4 On script

Visual culture in the Islamic world is often based around writing, rather than imagery. From its earliest days, writing the words of the divine was the most honourable method of visual communication, and great care was taken to produce beautiful script. This *tughra* is not a religious piece of text, but follows in the Islamic tradition of perfecting the appearance of written words to emphasize their importance and significance.

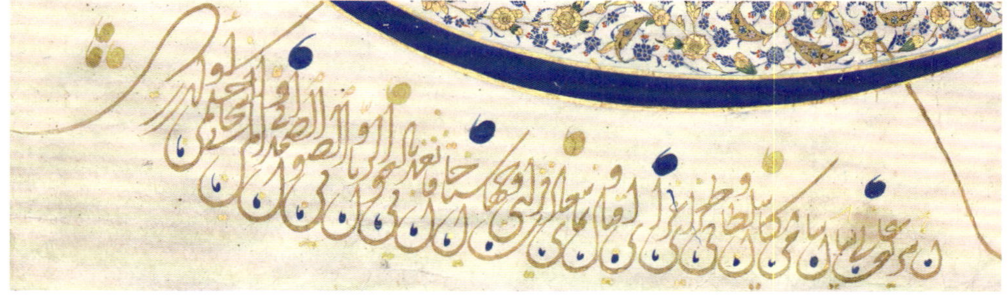

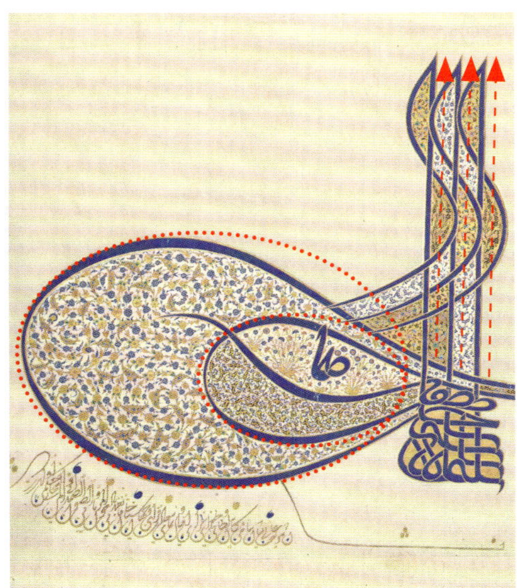

❼ Seal

By the time this example was created, *tughras* were made according to a standard composition comprising three vertical lines and two ovals that extended horizontally to the left. There are various theories about how this particular form came about:

- It derives from a fantastical bird known as the *tughri*, the symbol of the Oghuz tribe, who were ancestors of the Ottomans.
- It is an elaboration of the ancient hand-mark of the sultan, with the lines representing fingers and the ovals the thumb.
- It is a reference to the standards carried by ancient tribes of central Asia into battle, which were held in threes and had yak tails trailing from them.

❽ Ottoman arts

The arts and crafts of the Ottoman empire, including ceramics and textiles, and especially highly decorated rugs, were much sought after in the 15th and 16th centuries. All of these art forms incorporate patterns of flowers in garden-shaped enclosures into their designs, a visual motif adopted by the Ottomans from Persian art.

❾ The art of sophistication

Süleiman the Magnificent ruled over an immense kingdom that dominated the eastern Mediterranean, including parts of southern Italy and northern Africa, and was backed by a formidable navy. His *tughra* does not depict the usual symbols of power, but instead suggests wealth, influence and sophistication through its complex composition and rich colours.

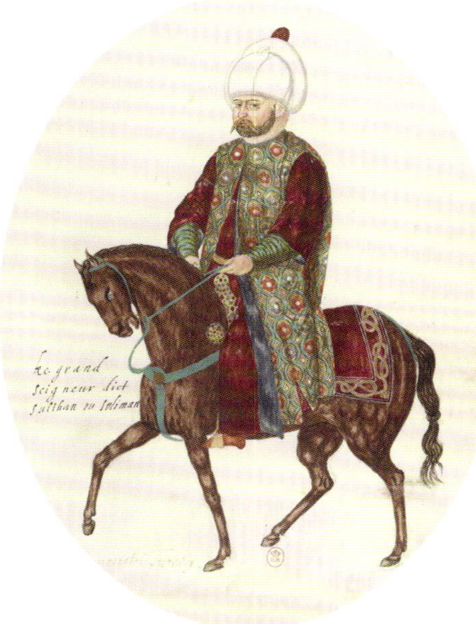

Süleiman the Magnificent, illustration from *Moeurs et costumes des pays Orientaux*, copy of a 1513 original

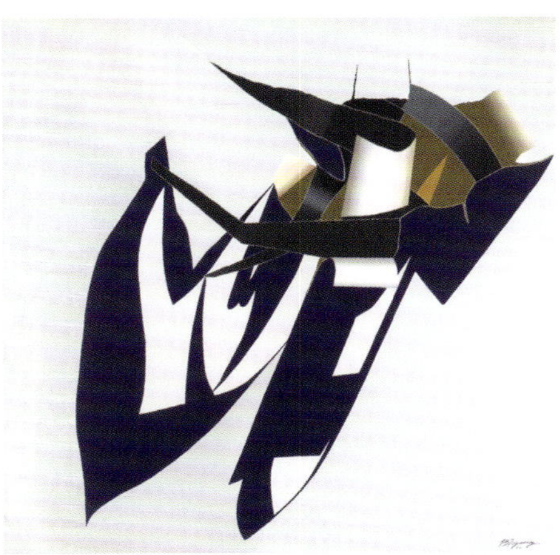

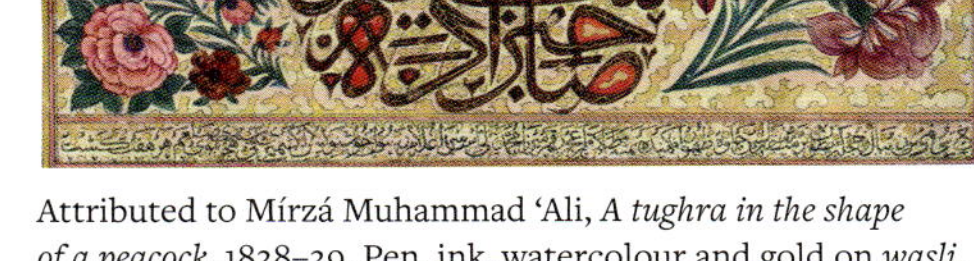

Attributed to Mírzá Muhammad ʻAli, *A tughra in the shape of a peacock*, 1828–29. Pen, ink, watercolour and gold on *wasli*, 30.2 × 39.4 cm, 12 × 15½ in.

❿ Choose your sign

Every *tughra* is different. At the start of his reign, each new sultan would be presented with a selection of prototypes designed by court calligraphers to choose from.

⓫ Influence

Burhan Doğançay and Asli Çavuşoğlu are two artists who have engaged with the style and subject matter of Ottoman art. *Ribbon Mania* appears to be a *tughra* in calligraphy, but closer inspection reveals that the shapes are formed from torn paper. In *Red/Red*, Çavuşoğlu used the motif of Ottoman-inspired flowers, here depicted in cochineal pigment.

← Burhan Doğançay, *Ribbon Mania*, 1982. Acrylic on canvas, 152.4 × 152.4 cm, 60 × 60 in.

→ Asli Çavuşoğlu, *Red/Red (Untitled) Diptych* 3, 2015. Paper, 100 × 70 cm, 39¼ × 27½ in.

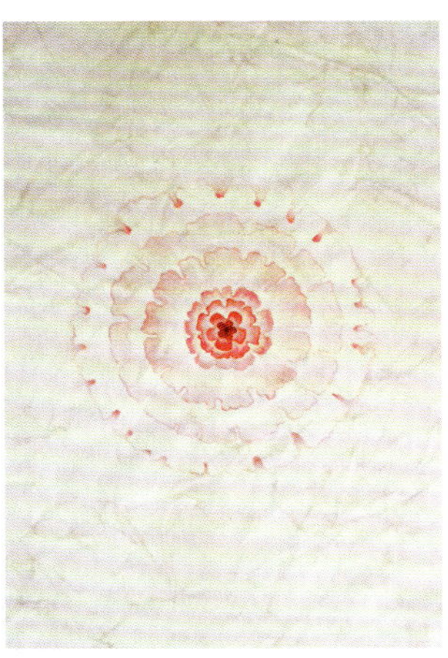

LINKED PRACTITIONERS

MODERN INSPIRATION:

Burhan Doğançay (1929–2013), TURKEY
Ali Omar Ermes (1945–2021), LIBYA
Ali Hüsrevoğlu (born 1956), TURKEY
Asli Çavuşoğlu (born 1982), TURKEY
Sami Savatli (born 1983), TURKEY

DECORATING WORDS:

Ismail Gulgee (1926–2007), PAKISTAN
Ed Ruscha (born 1937), USA
Michael Craig-Martin (born 1941), UK
Tracey Emin (born 1963), UK
Jason Revok (born 1977), USA

DEPICTING LEADERS:

Peter Paul Rubens (1577–1640), BELGIUM
Titian (c. 1488/90–1576), ITALY
Jacques-Louis David (1748–1825), FRANCE
Jean-Auguste-Dominique Ingres (1780–1867), FRANCE
Kehinde Wiley (born 1977), USA

21. Protection and Command

In the 16th century, when this mask was made, the kingdom of Benin in southwest Nigeria was a bustling city-state with international trading links and ateliers of skilled artists and craftspeople. Of these, ivory carvers were held in the highest esteem, because their works could only be possessed by members of the royal family.

The sculptors of objects such as this ivory pendant mask were provided with specialist studios at the court and belonged to an exclusive guild: the Igbesamwan. This particular mask represents Idia, the mother of the *oba* (king) of Benin, who ruled in the first half of the 16th century. It was designed to be worn at a ceremony in her honour, and served as a permanent reminder of her political acumen and spiritual guardianship over the kingdom.

Ivory, iron and copper (?)
23.8 × 12.7 × 6.4 cm, 9¼ × 5 × 2½ in.
Metropolitan Museum of Art, New York

Nigeria, Edo
Queen mother pendant mask
16th century

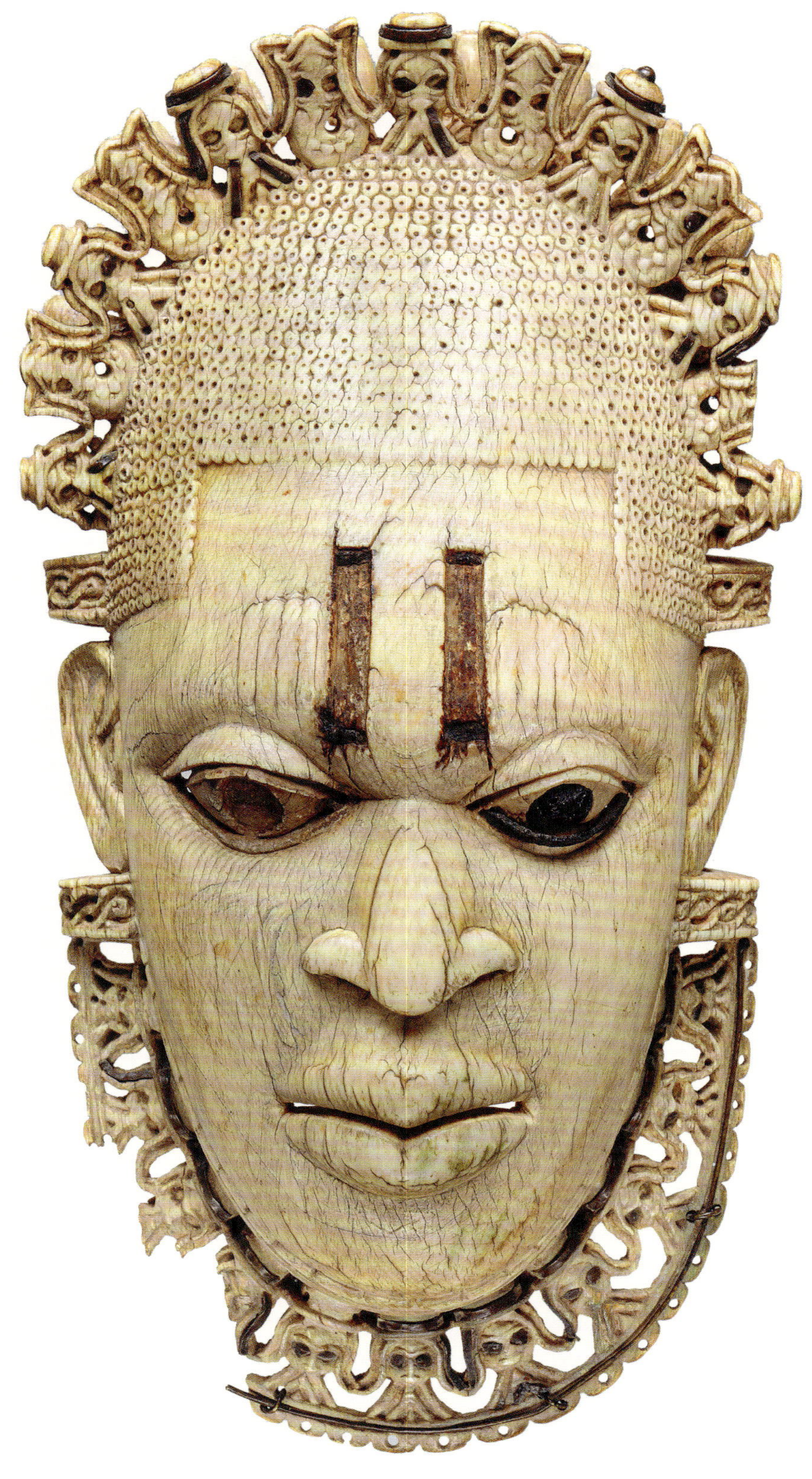

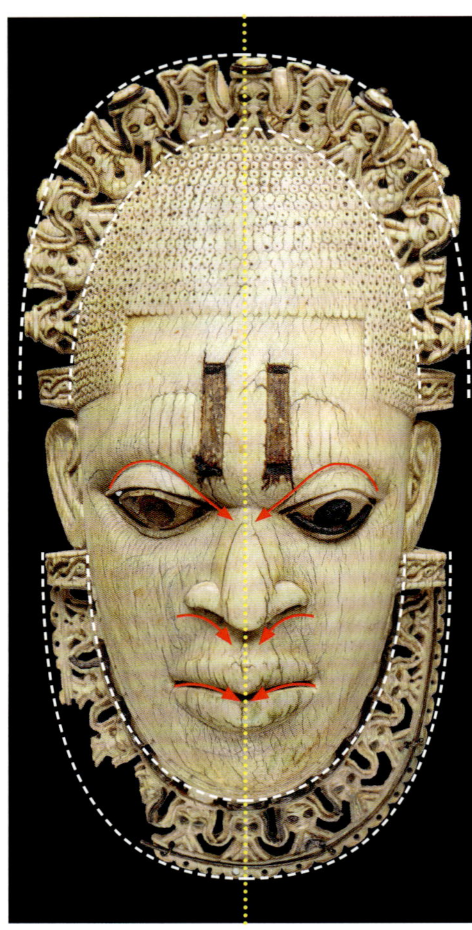

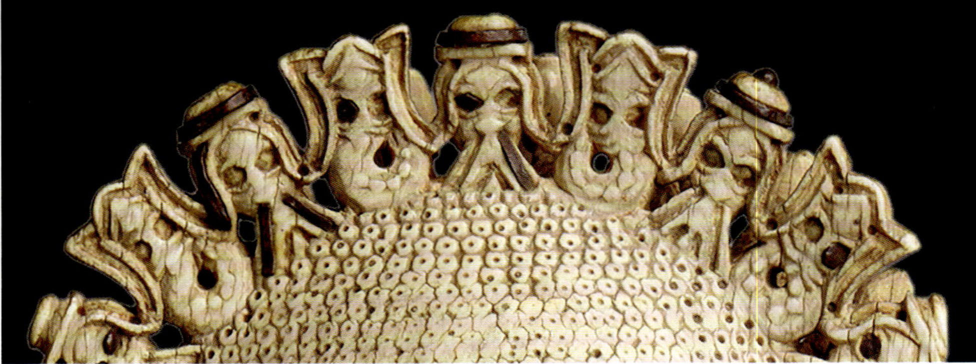

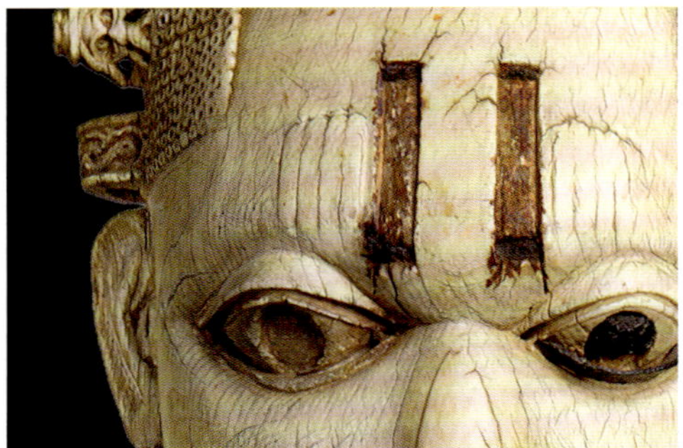

❶ Harmony of shape

The lips have been shaped to echo the form of the nostrils and eyebrows, while the tips of the woven hair mirror the collar below and the line of the chin corresponds with the shape of the head.

❷ Ivory

The ownership of ivory was an exclusive right of the Benin royal family. It was linked with the power of elephants and with the sea god Olokun, who was associated with spiritual purity and the colour white. It was also the focus of Portuguese traders, who had been present in the region since 1485, further raising its prestige.[46]

❸ Process

The artists probably used fresh ivory, which was oilier and easier to work with. They would have carved it using a special knife, afterwards polishing the surface to achieve a lustrous finish.

❹ Marks of femininity

Above each eye are four vertical marks, the result of scarification, a form of body art in which the skin is cut in a particular pattern and allowed to scar. In Benin, the number '4' was associated with women.

❺ Wise woman

Idia rose to prominence as the mother of Esigie, *oba* of Benin (r. 1504–50). Early in his reign, civil war erupted as the king and his half-brother Arhuaran battled for control. When Esigie emerged victorious, he credited his mother's tactical advice and insight as key to his success. Idia was given her own palace and a new title: *iyoba* (queen mother).[47]

❻ Protective gaze

The eyes are cast downwards beneath slightly hooded eyelids in a beneficent, transcendent gaze.

❼ Will of iron

Originally, the edges of the eyes would have been rimmed with iron, making the gaze appear softer and more animated. The pupils would have also been made from iron, as would the two strips above the nose.

❽ Symbols of power

The 'hair' is woven into stylized depictions of mudfish and Portuguese traders. Mudfish were powerful figures in Benin culture: they were able to survive on both land and sea, and were thus connected with the Benin royal family, who were believed to be able to straddle the realms of the earthly and the divine. Portuguese traders brought wealth and weapons to Benin, and appear as haloed figures, transmitting wisdom, strength and prosperity directly into Idia's mind.

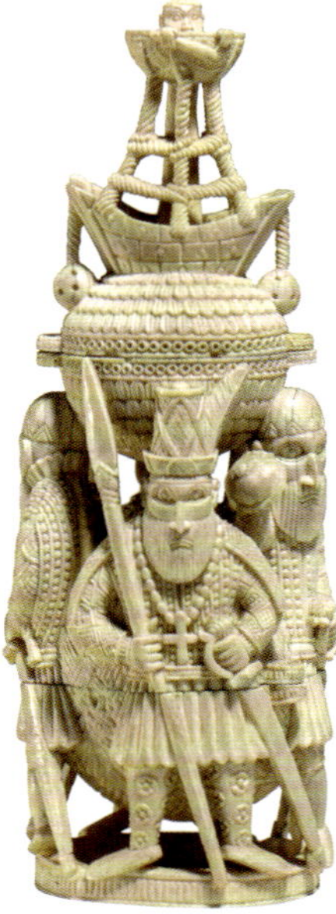

Saltcellar, Benin, Edo, 16th century. Ivory, height: 29.3 cm, 11½ in.

❾ Rulers of trade

By showing links with the Portuguese, the *oba* could demonstrate his control over the European trade in precious goods. As masters of seafaring, the Portuguese were also linked with the god Olokun, enhancing the *oba*'s divine standing. The belief that the afterlife would be found at the far side of the ocean also entwined the traders and mudfish with spiritual belief.

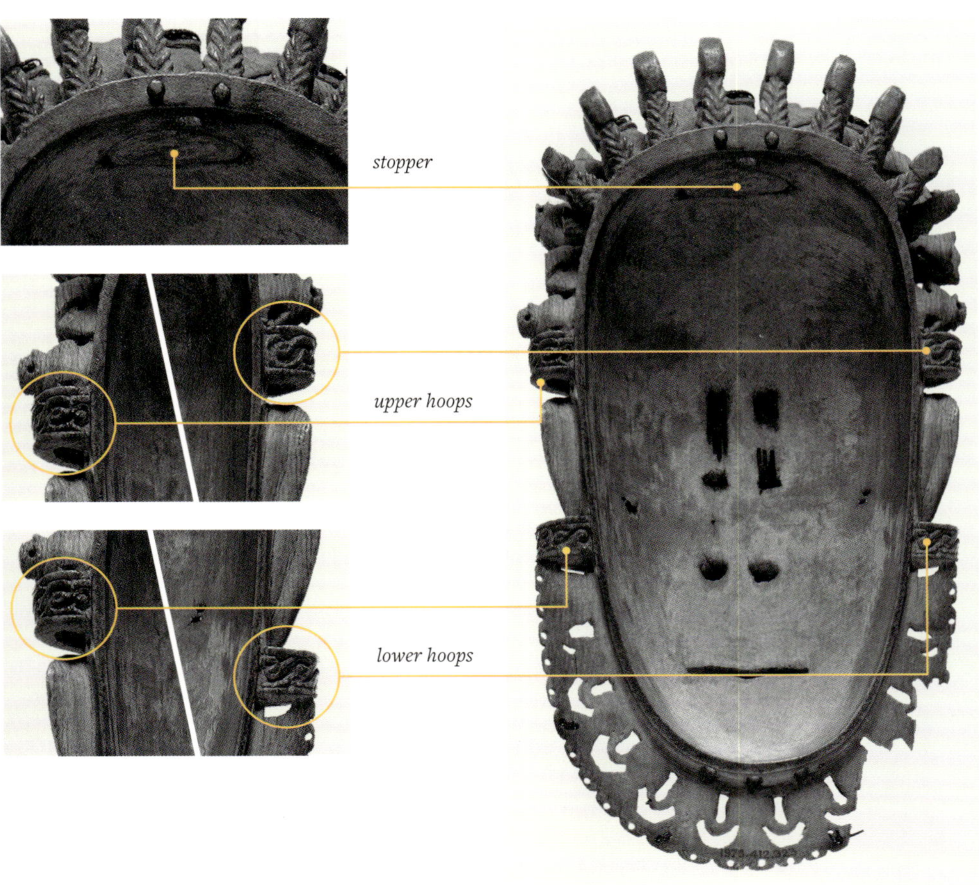

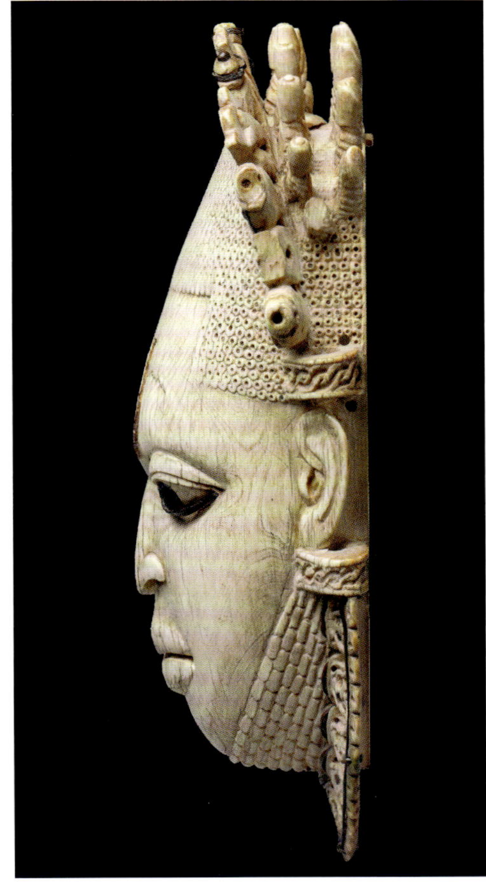

❿ Amulet

The mask has a stopper at the top, possibly to allow it be filled with potent materials so it that it became an amulet, or an object imbued with magical protective properties.

⓫ Safe from harm

The mask was designed to be worn by the *oba* at a ceremony honouring Idia's protection of the kingdom from malevolent spirits.[48]

→ Head of an *oba*, Benin, Edo, 19th century. Brass and iron, 45.7 × 29.2 × 29.8 cm, 18 × 11½ × 11¾ in.

→ Pendant mask, Benin, Edo, 16th century. Ivory, iron and copper alloy, 24.5 × 12.5 × 6 cm, 9¾ × 5 × 2¼ in.

⓬ Hoops

Hoops on either side of the mask enable it to be hung or suspended. It may have been worn from a belt, so that it rested at hip level, or attached to a necklace to be worn on the chest.

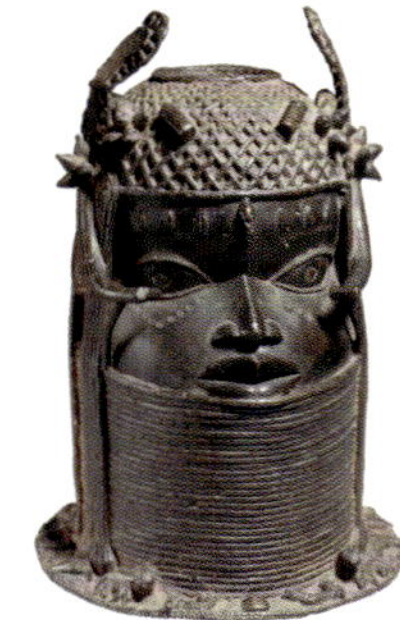

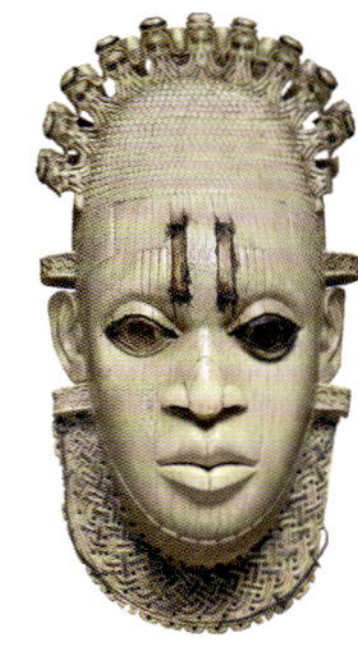

⓭ Pride

A similar mask in the British Museum was the official emblem of the Second World Black and African Festival of Arts and Culture in 1977, which took place in Lagos, Nigeria.

⓮ Dispossession

Both *iyoba* masks were seized by British forces during the notorious Benin Expedition in 1897, which sacked the palace, stripped the city of its artworks and artefacts, and brought an effective end to the kingdom of Benin. There are growing movements to repatriate the stolen objects: in 2021, the University of Aberdeen returned a bronze head to the Benin people.

LINKED PRACTITIONERS

PORTRAIT SCULPTORS:

Gian Lorenzo Bernini (1598–1680), ITALY
Louis-François Roubiliac (1702–1762), FRANCE
Franz Xaver Messerschmidt (1736–1783), GERMANY/AUSTRIA
Auguste Rodin (1840–1917), FRANCE
Camille Claudel (1864–1943), FRANCE

NIGERIAN ARTISTS:

Bruce Onobrakpeya (born 1932), NIGERIA
Tola Wewe (born 1959), NIGERIA
Ade Adekola (born 1966), NIGERIA
Victor Ehikhamenor (born 1970), NIGERIA
Njideka Akunyili Crosby (born 1983), NIGERIA

PORTRAITS OF QUEENS:

Nicholas Hilliard (1547–1619), UK
Peter Paul Rubens (1577–1640), BELGIUM
Vigilius Erichsen (1722–1782), DENMARK
Franz Xaver Winterhalter (1805–1873), GERMANY
Lucien Freud (1922–2011), UK

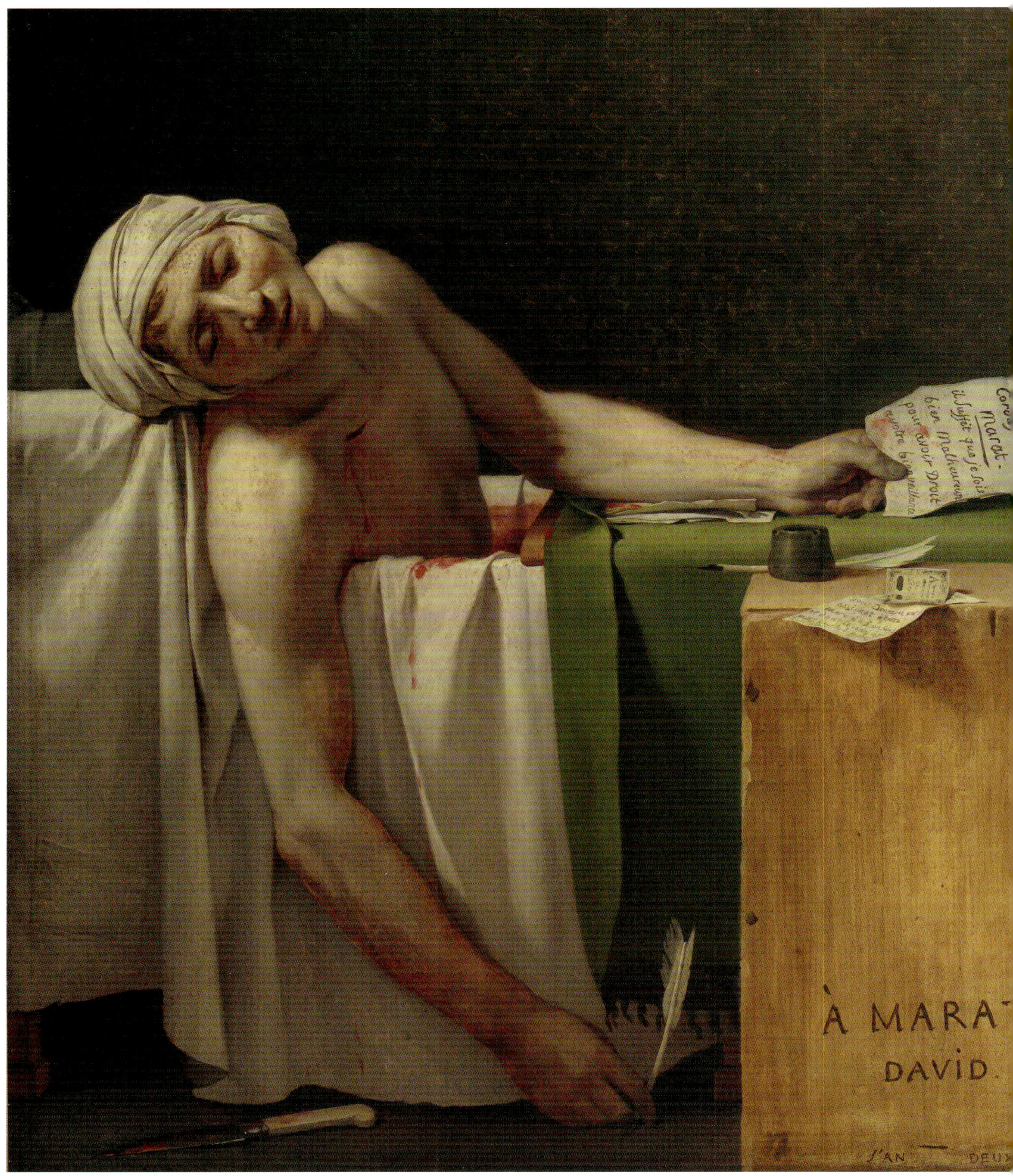
À MARA
DAVID.
L'AN
DEUX

3. The expansion of *vision*

1600 *to* 1799

Artists were beginning to introduce radical new approaches to creativity. They looked back to the innovations of their forebears for inspiration, but also tried to surpass them by pioneering new techniques and processes, depicting familiar scenes with extra complexities or previously unrepresented subjects.

1600 *to* 1799

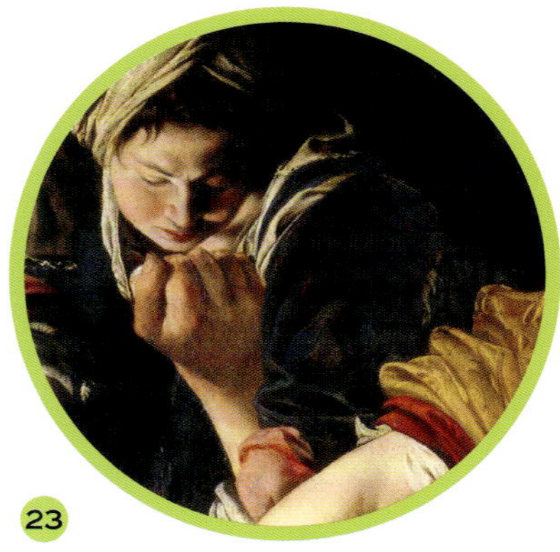

23

Baroque Violence

Artemisia Gentileschi
Judith Beheading Holofernes
c. 1620

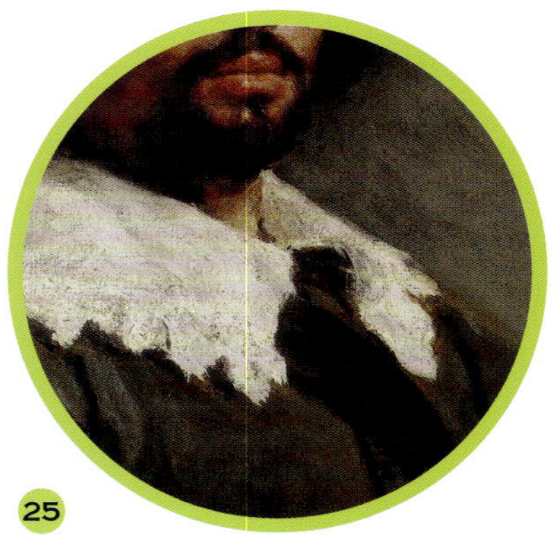

25

Subverting Expectations

Diego Velázquez
Juan de Pareja
1650

22

Flights of the Soul

Habiballah of Sava
The Concourse of the Birds
c. 1600

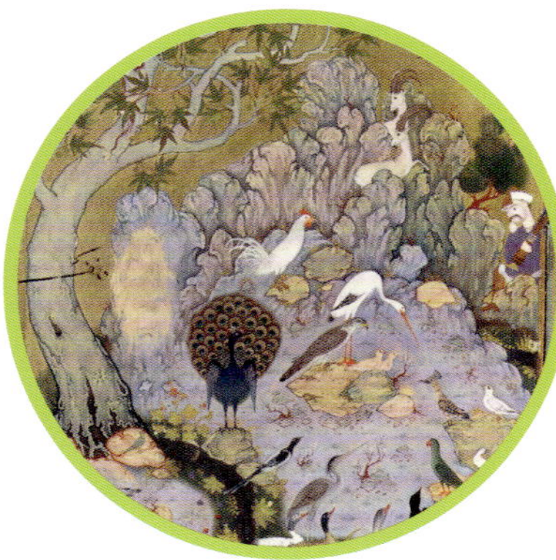

24

Dynamic Storytelling

Gian Lorenzo Bernini
David
1623–24

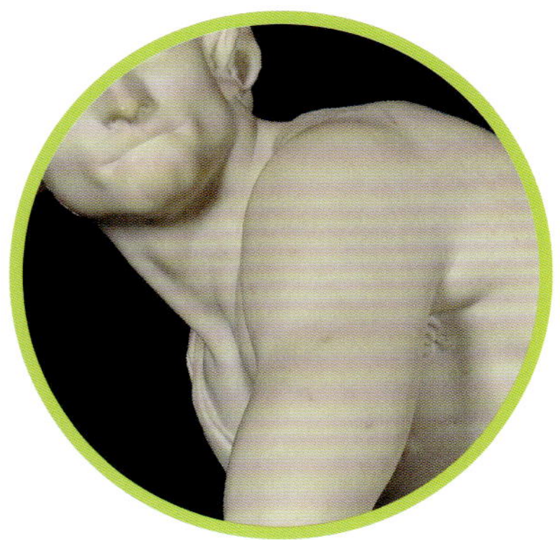

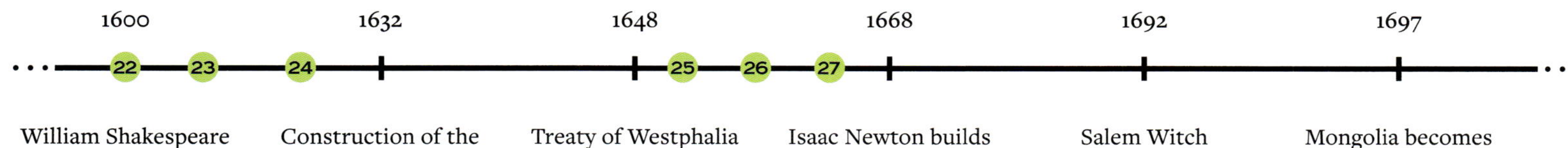

1600 — William Shakespeare writes *Hamlet*

1632 — Construction of the Taj Mahal begins

1648 — Treaty of Westphalia ends the Thirty Years' War

1668 — Isaac Newton builds the first reflecting telescope

1692 — Salem Witch Trials begin in Massachusetts

1697 — Mongolia becomes a province of the Qing dynasty

Timeline of events, artworks 22–31

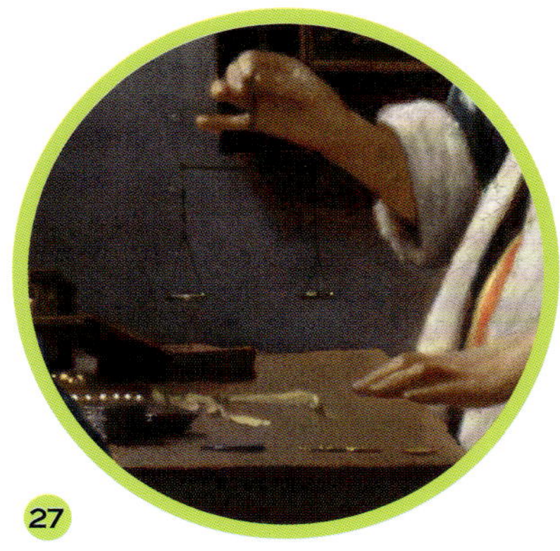

27

Hidden Messages

Johannes Vermeer
Woman Holding a Balance
c. 1664

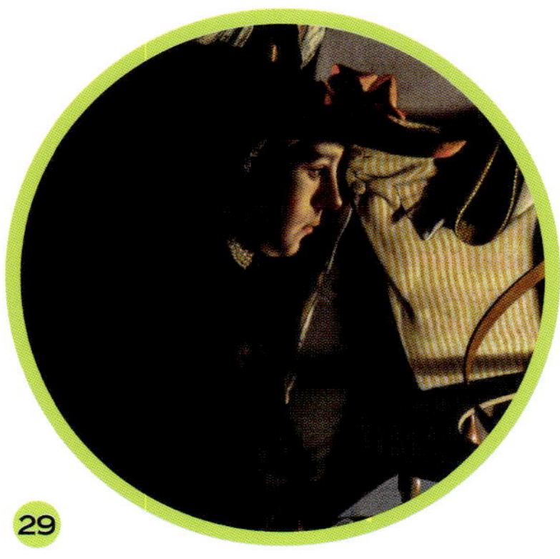

29

Enlightened Minds

Joseph Wright of Derby
A Philosopher Lecturing on the Orrery, *c.* 1764–66

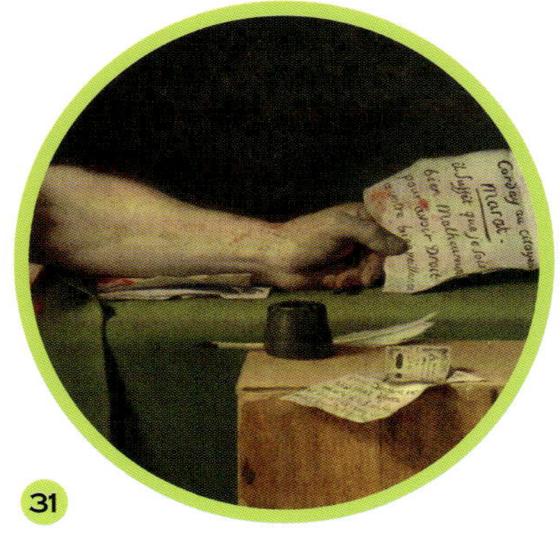

31

Art Crime

Jacques-Louis David
The Death of Marat
1793

26

A Technical Masterclass

Rembrandt van Rijn
The Three Crosses
third state, 1653

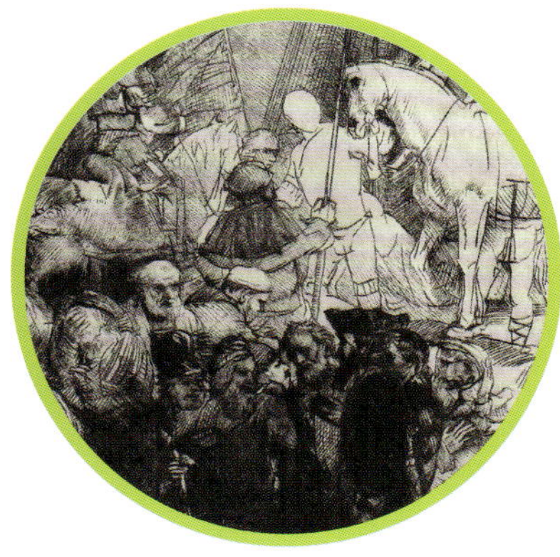

28

Radical Simplification

Ogata Kōrin
Red and White Plum Blossoms
c. 1712–16

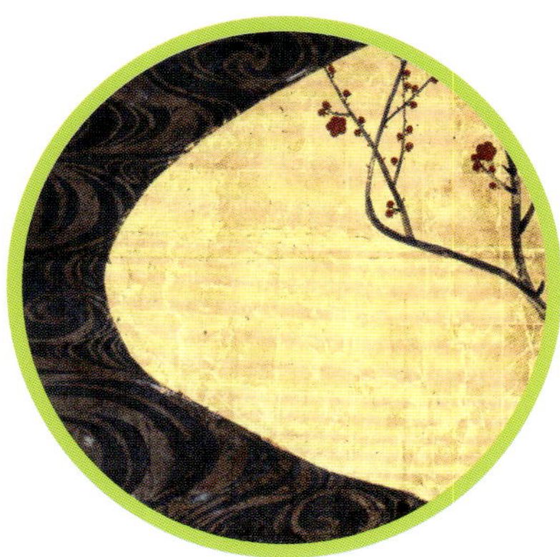

30

Making a Splash

Élisabeth Vigée Le Brun
Self-portrait in a Straw Hat
1782

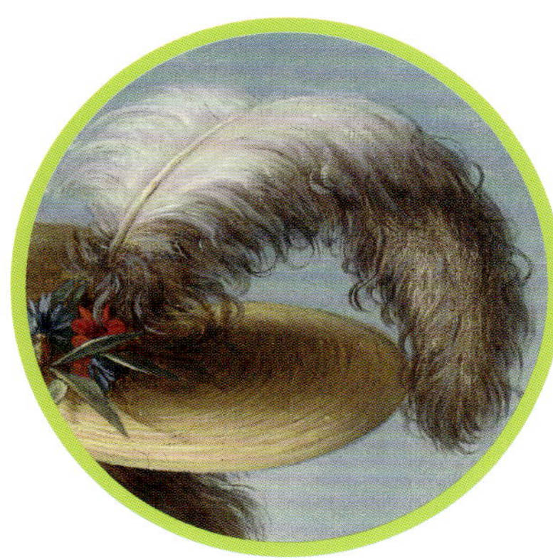

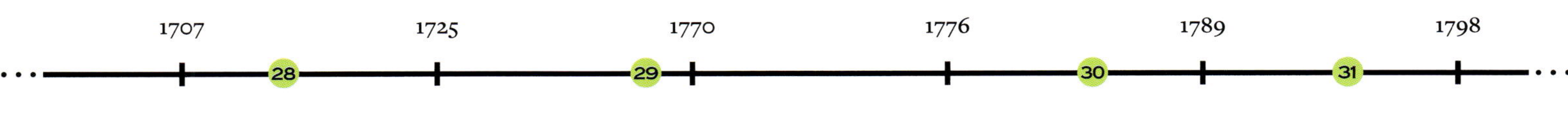

1707 — The Acts of Union unite England and Scotland

1725 — Completion of the *Gujin Tushu Jicheng* encyclopaedia in China

1770 — Great Bengal Famine, in which 7–10 million people perish

1776 — The United States declares independence from Britain

1789 — The French Revolution begins

1798 — Battle of Aboukir Bay is fought near Alexandria, Egypt

22. Flights of the Soul

This illustration for Mantiq al-Tayr *('language of the birds'), a poem written by Farid al-Din 'Attar in the 12th-century, was painted by Habiballah of Sava (fl. 1590–1610) nearly 500 years later in Isfahan, a prosperous city in what is now Iran, for a book of the poem produced in Afghanistan in 1483.*

Mantiq al-Tayr is a veiled allegory about the search for religious fulfilment and spiritual enlightenment, as told through a story about a congregation of birds who embark on a journey to find the mythical Simurgh and ask it to be their new leader. Habiballah of Sava's painting depicts the start of this tale, with the birds meeting to discuss their epic quest. The artist deliberately employed an old-fashioned style to create an atmosphere of mysticism and antiquity.

Ink, opaque watercolour, gold and silver on paper
25.4 × 11.4 cm, 10 × 4½ in.
Metropolitan Museum of Art, New York

Habiballah of Sava
The Concourse of the Birds
c. 1600

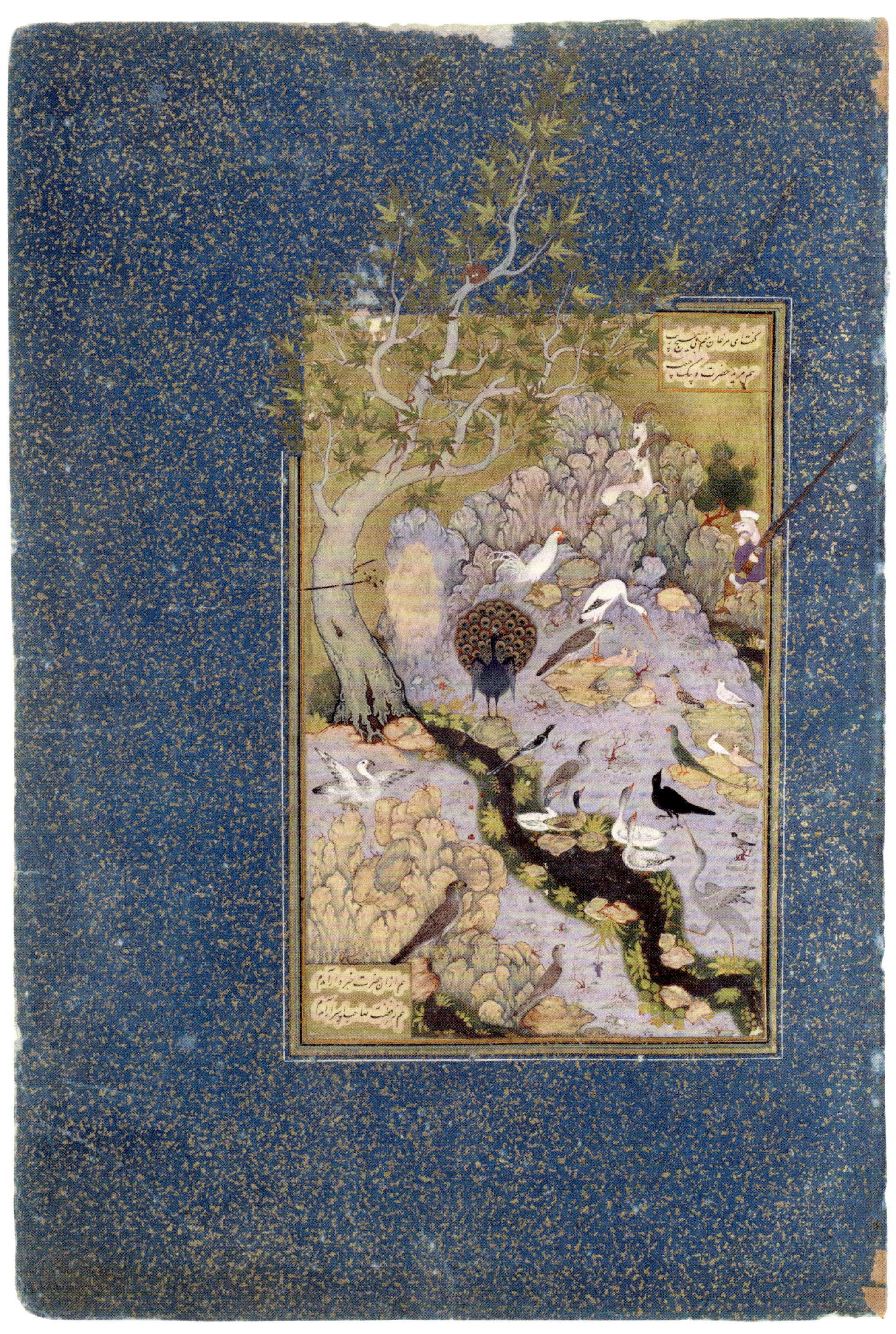

❶ Crossing boundaries

The barrel of a gun crosses over the frame of the image and into the border of the page. The hunter is not mentioned in Farid al-Din 'Attar's original poem, and is probably intended to connect the centuries-old poem with a contemporary audience.

❷ Time-traveller

The book was produced in Herat, Afghanistan, in 1483, and contains many illustrations made in the earlier, contemporary Timurid style. The musket depicted, however, dates to around 1550.

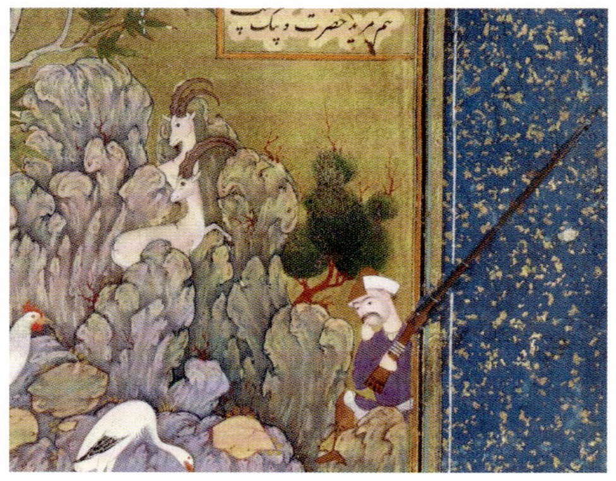

❹ Odyssey

The journey to find the Simurgh will be arduous, with the birds facing seven perilous valleys and challenged by distractions and obstacles along the way. Many will not survive, but those that do will ultimately experience a glorious unification with their king. At the end of the quest, just 30 birds out of the original multitude will remain. The words 'thirty' and 'birds' in Persian are '*si*' and '*murgh*': the birds, therefore, experience the mystical being as a reflection of themselves.

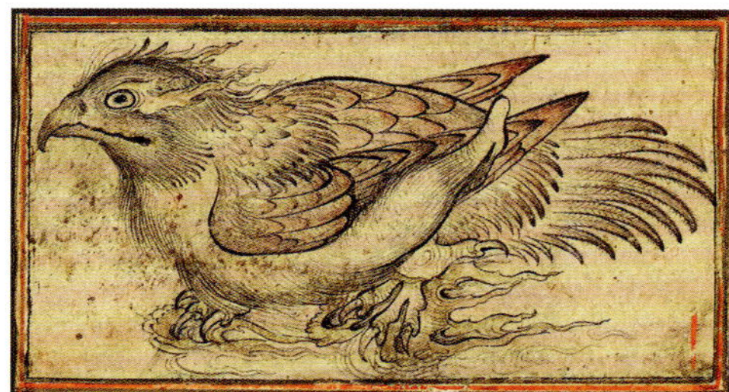

A Simurgh Chick, Persia, 17th century. Ink on paper, with inner borders of polychrome illumination heightened with gold, grey-green outer margins, 32.3 × 20.5 cm, 12¾ × 8 in.

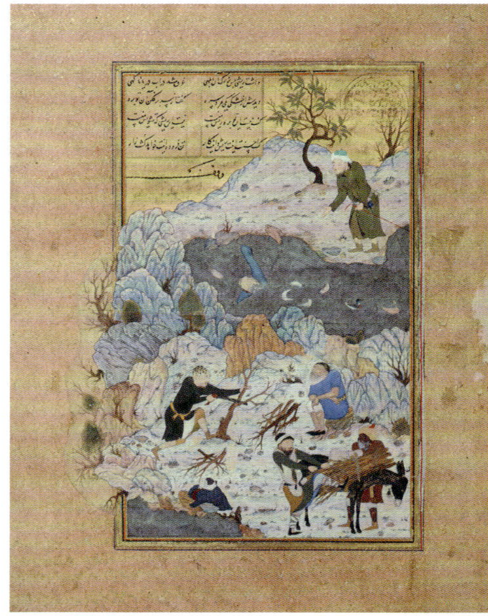

← Sultan 'Ali al-Mashhadi (calligrapher), *The Anecdote of the Man Who Fell into the Water*, folio 44r, from the *Mantiq al-Tayr*, *c.* 1487. Opaque watercolour, silver and gold on paper, 18.7 × 3 cm, 7¼ × 1¼ in.

↓ Riza yi-Abbasi, *The Lovers*, 1630. Opaque watercolour, ink and gold on paper, 17.5 × 11.1 cm, 7 × 4¼ in.

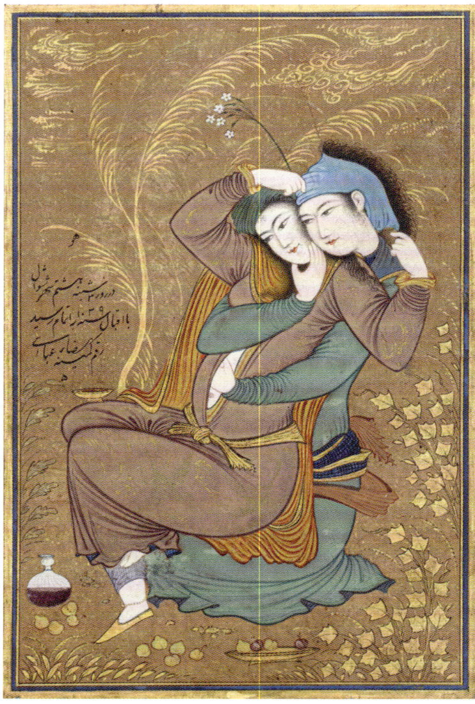

❸ Vintage style

After the book was brought to Isfahan from Herat by the Safavid dynasty in around 1600, Habiballah of Sava added new illustrations. He did so by imitating the earlier Timurid style to ensure the new paintings blended in, rather than in the modern style emerging in Isfahan at the time. *The Anecdote of the Man Who Fell into the Water* is a Timurid-era painting for the same book, while *The Lovers* by Riza yi-Abbasi, Habiballah's contemporary in Isfahan, was painted 150 years later in the Safavid style.

❺ Leader of the birds

The scene shows a hoopoe addressing the congregation of birds, in an attempt to persuade them to join him on his quest for the Simurgh, who will bring the birds spiritual enlightenment.

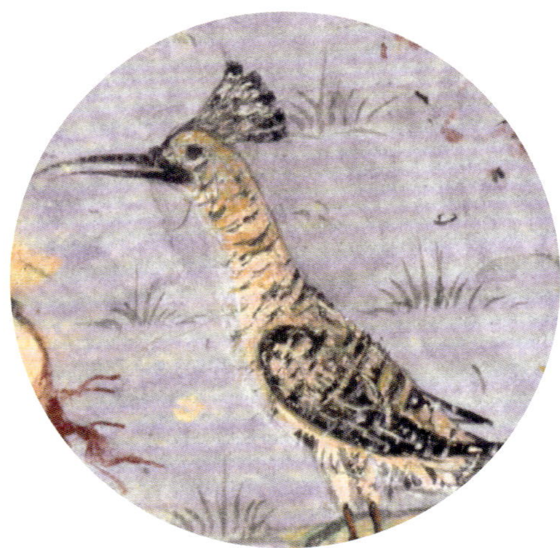

❻ Signature

Habiballah of Sava concealed his signature in the centre of the painting. It appears on a rock at the water's edge, with ducks and geese to either side.

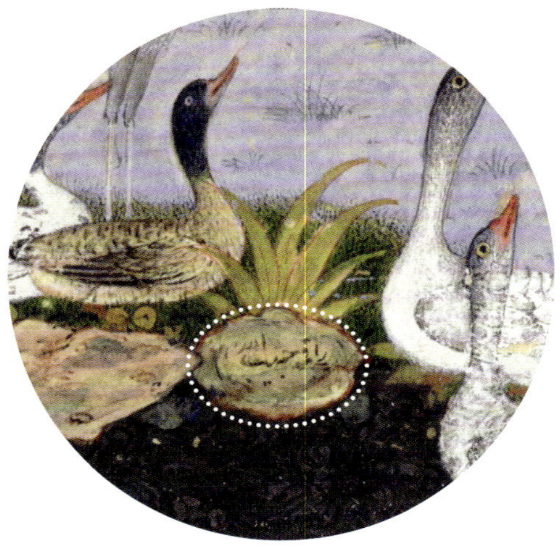

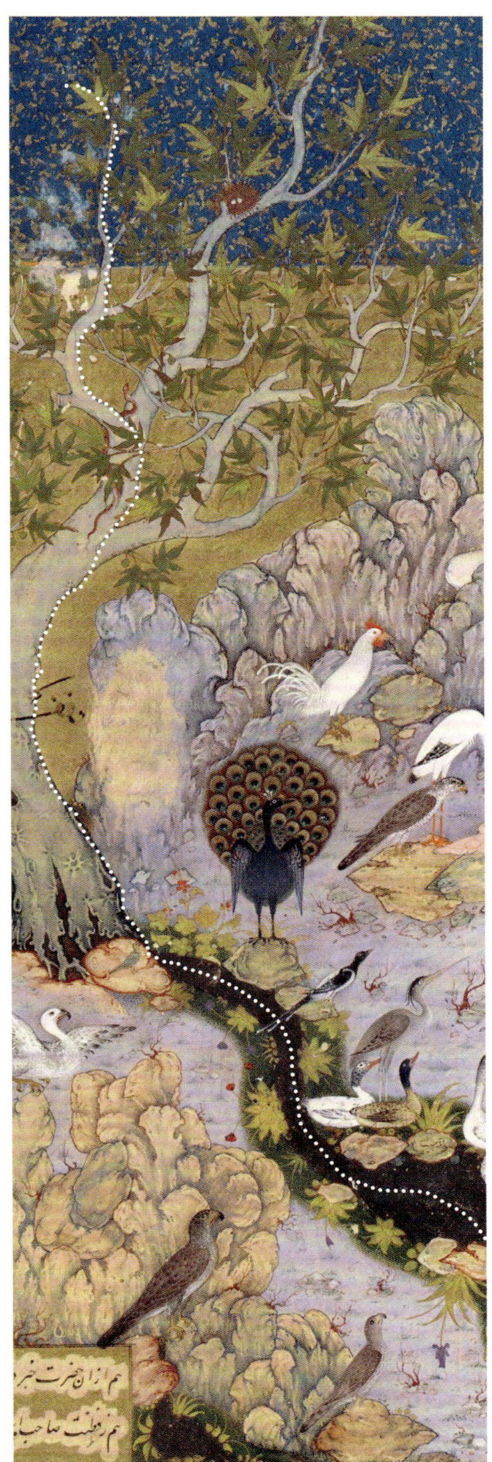

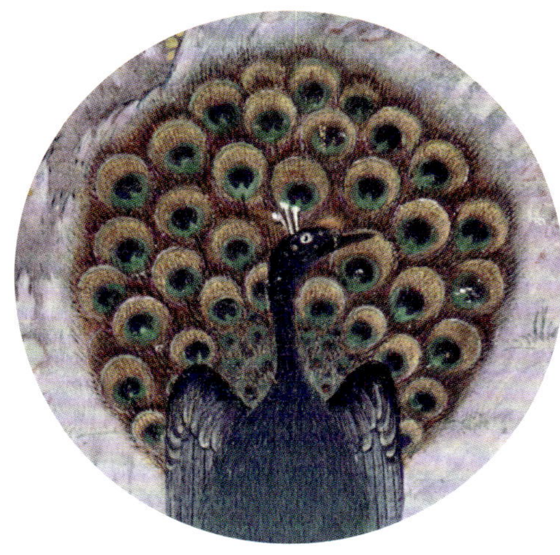

❼ Paradise

While trying to rally the throng into joining him on his quest, the hoopoe is given many excuses from the other birds as to why they cannot accompany him on the journey. The peacock explains that he was expelled from paradise because of his pride, and longs to return there, rather than apprehend the Simurgh.

❽ Snake

The peacock blames the serpent for his banishment. High above it, a snake slithers up a tree to raid a bird's nest – a detail that may have been added because it appeared in earlier Timurid paintings, and Habiballah wished to pay homage to his predecessors.

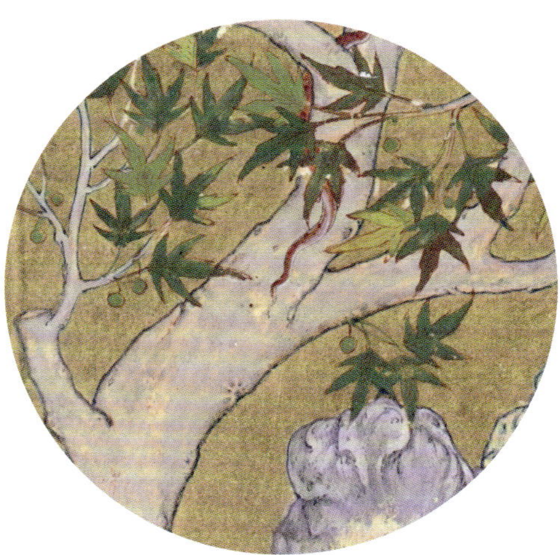

❾ Flow

The bends of the river extend into the sinuous form of the tree, leading our gaze from the bottom right to the upper left of the painting.

❿ Perspective

We see the river as if looking at it from above, but the landscape and birds are represented as though on the same level as ourselves. Paintings that were being made in Europe at the same time generally obeyed the laws of consistent perspective, but this mixing of viewpoints complements the mystical subject matter.

⓫ Sufism

Sufism is an Islamic belief rooted in mysticism, which emphasizes the search for the divine and a retreat from life's materialism. The *Language of the Birds* was written as a Sufi allegory, with the birds symbolizing the human soul and its journey to enlightenment. It has its origins in a story in the Qur'an about David and Solomon learning the meaning of birdsong. The poet Farid al-Din 'Attar expanded on this idea by using the birds as an allegory of the soul, which sheds its attachment to the self and soars up to heaven.

LINKED PRACTITIONERS

SAFAVID PAINTERS:

Riza yi-Abbasi (1565–1635), IRAN
Mo'en Mosavver (*c.* 1610/15–1693), IRAN
Shaykh 'Abbasi (fl. 1650–1684), IRAN
Aliquli Jabbadar (fl. 1666–1694), IRAN
Mohammad Zaman (fl. 1680–1700), IRAN

PAINTERS OF BIRDS:

Frans Snyders (1579–1657), BELGIUM
Jakob Bogdani (1658–1724), HUNGARY/UK
Karl Wilhelm de Hamilton (1668–1754), BELGIUM/GERMANY
Ferdinand Lucas Bauer (1760–1826), AUSTRIA
John James Audubon (1785–1851), USA

MANUSCRIPT ILLUMINATION:

Jean Fouquet (*c.* 1420–1481), FRANCE
Simon Marmion (*c.* 1425–1489), FRANCE
Simon Bening (1483–1561), BELGIUM
Manohar Das (fl. 1582–1624), INDIA
Ustad Mansur (fl. 1590–1624), INDIA

23. Baroque Violence

This gruesome scene was painted for Cosimo II de' Medici, Grand Duke of Tuscany (r. 1609–21), the patron of Galileo Galilei. It depicts a story from the Book of Judith, in which the eponymous heroine, an Israelite princess, exacts revenge upon the invading Assyrian army by seducing and murdering their general, Holofernes.

The story of Judith and Holofernes had been painted many times by other artists, among them Botticelli (ill. p. 114) and Caravaggio (p. 115), but the artist of this version – Artemisia Gentileschi (1593–1656), a young painter from Rome and the daughter of another artist – had the skill and personal motivation to outstrip them all in terms of the intensity and raw emotion she brought to her work. Today, the result stands as one of the great masterpieces of the Roman Baroque period of the 17th century.

Oil on canvas
146.5 × 108 cm, 57¾ × 42½ in.
The Uffizi, Florence

Artemisia Gentileschi
Judith Beheading Holofernes
c. 1620

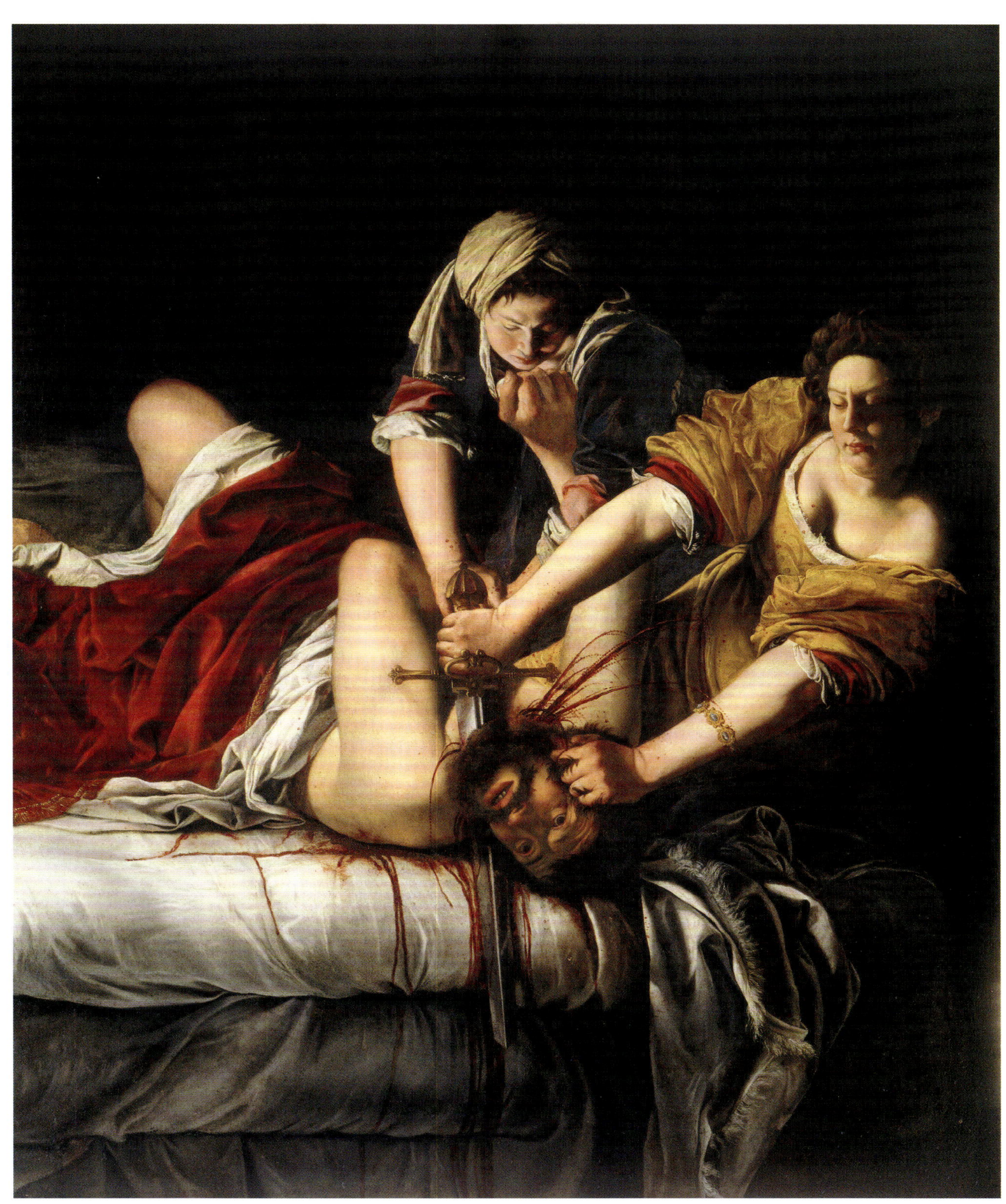

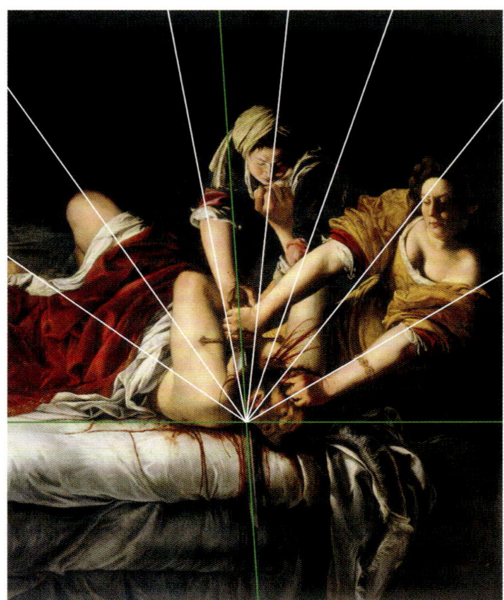

❶ An explosion of activity

The focus of the composition is the partially severed head of Holofernes. From this central point, several lines – articulated by limbs and eye lines – radiate outwards, creating a sensation of explosive dynamism.

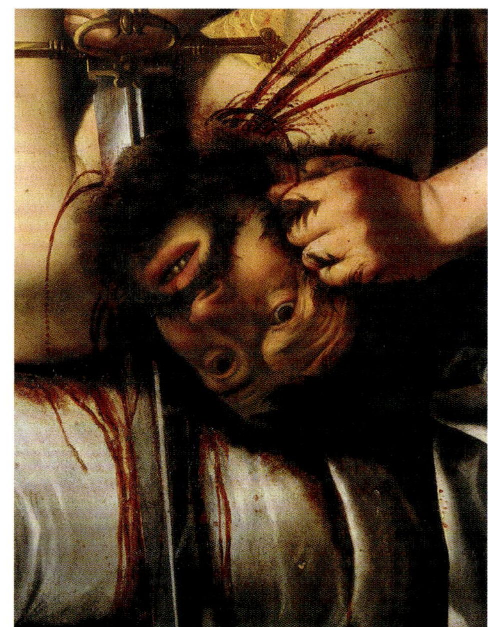

❷ Frozen action

Unlike other versions of the scene, which portray the aftermath of the event, Gentileschi has captured the bloody mid-point of the action, with Holofernes on the cusp of death and looking desperately out at the viewer.

❸ By the hand of a woman

According to the biblical story of Judith and Holofernes, the city of Bethulia was under attack by the Assyrian army. One resident was a young woman named Judith, who cast off her widow's weeds, adorned herself in jewelry and fine clothes, and went to confront the enemy in his campaign tent. After plying him with wine, she cut off his head with the help of her maid, Abra. 'Behold the head of Holofernes,' she proclaimed on her return to the city, 'and behold the canopy, wherein he did lie in his drunkenness; and the Lord hath smitten him by the hand of a woman.'

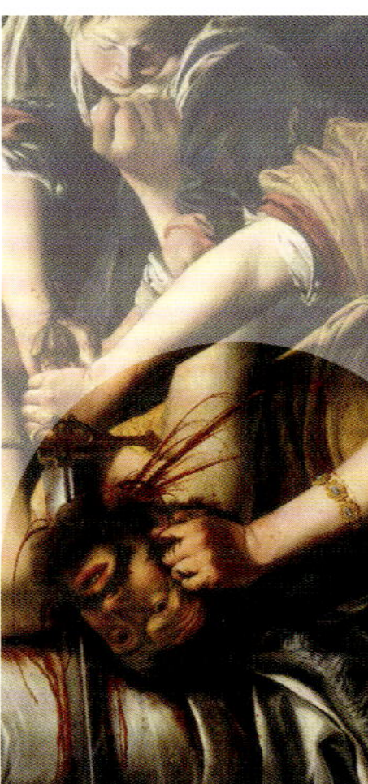

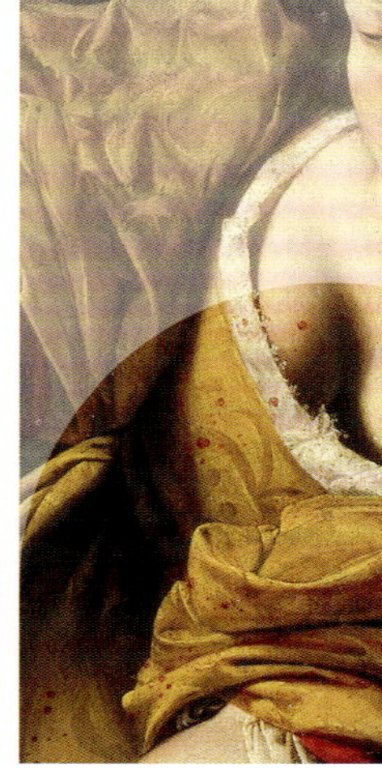

❼ Bloodstain pattern analysis

Gentileschi highlighted the goriness of the event by showing the blood spurting from Holofernes' neck in detail. Flecks of blood also appear on the women's arms and fine dresses.

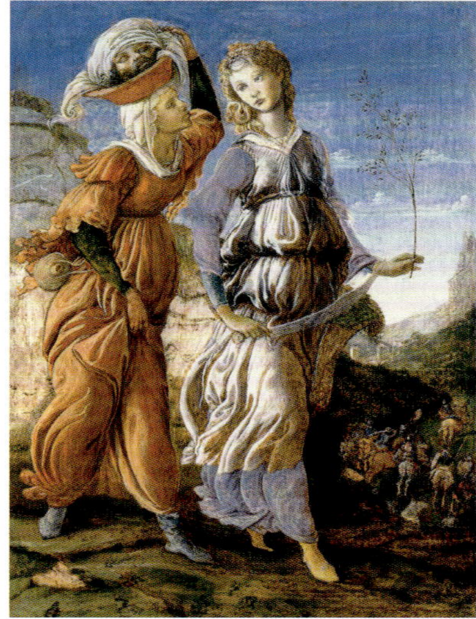

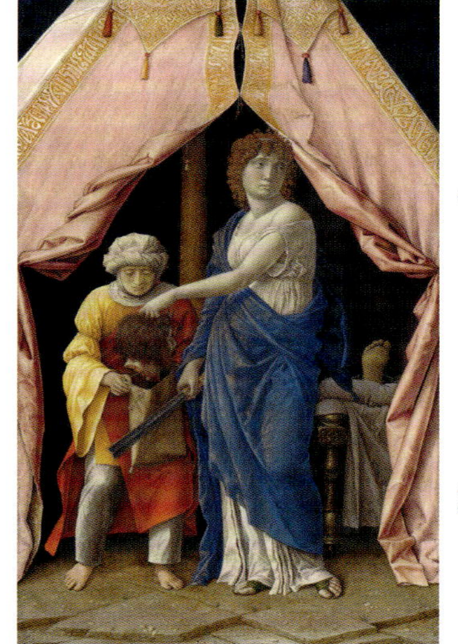

← Andrea Mantegna or follower (possibly Giulio Campagnola), *Judith with the Head of Holofernes*, c. 1495–1500. Tempera on poplar panel, 30.1 × 18.1 cm, 11¾ × 7 in.

←← Sandro Botticelli, *Judith with the Head of Holofernes*, c. 1469–70. Tempera on panel, 29.2 × 21.6 cm, 11½ × 8½ in.

❹ Revenge

Gentileschi had been sexually assaulted by Agostino Tassi, another artist, 10 years earlier. The case was brought to trial, and Tassi was convicted and imprisoned for two years. Most historians agree that the painting is related to this experience, with Holofernes standing in for Tassi, and Judith representing the artist herself.

❺ Art and science

Gentileschi may have learned how to represent the arcs of spurting blood by studying the analysis of projectile motion by Galileo Galilei, who would later assert that the earth orbited the sun, and not the other way around.[49]

❻ Light and dark

A beam of light cuts through the darkness, focusing attention on the action and creating a sensation of drama and threat. The contrast also symbolizes the fight of good against evil.

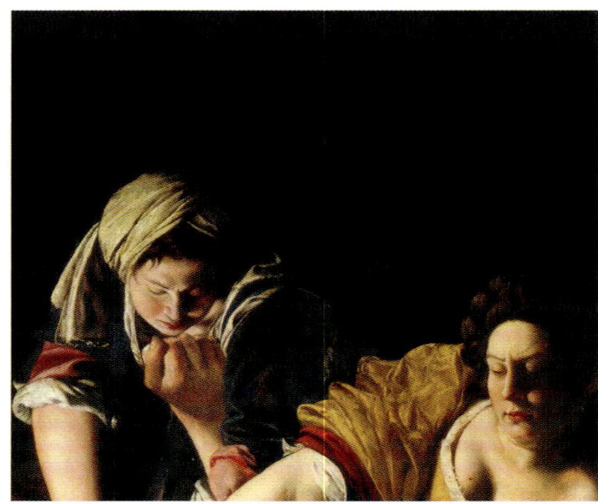

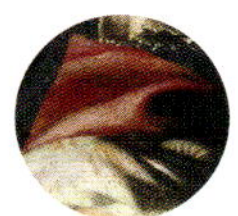
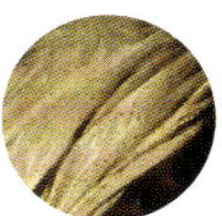
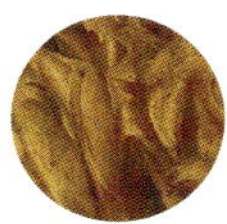
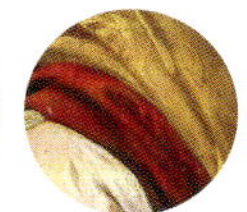

❽ Colours

The women's dresses are brightly coloured and made from expensive fabrics. Gentileschi's patron Cosimo II de' Medici resided in Florence, where works depicting sumptuous and refined objects and clothing were popular.[50] Scenes of extreme violence and realism were not, however, so the work was neglected for years after it was painted.

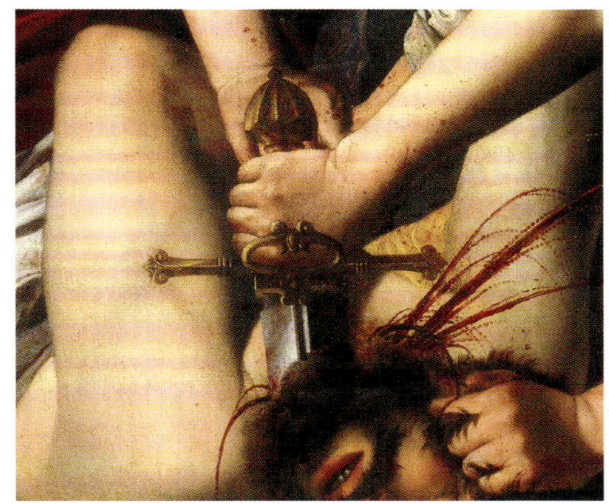

❾ Shapes

At the centre of the scene is the sword handle, which creates the shape of a cross, or crucifix, underscoring the religious theme.

❿ A bigger meaning

Gentileschi painted *Judith Beheading Holofernes* during the Counter-Reformation, a period of heightened antagonism between Catholics and Protestants. Painted in Catholic Italy, the work may have been seen by contemporary audiences as a reflection of these tensions. If so, Holofernes would embody the Protestants – or possibly the Ottoman Empire, with whom the Italian states were at war – and Judith the avenging Catholics.

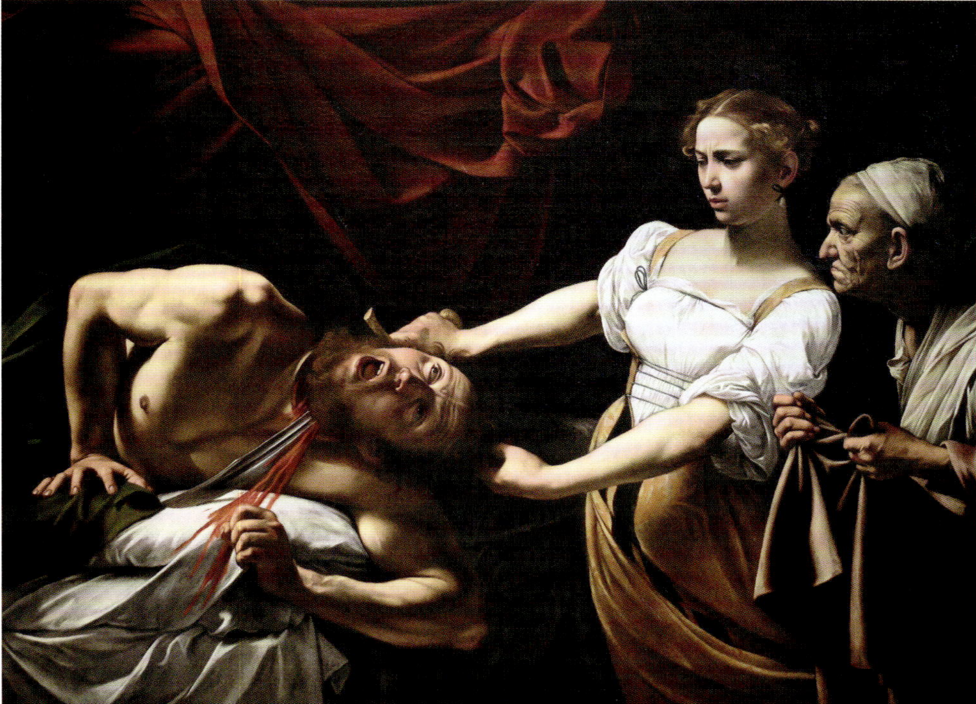

Caravaggio, *Judith Beheading Holofernes*, *c.* 1599. Oil on canvas, 145 × 195 cm, 57 × 76¾ in.

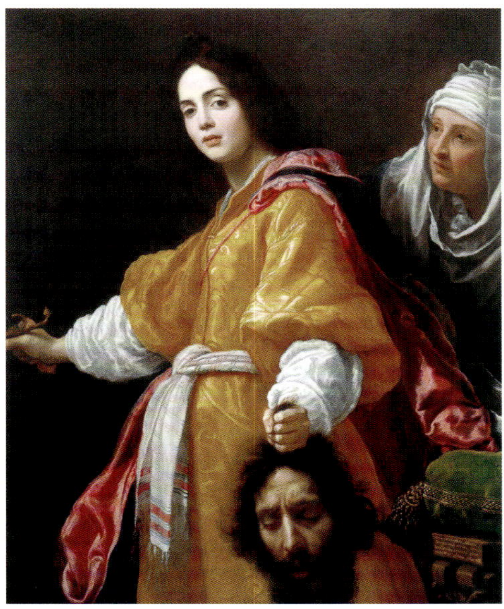

Cristofano Allori, *Judith with the Head of Holofernes*, 1613. Oil on canvas, 120.4 × 100.3 cm, 47½ × 39½ in.

⓫ Inspired by Caravaggio

The artist was trained by her father, Orazio Gentileschi, a follower of Caravaggio, whose own *Judith Beheading Holofernes* (above) was a direct inspiration for Artemisia's version. Her interpretation, however, shows Judith as more directly involved with the execution, mounting the side of the bed to get closer to her victim, whereas Caravaggio's Judith seems detached from the act of murder.

⓬ Ultra-violence

Compared to Cristofano Allori's version, painted a few years earlier in Florence, it is easy to see how shockingly violent Gentileschi's painting was. Although commissioned by Cosimo II de' Medici, it was considered so savage that it was hidden away in the family's art collection, and forgotten for decades.

LINKED PRACTITIONERS

JUDITH AND HOLOFERNES IN ART:

Andrea Mantegna (1431–1506), ITALY
Sandro Botticelli (*c.* 1445–1510), ITALY
Tintoretto (1518–1594), ITALY
Caravaggio (1571–1610), ITALY
Cristofano Allori (1577–1621), ITALY

FEMALE ARTISTS OF THE 16TH & 17TH CENTURIES:

Sofonisba Anguissola (*c.* 1532–1625), ITALY
Lavinia Fontana (1552–1614), ITALY
Maria van Oosterwijck (1630–1693), NETHERLANDS
Mary Beale (1633–1699), UK
Rachel Ruysch (1664–1750), NETHERLANDS

INFLUENCE OF CARAVAGGIO:

Hendrick ter Brugghen (1588–1629), NETHERLANDS
Simon Vouet (1590–1649), FRANCE
Jusepe de Ribera (1591–1652), SPAIN/ITALY
Gerard van Honthorst (1592–1656), NETHERLANDS
Virginia Vezzi (1600–1638), ITALY

24. Dynamic Storytelling

By 1623, Gian Lorenzo Bernini (1598–1680), aged only 24, had already achieved a reputation as an artistic prodigy among the cultural elite of Rome, a creator whose work was so skilled that it stretched the very limits of art. When he was offered a new sculptural commission that year, Bernini was determined to push those limits one step further.

The commission came from the artist's patron, Cardinal Scipione Borghese, and the brief was to carve David, the hero from the Old Testament, in marble. According to the story, David was a shepherd who defeated the mighty warrior Goliath with a stone launched from a humble slingshot. He was the archetypal hero: young and intelligent, fearless and pure of heart – and the perfect subject for Bernini, like Michelangelo (ill. p. 31), Donatello (p. 119) and Andrea del Verrocchio (p. 119) before him, to show off his artistic prowess.

Marble
Height: 170 cm, 67 in.
Galleria Borghese, Rome

Gian Lorenzo Bernini
David
1623–24

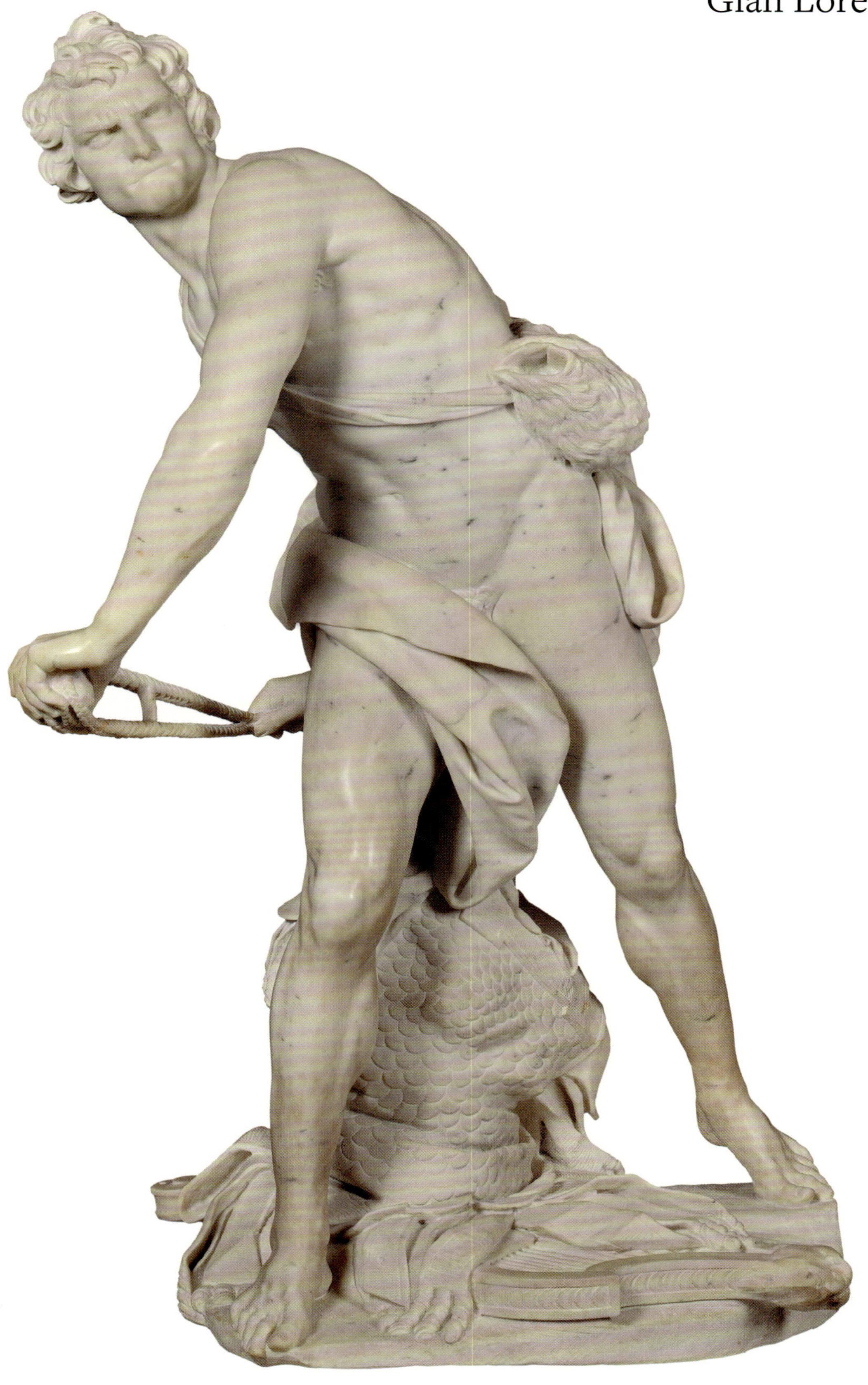

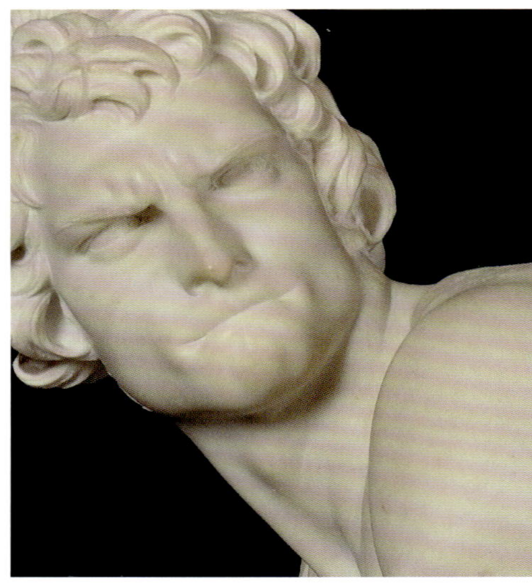

❶ Concentration

Bernini has captured an expression of deep concentration on David's face. The forehead is rippled with creases, the eyes intent and focused, and the mouth clenched.

❷ Self-portrait

The face of David is an idealized version of the artist's own craggy features. Bernini seems to be suggesting an affinity between himself and the hero's determination, ambition, fearlessness and youth.

❸ Self-reflection

Bernini's biographer Filippo Baldinucci claims the artist copied his face from a mirror held by Cardinal Maffeo Barberini (later Pope Urban VIII). The story may not be true, but in his lifetime Bernini was admired and respected by the most powerful leaders of the day, including Louis XIV of France.

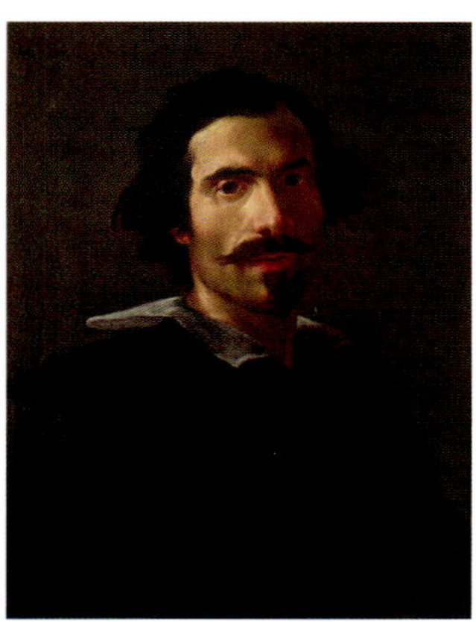

← *Self-portrait*, c. 1635. Oil on canvas, 62 × 46 cm, 24½ × 18 in.

→ *Bust of Louis XIV*, 1665. Marble, 105 × 95 × 46 cm, 41¼ × 37½ × 18 in.

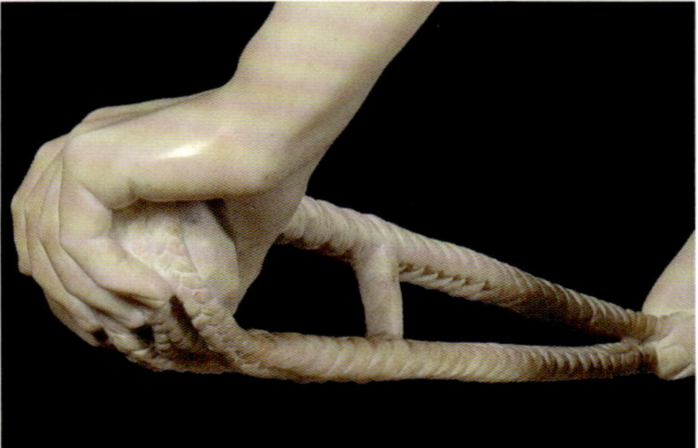

❹ Realism

Great attention has been paid to the various textures of the sculpture, with the rope that David holds in his hands the most striking example of Bernini's skill in rendering materials with scrupulous accuracy.

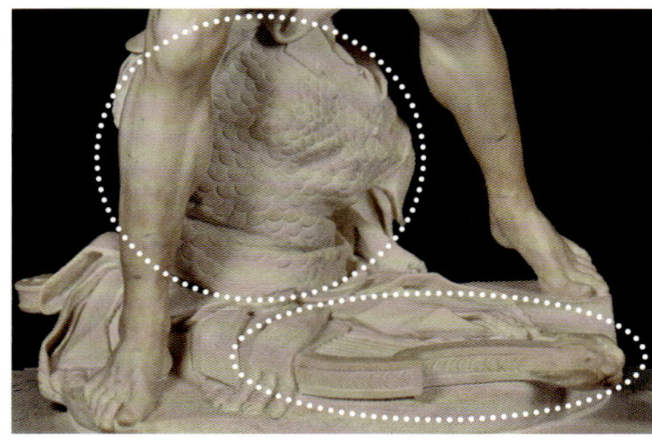

❺ Biblical hero

At the figure's feet are objects that allude to the description of David in the Book of Samuel. The cithara is evidence of his skills as a musician, and the discarded breastplate shown resting on the ground points to his refusal to wear armour for his fight with Goliath.

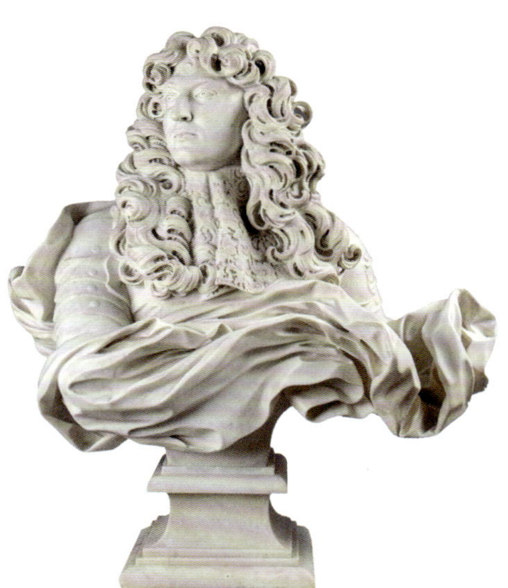

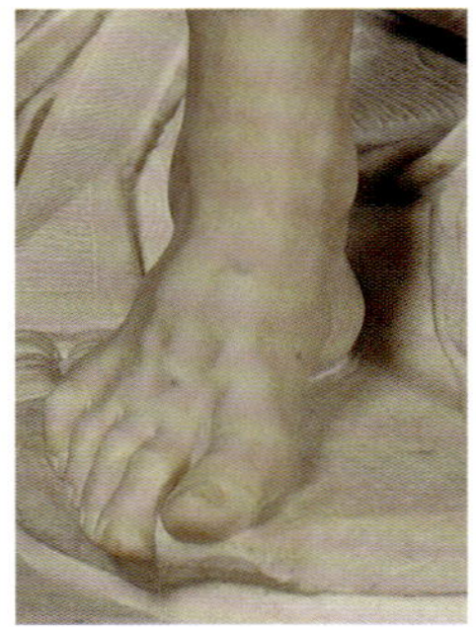

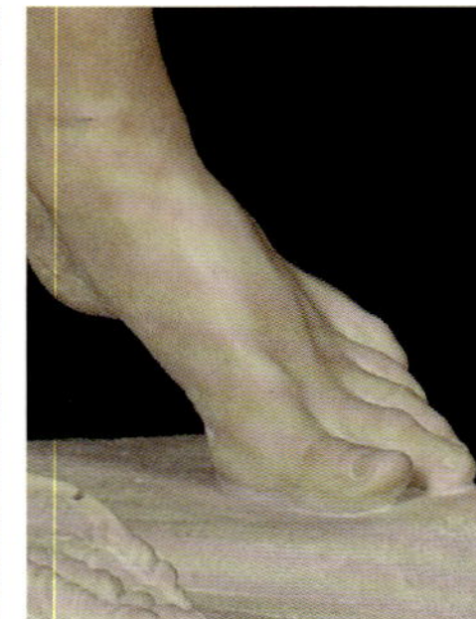

❻ Agility

David's nimbleness is suggested by the way his feet grip the floor. One of his toes extends beyond the base of the sculpture, crossing the boundary between art and real life.

❼ Tension

Veins stand out prominently on the feet, suggesting the adrenaline pumping through David's body in this pivotal moment.

❽ Master of matter

Marble, a prestigious and expensive material, was synonymous with classical sculpture. Its crystalline structure reflects light, and it is high in compressive, rather than tensile, strength. A marble column can resist weight from above, but shapes that extend horizontally into space are more likely to snap. Bernini's skill in carving the rope, therefore, is particularly impressive – as is the fact that, according to Baldinucci, he completed the statue in only seven months.

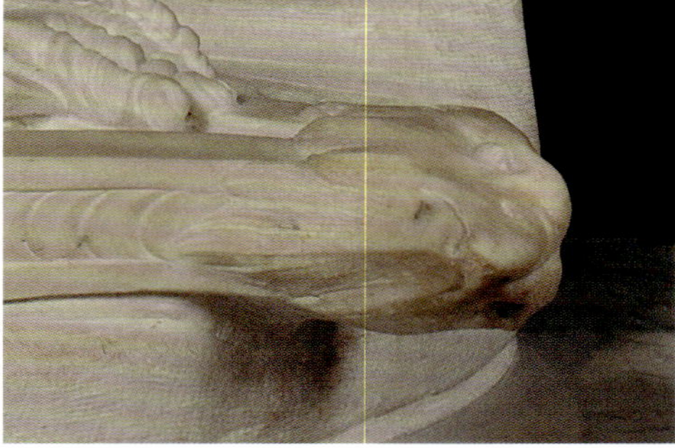

❾ The owner's share

The eagle's head on the cithara is a reference to the act of patronage: Bernini was tasked with making this sculpture by the wealthy and influential Cardinal Scipione Borghese, whose personal emblem was an eagle.

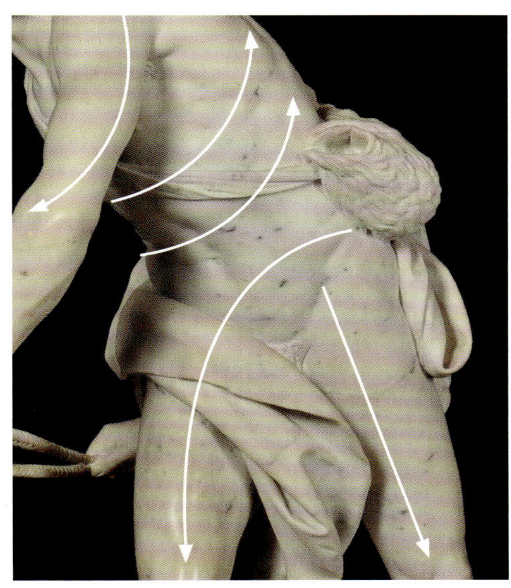

❿ A coiled spring

David's body is held in a tightly coiled, extremely dynamic pose. His legs face forwards, but his body is twisted dramatically in a taut spiral of latent energy.

⓫ Movement

Unlike previous depictions of David by Donatello, Verrocchio and Michelangelo (ill. p. 31), which show the hero either just before or after his fight with Goliath, Bernini has chosen to show David at the absolute climax of the event. We are witnessing the split-second before the attack is launched.

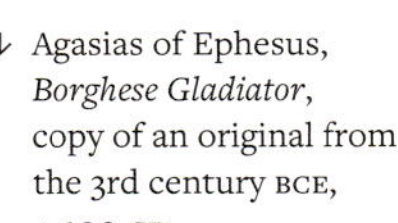

↓ Agasias of Ephesus, *Borghese Gladiator*, copy of an original from the 3rd century BCE, *c.* 100 CE

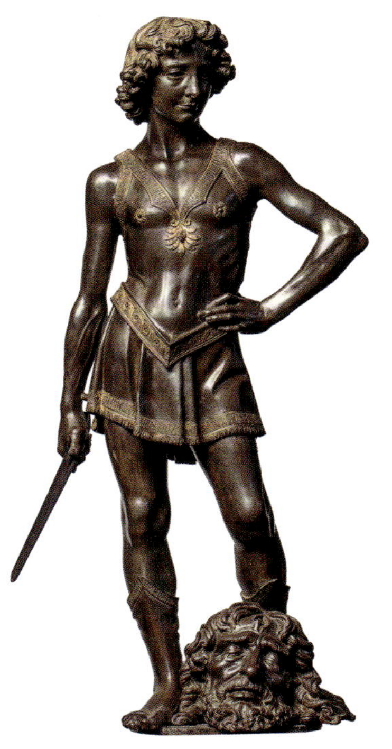

Andrea del Verrocchio, *David with the Head of Goliath*, *c.* 1465. Bronze with partial gilding

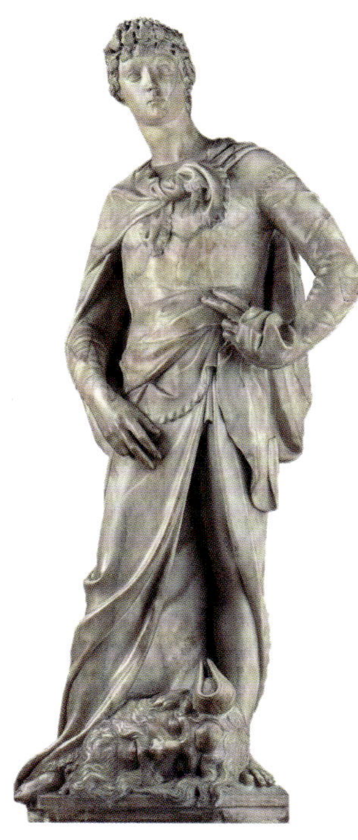

Donatello, *David*, 1408–9. Marble, height: 191 cm, 75¼ in.

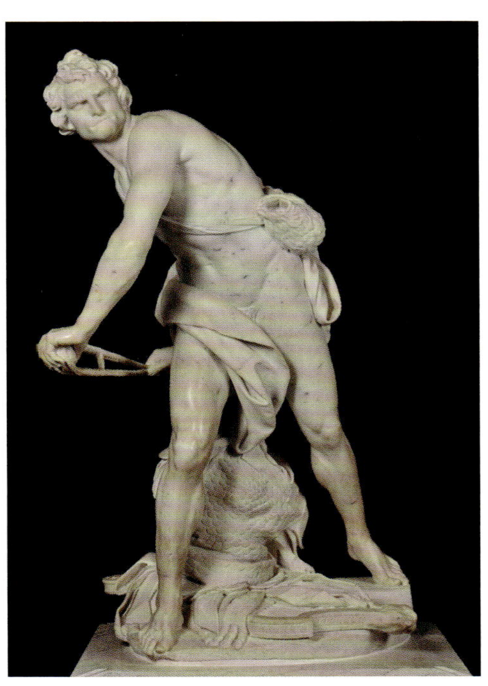

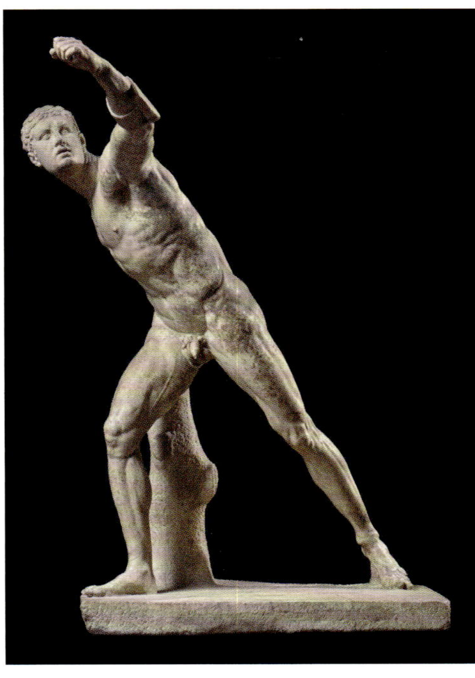

⓬ Outdoing the past

While Bernini's own David – with its heightened action and emotional intensity – could be seen as a challenge to the versions of the past, the artist is also paying homage to the sculpture of classical antiquity, specifically a work belonging to his patron Cardinal Scipione Borghese: the *Borghese Gladiator*.

⓭ Unpopularity

Bernini's work has not always been popular. The 19th-century sculptor Sir Richard Westmacott so disliked the heightened emotions of the artist's statues that he wrote in the *Handbook of Sculpture: Ancient and Modern* (1864): 'The variety of his pursuits, and his inordinate craving after picturesque effects, ruined the art he professed ... it would have been better for this art had Bernini never lived.'

LINKED PRACTITIONERS

SCULPTORS IN MARBLE:	DAVID REPRESENTED IN ART:	SELF-PORTRAITS HIDDEN IN ARTWORKS:
Phidias (*c.* 480–430 BCE), GREECE	*Donatello* (*c.* 1386–1466), ITALY	*Jan van Eyck* (before 1390–1441), NETHERLANDS
Michelangelo (1575–1564), ITALY	*Andrea del Castagno* (*c.* 1419–1457)	*Sandro Botticelli* (*c.* 1445–1510), ITALY
Antonio Canova (1757–1822), ITALY	*Andrea del Verrocchio* (*c.* 1435–1488), ITALY	*Raphael* (1483–1520), ITALY
Constantin Brâncuși (1876–1957), ROMANIA/FRANCE	*Michelangelo* (1475–1564), ITALY	*Diego Velázquez* (1599–1660), SPAIN
Marc Quinn (born 1964), UK	*Julian Schnabel* (born 1951), USA	*Clara Peeters* (fl. 1607–1621), BELGIUM

25. Subverting Expectations

Diego Velázquez (1599–1660) painted this portrait of his servant Juan de Pareja for an exhibition held on 19 March 1650 in Rome for an elite group of artists known as the Congregazione dei Virtuosi al Pantheon. The work was so technically accomplished that one contemporary exclaimed 'everything else looked like art; this alone like truth'.

It must have been especially striking that although the sitter stands confidently in the pose of an aristocrat, and the portrait itself was painted with as much care and attention as would be given to someone from the highest reaches of society, Juan de Pareja was in fact an enslaved person within Velázquez's own household. This was a radical departure from previous notions of what was deemed appropriate in portraiture, and poses questions about Velázquez's own intentions in his choice of subject.

Oil on canvas
81.3 × 69.9 cm, 32 × 27½ in.
Metropolitan Museum of Art, New York

Diego Velázquez
Juan de Pareja
1650

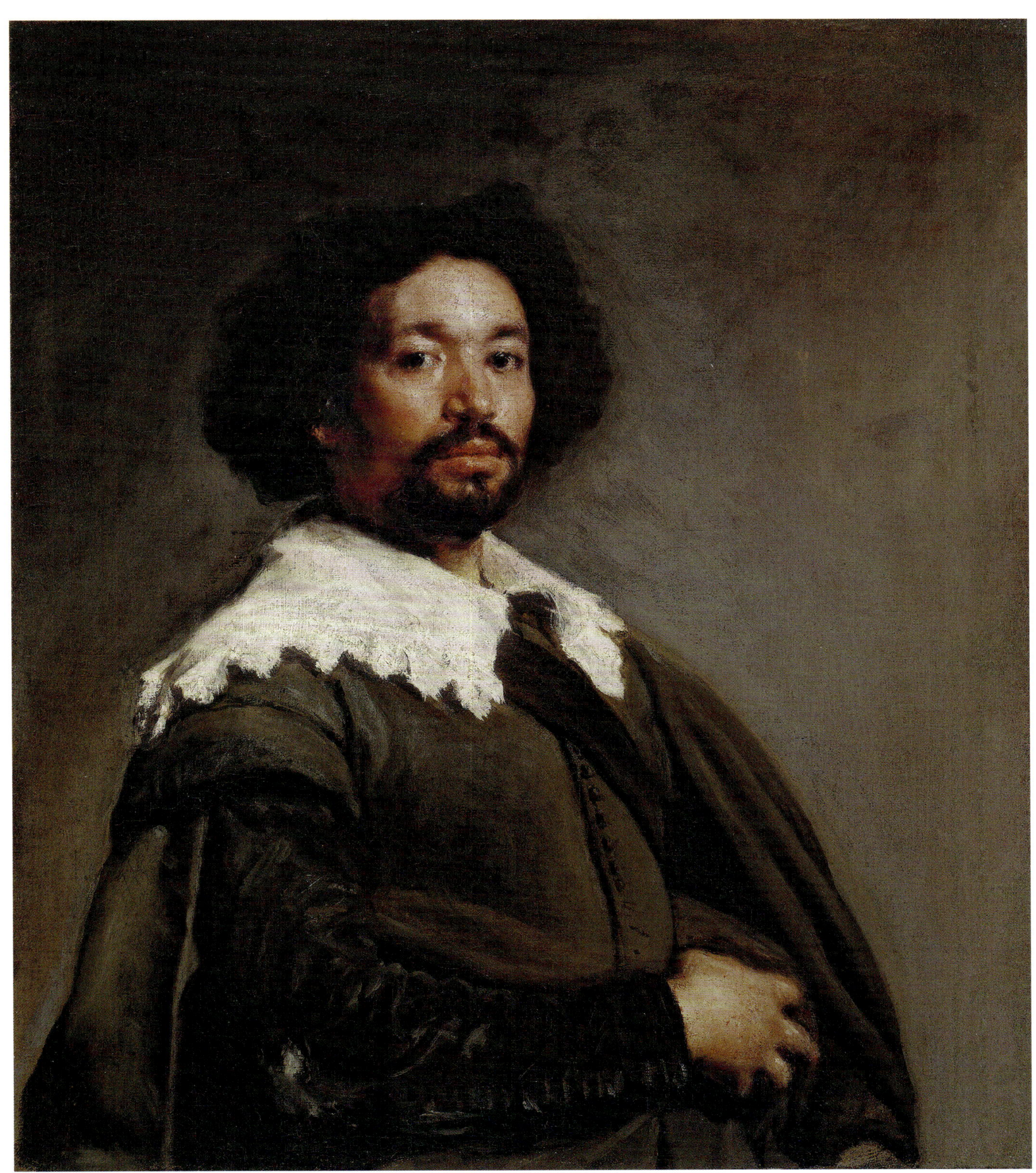

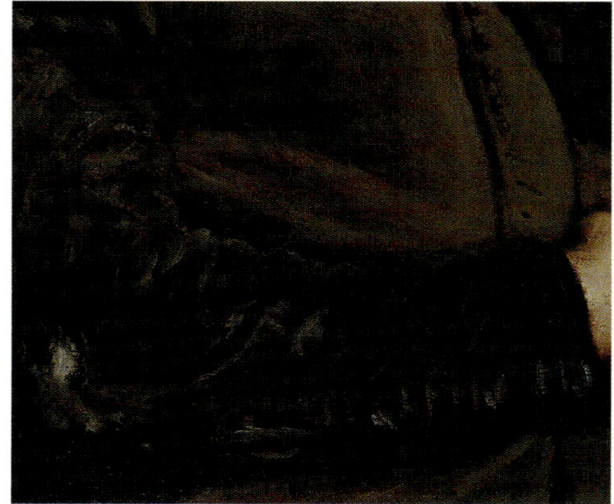

❶ Ripped elbow

The object that appears closest to the viewer is Juan de Pareja's elbow. The noticeable rip in his sleeve tells us that he is not wealthy, even if his body language is one of confident assurance. The pose was much used throughout the Renaissance to denote aristocratic ease, described by art historian Joaneath Spicer as 'indicative of boldness or control, and therefore of the self-defined masculine role'.[51]

❷ Sideways glance

The sitter is arranged in a pose known as the 'three-quarter view', set at an angle to the viewer. Like the jutting elbow, the pose serves to give him an air of informal authority. We, the viewers, are slightly below him; we can tell this because we can just see the underside of his nostrils and chin.

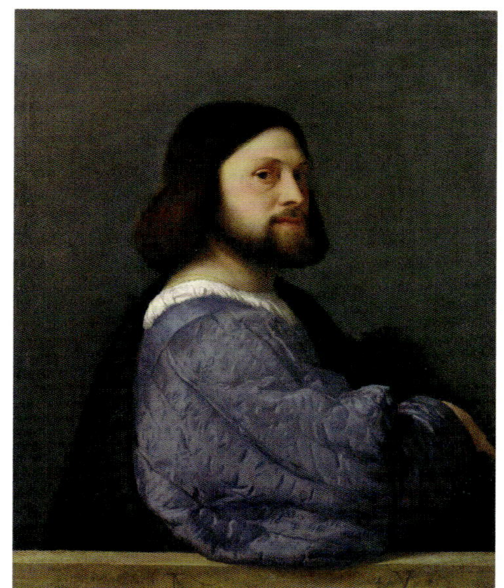

Titian, *Portrait of Gerolamo (?) Barbarigo*, c. 1510. Oil on canvas, 81.2 × 66.3 cm, 32 × 26 in.

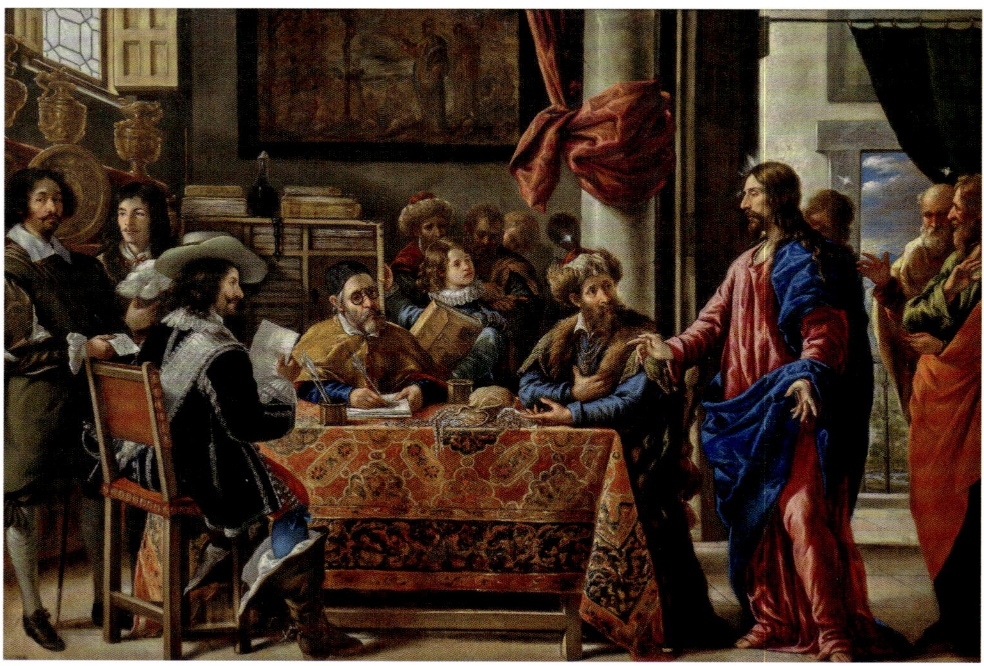

Juan de Pareja, *The Calling of Saint Matthew*, 1661. Oil on canvas, 225 × 325 cm, 88½ × 128 in.

❸ Sitter

Juan de Pareja was born to a Spanish father and a mother of African descent, and was an enslaved member of Velázquez's household in Spain. The artist taught Pareja to paint, and granted him his freedom in 1650, the year this portrait was painted. Pareja later went on to pursue his own artistic career (see above).

❹ Topsy-turvy

Throughout his career, Velázquez liked to depict contradictions in his art. The image of an enslaved person in the pose of an aristocrat is one such paradox, and prompts questions about the artist's attitudes and intentions regarding his servant. Did he wish to elevate Pareja's position through art, or just demonstrate his own talents?

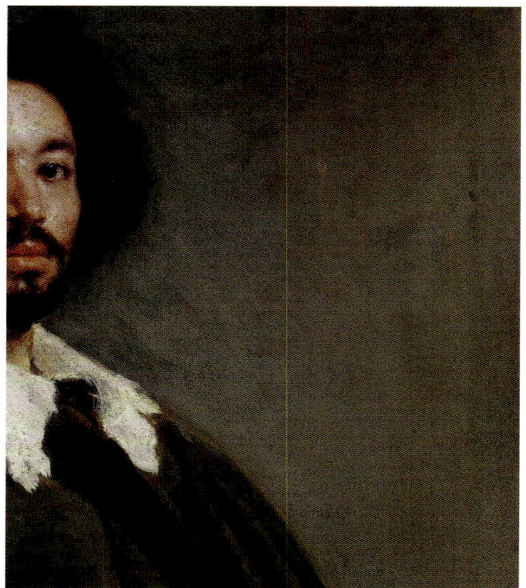

❺ Empty background

The empty background ensures that we are not distracted visually from the sitter. A faint glow draws our attention to Pareja's face.

LINKED PRACTITIONERS

SPANISH BAROQUE ARTISTS:

Francisco Ribaltá (1565–1628), SPAIN
Jusepe de Ribera (1591–1652), SPAIN
Francisco de Zurbarán (1598–1664), SPAIN
Bartolomé Esteban Murillo (1617–1682), SPAIN
Juan de Valdés Leal (1622–1690), SPAIN

DIRECT HOMAGE:

Salvador Dalí (1904–1989), SPAIN
Iba N'Diaye (1928–2008), SENEGAL
Rupert García (born 1941), USA
Kathleen Gilje (born 1945), USA
Omar Victor Diop (born 1980), SENEGAL

PORTRAITURE:

Anthony van Dyck (1599–1641), BELGIUM/UK
Élisabeth Vigée Le Brun (1755–1842), FRANCE
Tamara de Lempicka (1898–1980), POLAND/USA
Alice Neel (1900–1984), USA

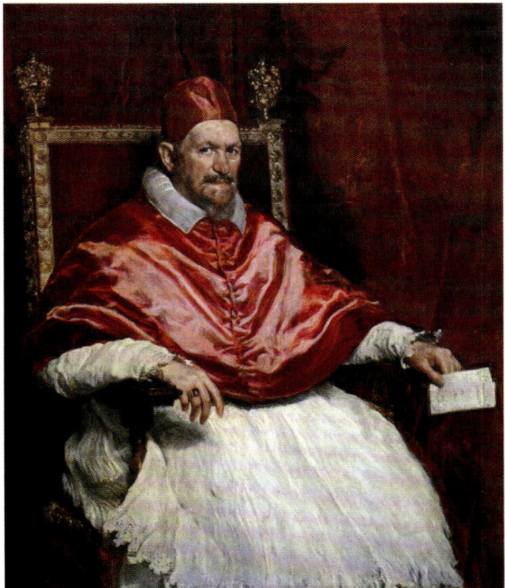

Pope Innocent X, c. 1650. Oil on canvas, 140 × 120 cm, 55 × 47¼ in.

❻ Two portraits

The Flemish painter Andreas Schmidt was in Rome at the same time as Velázquez, and told his version of events to the artist and writer Antonio Palomino, who published it in his three-volume treatise on the art of painting some 65 years later. According to Schmidt, Velázquez painted the portrait of Juan de Pareja in preparation for one of Pope Innocent X.[52] In contrast to Pareja, the pope was one of the most powerful men in the world, and yet both portraits present their subjects with the same level of technique and scrutiny. The portrait of Pareja was displayed at an exhibition held by the Congregazione dei Virtuosi al Pantheon in Rome on 19 March 1650, where its brilliance astonished Velázquez's fellow artists.

❼ Truth

According to Palomino, when Velázquez sent Pareja to show the painting to some colleagues for appraisal, 'they just stood looking at it and at the original in awe and wonder, not knowing to whom they should speak or who would answer them'. When it was exhibited in 1650, the portrait 'received such universal acclaim that in the opinion of all the painters of different nations everything else looked like art, this alone like truth'.[53] Even as a young artist, Velázquez was clearly interested in the relationship of art and truth. His final masterpiece, *Las Meninas* (1656), is widely considered to be a statement about the nature of vision and reality.

❽ A dab of paint

The painting technique is rapid, fluid and brilliantly abbreviated. Glints of light in the sitter's eyes and the bridge of his nose are single dabs of paint, which look thoroughly convincing from a distance. Velázquez's technique is miraculously skilled in suggesting the sheen of sweaty skin with an economy of means.

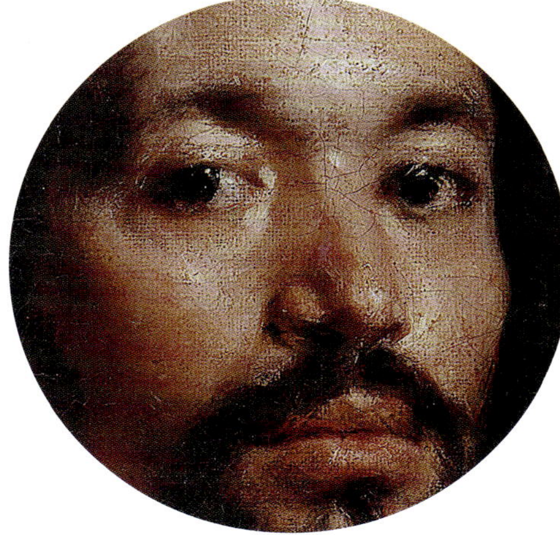

❾ Lace collar

Juan de Pareja wears a Flemish lace collar, which freemen were forbidden from wearing because of its sumptuousness.[54] It underscores the sitter's inherent humanity and style.

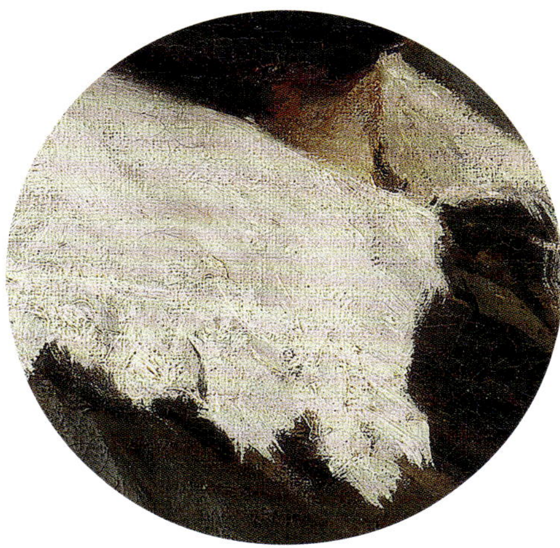

❿ A priceless object

The painting was bought by the Metropolitan Museum of Art in 1971 for $5,544,000, the highest amount paid for a work of art at auction at the time.

WORKS INFLUENCED BY VELÁZQUEZ

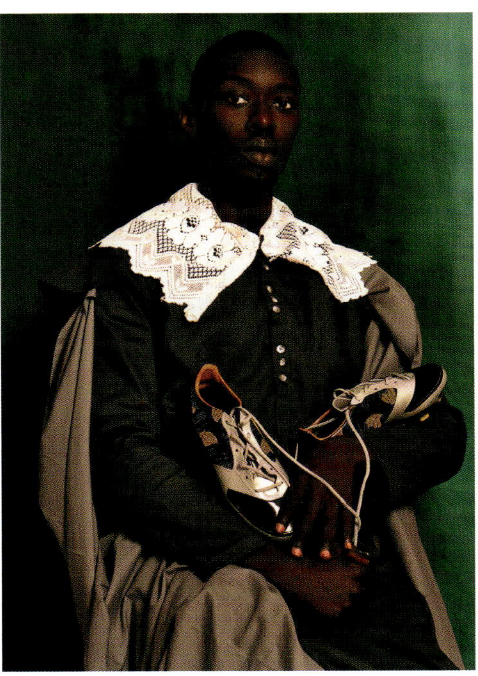

Omar Victor Diop, *Juan de Pareja*, from the *Diaspora* series, 2014. Pigment inkjet print on Harman By Hahnemühle paper, 120 × 80 cm, 47¼ × 31½ in.

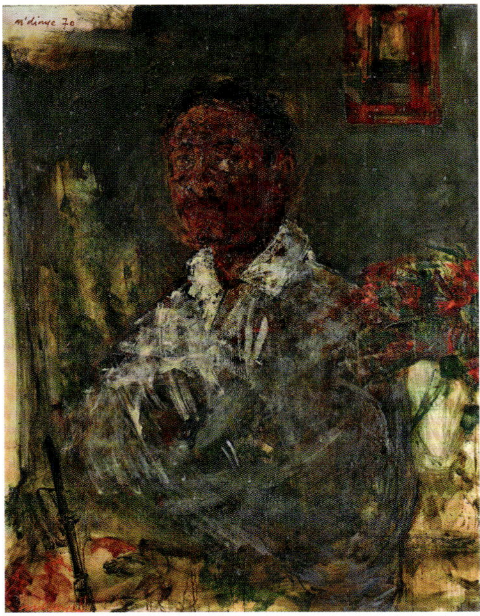

Iba N'Diaye, *Self-portrait*, 1970. Oil on canvas, 144 × 111 cm, 56¾ × 43¾ in.

26. A Technical Masterclass

In 1653, when he made this print, Rembrandt van Rijn (1606–1669) was living in an impressive townhouse on the Jodenbreestraat in Amsterdam. Although his surroundings may have suggested success and affluence to his contemporaries, he was encountering severe money troubles after over a decade of unwise investments and overspending.

It may have been more financially prudent at this stage to make a simple and easily reproducible print for a mass audience, but Rembrandt felt impelled to do the opposite. The technique he employed in *The Three Crosses* was especially difficult, laborious and not conducive to making a series of consistently accurate and detailed prints. He must have considered the effects as so perfect for the subject and function, however, that he persisted – resulting in a print that is among his finest works in any medium.

Drypoint
38.7 × 45.5 cm, 15¼ × 18 in.
Rijksmuseum, Amsterdam

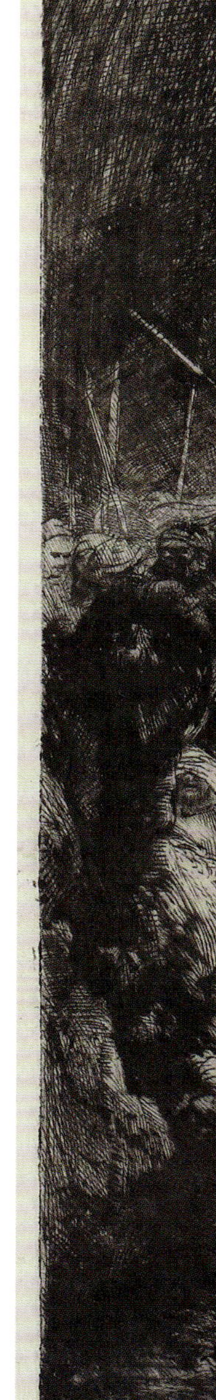

Rembrandt van Rijn
The Three Crosses
third state, 1653

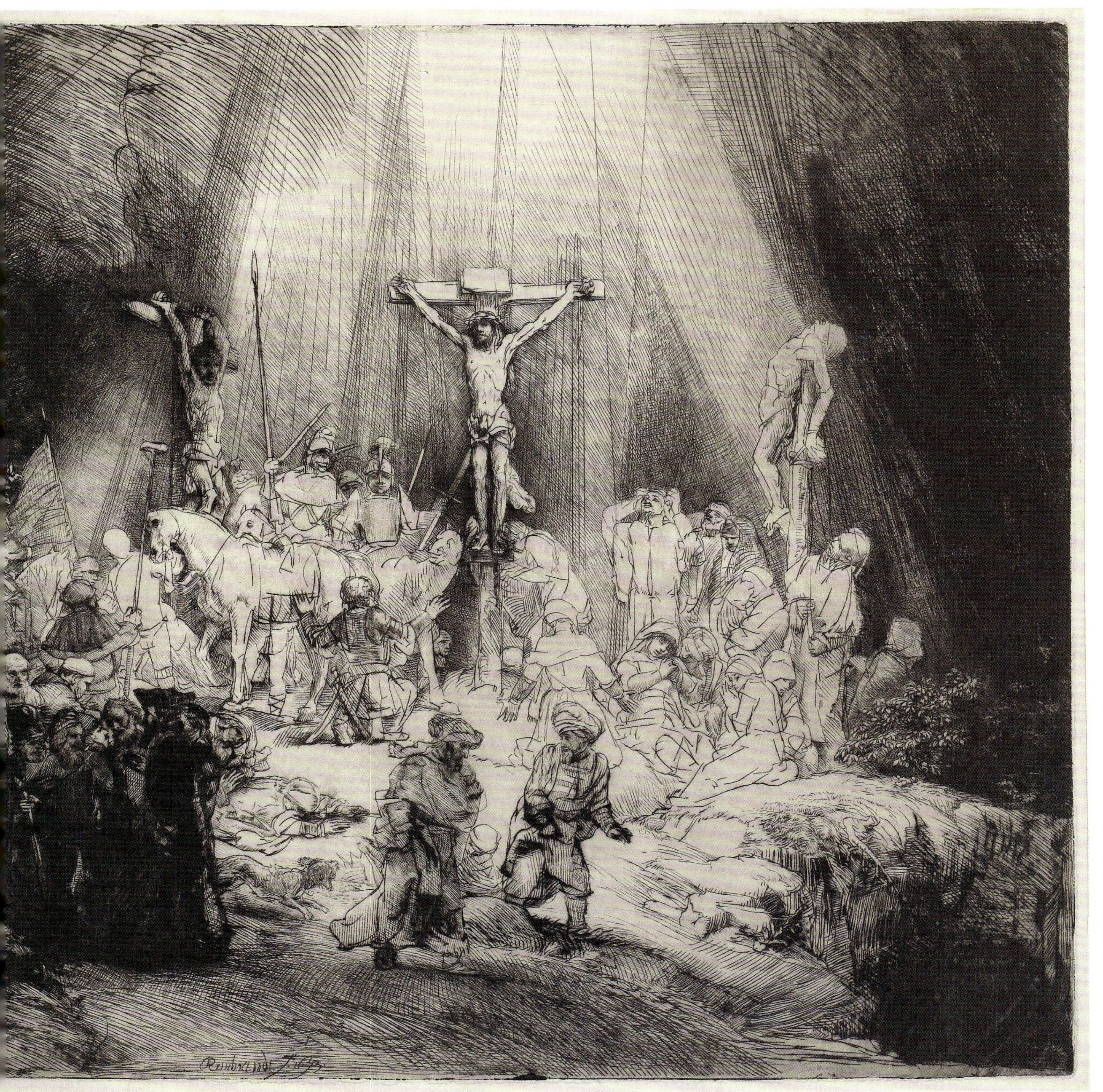

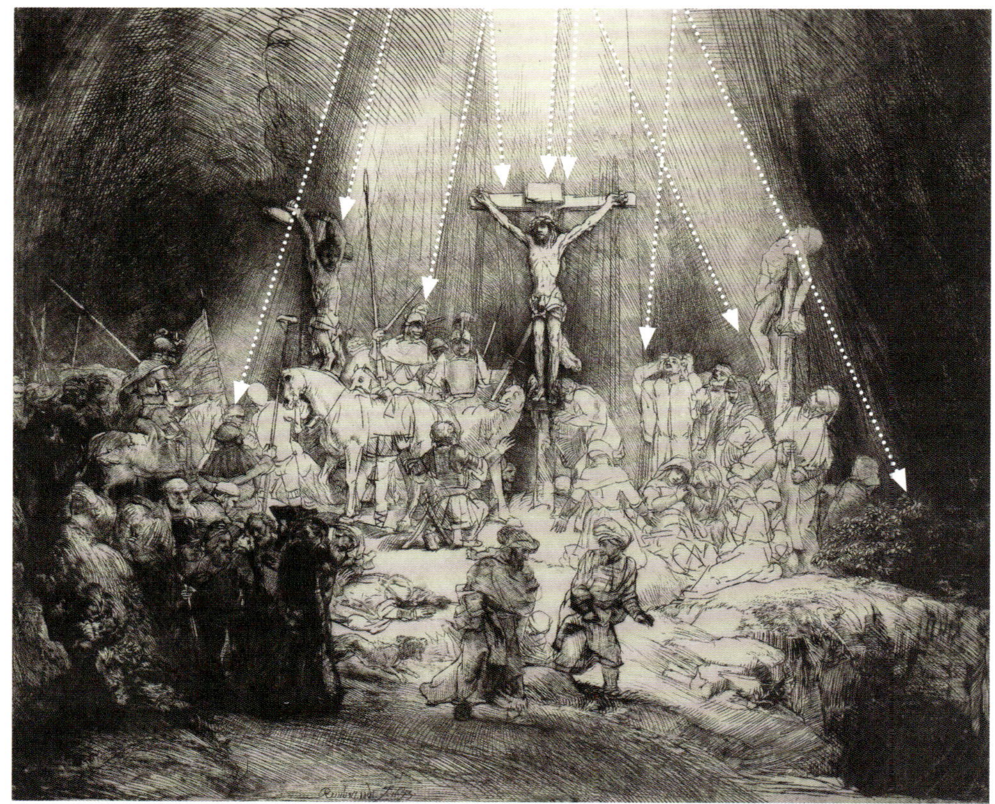

❶ Let there be light

Beams of blinding light pierce the surrounding darkness, spotlighting the characters below. Despite the lack of colour, Rembrandt has used the monochromatic nature of printing to his advantage in depicting divine illumination.

❷ Let there be darkness

The light splices the darkness, creating a theatrical atmosphere that dramatically illuminates the central action. This contrast of light and dark is known as 'chiaroscuro', manipulated here by Rembrandt to represent the celestial forces of good and evil.

❸ Drypoint

Unusually, this print was made entirely using the technique of drypoint, which Rembrandt had experimented with in the 1640s.[55] After drawing the image in reverse onto a copper plate rubbed with ink, the plate would be wiped with a cloth, leaving the ink in the incised lines, before pressing it onto a damp sheet of paper. Because the incising tool created fuzzy lines that wore out more quickly than in engraving or woodblocks, the number of editions that could be made from a single plate was limited.

❹ Rembrandt's evolutions

As the lines became less clear, Rembrandt scratched away whole sections of the plate and redrew them. He also left ink on the plates in key areas to create atmospheric chiaroscuro effects. Later editions of the print (the fourth and fifth stages) were thoroughly reworked, creating almost entirely different images.

❺ Hatching

The technique of using multiple parallel lines – occasionally overlapping to create grid-like patterns – to represent a three-dimensional form is known as hatching. The image is built up from thousands of individual lines, meticulously drawn in by Rembrandt.

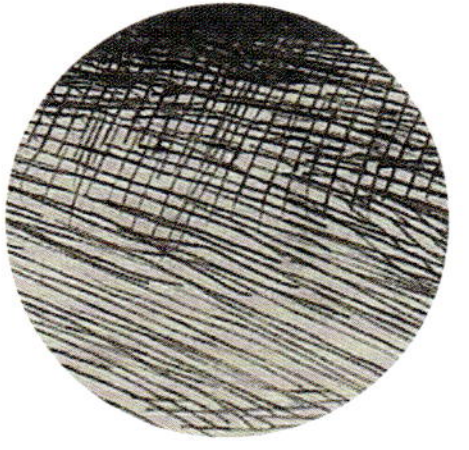

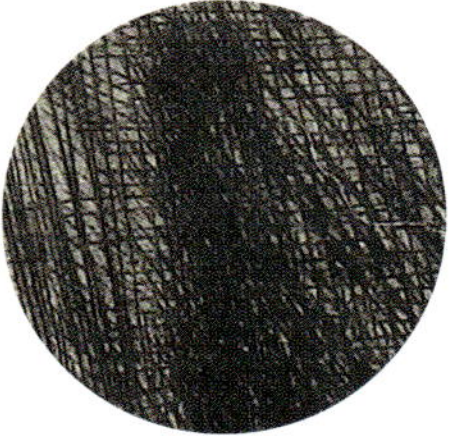

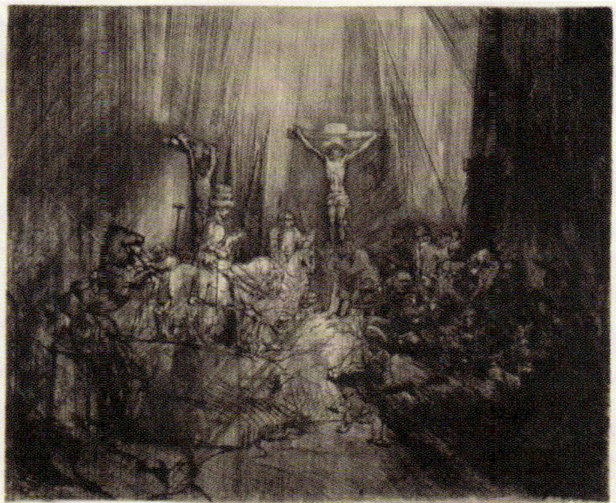

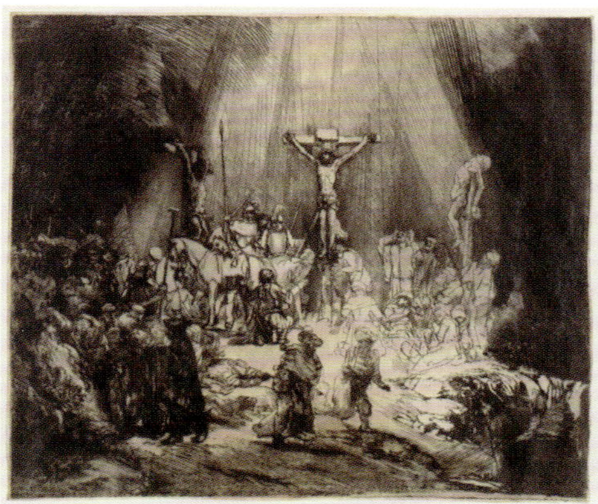

↑ *The Three Crosses*, second state, 1653. Drypoint, 38.1 × 43.8 cm, 15 × 17¼ in.
↑↑ *The Three Crosses*, first state, 1653. Drypoint, 37.8 × 43.4 cm, 15 × 17 in.

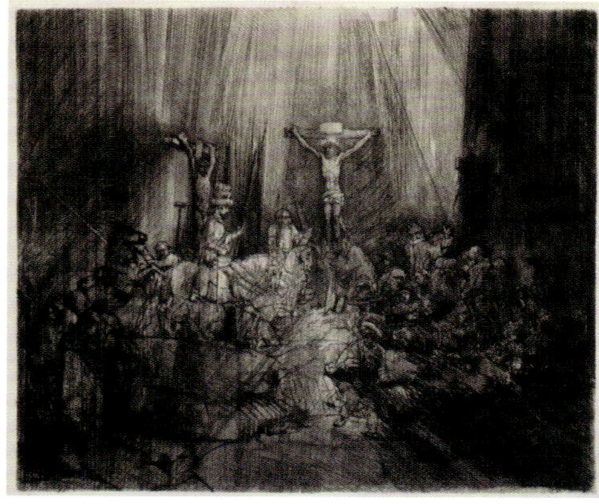

↑ *The Three Crosses*, fifth state, *c.* 1660. Drypoint, 38.5 × 44.9 cm, 15¼ × 17¾ in.
↑↑ *The Three Crosses*, fourth state, *c.* 1660. Drypoint, 38.2 × 44.4 cm, 15 × 17½ in.

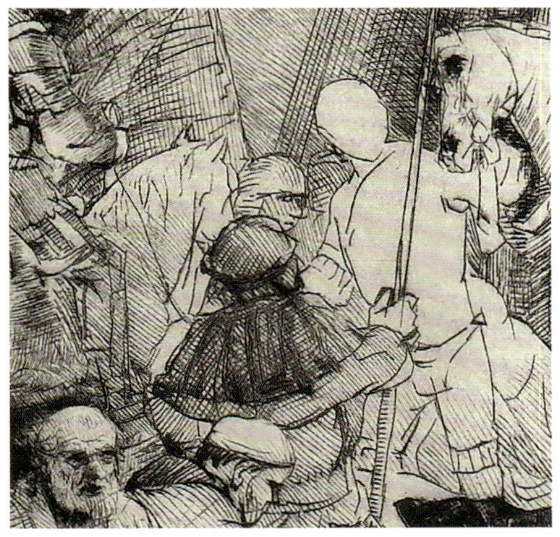

❻ Where is this man's face?

There is a sketchy quality to the print, with some sections appearing as if Rembrandt hasn't fully finished them. By not showing the details (the features of a face, for example), he is suggesting that the light from above is so intense that details are washed out.

❽ Longinus

The Gospel of John relates how one of the Roman soldiers pierced the side of the crucified Christ with his spear; he later became associated with the soldier who recognized Christ as the Son of God. The name 'Longinus' first appears in the Gospel of Nicodemus.

❾ Function

Because this work is a print, multiple versions of it would have been made. It was intended, therefore, as something that many people could buy and admire in their homes.

❿ Divisions

During the 16th and 17th centuries, religion in Europe was shaped fundamentally by the splitting of the Christian church into Catholic and Protestant, following Martin Luther's protests against the sale of indulgences in 1517 (see also p. 95). The two faiths had very different ways of looking at art, and inspired different philosophies of visual culture. In the Dutch Republic, churches were stripped of paintings and sculptures, and artists who had previously relied on church patronage had to look to other subjects. Rembrandt rose to the challenge and produced a private image of intense spirituality, despite the reduced scale and limitation to just two tones.

❼ Biblical subject

The scene depicts the crucifixion of Christ, when he is facing the final hours of his life. The two thieves who were crucified at the same time are shown on either side. In the Gospel of Luke, one is described as jeering Christ, the other as defending him – the reason why Rembrandt has shown one thief in darkness and the other bathed in light.

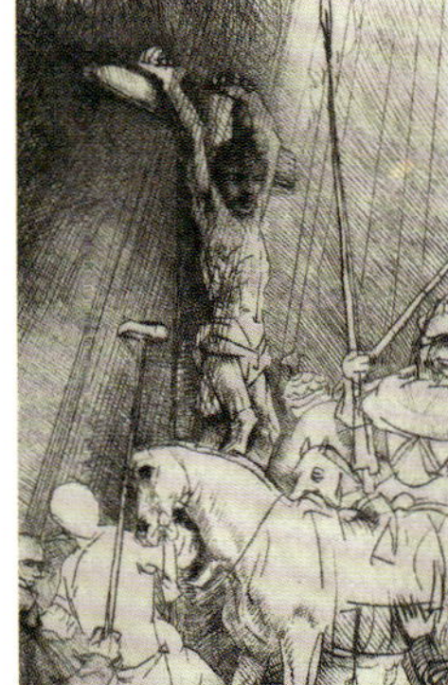

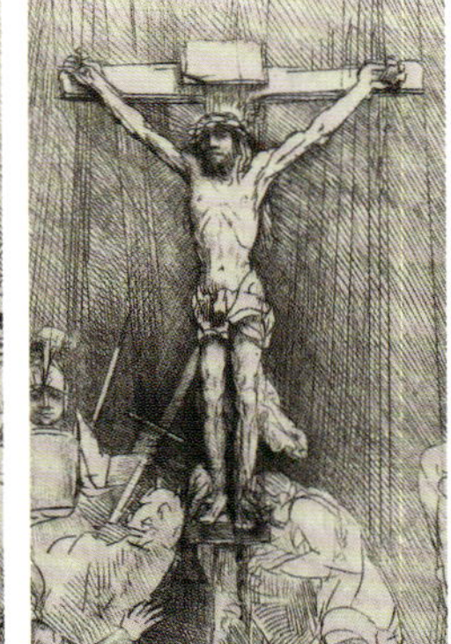

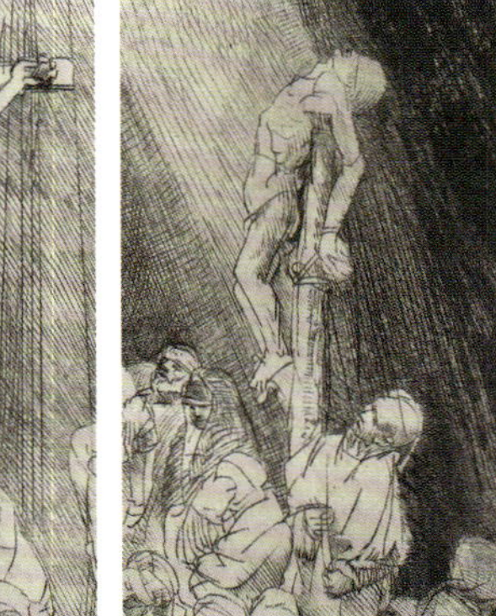

Mattia Preti, *The Martyrdom of St Peter*, late 1650s. Oil on canvas, 194.5 × 194.3 cm, 76½ × 76½ in.

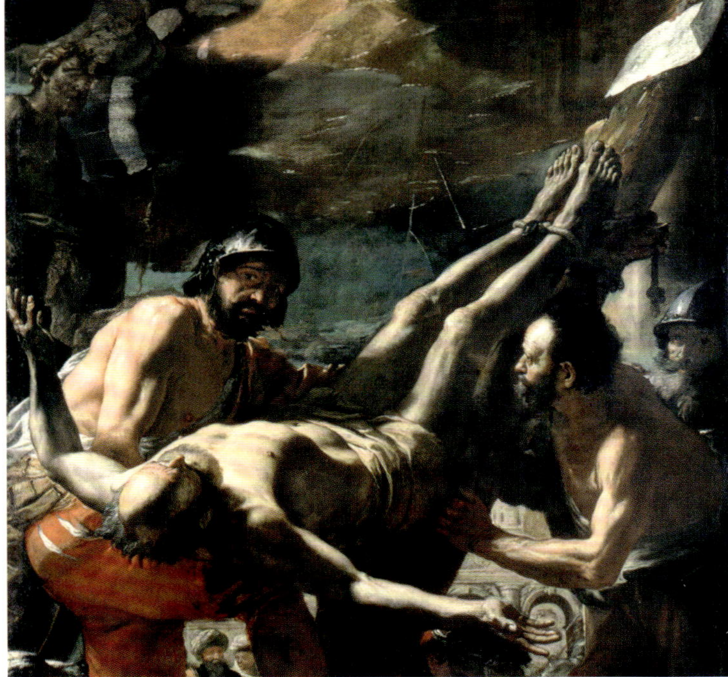

LINKED PRACTITIONERS

CRUCIFIXIONS:	HATCHING TECHNIQUE:	DRYPOINT:
Cimabue (*c.* 1240–1302), ITALY	*Martin Schongauer* (1450/3–1491), FRANCE/GERMANY	*Max Beckmann* (1884–1950), GERMANY/USA
Rogier van der Weyden (*c.* 1399–1464), BELGIUM	*Albrecht Dürer* (1471–1528), GERMANY	*Louise Bourgeois* (1911–2010), FRANCE/USA
Matthias Grünewald (*c.* 1470–1528), GERMANY	*Michelangelo* (1475–1564), ITALY	*Vija Celmins* (born 1938), LATVIA
Francis Bacon (1909–1992), IRELAND/UK	*Paula Rego* (1935–2022), PORTUGAL/UK	*Richard Spare* (born 1951), UK
Andres Serrano (born 1950), USA	*Il Lee* (born 1952), SOUTH KOREA/USA	*William Kentridge* (born 1955), SOUTH AFRICA

27. Hidden Messages

Johannes Vermeer (1632–1675) painted this serenely beautiful image in the Dutch city of Delft, where he lived and worked for the whole of his life. The painting was intended to dazzle the spectator with its compelling realism, which looks almost photographically accurate to the modern eye. That realism, however, is only one aspect of what makes this work so captivating.

Vermeer also introduced a sense of compositional harmony, making clever use of visual symbols that contain cryptic meanings. Beneath the surface, the painting is not just a simple representation of everyday life – a woman in a domestic interior, engaged in a mundane task – but also a vehicle for communicating a hidden message of devout religious belief: the reckoning that each of the faithful must make with their conscience.

Oil on canvas
39.7 × 35.5 cm, 15½ × 14 in.
National Gallery, Washington, DC

Johannes Vermeer
Woman Holding a Balance
c. 1664

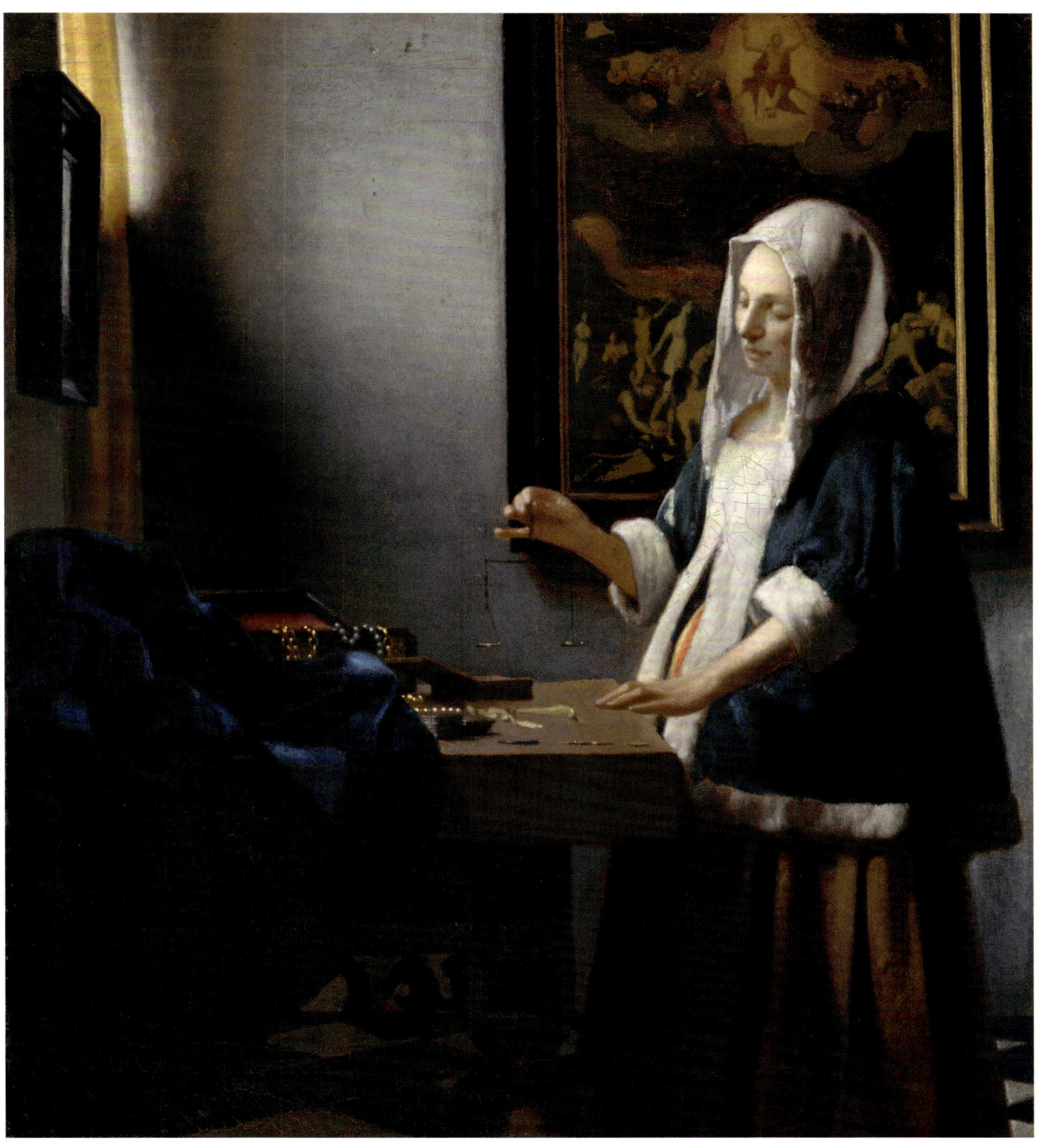

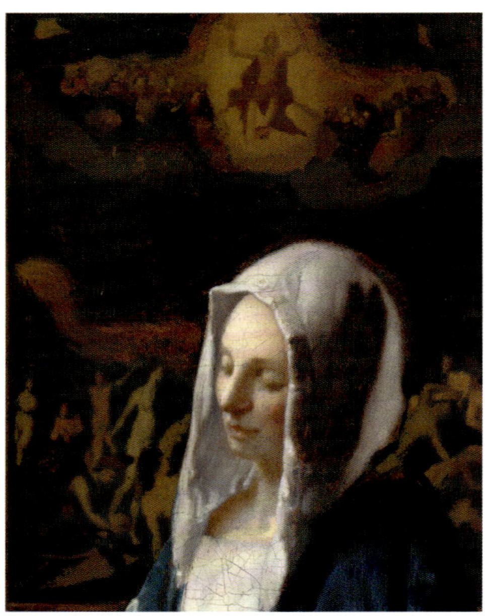

❶ Judgment

The painting that can be glimpsed on the wall behind the central figure depicts the Last Judgment, when Christ sends the virtuous to heaven and casts the sinners down into hell.

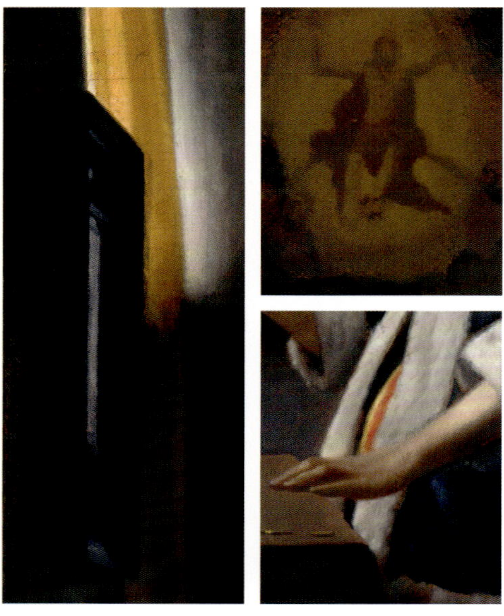

❷ Daylight glow

As daylight enters the room, it is given a golden tint through the yellow curtain. The colour is echoed by the gold of the mandorla around the figure of Christ.[56] It is also in the woman's dress, above her left hand. Vermeer has accurately recorded the way that light diffuses across the background wall using very subtle overlays of grey tones.

❸ Religion

Vermeer lived in the Protestant Dutch Republic, but was a practising Catholic. While religious art was largely discouraged, he included Catholic symbolism in many of his paintings.

❹ Jesuits

It is possible that Vermeer was married in a Jesuit church near his hometown of Delft. He also named one of his sons after the order's founder, St Ignatius of Loyola, whose popular book, *The Spiritual Exercises*, might hold the key to the painting's meaning. One passage reads:

> *I must rather be like the equalized scales of a balance, ready to follow the course which I feel is more for the glory and praise of God, our Lord, and the salvation of my soul.*[57]

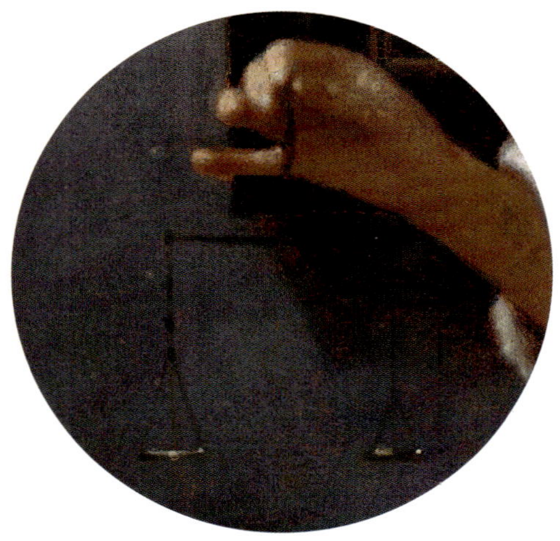

❺ Scales of justice?

If you look closely at the woman's weighing pans, it is clear that they are empty. She appears to be waiting for them to balance and attain equilibrium before weighing the gold and pearls that lie on the table in front of her.

❻ Mysterious figure

It is not clear who the woman represents, perhaps the Virgin Mary or an allegory of Conscience or Justice, or possibly a secular version of the Archangel Michael, who always holds a set of scales and typically stands below Christ in scenes of the Last Judgment.[58] Ultimately, the ambiguity around her identity, and how her actions relate to the painting on the wall behind her, have made the work a rich seam for art-historical debate.

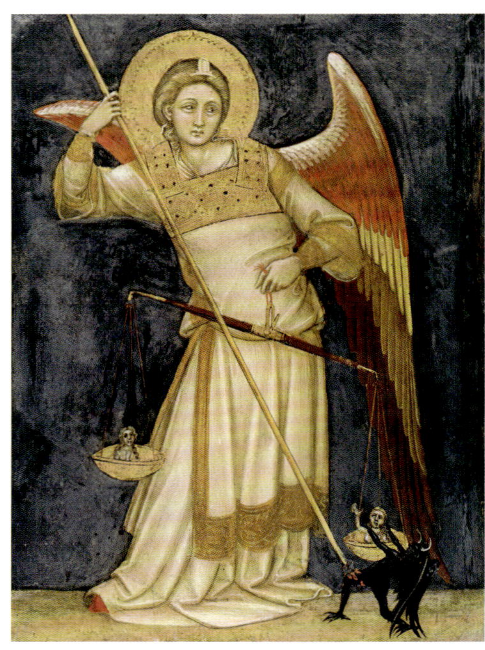

Guariento di Arpo, *Archangel Weighing Souls*, 14th century. Tempera on panel, 80 × 57 cm, 31½ × 22½ in.

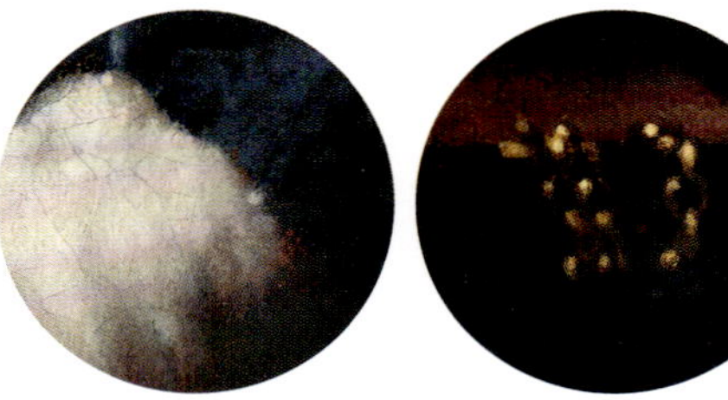

❼ Dots

Vermeer used a highly effective technique to show the fall of light: the application of dots of paint in various colours. This method would be reused by artists such as Georges Seurat in the 19th century and given a name: pointillism.

❽ Realism

The trompe-l'oeil effect is created by a realistic-looking nail in the wall and a hole left over by a previous nail.

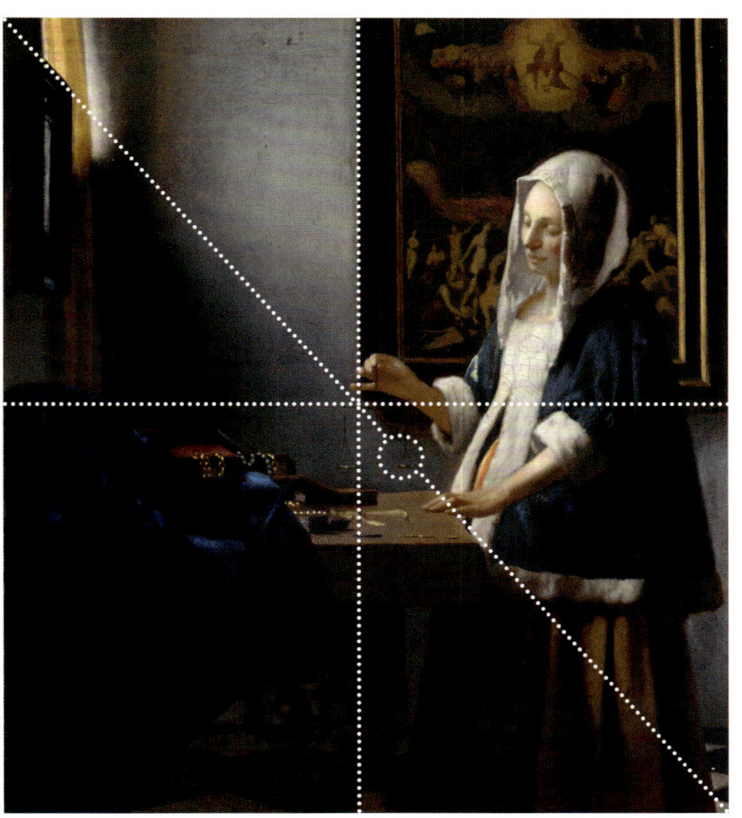

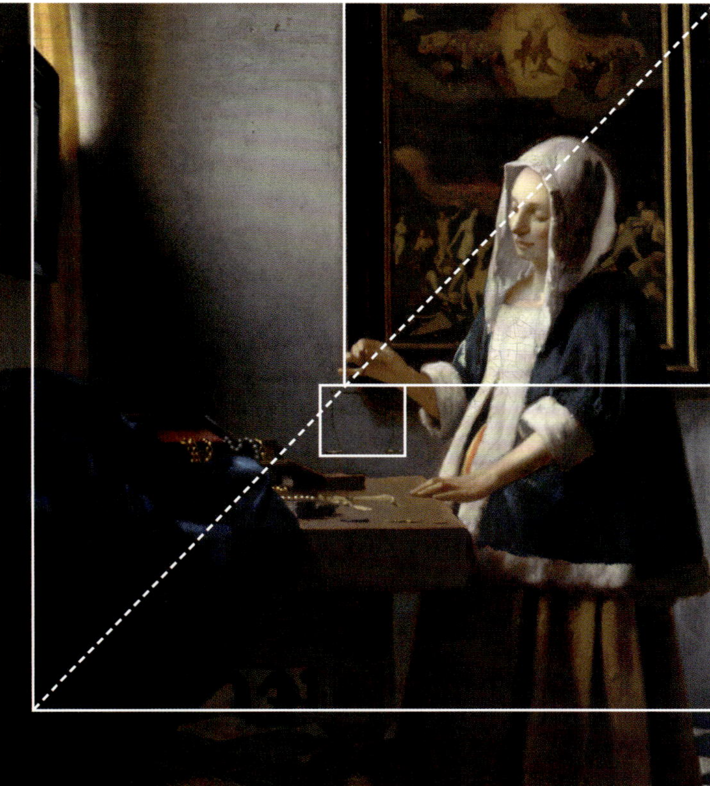

❾ Balance

The composition is perfectly balanced: the table leg is at the exact centre, and the top of the mirror forms a diagonal line, following the direction of light downwards to the right and passing the edge of the weighing pan.

❿ Imbalance

The vertical arm of the scales is *near* the centre, but just above it. The woman seems to be moving her right hand to the centre, giving the work a sense of movement and anticipation.

⓫ Riches

The pearls and gold represent wealth. In other paintings by Vermeer, such as *Allegory of the Catholic Faith*, they symbolize religious purity.

⓬ Proportion

The dimensions are in proportion to the painting of the Last Judgment on the wall. A smaller but identically proportioned rectangle defines the size and shape of the back wall. An even smaller rectangle establishes those of the scales.

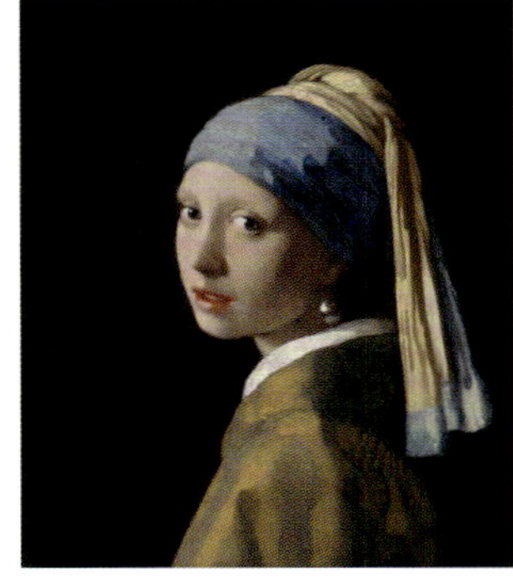

← *Girl with a Pearl Earring*, c. 1665. Oil on canvas, 44.5 × 39 cm, 17½ × 15¼ in.

→ *Allegory of the Catholic Faith*, c. 1670–72. Oil on canvas, 114.3 × 88.9 cm, 45 × 35 in.

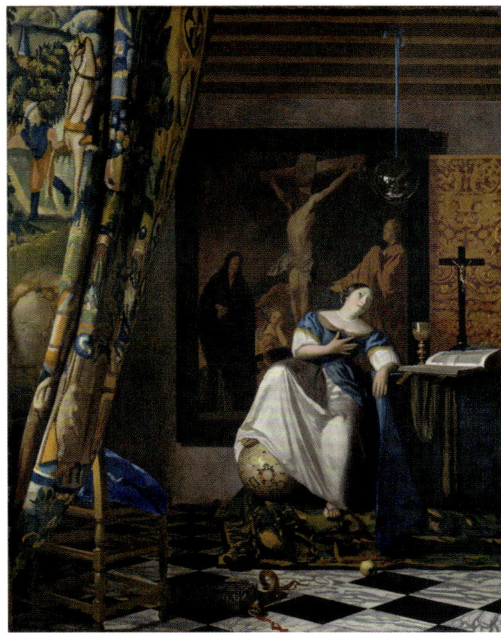

LINKED PRACTITIONERS

DUTCH GOLDEN AGE:

Frans Hals (1582–1666), NETHERLANDS
Judith Leyster (1609–1660), NETHERLANDS
Carel Fabritius (1622–1654), NETHERLANDS
Jan Steen (1626–1679), NETHERLANDS
Pieter de Hooch (1629–1684), NETHERLANDS

ALLEGORIES:

Sandro Botticelli (c. 1445–1510), ITALY
Bronzino (1503–1572), ITALY
Paolo Veronese (1528–1588), ITALY
Pietro da Cortona (1596–1669), ITALY
Sir Joshua Reynolds (1723–1792), UK

HIDDEN SYMBOLISM:

Robert Campin (c. 1375–1444), BELGIUM
Lucas Cranach the Elder (1472–1553), GERMANY
Hans Holbein the Younger (1497/8–1543), GERMANY/UK
Nicolas Poussin (1594–1665), FRANCE/ITALY
Dante Gabriel Rossetti (1828–1882), UK

28. Radical Simplification

In 1712, Ogata Kōrin (1658–1716) received a special delivery at his home in Kyoto, Japan: a pair of large wood-and-paper screens, covered in gold leaf. On them he would paint one of his last and most celebrated works.

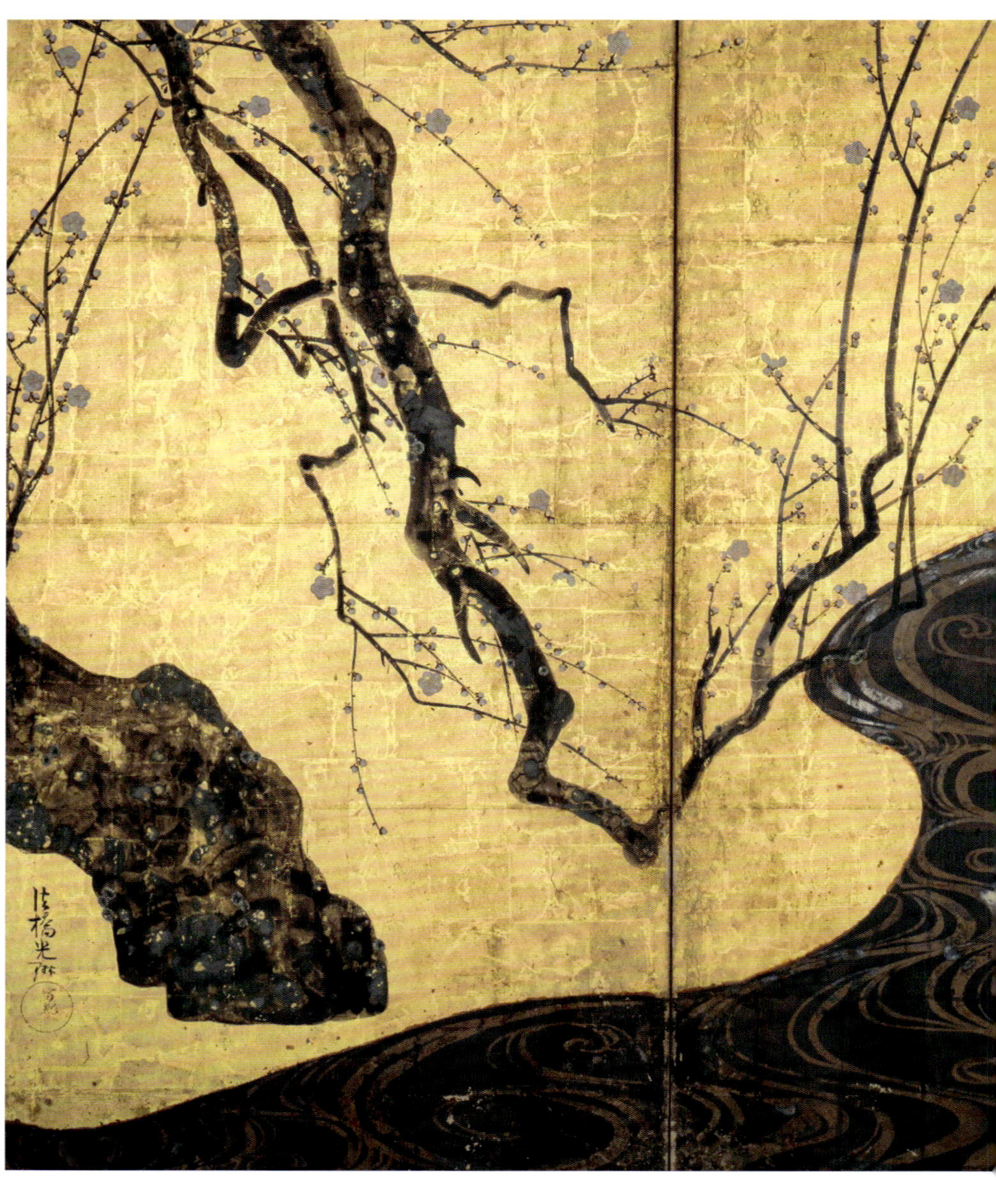

Pair of two-fold screens, colour and gold leaf on paper
156 × 172.2 cm, 61½ × 67¾ in. (each)
MOA Museum of Art, Shizuoka

Ogata Kōrin
Red and White Plum Blossoms
c. 1712–16

The screens were probably commissioned by a wealthy aristocrat, a high-ranking Samurai or a client from the merchant classes. Although Kōrin could not have known it at the time, *Red and White Plum Blossoms* would become his most famous work and the summation of the style with which his work would be synonymous: the Rinpa School.

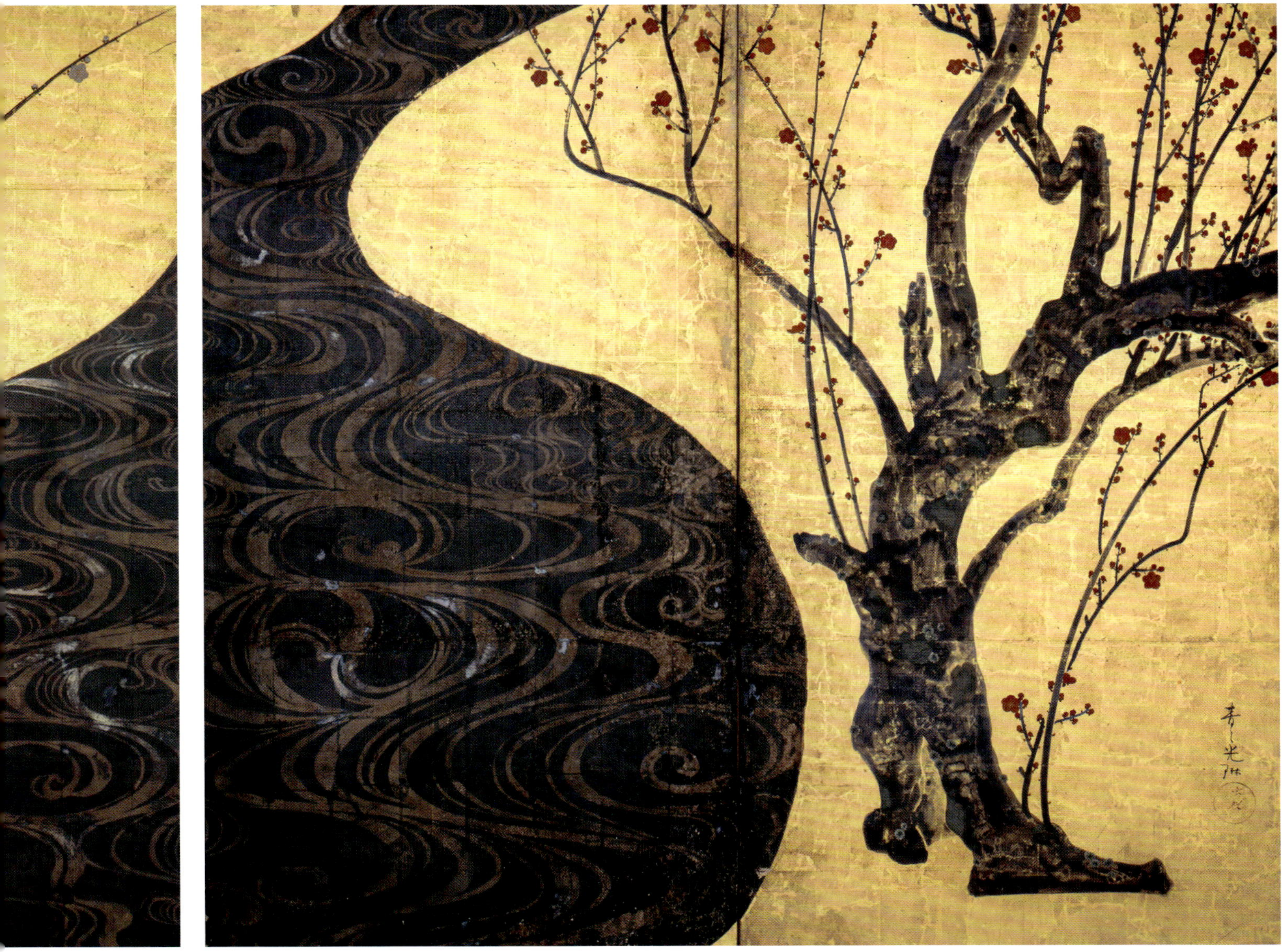

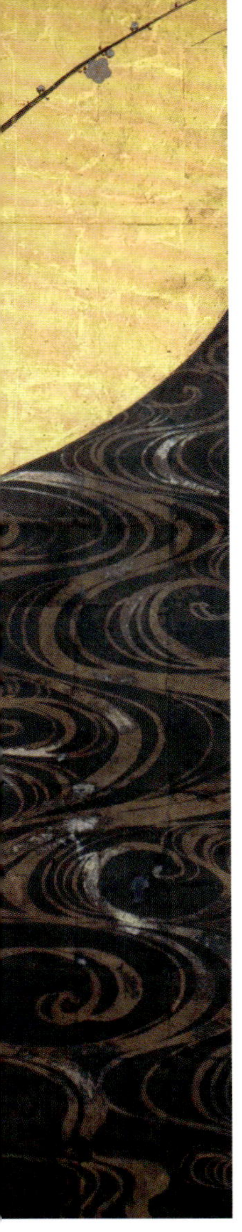

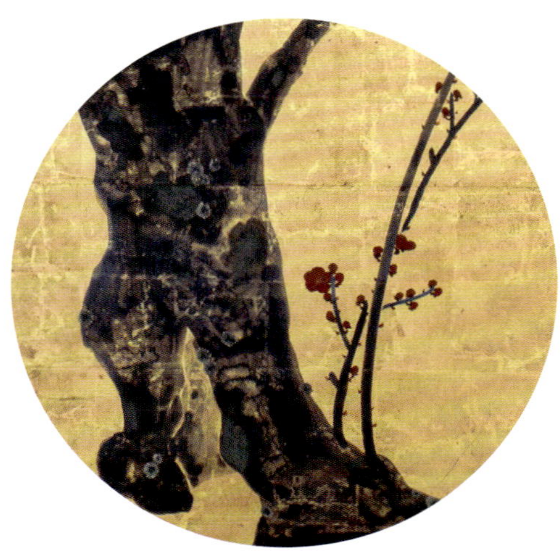
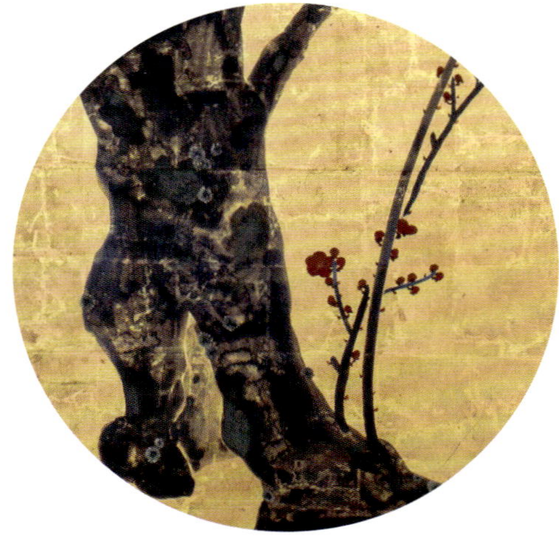

❶ Texture

In the design, a mottled pattern representing gnarled bark and lichen covers the trees. The artist has used a technique called *tarashikomi*, whereby one colour of paint is added to a wet surface covered with another colour to create a marbled effect. This technique was inherited from the processes of Chinese ink-painting.

❹ Influence

Despite this late start, Kōrin has inspired artists into the 21st century, including Kayama Matazō. Alongside the art of *ukiyo-e* (see pp. 152–5), the Rinpa style was hugely influential on European art and culture during the 19th and 20th centuries, notably the paintings of Gustav Klimt (right). *Red and White Plum Blossoms* has been designated a National Treasure in Japan, and *Irises* (opposite), another work by Kōrin, features on the modern 5,000 yen banknote.

❺ Harmony

Unlike the white plum tree on the left, with a trunk that deviates sharply out of the frame, then cuts back in with a branch that swerves diagonally down and then up, the tree on the right curves in a more graceful way. The shapes of the white plum tree are discordant in relation to the river, but the plum tree on the right echoes its shapes. The main trunk leans to the right in the same direction, and a smaller branch meanders left in harmony with the bend in the river.

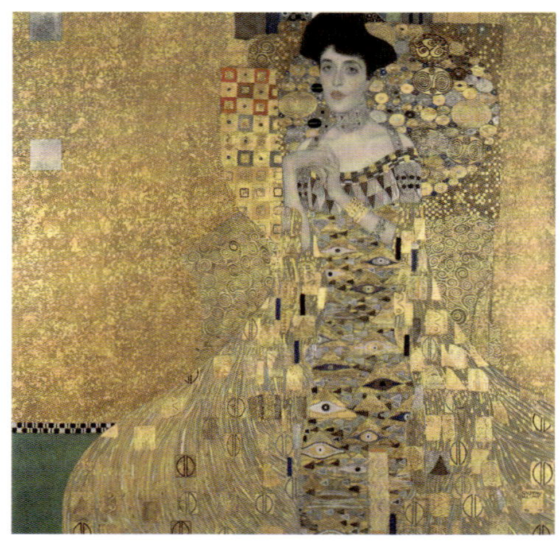

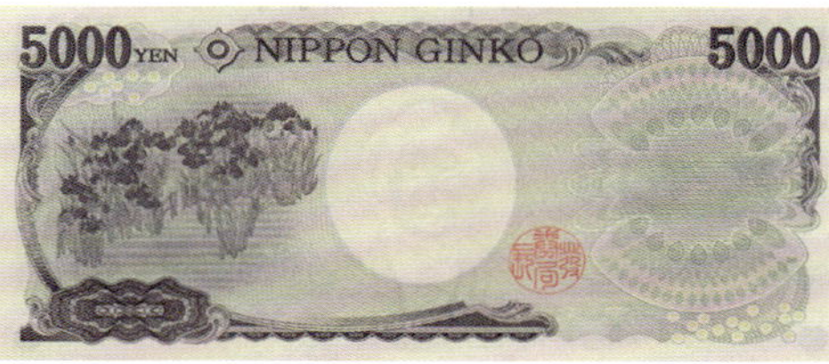

↑ 5,000 yen banknote (Series E), reverse

↑↑ Gustav Klimt, *Adele Bloch-Bauer I*, 1907. Oil, silver and gold on canvas, 140 × 140 cm, 55 × 55 in.

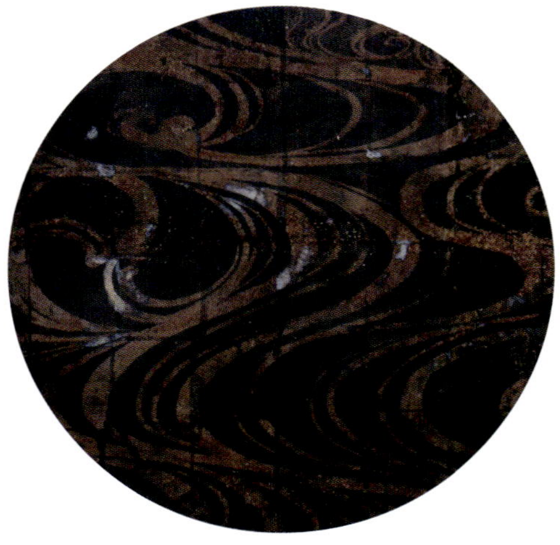

❷ Swirls

The surface of the river is represented with stylized curlicues. These shapes do not become smaller as they recede into the distance, making the river appear as if it is a piece of patterned fabric stuck to the screen.

❸ Late starter

Kōrin learned the basic principles of painting as a child, and was taught for a period by the artist Yamamoto Soken, but he did not become a professional artist until he reached his 30s.[59]

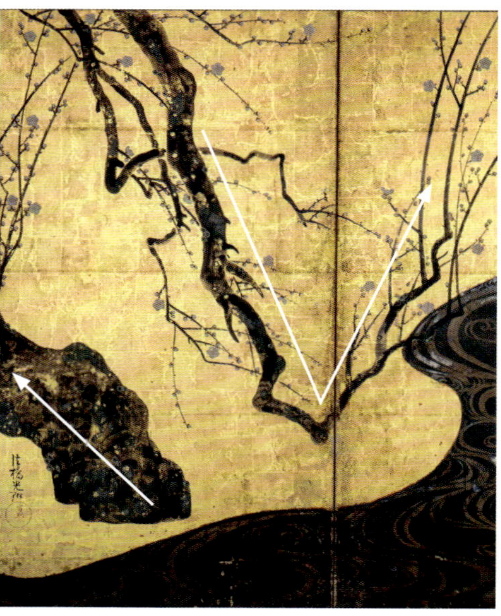

❻ Symbolism

Plum trees produce a blossom that has deep significance in Japan, symbolizing the arrival of spring and the transience of beauty and life. The beginning of the Rinpa style coincided with newfound medical, scientific and artistic fascination with trees in Japan, fuelled by the arrival of books on the subject from China and a growing interest in garden design.

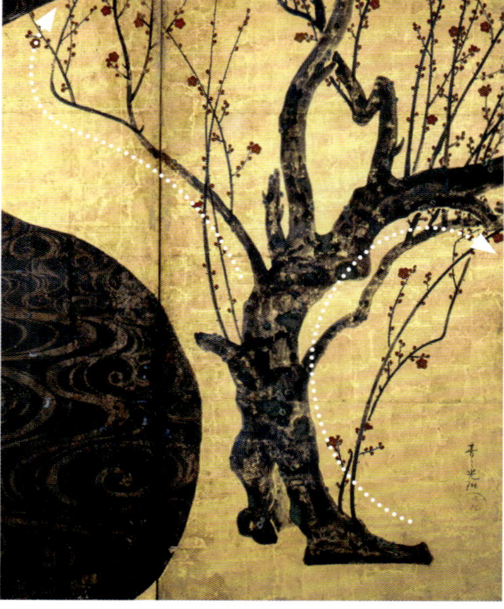

❼ Textiles

Kōrin was born into a wealthy family in Kyoto, Japan, and grew up surrounded by literature, art and the traditional Noh theatre. His father owned a prestigious textile shop, so he was also aware of the latest textile designs and fashions – an early exposure that perhaps influenced his later explorations of abstract patterning in his work.

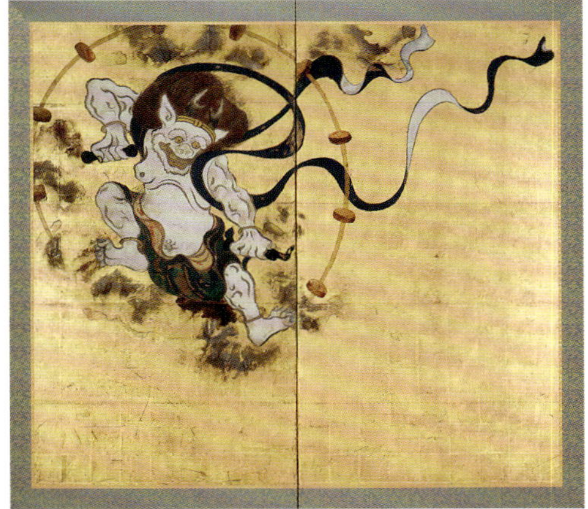

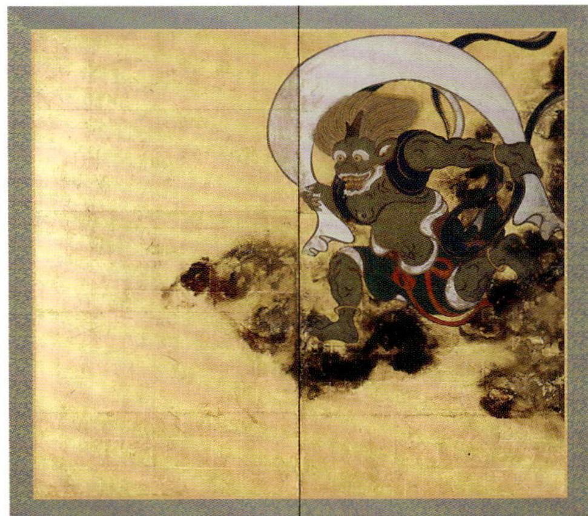

❽ Interpretations

The composition has led to various interpretations. Yamane Yûzô, for example, saw a perfect balance of opposites: red and white, vigour and reticence, a dualism that may be found in the character of the artist himself. Kōno Motoaki saw the oppositional forces as derived from Tawaraya Sōtatsu's *Wind God and Thunder God* (left), giving expression to Kōrin's competition with a great artist of the past. And finally, Kobayashi Taichirô has suggested that the white and red plum trees and the river represent the artist, his mistress San and his friend Nakamura Kuranosuke, who had embarked on a three-way love affair.[60]

↑ Tawaraya Sōtatsu, *Wind God and Thunder God Screens*, 17th century. Ink and colour on gold-foiled paper, each 169.8 × 154.5 cm, 66¾ × 60¾ in.

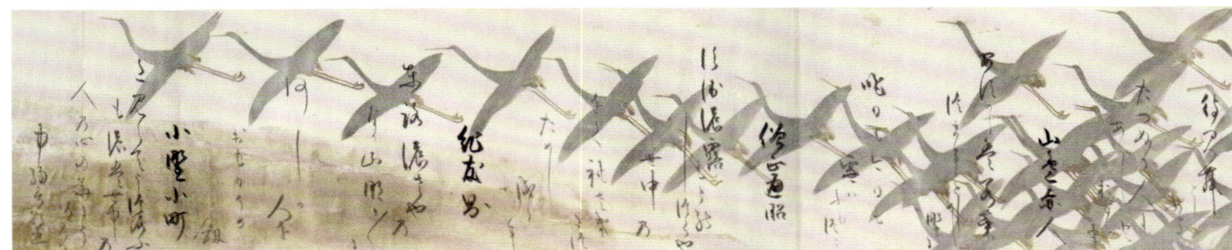

← Tawaraya Sōtatsu and Hon'ami Kōetsu, *Thirty-six Immortals of Poetry with Cranes*, 17th century. Gold and silver paint on paper, length: 130 cm, 51¼ in.

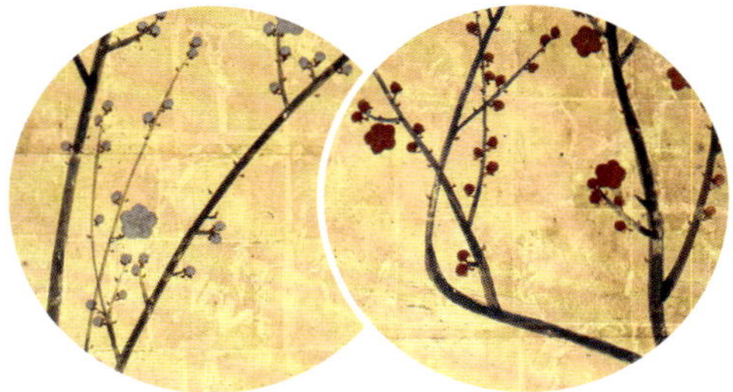

❾ Flat

There is no shading in this work: each blossom is rendered in a flat colour.

❿ Rinpa

The Rinpa painting style dates to the Edo period (1603–1868) and is defined by the radical simplification of shapes, careful placement and arrangement of compositions, bright colours, gold and silver fields, and a poetic stylization of forms. The term itself derives from the last three letters of Kōrin's name, showing how synonymous he was with the style.

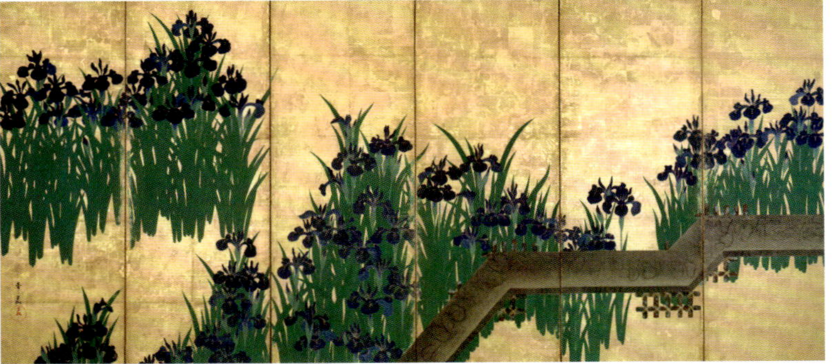

Irises at Yatsuhashi (Eight Bridges), after 1709. Ink, colour and gold leaf on paper, overall 179.1 × 371.5 cm, 70½ × 146¼ in.

⓫ Reinvigoration

Kōrin was inspired by the work of Tawaraya Sōtatsu, from whom he learned how to simplify forms and use both empty space and repetition for decorative effect.

⓬ Gold

There is no landscape setting, just a flat, gold surface, which gives a richly decorative and dreamlike feeling to the scene.

⓭ Function

The screen would have been used to divide or decorate a room, known as a *byōbu*. They had been popular as far back as the Muromachi period (1336–1573), and usually contained representations of nature in temples, castles and palaces.

⓮ Buyers

The Rinpa style was popular from the beginning of the *bakufu* (a military-run government), and its patrons were from the Samurai, aristocratic and merchant classes. *Red and White Plum Blossoms* was bought by Okada Mokichi in 1954 from the descendants of the *daimyô* (feudal overlords) of Tsugaru, a city in Aomori prefecture. It is in the collection of the MOA Museum of Art in Atami, Japan, which contains Okada's extensive art collection.

LINKED PRACTITIONERS

RINPA SCHOOL:	GOLD:	CONTINUING INSPIRATION:
Hon'ami Kōetsu (1558–1637), JAPAN	*Giotto di Bondone* (1267–1337), ITALY	*Kayama Matazō* (1927–2004), JAPAN
Ogata Kenzan (1663–1743), JAPAN	*Benvenuto Cellini* (1500–1571), ITALY	*Koichi Nabatame* (born 1933), JAPAN
Sakai Hōitsu (1761–1829), JAPAN	*Gustav Klimt* (1862–1918), AUSTRIA	*Nobuyoshi Watanabe* (born 1941), JAPAN
Suzuki Kiitsu (1796–1858), JAPAN	*Jeff Koons* (born 1955), USA	*Jun'ichi Hayashi* (born 1943), JAPAN
Kamisaka Sekka (1866–1942), JAPAN	*Marc Quinn* (born 1964), UK	*Yuji Tezuka* (born 1953), JAPAN

29. # Enlightened Minds

The subject of this work by Joseph Wright of Derby (1734–1797), painted in the city with which he has become synonymous, was unusual at the time. While most artists chose to paint biblical scenes, landscapes or portraits of the great and the good, Wright chose to turn the scientific discoveries of the age into an art form.

His decision to paint scientific progress reflects his contact with members of the Lunar Society, a group based in Birmingham that counted businessmen, inventors and engineers like Josiah Wedgwood, James Watt and Matthew Boulton among its members, and which would play a significant role in the inception of the Industrial Revolution a century later. Wright's scene illuminates the ideas and ambitions of a unique age of innovation.

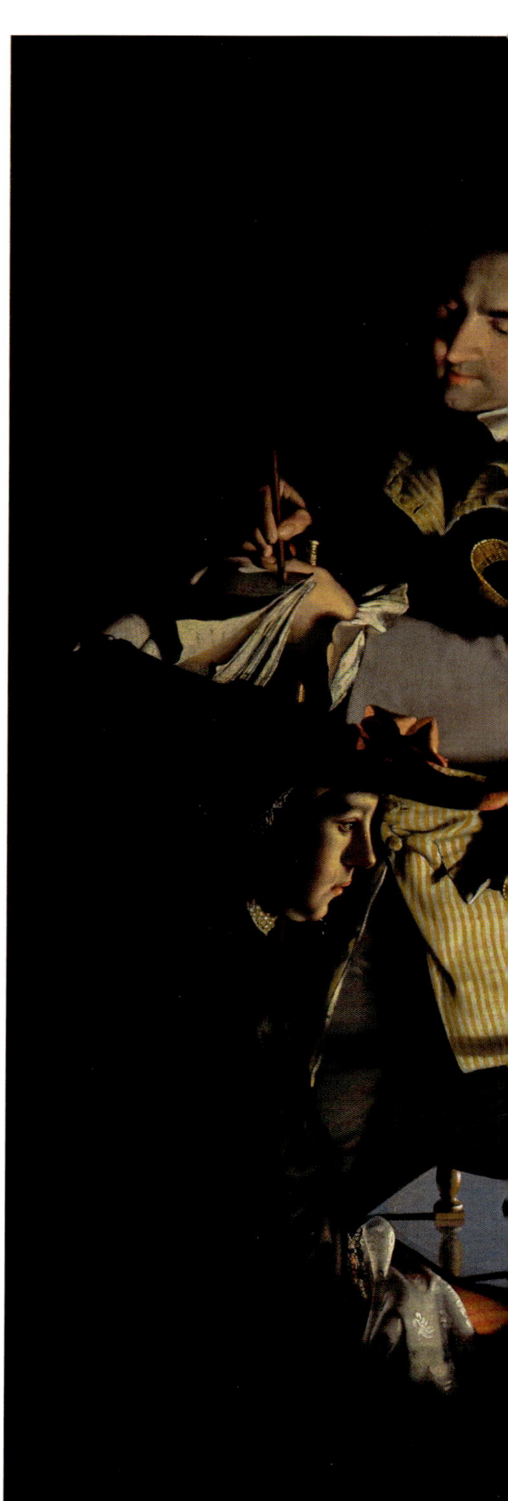

Oil on canvas
147.3 × 203.2 cm, 58 × 80 in.
Derby Museum and Art Gallery

Joseph Wright of Derby
A Philosopher Lecturing on the Orrery
c. 1764–66

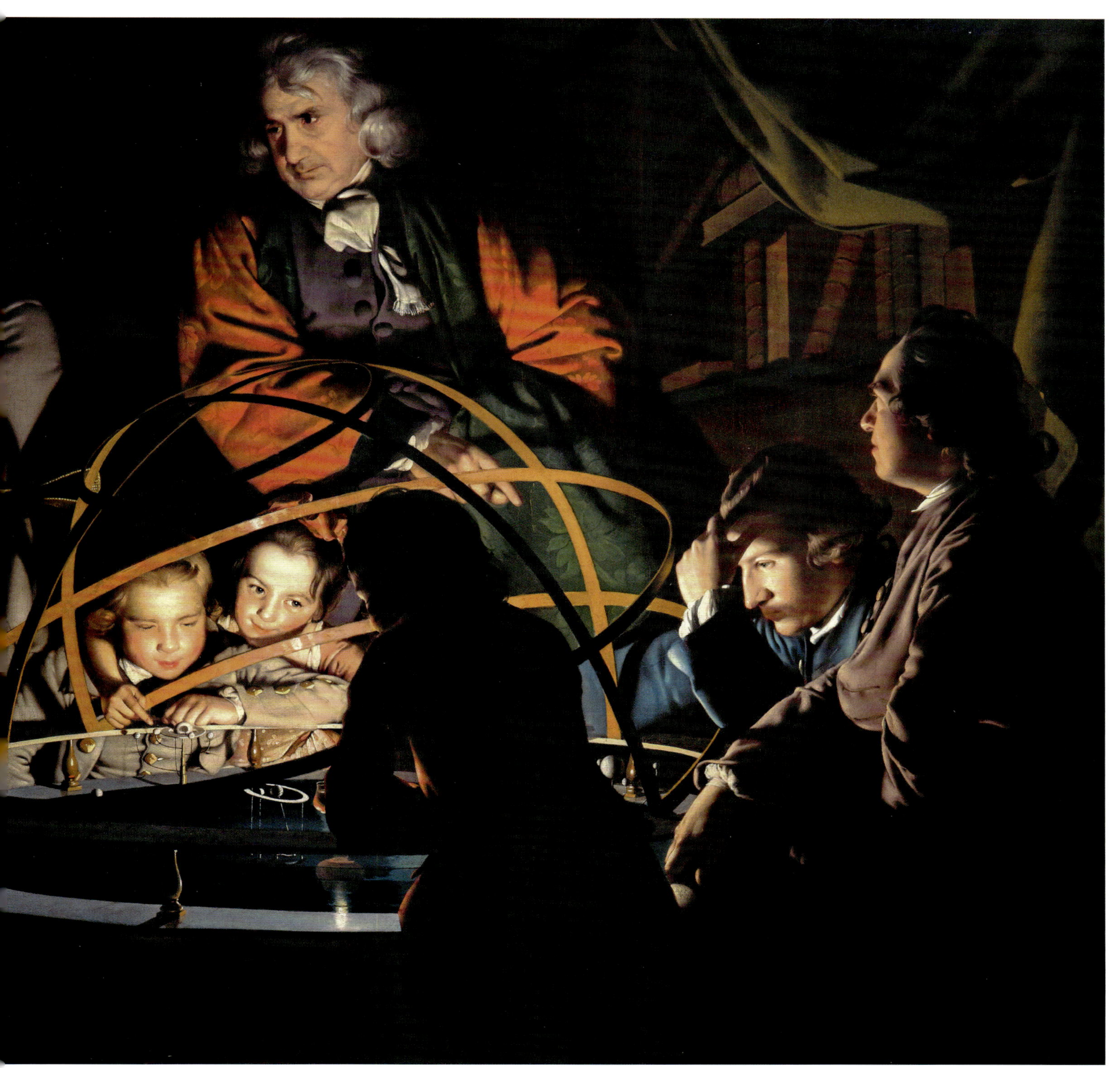

❶ Enlightenment

The Enlightenment was an intellectual movement in the 17th and 18th centuries that valued human reason over faith-based beliefs. Superstitions were displaced by scientific method, logic and explanations produced by data. Previously, an eclipse would have been seen as an act of God or the work of the Devil, but a scientific instrument like an orrery showed that it was governed by the positions of the planets in relation to the sun. Wright's style resembles that of Caravaggio (right) – except that Wright is depicting a scientific marvel, not a religious one.

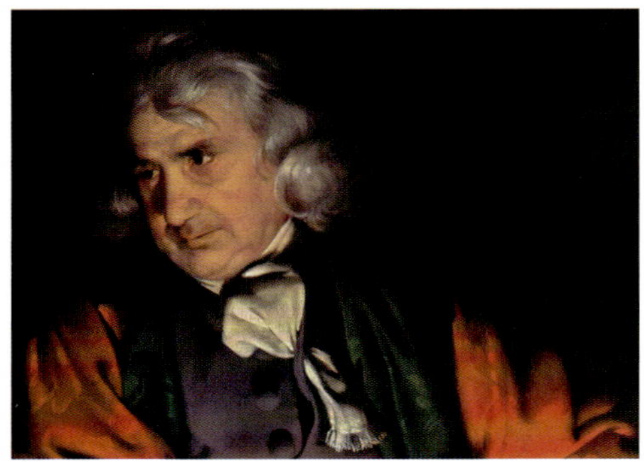

❷ Teacher

Wright has placed the main figure – the lecturer – at the top and centre of the composition. By doing so, he has organized the scene into a triangular formation. Compositions like this are common in art (see pp. 112–15, and 124–7).

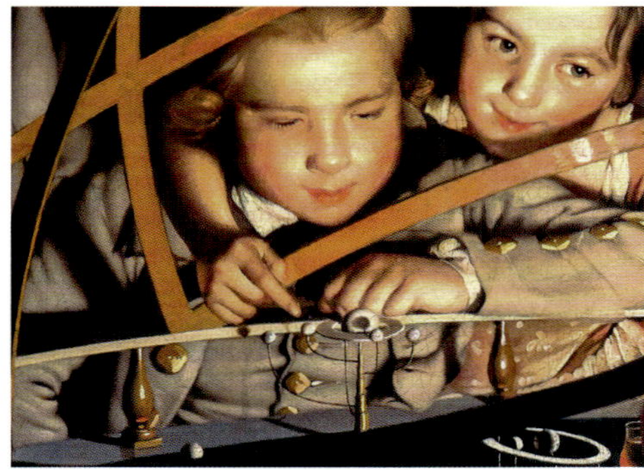

❸ Centre

The closest figures to the light source are the children, mesmerized by what is in front of them. We can see two faces; a third child stands with his back to us. The positioning of children at the centre of the painting and adults at the outer edges suggests that the composition is also defined by concentric circles.

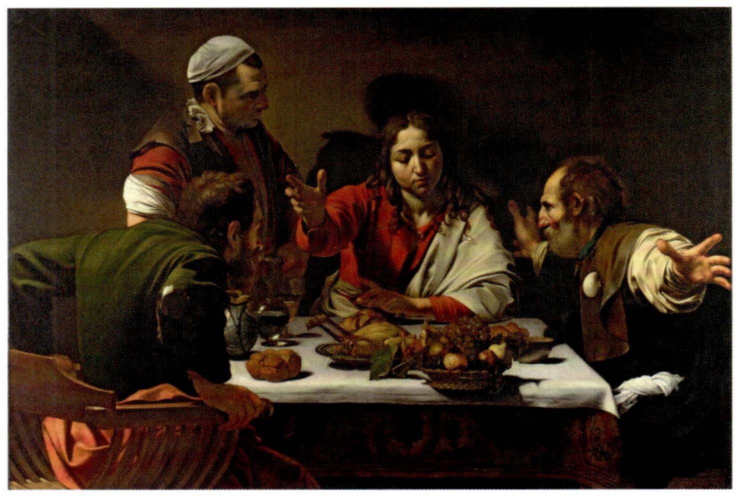

Caravaggio, *The Supper at Emmaus*, 1601.
Oil and tempera on canvas, 141 × 196.2 cm, 55½ × 77¼ in.

❹ Orbits

The girl in the centre of the scene points to the orbit of Saturn's moons on the orrery, while her young companion looks on.[61] Meanwhile, the faces of the other spectators are like the orbiting planets themselves, catching the light depending on their proximity and position in relation to the light source: a gas lamp on the table in front of them.

❺ Characters

Wright has included a variety of emotional responses to the central event. The woman on the left and the man in blue opposite her stare in rapt concentration at the mechanism in front of them. The man at the far right looks sceptically at the lecturer, while yet another makes notes. Together they frame the action and provide a dramatic narrative.

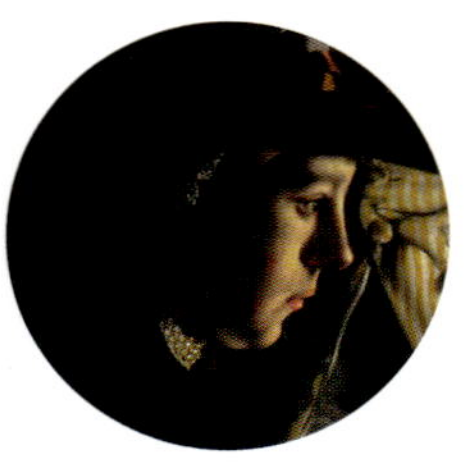

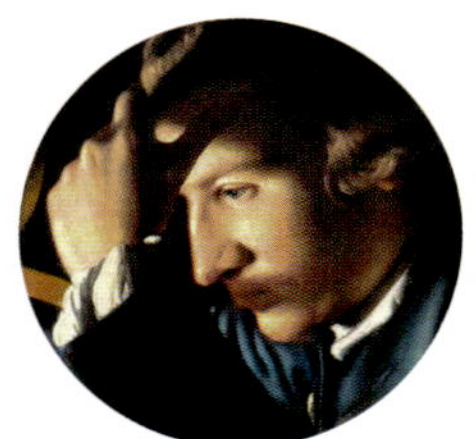

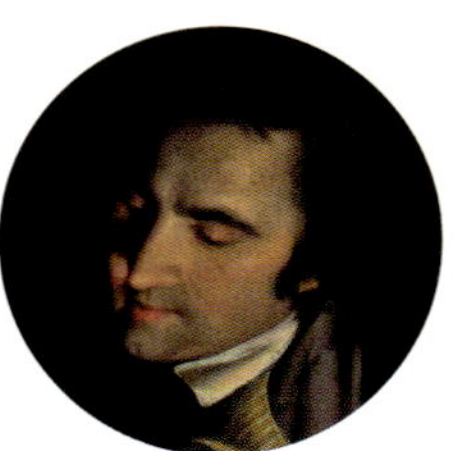

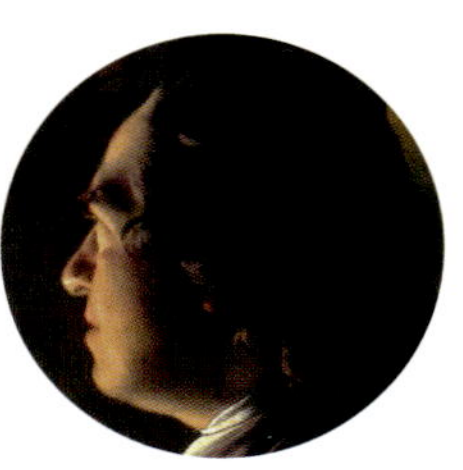

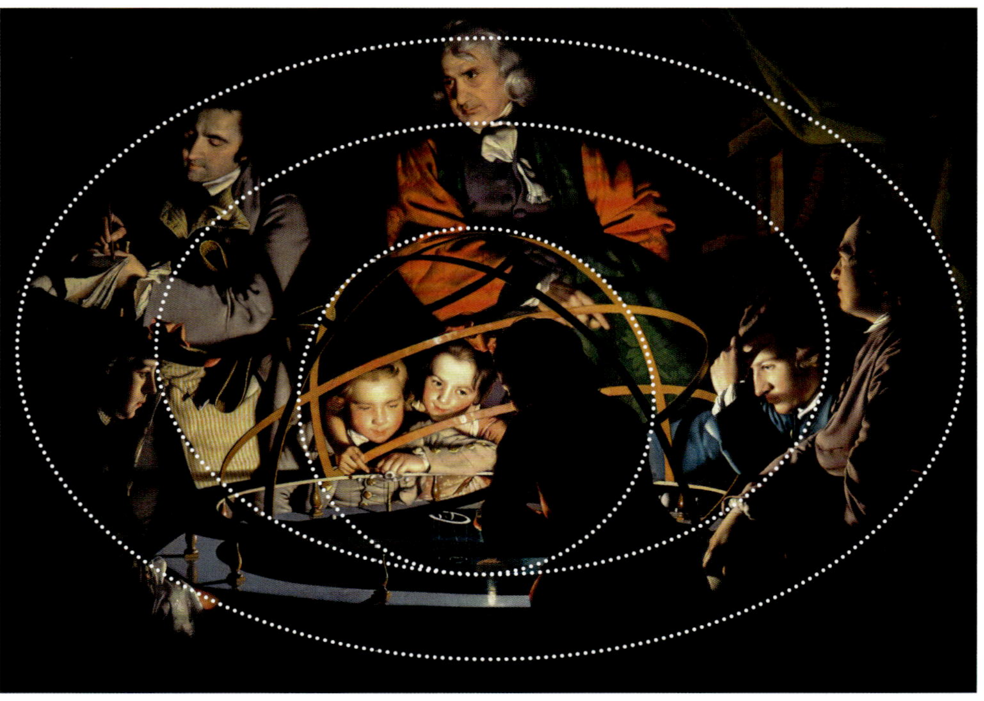

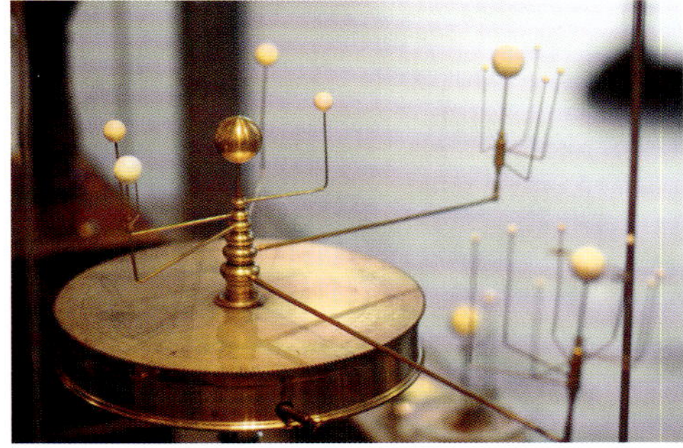

Benjamin Martin, Planetarium, *c.* 1765. Ivory, brass and steel, 45 × 53 × 33 cm, 17¾ × 20¾ × 13 in.

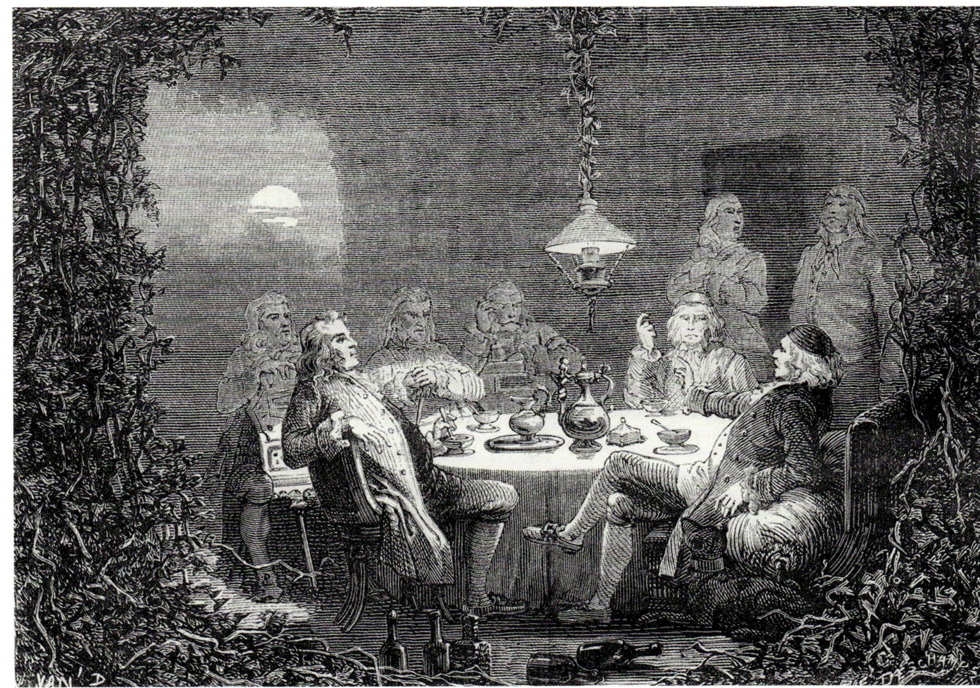

The Lunar Society, from *Les Merveilles de la science*, 1870

❻ Orrery

An orrery is a mechanical model of the universe, with a hand crank to rotate the various planets. It is named after the 4th Earl of Orrery, for whom clockmaker George Graham made one of the earliest modern versions in 1713.

❼ Science

Scientific demonstrations were a popular form of entertainment in England in the mid-18th century. One group – the Lunar Society – met every full moon in the city of Birmingham. Among its members were the pottery entrepreneur Josiah Wedgwood and the chemist Joseph Priestley, along with many other businessmen and engineers who laid the foundations for the Industrial Revolution.

❽ Theatre

The action is close to the picture plane, so that we feel like participants in the scene. The darkness adds to the drama, as does the addition of a green curtain, which has the effect of turning the lecture hall into a stage set.

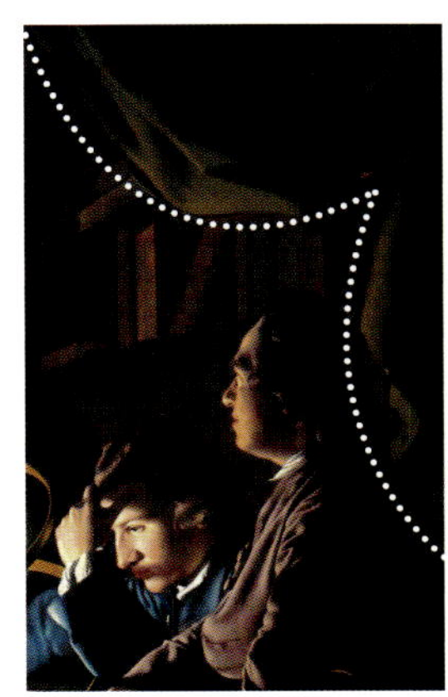

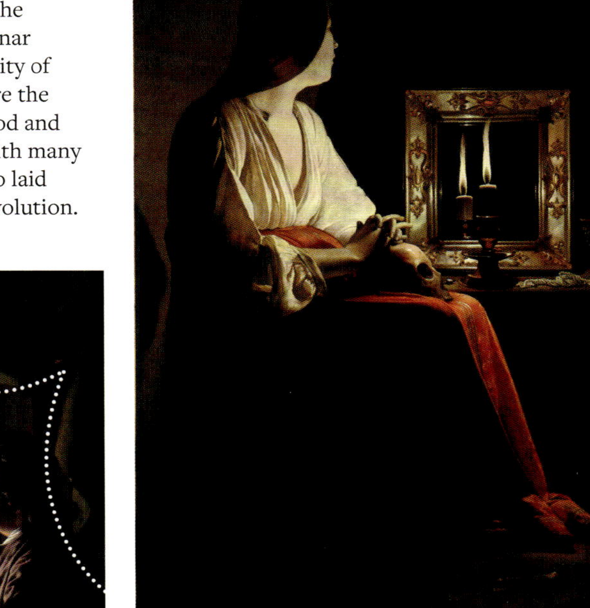

Georges de La Tour, *The Penitent Magdalen*, *c.* 1640. Oil on canvas, 133.4 × 102.2 cm, 52½ × 40¼ in.

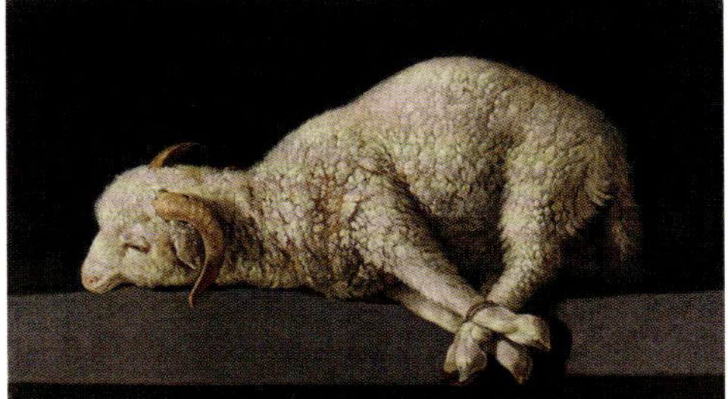

Francisco de Zurbarán, *Agnus Dei* (*The Lamb of God*), *c.* 1635–40. Oil on canvas, 37.3 × 62 cm, 14¾ × 24½ in.

❾ Tenebrism

Lit only by a single gas lamp, the illuminated faces against the black background create an intense atmosphere. This contrast of light and dark is called chiaroscuro, but when it is used with such intensity it is known as 'tenebrism', a technique used to great effect by artists such as Francisco de Zurbarán (above) and Georges de La Tour (left) in the 17th century. You can almost see the light shifting as the lamp gutters and spits with the gusts of air.

LINKED PRACTITIONERS

SCIENCE IN ART:

Leonardo da Vinci (1452–1519), ITALY
Tomás Saraceno (born 1973), ARGENTINA
Luke Jerram (born 1974), UK
Katie Paterson (born 1981), UK
Fabian Oefner (born 1984), SWITZERLAND

TENEBRISM:

Caravaggio (1571–1610), ITALY
Adam de Coster (*c.* 1586–1643), BELGIUM
Georges de La Tour (1593–1652), FRANCE
Artemisia Gentileschi (1593–*c.* 1656), ITALY
Francisco de Zurbarán (1598–1664), SPAIN

BRITISH ARTISTS OF THE 18TH CENTURY:

William Hogarth (1697–1764), UK
Sir Joshua Reynolds (1723–1792), UK
George Stubbs (1724–1806), UK
Thomas Gainsborough (1727–1788), UK
Henry Fuseli (1741–1825), SWITZERLAND/UK

30. Making a Splash

In 1782 Élisabeth Vigée Le Brun (1755–1842) painted a self-portrait that would be her breakthrough work, one that would assert her character, challenge tradition and showcase her superior skills with the paintbrush. The portrait, which was submitted to the Salon in 1783, had the desired effect, astounding visitors with its modern style and technical brilliance.

It was notoriously difficult for women to be admitted to the French Royal Academy: only four women could be members at any one time. But when Vigée Le Brun's self-portrait was exhibited, it was electrifying and she was admitted to the academy that same year. Vigée Le Brun was a favoured artist at the court of Louis XVI, and had achieved notoriety for her many portraits of his unpopular queen, Marie Antoinette. Following the French Revolution in 1789, she left Paris for over a decade, travelling across Europe with her daughter as a renowned, if sometimes controversial, artist/celebrity.

Oil on canvas
97.8 × 70.5 cm, 38½ × 27¾ in.
National Gallery, London

Élisabeth Vigée Le Brun

Self-portrait in a Straw Hat

1782

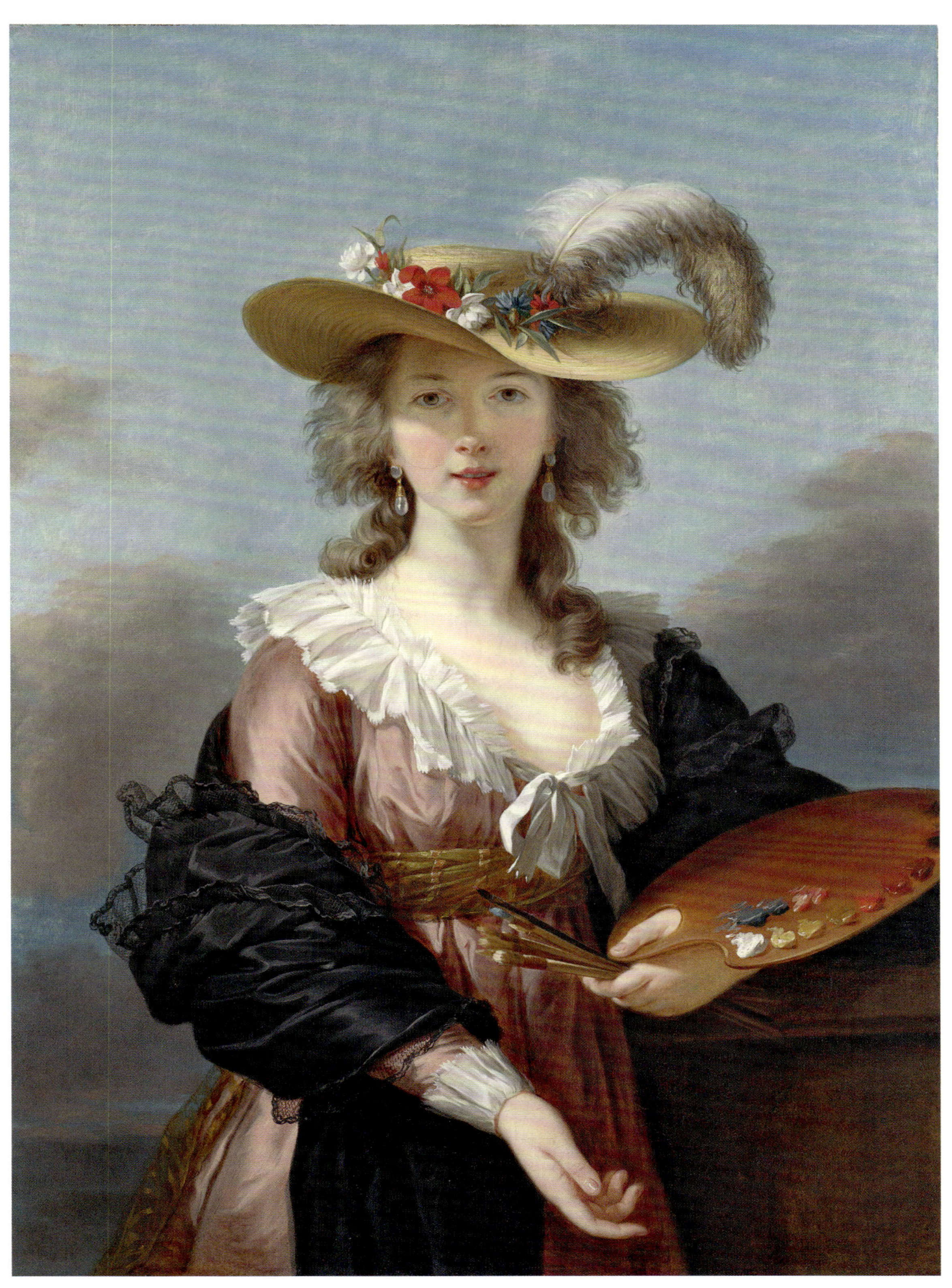

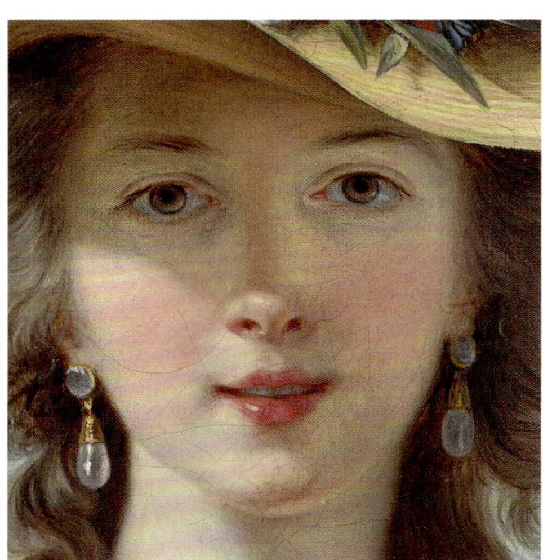

❶ A frank gaze

The sitter looks directly at the viewer, without arrogance or superiority. Her lower body is rotated subtly to the side, so that she appears to be turning casually, as if to greet us.

❷ Emulation

Vigée Le Brun's masterful treatment of light is also an act of homage to Peter Paul Rubens, whose work she saw first hand during a trip to Flanders in 1781. In particular she admired his *Portrait of Susanna Lunden* (right), which she had seen in the collection of the connoisseur Jean Michel van Havre, later writing:

> *[Its] great effect resides in the two different kinds of illumination which simple daylight and the light of the sun create ... This painting ... has inspired me to the point that I made my own portrait ... in search of the same effect.*[62]

❸ Teeth on display

The open-mouthed smile is a common sight in modern photographs, but was unusual in portraits painted in Europe before the 19th century. This is partly because of the frequently poor state of people's teeth in the past, but also because it is difficult to capture convincingly an unguarded, open-mouthed smile in art – something that Vigée Le Brun was able to master.

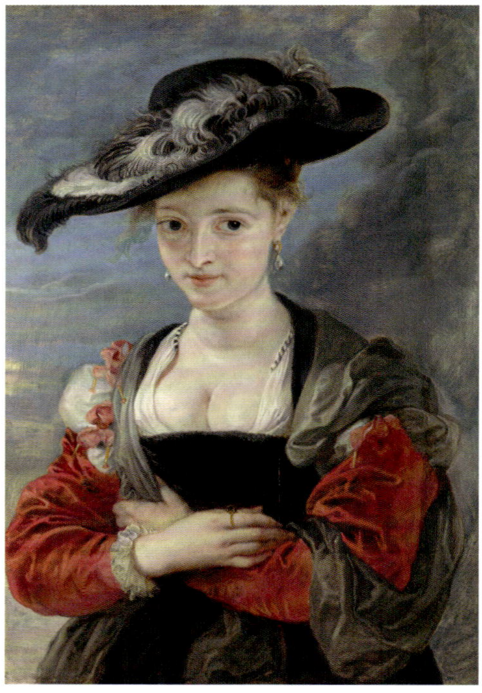

↑ Peter Paul Rubens, *Portrait of Susanna Lunden(?)*, 1622–25. Oil on oak, 79 × 54.6 cm, 31 × 21½ in.

↓ Joseph Wright of Derby, *An Experiment on a Bird in the Air Pump*, 1768. Oil on canvas, 183 × 244 cm, 72 × 96 in.

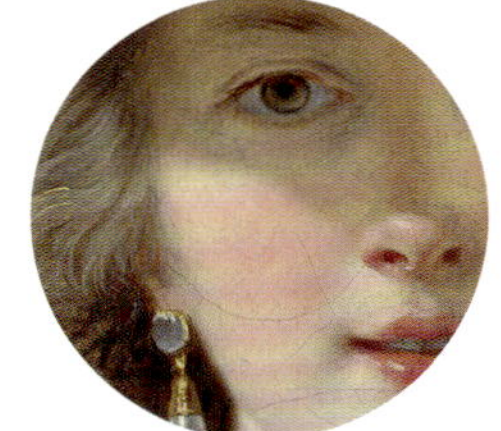

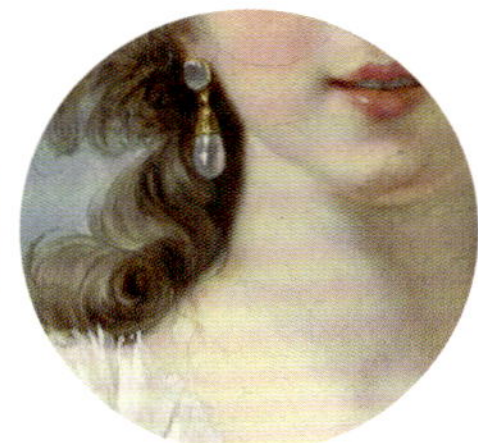

❹ Light

Another of her skills that the artist wished to showcase was her ability to handle the realistic fall of light on textures and forms. The light does not come from one angle alone: sunlight lights up the left side of the face, with the underside of her chin also gently illuminated by light reflected upwards by surrounding objects, such as her earrings.

❺ Alteration

Comparison of Rubens's portrait of Susanna Lunden and Vigée Le Brun's self-portrait shows some telling differences. Whereas Rubens looks at the female form from an elevated vantage point, representing the sitter with a passive facial expression and body language, Vigée Le Brun has painted herself as much more upright, assertive and active.

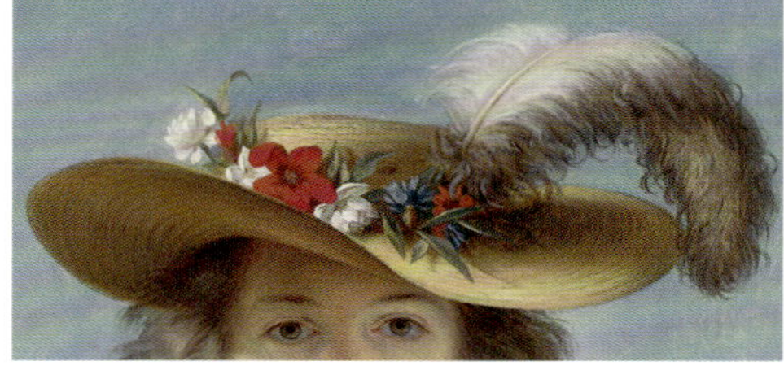

❻ Natural world

In the hat is an array of wildflowers alongside an ostrich feather. The freshly picked flowers indicate that Vigée Le Brun has been out in the meadows, engaging with nature.

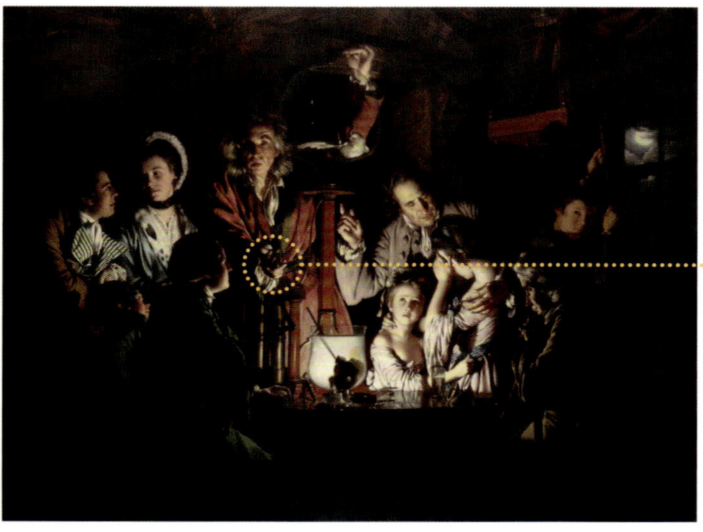

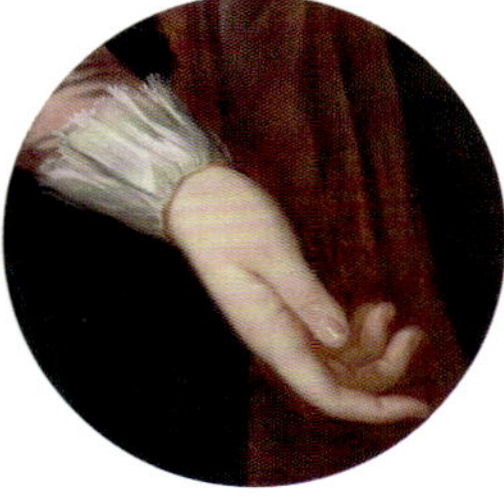

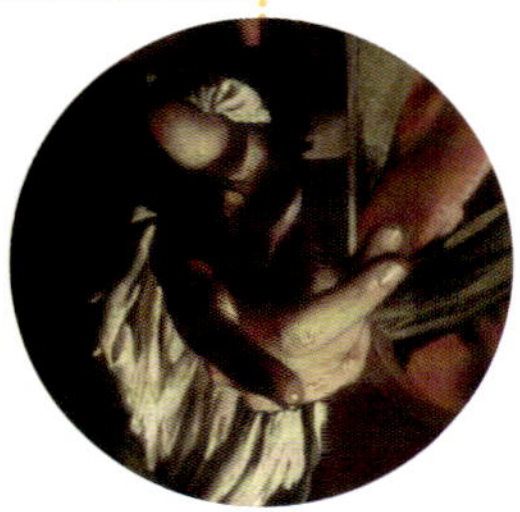

❼ Gesture

The hand unfurls at the base of the composition in a gesture that indicates an invitation to interaction and conversation. It is similar to the orator's gesture in the *Emperor as Philosopher, probably Marcus Aurelius* (pp. 28–31), and was a recognizable signal of invitation in art, visible in such paintings as Joseph Wright of Derby's *An Experiment on a Bird in the Air Pump* (left).

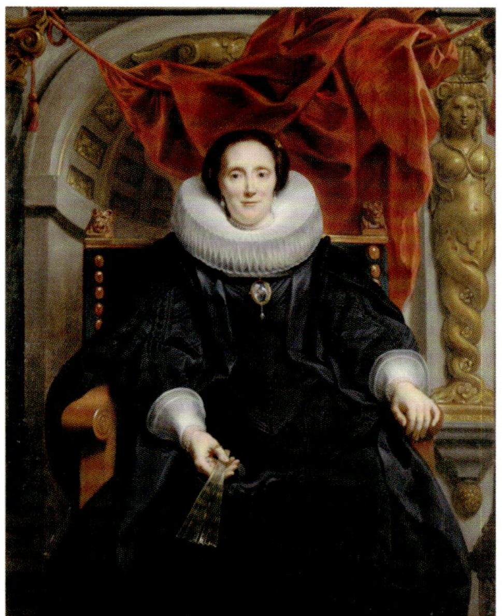

Jacob Jordaens, *Portrait of Catharina Behaghel*, 1635. Oil on canvas, 152 × 118 cm, 59¾ × 46½ in.

8 Painter to the Queen

Vigée Le Brun and Marie Antoinette met in 1778, an encounter that would lead to a mutually fruitful relationship, with the artist eventually producing over 30 portraits of the French queen (see below).

9 Influences

In 1781 Vigée Le Brun travelled to Flanders to study the art of the Low Countries. The self-portrait reveals how she adapted ideas from the past, including the hand gestures used by the Flemish painter Jacob Jordaens in his *Portrait of Catharina Behaghel* (left).

10 Clothing

Vigée Le Brun often portrayed women in a looser, informal style of dress called *à la grecque*. She herself wears a chemise dress with a low neckline and a lace ruffle fastened with a ribbon, a combination known as *parfait contentment*.[63] Although sitters in the 18th century were often shown in powdered wigs, the artist painted her hair falling freely to her shoulders.

11 Aging naturally

This radical embracing of relaxed informality was shared by Marie Antoinette, who even built a rustic hamlet at the Palace of Versailles so that she could live an unpretentious countryside existence. The 18th-century philosopher Jean-Jacques Rousseau wrote that humanity was at its best in a state of nature.

12 Composition

The artist positioned herself centrally within the composition. To avoid it looking too static, she introduced diagonal accents through light and shadow, and the position of the arms. A visual echo is also created between her palette, with its colourful blobs of paint, and her hat.

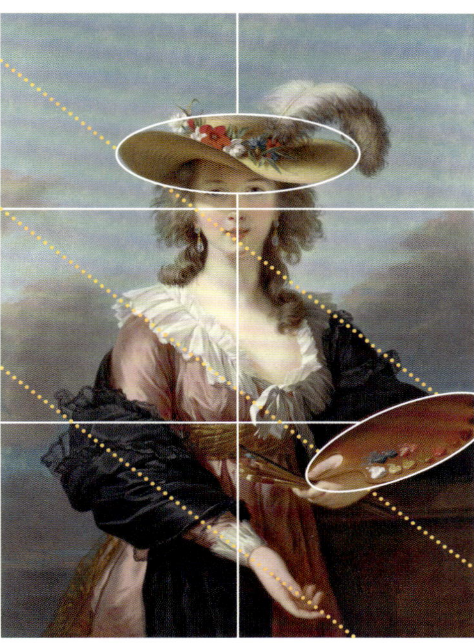

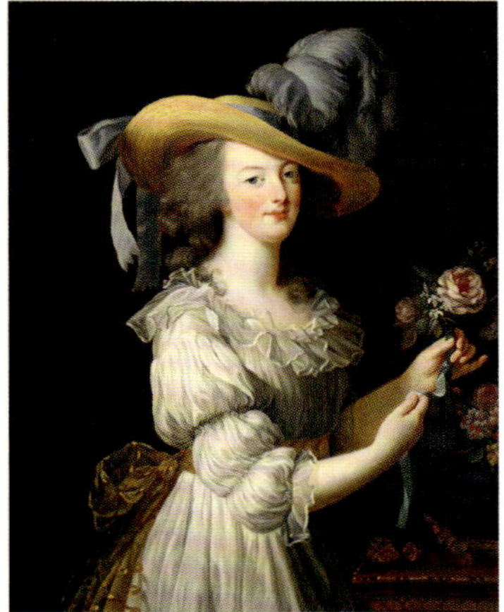

Marie Antoinette in a Chemise Dress (detail), 1783. Oil on canvas, 89.8 × 72 cm, 35¼ × 28¼ in.

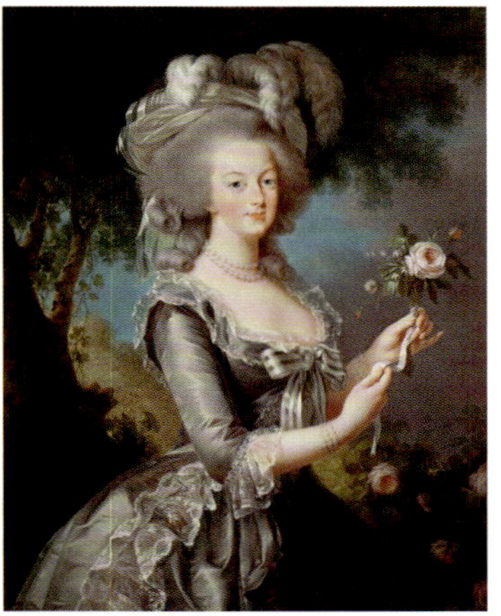

Marie Antoinette with a Rose (detail), 1783. Oil on canvas, 116.8 × 88.9 cm, 46 × 35 in.

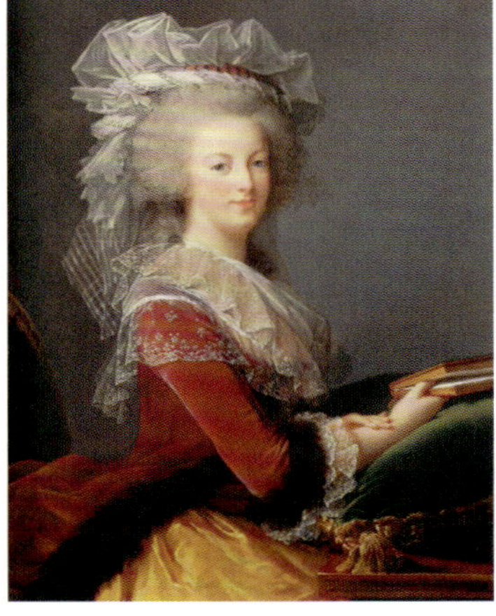

Portrait of Marie Antoinette, 1785. Oil on canvas, 93.3 × 74.8 cm, 36¾ × 29½ in.

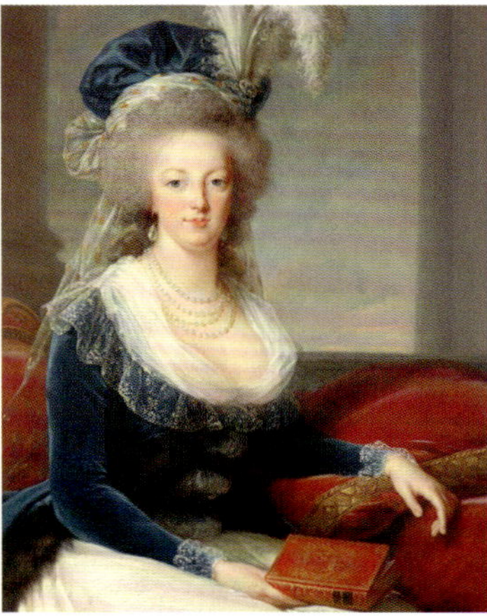

Marie Antoinette (detail), 1788. Oil on canvas, 271 × 195 cm, 106¾ × 76¾ in.

LINKED PRACTITIONERS

FRENCH ARTISTS OF THE 18TH CENTURY:

Jean-Marc Nattier (1685–1766), FRANCE
Jean-Baptiste-Siméon Chardin (1699–1779), FRANCE
François Boucher (1703–1770), FRANCE
Jean-Honoré Fragonard (1732–1806), FRANCE
Adélaïde Labille-Guiard (1749–1803), FRANCE

FEMALE SELF-PORTRAITS:

Artemisia Gentileschi (1593–c. 1656), ITALY
Angelika Kauffmann (1741–1807), SWITZERLAND/UK
Paula Modersohn-Becker (1876–1907), GERMANY
Frida Kahlo (1907–1954), MEXICO
Leonora Carrington (1917–2011), UK/MEXICO

ARTISTS INSPIRED BY PETER PAUL RUBENS:

Jean-Antoine Watteau (1684–1721), FRANCE
Eugène Delacroix (1798–1863), FRANCE
Paul Cézanne (1839–1906), FRANCE
Pablo Picasso (1881–1973), SPAIN/FRANCE
Jenny Saville (born 1970), UK

31. Art Crime

On 13 July 1793, a 24-year-old woman named Charlotte Corday walked into the Paris apartment of Jean-Paul Marat, a journalist and radical supporter of the French Revolution, drew a butcher's knife from her corset and stabbed him in the chest while he was at work in his bath. This was a calculated murder with a political motive.

A defender of the *sans-culottes*, Marat promoted the use of extreme aggression as an instrument for political change in his newspaper *L'Ami du peuple*, stating at one point that 'liberty must be established by violence'. His friend Jacques-Louis David (1748–1825) recast Marat from victim to noble hero, and turned a hurried and messy homicide into a grand and persuasive work of art – an effect he achieved through a skilful combination of style, composition, text, lighting and iconography.

Oil on canvas
165 × 128 cm, 65 × 50½ in.
Royal Museum of Fine Arts of Belgium, Brussels

Jacques-Louis David
The Death of Marat
1793

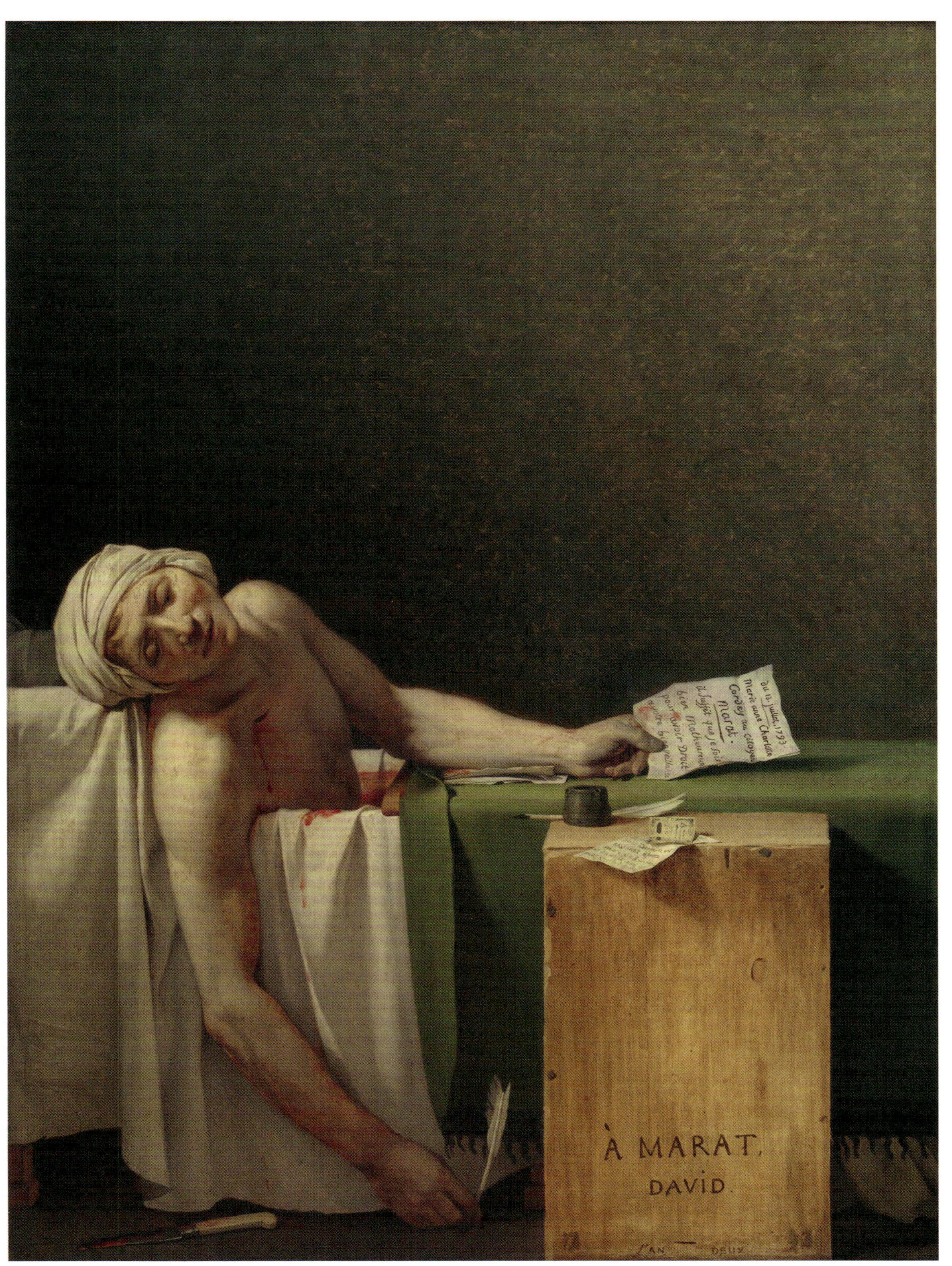

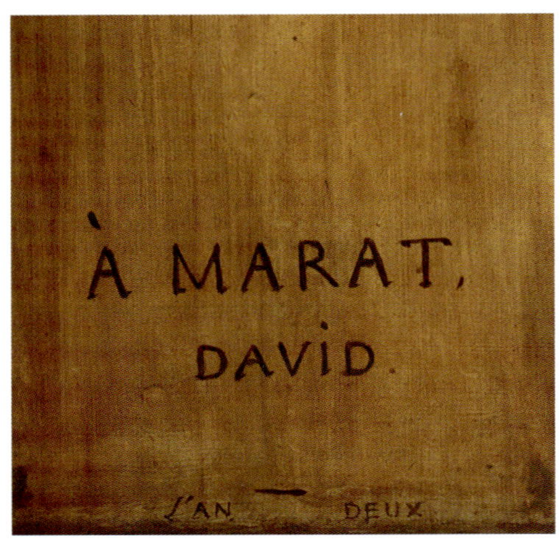

❶ Word and image #1

Words are integral to this painting, with image and text working in tandem to create meaning. David painted his own name on a wooden crate, the closest object to the spectator, giving it greater prominence. The words ('To Marat / David') reflect the personal relationship between the artist and his subject. The date below (*l'an deux*, or 'year two') alludes to the radical changes that occurred following the French Revolution; in this case, the overhaul of time itself. In the new Republican Calendar, 1789 was established as the new year zero. The crate resembles a tombstone, memorializing Marat's passing.[64]

❷ Revolutionary art

David was a member of the Jacobins, a radical political group, and an ardent supporter of the revolution. He voted for the execution of the former king, Louis XVI, and was friends with Maximilien Robespierre, one of the ringleaders behind the murder of tens of thousands of aristocrats during the Reign of Terror. The painting is a declaration of David's radical political stance, as it mourns the death of one of the revolution's key personalities.

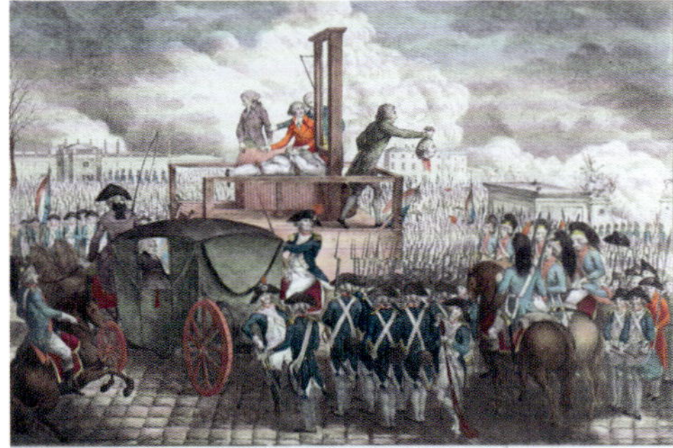

Execution of King Louis XVI, c. 1793. Hand-coloured etching, 43.5 × 58.5 cm, 17 × 23 in.

Michelangelo, *Pietà*, 1499. Marble, height: 174 cm, 68½ in.

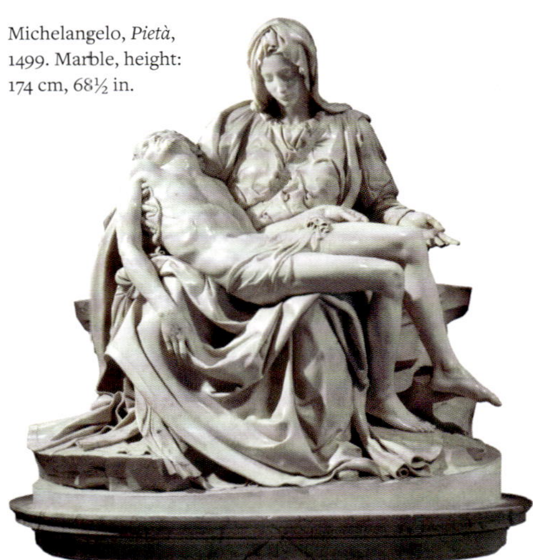

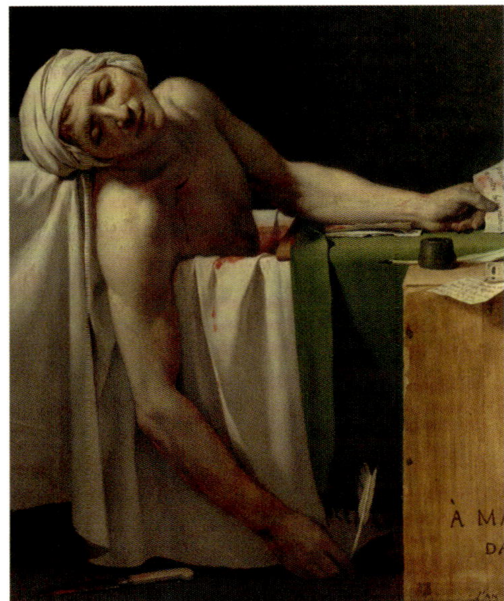

❸ The saintly Marat

After the revolution, there was a move to de-Christianize French society by deconsecrating churches; the famous Gothic cathedral of Notre Dame was renamed the 'Temple of Reason', for example. David appears to have portrayed Marat as a replacement for Christ in this new, secularized world, with the arrangement of the murdered journalist's body based on images of Christ by Michelangelo (top) and Caravaggio. The painting was even displayed on a temporary altar in the courtyard of the Louvre.

❹ Tainted art?

Is it acceptable to celebrate a work of art that venerates someone who championed the use of extreme violence for political gain?

❺ Word and image #2

On top of the crate is a banknote and a letter, which reads: 'You are to give this banknote to the mother of five whose husband died for his country'. David has placed it in a prominent location to persuade us of Marat's generosity.

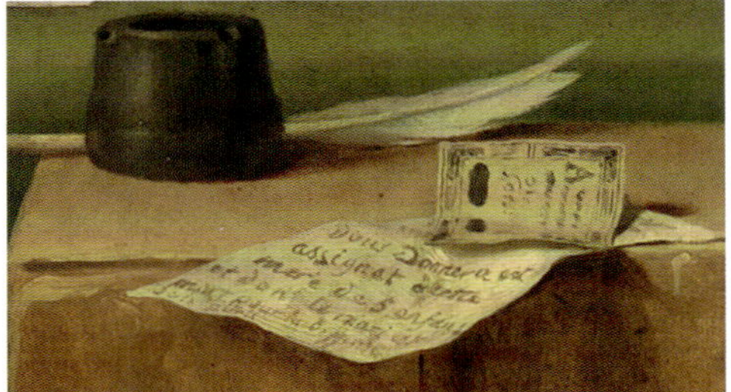

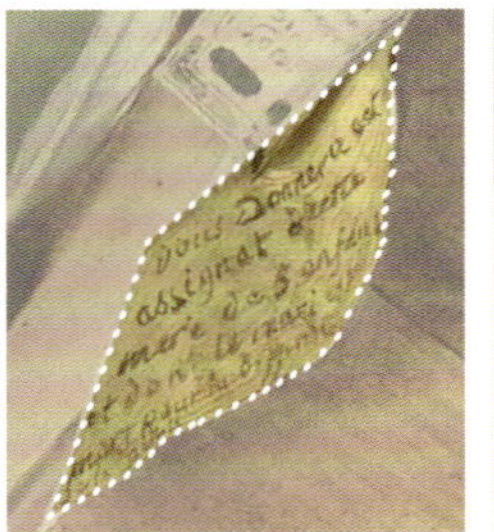

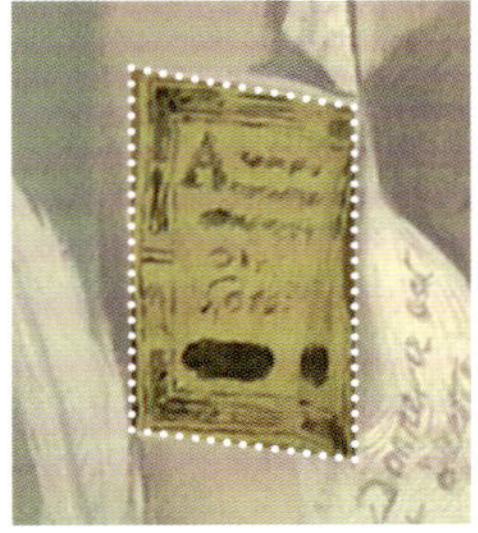

❻ Words and image #3

In Marat's bloodstained left hand is another letter, which reads: 'July 13 1793: Marie-Anne-Charlotte Corday to citizen Marat. It is enough for me to be truly wretched to have the right to your kindness.' The words are a fabrication by David to portray Corday as a ruthless and manipulative murderer.

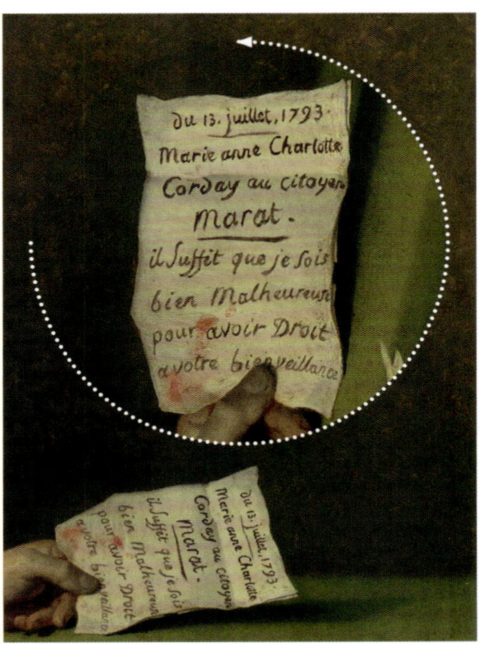

❼ Friend of the people?

Marat was physician, writer, politician and journalist, who used his position as editor of the newspaper *L'Ami du peuple* to urge violence against moderate factions of the post-revolutionary government during the Reign of Terror. He once wrote that 'liberty must be established by violence'.

❽ Murder most foul

Charlotte Corday believed that Marat was inciting widespread violence through journalism, and had travelled from Caen to kill him and thus end the bloodshed. She described herself as Judith, and her destiny was to slay the modern-day Holofernes, as represented by Marat (see also pp. 112–15). Corday pretended to be bringing Marat news of counter-revolutionary fighting in order to gain entry to his room.

❾ Empty space

The upper half of the painting is completely blank. It creates a solemn void and redirects our gaze to the figure below.

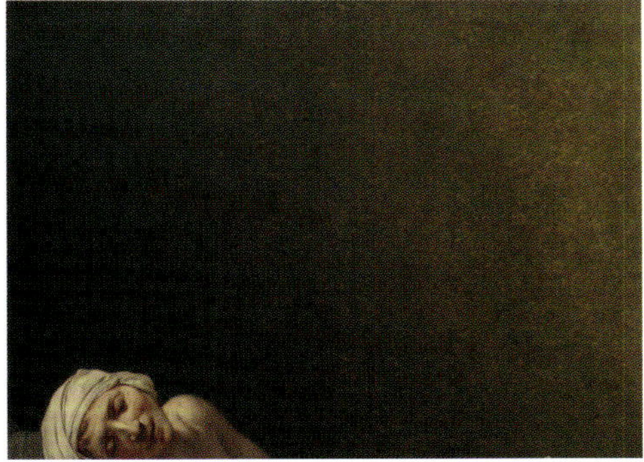

❿ Perfect body, perfect soul

The body of Marat seems flawless and smooth, like a marble statue. In reality, he suffered from a debilitating skin disease, which required him to bathe in a medicinal bath with his head wrapped in a vinegar-soaked turban.

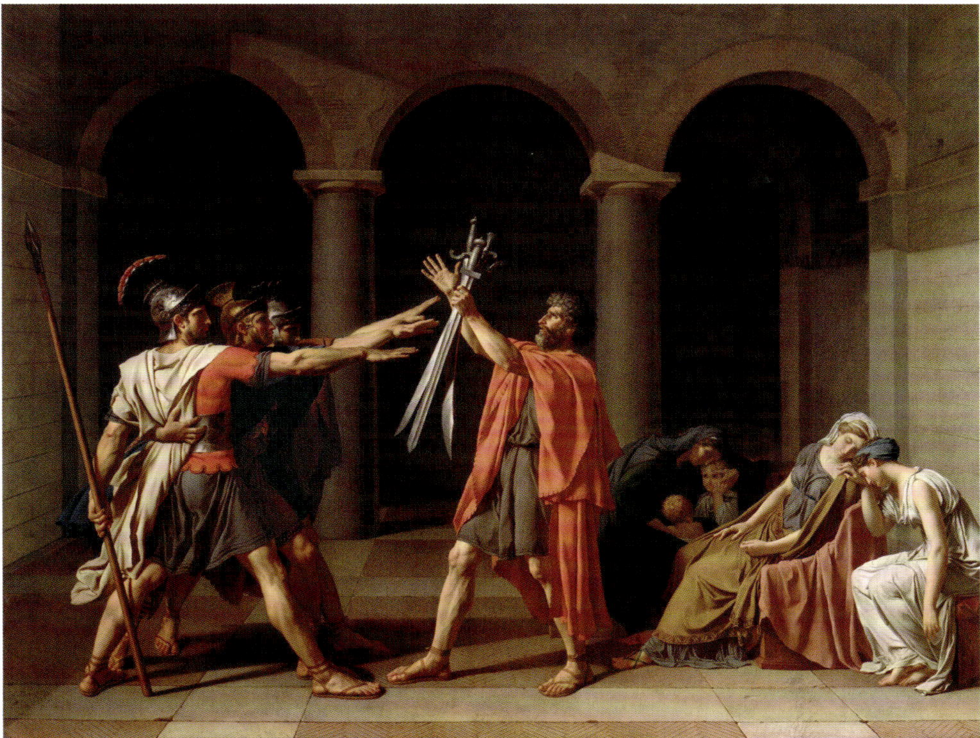

↑ *The Oath of the Horatii*, 1784. Oil on canvas, 330 × 425 cm, 130 × 167¼ in.

→ *The Death of Socrates*, 1787. Oil on canvas, 129.5 × 196.2 cm, 51 × 77¼ in.

⓫ Mightier than the sword

Marat is shown on the cusp of death, still holding a quill pen. The pen is juxtaposed with the knife that was used to kill him. David deliberately paired the two objects in this section of the painting to highlight the different characters of the drama: Marat, the defenceless writer, and Corday, the cold-blooded killer.

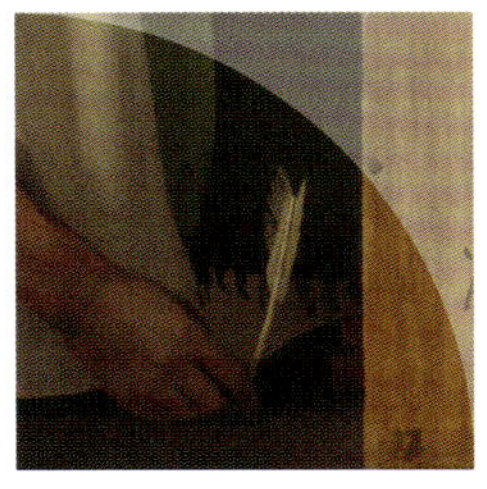

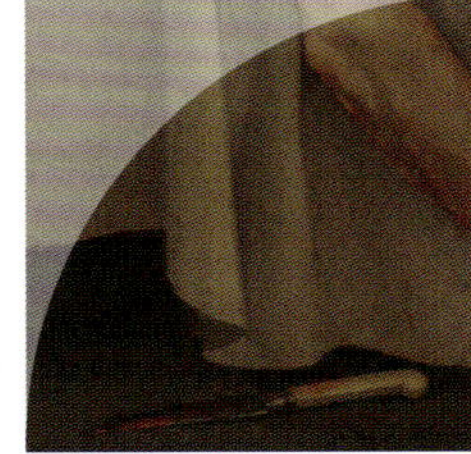

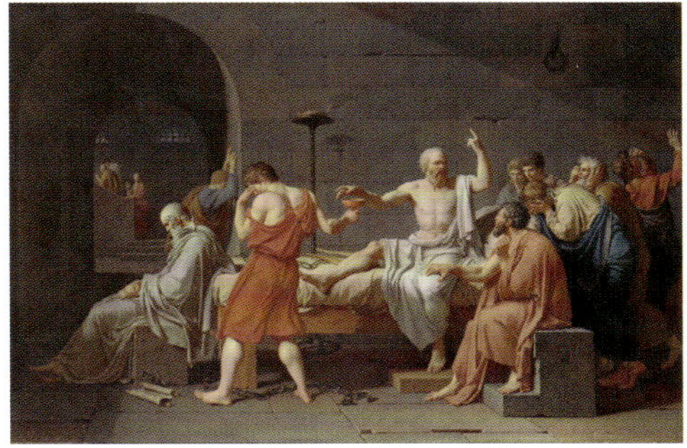

⓬ Neoclassicism

David is strongly associated with Neoclassicism, which drew inspiration from the visual style and ethics of ancient Greece and Rome. His work is characterized by simplicity, smooth surfaces and bold, austere compositions, coupled with heroic subject matter. This can be seen to great effect in *The Oath of the Horatii* (top), one of his most well-known paintings, painted nearly a decade before *The Death of Marat*, and *The Death of Socrates* (above).

LINKED PRACTITIONERS

NEOCLASSICISM:

Sir Joshua Reynolds (1723–1792), UK
Anton Raphael Mengs (1728–1779), GERMANY
Angelika Kauffmann (1741–1807), SWITZERLAND/UK
Antonio Canova (1757–1822), ITALY
Jean-Auguste-Dominique Ingres (1780–1867), FRANCE

DIRECT HOMAGE:

Edvard Munch (1863–1944), NORWAY
Andrzej Wajda (1926–2016), POLAND
Stanley Kubrick (1928–1999), USA
Derek Jarman (1942–1994), UK
Gavin Turk (born 1967), UK

MURDER AND DEATH IN ART:

Artemisia Gentileschi (1593–c. 1656), ITALY
Henry Wallis (1830–1916), UK
Walter Sickert (1860–1942), UK
René Magritte (1898–1967), BELGIUM
Francis Bacon (1909–1992), IRELAND/UK

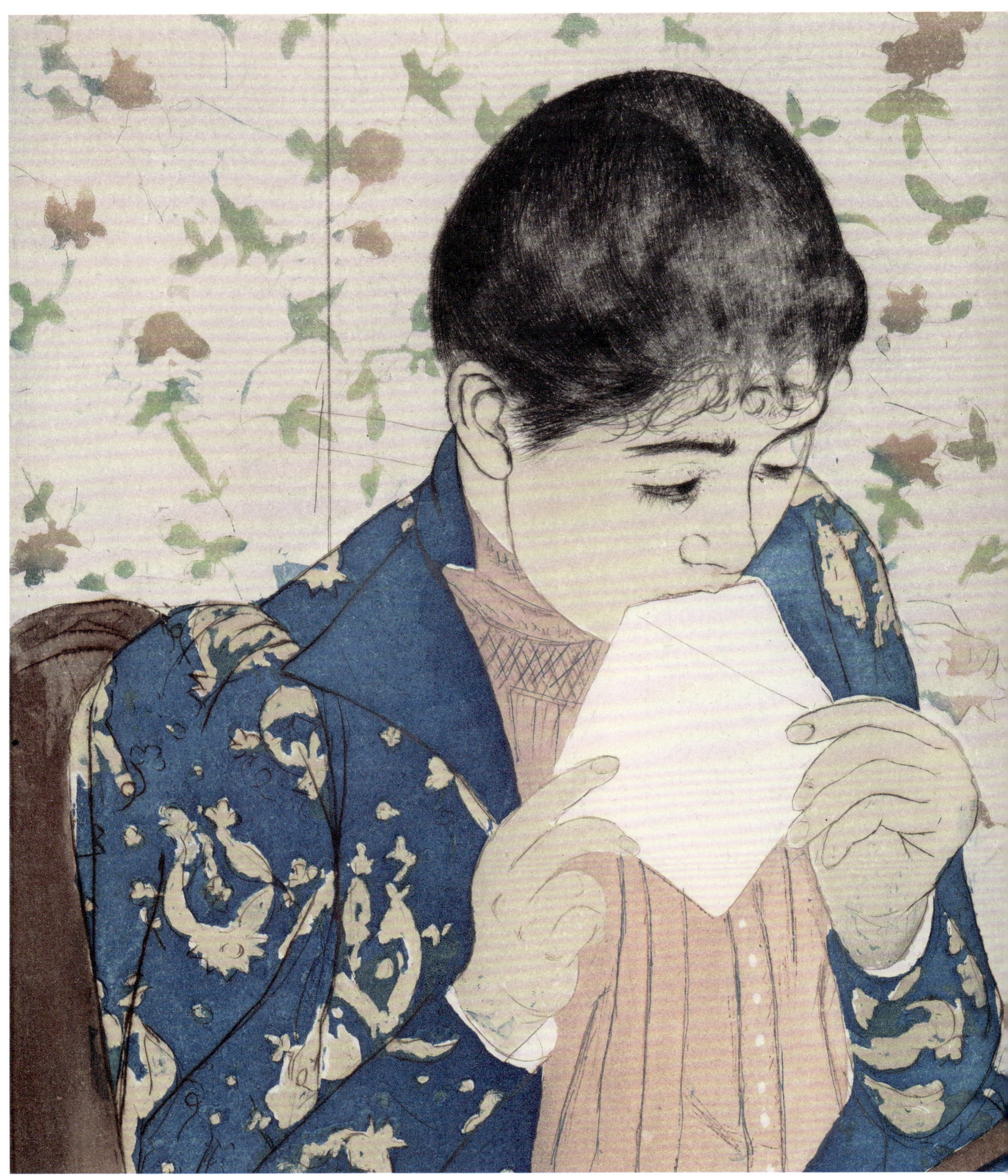

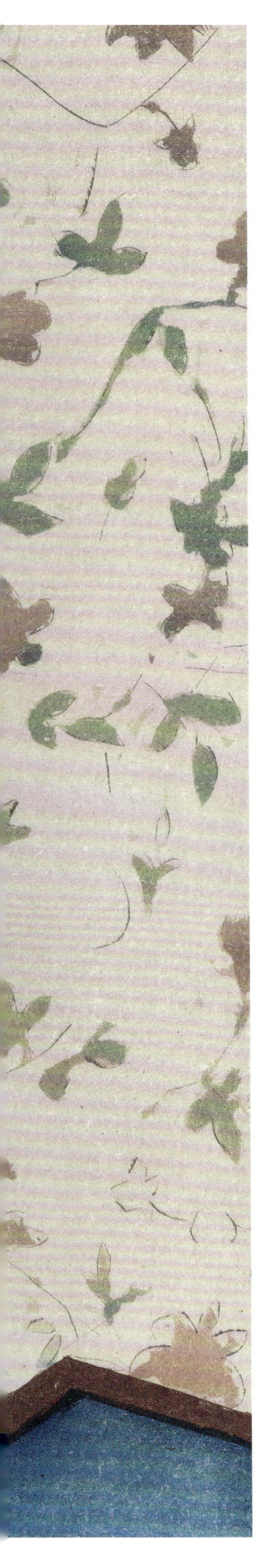

4. The modern *world*

1800 *to* 1945

Artists working during this century and a half of rapid change were trying to capture a world that was transforming before their eyes. New inventions in transport, seismic shifts in politics and ever-increasing globalization left an indelible mark on society. Art captured the excitement and fears of this new, modern world.

1800 *to* 1945

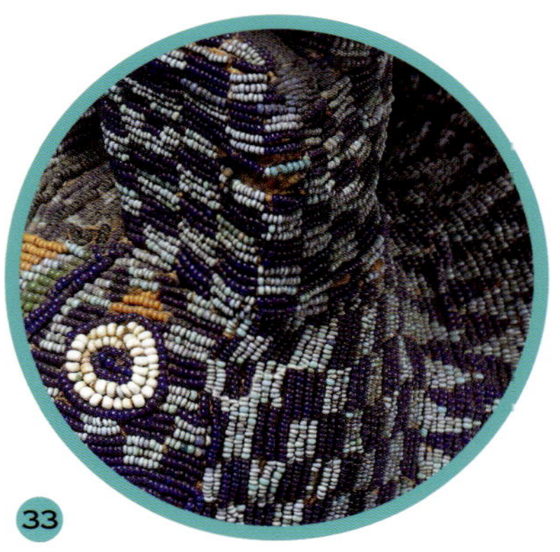

33

Supernatural Animals

Cameroon, Bamileke
Leopard caryatid stool
possibly 1800s

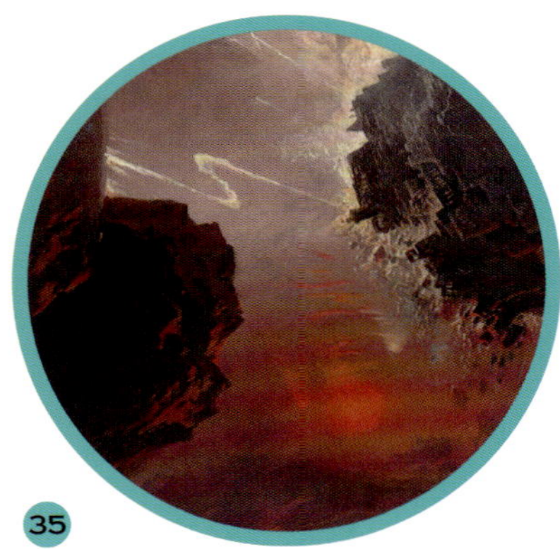

35

Apocalyptic Imagination

John Martin
The Great Day of His Wrath
1851–53

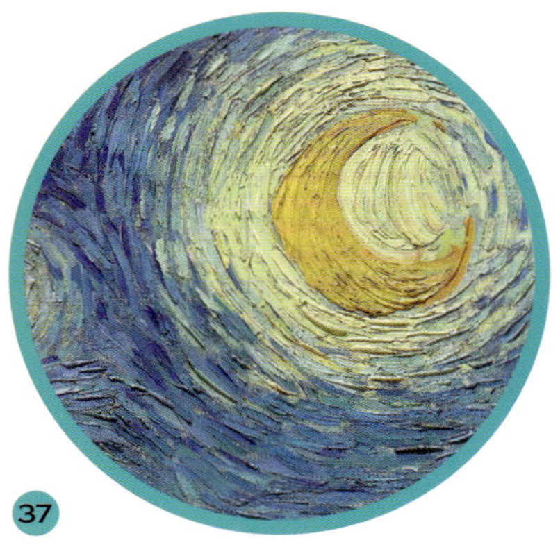

37

Searching the Stars

Vincent van Gogh
The Starry Night
1889

32

Engaging with the Elements

Katsushika Hokusai
Under the Wave off Kanagawa
c. 1830–32

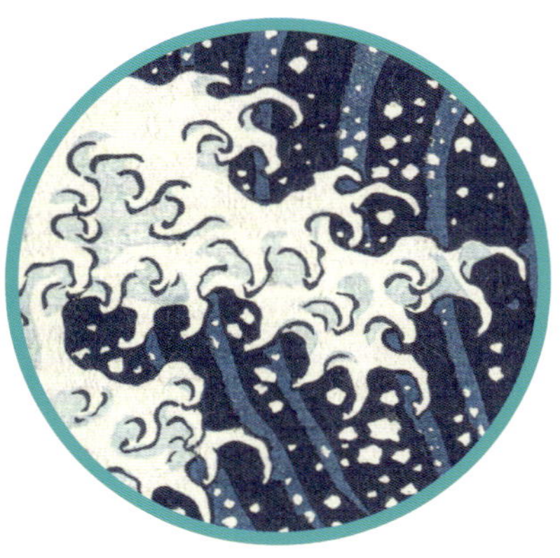

34

Threshold of Disaster

J.M.W. Turner, *Snow Storm – Steam-Boat off a Harbour's Mouth*, exhibited 1842

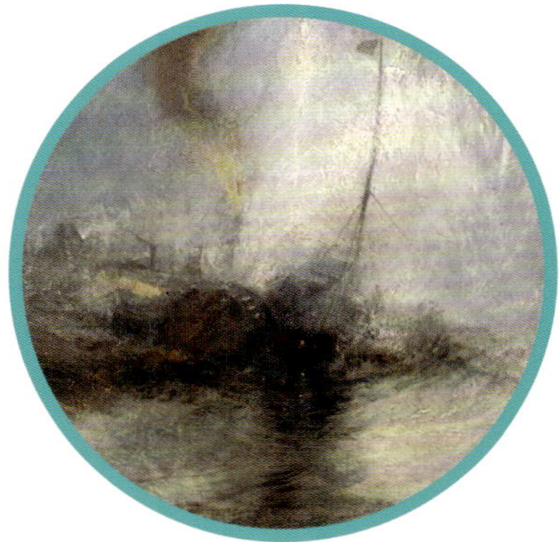

36

Paying Homage

Mary Cassatt
The Letter
1890–91

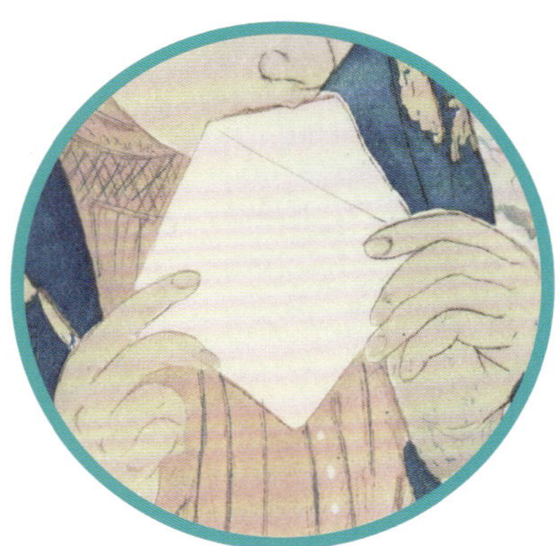

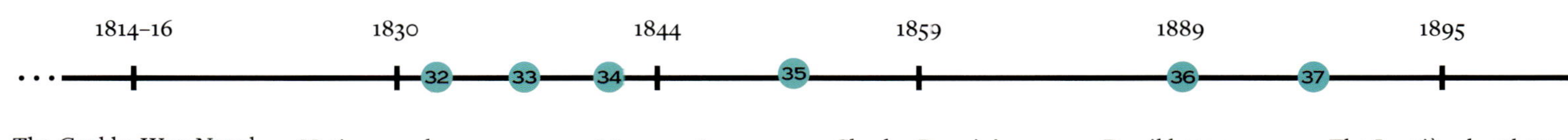

1814–16: The Gurkha War: Nepal cedes one-third of its territory to Britain

1830: Native peoples are forcibly moved west of the Mississippi

1844: Morse code is invented

1859: Charles Darwin's *On the Origin of Species* is published

1889: Brazil becomes a republic

1895: The Lumière brothers open the first public cinema in Paris

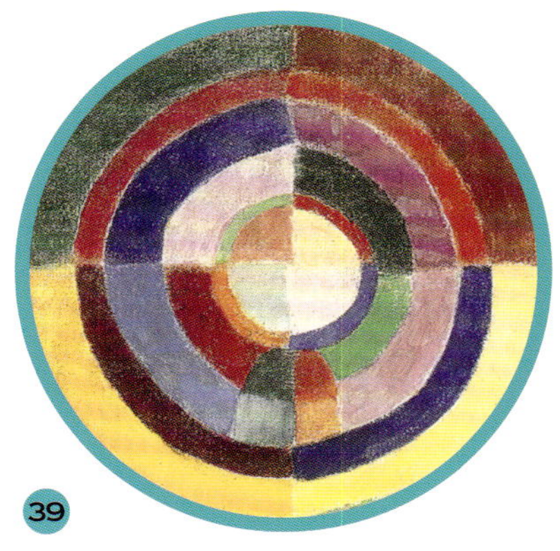

39

The Life of Colour

Sonia Delaunay
Prismes électriques
1914

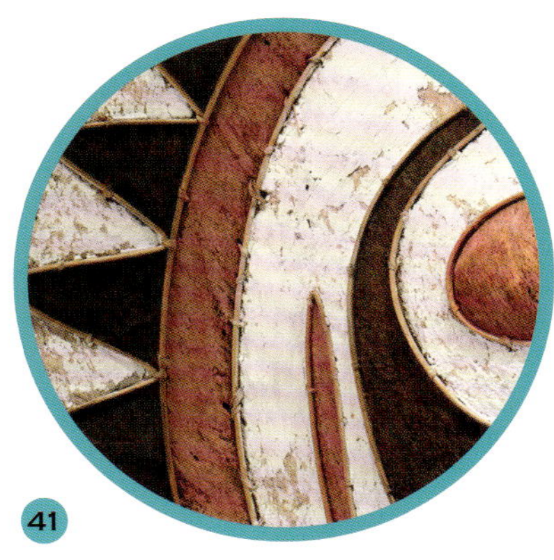

41

Creative Freedoms

Papua New Guinea, Elema
Eharo mask
early 20th century

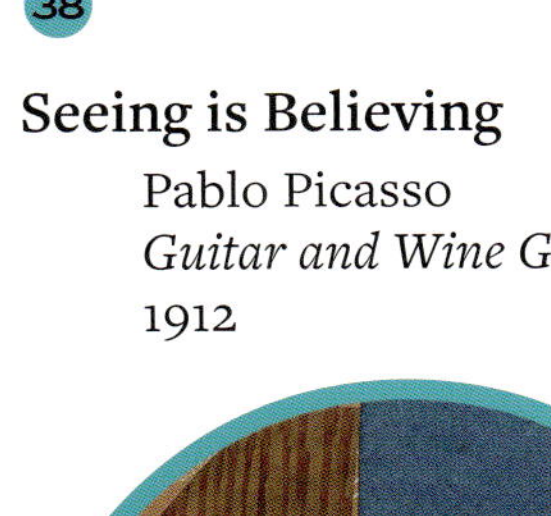

38

Seeing is Believing

Pablo Picasso
Guitar and Wine Glass
1912

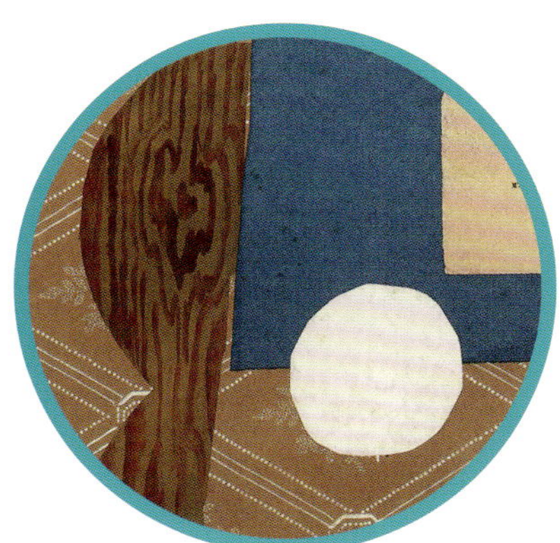

40

Culture is for Everyone

Aleksandr Rodchenko
Books!
1925

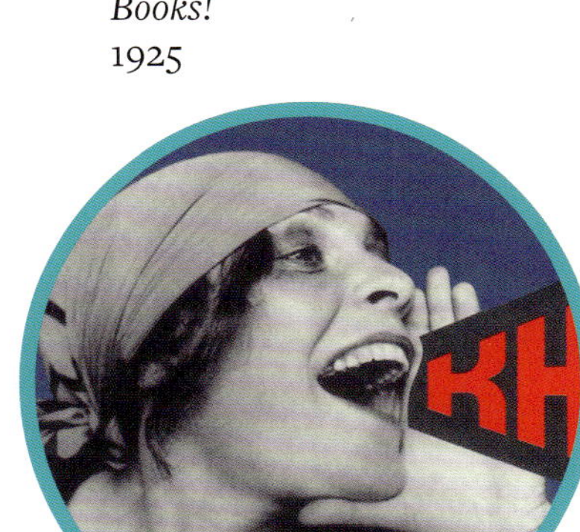

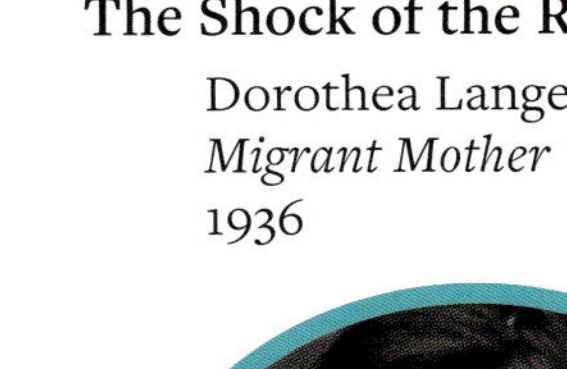

42

The Shock of the Real

Dorothea Lange
Migrant Mother
1936

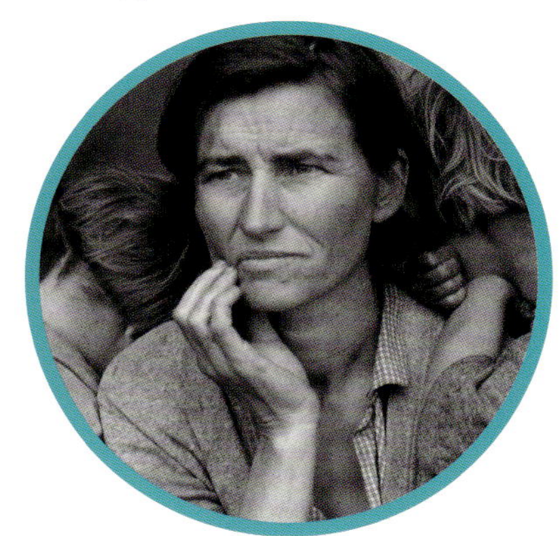

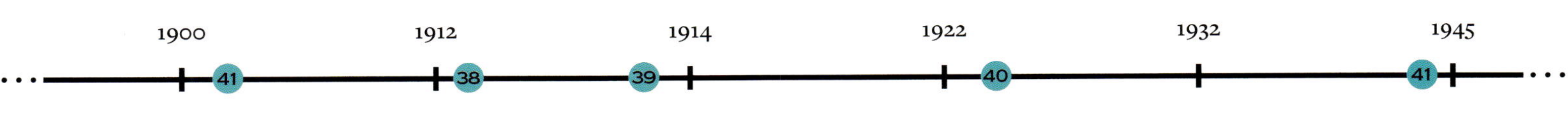

1900	1912	1914	1922	1932	1945
The Boxer Rebellion against foreign influence in China	The *Titanic* sinks on its maiden voyage in the North Atlantic	Archduke Franz Ferdinand is assassinated	Discovery of the tomb of Tutankhamun in Egypt	The kingdom of Saudi Arabia comes into being	Surrender of Japan marks the end of the Second World War

32. Engaging with the Elements

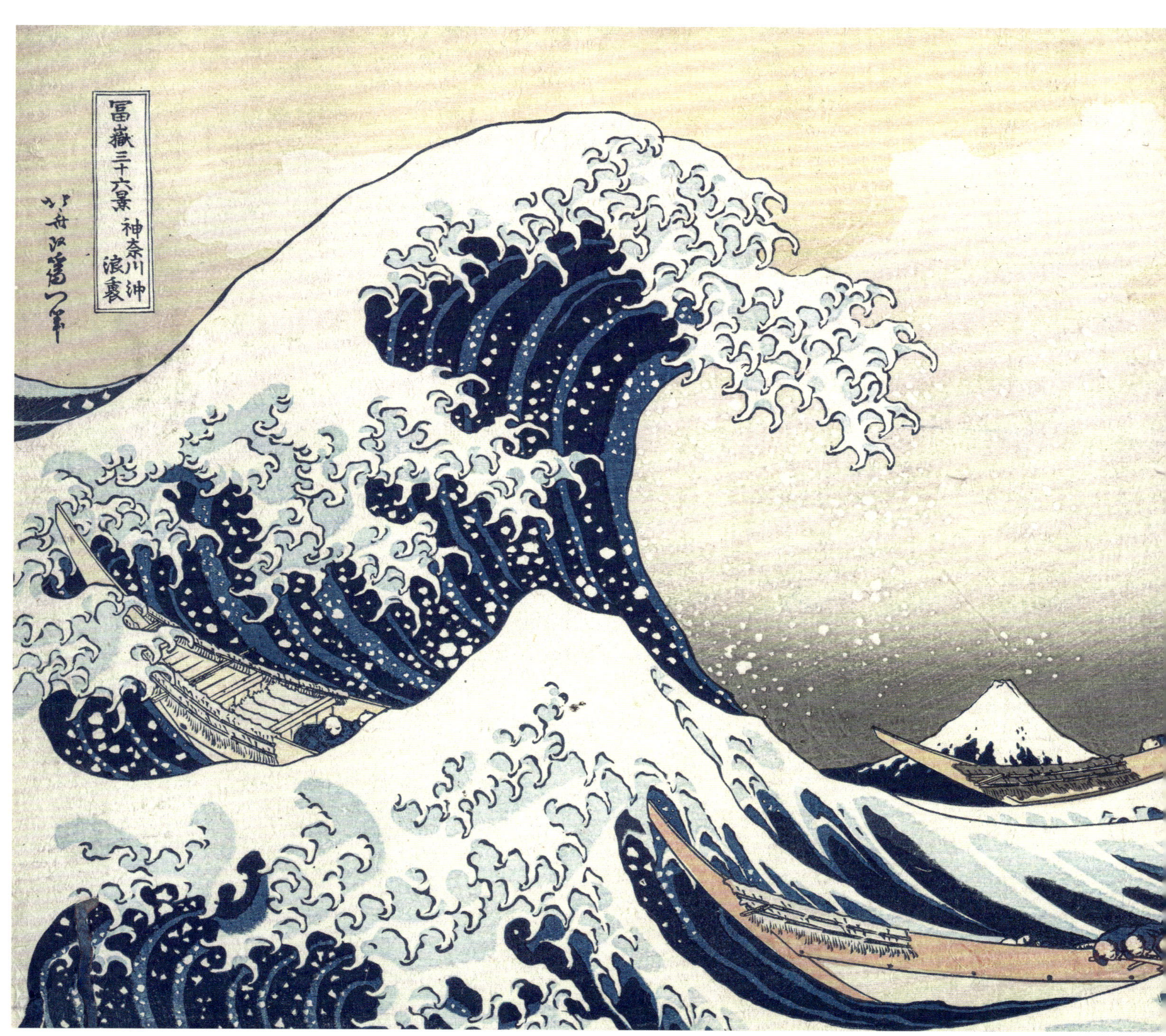

Katsushika Hokusai

Under the Wave off Kanagawa
c. 1830–32

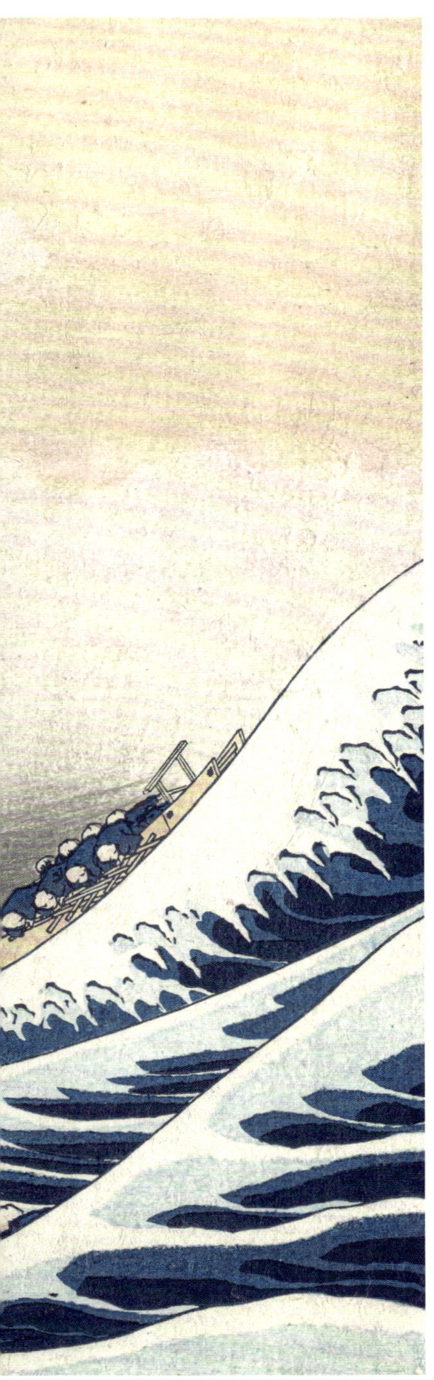

'No money, no clothing, barely enough to eat; if I can't make some arrangement by the middle of next month, I won't make it through the spring.' When Katsushika Hokusai (1760–1849) uttered these words, aged 70, he was at a moment of personal hardship, having recently suffered from a stroke and the death of his wife.

Hokusai made one last attempt to save himself from financial ruin and embarked on a new project: a series of 36 views of Mount Fuji. It worked – the series was so successful that he added a further 10 scenes and later created a book with 100 additional views. *Under the Wave off Kanagawa*, also known as *The Great Wave*, is one of the original 36 images: a scene of maritime disaster, in which a monster wave rips above three fragile boats.

Woodblock print, ink and colour on paper
25.7 × 37.9 cm, 10 × 15 in.
Metropolitan Museum of Art, New York

❶ Magic mountain

Mount Fuji, a volcano that had last erupted in 1707, was a Japanese national icon and sacred site in the Buddhist and Shinto religions. Its name means 'peerless one' according to one tradition, and 'deathless' in another. It was the focus of worship for various cults in Edo (modern-day Tokyo), where Hokusai lived.[65] The mountain would have been the first thing contemporary viewers searched for in the print, and was the true subject of each of Hokusai's scenes, despite the different activities occurring in the foreground.

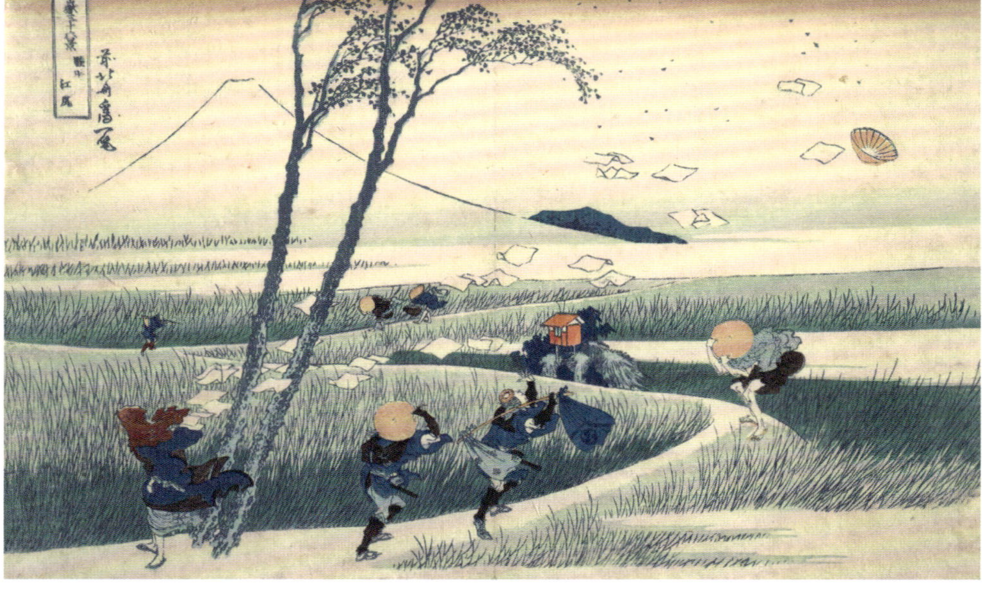

Ejiri in Suruga Province, from the series *Thirty-Six Views of Mount Fuji*, *c.* 1830–32. Woodblock print, ink and colour on paper, 25.1 × 37.5 cm, 10 × 14¾ in.

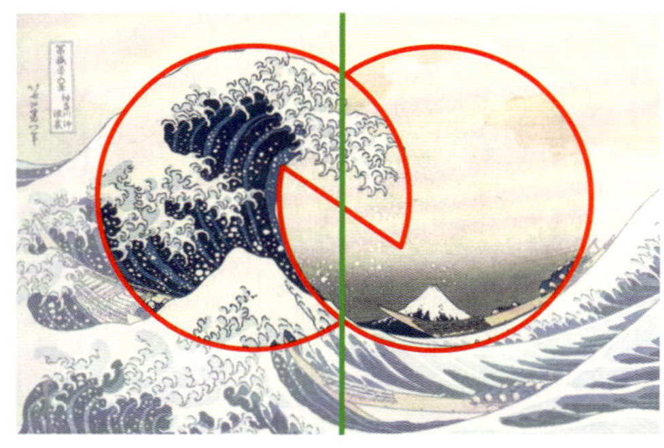

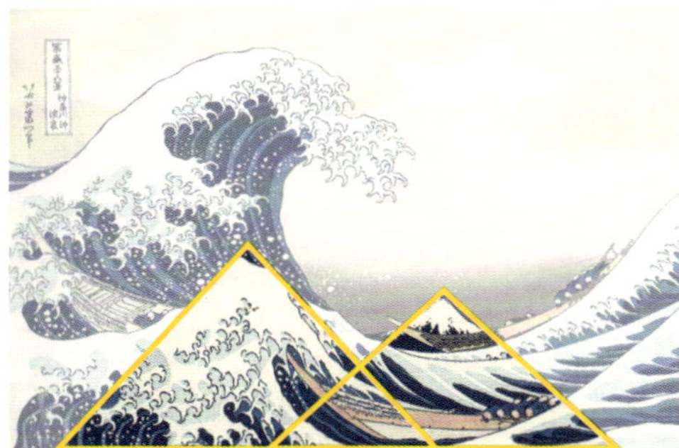

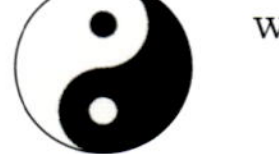

❷ A harmony of shape

Hokusai cleverly echoed the mountain's iconic triangular profile in one of the waves – even the colours are similar. At the same time, the circular shape of the top of the wave is echoed by the circular trough of the sea beneath it. The two circles, containing two elements – water and air – interlock with each other, as in the ancient Chinese *yin-yang* symbol.

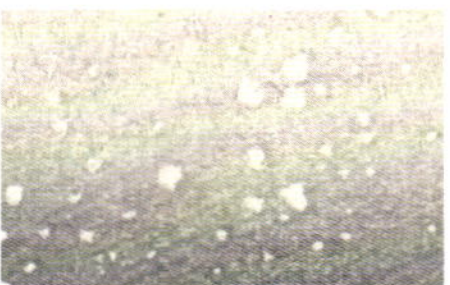

❸ Grain

Faint lines are visible in some areas. These are traces of the wood grain, evidence of the process used in creating the print. Hokusai would have drawn his design on a sheet of paper, which was then pasted onto a cherrywood block. Using chisels, the paper would be cut through into the wood, leaving fine ridges where the lines had been. The keyblock was then rubbed with indigo ink, defining the dark veins of blue in the waves, and creating a stamp with which to make multiple copies of the drawing. Seven further blocks had to be made for each colour. Around 8,000 copies were taken from the original blocks; these would deteriorate over time, so that the lines in later editions can appear worn out.

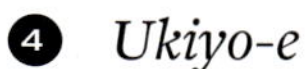

❹ *Ukiyo-e*

Ukiyo-e, which translates as 'pictures from the floating world', is a genre of Japanese art that represented pleasurable vignettes from daily life or history, including scenes from the theatre and well-known stories. The term reflects the style's focus on leisure and entertainment. Hokusai's series was innovative because the prints depicted an unusual subject at the time: landscape.[66]

❺ Pop Art

Hokusai's print was intended to be universally available and cheap to purchase – a popular art form that predated Pop Art by over two centuries. The print would have cost 20 *mon*, the equivalent of two helpings of soba noodles in Japan at the time, or roughly the cost of two Big Mac meals today. Such scenes would have been pasted into albums, hung on walls or kept carefully in boxes, to be brought out on special occasions.[67]

LINKED PRACTITIONERS

UKIYO-E:	MOUNTAINS:	THE POWER OF NATURE:
Hishikawa Moronobu (1618–1694), JAPAN	*Wang Meng* (*c.* 1308–1385), CHINA	*J.M.W. Turner* (1775–1851), UK
Kitagawa Utamaro (*c.* 1753–1806), JAPAN	*Giambologna* (1529–1608), ITALY	*John Martin* (1789–1854), UK
Utagawa Kunisada (1786–1865), JAPAN	*Jeong Seon* (1676–1759), SOUTH KOREA	*Walter Joseph De Maria* (1935–2013), USA
Utagawa Hiroshige (1797–1858), JAPAN	*Paul Cézanne* (1839–1906), FRANCE	*Hiroshi Sugimoto* (born 1948), JAPAN
Utagawa Kuniyoshi (1798–1861), JAPAN	*David Benjamin Sherry* (born 1981), USA	*Richard Misrach* (born 1949), USA

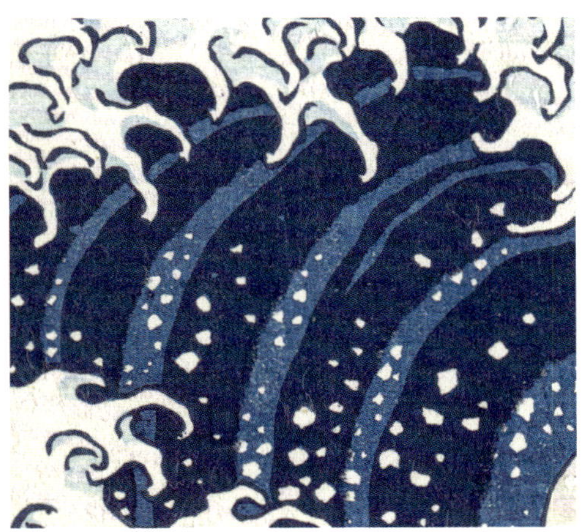

❻ Deep blue

One aspect of the print's fame when it was published was the colouration. It contains a large quantity of Prussian blue, a synthetic colour developed in Germany in the early 18th century. Previously, Japanese audiences would have only experienced blues derived from plants such as Asiatic dayflower, which were less intense and faded easily.

❼ Under attack

The vision of Mount Fuji being subsumed by a mega-wave may have had a political subtext. Japan had been isolated from the rest of the world since 1630, when foreign travel was banned and international trade all but ceased, apart from a heavily policed relationship with China and the Netherlands. During Hokusai's lifetime, there were increased antagonisms with countries whose ships had strayed too close to Japanese shores, and from 1825 aggressive naval engagements against foreigners were encouraged. Hokusai's scene may be about more than just the perils of nature.

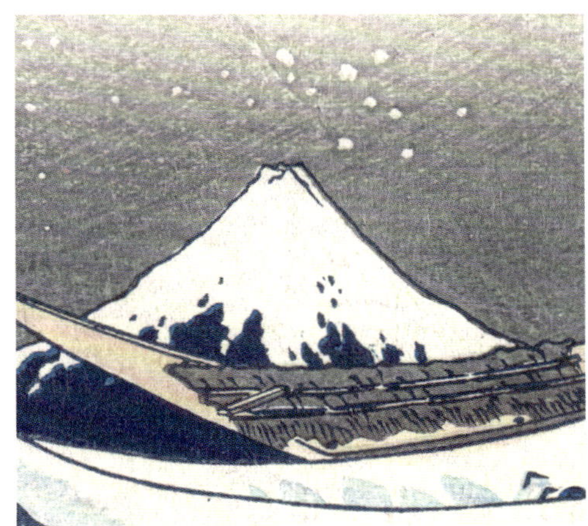

❽ Near and far

A boat's prow cuts dramatically in front of Mount Fuji. This radical juxtaposition of near and far creates a dynamic, plunging sense of distance. Our perspective is low, setting our view into a sinking valley below the waves, boats and mountain, and is suggestive of the original title of the work: *Under the Wave off Kanagawa*.

❾ Against the elements

The fight against nature's wrath is all in the name of money. The three boats are probably skiffs heading out to sea to rendezvous with a fishing fleet. Back in the Edo fish markets, fresh bonito could fetch a high price, and these narrow vessels were designed to zip back to the city at high speed: the fastest arrivals would achieve the highest prices. In the face of the epic wave, the rowers hunch against the onslaught. Their plight is not unlike Hokusai's own circumstances, whose series of prints was created at a time of personal hardship and financial despair.

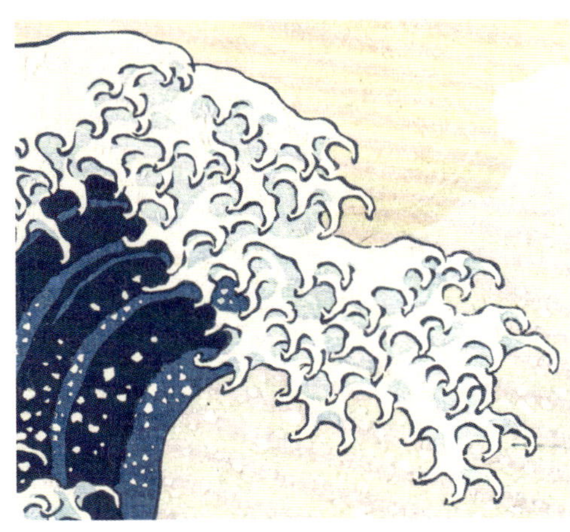

❿ Monsters of the deep

The representation of the wave as it begins to break into fractals is the print's most distinctive feature. The water looks like hands or the tentacles of a sea creature, giving the wave the appearance of a sentient force that is intent on destroying the boats and their occupants.

⓫ Inspirational

Hokusai's landscape scenes were highly influential for later Japanese *ukiyo-e* artists, including Utagawa Hiroshige. They became even more famous in Europe, inspiring artists like Paul Cézanne, whose repeated studies of a mountain – Mont Sainte-Victoire – echoed the shape of Mount Fuji in Hokusai's prints. Among the many other artists who paid homage to Hokusai's masterpiece were Paul Gauguin and Hergé, the author of *The Adventures of Tintin*, as well as modern Manga and street artists.

WORKS INFLUENCED BY HOKUSAI

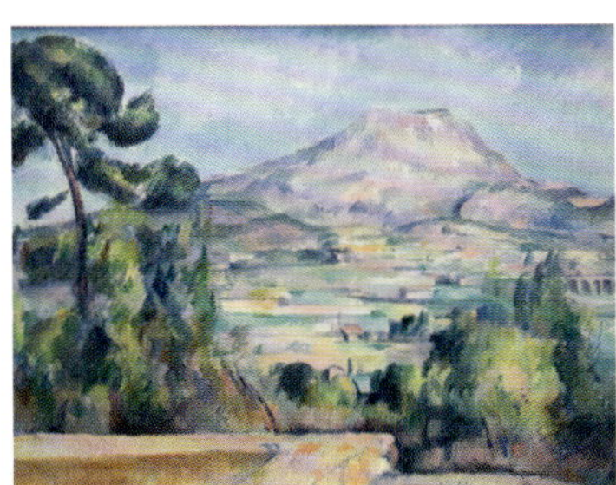

Paul Cézanne, *Montagne Sainte-Victoire*, c. 1890. Oil on canvas, 65 × 95.2 cm, 25½ × 37½ in.

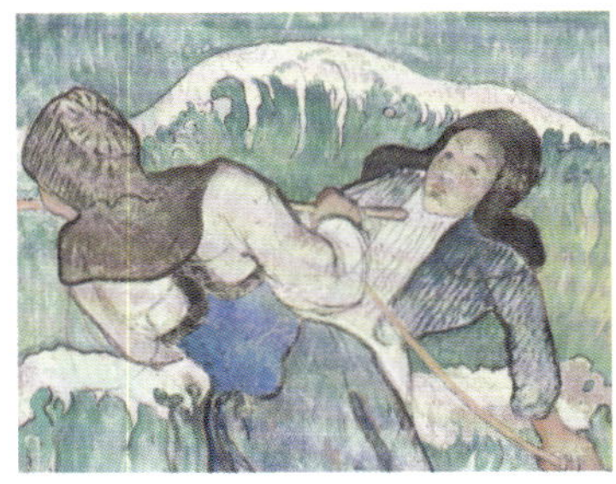

Paul Gauguin, *Les Pêcheuses de goëmon*, 1888–90. Gouache and graphite on grey board, 27.6 × 32.4 cm, 10¾ × 12¾ in.

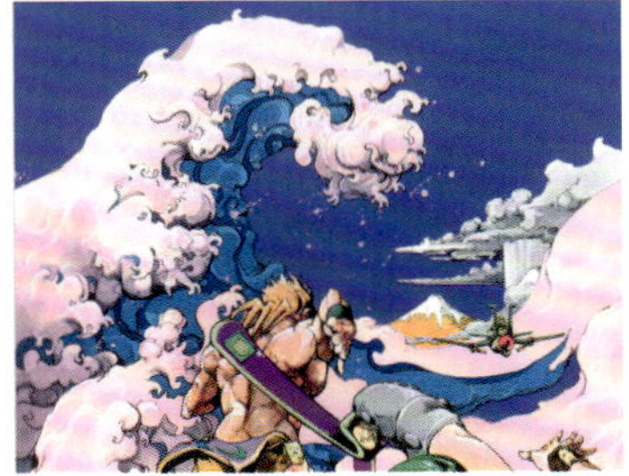

Hirohiko Araki, *The Sky Above the Great Wave off the Coast of Kanagawa*, poster, 2020 Tokyo Paralympics. Pencil, ink and oil on canvas

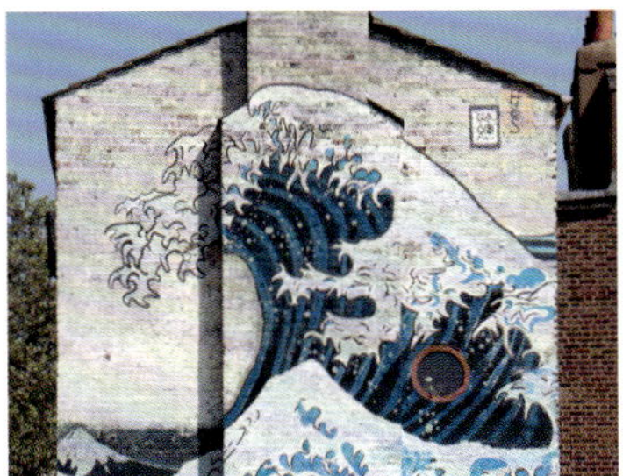

Dominic Swords, *Under the Wave*, mural in Camberwell, South London, 1998

33. Supernatural Animals

This stool, from the Grassfields region of central Africa, was produced to convey the authority of the king and his supernatural powers. Now part of Cameroon, the area was populated by numerous kingdoms, joined together through trade networks.

The various rulers of these realms needed to assert their leadership. Here, the might and authority of the king – possibly Fotso I or II – is embodied by the highly expressive form of a leopard, carved from wood and covered in beads, which bears the weight of the stool. Despite its power and role as hunter in the natural world, the leopard has been tamed and subdued into a seat-bearer for the human ruler of its environment.

Wood, cotton, plant fibre, glass beads and indigo
51 × 38 × 43 cm, 20 × 15 × 17 in.
Cleveland Museum of Art, Ohio

Cameroon, Bamileke
Leopard caryatid stool
possibly 1800s

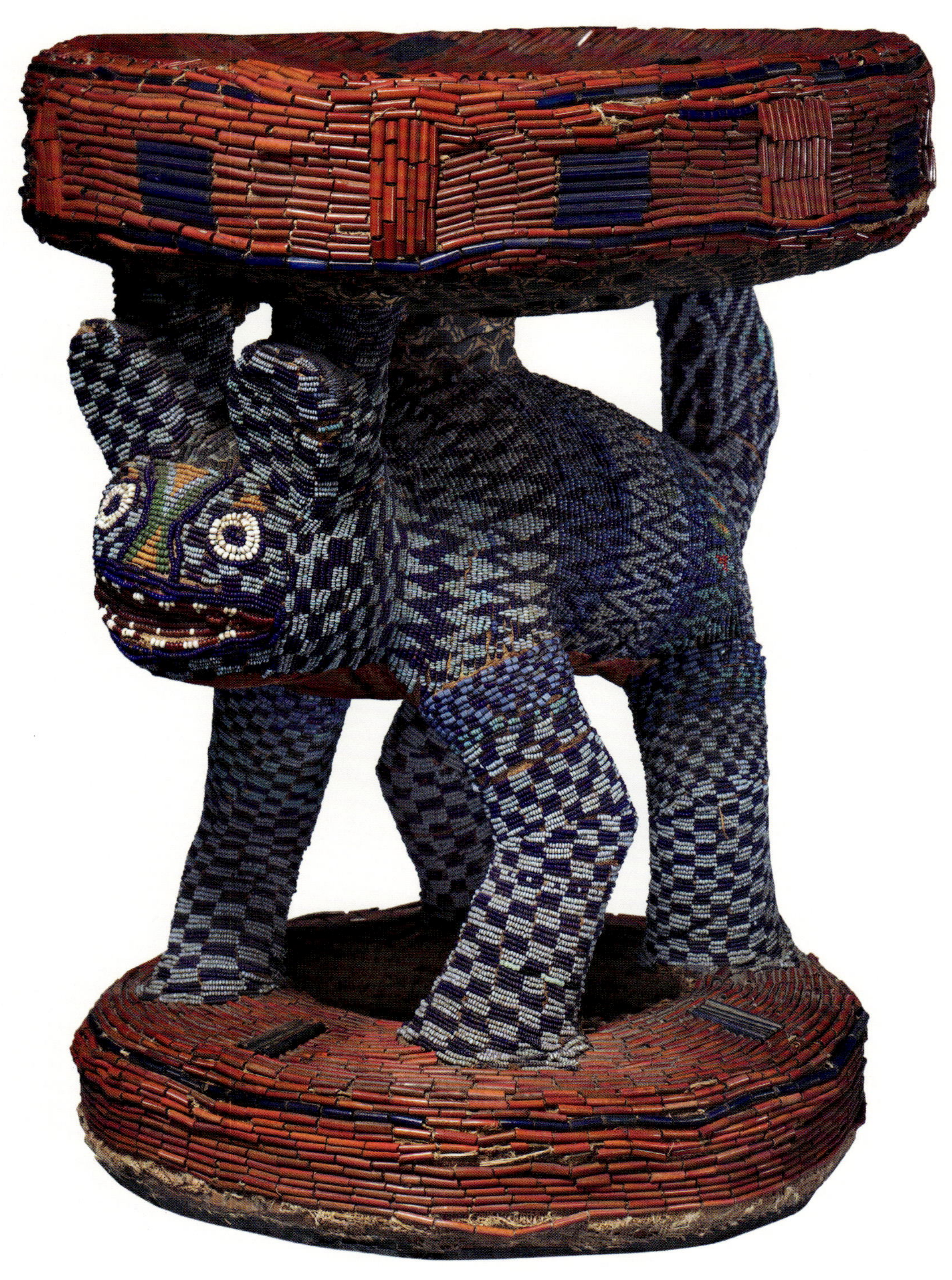

❶ Leadership

The stool was made for the ruler (*fon*) of the Bandjoun kingdom in what is now western Cameroon. Such items were important for indicating the *fon*'s power, and would also have been functional, serving as a travelling stool he could take with him on tours of the kingdom. It was owned by Kamga II Joseph (r. 1925–75), but may have been inherited from Fotso I or Fotso II. The stool projected the king's authority through its use of prized materials (beads) and animal symbolism. It represented the presence of the *fon*, even when he was absent.[68]

❷ Journey

A photograph taken in the 1920s shows the stool in the possession of Kamga II Joseph (right). The stool was later given as a diplomatic gift to the photographer, Frank Christol, a Catholic missionary. After being owned by various collectors in France, it was acquired by the Cleveland Museum of Art in 2006. Similar beaded objects are still in the possession of the kingdom's treasury in Cameroon, and continue to be used for ritual purposes.[69]

❸ Pattern

The spots of the leopard supporting the seat are depicted in an abstract way to create various patterns, yet still convey the distinctive markings of the animal. The face, ears and legs are covered in a chequerboard design, while the body and tail are decorated in diamond shapes and zig-zags.

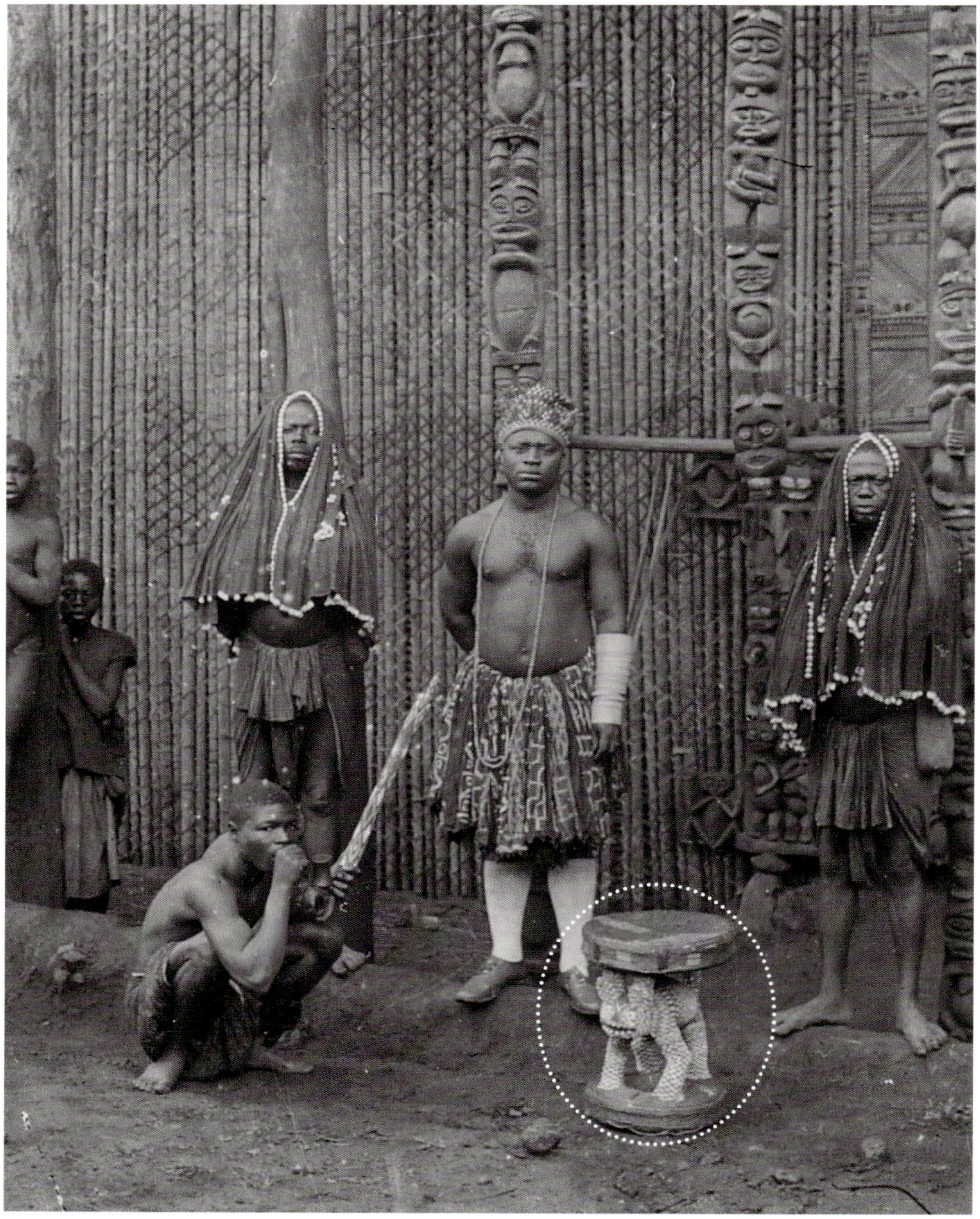

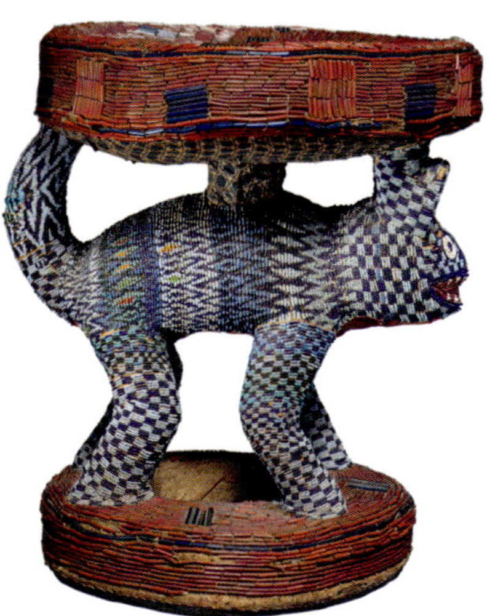

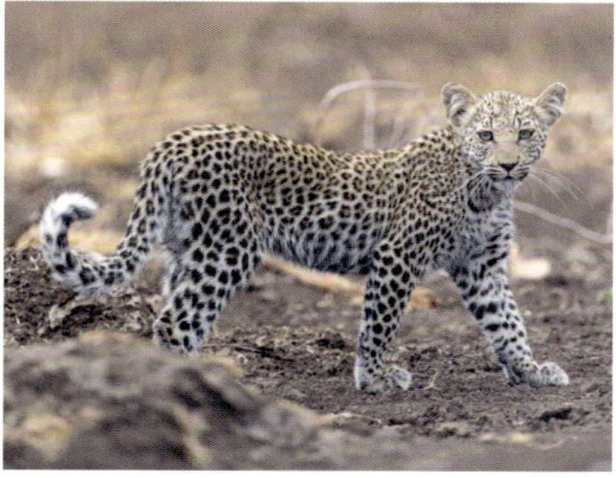

↑ Leopard cub, Kruger National Park, South Africa, 2019. Photo by Ozkan Ozmen

↑↑ King Kamga II Joseph of Bandjoun, with the leopard caryatid stool, *c*. 1925. Photo by Frank Christol

❹ War paint

The effect of these stylized geometric patterns is to give the leopard an enhanced dynamism. It is possible that the zig-zag motif may represent spear tips, and by extension the skills of a successful warrior.[70]

❺ Seat

Underneath the surface is an inner structure made from wood, designed to take the weight of a fully grown person. Covering the wood are thousands of beads, which give the stool its smooth contours and appearance of being entirely soft and pliable.

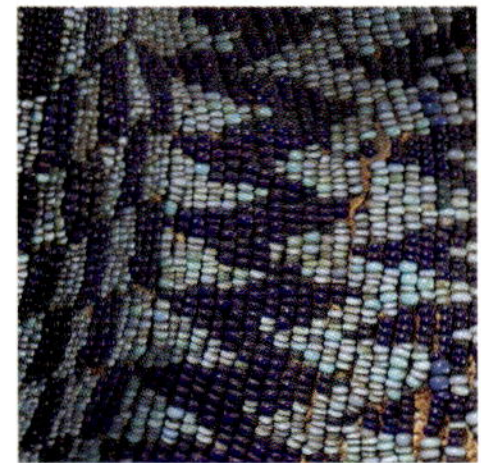

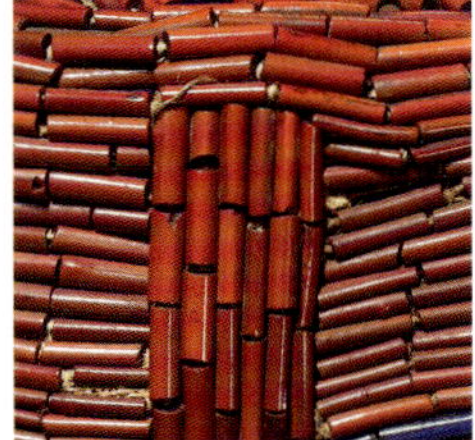

6 Beadwork

For this complex mosaic, two types of beads were used: seed beads for the leopard, and tubular beads for the red base and seat.

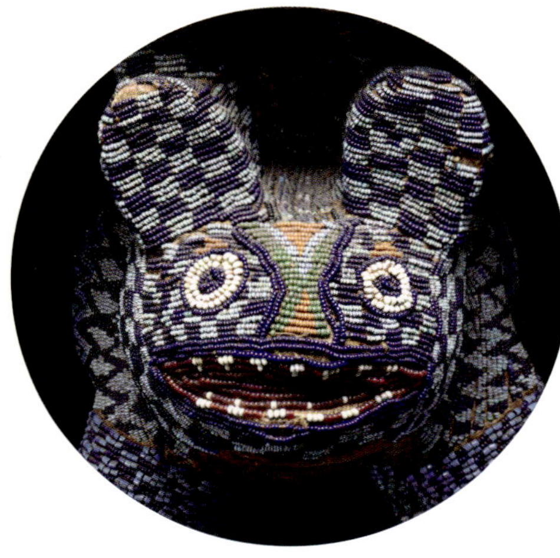

12 Expression

The crouching leopard is shown with teeth bared, ears alert and eyes wide open. Its features are stylized to convey maximum expression.

13 Status

Beads signified status in the Grassfields region. The beads on this stool were probably made in Venice or in what is now the Czech Republic, and imported to sell in Africa.[71] Initial contact between West Africa and European traders had occurred in the late 15th century (see pp. 80–3); previously, Arab merchants had traded in the region, selling among other goods coral, which could be turned into beads.

7 Beads as currency

Beads symbolized the *fon*'s control over international trade. They would also sometimes act as currency, with one teaspoon of beads the equivalent of a day's wages. Only the *fon* could use them for decoration; the more colour and pattern, the more valuable the objects they covered. It is possible that red beads were rarer and more valuable than blue ones.

8 Technique

The beads were threaded together and sewn onto pieces of fabric, which were then fixed to a wooden frame. The tiny seed beads allow the contours of the leopard's body to be articulated and appear smooth.

9 Influence

Should objects with ritual functions be treated like artworks? Artists of the Die Brücke group took inspiration from the shapes and colour of the Cameroonian sculptures they encountered in the Dresden Museum of Ethnology.

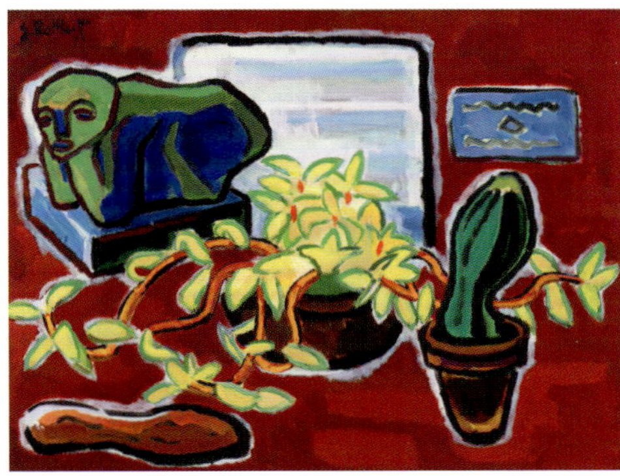

Karl Schmidt-Rottluff, *Still Life with Stone Sculpture*, 1960. Oil on canvas, 77.3 × 102 cm, 30½ × 40¼ in.

10 Imperialism

Such works were in German museum collections because Cameroon was one of the country's colonies at the time. The artists of Die Brücke may have been breaking the mould by bringing attention to the work of artists outside of Europe, but they paid scant attention to the cultural background of the art they depicted, nor did they highlight the cruelty and prejudice of western imperialism.

11 Symbolism

Leopards were both revered and feared among the people of the Grasslands. As well as being his personal emblem, it was believed that the *fon* could metamorphose into a leopard. In this guise, he could roam about the kingdom at night, meting out justice by killing those who had committed a crime or were capable of malevolence.

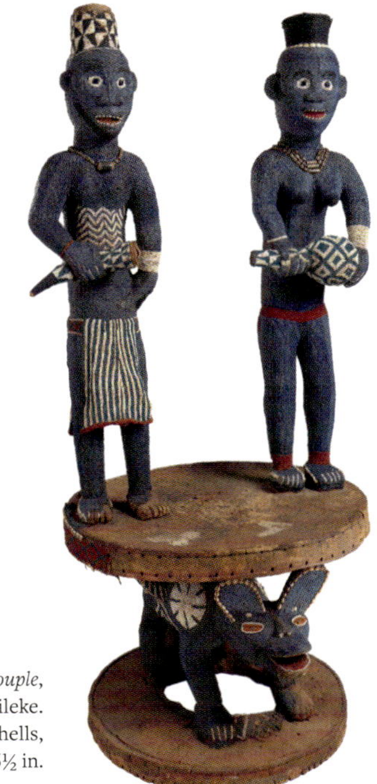

Throne of Njouteu: Royal Couple, late 19th–early 20th century. Cameroon, Bamileke. Wood, glass beads, cloth, cowrie shells, 163 × 74.3 × 67.3 cm, 64¼ × 29¼ × 26½ in.

LINKED PRACTITIONERS

BEADS IN ARTWORKS:

Joyce J. Scott (born 1948), USA
Hew Locke (born 1959), UK
Ran Hwang (born 1960), SOUTH KOREA
Liza Lou (born 1969), USA
Jeffrey A. Gibson (born 1972), USA

DIE BRÜCKE:

Emil Nolde (1867–1956), GERMANY
Ernst Ludwig Kirchner (1880–1938), GERMANY
Fritz Bleyl (1880–1966), GERMANY
Max Pechstein (1881–1955), GERMANY
Karl Schmidt-Rottluff (1884–1976), GERMANY

ANIMALS IN SCULPTURE:

Henri Gaudier-Brzeska (1891–1915), FRANCE
Barbara Hepworth (1903–1975), UK
Louise Bourgeois (1911–2010), FRANCE/USA
Barry Flanagan (1941–2009), UK/IRELAND
Jeff Koons (born 1955), USA

34. Threshold of Disaster

Of this work, J.M.W. Turner (1775–1851) is reported to have said: 'I did not paint it to be understood, but I wished to show what such a scene was like; I got the sailors to lash me to the mast to observe it; I was lashed for four hours, and I did not expect to escape, but I felt bound to record it if I did.'

Could the 67-year-old artist really have put himself at such risk, all for the sake of art? Whether the story is true or not, his claim does shed some light on his intentions for the painting. Turner wanted his audience to feel the sensations of the scene in front of them, which he achieved by evoking the pitiless fury of nature, with a moment of imminent human catastrophe at its core.

Oil on canvas
91.4 × 121.9 cm, 36 × 48 in.
Tate, London

J.M.W. Turner
Snow Storm – Steam-Boat off a Harbour's Mouth
exhibited 1842

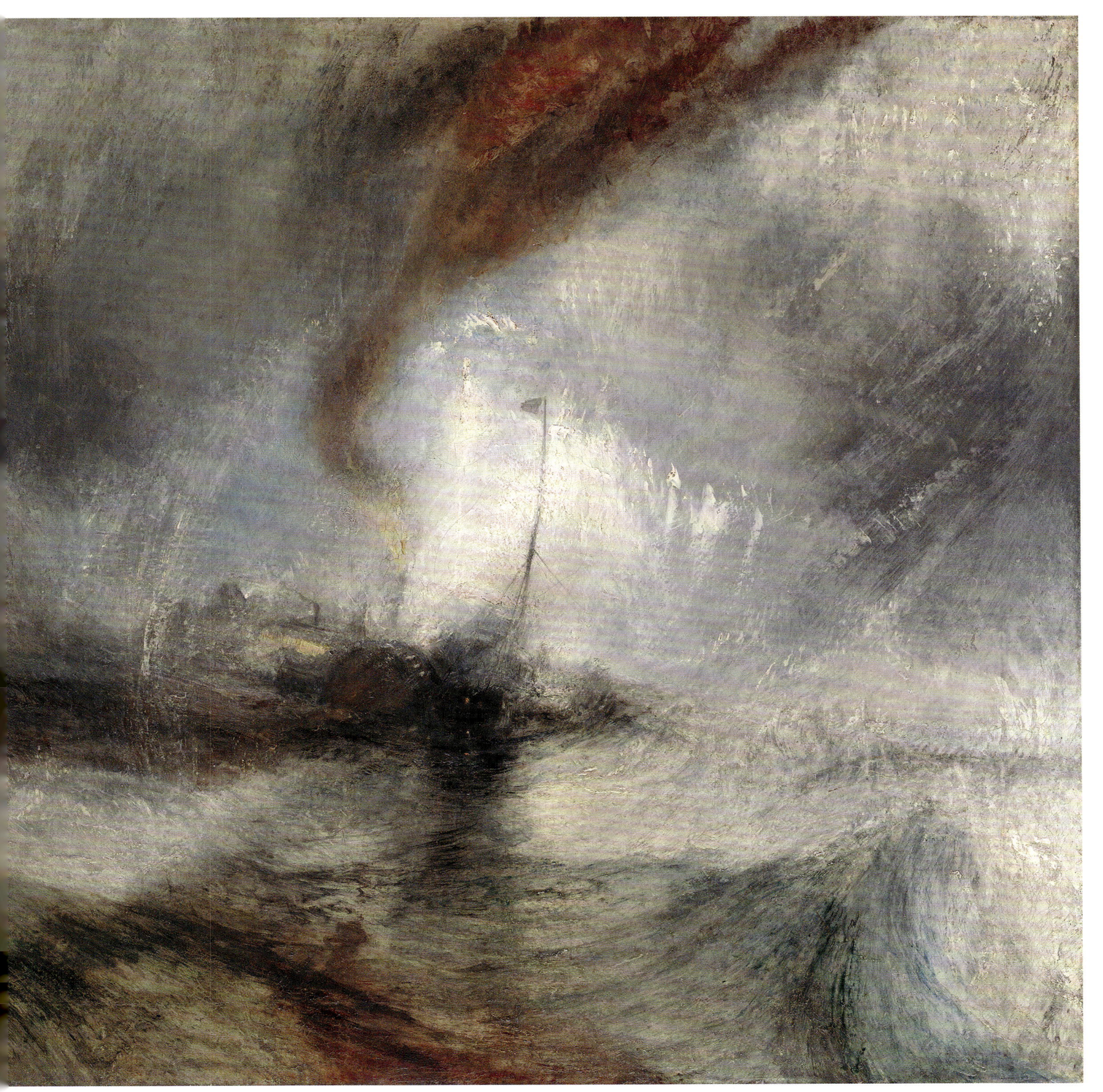

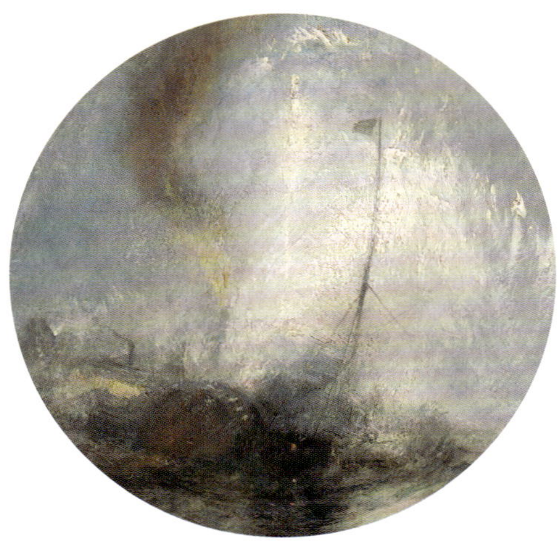

❶ Despair

Snow Storm – Steam-Boat off a Harbour's Mouth shows a ship caught in a violent storm. It is a battleground of humanity against nature, and hope against despair. The white line is a distress flare: a desperate cry for help, fighting to be noticed in the storm.

❷ Sublime

In *A Philosophical Enquiry into the Origin of Our Ideas of the Sublime and Beautiful* (1757), Edmund Burke asked why people thrill to see epic disasters represented in art. He identified this kind of subject matter as 'sublime', evoking feelings in spectators – whether in response to art or the real thing – of being overwhelmed by the immensity of nature. Generations of future artists, writers and film directors have, like Turner, represented the sublime in the form of natural and manmade disasters.

❸ Inspiration

Turner was inspired by, but re-imagined, earlier paintings by Dutch 17th-century masters of dramatic events at sea.

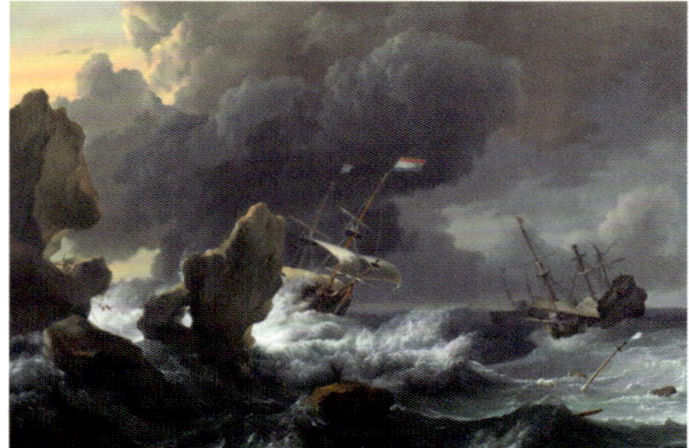

Ludolf Backhuysen, *Ships in Distress off a Rocky Coast*, 1667. Oil on canvas, 114.3 × 167.3 cm, 45 × 65¾ in.

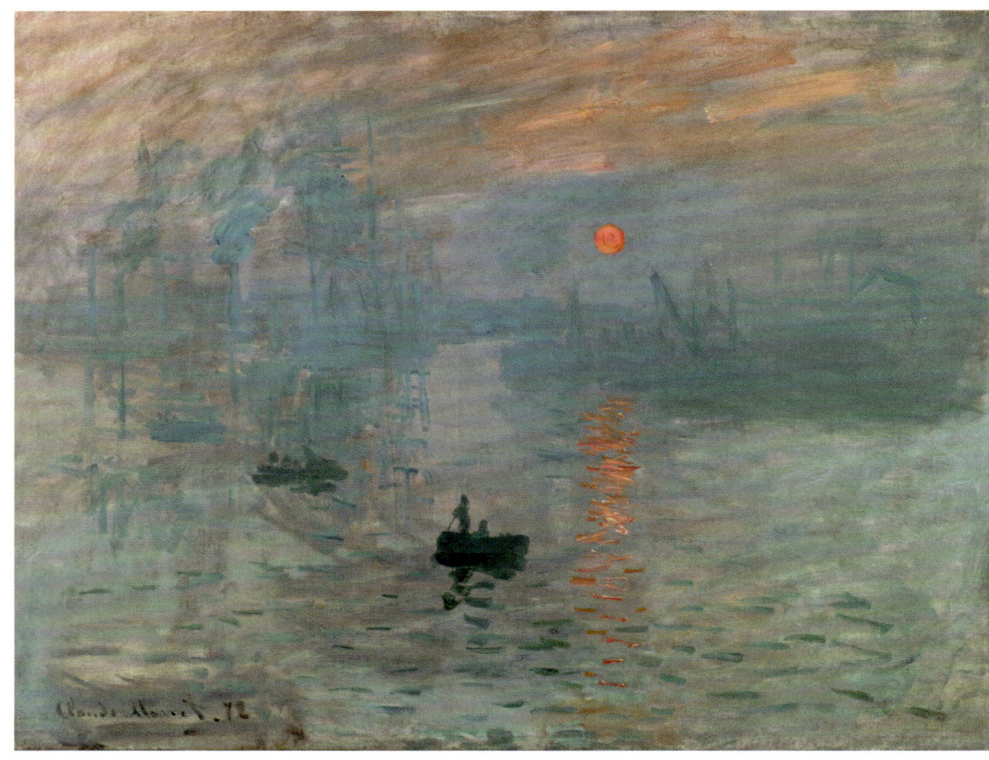

↑ Claude Monet, *Impression, Sunrise*, 1872. Oil on canvas, 50 × 65 cm, 19¾ × 25½ in.

↓ Jackson Pollock, *Number 4*, 1949. Oil, enamel and aluminium paint with pebbles on cut canvas, on composition board, 90.2 × 87.3 cm, 35½ × 34¼ in.

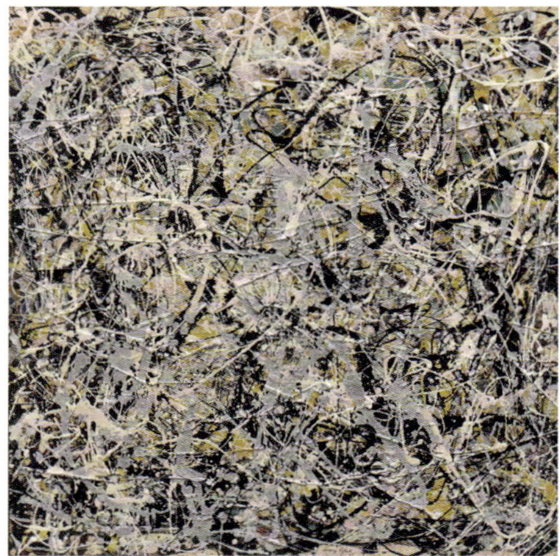

❹ Influence

In the 1870s, Claude Monet emulated Turner's ability to imitate nature with confident, bold brushstrokes. Seventy years later, the Abstract Expressionist artist Jackson Pollock dripped paint onto the canvas in a more exaggerated extension of Turner's original style. Pollock also wanted to express the natural world in a direct way. When asked if he painted nature, he simply replied: 'I am nature.'

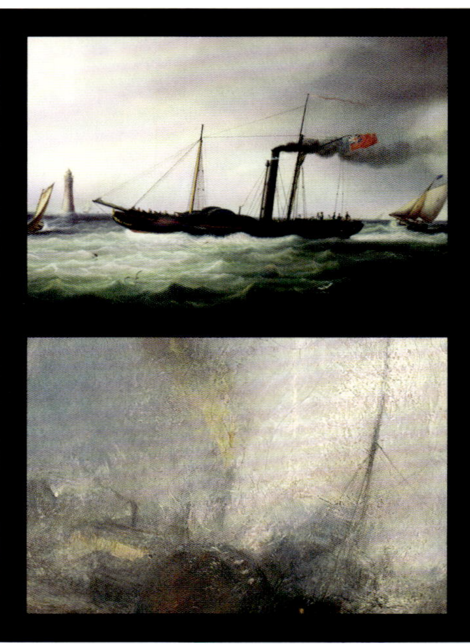

❺ New technology

Turner painted the ship's chimney, which spews out smoke, and the paddlewheel turning frantically against the surging waves. Coal-fuelled steamboats came into widespread use in Europe from 1812. Since the very first manmade boats, thousands of years earlier, ships had been powered by sails or oars. The beginning of the industrial age was a pivotal moment of change for both mankind and the natural world.

❻ Industrial Revolution

Between 1760 and 1840, manufacturers began using factories and new technologies like steam power. This sped up the rate of production, which led to growth in population, supply of goods and – for a few – great wealth. It also meant a huge increase in poverty and pollution. While many other artists chose to ignore the Industrial Revolution, Turner faced it head-on. But is he celebrating it, or criticizing?

❼ Chaos

Seascapes generally show the horizon line, allowing the viewer to establish a sense of space and scale. But you can't see one here, which increases the feeling of disorientation. It is almost impossible to discern the sea from the sky, with the cloud, smoke and snow all melded into a single, hostile system. The composition seems to be based around a vortex, with the ship at the centre and the elements circling around it like a whirlpool.

❽ Romanticism

Romanticism was an art movement that took hold at the beginning of the 1800s. It put the focus on emotional responses, the feelings of the individual and the power of nature. This contrasted with previous art movements, which had emphasized the intellect, collective responsibility and a person's ability to control emotions.

❾ Popularity

Many at the time couldn't understand Turner's work, and *Snow Storm* was dismissed as just 'soapsuds and whitewash'. But he did have some supporters: the art critic John Ruskin called it 'one of the very grandest statements of sea-motion, mist, and light, that has ever been put on canvas'.

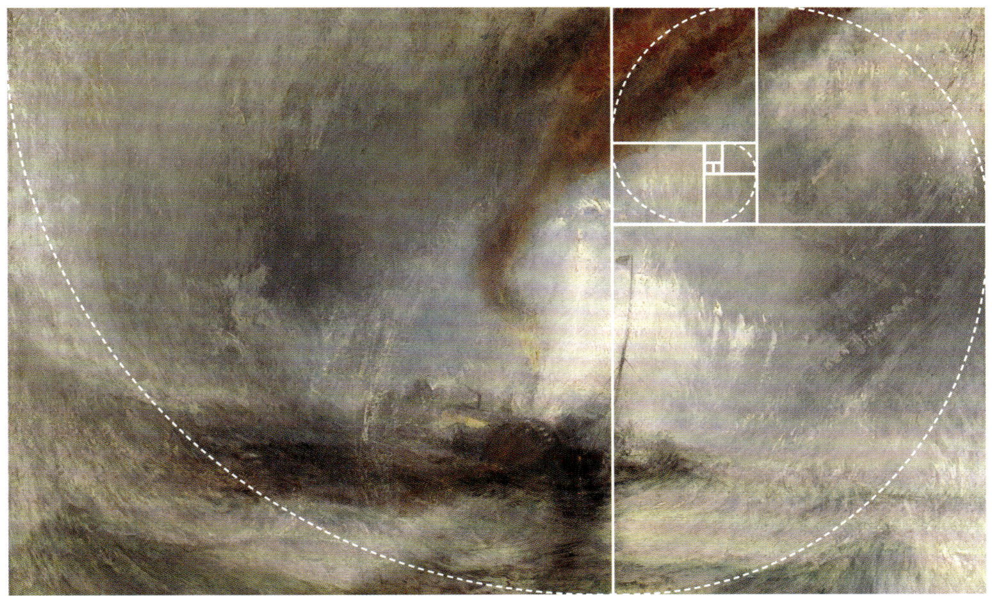

❿ Organization

Even though the scene has a heightened sensation of turmoil, there is an underlying order. The mast, for example, fits with the golden ratio, considered to be the most pleasing proportion to the human eye.

⓫ Hokusai

Painted at a similar time but never seen by Turner is *Under the Wave off Kanagawa* by Katsushika Hokusai (pp. 152–5). Unlike Turner, Hokusai represented the sea in a graphic, linear style, with bold outlines around the shapes.

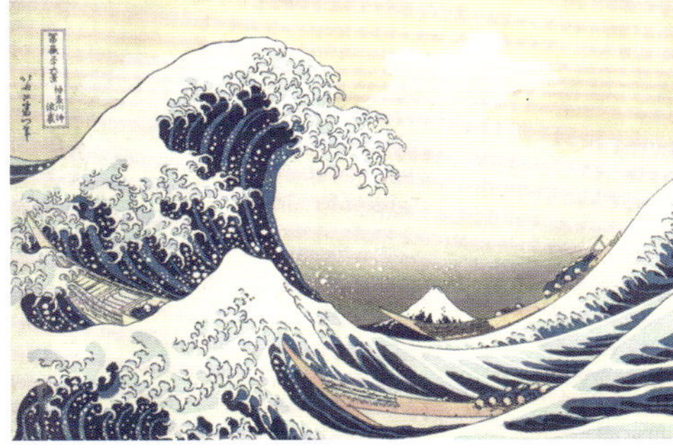

Katsushika Hokusai,
Under the Wave off Kanagawa,
c. 1830–32

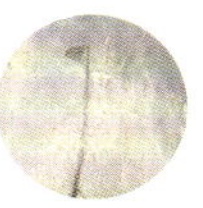
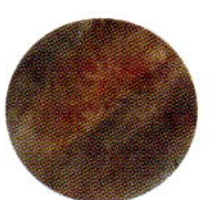

⓬ Balancing opposites

Cool tones of grey, blue and white paint intensify the perception of freezing conditions, while the plume of smoke introduces hints of warm brown to counteract the cold.

⓭ Technique

Turner's painting technique was viewed at the time as very unusual. He swiped, smeared and scratched at the surfaces he was working on, sometimes even spitting at them in an energetic frenzy. The lack of details effectively conveys the way vision is blurred in a storm.

⓮ Authenticity

Turner *claimed* to have strapped himself to the mast of a ship, asking the captain to sail into a storm so that he could represent the experience accurately.

LINKED PRACTITIONERS

SEA STORMS:

Rembrandt van Rijn (1606–1669), NETHERLANDS
Jacob van Ruisdael (1628–1682), NETHERLANDS
Ivan Aivazovsky (1817–1900), RUSSIA
Winslow Homer (1836–1910), USA
Tacita Dean (born 1965), UK

ROMANTIC PERIOD:

Jacob van Ruisdael (1628–1682), NETHERLANDS
John Constable (1776–1837), UK
Philipp Otto Runge (1777–1810), GERMANY
Théodore Géricault (1791–1824), FRANCE
Albert Bierstadt (1830–1902), USA

THE SUBLIME IN PHOTOGRAPHY AND LATER ART:

Timothy H. O'Sullivan (1840–1882), USA
Agnes Denes (born 1931), HUNGARY/USA
Anselm Kiefer (born 1945), GERMANY
Edward Burtynsky (born 1955), CANADA
Catherine Hyland, UK

35. Apocalyptic Imagination

John Martin (1789–1854) wanted his final project to be epic: a large-scale blockbuster that would wow the widest possible audience. The 62-year-old artist understood the appeal of disaster, so he decided to depict the ultimate catastrophe – the end of the world – in a series of three paintings, to be exhibited together.

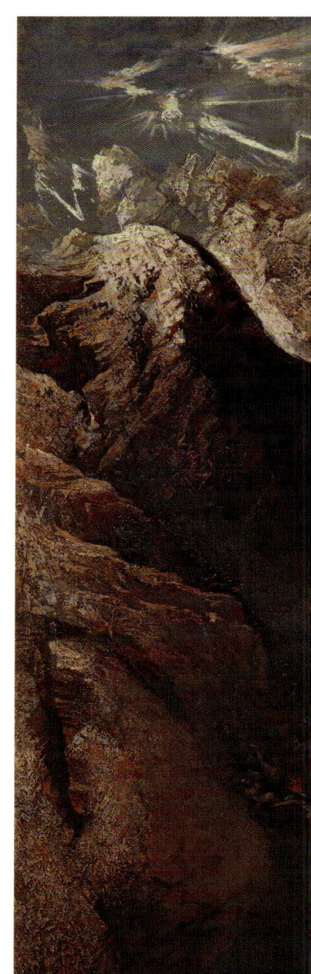

The series shows the biblical version of the apocalypse, with the sun obliterated and the earth buckling beneath titanic forces. To intensify the atmosphere for spectators, various light and sound effects were used to create a multisensory extravaganza. In 1853, the series was taken on a whirlwind tour of Britain before being shown across the US and Australia. It would travel almost continuously for two decades, stunning audiences with its vision of an earth-shattering cataclysm.

Oil on canvas
196.5 × 303.2 cm, 77¼ × 119¼ in.
Tate, London

John Martin
The Great Day of His Wrath
1851–53

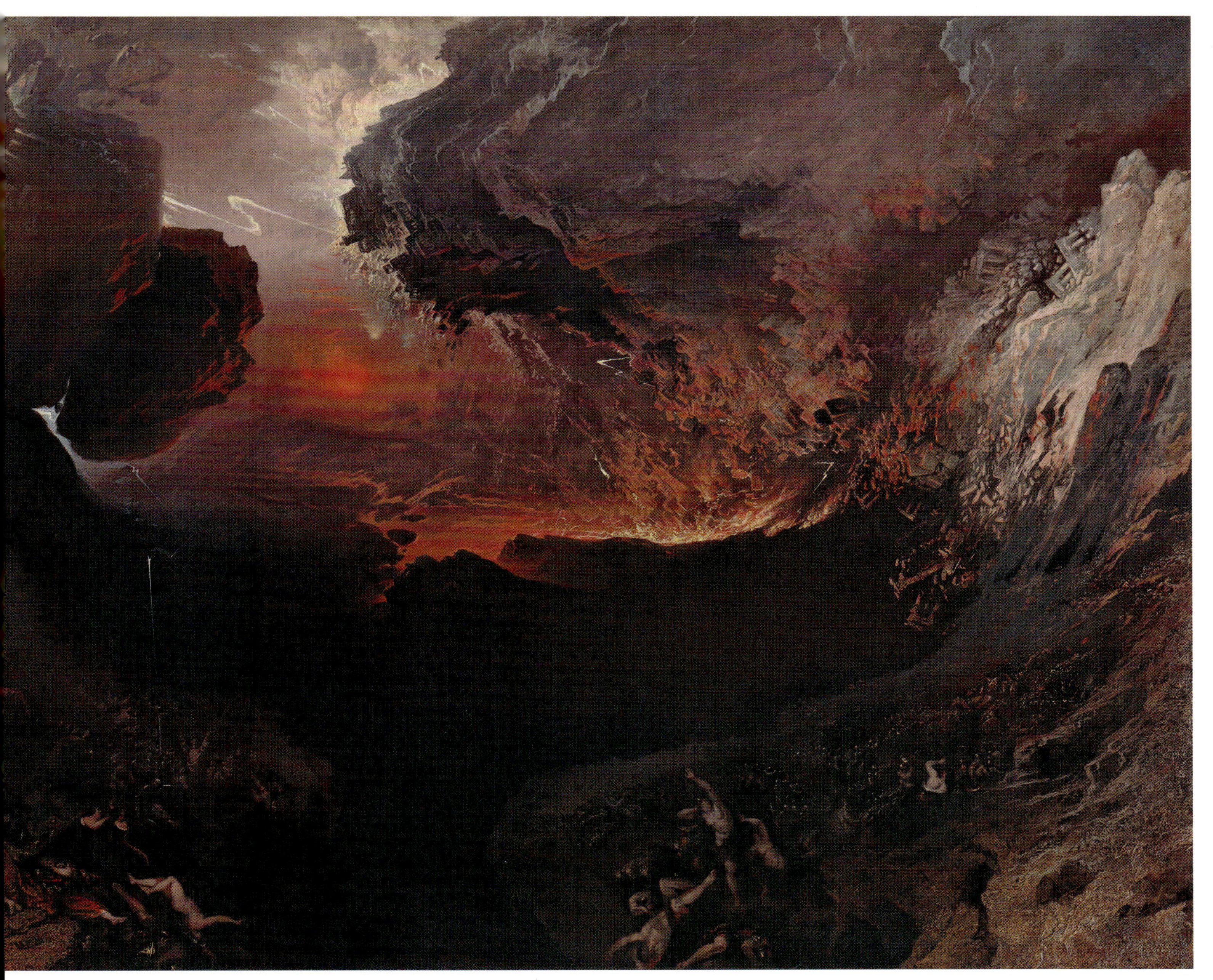

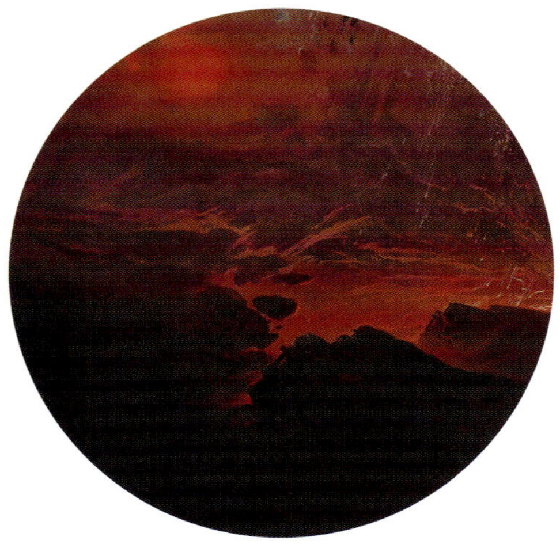

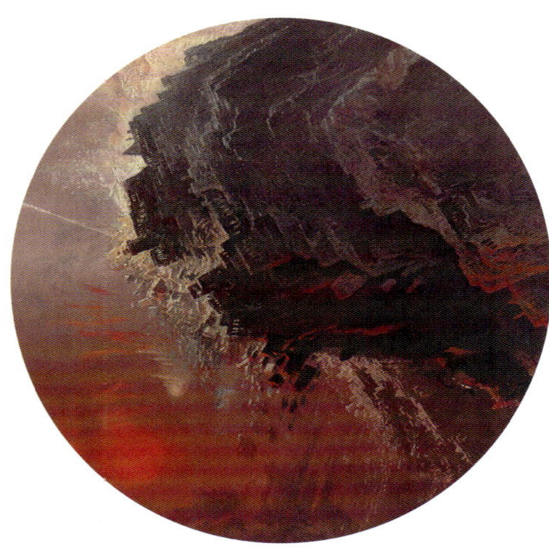

❶ Red

Red is a primary colour, its boldness and intensity setting the tone of the painting. It is also a 'warm' colour, and establishes the sensation of danger with its suggestion of broiling heat.

❷ Scale

In the background, a city is uprooted and flipped upside down. A sense of extreme distance is established by the contrast between the tiny scale of the buildings and the figures in the foreground.

❸ Triptych

Two other works – *The Last Judgment* and *The Plains of Heaven* – complete the triptych. Painted in the final years of his life (Martin died in 1854), the three paintings address themes of destruction and the end of the world.

❹ Millennialism

'Millennialism' is the belief that the end of the world is imminent. It is named for the 1,000-year-long rule of the saints on earth before the Last Judgment, as described in the Book of Revelation. It is not known if Martin adhered to these beliefs, but members of his family certainly did, along with many others in 19th-century Britain.

❺ Apocalypse

The Great Day of His Wrath depicts a scene from the Book of Revelation, which tells of the end of the world in seven stages, corresponding to the breaking of seven seals, with each seal linking to an apocalyptic event. The opening of the sixth seal prompts the terrifying climax:

> *... and, lo, there was a great earthquake; and the sun became black as sackcloth of hair, and the moon became as blood; fAnd the stars of heaven fell unto the earth ... and every mountain and island were moved out of their places*

❻ Royal Academy

The most prestigious art institution in Britain at the time was the Royal Academy. Martin was never accepted as a member, despite the huge popularity of his work, which was seen as emphasizing dramatic effect over intellectual content. Literary figures like William Hazlitt and Samuel Taylor Coleridge derided it as superficial. John Ruskin, too, thought it repetitive and lacking in imagination, noting: 'Martin's works are merely a common manufacture, as much makable to order as a tea-tray or coal scuttle.'[72]

❼ Weight

Impending doom is evoked with these enormous, tumbling rocks, and our anticipation of the aftermath of their descent.

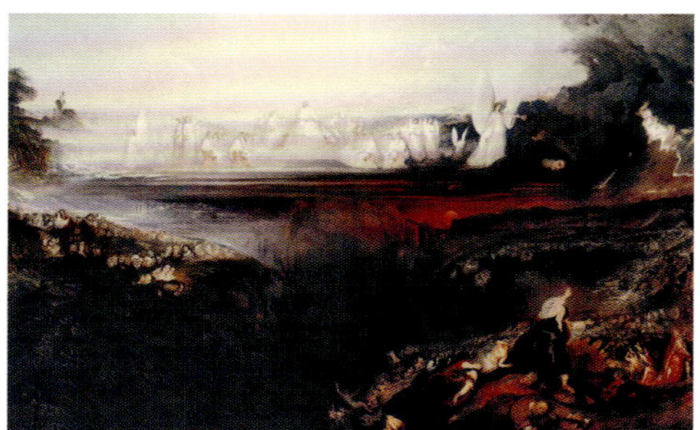

The Last Judgment, 1853. Oil on canvas, 196.8 × 325.8 cm, 77½ × 128¼ in.

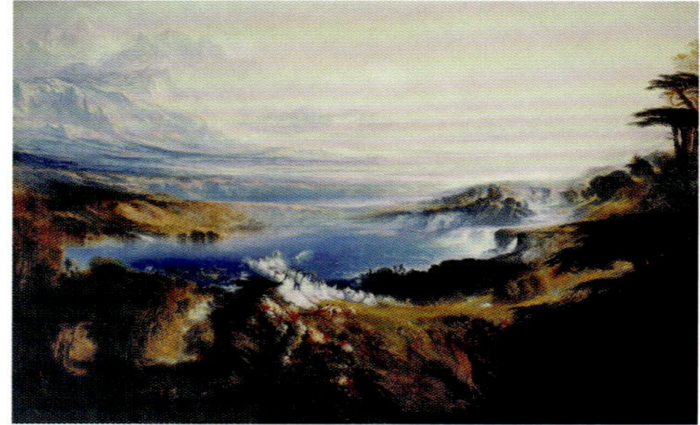

The Plains of Heaven, *c.* 1851. Oil on canvas, 198.8 × 306.7 cm, 78¼ × 120¾ in.

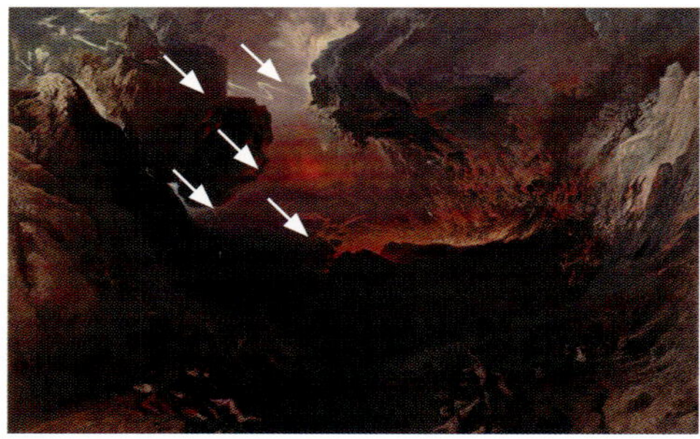

LINKED PRACTITIONERS

MAKERS OF DISASTER FILMS:

Felix E. Feist (1910–1965), USA
Kinji Fukasaku (1930–2003), JAPAN
George P. Cosmatos (1941–2005), ITALY/CANADA
Roland Emmerich (born 1955), GERMANY
Michael Bay (born 1965), USA

APOCALYPSE:

Hieronymus Bosch (1450–1516), NETHERLANDS
Michelangelo (1475–1564), ITALY
J.M.W. Turner (1775–1851), UK
Sebastião Salgado (born 1944), BRAZIL
Glenn Brown (born 1966), UK

THE SUBLIME:

Philip James de Loutherbourg (1740–1812), FRANCE/UK
Caspar David Friedrich (1774–1840), GERMANY
Johan Christian Dahl (1788–1857), NORWAY/GERMANY
Peder Balke (1804–1887), NORWAY
George Frederick Watts (1817–1904), UK

→ J.M.W. Turner, *Dido Building Carthage, or The Rise of the Carthaginian Empire*, 1815. Oil on canvas, 155.5 × 230 cm, 61¼ × 90½ in.

↓ Claude Lorrain, *Seaport with the Embarkation of the Queen of Sheba*, 1648. Oil on canvas, 149.1 × 196.7 cm, 58¾ × 77½ in.

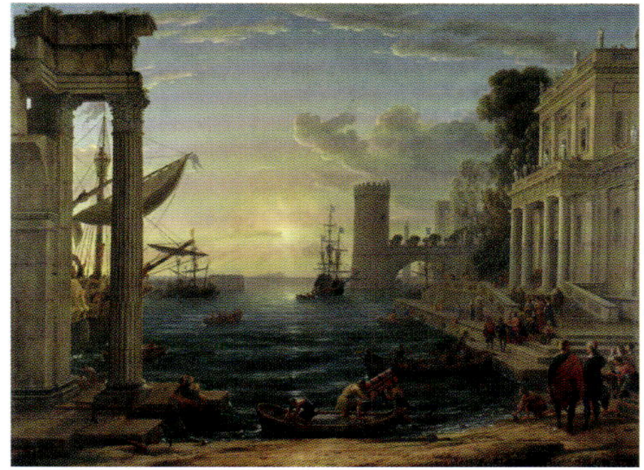

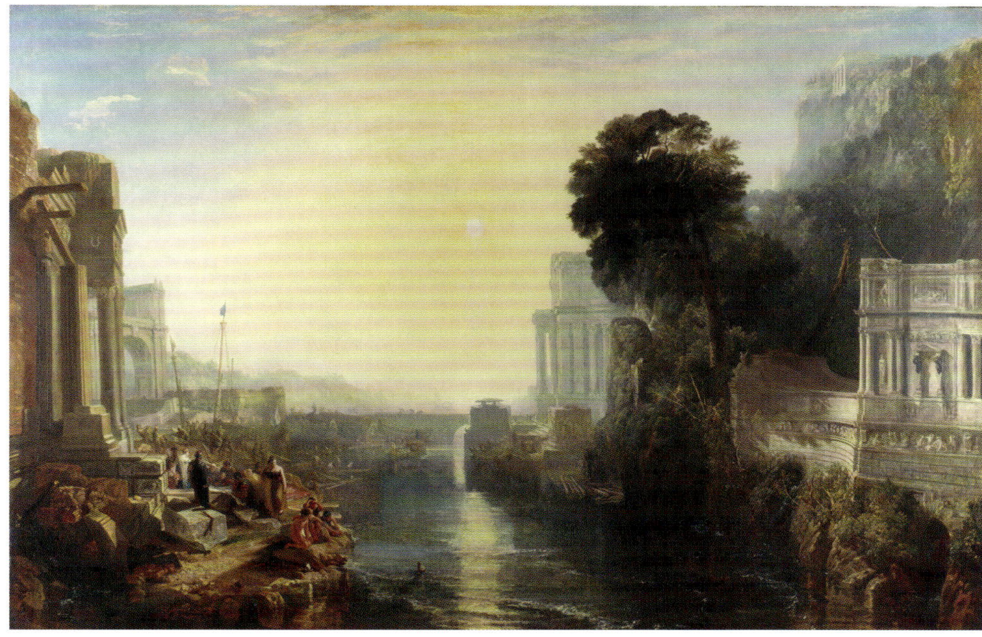

❽ Composition

The composition is based on a landscape format popularized by Claude Lorrain in the 17th century, and later perpetuated by J.M.W. Turner and others. This technique is known as *contre-jour* (looking into the sun). In the upper half of the composition, the scene is bracketed by tall forms (buildings, trees or mountains), with the centre opening to reveal a deep vista. In Martin's version, however, these restful scenes have been transformed into a landscape of epic demolition.

❾ Sublime

Martin's scene of epic disaster is a response to Edmund Burke's theory of the sublime (see p. 162).

❿ Size

The size of the work has a critical impact on its emotional effect. At approximately 2 × 3 m (6 × 10 ft), it is an overwhelming spectacle when seen in person.

⓫ Display

The painting was exhibited in a highly dramatic and immersive way. Audiences were seated in a darkened auditorium, while actors read from a script and stage lighting was pointed at the key areas of the scene.

Film stills from *Intolerance*, 1916, directed by D.W. Griffith

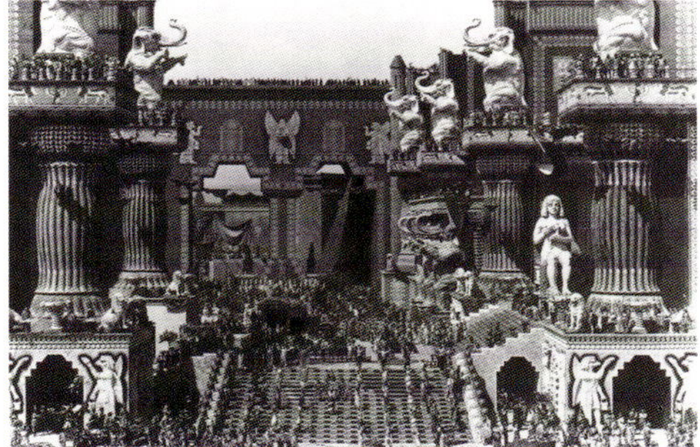

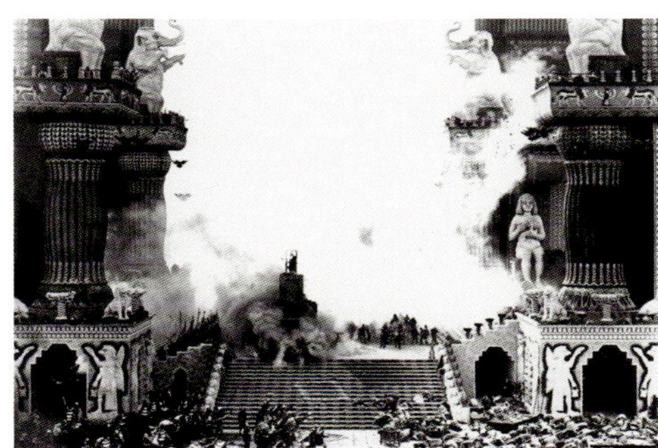

⓬ Cinematic drama

Martin's innovations are almost cinematic, despite his work predating film by several decades. His use of epic scale and dramatic scenes from history inspired many 20th-century film-makers, including D.W. Griffith (above) and the stop-motion animator Ray Harryhausen (*Jason and the Argonauts* and *Clash of the Titans*). Martin's paintings have also been compared to modern disaster movies like *2012* and *San Andreas* (above right).

Film poster for *San Andreas*, 2015, directed by Brad Peyton

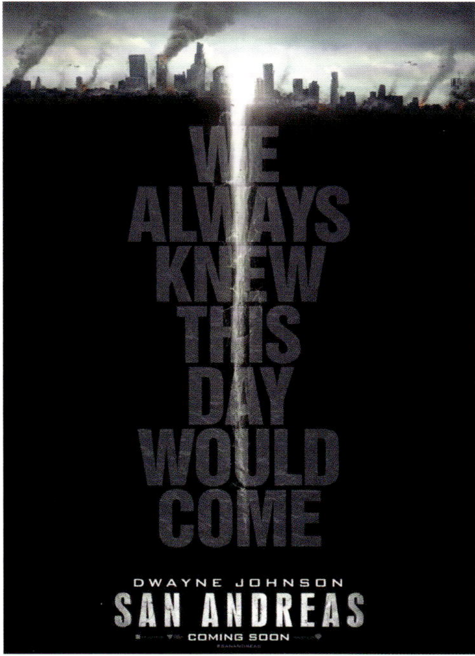

⓭ Entrepreneur

Martin's epic biblical scenes were famous around the world. He toured his works across Britain, displaying them in galleries, music halls and theatres. Most of his wealth came from making mezzotint prints of his work, which sold in vast quantities. His popularity during his lifetime is attested by the vast numbers who saw *The Great Day of His Wrath* while it was on tour. By 1861, three million people – one-third of the British population – had reportedly seen it.

36. Paying Homage

In the spring of 1890, the American artist Mary Cassatt (1844–1926) visited an exhibition of Japanese prints at the École des Beaux-Arts in Paris. Enthralled by what she saw, she wrote to her friend and fellow Impressionist, Berthe Morisot: 'You who want to make colour prints, you couldn't dream of anything more beautiful. I dream of it and don't think of anything else.'

Cassatt was particularly captivated by the prints of Kitagawa Utamaro, which depicted scenes of the everyday life of Japanese women, and plotted a new artistic project. She learned printing techniques under the tutelage of Félix Bracquemond and Edgar Degas, and rented the Château Bachivillers, a suitably large and inspirational space near Paris in which to launch her new venture.

Colour drypoint and aquatint
34.4 × 22.7 cm, 13½ × 9 in.
Philadelphia Museum of Art

Mary Cassatt
The Letter
1890–91

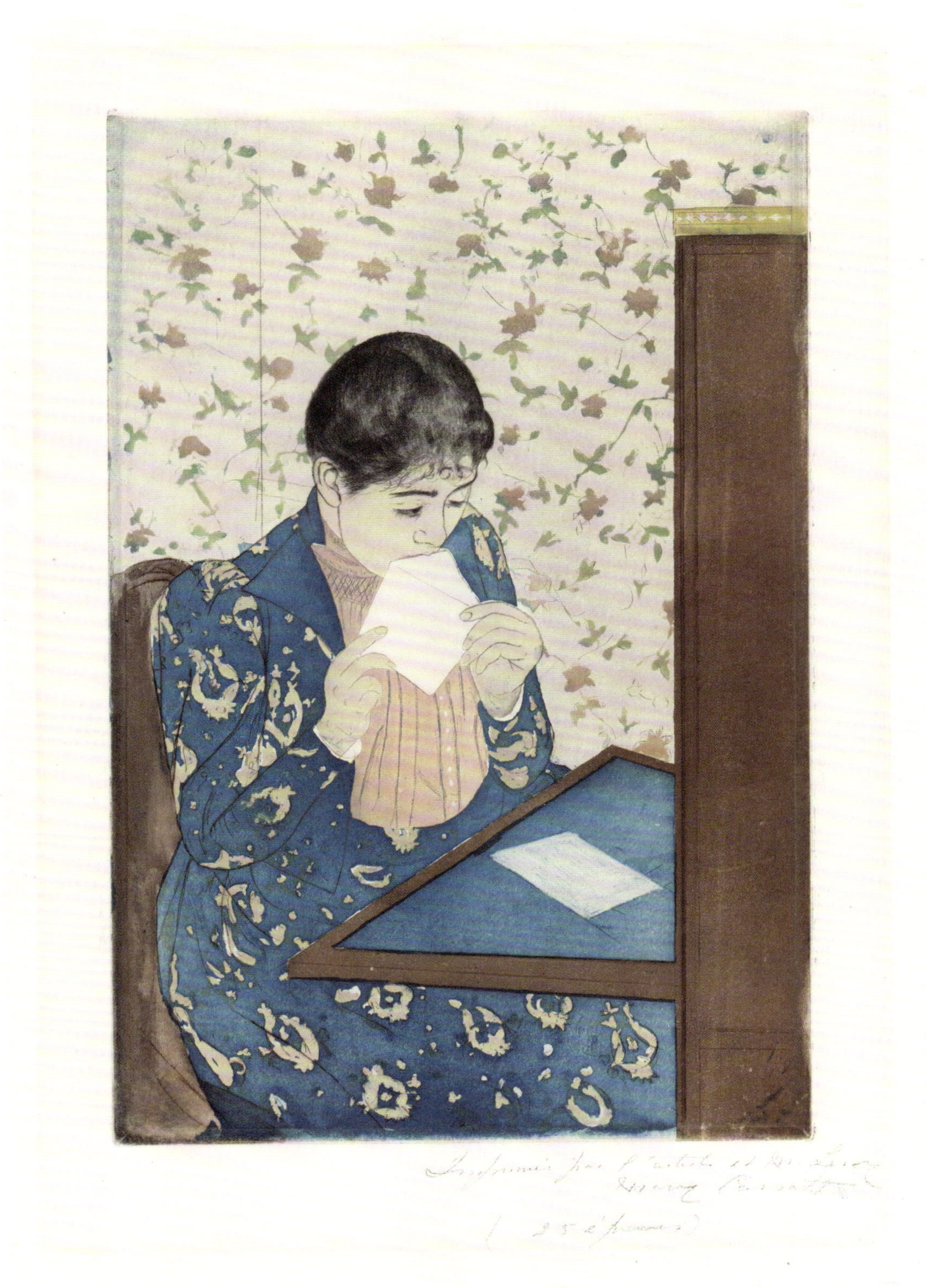

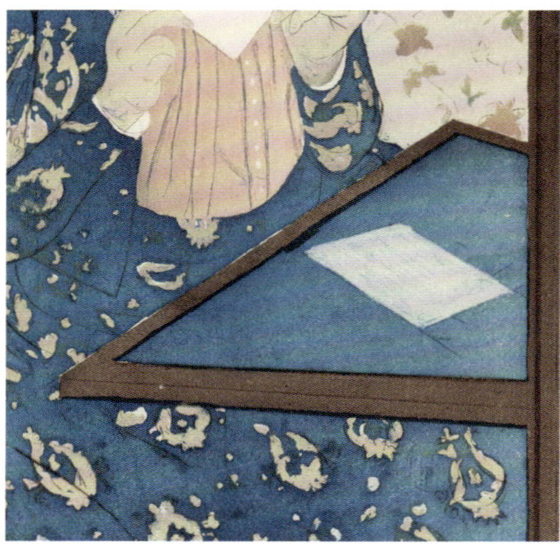

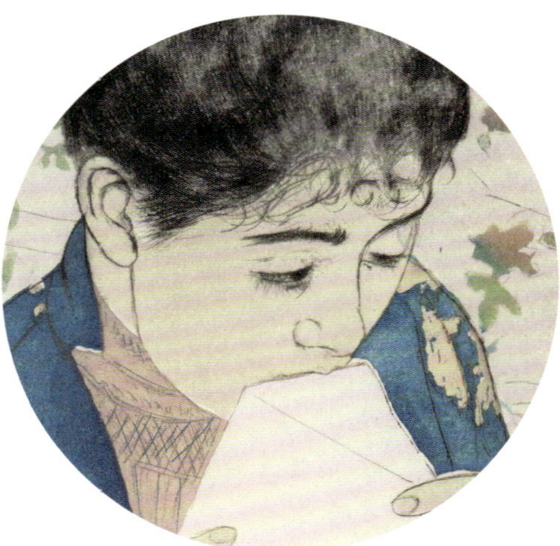

❶ Perspective

In an otherwise harmonious composition, the distorted perspective of the desk – with its non-parallel edges – is a disconcerting addition. It would have been jarring to a contemporary audience, who were by now accustomed to the spatial consistencies of photography.

❷ A modern approach

Techniques of photography had been invented in the 1830s by Louis Daguerre in France and William Henry Fox Talbot in Britain. As photographs became more popular and accessible, some artists chose deliberately unphotographic techniques, intensifying colours and exploring the effects of disjointed perspective. This paved the way for the more radical styles of art that were to follow.

❸ Japanese inspiration

The search for new ways of seeing led many artists to Japanese art, with its compositions, patterns and colouration that were utterly unlike European artistic traditions. Cassatt so admired *ukiyo-e* prints that she even replicated the *oban* format (38 × 25 cm, 10 × 15 in.).

❹ Technique

Like Rembrandt (pp. 124–7), Cassatt used the drypoint technique, which involved scratching lines directly onto copper plates. Three plates were used for a single image, each for a different colour applied by hand. Needing larger premises, she rented the Château Bachivillers and employed a specialist printer, Modeste Leroy, to assist her.

❺ Expression

The main focus of the image is the woman's face. It carries an ambiguous expression – the hooded eyes may indicate regret, weariness or indecision – and invites the viewer to engage with deciphering her emotional state.

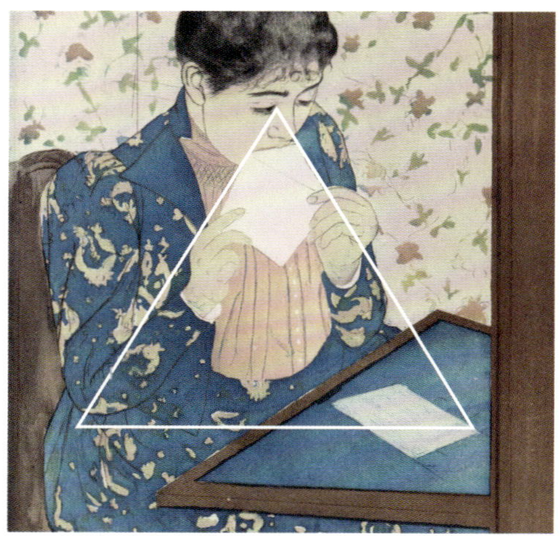

❻ Composition

Although seemingly illustrating a moment that has been captured spontaneously, the composition is logical and carefully structured. The edges of the envelope are the upper part of a triangle that has its apex at the woman's right eye. It guides our gaze up from the bottom left and down to the letter on the table.

❼ Blue and brown

Cassatt used blocks of unmodulated (or flat) colour in her print. The colour scheme is also simplified, so that the tone of blue in the dress is the same as the desktop, and the same brown is used in the desk and the chair.

❽ Line

One of Cassatt's aims was to create beauty through simplification. Her minimal use of line is a vital part of this visual economy. The lines defining the woman's form are abbreviated but evocative. For visual interest, straight lines (such as the edge of letter) counteract curved lines (such as the hands).

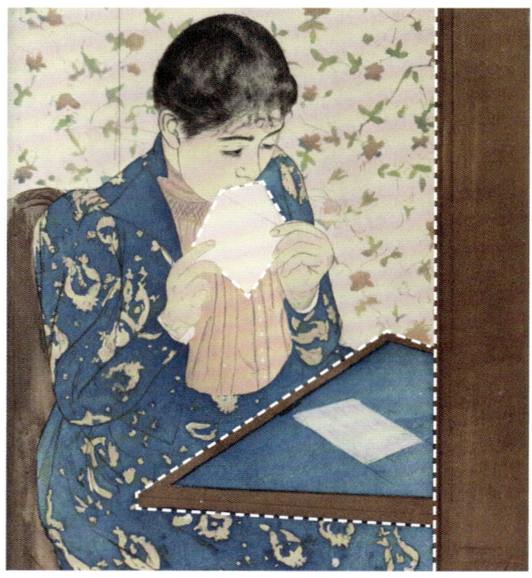

❾ Series

Cassatt made a total of 10 colour aquatints, 25 impressions of each. Because the plates were individually coloured for every impression, each version is subtly different. The prints were exhibited at Galerie Durand-Ruel, Paris, in 1891. One visitor, Camille Pissarro, grudgingly noted that the results were 'admirable, as beautiful as Japanese art'.[73]

❿ *Ukiyo-e*

Cassatt admired Japanese *ukiyo-e* prints for their ingenious compositions and bold use of colour and pattern. She was also attracted to the idea that the prints were a form of art that was widely available and inexpensive, later writing:

> *I believe [nothing] will inspire a taste for art more than the possibility of having it in the home. I should like to feel that amateurs in America could have an example of my work … for a few dollars. That is what they do in France. It is not left to the rich alone to buy art; the people – even the poor – have taste and buy according to their means, and here they can always find something they can afford.*[74]

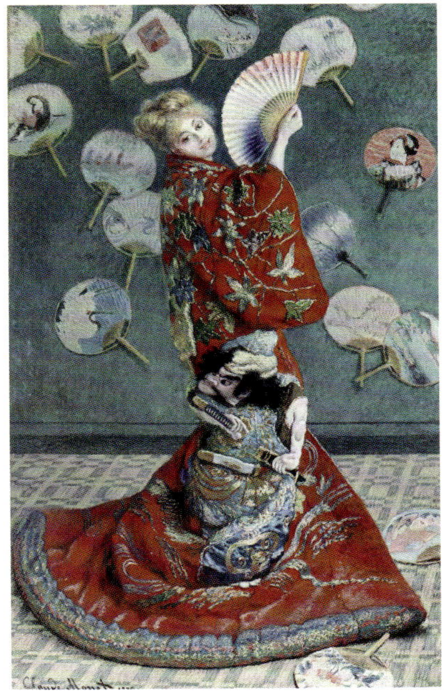

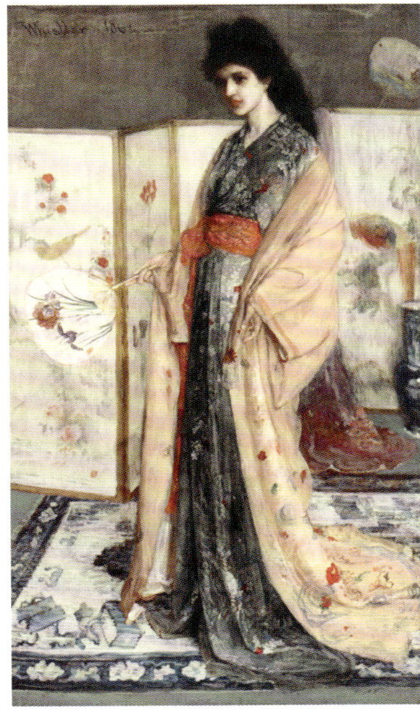

← J.A.M. Whistler, *The Princess from the Land of Porcelain*, 1865. Oil on canvas, 201.5 × 116.1 cm, 79¼ × 45¾ in.

←← Claude Monet, *La Japonaise (Camille Monet in Japanese Costume)*, 1876. Oil on canvas, 231.8 × 142.3 cm, 91¼ × 56 in.

⓭ Japonisme

The popularity of Japanese art in Europe in the later 19th century became known as 'Japonisme'. After two centuries of isolation, Japan opened its borders to international trade in 1854 and soon afterwards, artists – particularly in France – began to collect and imitate Japanese prints, which had often been used as packing material for ceramics and other goods. Among these artists were Édouard Manet, J.A.M. Whistler (left), Claude Monet (far left), Paul Gauguin and Vincent van Gogh (see pp. 172–5).

⓮ Narrative

This scene, one of a series of 10 showing the daily lives of well-heeled women, focuses on a humble episode, glorifying the humdrum aspect of life.

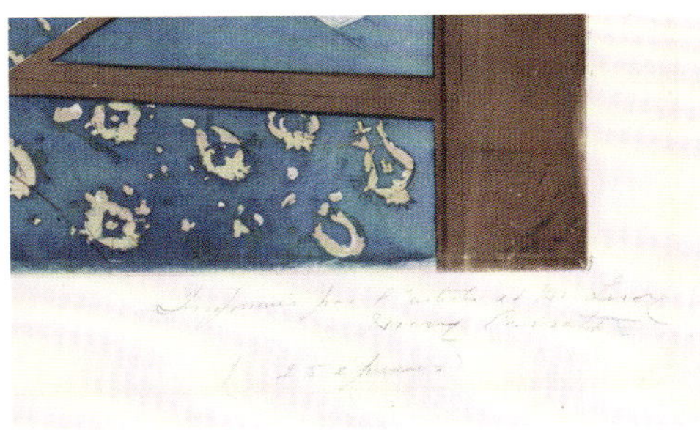

⓫ Writing

The writing at the bottom of the print gives the name of the artist (Cassatt) and the print-maker (Leroy). This follows the Japanese tradition of acknowledging both practitioners.

⓬ Tradition

Scenes of women reading or writing love letters was a popular subject for French Rococo artists in the late 18th century, including François Boucher and Jean Honoré Fragonard (above right). Cassatt's representation, however, is much less decadent and erotic.

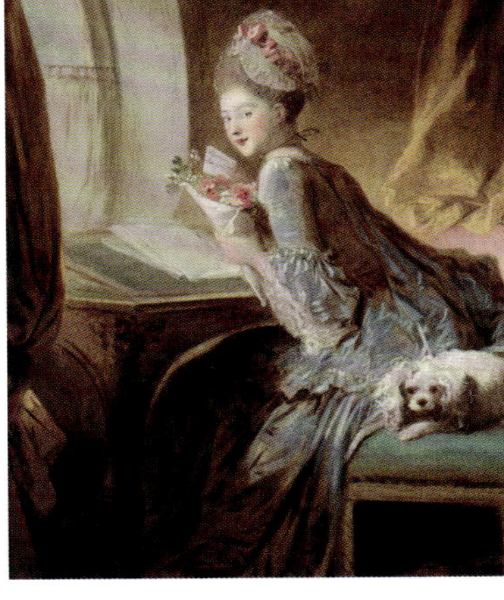

↑ Jean Honoré Fragonard, *The Love Letter*, early 1770s. Oil on canvas, 83.2 × 67 cm, 32¾ × 26¼ in.

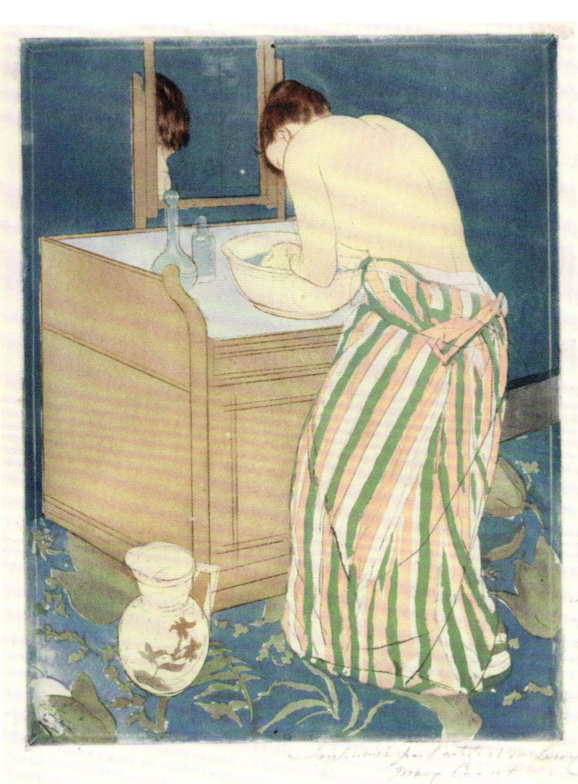

→ *Woman Bathing*, 1890–91. Colour drypoint and aquatint on laid paper, 36.4 × 26.7 cm, 14¼ × 10½ in.

LINKED PRACTITIONERS

PRINTMAKERS:

Albrecht Dürer (1471–1528), GERMANY
Rembrandt van Rijn (1606–1669), NETHERLANDS
William Blake (1757–1827), UK
Katsushika Hokusai (1760–1849), JAPAN
Tsukioka Yoshitoshi (1839–1892), JAPAN

IMPRESSIONIST ARTISTS:

Camille Pissarro (1830–1903), FRANCE
Edgar Degas (1834–1917), FRANCE
Claude Monet (1840–1926), FRANCE
Berthe Morisot (1841–1895), FRANCE
Pierre-Auguste Renoir (1841–1919), FRANCE

INSPIRED BY JAPANESE ART:

Alfred Stevens (1823–1906), BELGIUM/FRANCE
Vincent van Gogh (1853–1890), NETHERLANDS/FRANCE
Gustav Klimt (1862–1918), AUSTRIA
Pierre Bonnard (1867–1947), FRANCE
Bertha Lum (1869–1954), USA

37. Searching the Stars

One summer night in 1889, Vincent van Gogh (1853–1890) peered out at the moonlit Provençal landscape. 'I saw the countryside from my window a long time before sunrise with nothing but the morning star, which looked very big,' he wrote to his brother Theo. The Starry Night, *painted soon afterwards, shows a constellation of similarly glowing stars, connected by fluttering ribbons of clouds.*

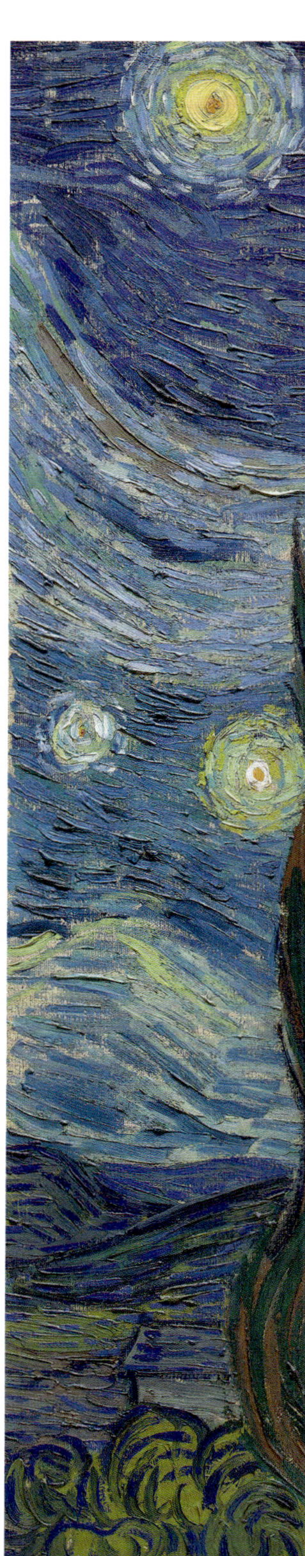

For Van Gogh, celestial bodies possessed a metaphysical symbolism. A year earlier, he had written to his fellow artist Émile Bernard, describing stars as the final destination of the soul, 'which, after death, would perhaps be no more unapproachable, inaccessible to us than the black dots that symbolize towns and villages on the map in our earthly life'. This agitated vision came from an agitated mind: Van Gogh was staring at the night sky from his room in the asylum at St-Paul-de-Mausole, where he had committed himself after a period of severe depression.

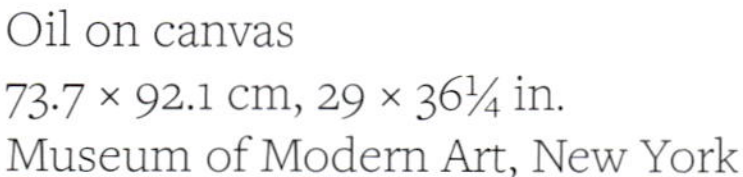

Oil on canvas
73.7 × 92.1 cm, 29 × 36¼ in.
Museum of Modern Art, New York

Vincent van Gogh
The Starry Night
1889

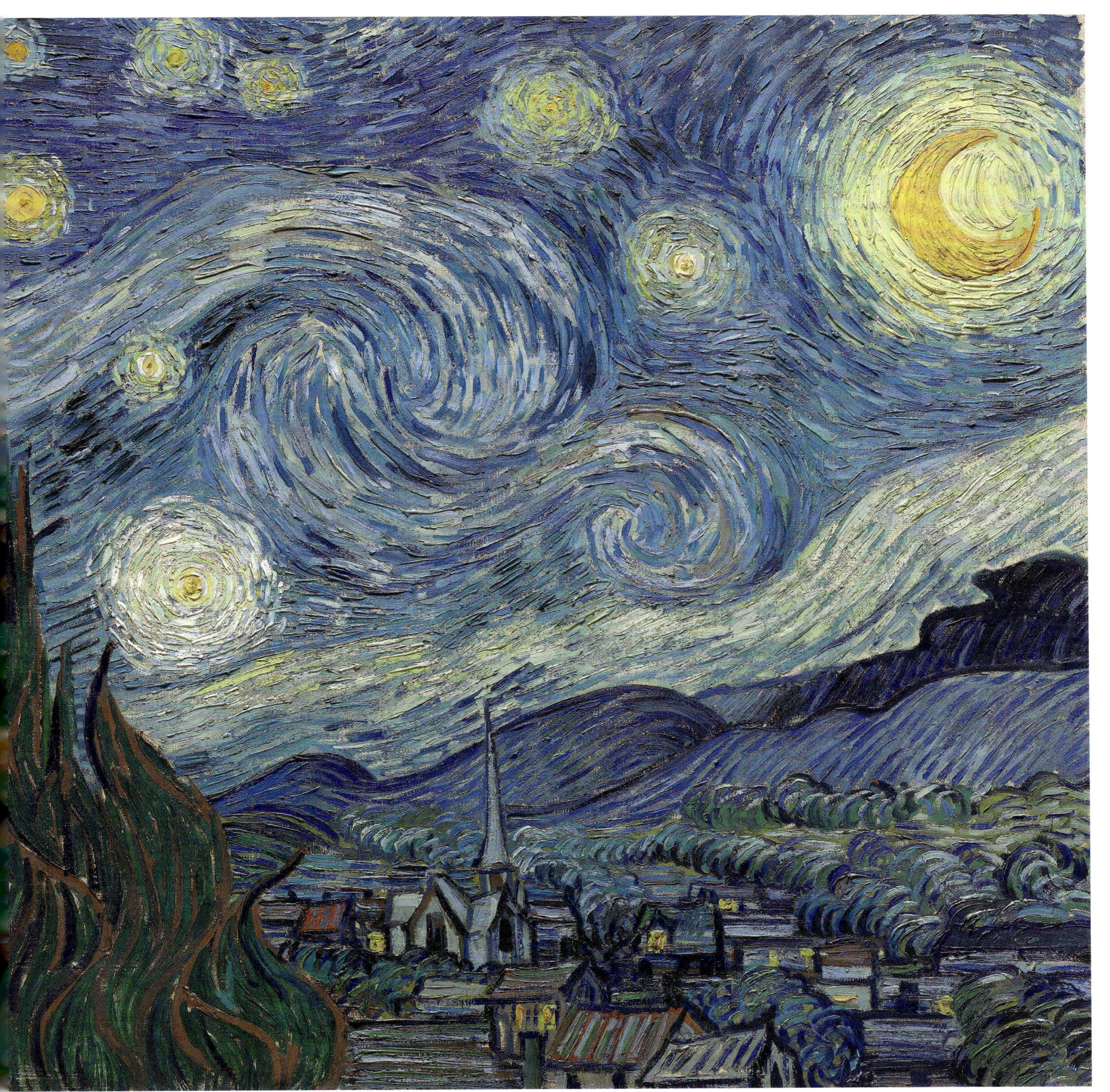

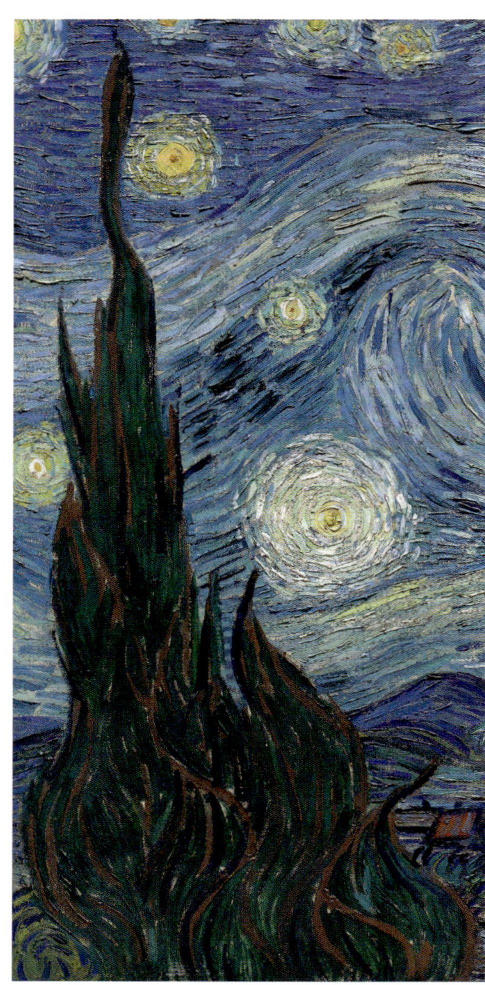

❶ Cypress

We are led into the painting from the left, where a large cypress tree is pushed right into the foreground. It balances out the moon, which dominates the right side of the work.

❷ Death

In the iconography of classical antiquity, the cypress tree was a symbol of mourning and death. Today, many cemeteries still feature cypress trees.

❸ Religion

Our gaze is drawn to the church spire. Like the cypress tree, it is rooted to the ground, but penetrates the sky. Van Gogh had been intensely religious earlier in his life, and had attempted to become a pastor – without success.

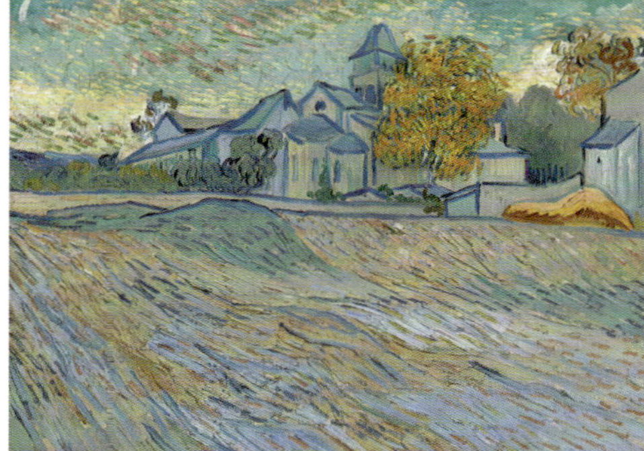

Church of St-Paul-de-Mausole, 1889. Oil on canvas, 45.2 × 60.3 cm, 17¾ × 23¾ in.

❹ Fantasy

The architecture of the church is Dutch in style, utterly unlike the location where the work was painted: the asylum at St-Paul-de-Mausole in Provence. The scene is not a faithful record of the landscape: there was no village in Van Gogh's eyeline from his bedroom, nor was there a cypress tree in the close foreground.

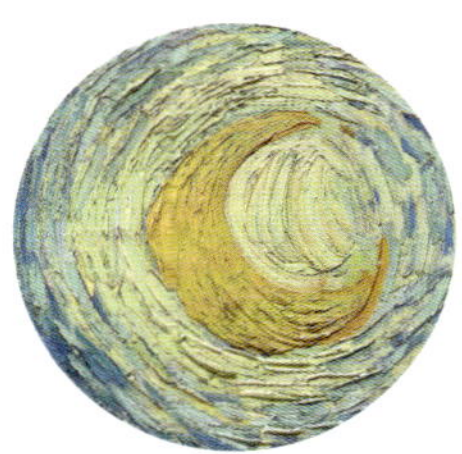

❺ Unity

The eddying of the clouds resembles the rolling hills and wave-like shapes of the cypress tree. Colours also unify the scene: the brown used around the edge of the tree is reused in the swirling clouds. The yellow of the moon reappears in the colour of the windows.

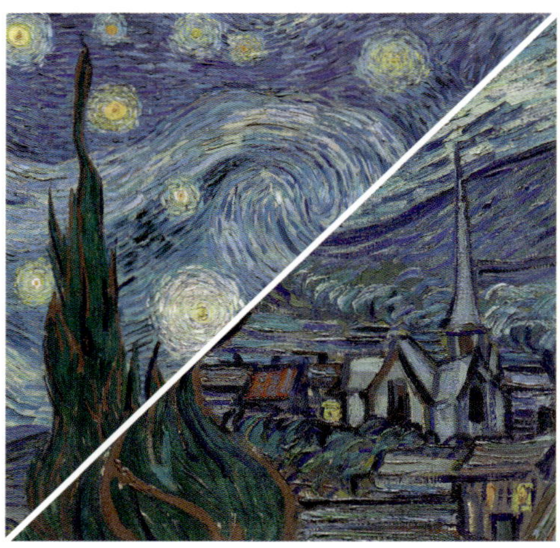

❻ Spire

The pointed spire at the centre of the composition also echoes the cypress tree. It creates a sense of visual harmony and leads our eye to the heart of the image, establishing depth.

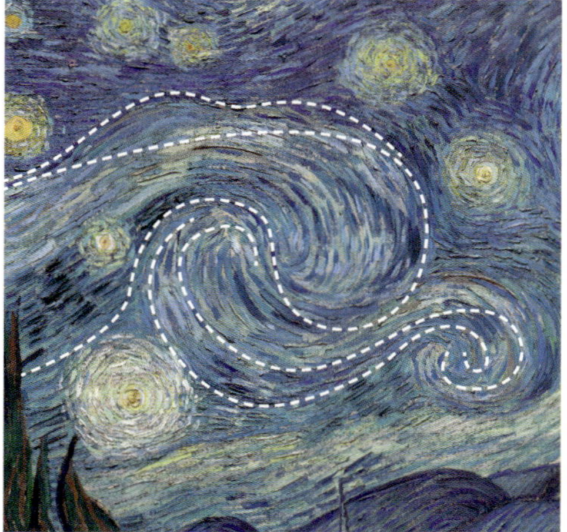

❼ Clouds

The clouds swirl overhead in a highly stylized, non-realistic manner, evoking the powerful mistral that buffets the region. A ball of cloud, resembling the Chinese *yin-yang* symbol, sits at the exact centre of the composition.

LINKED PRACTITIONERS

BLUE:	NIGHTTIME LANDSCAPES:	POST-IMPRESSIONISM:
Titian (*c.* 1488/90–1576), ITALY	*Adam Elsheimer* (1578–1610), GERMANY	*Paul Cézanne* (1839–1906), FRANCE
Wassily Kandinsky (1866–1944), RUSSIA	*Samuel Palmer* (1805–1881), UK	*Henri Rousseau* (1844–1910), FRANCE
Henri Matisse (1869–1954), FRANCE	*J.A.M. Whistler* (1834–1903), USA/UK	*Paul Gauguin* (1848–1903), FRANCE
Yves Klein (1928–1962), FRANCE	*Edward Hopper* (1882–1967), USA	*Georges Seurat* (1859–1891), FRANCE
Roger Hiorns (born 1975), UK	*Peter Doig* (born 1959), UK	*Maurice Prendergast* (1858–1924), USA

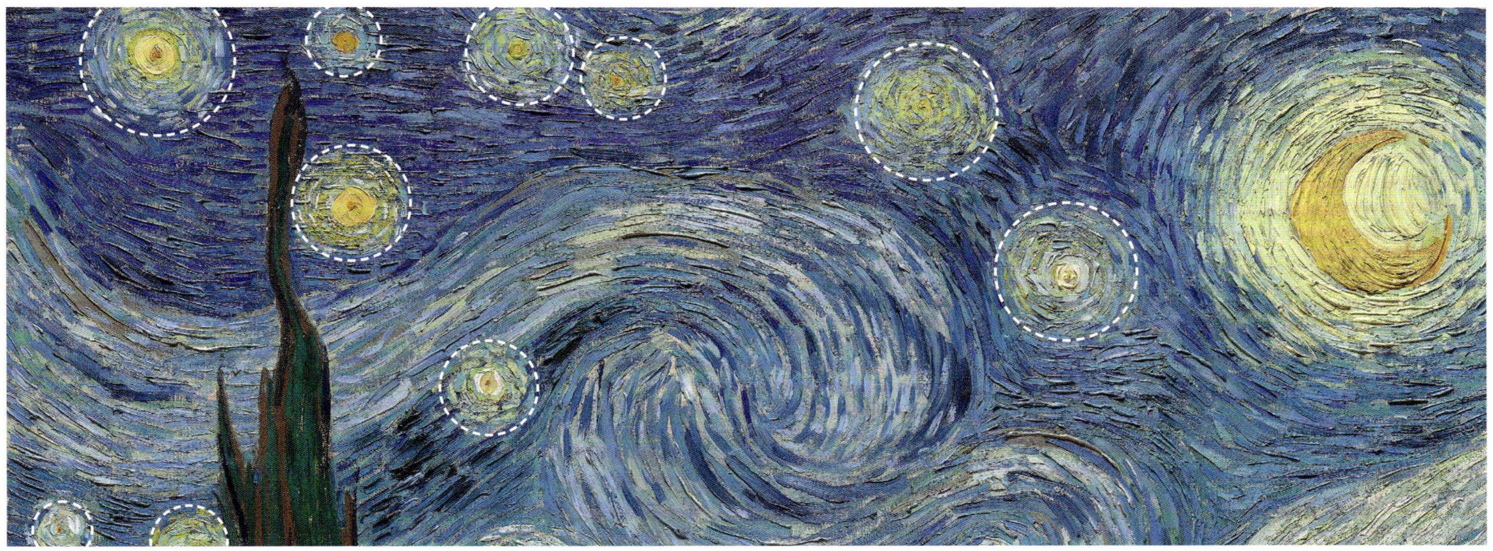

❽ Stars

Like other elements of the painting, Van Gogh has represented the stars in a non-realistic way, exaggerating their brightness and colour. This scene represents not a peaceful nocturne, but a sky with the explosive intensity of a firework display.

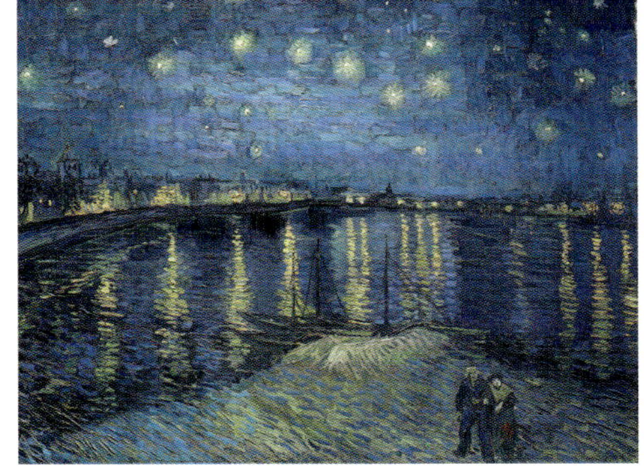

Starry Night Over the Rhône, 1888. Oil on canvas, 73 × 92 cm, 28¾ × 36¼ in.

❾ Sky

The horizon line is low, drawing our focus to the sky. This is a typical feature of the art of the Dutch Golden Age in the 17th century, especially landscapes by artists such as Jacob van Ruisdael (below).

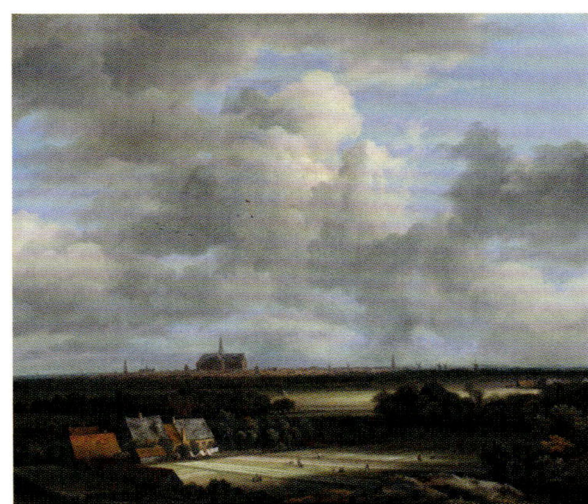

Jacob van Ruisdael, *View of Haarlem with Bleaching Grounds*, *c.* 1670–75. Oil on canvas, 55.5 × 62 cm, 21¾ × 24½ in.

❿ Blue

The painting has an overall feeling of consistency owing to the blue tones that feature in the sky, the hills of the background and the ground below.

Blue tones: sky

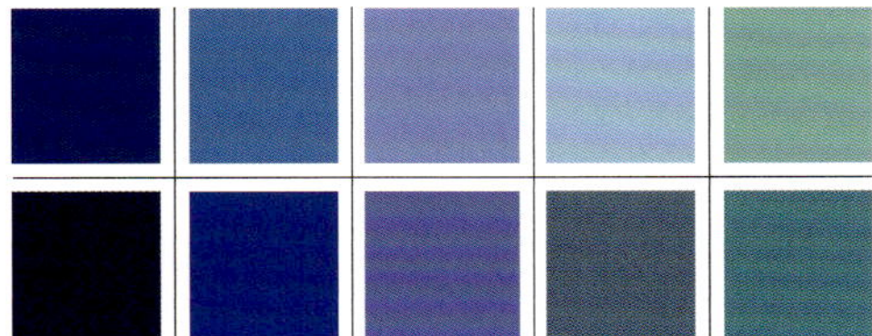

Blue tones: ground

⓫ Heavens

In his letters to his brother Theo, Van Gogh describes the stars as being the final destination of souls after death. The cypress tree in the foreground seems to reach upwards to connect with the highest star in the sky.

⓬ Inspiration

It has been suggested that Van Gogh was inspired to paint *The Starry Night* by Hokusai's *Under the Wave off Kanagawa* (pp. 152–5), a print he is known to have admired. Other elements of the canvas prove his knowledge of the work of other Japanese *ukiyo-e* artists, including Utagawa Hiroshige, whose style – particularly the placement of objects in the extreme foreground, and the use of intense colour – he emulates here.

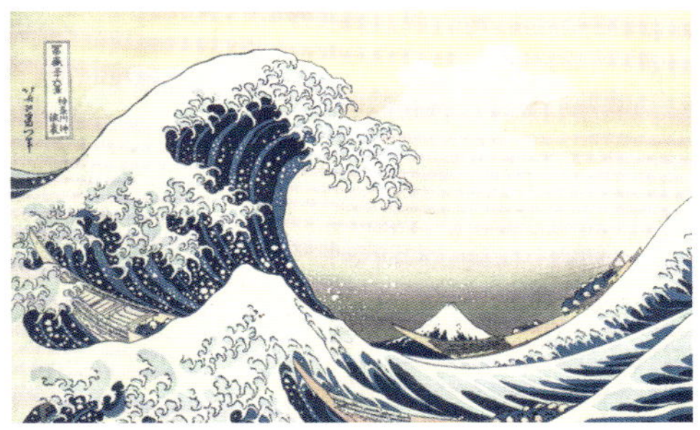

↑ Katsushika Hokusai, *Under the Wave off Kanagawa*, *c.* 1830–32

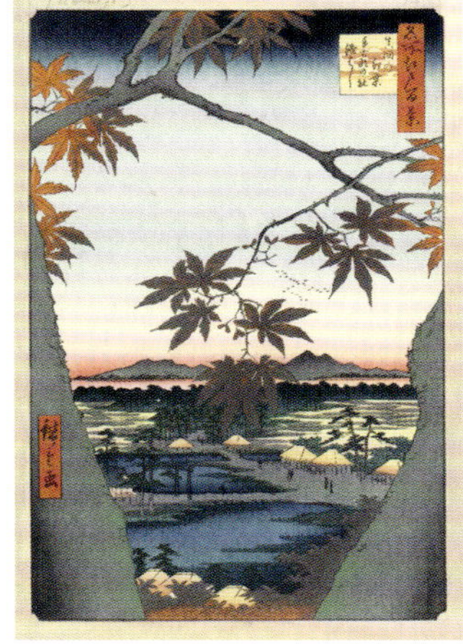

← Utagawa Hiroshige, *Maple Trees at Mama, Tekona Shrine and Linked Bridge*, no. 94 from *One Hundred Famous Views of Edo*, 1857. Woodblock print, 36 × 23.5 cm, 14¼ × 9¼ in.

38. Seeing is Believing

In 1912, Pablo Picasso (1881–1973) saw a work of art by his close friend and rival Georges Braque that impressed and challenged him. Braque had made a charcoal drawing of a fruit dish and glass in the Cubist style, but had then stuck strips of cheap imitation wood grain onto it to form the background of the scene (ill. p. 179).

This simple technique showed that even the most insignificant items could assume significance and be transformed into art. Picasso spent about a month working on his response: *Guitar and Wine Glass*. Part of his approach was to incorporate as many different modes of visual communication as he could find, calling into question the way that images create meanings. This included incorporating the written word, musical notation and everyday items like wallpaper into the composition.

Collage and charcoal on board
47.9 × 37.5 cm, 18¾ × 14¾ in.
McNay Art Museum, San Antonio

Pablo Picasso

Guitar and Wine Glass

1912

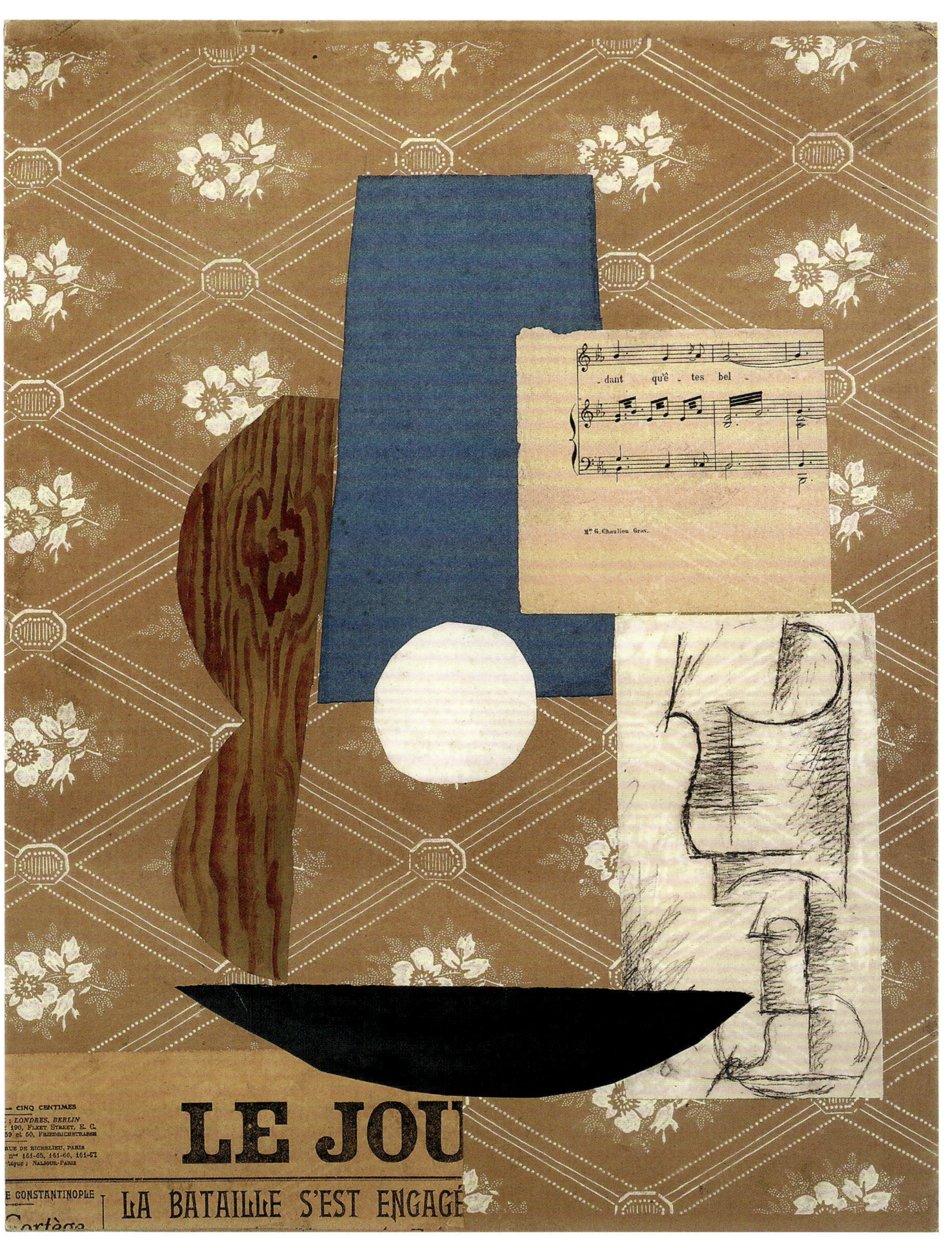

❶ Wallpaper

Guitar and Wine Glass is a still life, and does not represent depth in a conventional way. The background, for example, is simply a sheet of commercially produced wallpaper. Picasso soon became obsessed with finding old-fashioned wallpaper for his paintings, to achieve a suitably run-down atmosphere.

❷ Collage

This is one of the first works in which Picasso used the technique of collage, where pieces of paper and card are assembled and stuck down onto paper. After Braque led the way, collage was taken up by Picasso and his fellow Cubists, and adopted by succeeding generations of artists, including Kurt Schwitters (right).

❸ Simplification

This section of the collage indicates the side of the guitar. Along with the other pieces of black, white and blue cut paper, Picasso has made us imagine the guitar's presence by using the fewest possible shapes.

❹ Art and life

Rather than depicting the objects in his composition in the usual manner, Picasso has used the material itself (i.e., the wallpaper) to create the scene, bringing actual objects into the realm of 'art'.

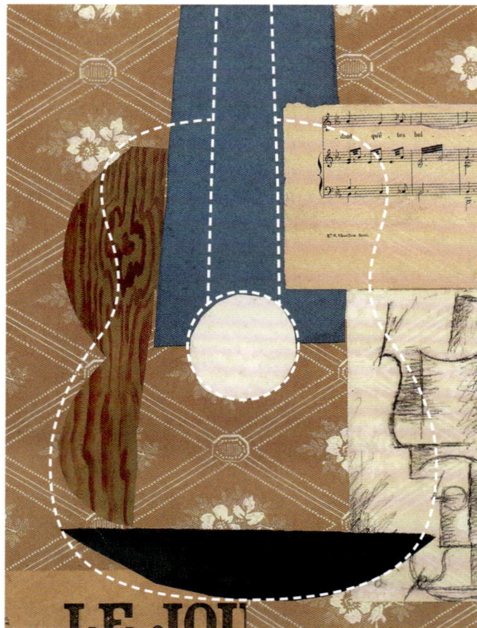

❺ Wood grain

The segment of faux-wood grain has the appearance of having been bought cheaply in a hardware store. In fact, it was painted by Picasso: a simulation of a simulation.

❻ Art within art

A glass sits beside the guitar, but it is not a real glass: it is a drawing of a glass, drawn in the Cubist style and stuck down onto the picture. Also present are a fragment of newspaper, some sheet music and pieces of paper arranged to suggest the shape of a guitar.

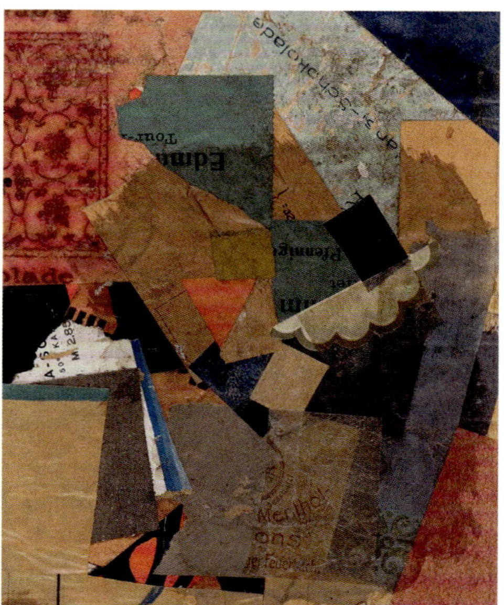

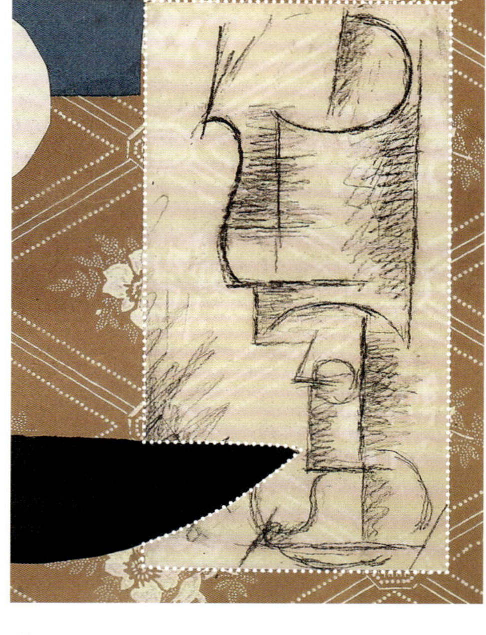

❼ Composition

The musical score is a popular song, which adds a suggestion of sound into an otherwise purely visual scene.

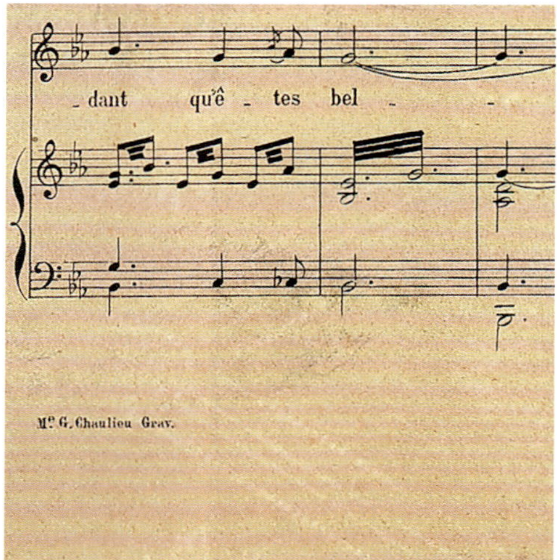

❽ 'While you are beautiful … '

Could Picasso's work be about desire? The musical annotation is for a song by popular French *chansonnier*, Marcel Legay, which contains the words *dans qu'êtes bel* ('while you are beautiful').[75]

Kurt Schwitters, *Mz 387. Kaltensundheim*, 1922. Collage, paper on paper, 33.1 × 26.9 cm, 13 × 10½ in.

9 News

The newspaper is placed at the foreground as if it is propped on a table in front of the guitar. It creates the atmosphere of a workers' café, where newspapers could be picked up for free.

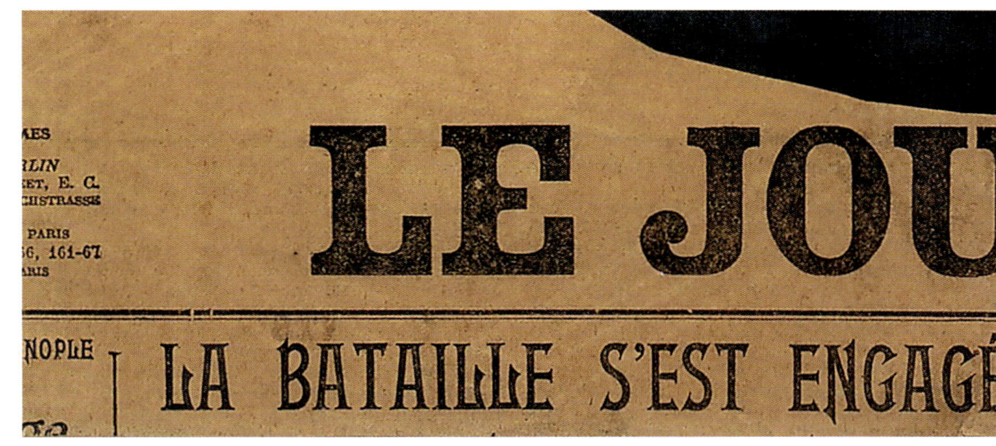

10 War

The headline *La battaille s'est engagé* ('The battle has been joined') refers to the ongoing Balkan Wars (1912–13), which many at the time feared could escalate into a large-scale conflict. What double meaning did Picasso have in mind? His personal competition with Braque, or the recent controversy about Cubism, which had caused arguments in the French Parliament? Or perhaps a more general anarchist sentiment detected by some in his work?[76]

11 Playful pun

The newspaper title – *Le Journal* – has been cut off in the middle, leaving the word *jou*, French for 'play'.

12 Against the old

In 1912 Guillaume Apollinaire, an enthusiastic defender of Cubism, wrote a poem entitled 'Zone'. Whereas other poets had tried to evoke timeless themes, Apollinaire embraced the language of the street: 'The handbills, catalogues, posters that sing out loud and clear, that's the morning's poetry, and for prose there are newspapers ... tabloids lurid with police reports.'[77] In the same year, Picasso also turned the language of the streets into art.

13 Revolution

Collage is a far cry from the more exalted art processes like drawing with charcoal or painting with oils. This was a deliberate signal by Picasso to demonstrate his desire to break with the art of the past.

→ *Violin, Bottle and Glass*, 1913. Oil, collage and charcoal on canvas, 65 × 50 cm, 25½ × 19¾ in.

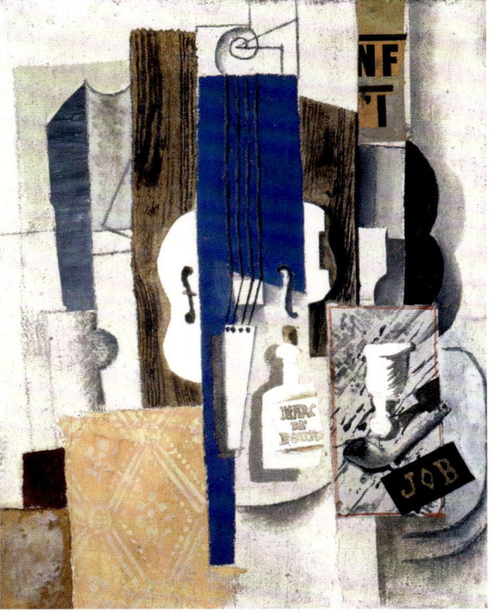

↓ Georges Braque, *Fruit Dish and Glass*, 1912. Charcoal and cut-and-pasted printed wallpaper with gouache on white laid paper; subsequently mounted on paperboard, 62.9 × 45.7 cm, 24¾ × 18 in.

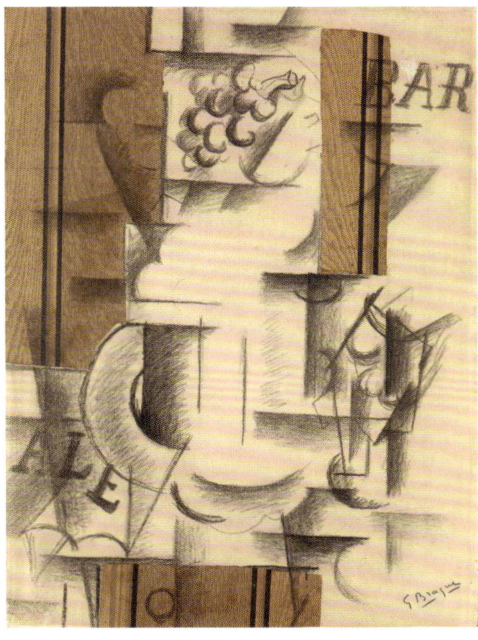

14 Guitars

In 1901 *Arte Joven*, a Barcelona journal of which Picasso was artistic editor, ran an article entitled 'The Psychology of the Guitar'. It linked the shape of the instrument to the shape of a woman's body, to be played by a male musician. This association of music and romance is well established in art history, and may account for the artist's frequent depiction of the guitar in his paintings and sculptures.

LINKED PRACTITIONERS

CUBISM:	COLLAGE:	STILL-LIFE PAINTINGS:
Fernand Léger (1881–1955), FRANCE	*Hannah Höch* (1889–1978), GERMANY	*Clara Peeters* (1594–1657), BELGIUM
Georges Braque (1882–1963), FRANCE	*Max Ernst* (1891–1976), GERMANY/FRANCE	*Rachel Ruysch* (1664–1750), NETHERLANDS
Jean Metzinger (1883–1956), FRANCE	*Eileen Agar* (1899–1991), UK	*Paul Cézanne* (1839–1906), FRANCE
Juan Gris (1887–1927), SPAIN/FRANCE	*Richard Hamilton* (1922–2011), UK	*Giorgio Morandi* (1890–1964), ITALY
Marcel Duchamp (1887–1968), FRANCE	*Wangechi Mutu* (born 1972), KENYA/USA	*Patrick Caulfield* (1936–2005), UK

39. The Life of Colour

Sonia Delaunay (1885–1979) moved to Paris from Germany in 1905, where she encountered some of the most avant-garde artists, writers and poets of the time, including her future husband, Robert Delaunay. They all shared a fascination with the momentous changes that were occurring in transport, science and technology, and experimented with the potential of composition and colour in art.

Travel by train, automobile and aeroplane had made far-flung places nearer, and telephones allowed instant communication between locations that were hundreds, even thousands, of miles apart. Time and space had changed shape, and artists like Delaunay and her contemporaries challenged themselves to devise new ways of representing this strange new world. The title of this painting – *Prismes électriques* – reflects the new modernity: electric lamps that pulsate energetic waves of colour, as if being split into every hue of the rainbow.

Oil on canvas
250 × 250 cm, 98½ × 98½ in.
Centre Pompidou, Paris

Sonia Delaunay

Prismes électriques

1914

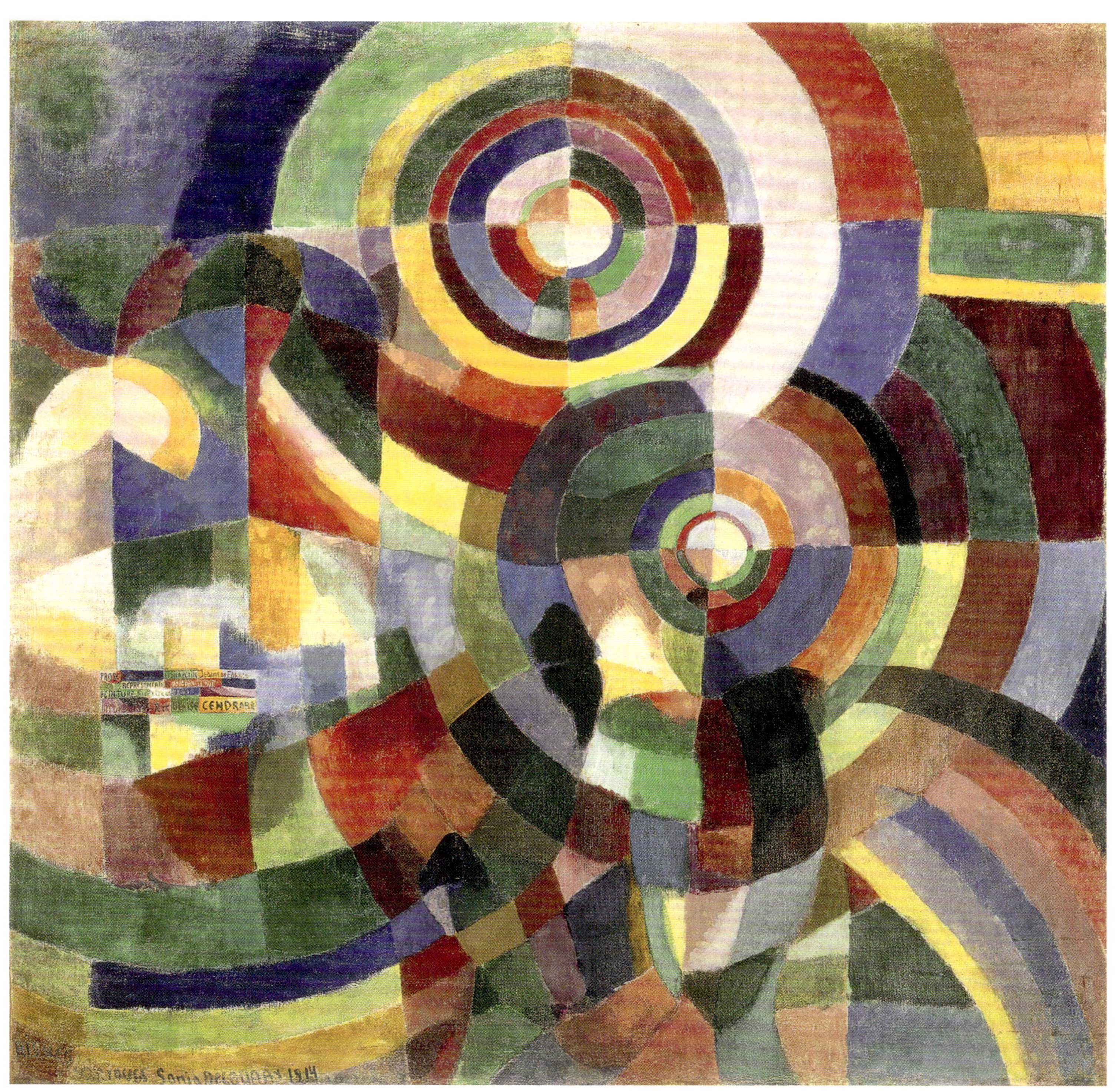

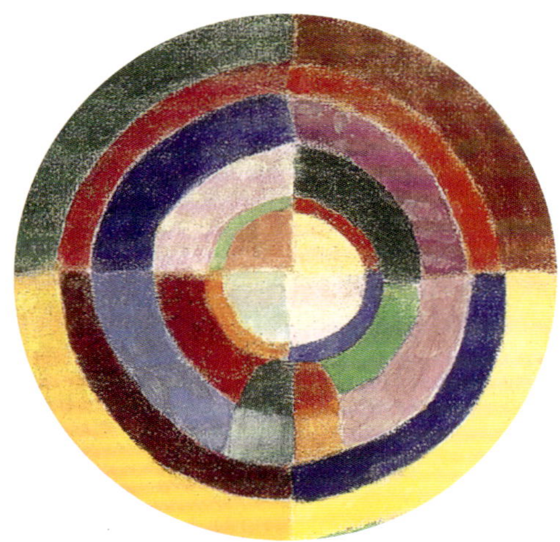

❶ Circles

The painting is dominated by two circles, which become the focal points. The centre of the upper circle sits in the middle of the composition, while the lower circle is dynamically off-centre. Rainbow shapes surge in from the bottom left and right, and other forms bend and distort the colour bands, which seem to radiate out from the circles' cores.

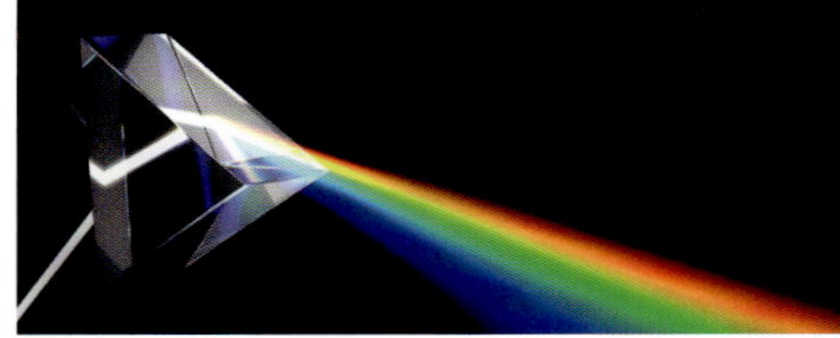

❷ Light

Whereas all art from the past represented the effects of either daylight or firelight (see pp. 16–19, 112–15, 124–7 and 136–9), Delaunay chose to tackle modern electric light. She was working in Paris, one of the first cities to adopt electric light in 1888, so the scene must be somewhere in that city – perhaps a street illuminated by two electric lamps. The painting's title suggests the diffraction of light through a prism, and the artist has exaggerated its explosion into sherds of colour.

❸ Cosmic movement

Delaunay was inspired by the contemporary poets Blaise Cendrars and Guillaume Apollinaire. They had written about how the human mind comprehends ideas, and likened consciousness to expanding circular ripples of light, engorging microscopic lifeforms and the orbital motions of the planets.[78]

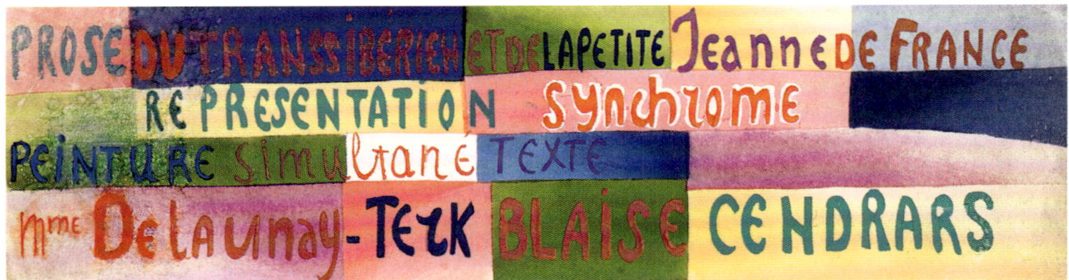

❹ Text

The painting contains a small section of writing, with the name 'Blaise Cendrars' prominently displayed. It mimics a work that Delaunay made to advertise a collaboration she had undertaken with the poet (below).

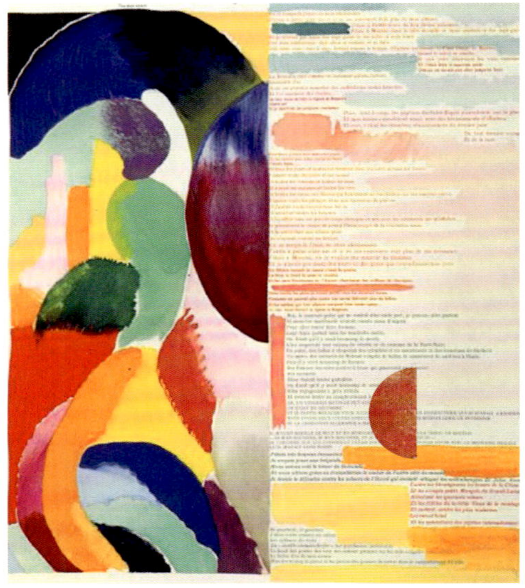

La prose du Transsibérien et de la petite Jehanne de France, 1913

❺ Multimedia

In 1913, Delaunay illustrated *La prose du Transsibérien et de la petite Jehanne de France* by Cendrars. She had spent her career working with different media, including textile design, drama, fashion and furniture – a pioneering attitude that was similar to the approach of the innovative Bauhaus art school in Germany during the 1920s and early '30s, where students were taught to abandon the traditional distinctions between such disciplines as design, painting, sculpture and textile design.

❻ Colour

Playing with colours and their artful contrasts is a fundamental aspect of the work, with its heavy use of the three primary colours: red, blue and yellow.

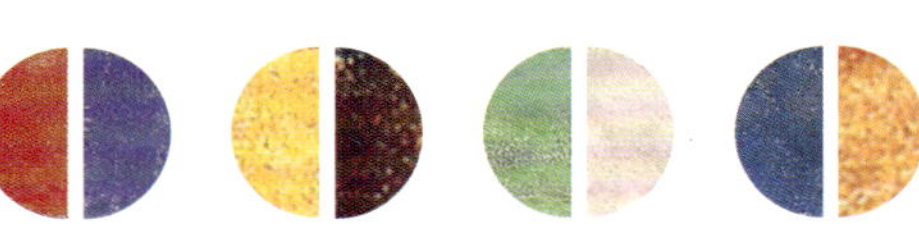

❼ Complementary colours

'Complementary colours' refer to colours from opposite sides of the colour wheel, set side by side to intensify each tone. The colour pairings are as follows: red/green, yellow/purple and green/red. Note the areas where complementary colours lie next to each other: these should be the painting's most intense areas.

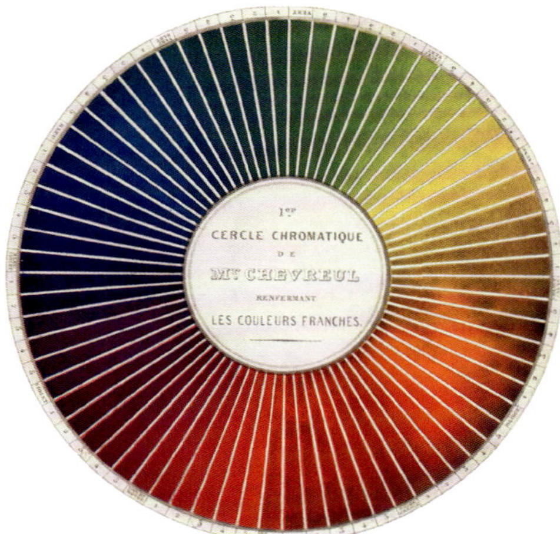

Chromatic circle, from *Exposé d'un moyen de définir et de nommer les couleurs*, 1861

❽ Colour theory

Delaunay was inspired by the colour theories put forward by Michel Eugène Chevreul in the mid-19th century. He showed how colours can appear more or less vibrant, depending upon how they are paired with one another. One of his books, *On the Law of the Simultaneous Contrast of Colours* (1839), gave Robert Delaunay the idea for the name of an art movement: Simultanism. This referred to the effect of colours seen simultaneously, and also indicated the subject matter of his art: the modern city, which can overwhelm with its overlapping sounds, tastes, feelings and sights.

❾ The language of colour

'The real new painting will begin when people understand that colour has a life of its own, that the infinite combinations of colour have poetry and a language much more expressive than the old methods,' Delaunay stated. 'It is a mysterious language in tune with the vibrations, the life itself, of colour. In this area, there are new and infinite possibilities.'[79]

❿ Patchwork

Delaunay's style was influenced by a patchwork quilt she made for her son in 1911 (below). In making it, she saw how this traditional technique created a modern, Cubist-like composition of two-dimensional colour planes.

⓫ Textiles

The use of needlework linked back to the crafts of Delaunay's native Ukraine. Russian avant-garde artists of the time also promoted the idea of returning to Arts and Crafts traditions.

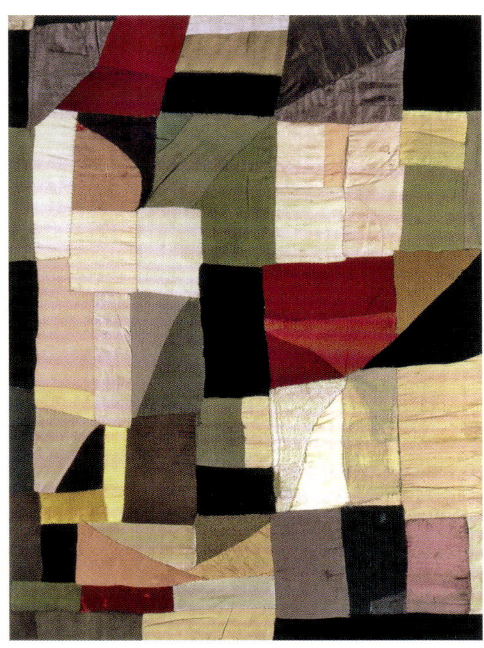

Quilt cover, 1911. Fabric on canvas, 111 × 82 cm, 43¾ × 32¼ in.

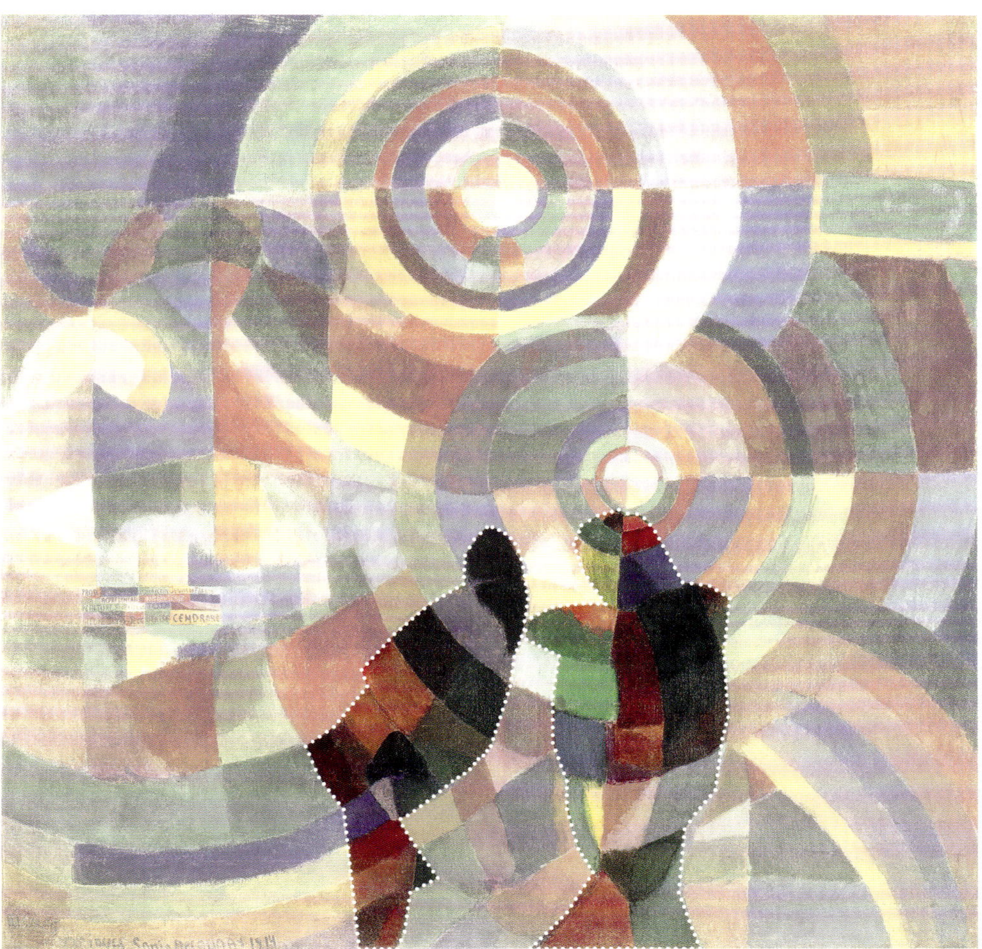

⓬ Hidden forms

There are strange forms in the foreground that look vaguely like bodies, heading towards the light. In earlier paintings Delaunay had also shown figures in patchwork clothes, set against patchwork settings.

⓭ Clothing

Delaunay pursued her interest in textiles by working as a fashion designer, as well as an artist. At home in Paris, she and Robert Delaunay hosted Simultanism parties, with their clothing and interior design based around colourful patchwork designs. She was also an entrepreneur, and in 1918 opened a boutique of her fashion designs, called Casa Sonia, in Madrid.[80]

Sonia Delaunay in Simultaneous dress, *c.* 1913. Photographer unknown

LINKED PRACTITIONERS

LIGHT EFFECTS:	MODERN LIFE:	INSPIRATION FROM POETRY:
Caravaggio (1571–1610), ITALY	*Frank Kupka* (1871–1957), CZECHIA/FRANCE	*Titian* (*c.* 1488/90–1576), ITALY
Claude Lorrain (1600–1682), FRANCE	*Francis Picabia* (1879–1953), FRANCE	*Édouard Manet* (1832–1883), FRANCE
Dan Flavin (1933–1996), USA	*Fernand Léger* (1881–1955), FRANCE	*John Williams Waterhouse* (1849–1917), UK
James Turrell (born 1943), USA	*Robert Delaunay* (1885–1941), FRANCE	*Charles Demuth* (1883–1935), USA
Mary Corse (born 1945), USA	*Anni Albers* (1889–1994), GERMANY/USA	*Cy Twombly* (1928–2011), USA

40. Culture is for Everyone

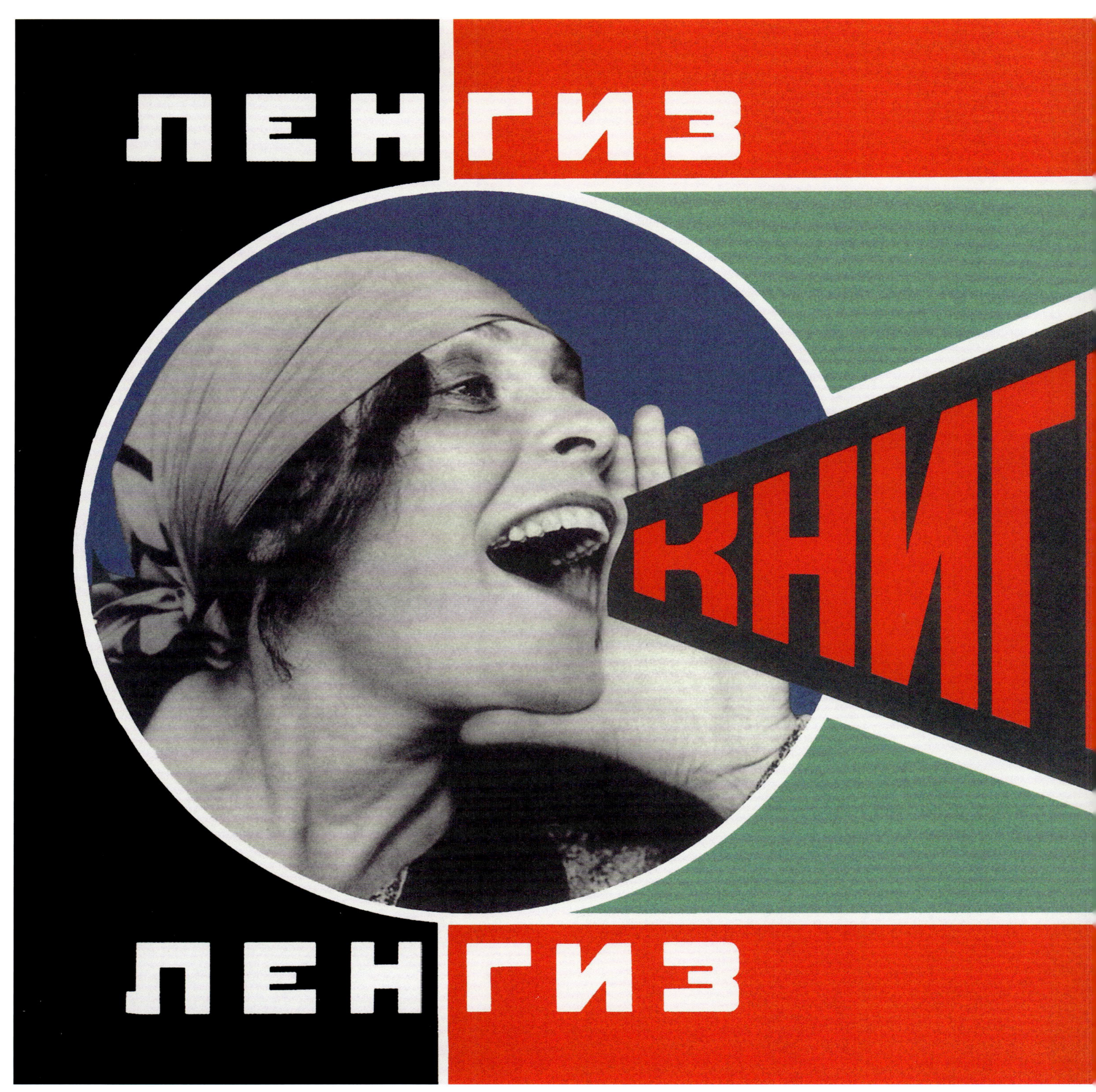

Aleksandr Rodchenko
Books!
1925

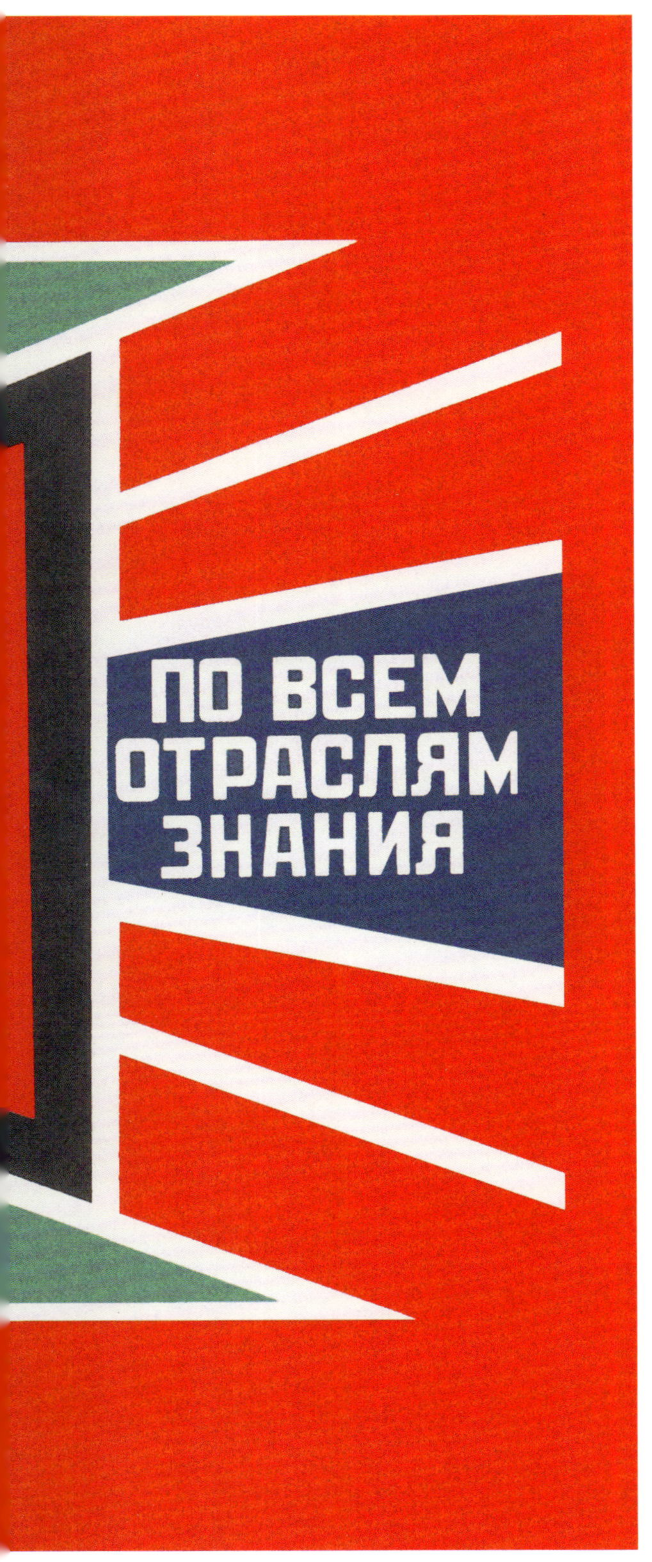

In 1924, the Leningrad State Publishing House (Lengiz) tasked the Constructivist artist Aleksandr Rodchenko (1891–1956) with designing an advertisement that would encourage the working classes towards a path of self-education.

Following the formation of a communist state in 1922, the Soviet government wanted to promote literacy among its proletariat power base. The image, therefore, needed to have clarity and maximum visual impact. The result is one of Rodchenko's most celebrated works and a globally recognized masterpiece of graphic design. Its innovative treatment of colour, shape, photography and text creates a sense of boldness and energy, ideally suited to its function.

Colour lithograph
48.9 × 69.8, 19¼ × 27½ in.
Private collection

❶ Colour

The red text spells out the word 'books'. The letters, shaped like a megaphone, give the typography energy and movement. The colour red has a political meaning associated with communism, but it is also a primary colour, which is attention-grabbing and emotive, perfect for articulating a shout.

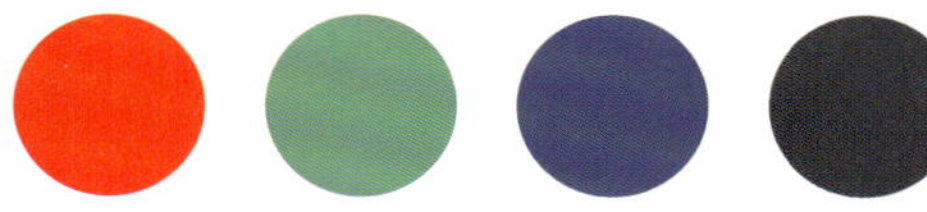

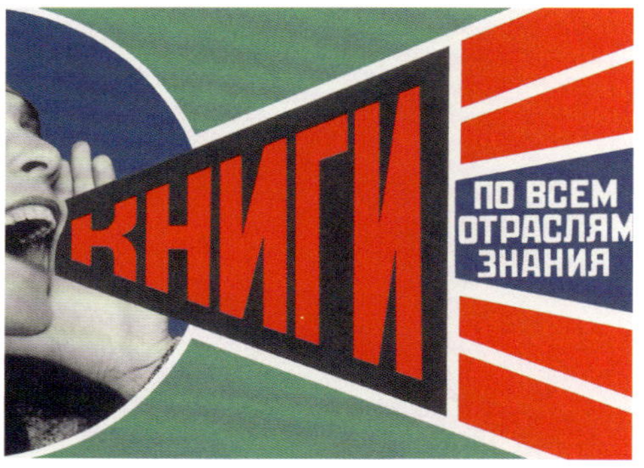

❷ Communism

Experimentations in art and design reflect the upheavals and revolutionary politics that rocked Russia in the five years between 1917 and 1922 – economic crisis, the First World War, the assassination of the imperial family, a civil war and the establishment of the communist Soviet Union.

❸ Inspiration

The Constructivists were inspired by Cubism, a movement that deconstructed the rules of shape and perspective, and Futurism, which celebrated technology and the modern world. In Russia, Wassily Kandinsky, Vladimir Tatlin and Kazimir Malevich were inspirational figures.

❹ Style

Constructivism reflected the industrialized modern world and aimed to be accessible to everyone. Artists abandoned old rulebooks: Rodchenko started out as a painter, but after declaring the 'death of painting' in 1921 became a graphic designer, photographer, typographer, film-maker and sculptor. He sought to radically rethink art and design, and educate people in new ways of seeing.

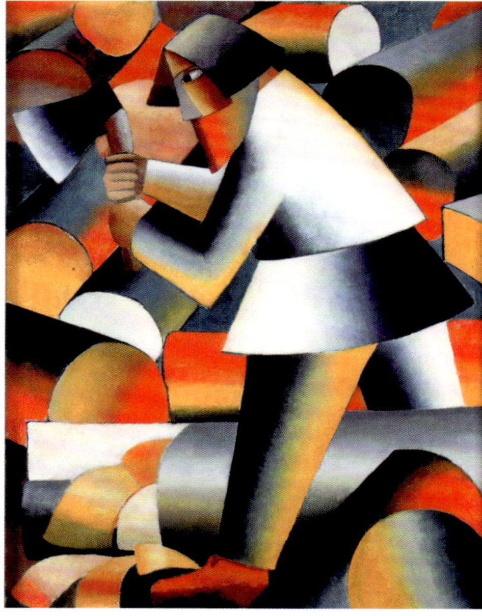

Kazimir Malevich, *The Woodcutter*, 1912. Oil on canvas, 76 × 99 cm, 30 × 39 in.

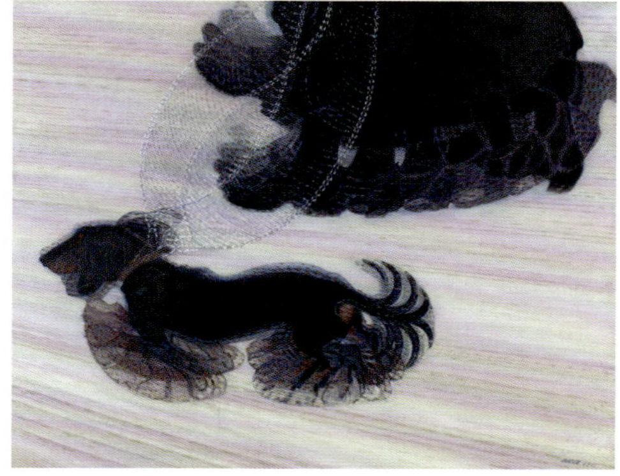

Giacomo Balla, *Dynamism of a Dog on a Leash*, 1912. Oil on canvas, 89.8 × 109.8 cm, 35¼ × 43¼ in.

❺ Shape

Rodchenko opted for basic shapes: a rectangular frame enclosing a circle, intersected by a triangle. Together with the use of primary colours, they keep the message simple, vivid and direct. The composition, too, is assertive and dynamic.

❻ Art for the masses

The word 'books' is followed by the phrase 'on all the branches of knowledge'. Rodchenko was commissioned to engage the public with learning, a message given edge by his use of aggressive colours and angular lines.

❼ Function

The white, blocky text spells out 'Lengiz', the name adopted by the Leningrad State Publishing House. It stands out clearly from the black and red backgrounds and echoes the colour of the border.

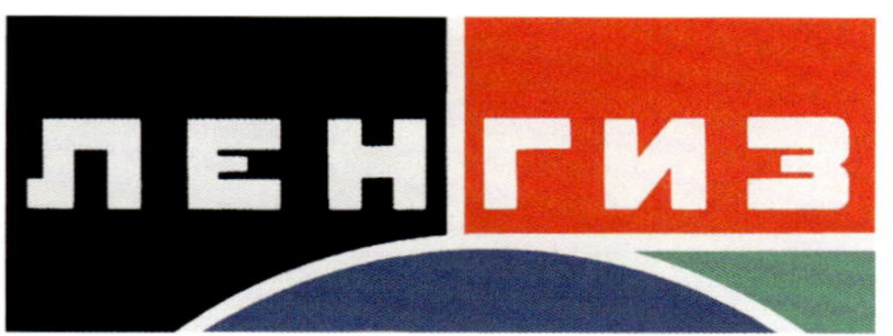

Lyubov Popova, *Painterly Architectonic*, 1917. Oil on canvas, 80 × 98 cm, 31½ × 38½ in.

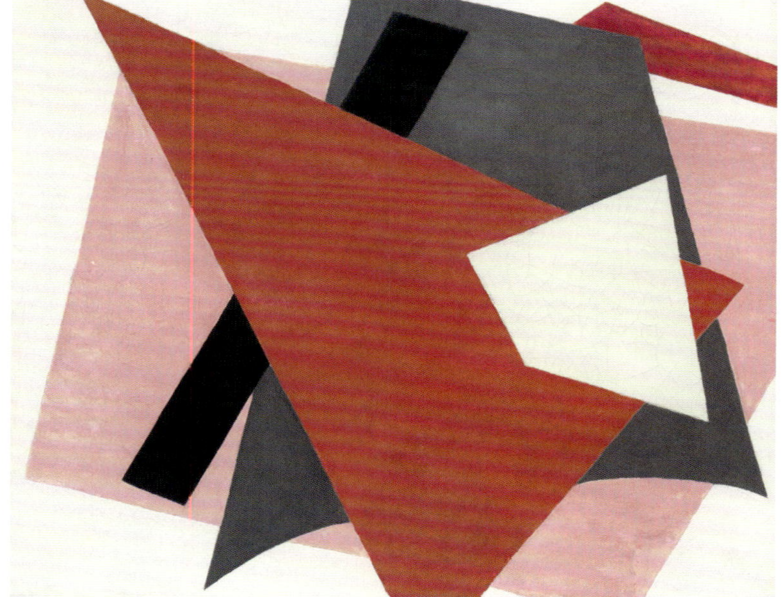

8 Expression

The poster's character comes from the facial expression of the woman, whose joyful call to arms animates the surrounding colours, shapes and text. This is an example of montage, in which different media (paint, typography and photography) have been mixed together in the same piece.

9 Muse to the avant-garde

The woman in the photo is Lilya Brik, an actress, writer and artist who was described by the poet Pablo Neruda as the 'muse of the Russian avant-garde'. Rodchenko incorporated photographs of her into several of his works, and her image has been used on album and poster artwork for the likes of Franz Ferdinand and Beyoncé.

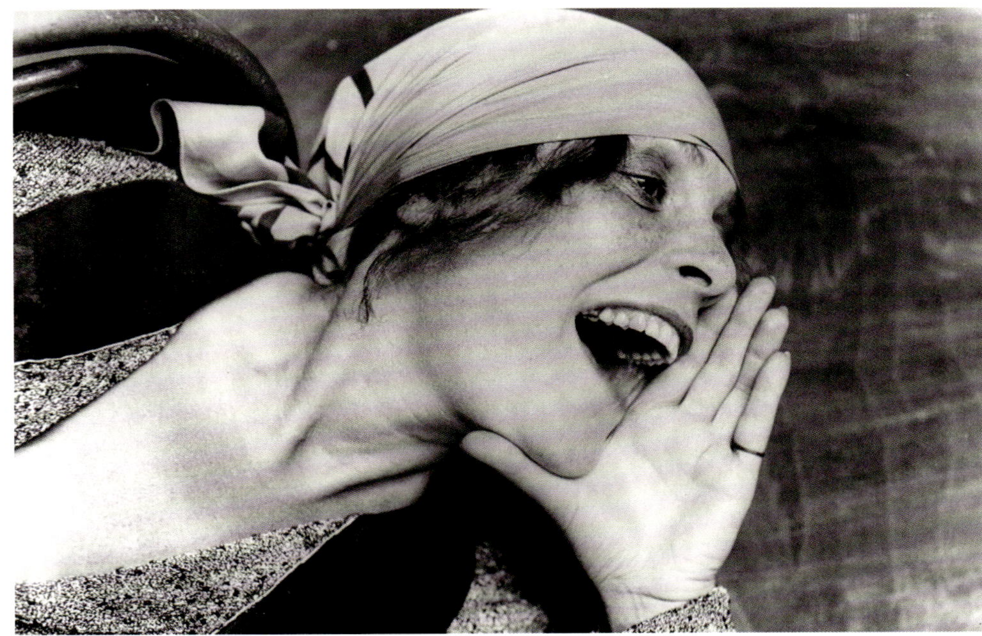

Lilya Brik, 1924. Gelatin silver print, photo by Aleksandr Rodchenko

10 Impact

The principles celebrated by Rodchenko have been a source of inspiration to thousands of designers. The influential Bauhaus art school was inspired by Constructivism, and in the later 20th century many posters, album-sleeve designs and magazine covers owe a debt to his bold experimentations.

→ Kraftwerk, *Man Machine* album cover, 1978. Designed by Karl Klefisch, photo by Günter Fröhling

→ Franz Ferdinand, *You Could Have It So Much Better* album cover, 2005. Designed by Matthew Cooper

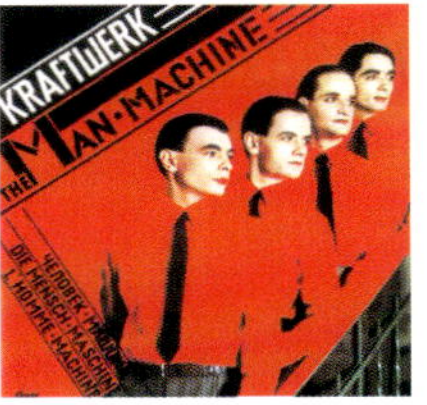

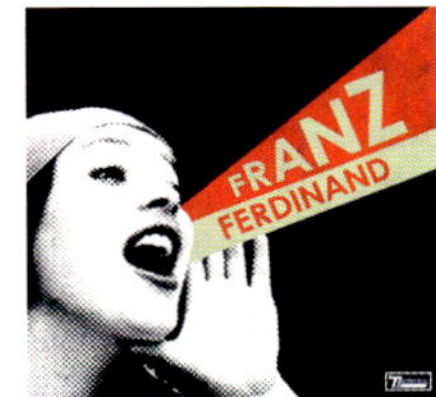

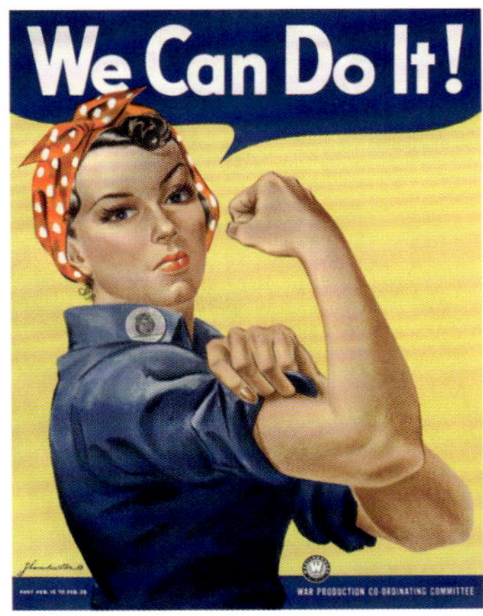

J. Howard Miller, *We Can Do It!* (*Rosie the Riveter*) poster, 1942–43. Lithograph, 55.9 × 43.2 cm, 22 × 17 in.

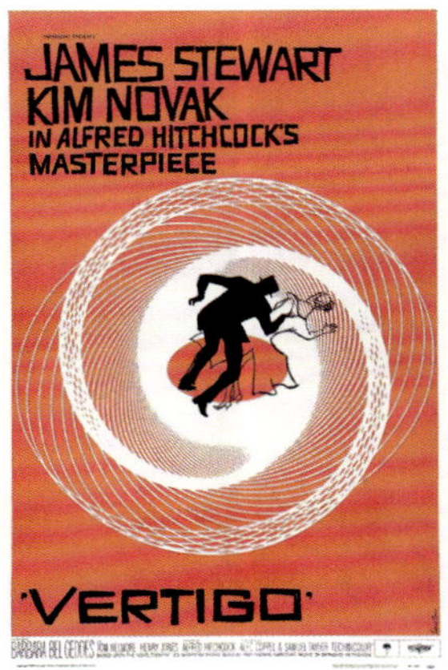

Saul Bass, *Vertigo* film poster, 1958

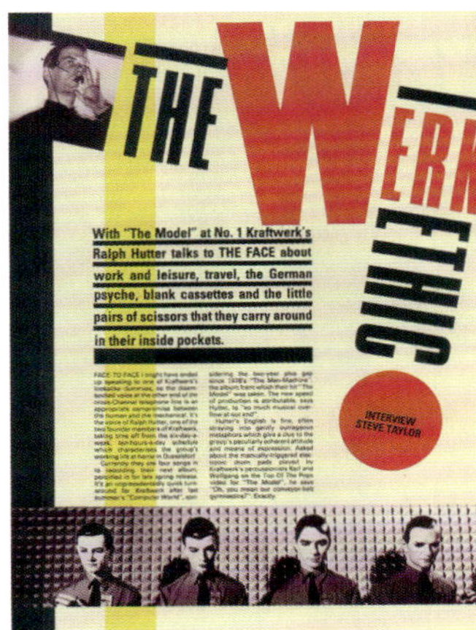

Neville Brody, 'The Werk Ethic', *The Face*, March 1982

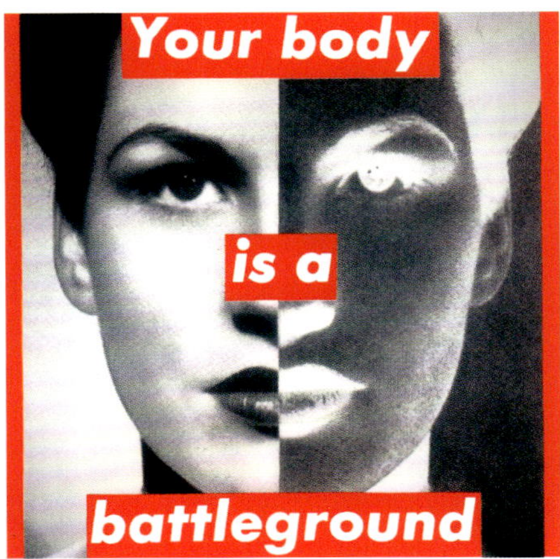

Barbara Kruger, *Untitled* (*Your body is a battleground*), 1989. Photographic silkscreen on vinyl, 284.5 × 284.5 cm, 112 × 112 in.

LINKED PRACTITIONERS

CONSTRUCTIVISM:

Vladimir Tatlin (1885–1953), RUSSIA
Lyubov Popova (1889–1924), RUSSIA
Naum Gabo (1890–1977), RUSSIA
Varvara Stepanova (1894–1958), RUSSIA
Katarzyna Kobro (1898–1951), POLAND

ART AND ADVERTISING:

Alphonse Mucha (1860–1939), CZECHIA
Henri de Toulouse-Lautrec (1864–1901), FRANCE
Norman Rockwell (1894–1978), USA
Salvador Dalí (1904–1989), SPAIN
Andy Warhol (1928–1987), USA

GRAPHIC DESIGN:

Saul Bass (1920–1996), USA
Barbara Kruger (born 1945), USA
Paula Scher (born 1948), USA
Neville Brody (born 1957), UK
Shepard Fairey (born 1970), USA

41. Creative Freedoms

The Elema people of Papua New Guinea have a long tradition of wearing ceremonial masks for ritual events. This example was designed as part of a festival in which participants could correspond with the sea spirits. Wearing the mask allowed them to inhabit other characters, leaving their own personalities behind.

The artists of this mask, which is made from painted barkcloth stitched around pliable canes, were not constrained by traditional conventions. Instead, they had the freedom to experiment with scale, colour and shape. Such creative expression opens the door onto a vibrant artistic practice, linked to deeply held spiritual and ceremonial beliefs.

Barkcloth, cane, paint, fibre
74.9 × 55.9 × 40.6 cm, 29½ × 22 × 16 in.
Metropolitan Museum of Art, New York

Papua New Guinea, Elema

Eharo mask

early 20th century

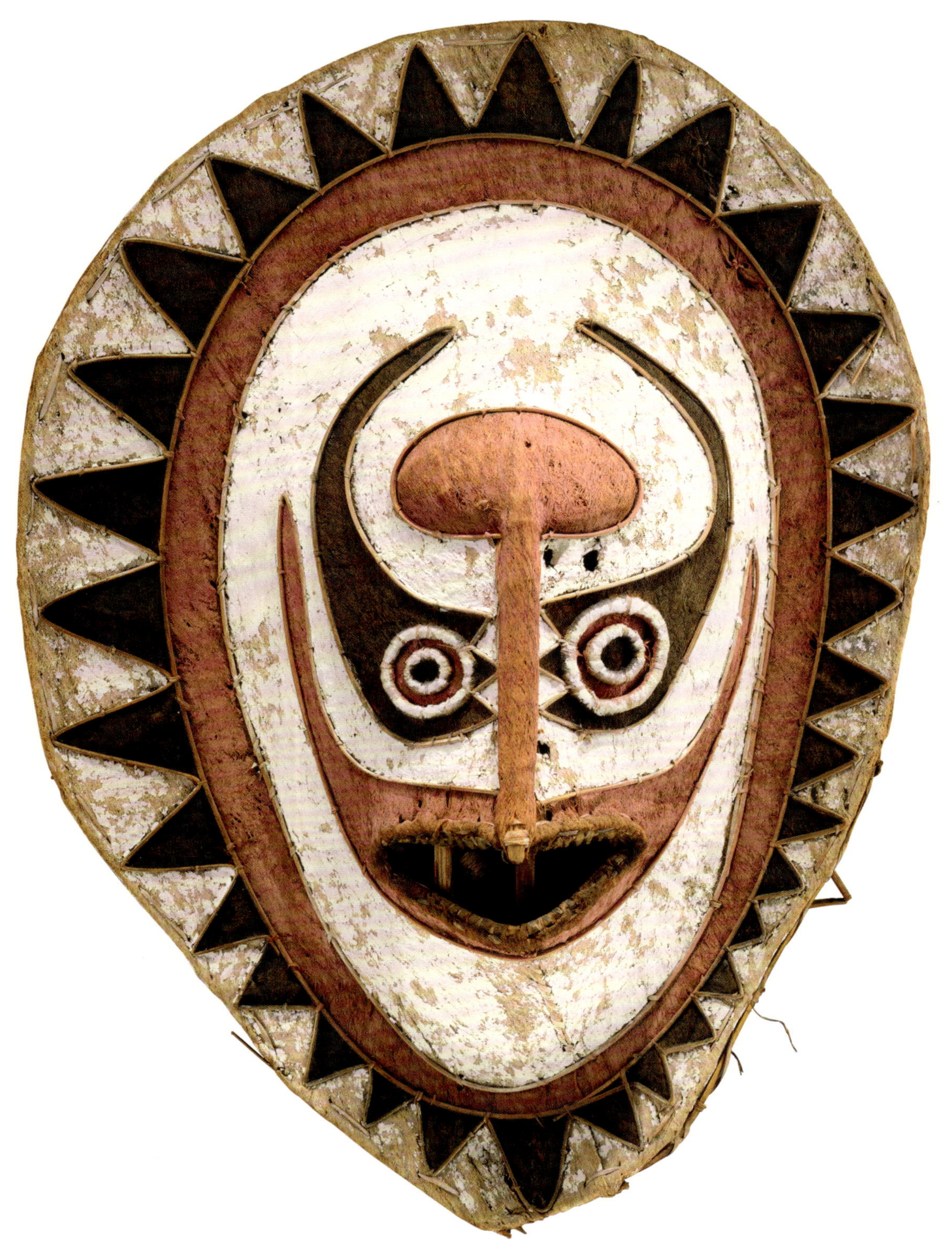

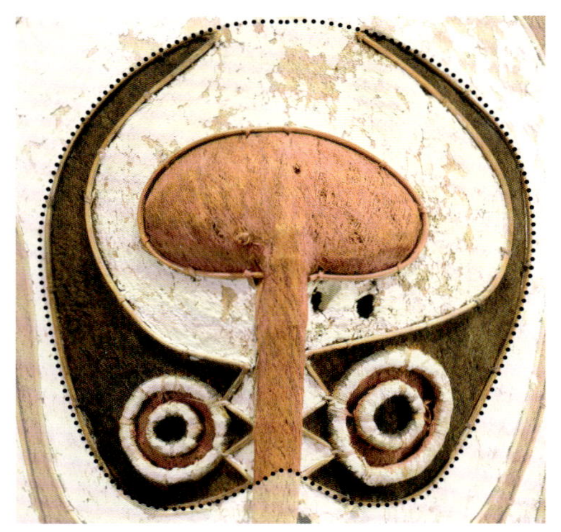

❶ Fixed stare

The mesmerizing, unequivocal and fixed gaze of the mask is established by its dilated mouth and gaping eyes, and the elongated shape of the head, resembling a blown-up balloon. The overall effect is one that hovers on the edge between horror and comedy.

❷ Whose face?

The intention of *eharo* masks was to make audiences laugh with delight and gasp with amazement. *Eharo* means 'dance head' or 'dance mask'.[81] The masks often depict characters from traditional fables, such as lewd old men or naïve youngsters, or clan spirits. But they could also depict entirely invented figures, figments of the artists' imaginations to provoke a reaction from a festival crowd.[82]

❸ Location

The Elema people come from a 480-km (300-mile) stretch of land along the Gulf of Papua, in what is now Papua New Guinea. This mask was made by men living separately from women in communal longhouses. In the Elema culture, men preserved ritual knowledge to do with communication with the spirit world, and women guarded the realms of childbearing and procreation.

❹ Fabric

The mask is made on a cane framework with barkcloth stretched over the top. The fabric, painted in white, red and black, is edged with canes stitched into place. Barkcloth is made from the inner bark of the elm, paper mulberry or ficus tree, which is boiled and beaten until the fibres become soft and pliable. Masks like these are very light, ideal for wearing during festivities, but generally did not have eye holes, so that the wearer would peer through the mesh of the barkcloth.

Upper, front

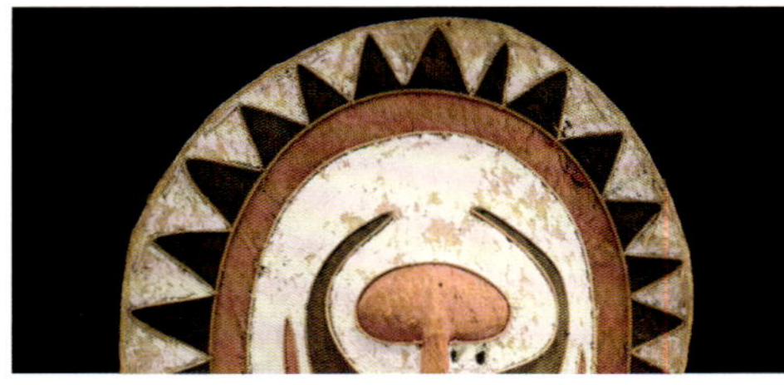

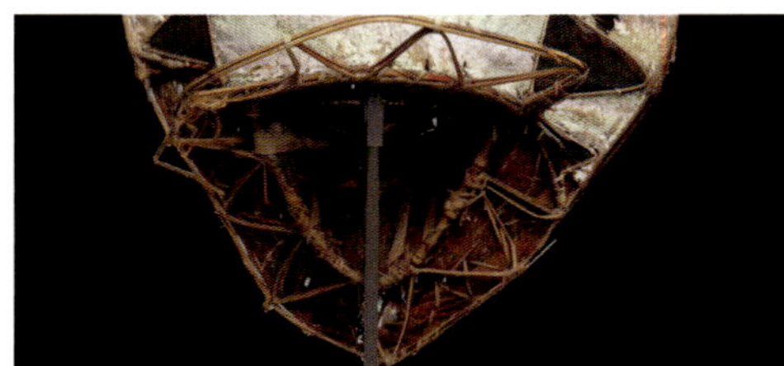

Lower, back

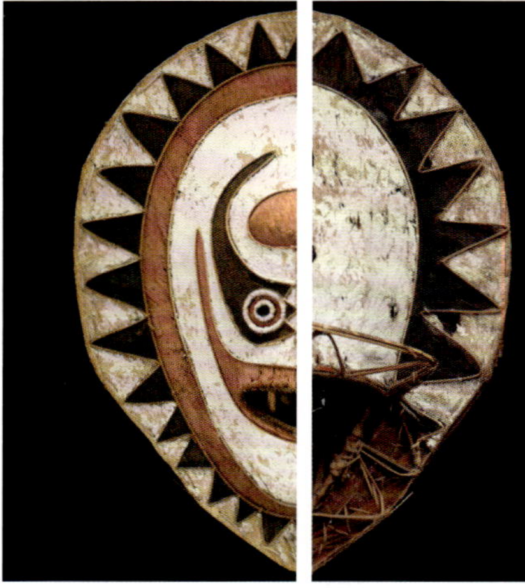

Left side, front *Left side, back*

❺ Repetition

The design is based on bold abstract patterns. The nose juts out from the forehead, and the corners of the mouth extend up the sides of the face, in an echo of the black pincers around the eyes. The serrated pattern along the edge resembles jagged teeth. The artist who came up with the design was not restricted by convention and could experiment freely.[83]

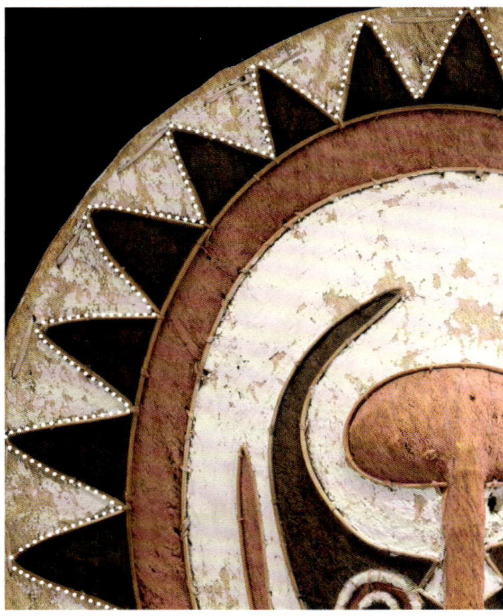

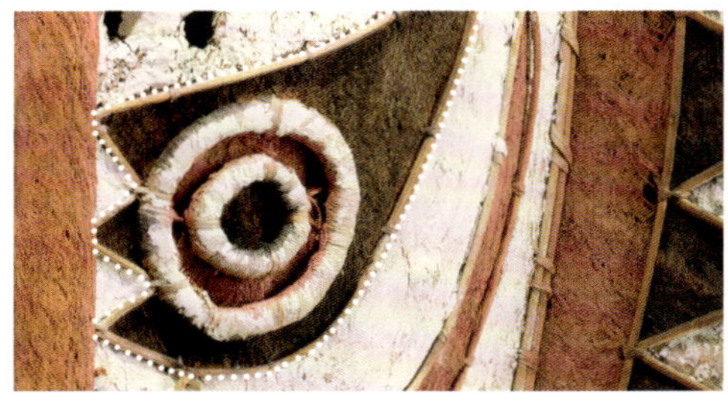

❻ Barkcloth zones

Barkcloth was once a prestigious material that was made and used extensively in the equatorial regions of the Pacific, Asia and Africa. It was gradually displaced by woven fabrics, and by the early 20th century Papua New Guinea was one of the few places still producing it for ritual use.

LINKED PRACTITIONERS

MASKS:

James Ensor (1860–1949), BELGIUM
Pablo Picasso (1881–1973), SPAIN/FRANCE
Rebecca Horn (born 1944), GERMANY
John Stezaker (born 1949), UK
Guerrilla Girls (established 1985), USA

DISTORTION:

Edvard Munch (1863–1944), NORWAY
Francis Bacon (1909–1992), IRELAND
Carol Rama (1918–2015), ITALY
George Condo (born 1957), USA
Jenny Saville (born 1970), UK

ART FROM TEXTILES:

Anni Albers (1899–1994), GERMANY/USA
Itchiku Kubota (1917–2003), JAPAN
Magdalena Abakanowicz (1930–2017), POLAND
Mrinalini Mukherjee (1949–2015), INDIA
Tracey Emin (born 1963), UK

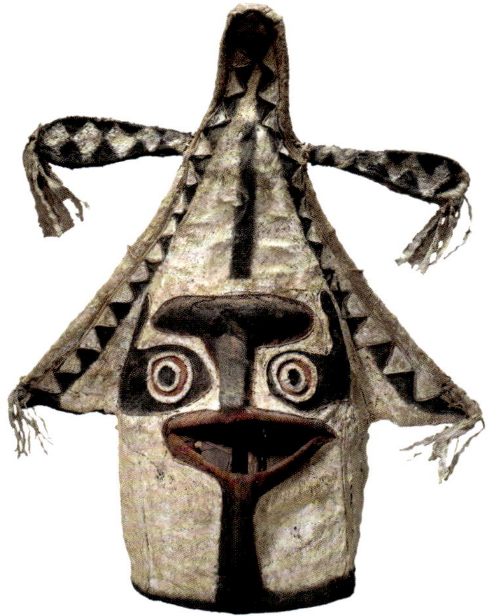

↑ *Eharo dance mask*, before 1930s. Tapa, rattan, pigment, 72.7 × 59 × 33 cm, 28½ × 23¼ × 13 in.

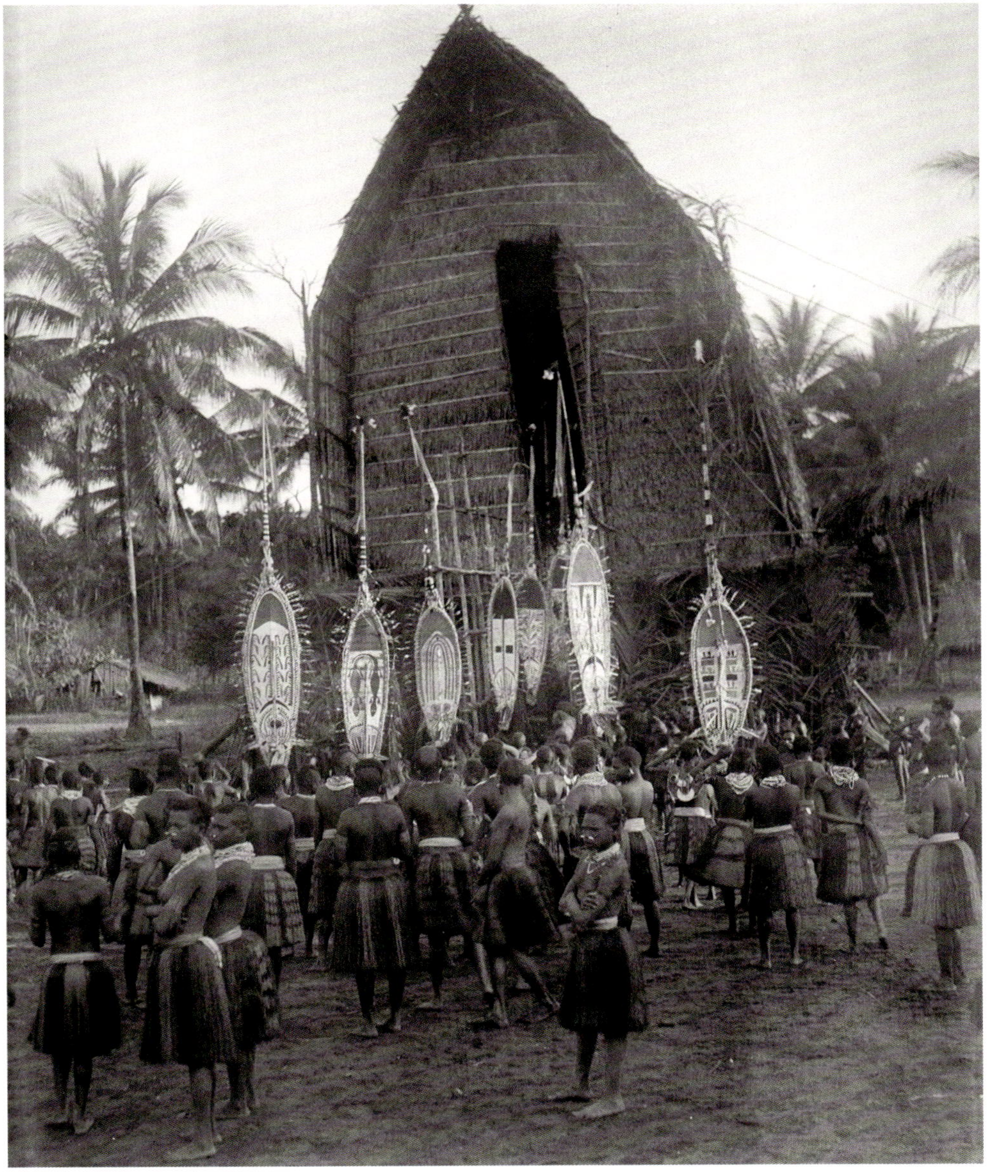

→ A group of Elema people standing in front of a men's longhouse, some holding *hevehe* masks, Papua New Guinea, late 19th century

7 Ceremony

The mask was one aspect of the *hevehe* ritual for communicating with and pacifying the dangerous sea spirits, a cycle that could last from 7 to 20 years. The centrepiece of the ceremony was the procession of *hevehe* masks, up to 7 m (23 ft) in height. They were made in secrecy by men in a specially made longhouse, accompanied by ritual feasting. Towards the end of the process, a new door would be cut into one of the walls, and the masks would ceremoniously emerge.

8 Doorway ready

The Elema people described masks as *maea morava eharu*, 'things of gladness'. They were made and worn by men from neighbouring villages, who would spend weeks preparing their masks and dances. A second outing of the *eharo* masks would occur just before the *hevehe* masks, as many as 100 of them, emerged from the longhouse in a spectacular procession.

9 Sound and vision

The wearers of the *eharo* masks would chant, beat drums and shake rattles. They performed their dances before host villagers, acting out various scenes.

10 Dangerous powers

The characters represented by the *eharo* masks were believed to be able to make the women of the host village fall in love with them. When the masked men arrived, the local women would throw confetti-like showers of shredded coconut at them, symbolically robbing the spirits of their powers of seduction.

11 Destruction

At the end of the ceremony, the masks would be burned to destroy the spirits. Missionaries had also encouraged the Elema to abandon their ceremonies and destroy ritual artefacts.[84] The *hevehe* cycle fell into disuse from the 1950s.

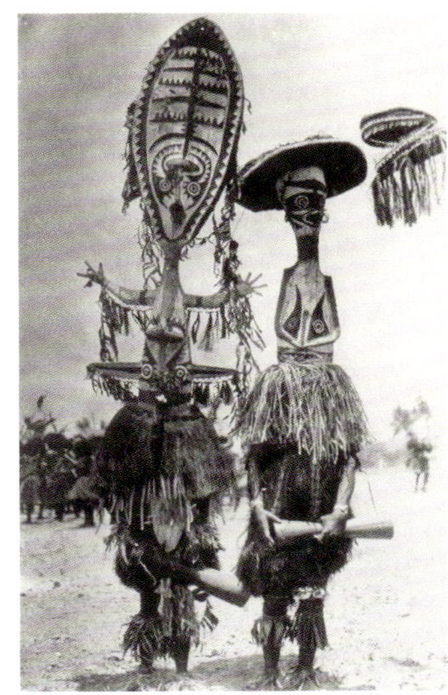

Elema people wearing *eharo* masks, Papua New Guinea, *c.* 1920s

42. The Shock of the Real

Dorothea Lange was travelling by car through California in March 1936, documenting rural poverty for the Resettlement Administration, a New Deal agency set up in 1935 to relocate families from agriculturally exhausted land to new planned communities. It was late in the day, but when she saw a crowd of pea-pickers camped in a field near Nipomo, she stopped the car, picked up her camera and walked towards the group.

Lange spent around 15 minutes at the site, mostly taking photographs of a mother and her children who were living in a makeshift tent. She took seven photographs in total, and then left. One of those shots, *Migrant Mother*, became the defining image of the Great Depression in America and one of the most famous images in the history of photography, even featuring on a United States postage stamp.

Digital photograph from original nitrate negative
Library of Congress Prints and Photographs Division, Washington, DC

Dorothea Lange
Migrant Mother
1936

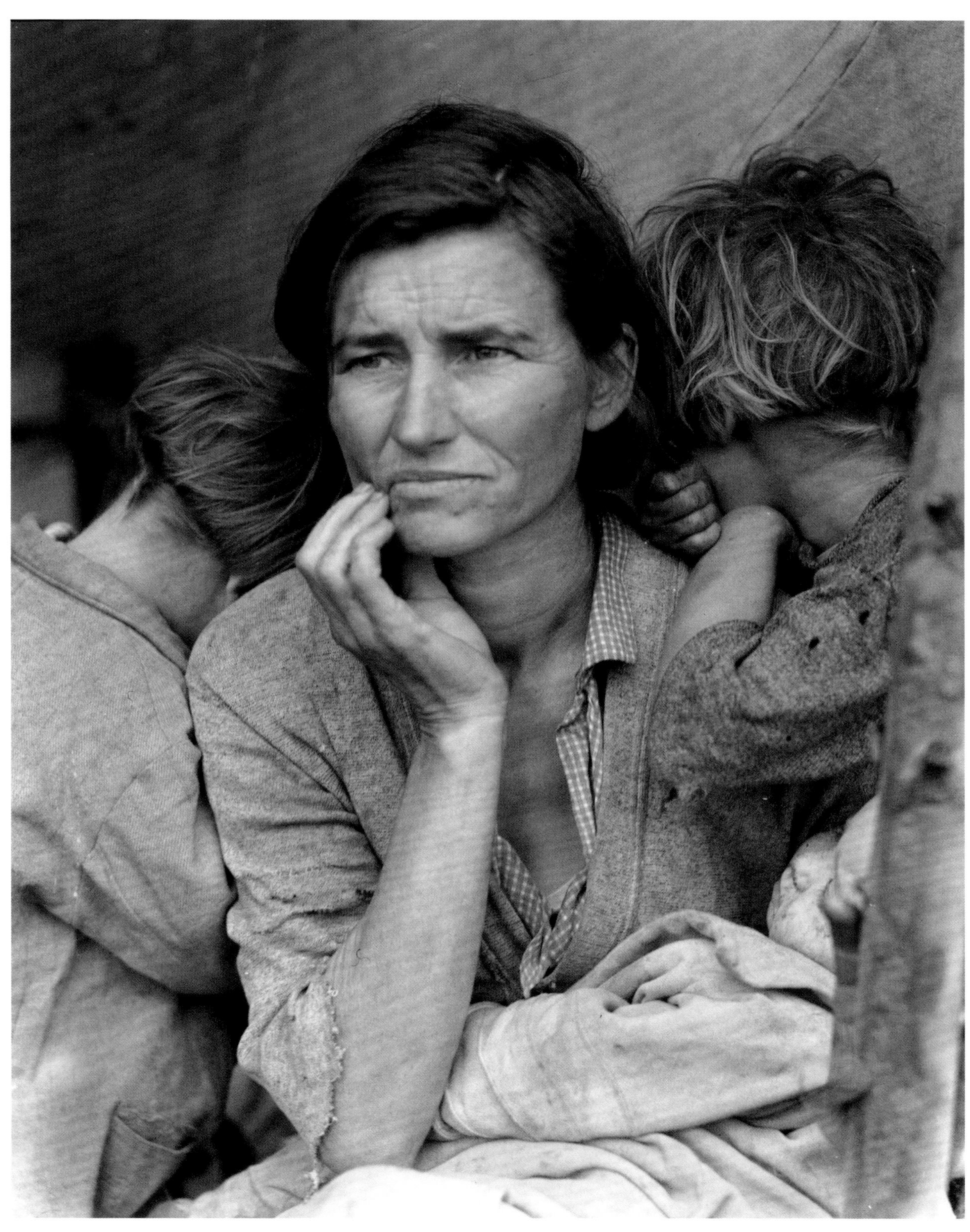

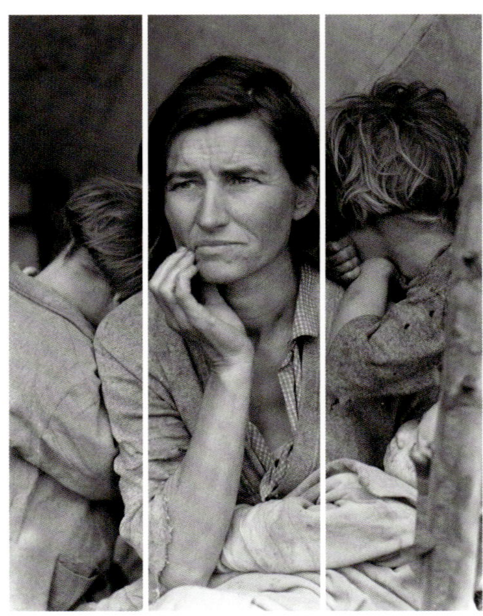

❶ Composition

The woman's body is framed by her two children, their poses mirroring each other and creating a three-part composition. It is not known whether the pose was directed in any way by Lange, or if it was just a happy coincidence. She took a total of seven photographs of the mother and her children in just 15 minutes, with *Migrant Mother* later selected as the best shot.

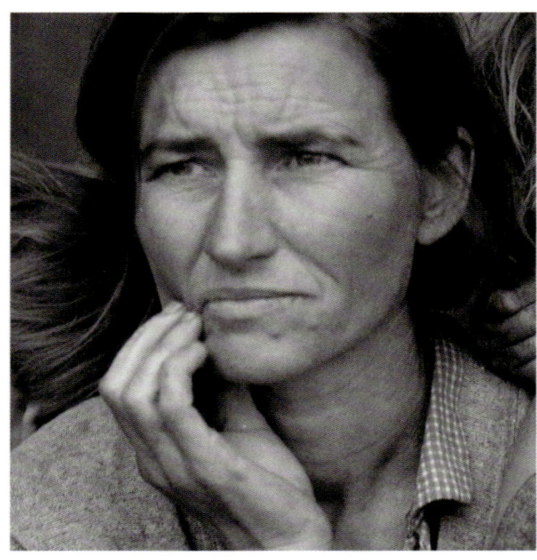

❷ Eyes and hands

The children's faces are all hidden, but the woman's eyes look outwards as if towards the future, avoiding the camera's gaze. Body language can often give away unconscious concerns: her hand is held to her face in a recognizable gesture of anxiety.

❸ History

The Wall Street Crash of 1929 sparked one of history's worst economic depressions. In America, the poverty was exacerbated by severe drought and dust storms in the Midwest, driving many agricultural labourers to California to seek work. This was the fate of the family in *Migrant Mother*. Lange was commissioned by the government-run Resettlement Administration to document the humanitarian crisis. The photograph was bought by the *San Francisco News*; when it was published, it became an icon of the Great Depression. It caused such an impact that the government soon afterwards delivered food supplies to the camp.

❹ Identity

Until 1978 the identity of the woman in the photograph was unknown. When Florence Owens Thompson was traced to Modesto, California and interviewed, she commented: 'I wish [Lange] hadn't taken my picture ... I can't get a penny out of it. She didn't ask my name. She said she wouldn't sell the pictures. She said she'd send me a copy. She never did.'

❺ Gender

Motherhood is a powerful and enduring theme – as seen in the endless variations of the Virgin and Child – although it was less common in the history of art for a woman to be both practitioner and subject. Feminist art historians from the 20th century onwards placed the role of women in art as a focus of research, a theme that had been largely ignored throughout art history.

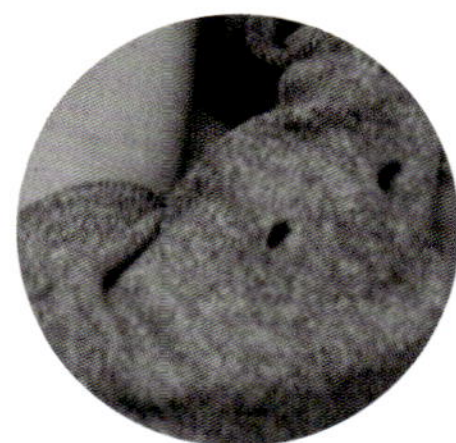

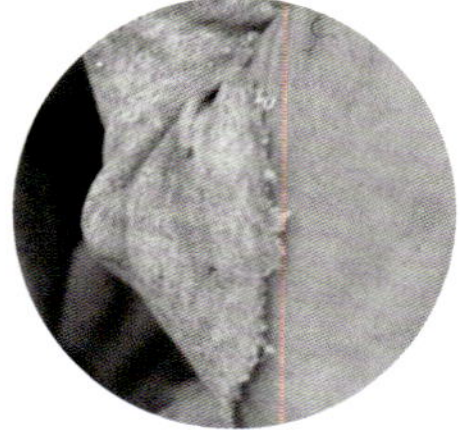

❽ Evidence or 'art'

The extent of the family's poverty can be seen in the details of the baby's dirty face and the ragged sleeves of the children's and the mother's clothes. The photograph's power comes from its presentation of such evidence, as much as its composition.

❻ Timelessness

Representations of the Virgin and Child are among the most widespread of Christian icons. Such images were hugely popular because of their focus on the better aspects of human nature: love and selflessness. Setting aside the immediate historical context of *Migrant Mother*, we are engaged by themes that have a universal human appeal: the instinctive bond between mother and child, and a mother's calm resilience in the face of calamity.

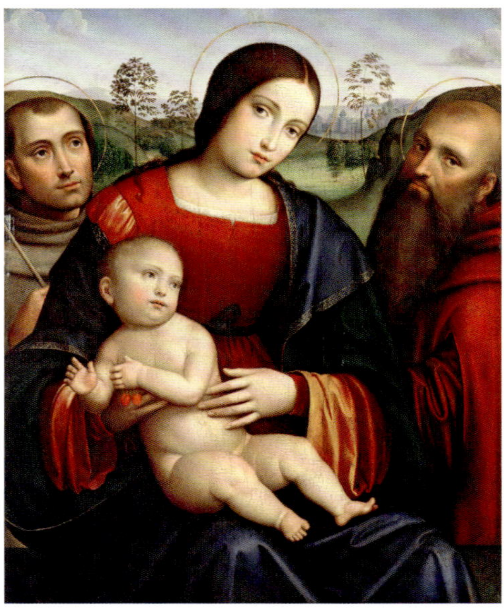

Francesco Francia, *Madonna and Child with Saints Francis and Jerome*, c. 1512–15. Oil and gold on wood, 74.9 × 57.2 cm, 29½ × 22½ in.

❼ Documentary photography

Documentary photography has recorded the great moments of history from the earliest days of the medium, including scenes from the battlefields of the American Civil War in the 1860s. Sometimes, like Lange, their work exposed social problems or depicted marginalized groups. Lange herself disliked the term because she didn't want her photographs to be thought of as merely scientific or factual; instead, she wanted them to affect people emotionally.

❾ Photographic memory

Lange was following in a tradition of photographers who recorded important historical events, subcultures and social issues, including Matthew Brady, Lewis Hine and Walker Evans.

⑩ Photography and truth

Even though the photograph is purportedly a documentary image, it has been cropped and altered. In the original exposure, a thumb and forefinger are visible on the post. In the final version, they have been erased. The Farm Security Administration, which succeeded the Resettlement Administration in 1937, worked like a photo agency. Photographers did not have control over their images, and the FSA could edit, crop and distribute them to the press.[85]

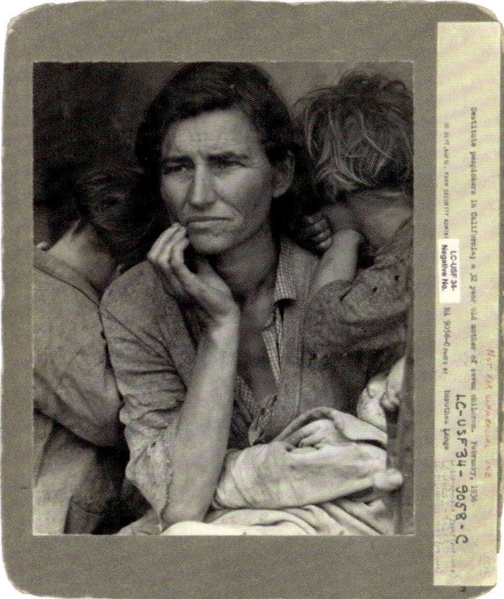

Migrant Mother, 1936 – FSA version

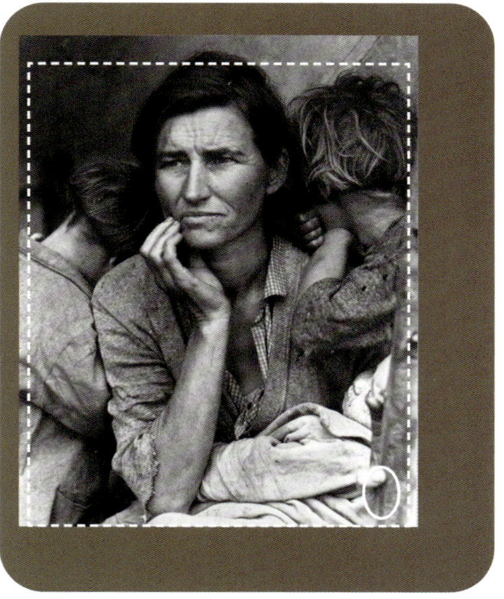

Migrant Mother, 1936 – unretouched version, highlighting edits

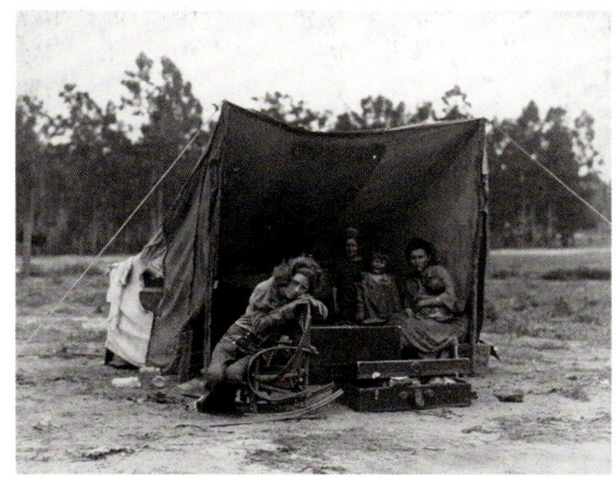

⑪ Depth of field

The setting is a makeshift tent constructed by the family. There is no background, and the restricted sense of space focuses the gaze on the human participants, creating a claustrophobic atmosphere.

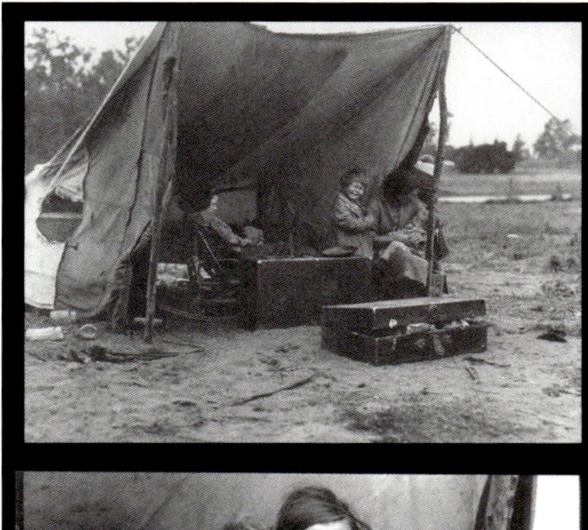

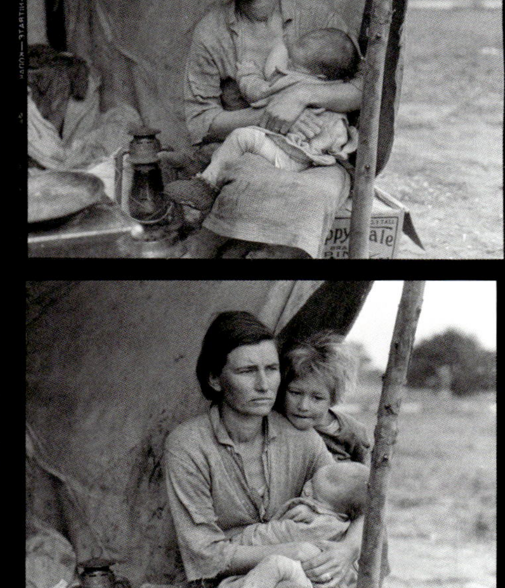

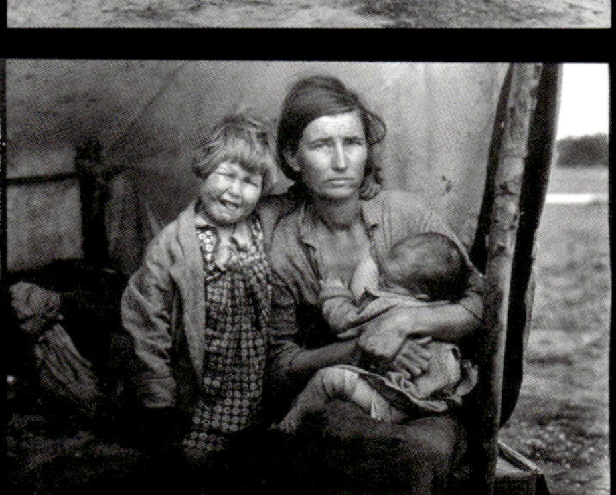

Additional photographs from the *Migrant Mother* series, 1936

⑫ Iconic

Migrant Mother has been copied and reproduced many times, appearing on postage stamps, T-shirts, posters, cartoons, advertisements and magazines.

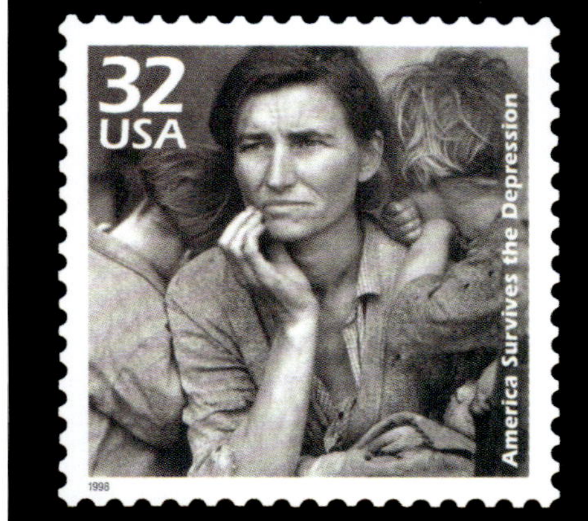

United States Postal Service stamp with Dorothea Lange's *Migrant Mother*, 1998

LINKED PRACTITIONERS

PHOTOJOURNALISM:	ART EXPOSING INEQUALITY:	DOCUMENTARY FILM-MAKERS:
Roger Fenton (1819–1869), UK	*Jean-François Millet* (1814–1875), FRANCE	*Dziga Vertov* (1896–1954), RUSSIA
Margaret Bourke-White (1904–1971), USA	*Gustav Courbet* (1819–1877), FRANCE	*Agnès Varda* (1928–2019), FRANCE
Robert Doisneau (1912–1994), FRANCE	*Ilya Repin* (1844–1930), RUSSIA	
Robert Capa (1913–1954), HUNGARY/USA	*Walter Sickert* (1860–1942), UK	
Susan Meiselas (born 1948), USA	*Tam Joseph* (born 1947), UK	

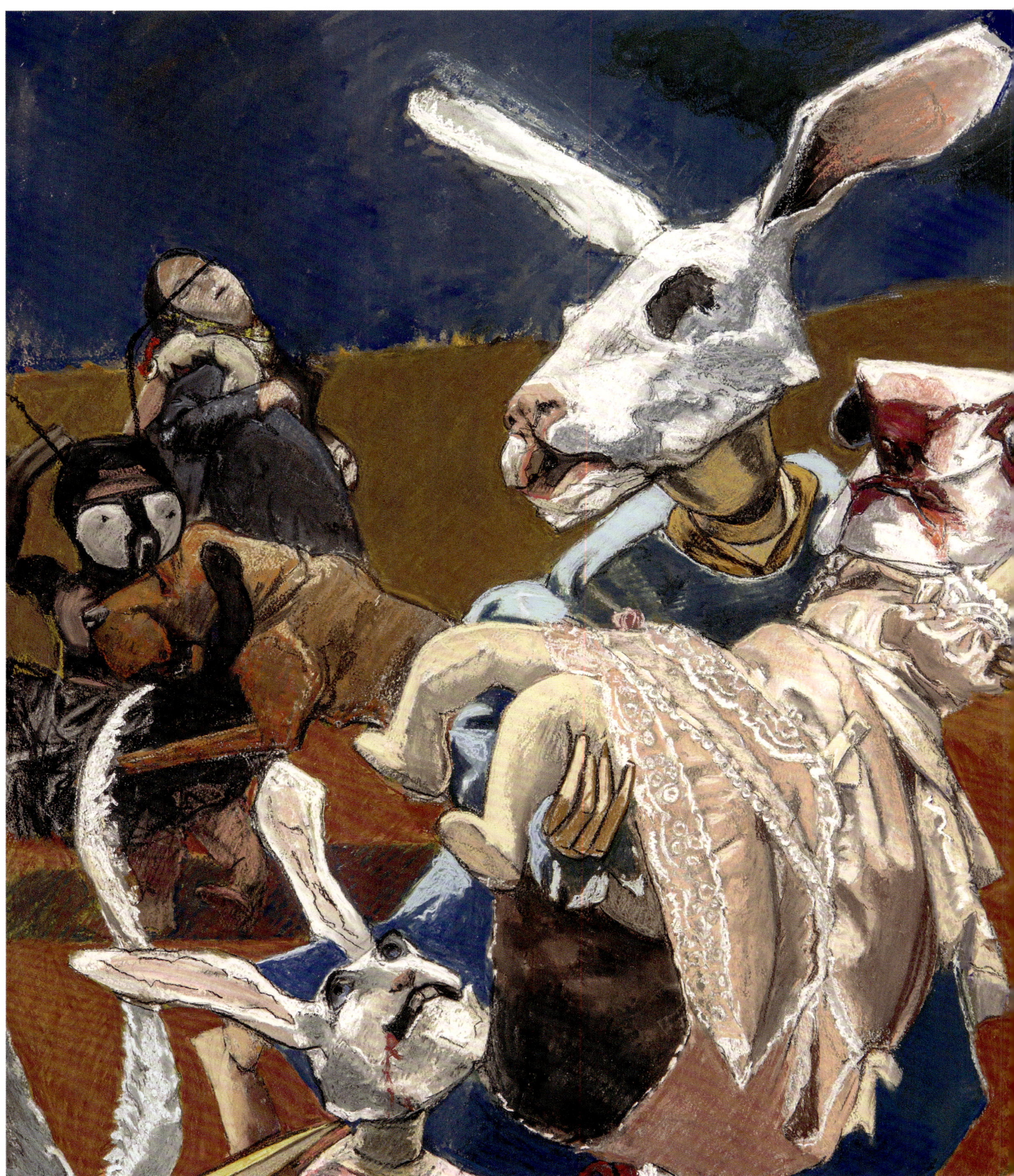

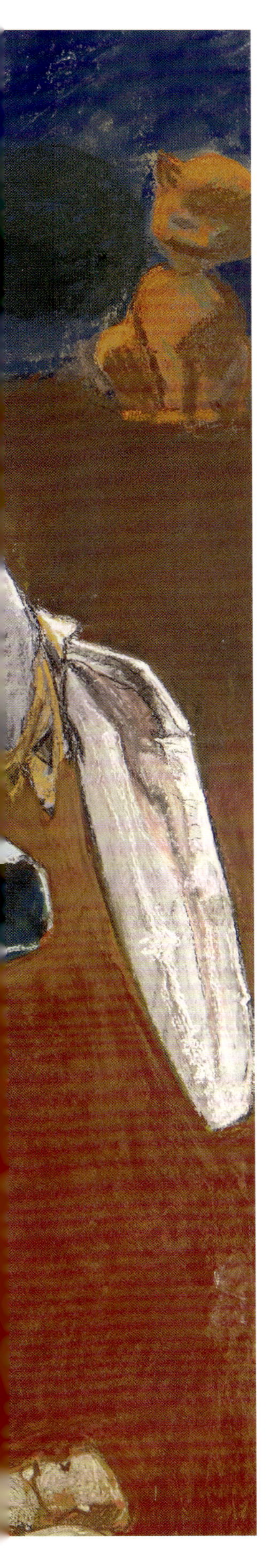

5. New practices and *beyond*

1946 onwards

The exploration of vital issues and new techniques has defined art since the middle of the 20th century. Artists adopted processes that were once considered non-artistic, with many engaging with concepts that had previously been underexplored, including race, gender and sexuality.

1946 *onwards*

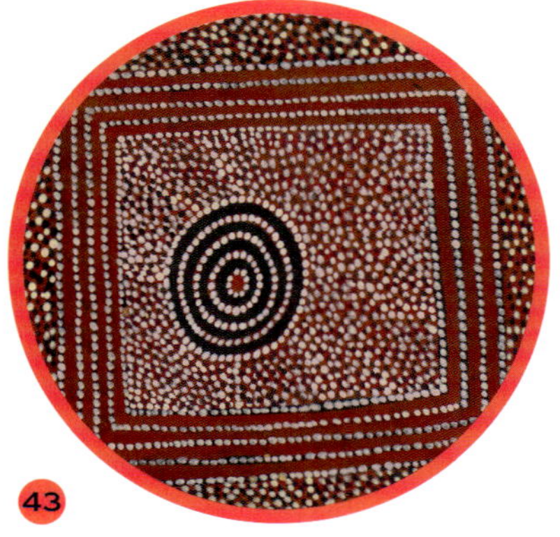

43

Memories of Home

Anatjari Tjakamarra
Story of the Women's Camp and the Origin of Damper, 1973

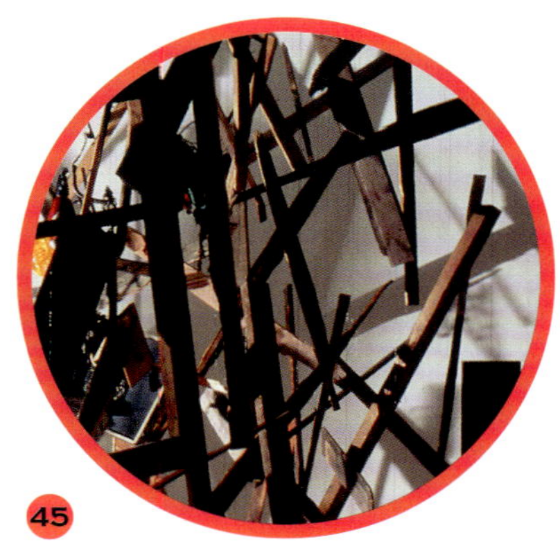

45

Creative Destruction

Cornelia Parker
Cold Dark Matter: An Exploded View, 1991

Using Humour Seriously

Guerrilla Girls
Do Women Have to be Naked to Get Into the Met. Museum?, 1989

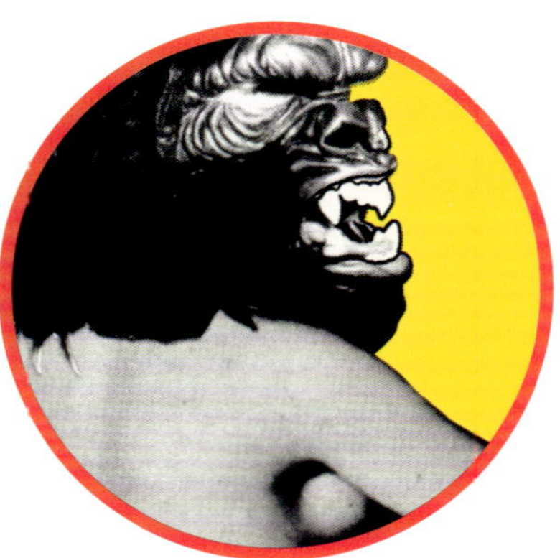

A Matter of Life and Death

Damien Hirst
The Physical Impossibility of Death in the Mind of Someone Living, 1991

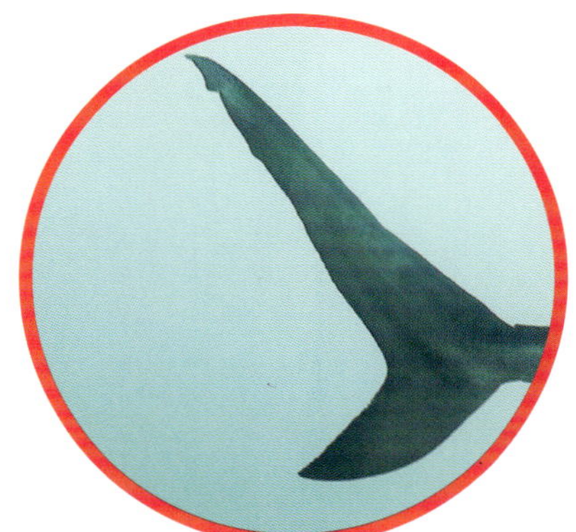

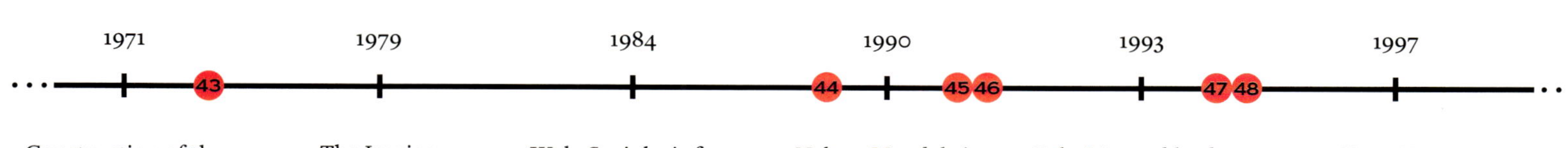

1971: Construction of the Aswan High Dam in Egypt is complete

1979: The Iranian Revolution begins

1984: Wole Soyinka is first African to win Nobel Prize in Literature

1990: Nelson Mandela is released from prison in South Africa

1993: Oslo I Accord leads to the formation of the Palestinian state

1997: Hong Kong is returned to Chinese rule

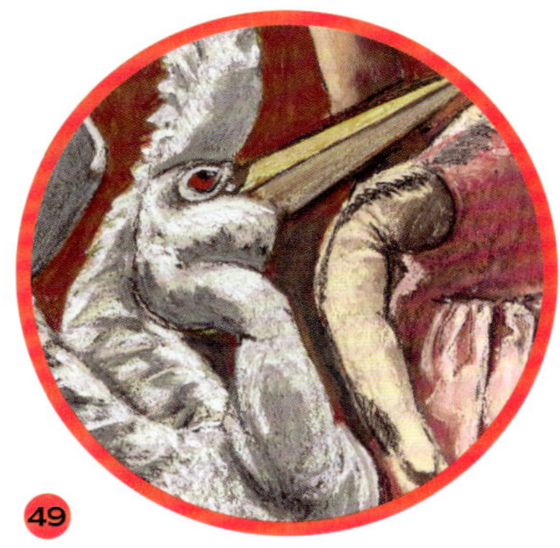

The Brutality of History

Kara Walker
Gone: An Historical Romance of a Civil War … , 1994

The Art of War

Paula Rego
War
2003

48

Conflicted Identities

Shirin Neshat
Rebellious Silence
Women of Allah, 1994

50

Crossing Boundaries

JR
Migrants, Picnic Across the Border
2017

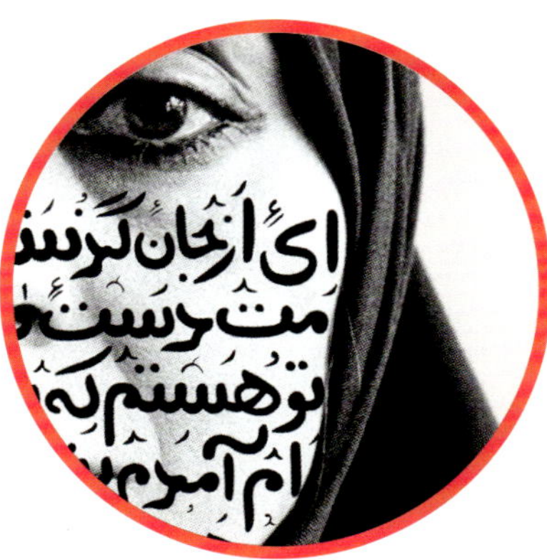

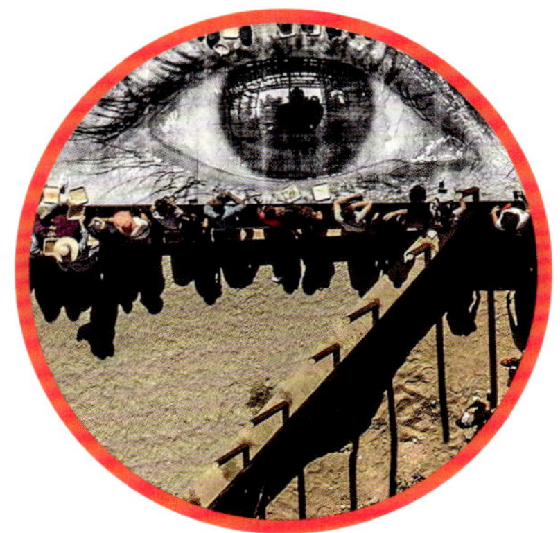

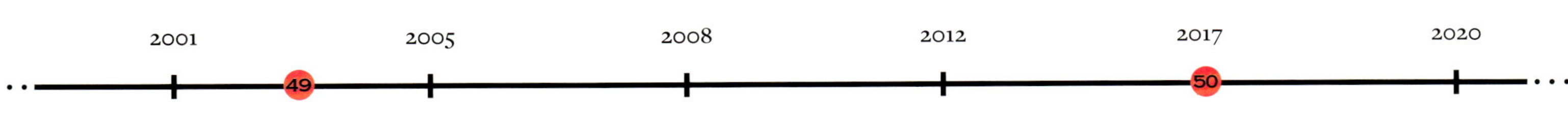

2001 — The Netherlands legalizes same-sex marriage

2005 — The first Amerindian president of Bolivia is elected

2008 — Lehman Brothers collapse leads to global banking crisis

2012 — The NASA rover *Curiosity* lands on Mars

2017 — Catalonia declares independence from Spain

2020 — The Covid-19 epidemic causes lockdowns worldwide

43. Memories of Home

This work by Anatjari Tjakamarra (1930–1992) was painted in Yayayi, a remote community in Australia's Northern Territory. Drawing on the artist's Aboriginal ritual knowledge, it is a representation of a landscape in which an ancestral 'Dreaming', or creation narrative, is played out.

The story told in the painting is of the invention of damper, a bread made from crushed seeds. Five women travel through a desert terrain, but no human figures are shown in the work. Instead, the narrative is told purely through the use of symbolic forms and colour. This type of storytelling and its symbolism forms part of the world's oldest tradition of artistic imagery, believed to have originated in Aboriginal culture around 50,000 to 60,000 years ago.

Acrylic paint on composition board
129.1 × 98.6 cm, 50¾ × 38¾ in.
National Museum of Australia, Canberra

Anatjari Tjakamarra
Story of the Women's Camp and the Origin of Damper
1973

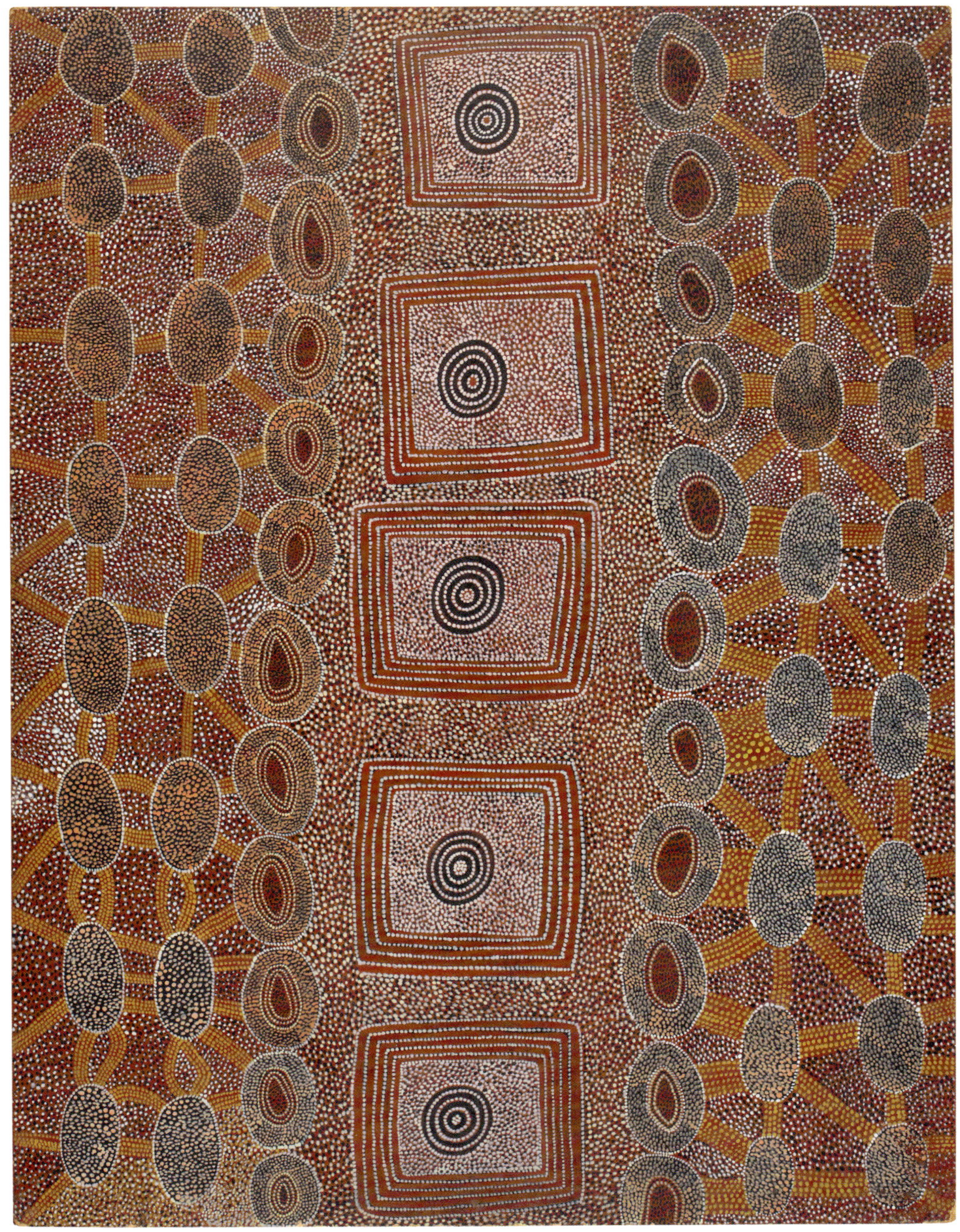

❶ Organization

Five red concentric squares run down the centre of the work, forming the backbone of the composition, with all of the other shapes creating a roughly symmetrical pattern to either side.

❷ Cell and nucleus

At first glance, the painting appears to depict a stylized view through a microscope, with the shapes resembling primary lifeforms such as amoebas or other unicellular organisms.

❸ Origins

The work is about the origins of life, but in a symbolic way. It tells the story of five women, represented by the red squares, and their route through their desert homeland. The circles within the squares represent the bread they made, known as 'damper' or 'bush bread'.

❹ Everything is connected

While the red squares are disconnected from one another, the ovals at the sides are linked by orange lines into a network of shapes.

❺ Scared sites, sacred people

These orange lines refer to the spread of ancestral knowledge and the connecting of past to present. The earthy colours emulate the natural pigments used by indigenous artists.

❻ Dots and ancient practices

Hundreds of dots of pigment cause the work to shimmer with speckles of colour. This technique echoes the practice of applying pigment to the skin for ceremonial purposes, to ground paintings, and in the decoration of sacred items.

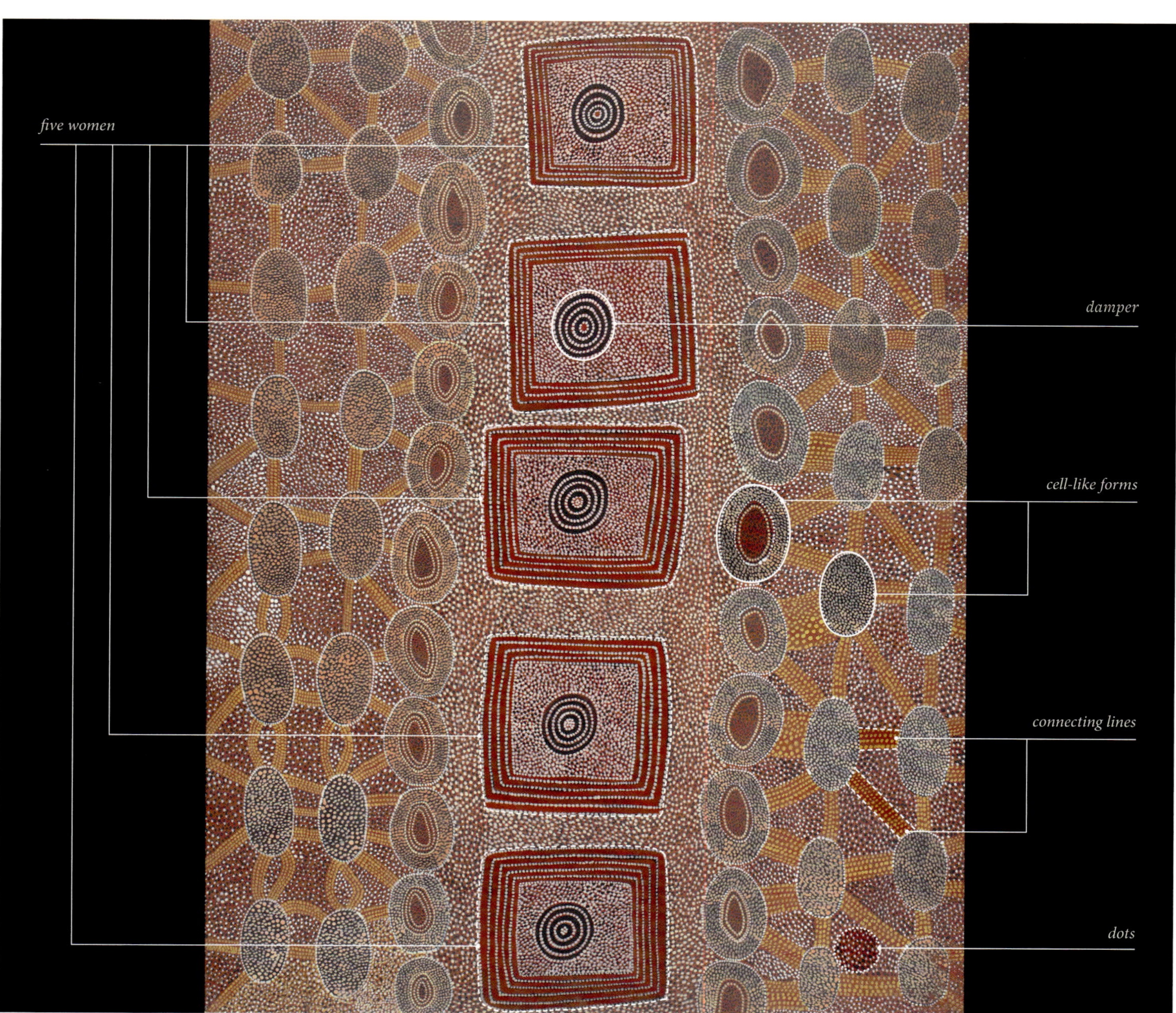

❼ After-effects

Tjakamarra applied Pintupi symbolism and techniques to easel painting, a move that would prove to be highly influential and ultimately contribute to the introduction of Aboriginal art to a wider audience. The work was included in the *Art of Aboriginal Australia* exhibition, which toured Canada in 1974–76.[86] The international exposure led to the acquisition of one of the artist's works by the Metropolitan Museum of Art in 1989.

❽ Iconoclasm

Aboriginal art is still neglected in other contexts, however. Works of art by indigenous peoples are the oldest extant examples of human visual culture, yet as recently as May 2020 the mining group Rio Tinto blew up the Juukan Gorge rock shelters, a sacred site that is 46,000 years old, to access the high-grade iron ore beneath it.[87]

❾ Landscape

Many artists over the centuries have painted landscapes, but Tjakamarra did not set out to replicate the appearance of a specific place. Unlike many landscapes in the European tradition, such as *Wivenhoe Park, Essex* by John Constable (below), his work does not portray the land as a status symbol or a commodity to be bought, owned or exploited. For indigenous Australians, the land is connected to humans' spiritual origins and is conceived as an extension of the human body.[88]

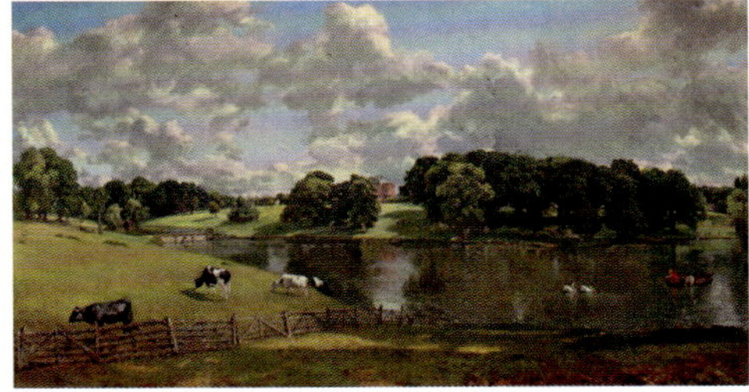

John Constable, *Wivenhoe Park, Essex*, 1816. Oil on canvas, 56.1 × 101.2 cm, 22 × 39¾ in.

→ *Men's Ceremony*, 1972. Synthetic polymer powder paint on composition board, 97 × 60.5 cm, 38¼ × 23¾ in.

↓ *Women's Dreaming at Tjukurla*, 1991. Synthetic polymer paint on canvas, 151.5 × 122.2 cm, 59¾ × 48 in.

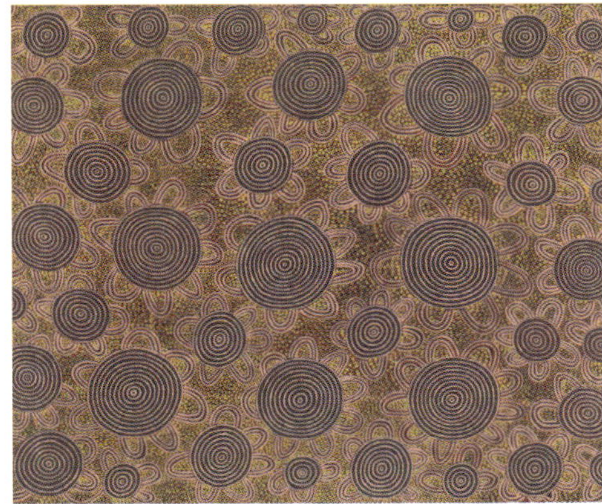

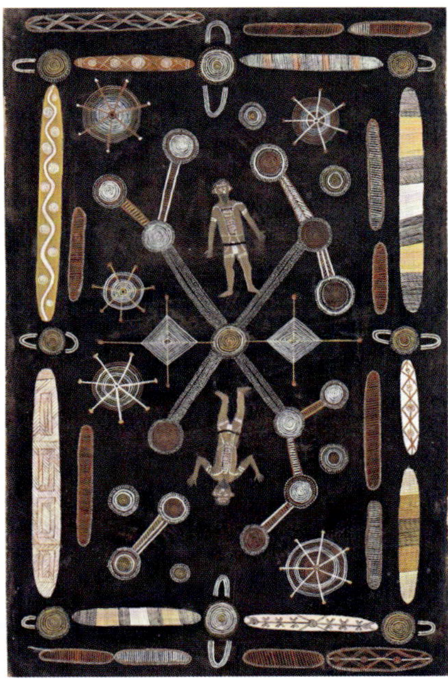

❿ Lost land

Tjakamarra was a ritual leader of the Pintupi group, who lived in the Gibson Desert of Western Australia. The Pintupi were among the last indigenous peoples to be encountered by colonizers, and Tjakamarra was among the last semi-nomadic people to be resettled in Papunya, a government-created township, in the 1960s.[89] The Pintupi's ancestral lands were repurposed to allow for mining, cattle farming and the testing of military equipment.

⓫ The art of the dispossessed

When the Pintupi men and women in the settlement spoke of the land they no longer had a connection to, Geoffrey Bardon, a teacher at Papunya, noticed that they would illustrate their stories by drawing patterns or images in the earth. Bardon supplied them with acrylic paints and boards, and urged them to make permanent records of their landscape and the symbolic language they used. This led to the creation of the Papunya Tula Artists' co-operative in 1972.

⓬ Back to the land

Bardon described Tjakamarra as a quiet, intently focused artist. In the 1980s, when the Tjukurla community was established, he returned to his homeland, where he continued to produce art.[90]

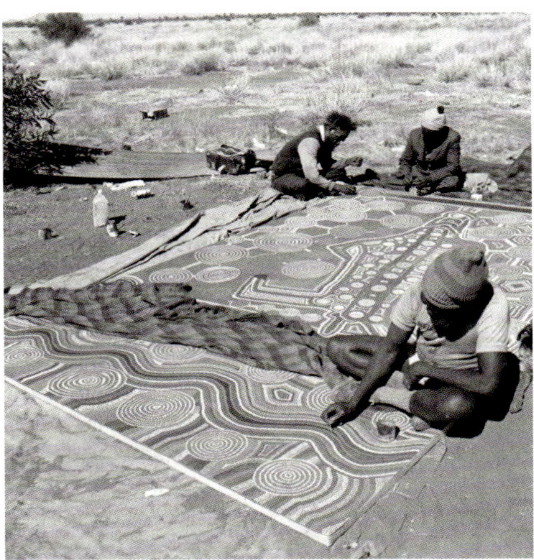

Anatjari Tjakamarra (foreground), John Tjakamarra and Uta Uta Tjangala, 1981. Gelatin silver print, photo by J.V.S Megaw

LINKED PRACTITIONERS

ABORIGINAL ART:

Albert Namatjira (1902–1959), AUSTRALIA
Emily Kame Kngwarreye (1910–1996), AUSTRALIA
Clifford Possum Tjapaltjarri (1932–2002), AUSTRALIA
Gloria Petyarre (1942–2021), AUSTRALIA
Dorothy Napangardi (1956–2013), AUSTRALIA

LANDSCAPE PAINTINGS:

Zhao Mengfu (1254–1322), CHINA
Jacob van Ruisdael (1628–1682), NETHERLANDS
Ogata Kōrin (1658–1716), JAPAN
Claude Monet (1840–1926), FRANCE
Georgia O'Keeffe (1887–1986), USA

ART AND NATURE:

Agnes Denes (born 1931), HUNGARY/USA
Nils-Udo (born 1937), GERMANY
Giuliano Mauri (1938–2009), ITALY
Alfio Bonanno (born 1947), ITALY/DENMARK
Andy Goldsworthy (born 1956), UK

44. Using Humour Seriously

How can art be used for change? Since 1984, the Guerrilla Girls have challenged museums, collectors and critics by bringing female and non-white artists to the fore.

Colour offset lithograph on illustration board
27.9 × 71.1 cm, 11 × 28 in.
National Gallery of Art, Washington, DC

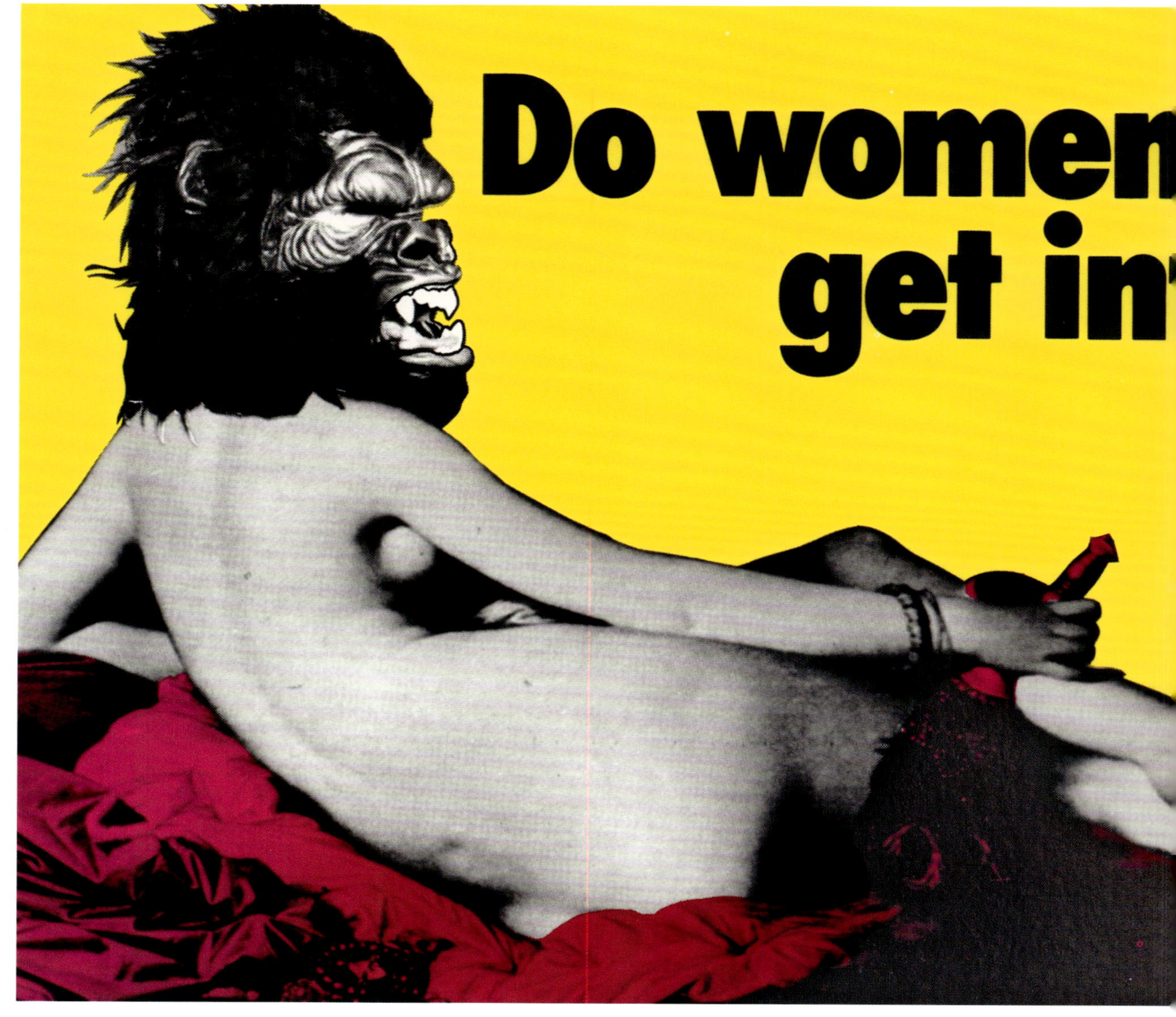

Guerrilla Girls
Do Women Have to be Naked to Get Into the Met. Museum?
1989

In 1989 the group was commissioned by the Public Art Fund in New York City to design a billboard. The artists seized the opportunity to draw attention to discrimination hidden in plain sight at the Metropolitan Museum of Art by using imagery, text, colour and composition – as well as humour.

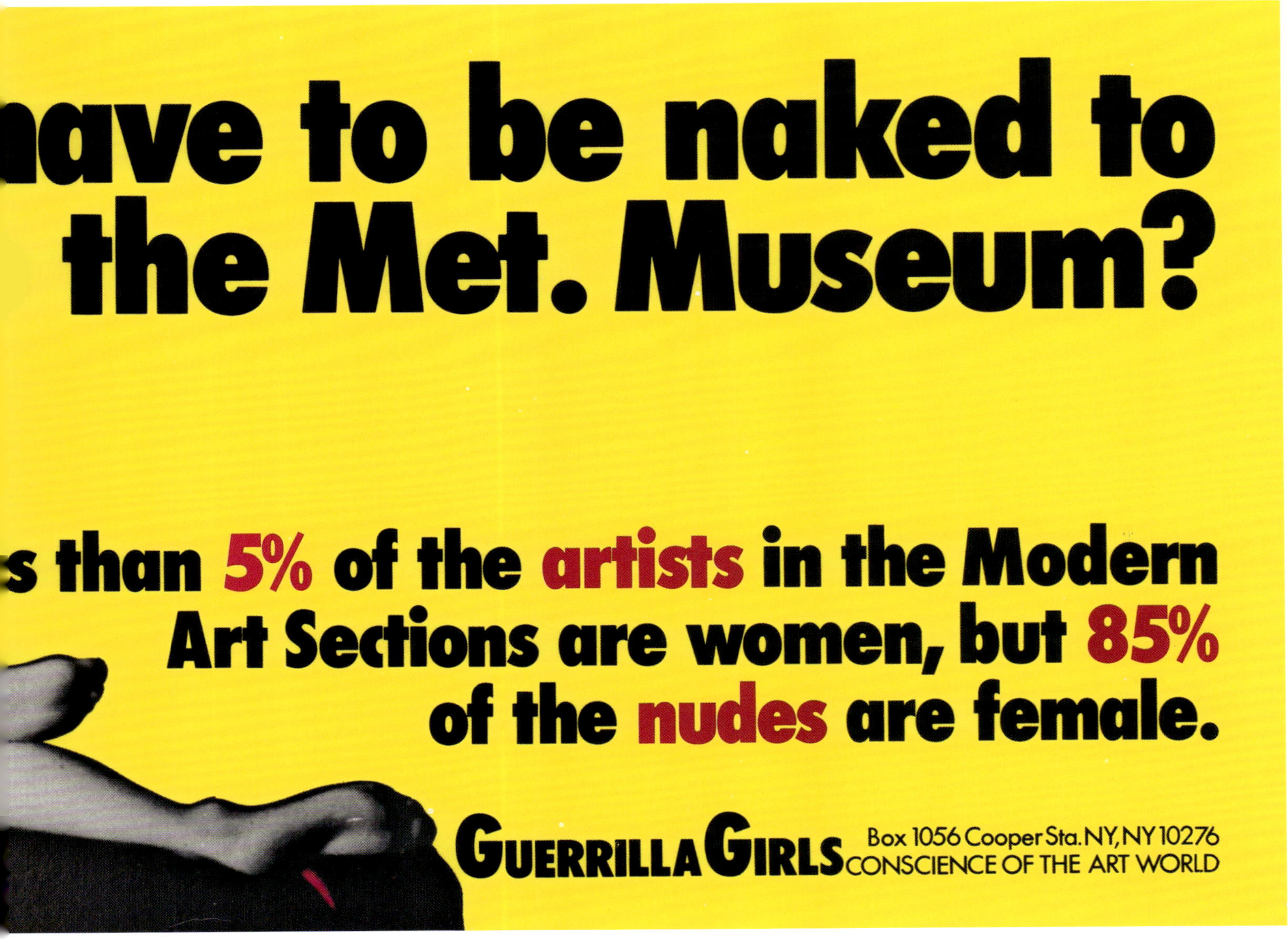

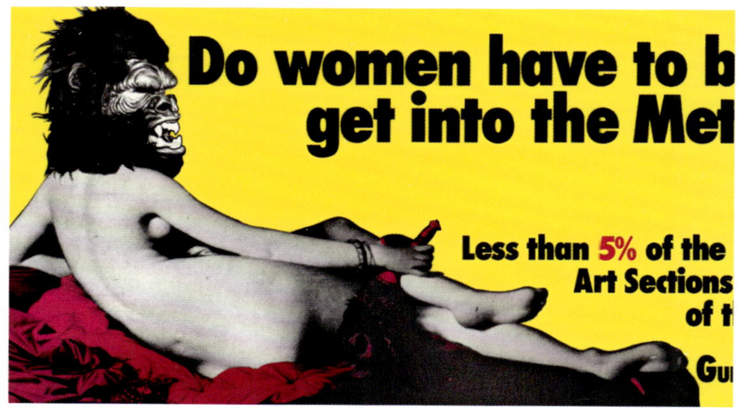

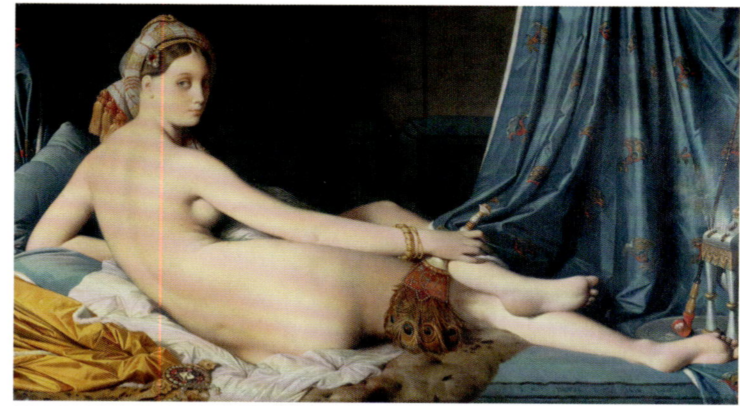

❶ Nude

The dominant figure in the image, which curves across the left-hand side of the composition, is a reproduction of a painting by Jean-Auguste-Dominique Ingres, crudely reproduced in magenta, black and white.

❷ Classical traditions

Ingres's painting, *La Grande Odalisque* (above), is kept in the Louvre in Paris. It was selected by the Guerrilla Girls because it is enshrined in high culture, while also objectifying and eroticizing the unclothed female form.

↑ Jean-Auguste-Dominique Ingres, *La Grande Odalisque*, 1819. Oil on canvas, 91 × 162 cm, 35¾ × 63¾ in.

↓ Let MoMA Know protest, 1984. Photo Clarissa Sligh

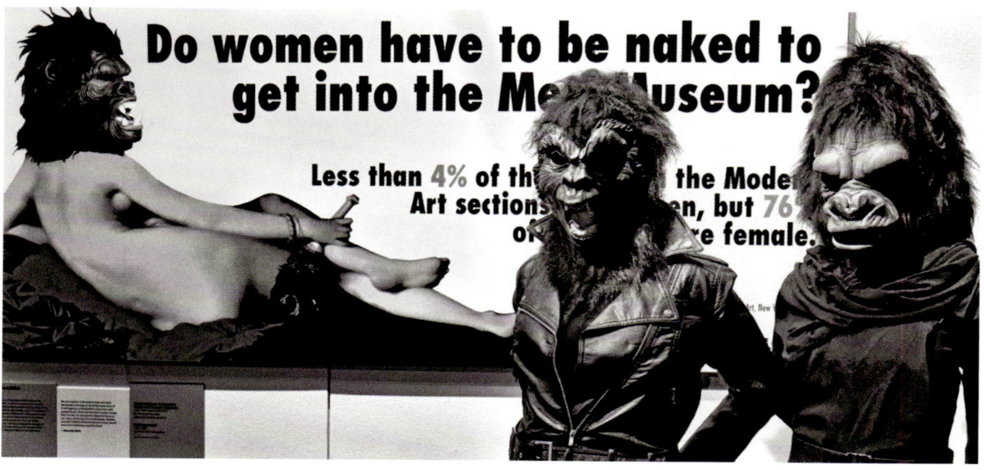

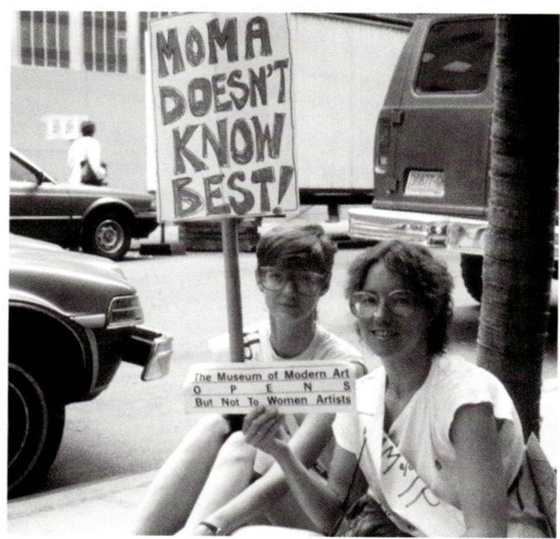

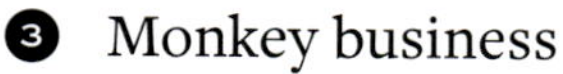

❸ Monkey business

From the start, the artists sported gorilla masks and used pseudonyms adopted from female artists such as Käthe Kollwitz and Frida Kahlo to maintain their anonymity. By hiding their identities, viewers are forced to focus on the issues, rather than on the artists. Here, the nude female body and gorilla mask provide a surreal juxtaposition, reminiscent of the collages of, among others, the Surrealist artist Max Ernst.

↑ Guerrilla Girls display within the exhibition *Disobedient Objects*, Victoria and Albert Museum, London, 2014

→ Max Ernst, *Untitled* (unpublished collage for *Une semaine de bonté*), 1934. Collage, 15.3 × 12.1 cm, 6 × 4¾ in.

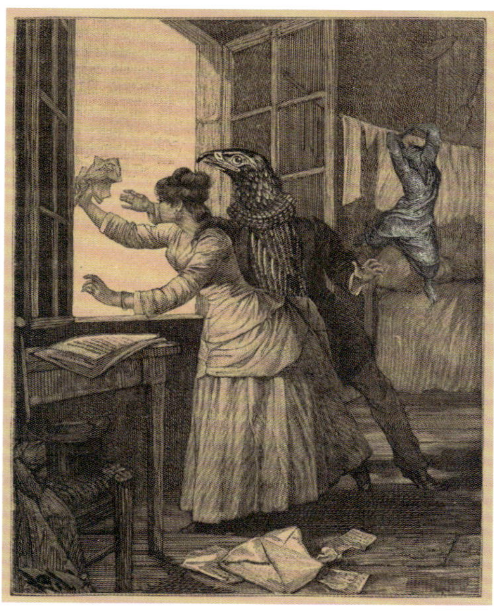

❹ Art-world discrimination

The origins of the Guerrilla Girls can be traced back to 1984. That year, an international survey of painting and sculpture at the Museum of Modern Art in New York presented 169 artists, only 13 of which were women.

❺ Feminism

The artists describe themselves as 'intersectional feminists', referring to the overlapping of different forms of discrimination, based on race, disability, sexuality or gender identity. Art in the 20th and 21st centuries has a rich vein of creativity and criticism linked to feminism, involving practitioners like Judy Chicago, Sherrie Levine, Martha Rosler and Cindy Sherman.

6 Word and image

The Guerrilla Girls took inspiration from other artists who combined text and imagery, such as Barbara Kruger (below) and Jenny Holzer. Other artists who used similar tactics to address political or social issues include Victor Burgin and David Wojnarowicz (bottom).

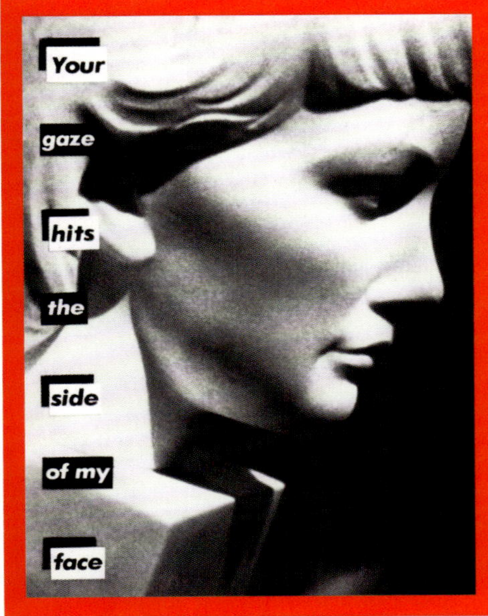

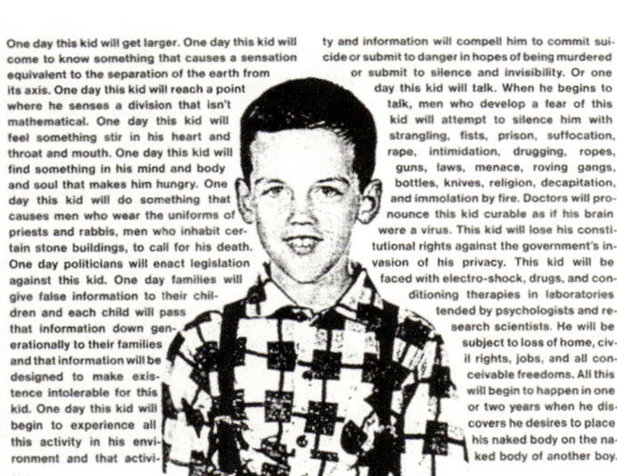

↑ David Wojnarowicz, *Untitled (One day this kid ...)*, 1990. Photostat, 78.1 × 104.1 cm, 30¾ × 41 in.

↑↑ Barbara Kruger, *Untitled (Your gaze hits the side of my face)*, 1981. Gelatin silver print, framed, 139.7 × 104.1 cm, 55 × 41 in.

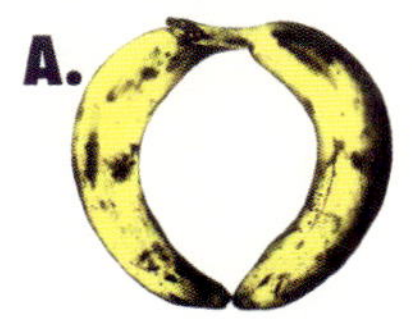

← *How Many Works by Women Artists Were in the Andy Warhol and Tremaine Auctions at Sotheby's?*, 1989. Colour offset lithograph, 43.2 × 56 cm, 17 × 22 in.

7 Print

The work was printed using the silkscreen process, an inexpensive and industrial way of reproducing images. It creates a slightly crude quality of print, as the technique involves ink being pressed through a fabric membrane. In certain areas, evidence of the grainy texture of the silkscreen fabric is visible. Versions of the original poster were reprinted alongside other members of the group under the title *Guerrilla Girls Talk Back*.

8 Information

The smaller text in the poster offers a change in tone from the headline. It delivers clear, simple words and statistics, with key words highlighted in magenta. The 'signature' at the bottom includes a phrase frequently used by the artists to advertise their motives and define their aims: 'conscience of the art world'.

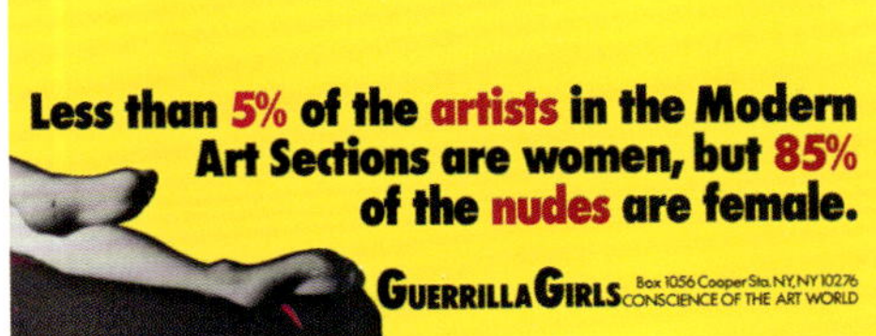

9 Attention-grabbing

The work was intended to be a billboard, and its bold imagery and plain-speaking text are all in keeping with design in advertising.

10 Headline

The title seems to emanate from the gorilla's open mouth and has a provocative and humorously ironic tone. It consciously mimics the style of tabloid headlines or attention-grabbing advertising slogans to make a serious point accessible and impossible to ignore.

11 Colour

The combative use of colours – with the magenta contrasting with the acid-yellow background and black against white – echoes the dissident message.

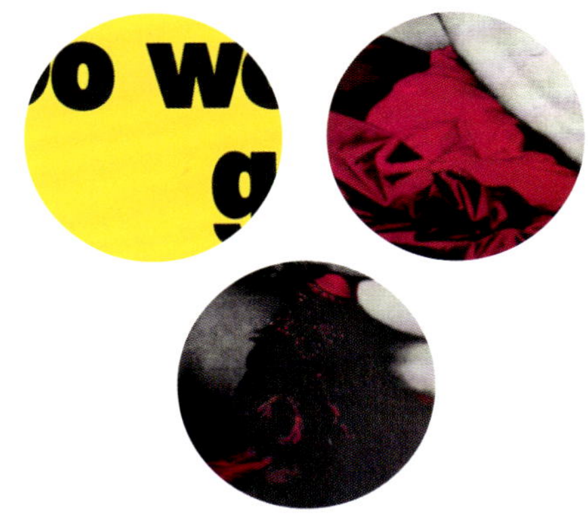

12 Commission

The work was originally commissioned by the Public Art Fund to appear on an advertising hoarding. The artists went to the Metropolitan Museum of Art to research the relative numbers of male and female nudes. In the 19th- and 20th-century galleries they discovered that the overwhelming majority of works on display containing nudity involved women, and that very few artists were female. The poster was rejected, citing a lack of clarity. This spurred the Guerrilla Girls to find an alternative platform, so they paid for the image to be emblazoned on the side of the city's buses for a period of time.

LINKED PRACTITIONERS

FEMINISM AND ART:

Frida Kahlo (1907–1954), MEXICO
Carolee Schneemann (1939–2019), USA
Judy Chicago (born 1939), USA
Martha Rosler (born 1943), USA
Linder (*Sterling*; born 1954), UK

IMAGE AND TEXT:

Victor Burgin (born 1941), UK
Barbara Kruger (born 1945), USA
Hamish Fulton (born 1946), UK
Jenny Holzer (born 1950), USA
David Wojnarowicz (1954–1992), USA

ACTIVIST ART:

Gustave Courbet (1819–1877), FRANCE
John Heartfield (1891–1968), GERMANY
Faith Ringgold (born 1930), USA
Yoko Ono (born 1933), JAPAN/USA

45. Creative Destruction

In 1991, Cornelia Parker was invited to create an artwork for the Chisenhale Gallery in East London by its then director, Jonathan Watkins. The space that she was due to work in was large and dark, with no natural light. Her first thought was to detonate an explosion inside the gallery's exhibition space.

Parker's work up until this point had often focused on the destruction and resurrection of objects. For *Thirty Pieces of Silver* (1988–89; ill. p. 211), she had placed a variety of items made from silver on a road, which were then driven over by a steamroller. The crushed objects were suspended in a gallery in 30 clusters that resembled serving trays. For the Chisenhale commission, the next stage was to work out what she would blow up, and how.

Wood, metal, plastic, ceramic, paper, textile and wire
400 × 500 × 500 cm, 157½ × 196¾ × 196¾ in.
Tate, London

Cornelia Parker

Cold Dark Matter: An Exploded View

1991

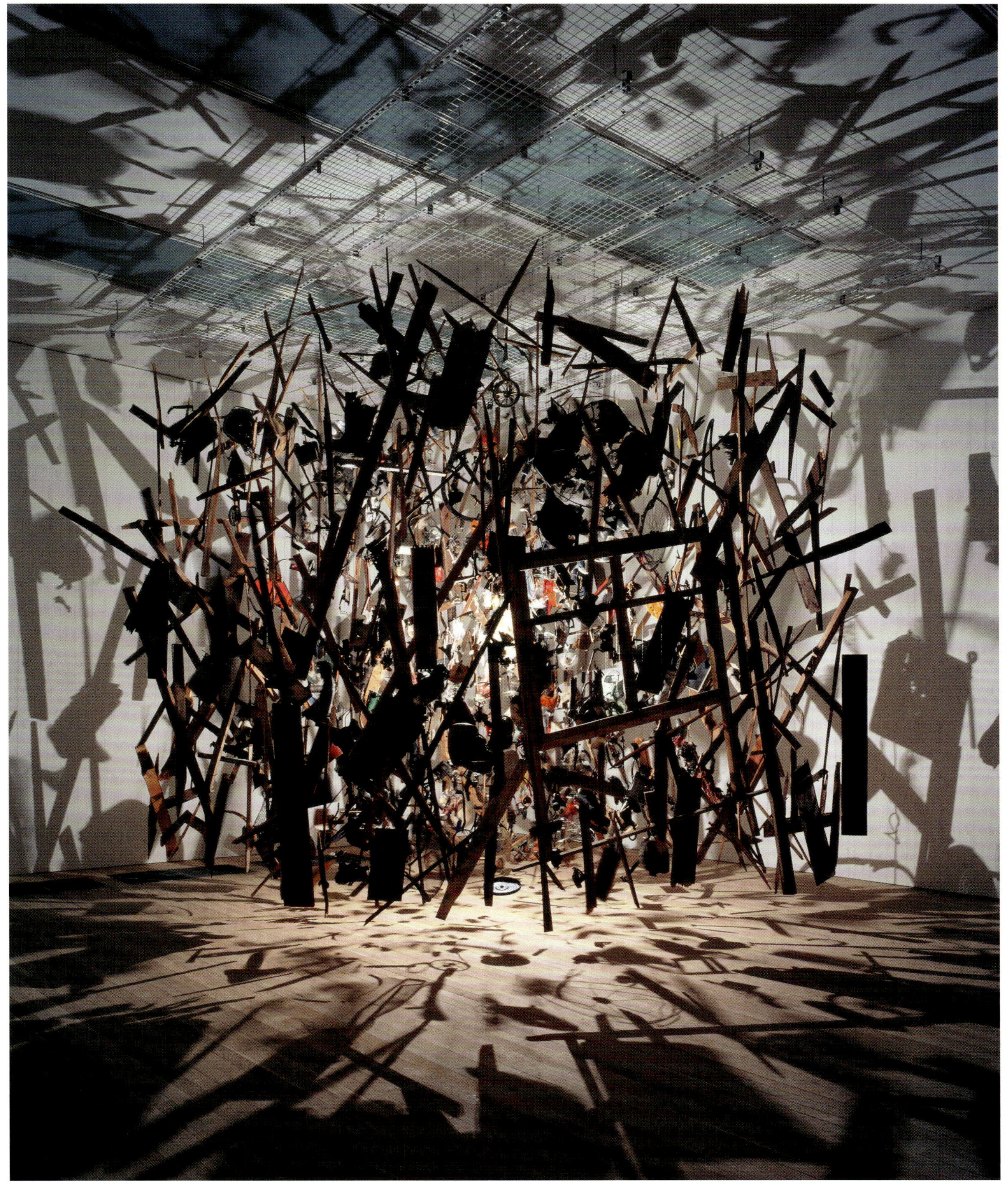

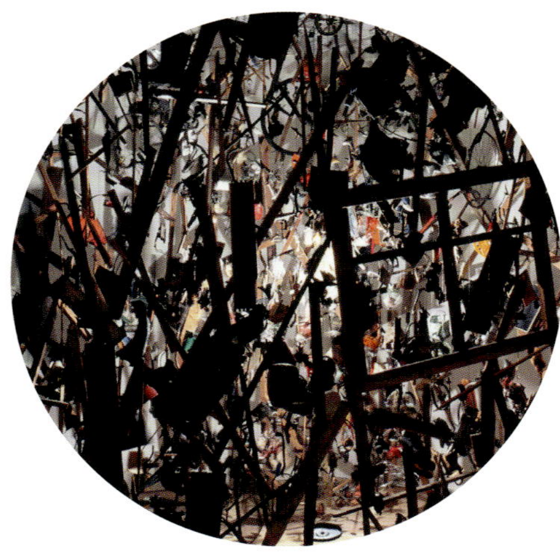

❶ Reminders of past things

The work is made up of a cluster of objects that were deliberately destroyed in the explosion of a garden shed. Along with the shredded wood, there is a toy Spider-Man, a plastic bucket, a bicycle wheel, a puppet of Queen Elizabeth II, a Coca-Cola can and two books: *The Artist's Dilemma* by James Boswell and Marcel Proust's *Remembrance of Things Past*.

❷ Before and after

When *Cold Dark Matter* was originally displayed at the Chisenhale Gallery, Parker included a photograph of the shed before the explosion, so that viewers could see the 'before' and 'after' of the detonation.

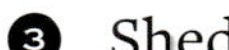

❸ Shed

Parker identifies the shed as a place for tools and an archive of private possessions. With the cosmic implications of the work's title, the shed is also teasingly implied as a kind of personal universe: memories made solid, then torn apart.

❹ A blast of light

The epicentre of the work is a 200-watt bulb that casts light from the inside out, mimicking the explosion.

❺ A big bang

The title refers to two things. The first, 'cold dark matter', is a component of the universe that is known to exist but cannot be measured or perceived. The second is the 'exploded view', a diagram of a building or piece of machinery that shows its components extrapolated and labelled separately.[91] Parker's sculpture is reminiscent of the Big Bang, and the origins of the cosmos.

❻ Military aid

Parker enlisted the British Army to blow up her shed. It was stuffed with possessions, and a pack of Semtex was placed in the middle. After it was blown to smithereens, she collected the scattered fragments, filled a van with them and then drove back home.

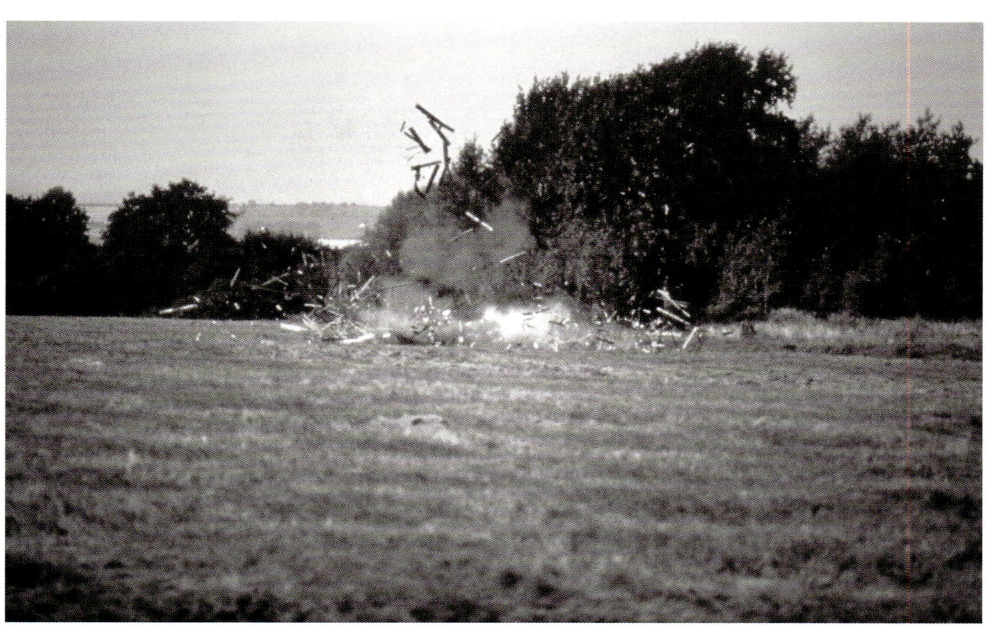

Cold Dark Matter: An Exploded View (work in progress), 1991. Photo by Hugo Glendinning

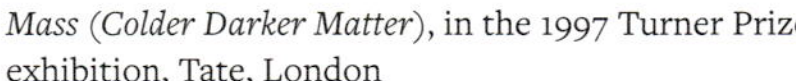

Mass (Colder Darker Matter), in the 1997 Turner Prize exhibition, Tate, London

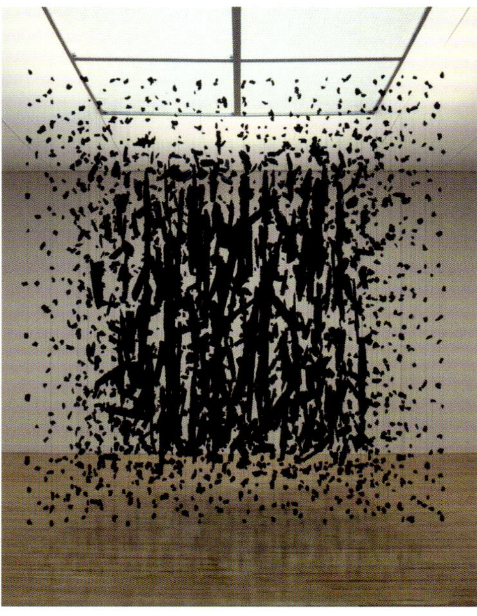

❼ Installation

This is an example of an art installation, which requires spectators to move into and around the space in which the work is exhibited to engage with it.

❽ Budget

The concept was always intended to cost very little, and Parker estimated that the materials added up to about £250 ($330).

❾ Abstraction

Before you are aware of how it was constructed, *Cold Dark Matter* looks like an abstract work of art. Parker has said that she makes abstract works out of real things – a reversal of the original aim of abstract art, which was to make distorted images that suggested real objects.

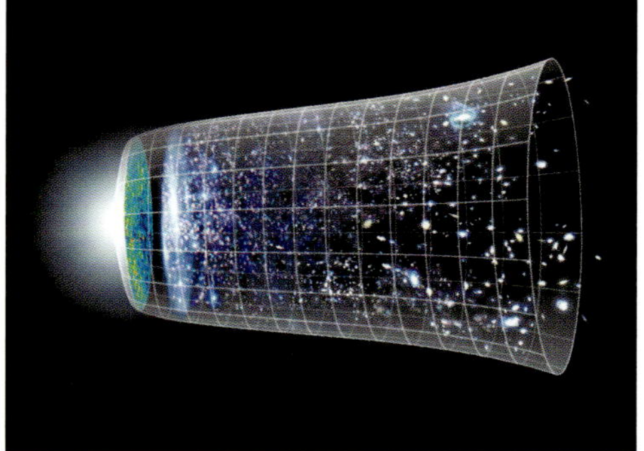

Timeline of the Big Bang

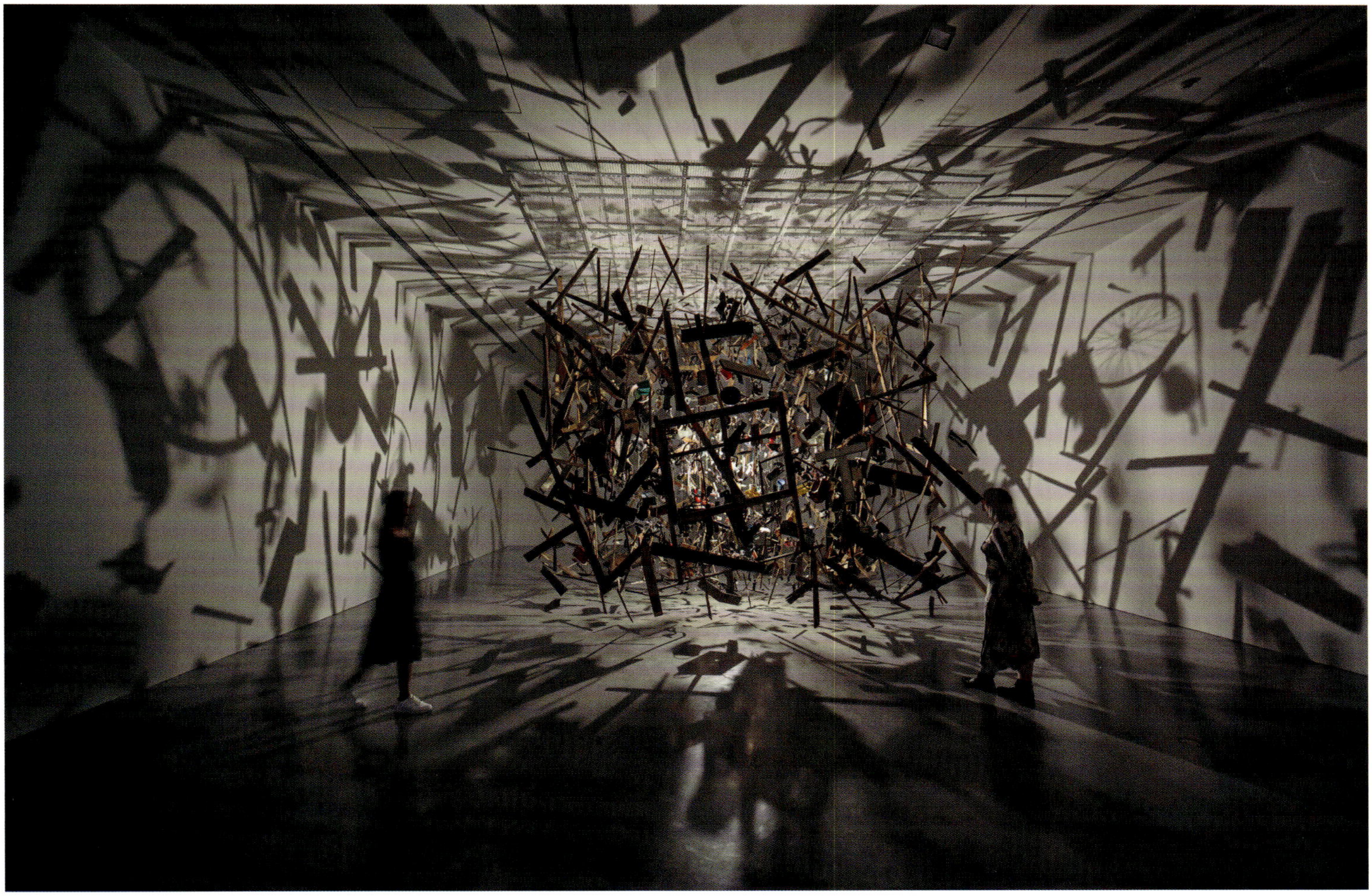

⑩ Viewer becomes artwork

As visitors to the gallery move around the work, their shadows are cast on the walls alongside those of the suspended group of objects. The very act of viewing the artwork, therefore, has the effect of changing it.

⑪ Dynamism

The feeling of explosive outward energy is generated by the positioning of objects. The smallest elements are hung nearest the centre, with larger pieces, including the shed's outer walls, at the periphery.

⑫ Appetite for destruction

Many of Parker's other artworks involve destroying objects. In a work that was shortlisted for the Turner Prize in 1997 (opposite, above right), she took the charred remnants of a chapel that had been struck by lightning and suspended them in a cube formation. The destructions have a dark comedy about them, which leavens the serious themes Parker addresses in her work. 'I am particularly interested in cartoon deaths,' she has said, 'where Tom and Jerry are shot full of holes or blown apart.' Her art presents us with things that have been obliterated but reconfigured, order re-established from chaos.

↑ Viewers interacting with *Cold Dark Matter: An Exploded View*, Museum of Contemporary Art, Chicago, 2019

↓ *Thirty Pieces of Silver*, 1988–89. Silver and copper wire

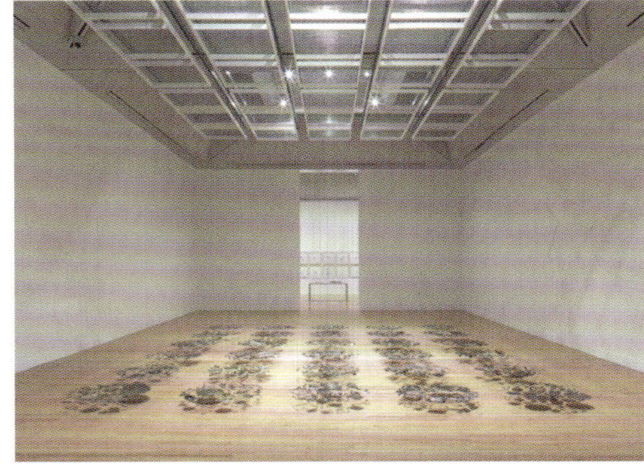

LINKED PRACTITIONERS

INSTALLATION ART:

Kurt Schwitters (1887–1948), GERMANY
Yayoi Kusama (born 1929), JAPAN
Thomas Hirschhorn (born 1957), SWITZERLAND
Doris Salcedo (born 1958), COLOMBIA
Olafur Eliasson (born 1967), DENMARK

FOUND OBJECTS:

Marcel Duchamp (1887–1968), FRANCE
Salvador Dalí (1904–1989), SPAIN
Carl Andre (born 1935), USA
El Anatsui (born 1944), GHANA
Tony Cragg (born 1949), UK

ARTISTS WHO CREATE BY DESTROYING:

Lucio Fontana (1899–1968), ARGENTINA/ITALY
Gustav Metzger (1926–2017), GERMANY/UK
Yoko Ono (born 1933), JAPAN/USA
Raphael Ortiz (born 1934), USA
Michael Landy (born 1963), UK

46. A Matter of Life and Death

The year 1991 was a pivotal one for Damien Hirst: he held his first solo exhibition in London and secured the backing of an influential and supportive patron, the businessman and art collector Charles Saatchi.

Hirst had been building a keen following among collectors and curators since 1988. Saatchi was particularly impressed with *A Thousand Years* (1990), a large glass case filled with flies, a rotting cow's head (in which the flies' larvae grew) and an electronic insect-killer (which executed them). He offered Hirst the financial backing to create a new piece, and the result was the now iconic *The Physical Impossibility of Death in the Mind of Someone Living.*

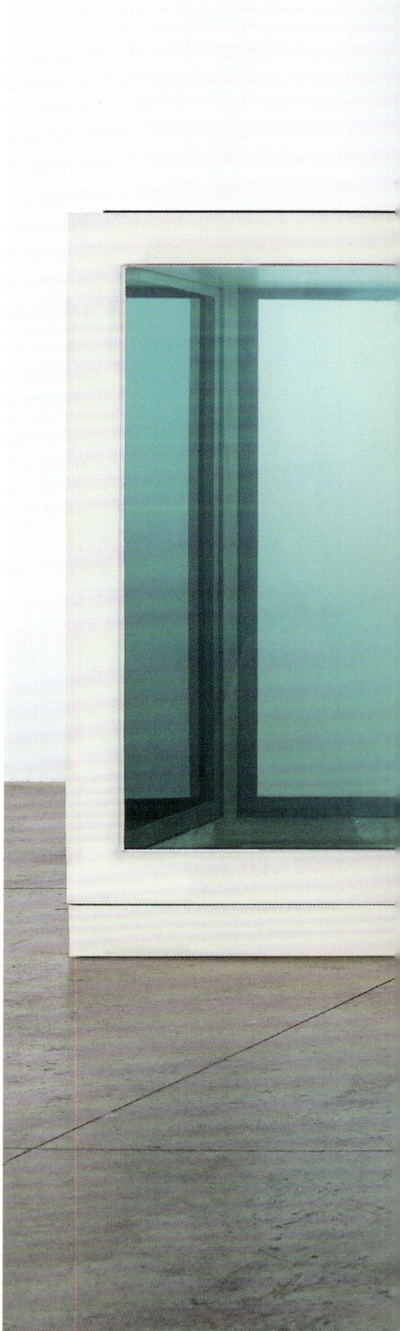

Glass, painted steel, silicone, monofilament, shark and formaldehyde solution
217 × 542 × 180 cm, 85½ × 213¼ × 70¾ in.

Damien Hirst

The Physical Impossibility of Death in the Mind of Someone Living

1991

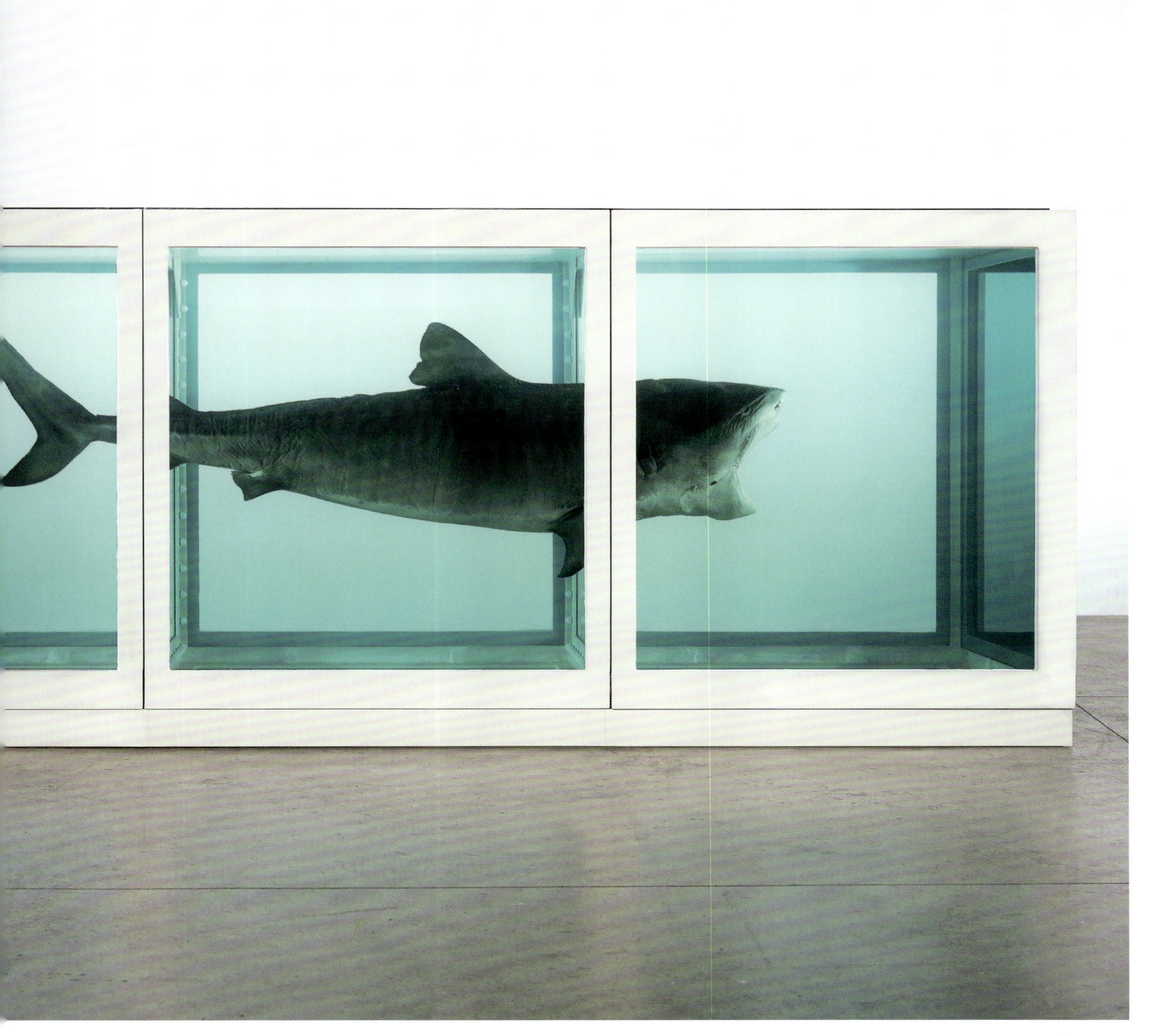

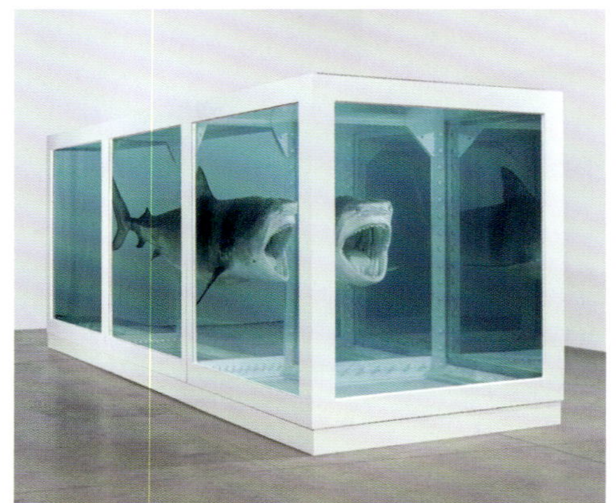

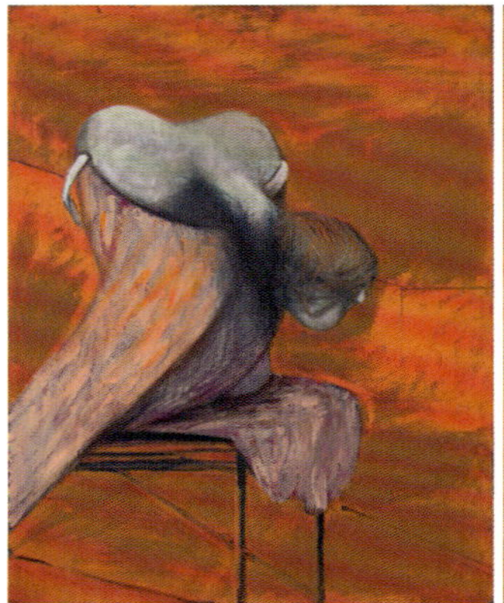

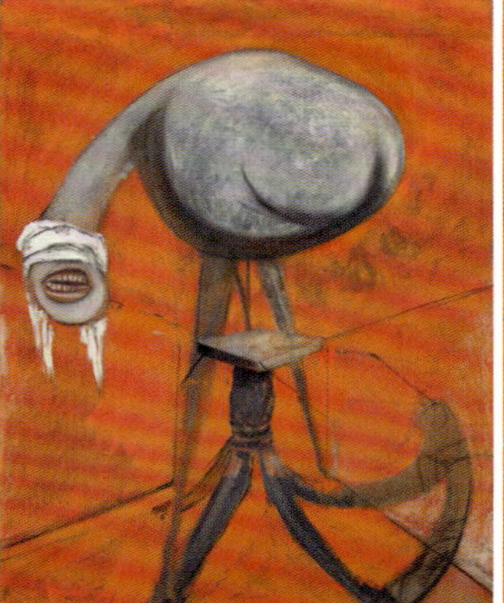

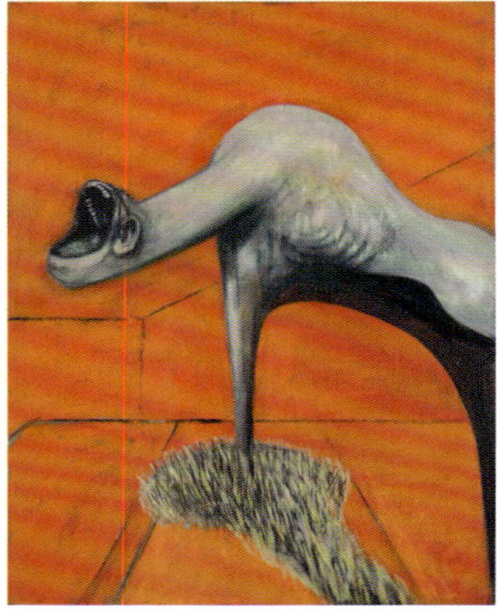

Francis Bacon, *Three Studies for Figures at the Base of a Crucifixion*, 1944. Oil on three boards, each 94 × 73.7 cm, 37 × 29 in.

❶ Frame

A thick case contains the glass vitrine and splits the sculpture into three parts, suggestive of a triptych – a format used in paintings by Francis Bacon (above right), whom Hirst admired.[92] The frame and vitrine create angular lines in standardized units, which contrast with the shark's curved silhouette.

❷ Display case

The industrial-looking, pure-white case is at odds with the natural subject that it frames. It resembles a trophy cabinet, containing a hunter's victim.

❸ Predator

The shark is a real, 4 m (13 ft)-long, 23-ton tiger shark. It is placed centrally within the case, with the transparent suspension liquid enabling it to be seen from all angles.

❹ Commission

The work was commissioned by the art collector Charles Saatchi in 1991, who granted the artist money to create whatever he wished.

❺ Creation

The original shark was caught by an Australian fisherman and transported to London, where it was mounted in its case under Hirst's direction. The whole thing cost £50,000 to make.

❻ Impact

The shark is suspended in a vitrine of formaldehyde. The simplicity of the work gives it impact, turning the dead shark into a confrontational gesture.

❼ Controversy

When it was first displayed, the piece caused an uproar. *The Sun* newspaper ran a story titled '£50,000 for fish without chips', and criticized the large sums of money spent on a work of art that seemed to show little or no evidence of creative input from the artist himself. The notion of using a 'found' object is not unique in the history of western art, however (a significant example is Marcel Duchamp's *Fountain* from 1917; below), nor is the use of a vitrine to suspend an object for aesthetic contemplation (see Jeff Koons's suspended basketballs from 1985; right).

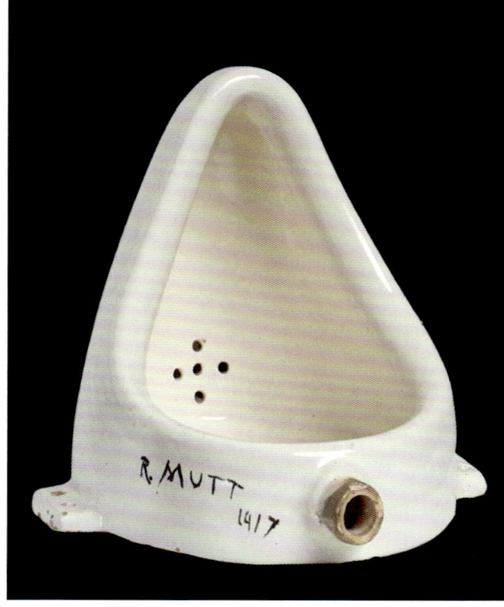

❽ Display

The work was originally displayed at the Saatchi Gallery in London as part of the *Young British Artists I* exhibition in 1992. Later it was included in a much more prominent exhibition – *Sensation* – at the Royal Academy in 1997. Hirst is one of the Young British Artists (YBAs) who emerged in the 1990s, along with Tracey Emin, Sarah Lucas and the brothers Jake and Dinos Chapman.

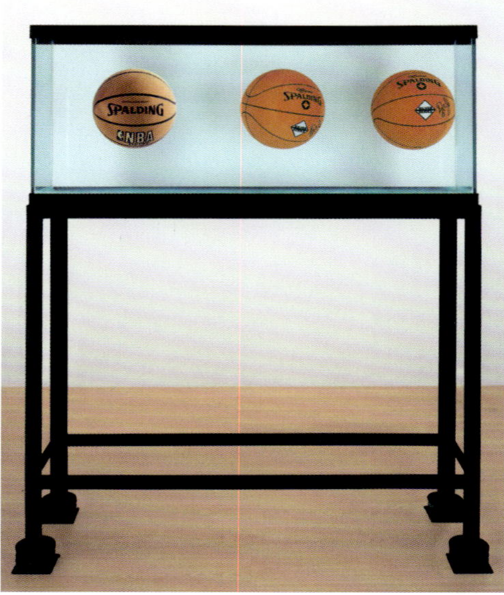

← Marcel Duchamp, *Fountain*, 1950 (replica of 1917 original). Porcelain urinal, 30.5 × 38.1 × 45.7 cm, 12 × 15 × 18 in.

↑ Jeff Koons, *Three Ball Total Equilibrium Tank (Two Dr J Silver Series Spalding NBA Tip-Off)*, 1985. Glass, steel, pneumatic feet, three rubber basketballs and water, 153.6 × 123.8 × 33.6 cm, 60½ × 48¾ × 13¼ in.

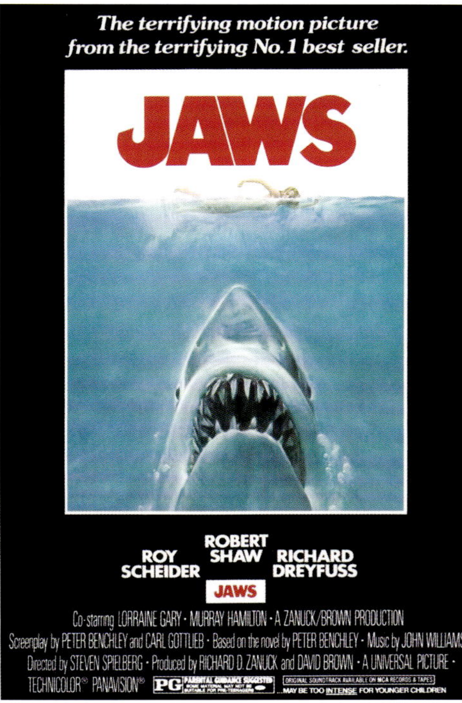

Jaws film poster, 1975

Barnett Newman, *Vir Heroicus Sublimis*, 1950–51.
Oil on canvas, 242.2 × 541.7 cm, 95¼ × 213¼ in.

9 Influences

Hirst may have been inspired by Bacon, Duchamp and Koons, but his work often betrays pop-cultural references, as well. Here, the open-mouthed shark evokes the blockbuster film, *Jaws* (1975). Art historian Luke White has commented: 'Hirst's shark is more Steven Spielberg than it is Barnett Newman.'[93] In using such subjects, Hirst intended to open art to a wider audience; as he put it, to 'make art that everybody could believe in'.

10 Deterioration

The shark has deteriorated over time, and the formaldehyde has become cloudy. In 2006, the whole shark was replaced and treated with different preservation techniques.

11 Death

Hirst has commented on the underlying meaning of the sculpture, noting: 'You try and avoid [death], but it's such a big thing that you can't. That's the frightening thing, isn't it?'[94] As a representation of death, the sculpture is a variant on the *memento mori* theme. A curator at the Tate Gallery in London described Hirst as 'brutally honest and confrontational ... [drawing] attention to the paranoiac denial of death that permeates our culture'.[95]

12 Title

The title – *The Physical Impossibility of Death in the Mind of Someone Living* – invites the contemplation of mortality and the extent to which we can come to terms with the enormity of the notion of death. The pathos is linked to the subject matter. In the wild, we would fear such a powerful and deadly creature; following Hirst's intervention, however, its powers have evaporated.

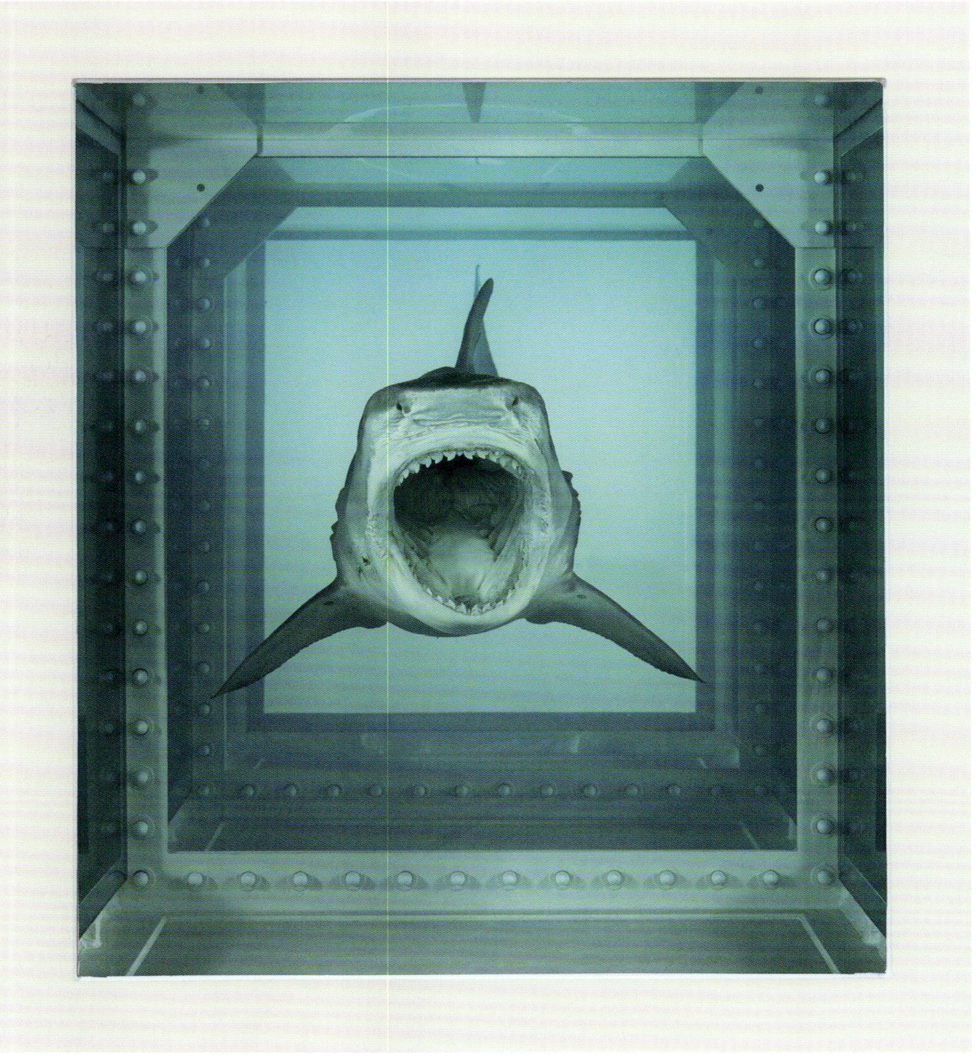

LINKED PRACTITIONERS

OTHER YBAS:

Gary Hume (born 1962), UK
Sarah Lucas (born 1962), UK
Tracey Emin (born 1963), UK
Jake (born 1966) *& Dinos Chapman* (born 1962), UK
Chris Ofili (born 1968), UK

ANIMALS IN ART:

Albrecht Dürer (1471–1528), GERMANY
Tawaraya Sōtatsu (c. 1570–c. 1640), JAPAN
George Stubbs (1724–1806), UK
Henri Rousseau (1844–1910), FRANCE
Cai Guo-Qiang (born 1957), CHINA

CONCEPTUAL ART:

Joseph Beuys (1921–1986), GERMANY
On Kawara (1932–2014), JAPAN
Michael Craig-Martin (born 1941), UK
Joseph Kosuth (born 1945), USA
Sophie Calle (born 1953), FRANCE

47. The Brutality of History

In 1994 Kara Walker was asked to enter an artwork for a group exhibition at the Drawing Center in New York. She was 24, and this was her first big break.

Cut paper on wall
396.2 × 1,524 cm, 156 × 600 in.
Installation view, Hamner Museum, Los Angeles

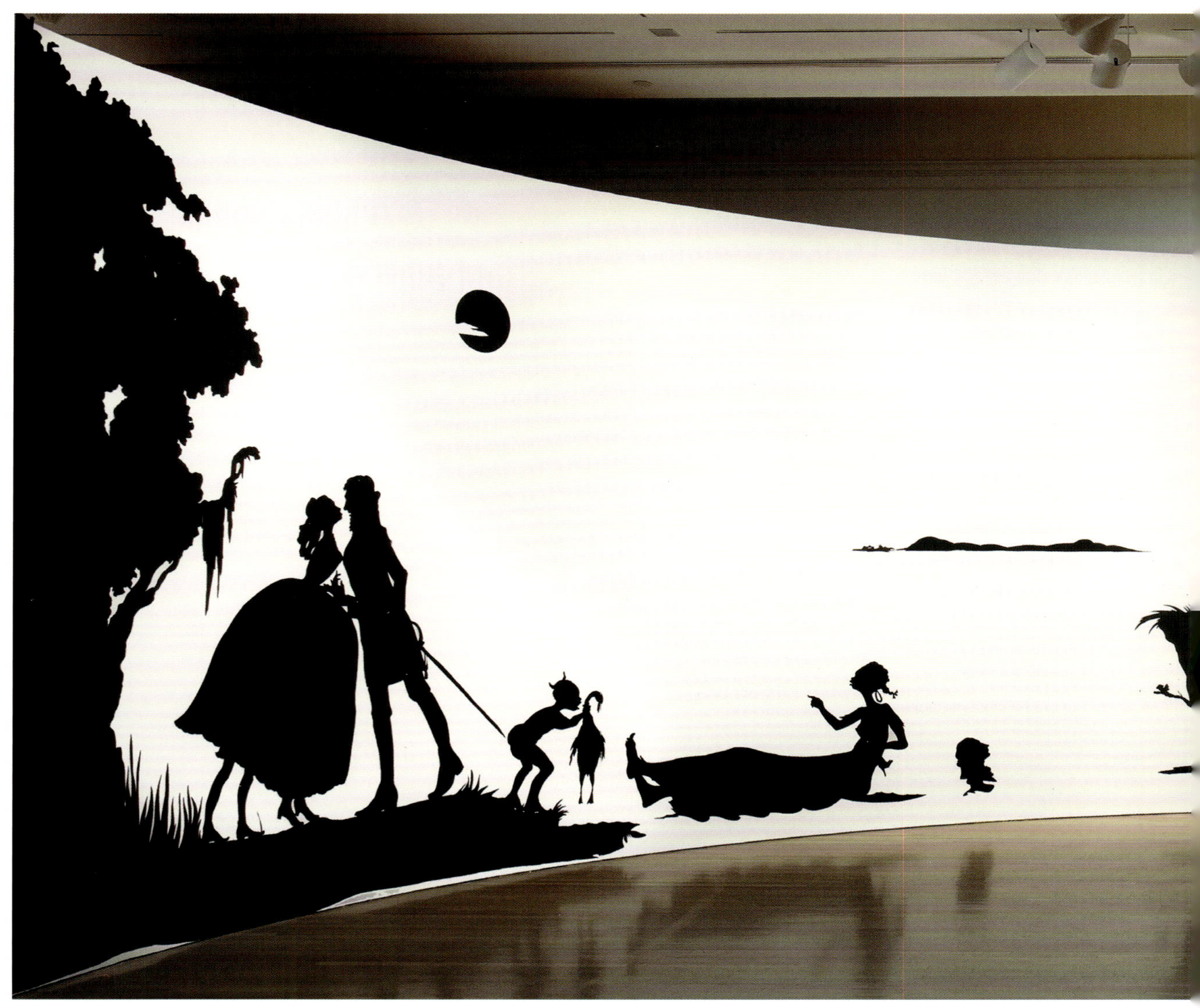

Kara Walker

Gone: An Historical Romance of a Civil War as it Occurred between the Dusky Thighs of One Young Negress and Her Heart

1994

Walker decided to create a monumental piece, 15 m (50 ft) in length, made entirely from cut-paper silhouettes. She chose a visual style and title that evoked antebellum romance, but paired it with themes of racial violence and sexual exploitation. The exhibition became the launchpad for her career.

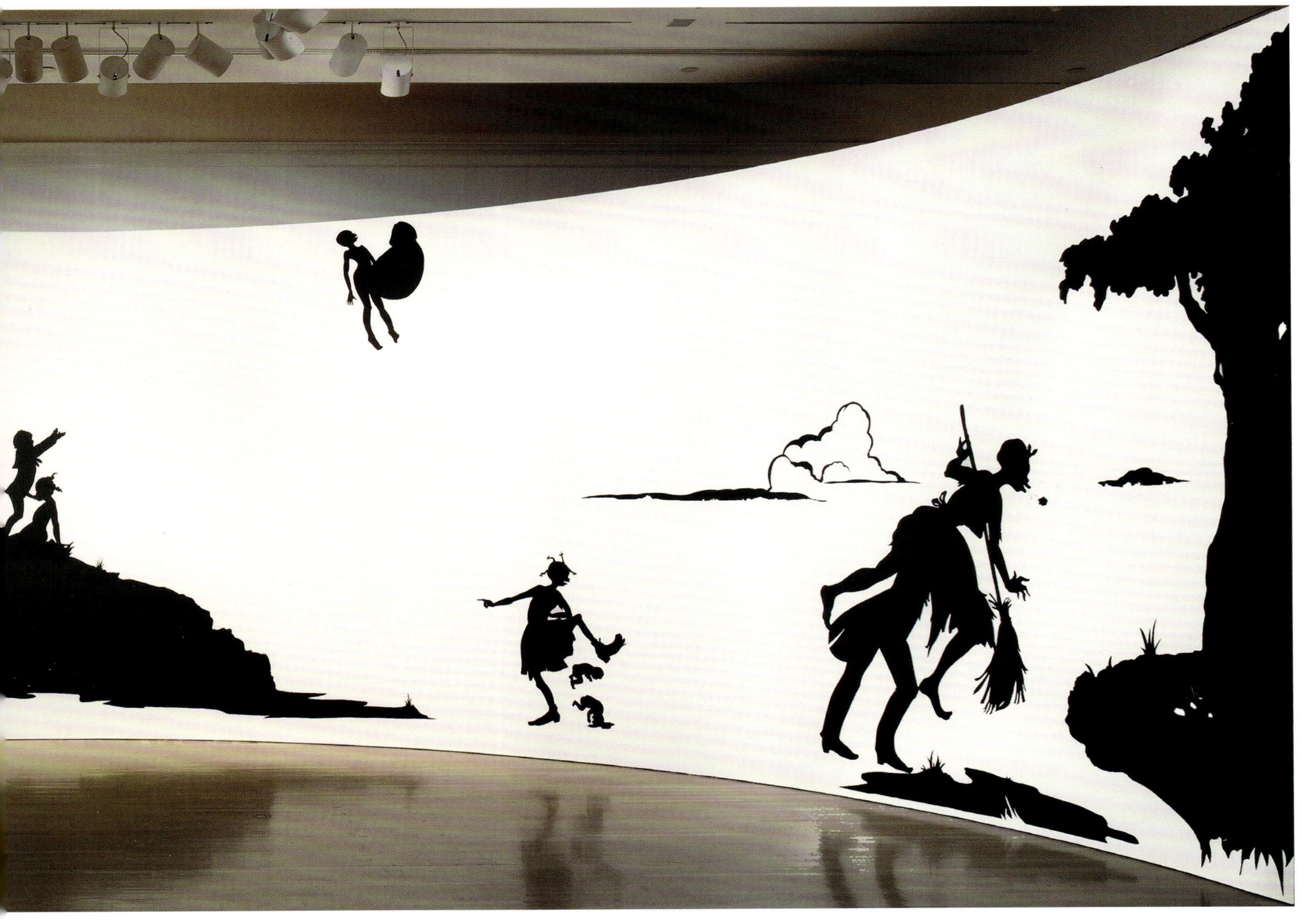

❶ Romance

Starting at the left, we are led into the story by a genteel-looking couple, poised for a kiss. The romantic scene harks back to the Rococo style of art in the 18th century, such as Jean-Honoré Fragonard's *The Progress of Love: Love Letters* (far right). Walker's lovers are set within a bayou-type landscape, indicating that they are from a plantation-owning family and thus the keepers of enslaved people.

❷ Space

The use of cut-paper silhouettes means that each form is flat and there is no definition of pictorial space. It is difficult to establish the relative positions of people or objects when they overlap. The artist has used this for comic effect: the woman has two pairs of legs, so we are uncertain if there is a child in front of or behind her, or beneath her skirts.

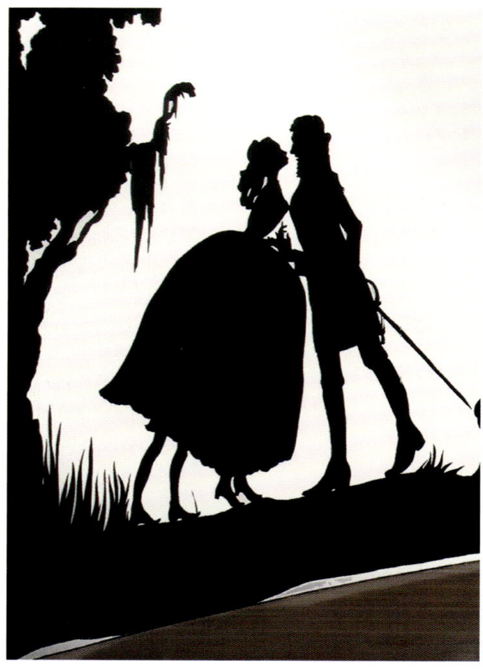

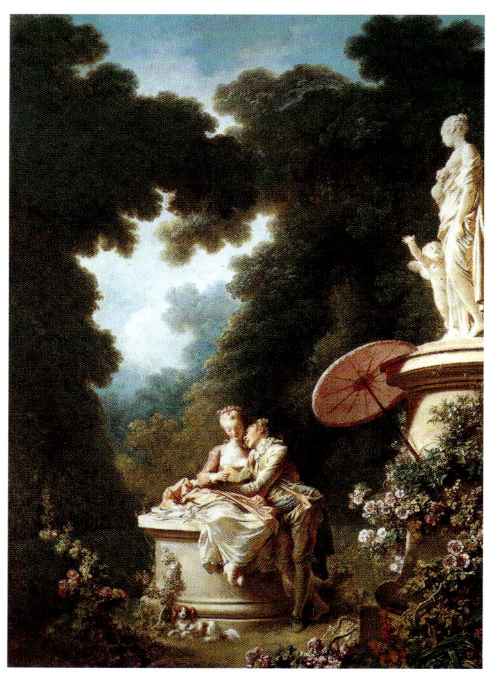

Jean-Honoré Fragonard, *The Progress of Love: Love Letters*, 1771–72. Oil on canvas, 317.2 × 216.9 cm, 124¾ × 85½ in.

❸ Stereotypes

By using a monochromatic palette, Walker highlights racial division between black and white. To the right of the kissing couple is an enslaved person, apparently lying on the water. In art, it is usually Venus, the goddess of love, who is shown in this pose. This parodies the racist stereotype of the enslaved woman as a temptress capable of corrupting white power, as put forward in novels like *The Clansman* (1905) by Thomas Dixon, Jr.[96]

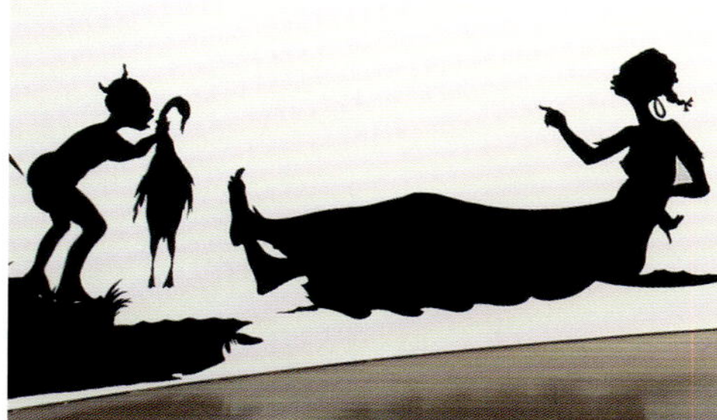

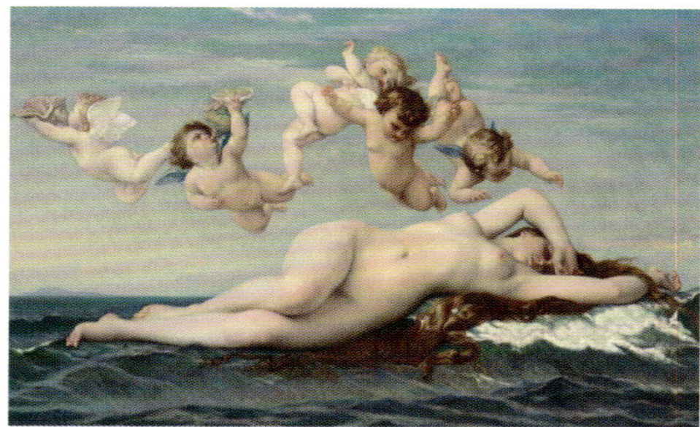

Alexandre Cabanel, *The Birth of Venus*, 1875. Oil on canvas, 106 × 182.6 cm, 41¾ × 71¾ in.

❹ Dead centre

Counterbalancing the romantic tryst at the left, the central part of the composition reveals a graphic sexual act between an underaged couple. The shock factor of this vignette is intensified by its juxtaposition with the visual style and association with the refined and straitlaced society of the 19th century.

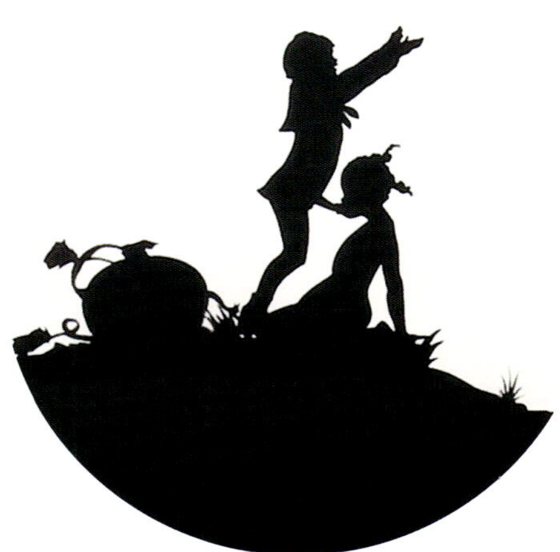

❺ *Gone with the Wind*

Walker took the title and aspects of the narrative from *Gone with the Wind* (1936) by Margaret Mitchell. Along with other examples of 'plantation literature', the novel was written from a white perspective, rather than from that of enslaved persons, providing Walker with a platform for her satirical artwork.

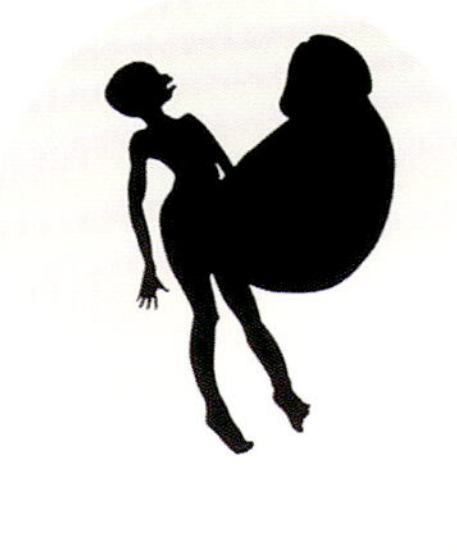

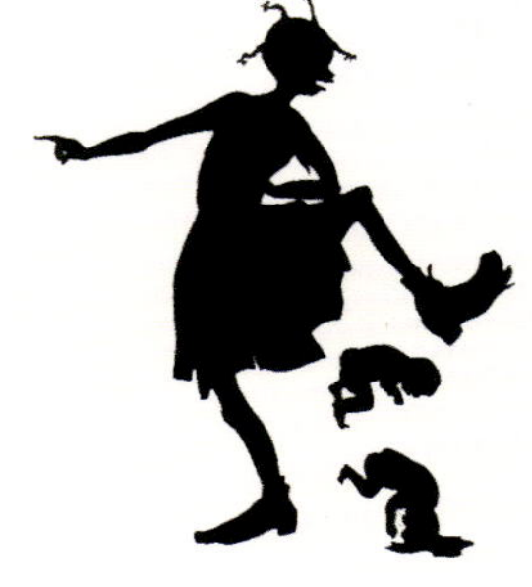

❻ Motherhood

Perhaps the most disturbing aspect is the scene of an enslaved woman with legs akimbo, apparently giving birth to two foetuses that crash to the floor. She is below a male figure, who floats to the sky, attached to a large, inflated penis. These details add a dreamlike element, enhancing the volatile atmosphere. The rosy-tinted melodrama of *Gone with the Wind* has been metamorphosed by the artist into a vision of sexual exploitation.[97]

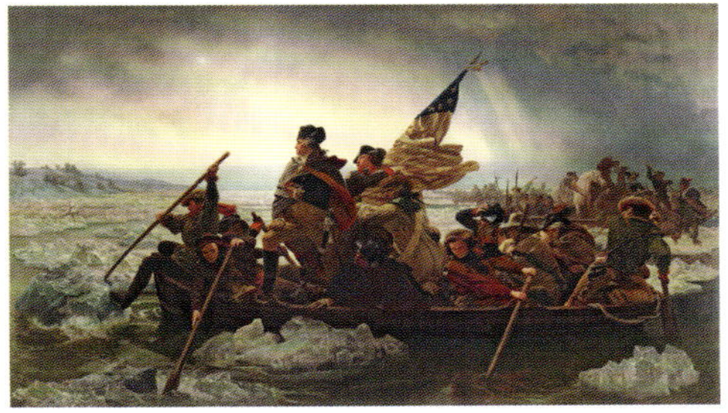

Emanuel Leutze, *Washington Crossing the Delaware*, 1851. Oil on canvas, 378.5 × 647.7 cm, 149 × 255 in.

Illustration from Johann Kaspar Lavater, *Essays on Physiognomy; designed to promote the knowledge and the love of mankind*, 1789–98

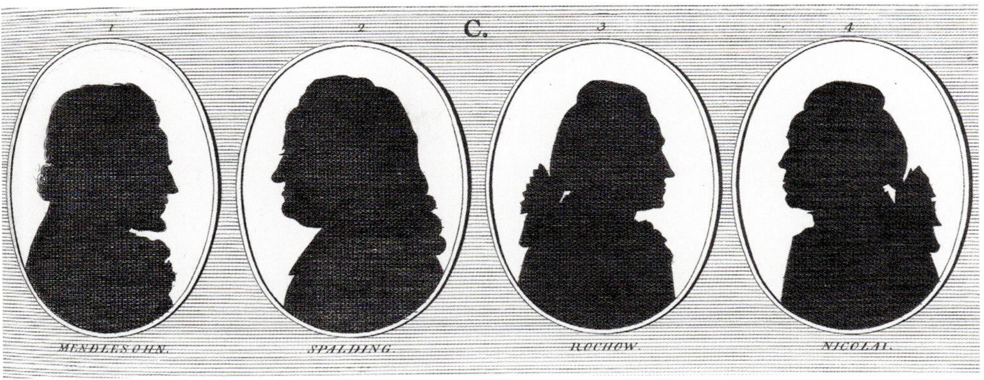

7 Storyline

In its size and narrative style, the work is reminiscent of history painting, once seen as one of the most prestigious genres in art. Works like *Washington Crossing the Delaware* by Emanuel Leutze (above) depicted stories from mythology and religion, and historic events.

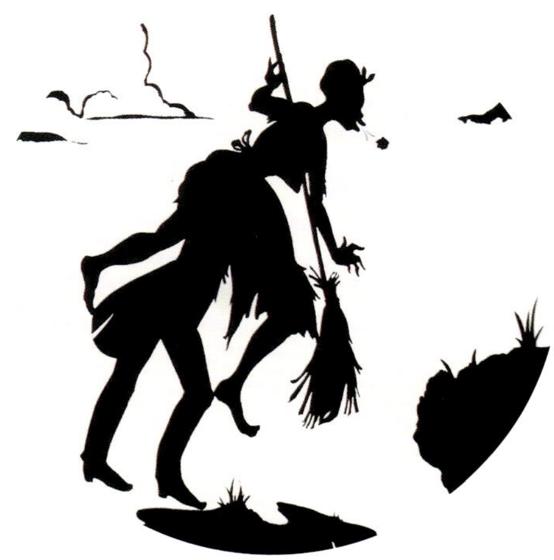

8 Old maid

In the last scene, the plantation owner and an older maid are shown in a surreal and disturbing conjunction. She spits out a wad of tobacco and drops her broom as his upper body apparently disappears up her skirt.

9 Phrenology

The characters of Walker's epic work recall a sinister application of silhouette portrait images from the 18th and 19th centuries. In *Essays on Physiognomy* (above), the Swiss poet and philosopher Johann Kaspar Lavater set out to prove that an individual's intelligence and moral character could be judged by the shape of the head.[98] Known as phrenology, the practice is seen today as an entirely discredited pseudo-science, and one that has contributed to racist stereotyping in the past.

10 Silhouettes

Cut-paper silhouettes have historically fallen into the category of folk art, or self-taught crafts based on traditional styles and techniques. They were fashionable in the 18th and 19th centuries, sometimes made by professional artists, but mostly by amateurs at home making family portraits or items such as Valentine's Day cards.[99] Walker's process is simple: the figures are drawn on large sheets of black paper, cut out with a scalpel, and applied to a white wall.

Frederick Frith and Henry A. Frith, *Silhouette of a Girl*, 1843. Paint, ink and pencil on paper, 22.9 × 16.5 cm, 9 × 6½ in.

11 Process and meaning

The technique of cut-paper silhouettes is meaningful for Walker on several levels. This type of imagery was popular in the 19th century, aligning with the historical subject matter. The flatness of the figures also alludes to the lack of depth with which traditional histories have told the story of enslaved people in America.

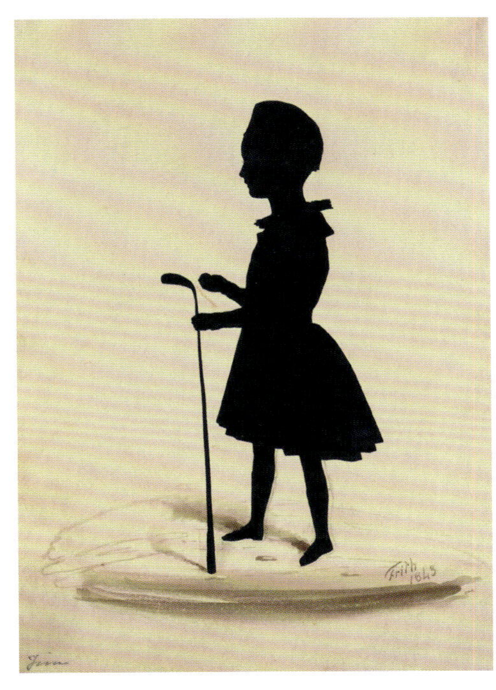

LINKED PRACTITIONERS

SATIRE:

William Hogarth (1697–1764), UK
James Gillray (1756–1815), UK
Honoré Daumier (1808–1879), FRANCE
Philip Guston (1913–1980), USA
Maurizio Cattelan (born 1960), ITALY

RECALLING PAST ART STYLES:

John Everett Millais (1829–1896), UK
Masami Teraoka (born 1936) JAPAN/USA
Cindy Sherman (born 1954), USA
Glenn Brown (born 1966), UK
Kehinde Wiley (born 1977), USA

HISTORY PAINTING:

Peter Paul Rubens (1577–1640), BELGIUM
Diego Velázquez (1599–1660), SPAIN
Jean-Baptiste Greuze (1725–1805), FRANCE
Benjamin West (1738–1820), USA/UK
Jacques-Louis David (1748–1825), FRANCE

48. Conflicted Identities

In 1975, three years before the outbreak of the Iranian Revolution, Shirin Neshat emigrated to the United States as a 17-year-old. In 1991 she returned to her homeland to see for herself the profound changes that had taken place there since the events over a decade earlier. What she witnessed during her visit inspired the Unveiling *series from 1993.*

One of the photographs from that series was *Offered Eyes* (ill. p. 223), which shows an eye with text surrounding the iris in concentric circles. It became the impetus for a new series, *Women of Allah* (1993–97), which again combined text and photography. The project became a watershed in Neshat's career, with *Rebellious Silence* – depicting a woman wearing a *chador* and holding a rifle – its most well-known image, as well as an eloquent encapsulation of the events that shaped Neshat's work.

RC print and ink
Photo by Cynthia Preston

Shirin Neshat
Rebellious Silence
Women of Allah, 1994

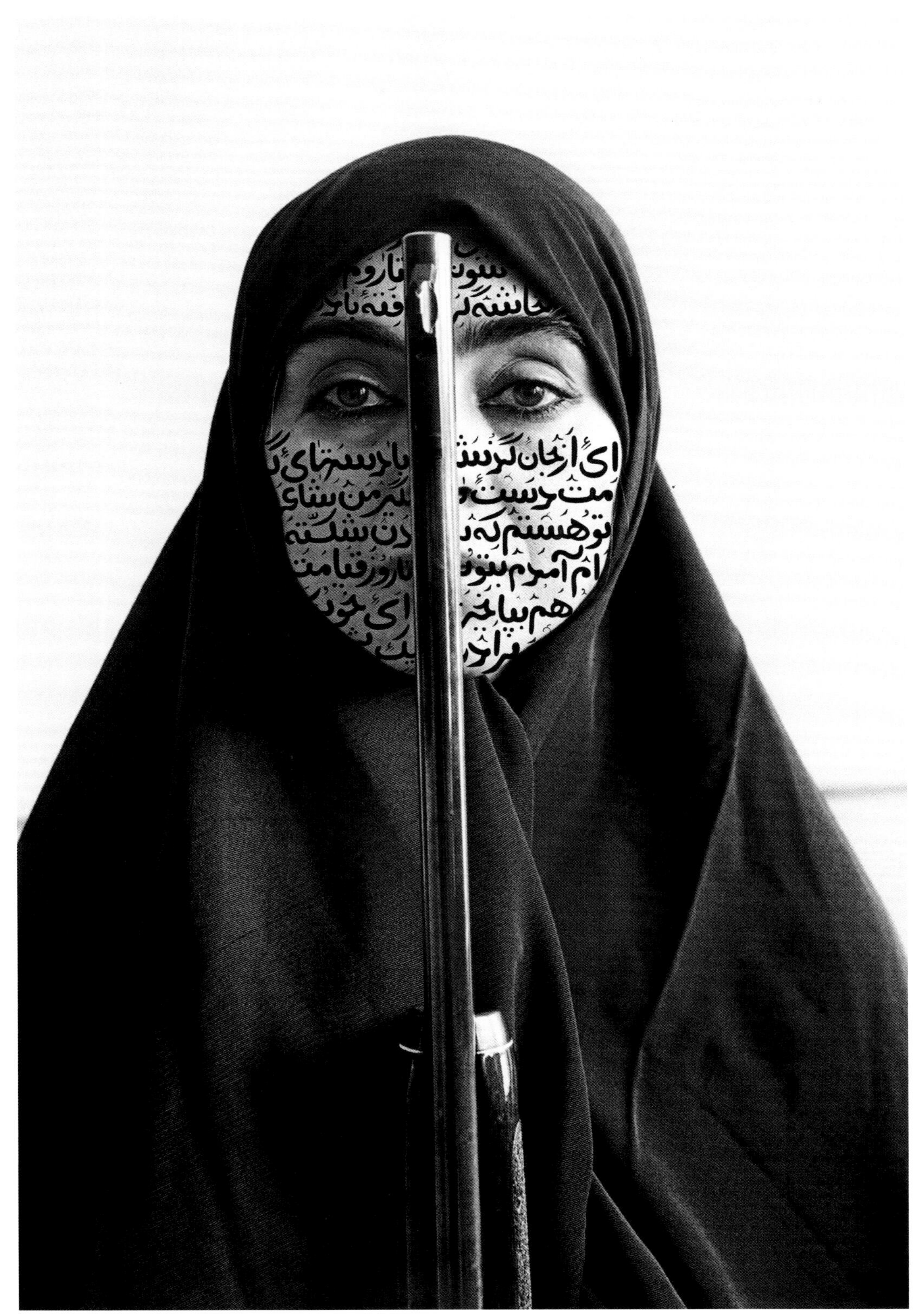

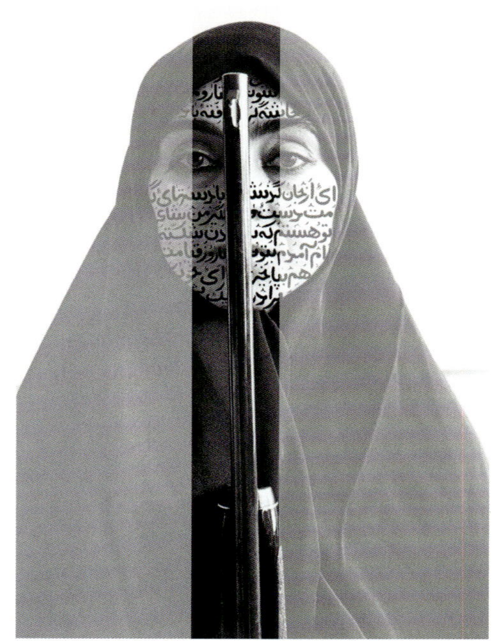

❶ Symmetry

The object in the photograph closest to the viewer is the rifle, pointed to the heavens and placed so that the stock and trigger are not visible. The barrel is aligned down the front of the woman's body, as if she is obeying a military command to present arms. The gun bisects her face, creating an almost perfectly symmetrical composition.

❷ Frozen in time

It is a common reaction to see symmetrical images as harmonious. It is rare in everyday photography, however, to see such carefully contrived balance, which gives works like this a mesmeric or monumental quality.

❸ Division

The gun establishes a bold visual split down the centre of the photograph. Neshat did this deliberately to establish an atmosphere of division and rupture, and to allude to recent political events in Iran. The Iranian Revolution (1978–79) overthrew the Shah of Iran, who had embraced elements of western modernization but ruled as an authoritarian, and established an Islamic Republic. Women became subjected to increased restrictions on what they could wear and how much they interacted with men in public.

❹ Text

Lines of writing cover the woman's face, apart from a section across her eyes. The text is from 'Allegiance with Wakefulness', a poem by Tahereh Saffarzadeh, which describes religious martyrdom and celebrates the Iranian Revolution. The poem includes the lines:

> *O, you martyr,*
> *hold my hands*
> *With your hands*
> *Cut from earthly means*
> *Hold my hands,*
> *I am your poet.*
> *With an inflicted body.*
> *I've come to be with you*
> *and on the promised day,*
> *We shall rise again.*[100]

❺ Calligraphy

Neshat's work appears to allude to a shared cultural heritage between Iranian poetry and calligraphy. Some may see the writing as something that dehumanizes the woman, concealing her individuality with a shroud of ideology. Its power derives from the provocative relationship between the reality the words create and what we see.

❻ Handwriting

Neshat devised the concept for *Rebellious Silence* and employed a professional photographer to take the picture. Once a large-scale print was produced, she handpainted the text over the woman's face.

Four Grenadier Guards presenting arms

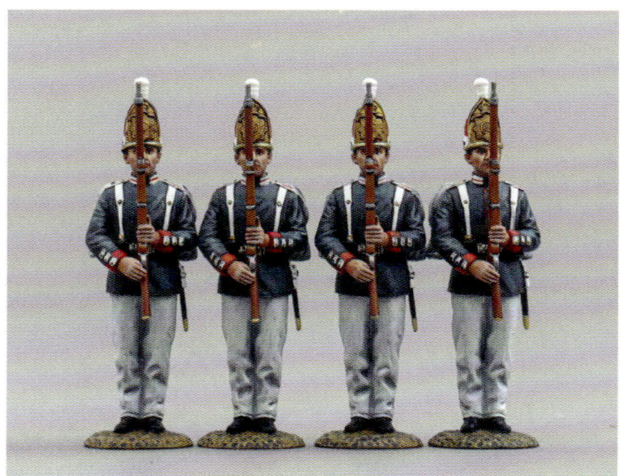

Habiballah of Sava, *The Concourse of the Birds* (detail), *c.* 1600

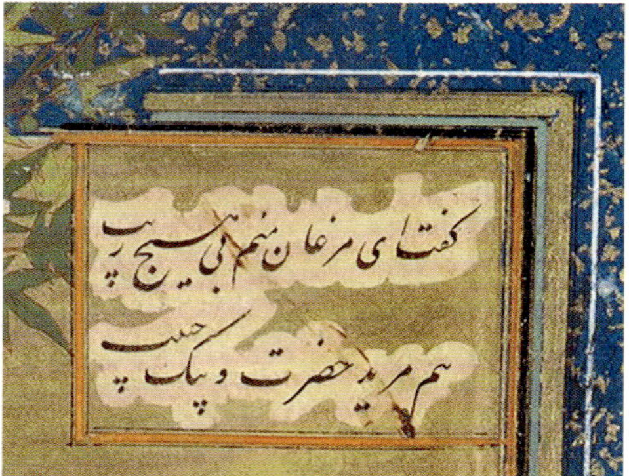

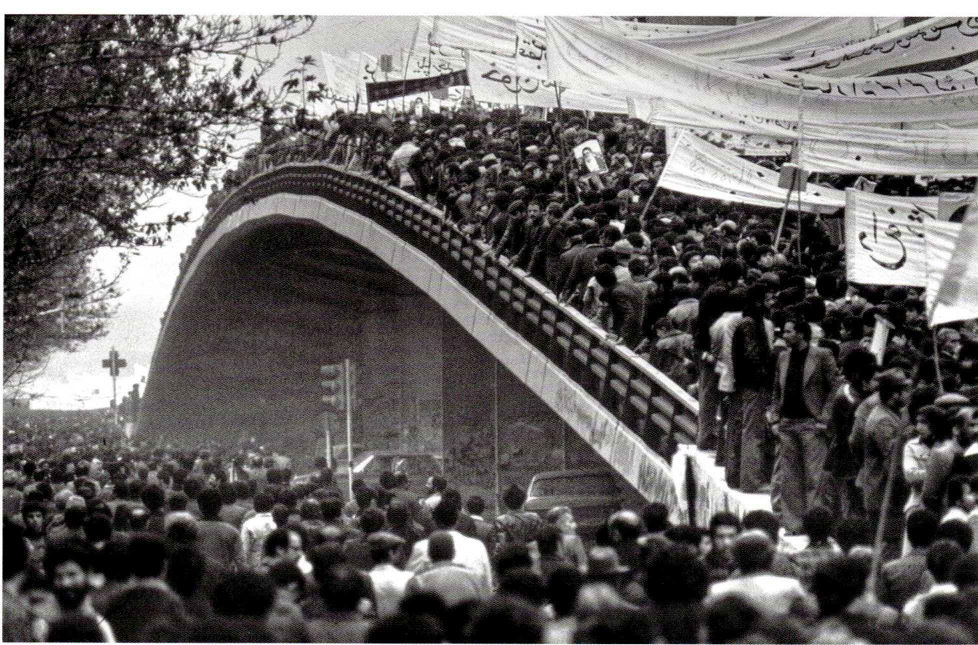

Protests during the Iranian Revolution, 1979. Photo by Ahmad Kavousian

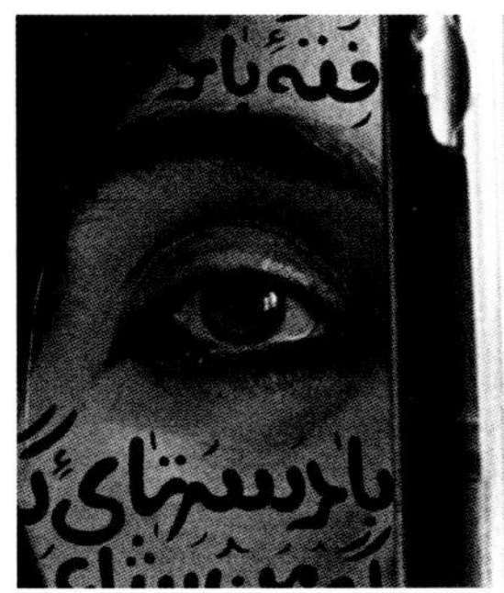
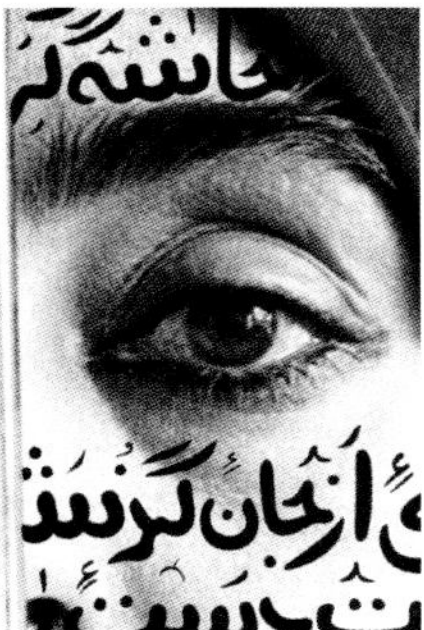

❼ Gaze

The woman's head is posed frontally and close to the viewer. With no emotional clues in her expression, it is impossible to read her state of mind. Her soft, hooded eyes contrast with the sharp edge of the gun barrel.

❽ Fear

Neshat has stated that the underlying theme of the photograph was one of conflicted loyalties. 'The woman may be armed and very dangerous,' she said, 'but her eyes are vulnerable and fearful and full of uncertainty.'[101]

❾ Chador

The woman wears a *chador*, which covers the upper body and head. In post-revolutionary Iran, this became the accepted mode of dress for women as it concealed the hair. The text covers most of the rest of the face, imitating the *niqab*, another type of garment that leaves only the eyes visible.[102]

❿ Perspectives

When she was 17, Neshat emigrated to the US, where she has lived ever since. Her view of Iranian society has, therefore, been informed by the perspective of an insider and an outsider.

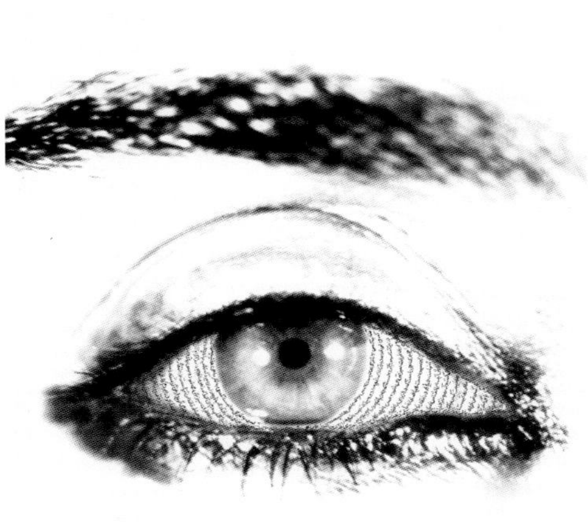

Offered Eyes, from the *Unveiling* series, 1993.
RC print and ink, photo by Plauto

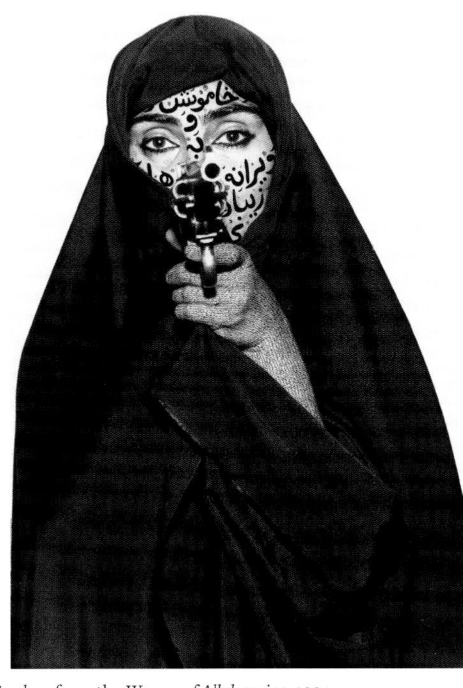

Faceless, from the *Women of Allah* series, 1994.
Black and white RC print and ink,
photo by Cynthia Preston

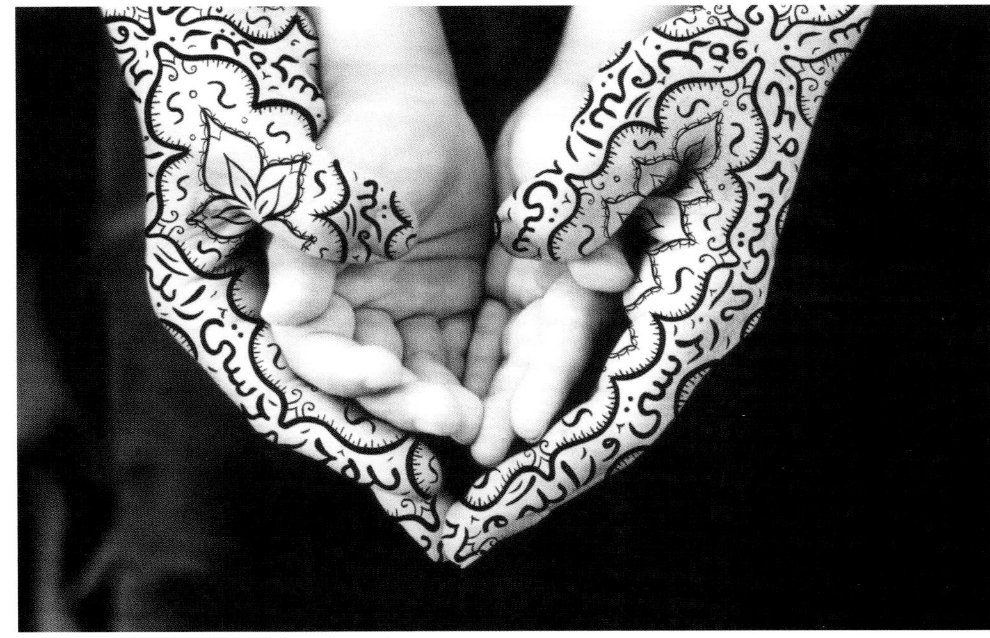

Bonding, from the *Women of Allah* series, 1995.
Gelatin silver print and ink, photo by Kyong Park

LINKED PRACTITIONERS

PHOTOGRAPHERS AND SOCIAL ISSUES:

Yau Leung (1941–1997), CHINA
Jeff Wall (born 1946), CANADA
Dawoud Bey (born 1953), USA
Shahidul Alam (born 1956), BANGLADESH
Tish Murtha (1956–2013), UK

SELF-PORTRAITURE:

Claude Cahun (1894–1954), FRANCE
Valie Export (born 1940), AUSTRIA
Gilbert (*Prousch*; born 1943) & *George* (*Passmore*; born 1942), ITALY/UK
Cindy Sherman (born 1954), USA
Sarah Lucas (born 1962), UK

CONTEMPORARY IRANIAN ARTISTS:

Monir Shahroudy Farmanfarmaian (1922–2019), IRAN
Reza Derakshani (born 1952), IRAN
Parastou Forouhar (born 1962), IRAN
Simin Keramati (born 1970), IRAN
Abbas Kowsari (born 1970), IRAN

49. The Art of War

In 2003 an exhibition of prints and pastels by Paula Rego, all relating to Charlotte Brontë's novel Jane Eyre, *originally published in 1847, was held at Marlborough Fine Art in London. One of the works on display was this pastel drawing, entitled* War.

The work immediately pivoted the mood of the exhibition from an homage to a literary classic to a critique of contemporary warfare. Rego's inspiration had come from a photograph she had seen in a newspaper, which showed a young girl caught up in the horrors of the Second Gulf War, the military campaign led by US forces in Iraq from 2003 to 2011. Through several innovative artistic choices, Rego manages to make a direct appeal to viewers' hearts and minds.

Pastel on paper mounted on aluminium
160 × 120 cm, 63 × 47¼ in.
Tate, London

Paula Rego
War
2003

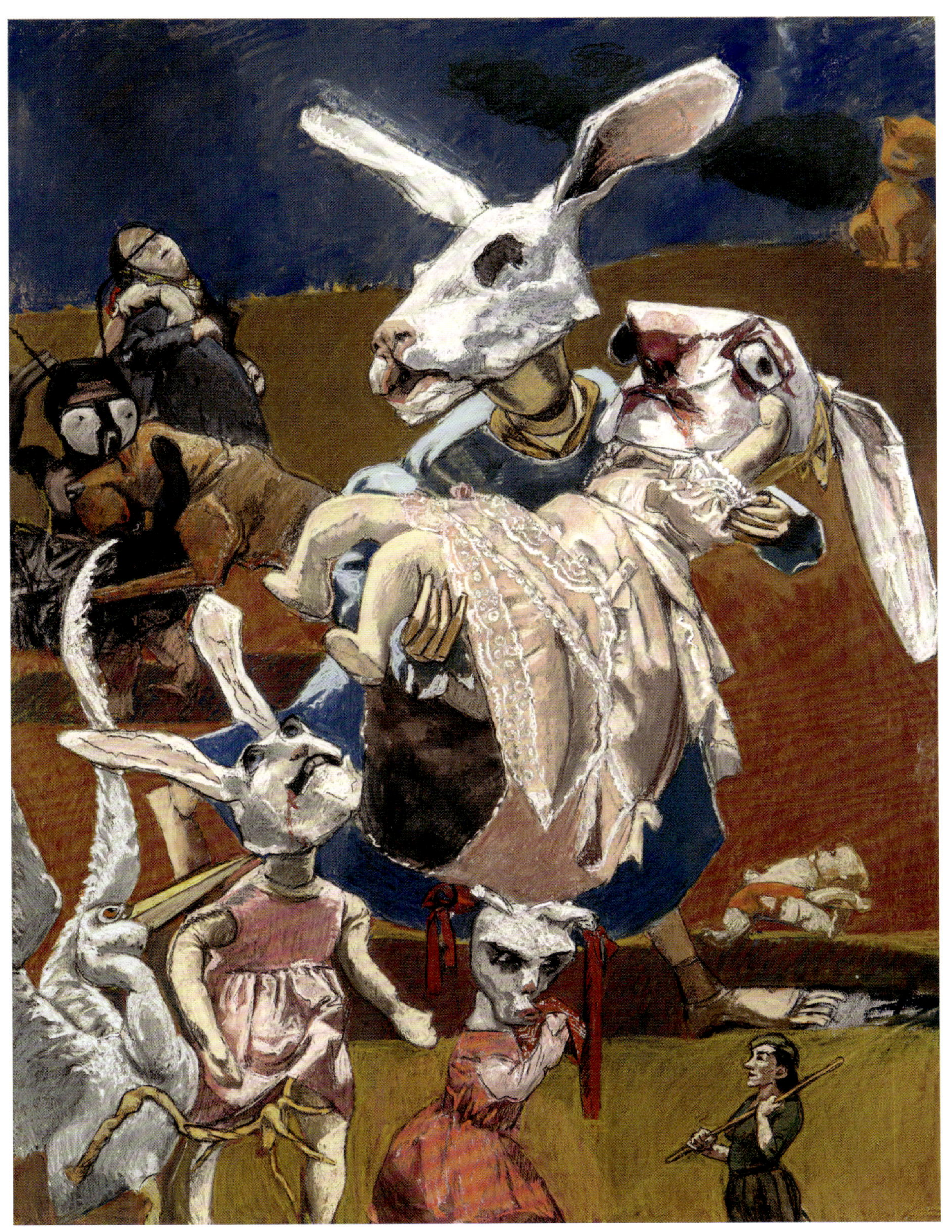

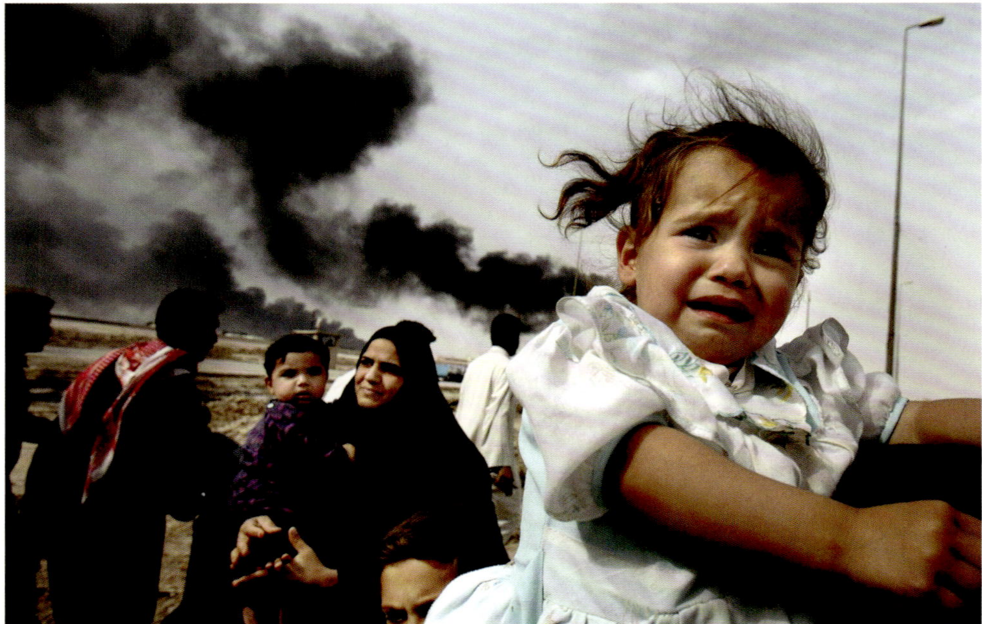

Families fleeing the city of Basra, Iraq, 2003. Photo by Dan Chung

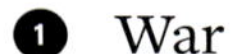

❶ War

Paula Rego painted *War* after seeing a photograph by Dan Chung in *The Guardian* in 2003. The photograph shows families fleeing the Iraqi city of Basra. Two mothers are seen carrying their children with a young girl in a white dress, crying and frightened, in the foreground, set against the background of an ominously smoke-filled sky. As in the painting, the facial expression and distress of the child is the emotional focus of the image.

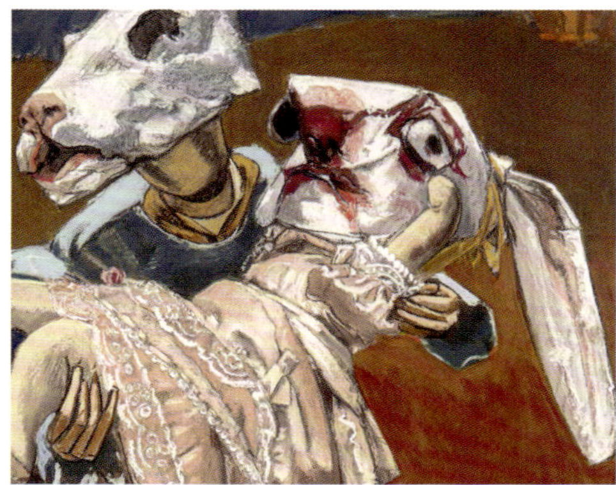

❷ Victim

Our gaze is drawn to the figure with the head of a baby rabbit. She has drooped ears, a bloodied nose and hands raised to wipe tears from her cheeks. With her exaggeratedly large eyes, she is reminiscent of a character from a Beatrix Potter book or a Disney film, recast by the artist in a surreal world of adult violence.

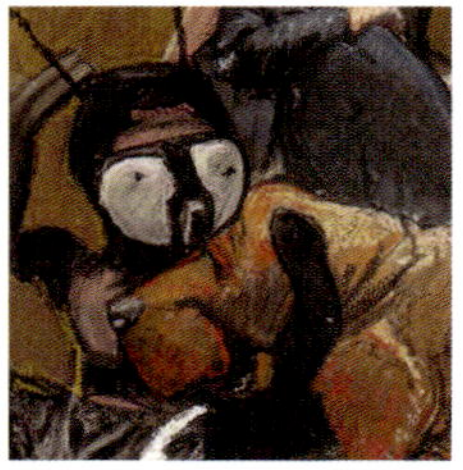

❸ Animal characters

Animals, or humanoid figures with animal heads, dominate the composition. An ant-like figure on the left embraces a dog, mirroring the action of the central rabbit-headed characters. A cat perches in the upper-right corner, and a stork strides forward at the bottom left.

❹ Pure cruelty

By using animals in place of humans, Rego makes us see the horror of war from the perspective of a war-affected child, understanding events through their eyes.

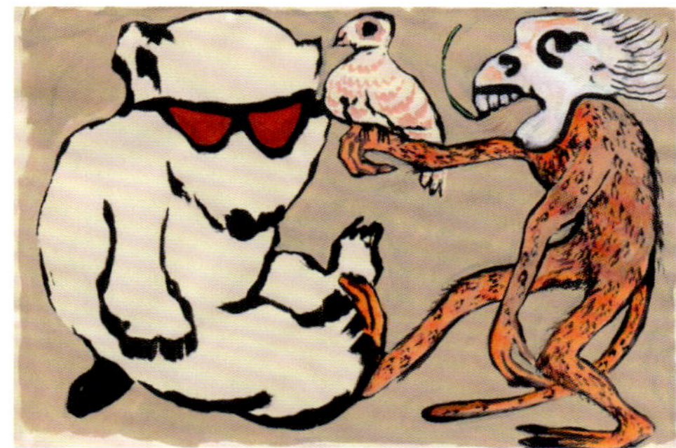

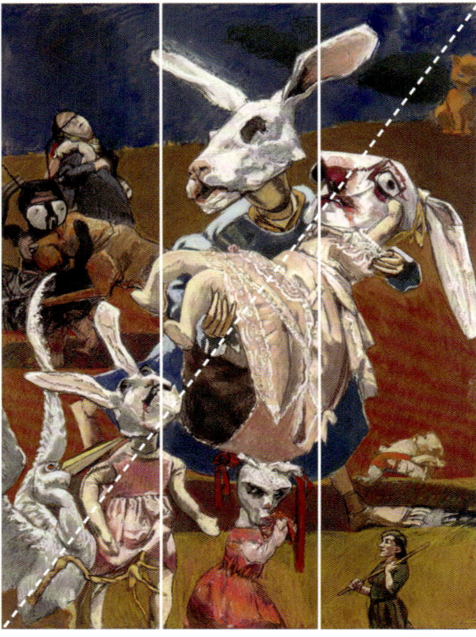

❺ Composition

The various figures have been placed carefully within the composition, which is divided into thirds. A clear diagonal axis is established by the upward gaze of the figures in the lower left, including the marching stork and a child rabbit in a pink dress.

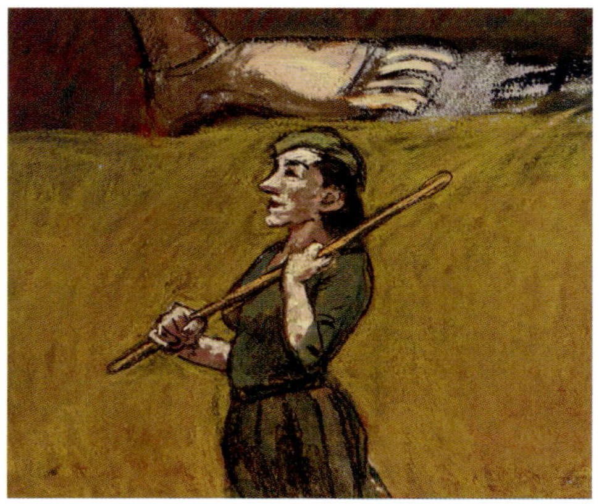

❻ Humanity

There are only two human figures in the painting. The figure at the bottom right is Miss Cook, the artist's childhood dance teacher, who came from England. During the Second World War, Rego's hometown of Estoril, Portugal, became a haven from the conflict for people from all over the world.[103]

Red Monkey Offers Bear a Poisoned Dove, 1981. Acrylic on paper, 69 × 101 cm, 27¼ × 39¾ in.

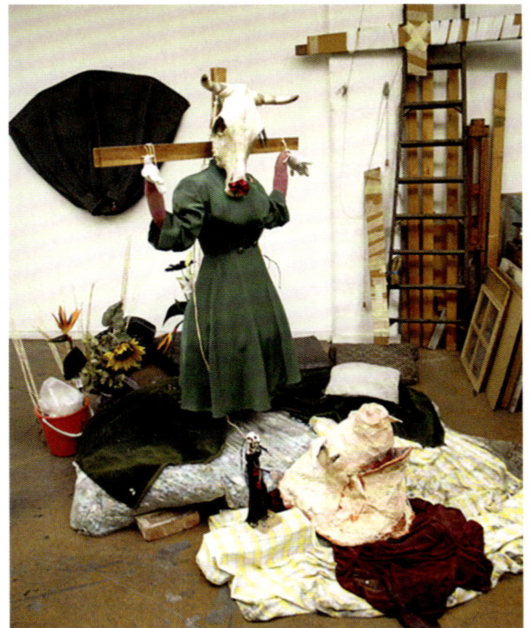

Paula Rego's studio in Kentish Town. Photo by Luke Watson

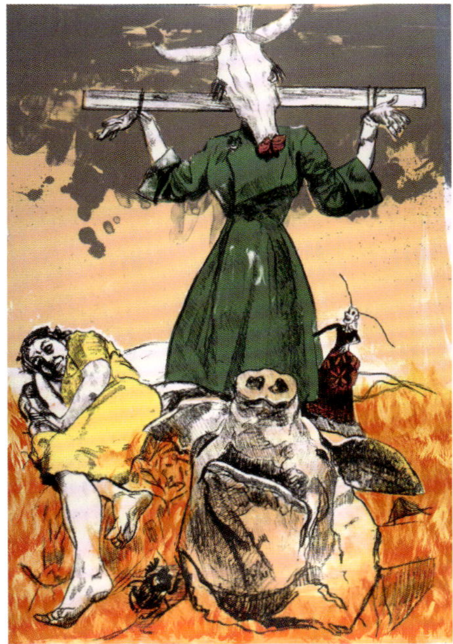

Scarecrow, 2006. Lithograph, 102 × 71 cm, 40¼ × 28 in.

❼ Setting the scene

Rego's technique for creating her work is to arrange a tableau of puppets and mannequins with enlarged heads, made from papier-mâché or clay, into her chosen composition. For this piece, the stork was carved from foam by her son-in-law, the artist Ron Mueck.

❽ Studio

Her studio is stocked full of props, mannequins and costumes. The process of arranging the figures and sets is similar to that of a theatre or film director creating a *mise en scène*. Some costumes were made from bought fabrics, others hired from theatrical agencies, including the Royal Opera House.

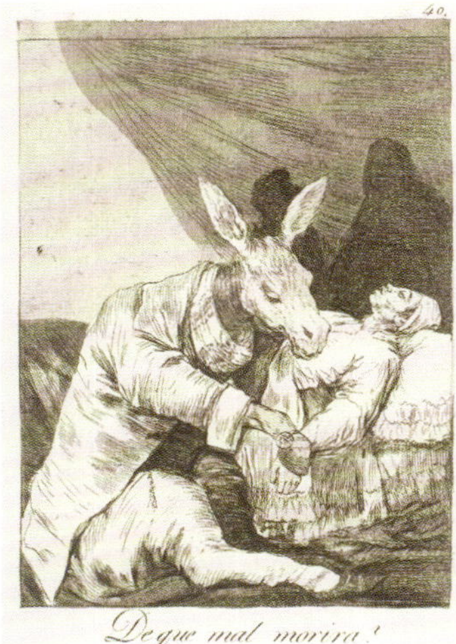

Francisco José de Goya y Lucientes, *Of what ill will he die?*, plate 40 from *Los Caprichos*, 1797–98, published 1799. Etching and aquatint in brown on ivory laid paper, 18.5 × 13.1 cm, 7¼ × 5¼ in.

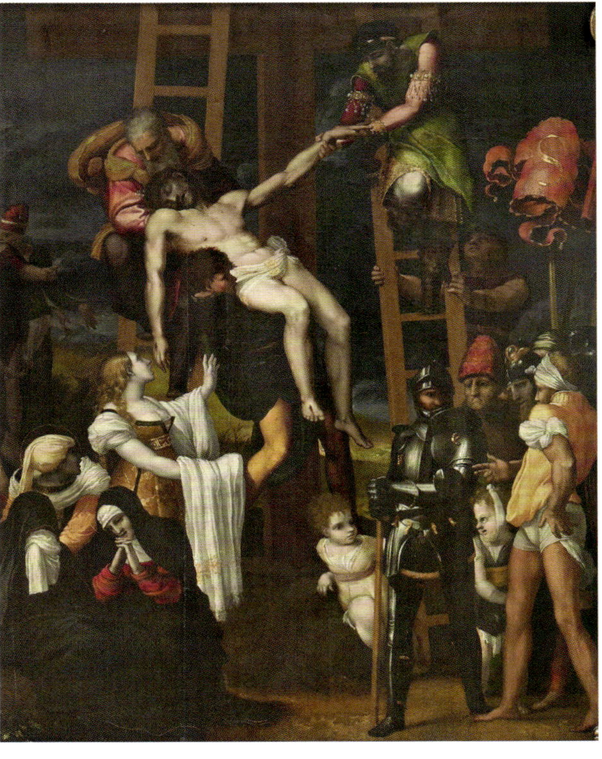

❾ Process

By using this technique of arranging tableaux with props and figurines, Rego does away with the need for live models or mapping out her compositions on paper. She has also stated that she prefers pastels to oil paint, as they have a sketchier quality that emphasizes the discipline of drawing and feels more immediate and personal.

❿ Art history

The work appears to have been inspired by scenes from the history of art, including the Deposition of Christ (left), in which Christ's body is lowered from the cross – usually by Nicodemus – to the grieving figures of the Virgin and Mary Magdalene below. Goya's highly imaginative prints were also an important source of inspiration (far left), with their grotesque distortions of human forms and use of animals for emotional impact.

Pedro Machuca, *The Descent from the Cross* (detail), 1547. Oil on panel, 141 × 128 cm, 55½ × 50½ in.

LINKED PRACTITIONERS

ART DEPICTING WAR:

Peter Paul Rubens (1577–1640), BELGIUM
Jacques Callot (1592–1635), FRANCE
Pablo Picasso (1881–1973), SPAIN/FRANCE
Paul Nash (1889–1946), UK
Otto Dix (1891–1969), GERMANY

PASTELS AS A MEDIUM:

Hans Holbein the Younger (*c.* 1497–1543), GERMANY/UK
Edgar Degas (1834–1917), FRANCE
Odilon Redon (1840–1916), FRANCE
Elizabeth Blackadder (1931–2021), UK
Peter Howson (born 1958), UK

ANIMAL-HUMAN HYBRIDS:

Hieronymus Bosch (1450–1516), NETHERLANDS
Francisco Goya (1746–1828), SPAIN
Leonora Carrington (1917–2011), UK
Jane Alexander (born 1959), SOUTH AFRICA
Matthew Barney (born 1967), USA

50. Crossing Boundaries

Global attention was focused on the border between the United States and Mexico in 2017 following the signing of Executive Order 13767 in Washington, DC. The directive initiated the construction of a permanent wall between the two countries to prevent people crossing illegally from Mexico into the US.

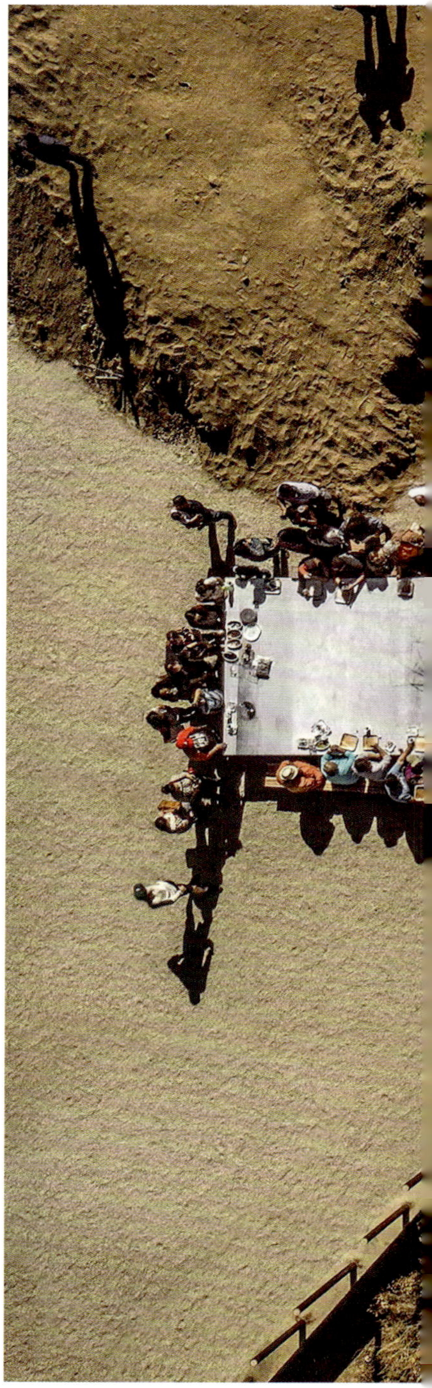

Later that year, the French street artist JR arrived in Mexico to begin a project based around a section of the existing fence near the city of Tecate, located south of the border on the Baja peninsula. The world's media turned its gaze on his work, which explored the simmering tensions of this fraught border zone, using photography, paper and paste – and social media.

Wheat-pasted poster on table
Temporary installation
Tecate, Mexico–USA border

JR

Migrants, Picnic Across the Border

2017

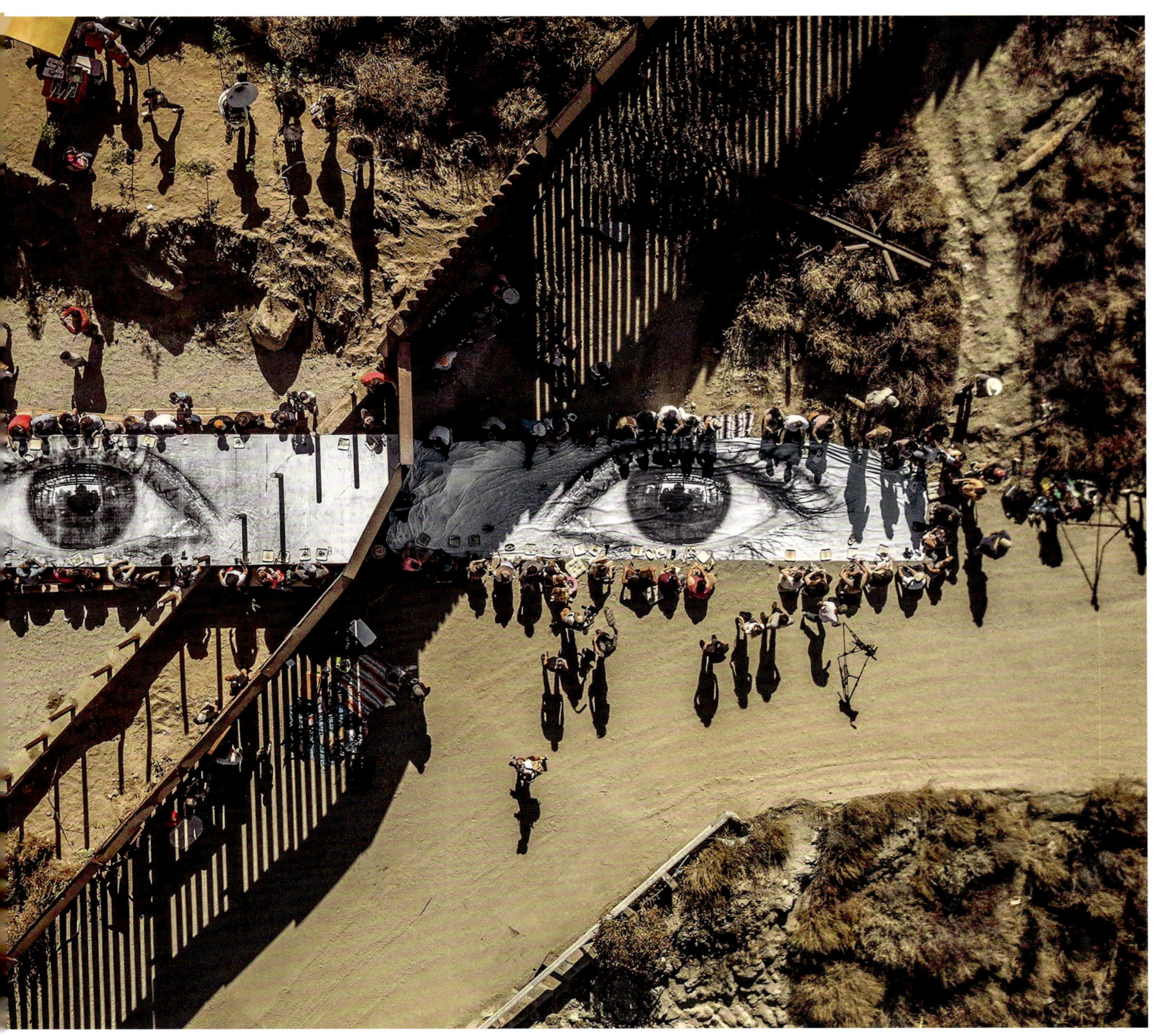

❶ Tabletop

The eye on the left of the image is a photograph that has been enlarged and pasted to a tabletop. Surrounding it are a group of visitors eating a meal. They cannot see the eye clearly since the work was intended to be seen from above. Our view is from an aerial drone, which was taking pictures overhead.

❷ Kikito

JR's main project in Tecate was *Giants, Kikito*, a vast billboard on the Mexican side of the border, bearing a hugely enlarged photograph of a toddler. It was taken by the artist while visiting a family in Tecate, and captures their young son peeping over the side of his crib. The work was a temporary installation and remained in place for just one month.

❸ Improvisation

Giants, Kikito was not commissioned by a local authority, and JR had not been granted official approval to build it. Once he found a suitable site, he simply hired a digger to level a section of ground, and then got a company to build a scaffold to support the billboard. No one challenged the artist throughout the process, or asked him if he had a permit for the work. Pasting the enormous photograph onto the billboard took a single day, with friends helping with the work.

❹ Child is father

Unlike a political poster or commercial advertising, JR's billboard just represents an ordinary boy from the local community. By depicting a toddler, he also drew attention to the shamefulness that children can be born into a world of arbitrary political and ethnic divisions represented by the fence.

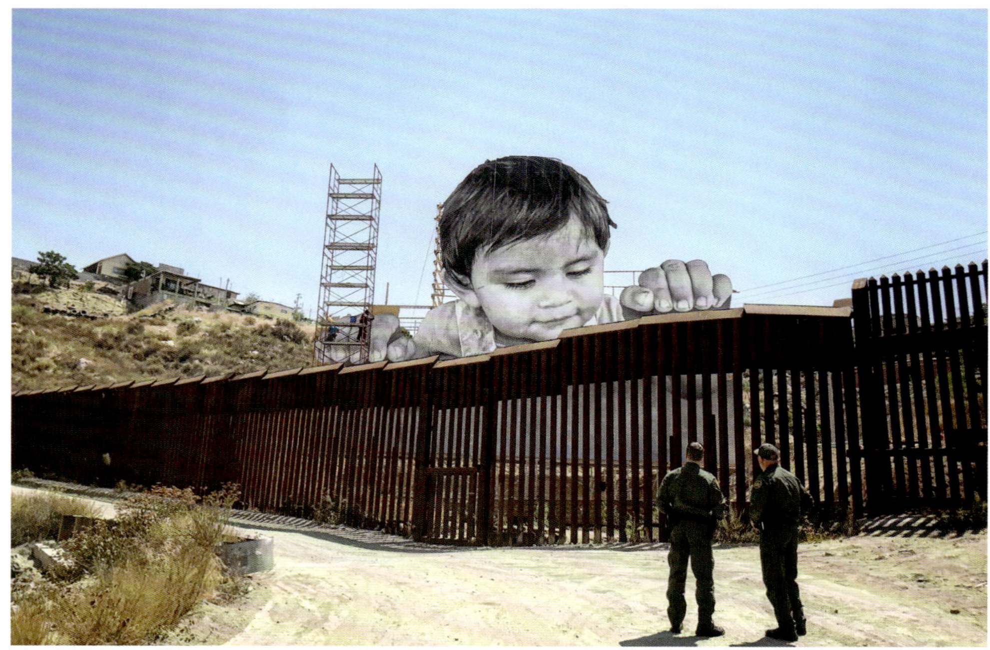

↑ *Giants, Kikito* and the US Border Patrol, Tecate, Mexico–USA border, 2017

↓ *Giants, Kikito* on scaffolding, Tecate, Mexico–USA border, 2017

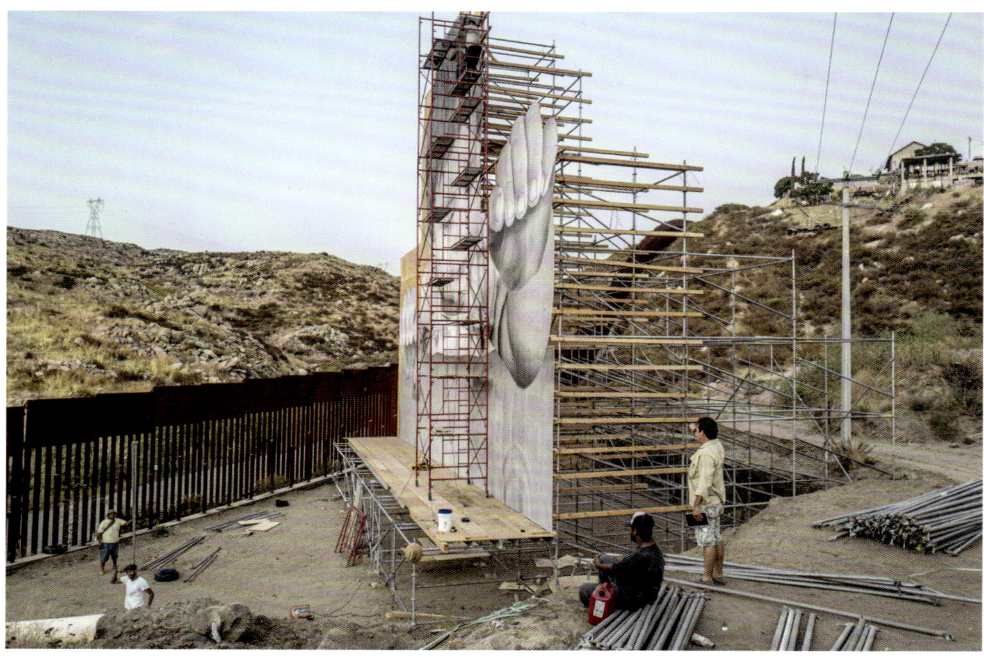

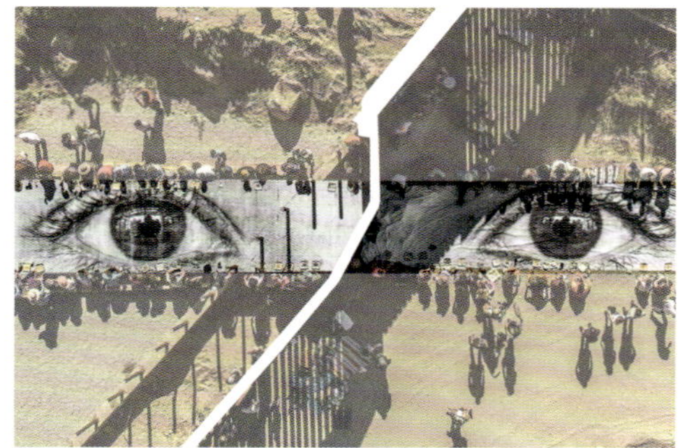

❺ Eyes

From above we can see an enormous pair of eyes, divided down the middle by the fence separating the USA and Mexico. The eyes are from a photograph JR had taken of a young woman named Mayra, who had migrated from Mexico at the age of seven and was currently living in San Francisco.

❻ Dreamer

Mayra was classed as a 'dreamer', to use US immigration parlance. The term refers to juvenile immigrants who qualify for the Deferred Action for Childhood Arrivals programme. JR used Mayra to bring attention to the difficulties faced by migrants, along with their ambitions and courage. Although we can't see her whole face, the disembodied eyes nonetheless assert a real human presence.

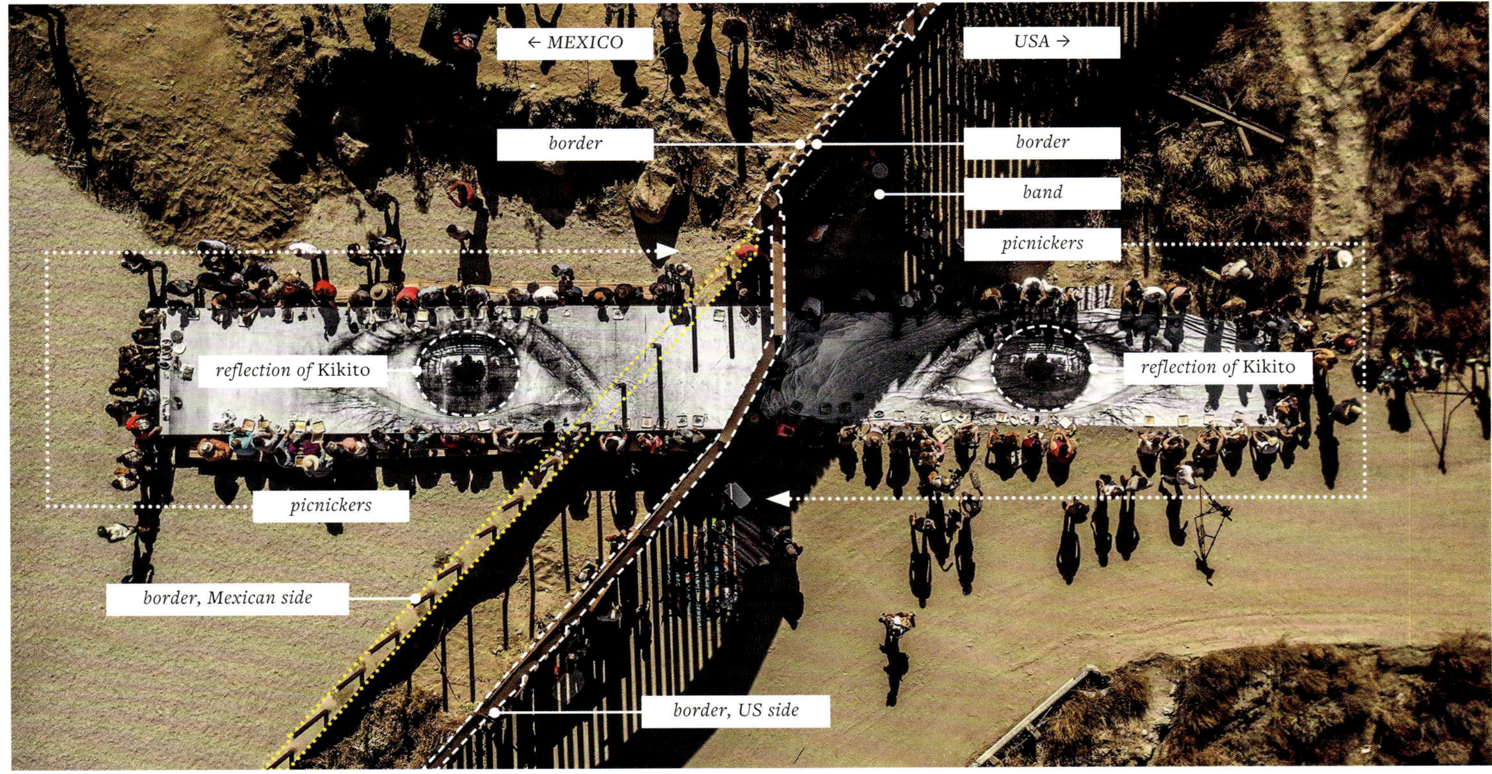

❼ Clear vision

As a young woman, Mayra suffered from ptosis, an eye condition that causes migraines and visual impairment. It was successfully treated in the US. As an adult, Mayra went on to work for the public health services.[104]

❽ Fence

Diagonally cutting across the image like a rip in a sheet of paper is the fence that divides Mexico and the USA. The border, extending from the Pacific Ocean to the Gulf of Mexico, is over 3,000 km (nearly 2,000 miles) long. It was decided after the Mexican–American war (1846–48), and completed with the Gadsden Purchase in 1854, which included parts of southern Arizona and New Mexico. It is the most frequently crossed border in the world.

❾ Across the border

Even though JR's original project was the *Kikito* billboard, he was inspired to create a final piece – *Migrants, Picnic Across the Border* – when he saw how many people visited the site and shared their photographs on Instagram. Mexican visitors who couldn't see *Kikito* from their side of the fence passed their phones to those on the US side to take pictures for them.

❿ Picnic

People are seen enjoying a picnic on both sides of the border. It is a communal meal, despite the fence separating one group of picnickers from another. There is a table on the Mexican side, but JR's application for a permit to have a table on the US side was turned down, and the picknickers are seated around a tarp instead.

⓫ Last supper

The picnic was organized by JR on 8 October 2017 to celebrate the final day before *Kikito* would be taken down. Kikito and his family attended on the Mexican side, and Mayra (whose eyes peer out from either side of the fence) attended the US side. A band played music, and food cooked on site was shared on both sides, passed through the bars of the fence.

⓬ Community

US Border Patrol officers had noticed the picnic early on and decided not to intervene. One official even joined in the event and shared a cup of tea with JR. 'It was a joyous occasion,' the artist notes on his website. 'For a few hours, divisions disappeared.'

LINKED PRACTITIONERS

SITE-SPECIFIC ART:

Christo (*Javacheff*; 1935–2020) BULGARIA/USA, and *Jeanne-Claude* (*Denat de Guillebon*; 1935–2009), FRANCE/USA
Robert Smithson (1938–1973), USA
Richard Serra (born 1938), USA
Antony Gormley (born 1950), UK

STREET ART:

Blek le Rat (*Xavier Prou*; born 1951), FRANCE
Lady Pink (born 1964), ECUADOR/USA
Invader (born 1969), FRANCE
Shepard Fairey (born 1970), USA
Banksy (fl. 1990s–present), UK

EPHEMERAL ART:

Joseph Beuys (1921–1986), GERMANY
Piero Manzoni (1933–1963), ITALY
Richard Long (born 1945), UK
Anya Gallaccio (born 1963), UK
Urs Fischer (born 1973), SWITZERLAND/USA

Notes

1 Judith Thurman, 'First impressions', *The New Yorker*, 16 June 2008; https://www.newyorker.com/magazine/2008/06/23/first-impressions

2 Joshua Hammer, 'Finally, the beauty of France's Chauvet cave makes its grand public debut', *Smithsonian Magazine*, April 2015; https://www.smithsonianmag.com/history/france-chauvet-cave-makes-grand-debut-180954582/

3 Dr Elizabeth Cummins, 'Tutankhamun's tomb (innermost coffin and death mask)', Khan Academy, Lesson 2: Ancient Egypt, https://www.khanacademy.org/humanities/ap-art-history/ancient-mediterranean-ap/ancient-egypt-ap/a/tutankhamuns-tomb

4 Ministry of Tourism and Antiquities, 'The large gilded coffin of King Tutankhamun', 2019; https://egymonuments.gov.eg/news/gilded-coffin-of-king-tutankhamun

5 Jarrett A. Lobell, 'Magical beasts of Babylon', *Archaeology* 72:6 (November/December 2019): 47

6 Kim Benzel, et al., *The Art of the Ancient Near East: A Resource for Educators* (New York, 2010), p. 96

7 I.L. Finkel and M.J. Seymour (eds), *Babylon: Myth and Reality* (London, 2008), p. 50

8 Lobell, p. 45

9 Oriana Baddeley (ed.), *The Art of Ancient Mexico*, exh. cat., Hayward Gallery, London, 1992, p. 181

10 Matthew Wilson, *The Hidden Language of Symbols* (London, 2022), p. 87

11 Christopher de Hamel, *Meetings with Remarkable Manuscripts* (London, 2016), p. 118

12 David Wilkins, Bernie Schultz and Katheryn M. Linduff (eds), *Art Past, Art Present* (Hoboken, New Jersey, 2005), p. 171; Julian Bell, *Mirror of the World* (London, 2007), p. 98

13 De Hamel, p. 122

14 Kurt Behrendt, *How to Read Buddhist Art* (New Haven and London, 2019), p. 13

15 *The Metropolitan Museum of Art: Asia*, vol. 10; introduction by Richard M. Barnhart (New York, 1987), p. 82

16 Jessica Harrison-Hall, *China: A History in Objects* (London, 2017), p. 114

17 *The Metropolitan Museum of Art: Recent Acquisitions, A Selection: 1986–1987* (New York, 1987), p. 105

18 Steve Kossak, 'The arts of South and Southeast Asia', *The Metropolitan Museum of Art Bulletin* (Spring 1994): 44

19 James Doyle, 'Arte del mar: Art of the early Caribbean', *The Metropolitan Museum of Art Bulletin* (Winter 2020): 9

20 Julie Jones and Heidi King, 'Gold of the Americas', *The Metropolitan Museum of Art Bulletin* (Spring 2002): 43

21 'Head, possibly of a King, 12th–14th century, Ife', Kimbell Art Museum, Fort Worth; https://kimbellart.org/collection/ap-199404

22 Alisa LaGamma, *Heroic Africans: Legendary Leaders, Iconic Sculptures* (New Haven and London, 2011), p. 44

23 M. Akin-Makinde, 'An African concept of human personality: the Yoruba example', *Ultimate Meaning and Reality* 7:3 (September 1984): 190

24 Suzanne Preston Blier, 'Art in ancient Ife, birthplace of the Yoruba', *African Arts* 45:4 (2012): 76

25 Ezio Bassani, *African Art* (Milan, 2012), p. 48

26 Alfreda Murck and Wen C. Fong (eds), *Words and Images: Chinese Poetry, Calligraphy and Painting* (New York, 1991), p. 183

27 Maxwell K. Hearn, *How to Read Chinese Paintings*, exh. cat., Metropolitan Museum of Art, New York, 2008, p. 78

28 Richard M. Barnhart, *Along the Border of Heaven: Sung and Yüan Paintings from the C.C. Wang Family Collection* (New York, 1983), p. 119

29 Wen C. Fong, *Beyond Representation: Chinese Painting and Calligraphy, 8th–14th Century* (New York, 1992), pp. 438, 440

30 Stefano Carboni and Masuya Tomoko, *Persian Tiles* (New York, 1993), p. 36

31 *The Metropolitan Museum of Art: The Islamic World*, vol. 2; introduction by Stuart Cary Welch (New York, 1987), p. 77

32 Stephanie Porras, *Art of the Northern Renaissance: Courts, Commerce and Devotion* (London, 2018), p. 61

33 Wilson, p. 144

34 Jill Burke, *The Renaissance Nude* (New Haven and London, 2018), pp. 17, 110

35 Martin Kemp, *Leonardo* (Oxford, 2004; rev. ed. 2011), p. 67

36 'Study of the proportions of the human body', Gallerie Accademia, Venice; https://www.gallerieaccademia.it/en/study-proportions-human-body-known-vitruvian-man

37 Domenico Laurenza, *Art and Anatomy in Renaissance Italy: Images from a Scientific Revolution* (New Haven and London, 2012), p. 16

38 Burke, p. 95

39 Carmen C. Bambach (ed.), *Leonardo da Vinci: Master Draftsman* (New Haven and London, 2003), p. 36

40 Christine M. Kralik, *A Matter of Life and Death: Forms, Functions and Audiences for 'The Three Living and the Three Dead' in Late Medieval Manuscripts*, PhD thesis, University of Toronto, 2013, p. 112

41 De Hamel, p. 557

42 'Deathbed Scene', Getty, Los Angeles; https://www.getty.edu/art/collection/object/103S80

43 Roger S. Wieck, *The Book of Hours in Medieval Art and Life* (London, 1988), p. 27

44 Elizabeth Morrison and Thomas Kren (eds), *Flemish Manuscript Painting in Context: Recent Research* (Los Angeles, 2007), p. 66

45 Matthew Wilson, *Symbols in Art* (London, 2020), p. 114

46 Christa Clarke, *The Art of Africa: A Resource for Educators* (New York, 2006), pp. 35, 119

47 LaGamma, p. 29

48 Diana Craig Patch and Alisa LaGamma, 'The African origin of civilization', *The Metropolitan Museum of Art Bulletin* (Spring 2022): 43

49 David Topper and Cynthia Gillis, 'Trajectories of blood: Artemisia Gentileschi and Galileo's parabolic path', *Woman's Art Journal* 17:1 (1996): 10–13; https://doi.org/10.2307/1358523.

50 Marjorie Och, review of Eve Straussman-Pflanzer, *Violence and Virtue: Artemisia Gentileschi's Judith Slaying Holofernes*, *Woman's Art Journal* 35:2 (Autumn/Winter 2014): 63–4; http://www.jstor.org/stable/24395426

51 Joaneath Spicer, 'The Renaissance elbow', in H. Roodenburgh (ed.), *A Cultural History of Gesture* (Oxford, 1991), pp. 84–128

52 Theodore Rousseau, 'Juan de Pareja by Diego Velázquez: An appreciation of the portrait', *The Metropolitan Museum of Art Bulletin* 29:10 (1971): 450

53 'Juan de Pareja (*c.* 1608–1670)', Metropolitan Museum of Art, New York; https://www.metmuseum.org/art/collection/search/437869

54 Antonio Domínguez Ortiz, Alfonso E. Pérez Sánchez and Julián Gállego, *Velázquez* (New York, 1989), p. 234

55 'Christ Crucified between the Two Thieves (The Three Crosses), 1653–55', Princeton University Art Museum, Princeton; https://artmuseum.princeton.edu/collections/objects/11023

56 Edward Snow, *A Study of Vermeer* (Berkeley, California: 1979), p. 138

57 Arthur K. Wheelock, Jr, 'Johannes Vermeer, Woman Holding a Balance, *c.* 1664,' in *Dutch Paintings of the 17th Century*, NGA Online Editions, https://purl.org/nga/collection/artobject/1236; Eugene R. Cunnar, 'The viewer's share: Three sectarian readings of Vermeer's *Woman with a Balance*,' *Exemplaria* 2 (1990): 518

58 Marjorie E. Wieseman, Wayne E. Franits and H. Perry Chapman, *Vermeer's Women: Secrets and Silence* (New Haven and London, 2011), pp. 82–5

59 John T. Carpenter, *Designing Nature: The Rinpa Aesthetic in Japanese Art* (New York, 2012), p. 23

60 Cynthia Daugherty, 'Historiography and iconography in Ogata Korin's *Iris* and *Plum* screens', *Ningen Kagaku Hen* 16 (2003): 67–73

61 Jenny Uglow, *The Lunar Men* (London, 2002), p. 123

62 Erika Langmuir, *The National Gallery Companion Guide* (London, 1994), p. 343

63 Katharine Baetjer, et al., *Vigée Le Brun: Woman Artist in Revolutionary France* (New York, 2016), p. 78

64 Simon Lee, *David* (London, 1999), p. 172

65 Timothy Clark, *Hokusai: Beyond the Great Wave* (London, 2017), p. 25

66 Andrea Marks, *Hokusai: Thirty-Six Views of Mount Fuji* (Cologne, 2022) p. 11

67 Clark, pp. 9, 13

68 Andrzej Gutek, *More than a Seat: Numbers and Symbols in the Cameroon Grasslands* (Cookeville, Tenessee, 2004), p. 2

69 'Prestige Stool' (*Kuo*), Cleveland Museum of Art, Cleveland, Ohio; https://www.clevelandart.org/art/2006.138#

70 Christraud M. Geary, 'Art and political process in the kingdoms of Bali-Nyonga and Bamum (Cameroon Grassfields)', *Canadian Journal of African Studies* 22:1 (1988): 17

71 Pierre Harter, 'The beads of Cameroon', *Beads: Journal of the Society of Bead Researchers* 4 (1992): 6

72 Martin Myrone, *John Martin: Apocalyse* (London, 2011), p. 13

73 Colta Feller Ives, *The Great Wave: The Influence of Japanese Woodcuts on French Prints* (New York, 1974), p. 45

74 Nancy Mowll Mathews, *Mary Cassatt: A Life* (New Haven and London, 1998), p. 234

75 Neil Cox, *Cubism* (London, 2000), p. 294

76 John Richardson, *A Life of Picasso, vol. 2: The Painter of Modern Life, 1907–1917* (London, 1996), p. 250

77 Hal Foster, et al. (eds), *Art Since 1900* (London, 2004), p. 112

78 Virginia Spate, 'Orphism', in Nikos Stang (ed.), *Concepts of Modern Art* (London, 1981), p. 89

79 Stanley Baron and Jacques Damase, *Sonia Delaunay: The Life of an Artist* (London, 1995), p. 199

80 Jane Alison and Coraline Malissard (eds), *Modern Couples* (Munich, 2018), p. 107

81 Eric Kjellgren, *Oceania: Art of the Pacific Islands in the Metropolitan Museum of Art* (New Haven and London, 2007), p. 127

82 Francis Edgar Williams, *Drama of Orokolo: The Social and Ceremonial Life of the Elema* (Oxford, 1940), p. 266

83 'Ebaro dance mask', Museum of New Zealand, Wellington; https://collections.tepapa.govt.nz/object/163386

84 National Museums Scotland, Edinburgh, https://www.nms.ac.uk/explore-our-collections/stories/global-arts-cultures-and-design/understanding-barkcloth-at-national-museums-scotland/

85 Wells, Liz (ed.), *Photography: A Critical Introduction* (Milton Park, Oxfordshire, 2015), p. 49

86 'Story of the Women's Camp and the Origin of Damper', National Museum of Australia, Canberra; https://collectionsearch.nma.gov.au/icons/images/kaui2/index.html#/home?usr=CE

87 Jennifer Higgie, 'Stories we missed in 2020: Rio Tinto's destruction of the Juukan Gorge proved (again) nothing is sacred except profit', *Frieze*, 22 December 2020; https://www.frieze.com/article/stories-we-missed-2020-rio-tintos-destruction-juukan-gorge-proved-again-nothing-sacred

88 Kathleen Soriano, et al., *Australia*, exh. cat., Royal Academy of Arts, London, 2013, p. 23

89 Anatjari (Yanyatjarri) Tjakamarra, *Untitled, Body Paint for Initiation*, Sotheby's, London, 21 September 2016 (52); https://www.sothebys.com/en/auctions/ecatalogue/2016/aboriginal-art-l16321/lot.52.html

90 'Styles: Kulkuta', Cooee Art, Redfern, New South Wales; https://www.cooeeart.com.au/styles/kulkuta/

91 Polly Staple, interview with Cornelia Parker, Chisenhale Gallery, London, September 2016; https://chisenhale.org.uk/wp-content/uploads/Chisenhale_Interviews_Cornelia_Parker-1.pdf

92 Virginia Button, *The Turner Prize* (London, 2005), p. 114

93 Luke White, 'Damien Hirst's shark: Nature, capitalism and the sublime', *Tate Papers* 14 (Autumn 2010); https://www.tate.org.uk/art/research-publications/the-sublime/luke-white-damien-hirsts-shark-nature-capitalism-and-the-sublime-r1136828

94 Alistair Sooke, 'Damien Hirst: "We're here for a good time, not a long time"', *The Daily Telegraph* (8 January 2011)

95 Julian Stallabrass, *High Art Lite: British Art in the 1990s* (London, 1999), p. 20

96 'The melodrama of *Gone with the Wind*', interview with Kara Walker, PBS.org, September 2003 (republished on Art21, November 2011); https://art21.org/read/kara-walker-the-melodrama-of-gone-with-the-wind/

97 Kim Wickham, '"I undo you, master": Uncomfortable encounters in the work of Kara Walker', *The Comparatist* 39 (October 2015): 340

98 Leesa Rittelmann, 'Winold Reiss to Kara Walker: The silhouette in Black American art', in Maria I. Diedrich and Jürgen Heinrichs (eds), *Black to Schwarz: Cultural Crossovers Between African America and Germany* (East Lansing, Michigan, 2011), p. 292

99 Penley Knipe, 'Paper profiles: American portrait silhouettes,' *Journal of the American Institute for Conservation* 41:3 (Autumn/Winter 2002): 209

100 Sussan Babaie, Rebecca R. Hart and Nancy Princenthal, *Shirin Neshat* (Detroit, 2013)

101 Kelly Grovier, 'Shirin Neshat: A stare that challenges us to look away', 4 November 2019; BBC Culture; https://www.bbc.com/culture/article/20191104-shirin-neshat-a-stare-that-challenges-us-to-look-away

102 Iftikhar Dadi, 'Shirin Neshat's photographs as postcolonial allegories', *Signs: Journal of Women in Culture and Society* 34:1 (2008)

103 John McEwan, *Paula Rego: Behind the Scenes* (London, 2008), p. 134

104 Lauren Powell Jobs, 'What a work of art can teach us about dishonest portrayals of immigrants', *Time*, 9 November 2017; https://time.com/5016079/dreamers-jr-immigration/

List of illustrations

t = top; b = bottom; m = middle; l = left; r = right

pages 1–126

List of illustrations (*continued*)

pages 127–230

187bl National Archives at College Park. Still Picture Records Section, Special Media Archives Services Division

187bm Photo Saul Bass/Paramount/Kobal/Shutterstock

187bm © design Neville Brody

187br The Broad, Los Angeles. Courtesy the artist, The Broad Art Foundation and Sprüth Magers

189 The Metropolitan Museum of Art, New York. The Michael C. Rockefeller Memorial Collection, Gift of Nelson A. Rockefeller, 1972. Photo The Metropolitan Museum of Art/Art Resource/Scala, Florence

190m The Metropolitan Museum of Art, New York. The Michael C. Rockefeller Memorial Collection, Gift of Nelson A. Rockefeller, 1972. Photo The Metropolitan Museum of Art/Art Resource/Scala, Florence

191tl Minneapolis Institute of Art. The John Cowles Family Fund

191tr The British Museum, London. Photo The Trustees of the British Museum

191b Photo Chronicle/Alamy Stock Photo

193 Library of Congress Prints and Photographs Division, Washington, DC. Farm Security Administration – Office of War Information Photograph Collection

194r The Metropolitan Museum of Art, New York. Robert Lehman Collection, 1975

195tl Library of Congress Prints and Photographs Division, Washington, DC. Farm Security Administration – Office of War Information Photograph Collection

195tr Library of Congress Prints and Photographs Division, Washington, DC. Farm Security Administration – Office of War Information Photograph Collection

195ml Oakland Museum. Gift of Paul S. Taylor

195mr Library of Congress Prints and Photographs Division, Washington, DC. Farm Security Administration – Office of War Information Photograph Collection

195b National Postal Museum, Washington, DC. Copyright United States Postal Service. All rights reserved. Photo MMphotos/Alamy Stock Photo

201 National Museum of Australia, Canberra. © Estate of the artist licensed by Aboriginal Artists Agency Ltd

203tl National Gallery of Victoria, Melbourne. Gift of The Hon. Justice David Angel through the Australian Government's Cultural Gifts Program, 2004. © Estate of the artist licensed by Aboriginal Artists Agency Ltd

203tr Private collection. Courtesy of Deutscher and Hackett. © Estate of the artist licensed by Aboriginal Artists Agency Ltd

203bl National Gallery of Art, Washington, DC. Widener Collection

203br The British Museum, London. Photo J.V.S. Megaw. Uta Uta Tjangala © Estate of the artist licensed by Aboriginal Artists Agency Ltd

204–5 National Gallery of Art, Washington, DC. Gift of the Gallery Girls in support of the Guerrilla Girls. © Guerrilla Girls, courtesy guerrillagirls.com

206tr Musée du Louvre, Paris. Photo Musée du Louvre, Dist. RMN-Grand Palais/Angèle Dequier

206ml Photo Eric Huybrechts. Artwork © Guerrilla Girls, courtesy guerrillagirls.com

206mr Duke University Sallie Bingham Center for Women's History and Culture. © Clarissa Sligh

206b Scottish National Gallery of Modern Art, Edinburgh. Purchased with assistance from the Patrons of the National Galleries of Scotland, 2002. Ernst © ADAGP, Paris and DACS, London 2023

207t National Gallery of Victoria, Melbourne. Purchased with funds donated by Susan Jones and James McGrath, 2018. © Guerrilla Girls, courtesy guerrillagirls.com

207m Courtesy the artist and Sprüth Magers

207bl Courtesy of the Estate of David Wojnarowicz and P·P·O·W, New York

209 Tate. Photo Tate. Courtesy the artist and Frith Street Gallery, London. © Cornelia Parker

210tr Tate. Photo Tate. Courtesy the artist and Frith Street Gallery, London. © Cornelia Parker

210bl © Hugo Glendinning. All Rights Reserved, DACS 2023

210br Photo NASA/WMAP Science Team

211t Courtesy the artist and Frith Street Gallery, London. Photo Anna Kucera. © Cornelia Parker

211b Tate. Photo Tate. Courtesy the artist and Frith Street Gallery, London. © Cornelia Parker

212–13 Photo Prudence Cuming Associates Ltd. © Damien Hirst and Science Ltd. All rights reserved, DACS/Artimage 2023

214tl Photo Prudence Cuming Associates Ltd. © Damien Hirst and Science Ltd. All rights reserved, DACS/Artimage 2023

214tr Tate. Photo Tate. © The Estate of Francis Bacon. All rights reserved. DACS 2023

214bl Philadelphia Museum of Art. 125th Anniversary Acquisition. Gift (by exchange) of Mrs Herbert Cameron Morris, 1998. © Association Marcel Duchamp/ADAGP, Paris and DACS, London 2023

214br Tate. © Jeff Koons

215tl Photo Universal/Kobal/Shutterstock

215bl The Museum of Moden Art, New York. Gift of Mr and Mrs Ben Heller. © The Barnett Newman Foundation, New York/DACS, London 2023

215r Photo Prudence Cuming Associates Ltd. © Damien Hirst and Science Ltd. All rights reserved, DACS/Artimage 2023

216–17 Installation view: *Kara Walker: My Complement, My Enemy, My Oppressor, My Love*. Hammer Museum, Los Angeles, 2008. Photo Joshua White. Courtesy of Sikkema Jenkins & Co. and Sprüth Magers. Artwork © Kara Walker

218tr The Frick Collection, New York. Henry Clay Frick Bequest. Photo DeAgostini Picture Library/Scala, Florence

218bl The Metropolitan Museum of Art, New York. Gift of John Wolfe, 1893

219tl The Metropolitan Museum of Art, New York. Gift of John Stewart Kennedy, 1897

219tr Wellcome Collection, London

219bl The J. Paul Getty Museum, Los Angeles

221 Courtesy of the artist and Gladstone Gallery. © Shirin Neshat

222ml Figurines and photo courtesy Thomas Gunn Miniatures

222mr The Metropolitan Museum of Art, New York. Fletcher Fund, 1963

222b Photo Ahmad Kavousian/Moment Editorial/Getty Images

223tm Courtesy of the artist and Gladstone Gallery. © Shirin Neshat

223tr Courtesy of the artist and Gladstone Gallery. © Shirin Neshat

223b Courtesy of the artist and Gladstone Gallery. © Shirin Neshat

225 Tate. Courtesy Ostrich Arts Ltd and Victoria Miro. © Ostrich Arts Ltd

226tl Photo Dan Chung/PA Images/Alamy Stock Photo

226b Courtesy Ostrich Arts Ltd and Victoria Miro. © Ostrich Arts Ltd

227tl Photo Luke Watson

227tr Courtesy Ostrich Arts Ltd and Victoria Miro. © Ostrich Arts Ltd

227bl Art Institute of Chicago. Clarence Buckingham Collection

227br Museo del Prado, Madrid

228–9 © JR

230t © JR

230m © JR

Index of artists

Page numbers in **bold** refer to illustrations

Acknowledgments

To Ben Wilson, my inspirational brother.

Truly, this book's identity was crafted in the hands of the talented editorial and design team at Thames & Hudson: Elain McAlpine, Tristan de Lancey and Susanna Ingram. It wouldn't exist without the original guidance of Roger Thorp and Mohara Gill, who have been a constant source of help and encouragement. Thanks also to picture researcher Nikos Kotsopoulos, to Jake Murray and Maria Kelesidi for design concepts, and Fiona Macdonald for her generosity and belief. As ever, the wise counsel of my parents Marney and Chris, and the moral support of Jo Rayner, George and Orla Wilson have been invaluable.

Matthew Wilson is an art historian, educator and writer. He has written for numerous publications and media on art and culture, and is an examination specialist in art history. He is the author of *Symbols in Art* (2020) and *The Hidden Language of Symbols* (2022), both published by Thames & Hudson.

On the cover:
Front Johannes Vermeer,
Woman Holding a Balance, *c.* 1664,
National Gallery of Art,
Washington, DC

Back Katsushika Hokusai,
Under the Wave off Kanagawa, 1830–32,
The Metropolitan Museum of Art,
New York

First published in the United Kingdom in 2023 by
Thames & Hudson Ltd, 181A High Holborn, London WC1V 7QX

First published in the United States of America in 2023 by
Thames & Hudson Inc., 500 Fifth Avenue, New York, New York 10110

Art Unpacked: 50 Works of Art: Uncovered, Explored, Explained

British Library Cataloguing-in-Publication Data
A catalogue record for this book is available from the British Library

Library of Congress Control Number 2023939220

ISBN 978-0-500-02567-3

Printed and bound in China by C & C Offset Printing Co. Ltd

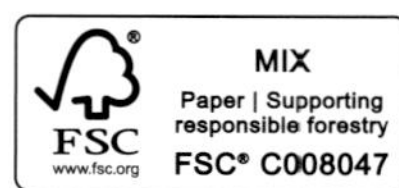